A

HISTORY

OF

THE UNITED STATES.

FOR FAMILIES AND LIBRARIES.

BY

BENSON J. LOSSING,

AUTHOR OF "PICTORIAL FIELD-BOOK OF THE REVOLUTION," "HISTORY OF THE UNITED STATES FOR SCHOOLS;" "LIVES OF EMINENT AMERICANS," ETC.

ILLUSTRATED BY NEARLY THREE HUNDRED ENGRAVINGS.

NEW YORK:
MASON BROTHERS,
1859.

ELECTROTYPED BY
THOMAS B. SMITH,
82 & 84 Beekman Street, N. Y.

PRINTED BY
C. A. ALVORD,
15 Vandewater-st., N.Y.

PREFACE.

THIS work has been prepared with great care, for the purpose of supplying a want long felt by the reading public, and especially by Heads of Families. Every important event in the history of the United States, from the Aboriginal period to the present time, is presented in a concise, but perspicuous and comprehensive manner, without giving those minute and often tedious details, which are valuable to the student, but irksome to the common reader. The History of our Republic is herein popularized, and adapted to the use of those who may not find leisure to peruse more extensive works upon the subject. The materials have been drawn from the earlier, most elaborate, and most reliable historians and chroniclers of our continent. The work is constructed upon a new plan, which, it is believed, will be found to be the most acceptable yet offered to the public, for obtaining, with facility, and fixing in the memory, a knowledge of the great events of our truly wonderful history. And having visited a greater portion of the localities made memorable by important occurrences in our country, the writer claims, in that particular, an advantage over his predecessors in this special field, for he has been able to correct errors and give truthful impressions of things and events. An endeavor has also been made to show the cause of every important event, and thus, by developing the philosophy of our history, to make it more attractive and instructive than a bald record of facts. And wherever the text appeared to need further elucidation, additional facts have been given in foot-notes.

The arrangement of the work is new. It is in six Periods, each commencing where the history naturally divides into distinct epochs. The first Period exhibits a general view of the *Aboriginal* race who occupied the continent when the Europeans came. The second is a record of all the *Discoveries* and preparations for settlement, made by individuals and governments. The third delineates the progress of all the *Settlements* until colonial governments were formed. The fourth tells the story of these *Colonies* from their infancy to maturity, and illustrates the continual development of Democratic ideas and Republican tendencies which finally resulted in a political confederation. The fifth has a full account of the important events of the *War for Independence*, and the sixth gives a concise history of the *Republic*, from its formation to the present time. The Supplement is composed of the most important State Papers connected with that formation, such as the Stamp Act, and papers put forth by the Stamp Act Congress; the papers presented to the consideration of the world by the First and Second Continental Congresses; the Declaration of Independence; the Articles of Confederation; and the Federal Constitution, with the admirable Farewell Address of Washington. These documents, thus grouped and preserved, will be found valuable as embodying the principles of our government. The original draft, with the amendments, of the Declaration of Independence, is given; and, in foot-notes, every charge made against the king of Great Britain, in that manifesto, is proven from History. The Federal Constitution is also accompanied by important commentaries.

The system of concordance interwoven with the notes throughout the entire work, is of great importance to the reader. When a fact is named which bears a relation to another fact elsewhere recorded in the volume, a reference is made to the *page* where such fact is mentioned. A knowledge of this relationship of separate events is often essential to a clear view of the subject, and without this concordance, a great deal of time would be spent in searching for that relationship. With the concordance the matter may be found in a moment. Favorable examples of the utility of this new feature may be found on page 289. If strict attention shall be given to these references, the whole subject will be presented to the mind of the reader in a comprehensive aspect-of unity not to be obtained by any other method.

The engravings are introduced not for the sole purpose of embellishing the volume, but to enhance its utility as an instructor. Every picture is intended to illustrate a fact, not merely to beautify the page. Great care has been taken to secure accuracy in all the delineations of men and things, so that they may not convey false instruction. Geographical maps have been omitted, because they must necessarily be too small to be of essential service. History may be *read* for the purpose of obtaining general information on the subject, without maps, but it should never be *studied* without the aid of an accurate Atlas.

The author has endeavored to make this work essentially a FAMILY HISTORY, attractive and instructive; and the Publishers have generously co-worked with him in producing a volume that may justly claim to be excellent in every particular. With these few observations concerning the general plan and merits of the work, it is presented to the public, with an entire willingness to have its reputation rest upon its own merits.

ILLUSTRATIONS.

HISTORY

OF

THE UNITED STATES.

SIOUX INDIANS.

RED JACKET.

FIRST PERIOD.

THE ABORIGINALS.

CHAPTER I.

EVERY cultivated nation had its heroic age—a period when its first physical and moral conquests were achieved, and when rude society, with all its impurities, was fused and refined in the crucible of progress. When civilization first set up its standard as a permanent ensign, in the western hemisphere, northward of the Bahamas and the great Gulf, and the contests for possession began between the wild Aboriginals, who thrust no spade into the soil, no sickle into ripe harvests, and those earnest delvers from the Old World, who came with the light of Christianity, to plant a new empire, and redeem the wilderness by cultivation—then commenced the heroic age of America. It ended when the work of the Revolution in the eighteenth century was accomplished—when the bond of vassalage to Great Britain was severed by her colonies, and when thirteen confederated States ratified a Federal Constitution, and upon it laid the broad foundation of our Republic.[1]

Long anterior to the advent of Europeans in America, a native empire, little inferior to old Rome in civilization, flourished in that region of our Continent which now forms the south-western portion of our Republic, and the adjoining States of Central America. The Aztec Empire, which reached the acmé of its refinement during the reign of Montezuma, and crumbled into fragments beneath the heel of Cortez, when he dethroned and destroyed that monarch,[2] extended over the whole region from the Rio Grande to the Isthmus of Darien; and when the Spaniards came, it was gradually pushing its conquests northward, where all was yet darkness and gloom. To human apprehension, this people, apparently allied by various ties to the wild nations of North America, appeared to be the most efficient instruments in the hands of Providence, for spreading the light of dawning civilization over the whole Continent. Yet, they were not only denied this glorious privilege, but, by the very race which first attempted to plant the seeds of European society in Florida, and among the Mobilian tribes,[3] and to shed the illumination of their dim Christianity over the dreary region of the North, was their own bright light extinguished. The Aztecs and their neighbors were beaten into the dust of debasement by the falchion blows of avarice and bigotry, and nothing remains to attest their superiority but the magnificent ruins of their cities and temples, and their colossal statuary, which has survived the fury of the Spanish iconoclast and the tooth of decay. They form, apparently, not the most insignificant atom of the chain of events which connects the history of the Aboriginal nations of America with that of our Republic. The position of the tribes of the North is different. From the beginning of European settlements, they have maintained, and do still maintain, an important relation to the white people.

The first inhabitants of a country properly belong to the history of all subsequent occupants of the territory. The several nations of red or copper-colored people who occupied the present domain of the United States, when Europeans first came, form as necessary materials for a portion of the history of our Republic, as the Frenchmen[4] and Spaniards,[5] by whom parts of the territory were settled, and from whom they have been taken by conquest or purchase.

The history of the Indian[6] tribes, previous to the formation of settlements among them, by Europeans,[7] is involved in an obscurity which is penetrated

---

[1] Page 360. [2] Page 43. [3] Page 29. [4] Page 180.
[5] Page 51. [6] Page 40. [7] Before the year 1607.

only by vague traditions and uncertain conjectures. Whence came they? is a question yet unanswered by established facts. In the Old World, the monuments of an ancient people often record their history. In North America, such intelligible records are wanting. Within almost every State and Territory remains of human skill and labor have been found,[1] which seem to attest the existence here of a civilized nation or nations, before the ancestors of our numerous Indian tribes became masters of the Continent. Some of these appear to give indisputable evidence of intercourse between the people of the Old World and those of America, centuries, perhaps, before the birth of Christ, and at periods soon afterward.[2] The whole mass of testimony yet discovered does not prove that such intercourse was extensive; that colonies from the eastern hemisphere ever made permanent settlements in America, or remained long enough to impress their character upon the country or the Aboriginals, if they existed; or that a high degree of civilization had ever prevailed on our Continent.

The origin of the Indian tribes is referred by some to the Phœnicians and other maritime nations, whose extensive voyages have been mentioned by ancient writers, and among whom tradition seemed to cherish memories of far-off lands beyond the sea, unknown to the earlier geographers. Others perceive evidences of their Egyptian or Hindoo parentage; and others find their ancestors among the "lost tribes of Israel," who "took counsel to go forth into a further country where never mankind dwelt,"[3] and crossed from north-eastern Asia to our Continent, by way of the Aleutian Islands, or by Behring's Straits.[4] These various theories, and many others respecting settlements of Europeans and Asiatics here, long before the time of Columbus, unsupported as they are by a sufficiency of acknowledged facts, have so little practical value

---

[1] Remains of fortifications, similar in form to those of ancient European nations, have been discovered. An idol, composed of clay and gypsum, representing a man without arms, and in all respects resembling one found in Southern Russia, was dug up near Nashville, in Tennessee. Also fireplaces, of regular structure; weapons and utensils of copper; catacombs with mummies; ornaments of silver, brass, and copper; walls of forts and cities, and many other things which only a people advanced in civilization could have made. The Aboriginals, themselves, have various traditions respecting their origin—each nation having its distinct records in the memory. Nearly all have traditional glimpses of a great and universal deluge; and some say their particular progenitor came in a bark canoe after that terrible event. This belief, with modifications, was current among most of the northern tribes, and was a recorded tradition of the half-civilized Aztecs. The latter ascribed all their knowledge of the arts, and their religious ceremonies, to a white and bearded mortal who came among them; and when his mission was ended, was made immortal by the Great Spirit.

[2] A Roman coin was found in Missouri; a Persian coin in Ohio; a bit of silver in Genesee county, New York, with the year of our Lord, 600, engraved on it; split wood and ashes, thirty feet below the surface of the earth, near Fredonia, New York; and near Montevideo, South America, in a tomb, were found two ancient swords, a helmet and shield, with Greek inscriptions, showing that they were made in the time of Alexander the Great, 330 years before Christ. Near Marietta, Ohio, a silver cup, finely gilded within, was found in an ancient mound. Traces of iron utensils, wholly reduced to rust, mirrors of isinglass, and glazed pottery, have also been discovered in these mounds. These are evidences of the existence of a race far more civilized than the tribes found by modern Europeans.

[3] 2 Esdras, xiii. 40–45.

[4] The people of north-eastern Asia, and on the north-west coast of America, have a near resemblance in person, customs, and languages; and those of the Aleutian Islands present many of the characteristics of both. Ledyard said of the people of Eastern Siberia, "Universally and circumstantially they resemble the Aborigines of America."

for the student of our history, that we will not occupy space in giving a delineation of even their outlines. There are elaborately-written works specially devoted to this field of inquiry, and to those the curious reader is referred. The proper investigation of such subjects requires the aid of varied and extensive knowledge, and a far wider field for discussion than the pages of a volume like this. So we will leave the field of conjecture for the more useful and important domain of recorded history.

The New World, dimly comprehended by Europeans, afforded materials for wonderful narratives concerning its inhabitants and productions. The few natives who were found upon the seaboard, had all the characteristics common to the human race. The interior of the Continent was a deep mystery, and for a long time marvelous stories were related and believed of nations of giants and pigmies; of people with only one eye, and that in the centre of the forehead; and of whole tribes who existed without eating. But when sober men penetrated the forests and became acquainted with the inhabitants, it was discovered that from the Gulf of Mexico to the country north of the chain of great lakes which divide the United States and the British possessions, the people were not remarkable in persons and qualities, and that a great similarity in manners and institutions prevailed over that whole extent of country.

The Aboriginals spoke a great variety of dialects, but there existed not more than eight radically distinct languages among them all, from the Atlantic to the Mississippi, and westward to the Rocky Mountains, namely: ALGONQUIN, HURON-IROQUOIS, CHEROKEE, CATAWBA, UCHEE, NATCHEZ, MOBILIAN, and DAHCOTAH or SIOUX. These occupied a region embraced within about twenty-four degrees of latitude and almost forty degrees of longitude, and covering a greater portion of the breadth of the north temperate zone.

All the nations and tribes were similar in physical character, moral sentiment, social and political organization, and religious belief. They were all of a copper color; were tall, straight, and well-proportioned; their eyes black and expressive; their hair black, long, coarse, and perfectly straight; their constitutions vigorous, and their powers of endurance remarkable. Bodily deformity was almost unknown, and few diseases prevailed. They were indolent, taciturn, and unsocial; brave, and sometimes generous in war; unflinching under torture; revengeful, treacherous, and morose when injured or offended; not always grateful for favors; grave and sagacious in council; often eloquent in speech; sometimes warm and constant in friendship, and occasionally courteous and polite.

The men were employed in war, hunting and fishing. The women performed all menial services. In hunting and fishing the men were assiduous and very skillful. They carried the knowledge of woodcraft to the highest degree of perfection; and the slightest indication, such as the breaking of a twig, or the bending of grass, was often sufficient to form a clew to the pathway of an enemy or of game. The women bore all burdens during journeys; spread the tents; prepared food; dressed skins for clothing; wove mats for beds, made of the bark of trees and the skins of animals; and planted and gathered the scanty crops of corn, beans, peas, potatoes, melons, and tobacco. These constituted the chief agricultural productions of the Aboriginals, under the most favorable circumstances. In these labors the men never engaged; they only manufactured their implements of war. Their wigwams, or houses, were rude huts, made of poles covered with mats, skins, or bark of trees; and all of their domestic arrangements were very simple.

A WIGWAM.

And simple, too, were their implements of labor. They were made of stones, shells, and bones, with which they prepared their food, made their clothing and habitations, and tilled their lands. Their food consisted of a few vegetables, and the meat of the deer, buffalo, and bear, generally roasted upon the points of sticks; sometimes boiled in water heated by hot stones, and always eaten without salt. Their dress in summer was a slight covering around the loins. In winter they were clad in the skins of wild beasts,[1] often profusely ornamented with the claws of the bear, the horns of the buffalo, the feathers of birds, and the bones of fishes. Their faces were often tattooed, and generally painted with bright colors in hideous devices. Their money was little tubes made of shells, fastened upon belts or strung in chains, and called *wampum.*[2] It was used in traffic, in treaties, and as a token of friendship or alliance. Wampum belts constituted records of public transactions in the hands of a chief.

WAMPUM.

There was no written language in all the New World, except rude hieroglyphics, or picture writings. The history of the nations, consisting of the records of warlike achievements, treaties of alliance, and deeds of great men, was, in the form of traditions, carefully handed down from father to son, especially from chief to chief. Children were taught the simple

INDIAN HIEROGLYPHICS.[3]

[1] The engraving at the head of this chapter represents some Sioux Indians, in their winter and fanciful costumes.

[2] Wampum is yet in use, as money, among some of the Western tribes, and is manufactured, we believe, as an article of commerce on the sea-shore of one of the counties of New Jersey. It is made of the clear parts of the common clam-shell. This part being split off, a hole is drilled in it, and the form, which is that of the bead now known as the *bugle*, is produced by friction. They are about half an inch long, generally disposed in alternate layers of white and bluish black, and valued, when they become a circulating medium, at about two cents for three of the black beads, or six of the white. They were strung in parcels to represent a penny, three pence, a shilling, and five shillings, of white; and double that amount in black. A fathom of white was worth about two dollars and a half, and black about five dollars. They were of less value at the time of our war for independence. The engraving shows a part of a *string* and a *belt* of wampum.

[3] This is part of a record of a war expedition. The figures on the right and left—one with a gun and the other with a hatchet—denote prisoners taken by a warrior. The one without a head, and holding a bow and arrow, denotes that one was killed; and the figure with a shaded part below the cross indicates a female prisoner. Then he goes in a war canoe, with nine companions, denoted by the paddles, after which a council is held by the chiefs of the Bear and Turtle tribes, indicated by rude figures of these animals on each side of a fire.

arts practiced among them, such as making wampum, constructing bows, arrows, and spears, preparing matting and skins for domestic use, and fashioning rude personal ornaments.

Individual and national pride prevailed among the Aboriginals. They were ambitious of distinction, and therefore war was the chief vocation, as we have said, of the men.[1] They generally went forth in parties of about forty bowmen. Sometimes a half-dozen, like knights-errant,[2] went out upon the war-path to seek renown in combat. Their weapons were bows and arrows, hatchets (tomahawks) of stone, and scalping-knives of bone. Soon after they became acquainted with the Europeans, they procured knives and hatchets made of iron, and this was a great advance in the increase of their power. Some wore shields of bark; others wore skin dresses for protection. They were skillful in stratagem, and seldom met an enemy in open fight. Ambush and secret attack were their favorite methods of gaining an advantage over an enemy. Their close personal encounters were fierce and bloody. They made prisoners, and tortured them, and the scalps[4] of enemies were their trophies of war. Peace was arranged by sachems[5] in council; and each smoking the same "pipe of peace," called *calumet*,[6] was a solemn pledge of fidelity to the contract.

INDIAN WEAPONS.[3]

CALUMETS.

With the Indians, as with many oriental nations, women were regarded as inferior beings. They were degraded to the condition of abject slaves, and they never engaged with the men in their amusements of leaping, dancing, target-shooting, ball-playing, and games of chance. They were allowed as spectators, with their children, at war-dances around fires, when the men recited the feats of their ancestors and of themselves. Marriage, among them, was only a temporary contract—a sort of purchase—the father receiving presents from the

[1] It was offensive to a chief or warrior to ask him his name, because it implied that his brave deeds were unknown. Red Jacket, the great Seneca chief (whose portrait is at the head of this chapter), was asked his name in court, in compliance with a legal form. He was very indignant, and replied, "Look at the papers which the white people keep the most carefully"—(land cession treaties)—"they will tell you who I am." Red Jacket was born near Geneva, New York, about 1750, and died in 1830. He was the last great chief of the *Senecas*. For a biographical sketch of him, see Lossing's "Eminent Americans."

[2] Knights-errant of Europe, six hundred years ago, were men clothed in metal armor, who went from country to country, to win fame by personal combats with other knights. They also engaged in wars. For about three hundred years, knights-errant and their exploits formed the chief amusement of the courts of Europe. It is curious to trace the connection of the spirit of knighthood, as exhibited by the one hundred and thirty-five orders that have existed, at various times, in the Old World, with some of the customs of the rude Aboriginals of North America

[3] *a*, bow and arrow; *b*, a war club; *c*, an iron tomahawk; *d*, a stone one; *e*, a scalping-knife.

[4] They seized an enemy by the hair, and by a skillful use of the knife, cut and tore from the top of the head a large portion of the skin.

[5] *Sachems* were the civil heads of nations or tribes; *chiefs* were military leaders.

[6] Tobacco was in general use among the Indians for *smoking*, when the white men came. The more filthy practice of *chewing* it was invented by the white people. The *calumet* was made of pipe-clay, and was often ornamented with feathers.

husband, in exchange for the daughter, who, generally, after being fondled and favored for a few months, was debased to the condition of a domestic servant, at best. The men had the right to take wives and dismiss them at pleasure; and, though polygamy was not very common, except among the chiefs, it was not objectionable. Every Indian might have as many wives as he could purchase and maintain. The husband might put his wife to death if she proved unfaithful to him. The affections were ruled by custom, and those decorous endearments and attentions toward woman, which give a charm to civilized society, were wholly unknown among the Indians; yet the sentiment of conjugal love was not always wanting, and attachments for life were frequent. There was no society to call for woman's refining qualities to give it beauty, for they had but few local attachments, except for the burial-places of their dead.

From the frozen North to the tropical South, their funeral ceremonies and methods of burial were similar. They laid their dead, wrapped in skins, upon sticks, in the bottom of a shallow pit, or placed them in a sitting posture, or occasionally folded them in skins, and laid them upon high scaffolds, out of the reach of wild beasts. Their arms, utensils, paints, and food, were buried with them, to be used on their long journey to the spirit-land. By this custom, the doctrine of the immortality of the soul was clearly and forcibly taught, not as distinctively spiritual, but as possessing the two-fold nature of matter and spirit. Over their graves they raised mounds, and planted beautiful wild-flowers upon them. The Algonquins, especially, always lighted the symbolical funeral pyre, for several nights, upon the grave, that the soul might perceive and enjoy the respect paid to the body. Relatives uttered piercing cries and great lamentations during the burial, and they continued mourning many days.

BURIAL-PLACE.

Like that of the earlier nations of the world, their religion was simple, without many ceremonies, and was universally embraced. They had no infidels among them. The *duality of God* is the most ancient tenet of Indian faith—a prominent tenet, it will be observed, in the belief of all of the more advanced oriental nations of antiquity. They believed in the existence of two Great Spirits: the one eminently great was the Good Spirit,[1] and the inferior was an Evil one. They also deified the sun, moon, stars, meteors, fire, water, thunder, wind, and every thing which they held to be superior to themselves, but

[1] They believed every animal to have had a great original, or father. The first *buffalo*, the first *bear*, the first *beaver*, the first *eagle*, etc., was the *Manitou* of the whole race of the different creatures. They chose some one of these originals as their special *Manitou*, or guardian, and hence arose the custom of having the figure of some animal for the arms or symbol of a tribe, called *totum*. For example, each of the FIVE NATIONS (see page 12) was divided into several tribes, designated The Wolf, The Bear, The Turtle, etc., and their respective *totums* were rude representations of these animals. When they signed treaties with the white people, they sometimes sketched outlines of their *totums*. The annexed cut represents the *totum* of Teyendagages, of the Turtle tribe of the Mohawk nation, as affixed by him to a deed. It would be a curious and pleasant task to trace the intimate connection of this totemic system with the use of symbolical signet-rings, and other seals of antiquity, and, by succession, the heraldic devices of modern times.

TOTUM.

they never exalted their heroes or prophets above the sphere of humanity. They also adored an invisible, great Master of life, in different forms, which they called *Manitou*, and made it a sort of tutelar deity. They had vague ideas of the doctrine of atonement for sins, and made propitiatory sacrifices with great solemnity. All of them had dim traditions of the creation, and of a great deluge which covered the earth. Each nation, as we have observed, had crude notions, drawn from tradition, of their own distinct origin, and all agreed that their ancestors came from the North.

It can hardly be said that the Indians had any true government. It was a mixture of the patriarchal and despotic. Public opinion and common usage were the only laws of the Indian.[1] All political power was vested in a sachem or chief, who was sometimes an hereditary monarch, but frequently owed his elevation to his own merits as a warrior or orator. While in power, he was absolute in the execution of enterprises, if the tribe confided in his wisdom. Public opinion, alone, sustained him. It elevated him, and it might depose him. The office of chief was often hereditary, and its duties were sometimes exercised even by women. Unlike the system of lineal descent which prevails in the Old World, the heir to the Indian throne of power was not the chief's own son, but the son of his sister. This usage was found to be universal throughout the continent. Yet the accident of *birth* was of little moment. If the recipient of the honor was not worthy of it, the *title* might remain, but the *influence* passed into other hands. This rule might be followed, with benefit, by civilized communities. Every measure of importance was matured in council, which was composed of the elders, with the sachem as umpire. His decision was final, and wherever he led, the whole tribe followed. The utmost decorum prevailed in the public assemblies, and a speaker was always listened to with respectful silence.

We have thus briefly sketched the general character of the inhabitants of the territory of the United States, when discovered by Europeans. Although inferior in intellectual cultivation and approaches to the arts of civilization, to the native inhabitants of Mexico[2] and South America, and to a race which evidently occupied the continent before them, they possessed greater personal manliness and vigor than the more southern ones discovered by the Spaniards. They were almost all wanderers, and roamed over the vast solitudes of a fertile continent, free as the air, and unmindful of the wealth in the soil under their feet. The great garden of the western world needed tillers, and white men came. They have thoroughly changed the condition of the land and the people. The light of civilization has revealed, and industry has developed, vast treasures in the soil, while before its radiance the Aboriginals are rapidly melting like snow in the sunbeams. A few generations will pass, and no representative of the North American Indian will remain upon the earth.

---

[1] It was said of McGillivray, the half-breed emperor of the Creeks, who died in 1793, that, notwithstanding he called himself "King of kings," and was idolized by his people, "he could neither restrain the meanest fellow of his nation from the commission of a crime, nor punish him after he had committed it. He might persuade, or advise—all the good an Indian king or chief can do."

[2] Page 43.

CHAPTER II.

THE ALGONQUINS.

THE first tribes of Indians, discovered by the French in Canada,[1] were inhabitants of the vicinity of Quebec, and the adventurers called them Montagners, or Mountain Indians, from a range of high hills westward of that city. Ascending the St. Lawrence, they found a numerous tribe on the Ottawa River, who spoke an entirely different dialect, if not a distinct language. These they called ALGONQUINS, and this name was afterward applied to that great collection of tribes north and south of Lakes Erie and Ontario, who spoke dialects of the same language. They inhabited the territory now included in all of Canada, New England, a part of New York and Pennsylvania, the States of New Jersey, Delaware, Maryland, and Virginia, eastern North Carolina above Cape Fear, a large portion of Kentucky and Tennessee, and all north and west of these States, eastward of the Mississippi.

The ALGONQUIN nation was composed of several powerful tribes, the most important of which were the Knisteneaux and Athapascas, in the far north, the Ottawas, Chippewas, Sacs and Foxes, Menomonees, Miamies, Piankeshaws, Pottowatomies, Kickapoos, Illinois, Shawnees, Powhatans, Corees, Nanticokes, Lenni-Lenapes, or Delawares, Mohegans, the New England Indians, and the Abenakes. There were smaller, independent tribes, the principal of which were the Susquehannocks, on the Susquehanna in Pennsylvania; the Mannahoacks, in the hill country between the York and Potomac Rivers, and the Monocans, on the head waters of the James River in Virginia. All of these tribes were divided into cantons or clans, sometimes so small as to afford only a war party of forty bowmen.

The KNISTENEAUX yet [1856] inhabit a domain extending across the continent from Labrador to the Rocky Mountains, and are the hereditary enemies of the ESQUIMAUX, their neighbors of the Polar Circle. The Athapascas inhabit a belt of country from Churchill's River and Hudson's Bay to within a hundred miles of the Pacific coast, and combine a large number of tribes who speak a similar language. They, too, are the enemies of the Esquimaux. The extensive domain occupied by these tribes and the Esquimaux, is claimed by the British, and is under the control of the Hudson's Bay Company. The orginal land of the OTTAWAS was on the west side of Lake Huron, but they were seated upon the river in Canada bearing their name, when the French discovered them. They claimed sovereignty over that region, and exacted tribute from those who passed to or from the domain of the Hurons.[2] They assisted

---

[1] Page 48.

[2] Between the Ottawas and Hurons, was a tribe called Mississaguies, who appear to have left the ALGONQUINS, and joined the FIVE NATIONS, south of Lake Ontario. Remnants of this tribe are still found in Canada.

the latter in a war with the FIVE NATIONS[1] in 1650, and suffered much. The Hurons were almost destroyed, and the OTTAWAS were much reduced in numbers. Some of them, with the Huron remnant, joined the Chippewas, and, finally, the whole tribe returned to their ancient seat [1680] in the northern part of the Michigan peninsula. Under their great chief, Pontiac, they were confederated with several other ALGONQUIN tribes of the north-west, in an attempt to exterminate the white people, in 1763.[2] Within a fortnight, in the summer of that year, they took possession of all the English garrisons and trading posts in the West, except Detroit, Niagara,[3] and Fort Pitt.[4] Peace was restored in 1764–5, the confederation was dissolved, and Pontiac took up his abode with the Illinois, where he was murdered.[5] "This murder," says Nicollet, "which roused the vengeance of all the Indian tribes friendly to Pontiac, brought about the successive wars, and almost extermination of the Illinois nation." His broken nation sought refuge with the French, and their descendants may yet [1856] be found in Canada.

Those two once powerful tribes, the CHIPPEWAS and POTTAWATOMIES, were closely allied by language and friendship. The former were on the southern shores of Lake Superior; the latter occupied the islands and main land on the western shores of Green Bay, when first discovered by the French in 1761. They afterward seated themselves on the southern shore of Lake Michigan [1701], where they remained until removed, by treaty, to lands upon the Little Osage River, westward of Missouri. They are now [1856] the most numerous of all the remnants of the ALGONQUIN tribes. The Chippewas and the Sioux, west of the Mississippi, are their deadly enemies.

The Sacs and Foxes are really one tribe. They were first discovered by the French at the southern extremity of Green Bay, in 1680. In 1712 the French garrison of twenty men at Detroit,[6] was attacked by the Foxes. The French repulsed them, with the aid of the Ottawas, and almost destroyed the assailants. They joined the Kickapoos in 1722, in driving the Illinois from their lands on the river of that name. The Illinois took refuge with the French, and the Kickapoos remained on their lands until 1819, when they went to the west bank of the Missouri in the vicinity of Fort Leavenworth. The Sacs and Foxes sold their lands to the United States in 1830. Black Hawk, a Sac chief, who, with his people, joined the English in our second war with Great Britain,[7] demurred, and commenced hostilities in 1832.[8] The Indians were defeated, and Black Hawk,[9] with many of his warriors, were made prisoners.

BLACK HAWK.

Among the very few Indian tribes who have remained upon their ancient

[1] Chapter III., p 23. [2] Page 205. [3] Page 200. [4] Page 198.

[5] He was buried on the site of the city of St. Louis, in Missouri. "Neither mound nor tablet," says Parkman, "marked the burial-place of Pontiac. For a mausoleum, a city has risen above the forest hero, and the race whom he hated with such burning rancor, trample with unceasing footsteps over his forgotten grave."

[6] Page 180. [7] Page 409. [8] Page 463.

[9] This picture is from a plaster-cast of the face of Black Hawk, taken when he was a prisoner in New York, in 1832. See page 463.

territory, during all the vicissitudes of their race, are the MENOMONEES, who were discovered by the French, upon the shores of Green Bay, in 1699. They yet [1856] occupy a portion of their ancient territory, while their southern neighbors and friends, the Winnebagoes, have gone westward of the Mississippi.[1]

The MIAMIES and PIANKESHAWS inhabited that portion of Ohio lying between the Maumee River of Lake Erie, and the ridge which separates the head waters of the Wabash from the Kaskaskias. They were called Twightwees by the FIVE NATIONS, and English. Of all the Western tribes, these have ever been the most active enemies of the United States.[2] They have ceded their lands, and are now [1856] far beyond the Mississippi.

The ILLINOIS formed a numerous tribe, twelve thousand strong, when discovered by the French. They were seated upon the Illinois River, and consisted of a confederation of five families, namely, Kaskaskias, Cahokias, Tamaronas, Michigamias, and Peorias. Weakened by internal feuds, the confederacy was reduced to a handful, by their hostile neighbors. They ceded their lands in 1818, when they numbered only three hundred souls. A yet smaller remnant are now [1856] upon lands west of the Mississippi. It can not properly be said that they have a tribal existence. They are among the many extinct communities of our continent.

The once powerful SHAWNEES occupied a vast region west of the Alleghanies,[3] and their great council-house was in the basin of the Cumberland River. At about the time when the English first landed at Jamestown[4] [1607], they were driven from their country by more southern tribes. Some crossed the Ohio, and settled on the Sciota, near the present Chilicothe; others wandered eastward into Pennsylvania. The Ohio division joined the Eries and Andastes against the FIVE NATIONS in 1672. Suffering defeat, the Shawnees fled to the country of the Catawbas, but were soon driven out, and found shelter with the Creeks.[5] They finally returned to Ohio, and being joined by their Pennsylvania brethren, they formed an alliance with the French against the English, and were among the most active allies with the former, during the long contest known in America as the French and Indian War. They continued hostilities, in connection with the Delawares, even after the conquest of the Canadas by the English.[6] They were subdued by Boquet in 1763,[7] and again by Virginians, at Point Pleasant, at the mouth of the Great Kenawha, in 1774.[8] They aided the British during the Revolution, and continued to annoy the Americans until 1795, when permanent peace was established.[9] They were the enemies of the Americans during their second war with Great Britain, a part of them fighting with the renowned Tecumseh. Now [1856] they are but

---

[1] The Winnebagoes are the most dissolute of all the Indian remnants. In August, 1853, a treaty was made with them to occupy the beautiful country above St. Paul, westward of the Mississippi, between the Crow and Clear Water Rivers.

[2] Page 408.

[3] The Alleghany or Appalachian Mountains extend from the Catskills, in the State of New York, in a south-west direction, to Georgia and Alabama, and have been called "the backbone of the country." Some geographers extend them to the White Mountains of New Hampshire.

[4] Page 64. [5] Page 30. [6] Page 203.

[7] Note 7, page 205. [8] Note 4, page 237. [9] Page 374.

a miserable remnant, and occupy lands south of the Kansas River. The road from Fort Independence[1] to Santa Fé passes through their territory.[2]

The POWHATANS constituted a confederacy of more than twenty tribes, including the Accohannocks and Accomacs, on the eastern shore of the Chesapeake Bay. Powhatan (the father of Pocahontas[3]), was the chief sachem or emperor of the confederacy, when the English first appeared upon the James River, in 1607. He had arisen, by the force of his own genius, from the position of a petty chief to that of supreme ruler of a great confederacy. He governed despotically, for no man in his nation could approach him in genuine ability as a leader and counselor. His court exhibited much barbaric state. Through fear of the English, and a selfish policy, he and his people remained nominally friendly to the white intruders during his lifetime, but after his death, they made two attempts [1622, 1644] to exterminate the English. The Powhatans were subjugated in 1644,[4] and from that time they gradually diminished in numbers and importance. Of all that great confederacy in Lower Virginia, it is believed that not one representative on earth remains, or that one tongue speaks their dialect.

On the Atlantic coast, south of the Powhatans, were the Corees, Cheraws, and other small tribes, occupying the land once inhabited by the powerful Hatteras Indians.[5] They were allies of the Tuscaroras in 1711, in an attack upon the English,[6] suffered defeat, and have now disappeared from the earth. Their dialect also is forgotten.

Upon the great peninsula between the Chesapeake and Delaware Bays, were the NANTICOKES. They were early made vassals, and finally allies, on compulsion, of the FIVE NATIONS. They left their ancient domain in 1710, occupied lands upon the Susquehanna, in Pennsylvania, until the Revolutionary War commenced, when they crossed the Alleghanies, and joined the British in the west. They are now [1856] scattered among many tribes.

The Original People,[7] as the LENNI-LENAPES (who are frequently called Del-

---

[1] United States fort on the Missouri. Santa Fé is in New Mexico, 765 miles south-west of Fort Independence.

[2] One of the most eminent of the Shawnee chiefs, was Cornstalk, who was generally friendly to the Americans, and was always ready to assist in negotiating an honorable peace between them and his own people. But he cordially united with Logan, the Mingo chief, against the white people in 1774; and during the same battle at Point Pleasant, his voice, stentorian in volume, was frequently heard, calling to his men, "Be strong! be strong!" He made his warriors fight without wavering, and actually sunk his tomahawk deep into the head of one who endeavored to escape. He was murdered by some exasperated soldiers at Point Pleasant. When he perceived their intent, he calmly said to his son, who had just joined him, "My son, the Great Spirit has seen fit that we should die together, and has sent you hither for that purpose. It is His will; let us submit." Turning to the soldiers, he received the fatal bullets, and his son, who was sitting near him, was shot at the same time. The celebrated Tecumseh—meaning a tiger crouching for his prey—who endeavored to confederate all the Western tribes in opposition to the white people, was also a Shawnee chief. See page 408.

[3] Page 66. [4] Page 108.

[5] This tribe numbered about three thousand warriors when Raleigh's expedition landed on Roanoke Island in 1584; when the English made permanent settlements in that vicinity, eighty years later, they were reduced to about fifteen bowmen. [6] Page 168.

[7] This name has been applied to the whole ALGONQUIN nation. The Lenni-Lenapes claimed to have come from beyond the Mississippi, conquering a more civilized people on the way, who inhabited the great valleys beyond the Alleghany Mountains.

awares) named themselves, comprised two powerful nations, namely, the Minsi and the Delawares proper. The former occupied the northern part of New Jersey, and a portion of Pennsylvania, and the latter inhabited lower New Jersey, the banks of the Delaware below Trenton, and the whole valley of the Schuylkill. The FIVE NATIONS subjugated them in 1650, and brought them under degrading vassalage. They gradually retreated westward before the tide of civilization, and finally a portion of them crossed the Alleghanies, and settled in the land of the Hurons,[1] on the Muskingum, in Ohio. Those who remained in Pennsylvania joined the Shawnees,[2] and aided the French against the English, during the French and Indian War.[3] In 1768, they all went over the mountains, and the great body of them became friends of the British during the Revolution. They were at the head of the confederacy of Western tribes who were crushed by Wayne in 1794,[4] and the following year they ceded all their lands on the Muskingum, and seated themselves near the Wabash. In 1819, they ceded those lands also, and the remnant now [1856] occupy a territory north of the Kansas River, near its mouth.

The MOHEGANS were a distinct tribe, on the Hudson River, but the name was given to the several independent tribes who inhabited Long Island, and the country between the Lenni-Lenapes and the New England Indians.[5] Of this family, the Pequods,[6] inhabiting eastern Connecticut, on the shores of Long Island Sound, were the most powerful. They exercised authority over the Montauks and twelve other tribes upon Long Island. Their power was broken by the revolt of Uncas against his chief, Sassacus,[7] a short time before the appearance of the white people. The Manhattans were seated upon the Hudson, in lower Westchester, and sold Manhattan Island, whereon New York now stands, to the Dutch.[8] The latter had frequent conflicts with these and other River Indians.[9] The Dutch were generally conquerors. The Mohawks, one of the FIVE NATIONS,[10] were pressing hard upon them, at the same time, and several of the Mohegan tribes were reduced to the condition of vassals of that confederacy. Peace was effected, in 1665, by the English governor at New York. In the mean while, the English and Narragansets had smitten the Pequods,[11] and the remaining independent Mohegans, reduced to a handful, finally took up their abode upon the west bank of the Thames, five miles below Norwich,[12] at a place still known as *Mohegan Plain*. Their burial-place was at Norwich, and there a granite monument rests upon the grave of Uncas. The tribe is now almost extinct—"the last of the Mohicans" will soon sleep with his fathers.[13]

UNCAS' MONUMENT.

[1] Page 23. [2] Page 19. [3] Fourth Period, Chap. XII. [4] Page 374.
[5] Page 22. [6] Page 86. [7] Page 87. [8] Page 139.
[9] Page 140. [10] Page 23. [11] Page 87. [12] Note 4, page 340.

[13] The last known lineal descendant of Uncas, named Mazeon, was buried in the Indian cemetery, at Norwich, in 1827, when the remnant of the Mohegan tribe, then numbering about sixty, were present, and partook of a cold collation prepared for them by a lady of that city. The most noted leaders among the New England Indians known to history, are Massasoit, the father of the renowned King Philip; Caunbitant, a very distinguished captain; Hobomok; Canonicus; Miastonomoh; Ninigret, his cousin; King Philip, the last of the Wampanoags; Canonchet, and Annawan. We shall meet them in future pages.

The Aboriginals who inhabited the country from Connecticut to the Saco River, were called the NEW ENGLAND INDIANS. The principal tribes were the Narragansets in Rhode Island, and on the western shores of Narraganset Bay; the Pokonokets and Wampanoags on the eastern shore of the same bay, and in a portion of Massachusetts; the Nipmucs in the center of Massachusetts; the Massachusetts in the vicinity of Boston and the shores southward; and the Pawtuckets in the north-eastern part of Massachusetts, embracing the Pennacooks of New Hampshire. These were divided into smaller bands, having petty chiefs. The Pokonokets, for example, were divided into nine separate cantons or tribes, each having its military or civil ruler, but all holding allegiance to one Grand Sachem. They were warlike, and were continually engaged in hostilities with the FIVE NATIONS, or with the Mohegans. The English and Dutch effected a general peace among them in 1673. Two years afterward [1675], Metacomet (King Philip) aroused most of the New England tribes against the English. A fierce war ensued, but ended in the subjugation of the Indians and the death of Philip, in 1676.[1] The power of the New England Indians was then completely broken. Some joined the more eastern tribes, and others took refuge in Canada, from whence they frequently came to the border settlements on errands of revenge.[2] These incursions ceased when the French dominion in Canada ended in 1763.[3] When the Puritans came[4] [1620], the New England Indians numbered about ten thousand souls; now [1856] probably not three hundred representatives remain; and the dialects of all, except of the Narragansets, are forgotten.

Eastward of the Saco River were the Abenakes. The chief tribes were the Penobscots, Norridgewocks, Androscoggins, and Passamaquoddies. These, with the more eastern tribes of the Micmacs and Etchemins, were made nominal Christians by the French Jesuits;[5] and they were all firm allies of the French until the conquest of Canada by the English, in 1760.[6] Most of the ABENAKES, except the Penobscots, withdrew to Canada in 1754. A few scattered families of the latter yet [1856] dwell upon the banks of the Penobscot River, and wanderers are seen on the St. Lawrence. Like other New England tribes, they are rapidly fading, and will, doubtless, be extinct before the dawn of another century.

CHAPTER III.

THE HURON-IROQUOIS.

WE now come to consider the most interesting, in many respects, of all the aboriginal tribes of North America, called IROQUOIS by the French. The prefix "Huron" was given, because that people seemed, by their language, to form

[1] Page 128. [2] Page 130. [3] Page 202. [4] Page 114. [5] Page 130. [6] Page 203.

a part of the IROQUOIS nation, and like them, were isolated in the midst of the ALGONQUINS, when discovered by the Europeans. The great body of the IROQUOIS occupied almost the whole territory in Canada, south-west of the Ottowa River, between Lakes Ontario, Erie and Huron; a greater portion of the State of New York, and a part of Pennsylvania and Ohio along the southern shores of Lake Erie. They were completely surrounded by the ALGONQUINS, in whose southern border in portions of North Carolina and Virginia, were the Tuscaroras and a few smaller Iroquois tribes.[1] The Hurons occupied the Canadian portions of the territory, and the land on the southern shore of Lake Erie, and appeared to be a distinct nation; but their language was found to be identical with that of the Iroquois. The Hurons consisted of four smaller tribes, namely, the Wyandots or Hurons proper, the Attiouandirons,[2] the Eries, and the Andastes. The two latter tribes were south of the lake, and claimed jurisdiction back to the domains of the Shawnees.[3]

Those "Romans of the Western World," the FIVE NATIONS, or IROQUOIS proper, formed a confederacy composed of the Seneca, Cayuga, Onondaga, Oneida, and Mohawk tribes, all occupying lands within the present State of New York. They fancifully called their confederacy the Long House. The eastern door was kept by the Mohawks; the western by the Senecas; and the Great Council fire was with the Onondagas, at the metropolis, or chief village, near the present city of Syracuse. The French, as we have observed, gave them the name of Iroquois; the ALGONQUINS called them Mingoes.[4] At what time the confederacy was formed, is not known. It was strong and powerful when the French discovered them, in 1609, and they were then engaged in bloody wars with their kinsmen, the Wyandots.[5]

---

1 The Southern Iroquois were the Tuscaroras, Chowans, Meherrins, and Nottoways. The three latter were upon the rivers in lower Virginia, called by their respective names, and were known under the general title of Tuscaroras.

2 Neutral Nation. When the Hurons and FIVE NATIONS were at war, the Attiouandirons fled to the Sandusky, and built a fort for each of the belligerents when in that region. But their neutrality did not save them from internal feuds which finally dismembered the tribe. One party joined the Wyandots; the other the Iroquois.

3 Page 19.

4 Mingoes, Minquas, and Maquas, were terms more particularly applied to the Mohawk tribe, who called themselves Kayingehaga, "possessors of the flint." The confederation assumed the title of Aquinuschioni, "united people;" or as some say, Konoshioni, "cabin builders."

5 The time of the formation of the confederation is supposed to have been at about the year 1539. According to their own tradition, it was about two generations before the white people came to trade with them. Clarke, in his history of Onondaga county, has given, from the lips of an old chief of the Onondaga tribe, that beautiful legend of the formation of the great confederacy, which forms the basis of Longfellow's Indian Edda, "HI-A-WAT-HA." Centuries ago, the story runs, the deity who presides over fisheries and streams, came from his dwelling-place in the clouds, to visit the inhabitants of earth. He was delighted with the land where the tribes that afterward formed the confederacy, dwelt; and having bestowed many blessings on that land, he laid aside his Divine character, and resolved to remain on earth. He selected a beautiful residence on the shore of Te-ungk-too (Cross lake), and all the people called him Hi-a-wat-ha, "the wise man." After a while, the people were alarmed by the approach of a ferocious band of warriors from the country north of the great lakes. Destruction seemed inevitable. The inhabitants thronged around the lodge of Hi-a-wat-ha, from all quarters, craving his wise advice in this hour of great peril. After solemn meditation, he told them to call a grand council of all the tribes. The chiefs and warriors from far and near, assembled on the banks of Lake Oh-nen-ta-ha (Onondaga). The council-fire blazed three days before the venerable Hi-a-wat-ha arrived. He had been devoutly praying, in silence, to the Great Spirit, for guidance. Then, with his darling daughter, a virgin of twelve years, he entered his white canoe, and, to the great joy of the people, he appeared on the Oh-nen-

In the year 1649, the FIVE NATIONS resolved to strike a final and decisive blow against their western neighbors, and, gathering all their warriors, they made a successful invasion of the Wyandot, or Huron country. Great numbers of the Wyandots were slain and made prisoners, and the whole tribe was dispersed. Some of the fugitives took refuge with the Chippewas; others fled to Quebec, and a few were incorporated into the Iroquois confederacy. Yet the spirit of the Wyandots was not subdued, and they claimed and exercised sovereignty over almost the whole of the Ohio country. They had great influence among the ALGONQUIN tribes,[1] and even as late as the treaty of Greenville, in 1795, the principal cession of lands in Ohio to the United States was made by the Wyandot chiefs in council.[2] They, too, are reduced to a mere remnant of less than five hundred souls, and now [1856] they occupy lands on the Neosho River, a chief tributary of the Arkansas.

Being exceedingly warlike, the FIVE NATIONS made hostile expeditions against the New England Indians[3] in the East, the Eries, Andastes, and

---

ta-ha. A great shout greeted him, and as he landed and walked up the bank, a sound like a rushing wind was heard; a dark spot, every moment increasing in size, was descending from the clear sky. Fear seized the people; but Hi-a-wat-ha stood unmoved. The approaching object was an immense bird. It came swiftly to earth, crushed the darling daughter of Hi-a-wat-ha—was itself destroyed, but the wise man was unharmed. Grief for his bereavement prostrated him in the dust for three days. The council anxiously awaited his presence. At length he came: the subject of the peril from invaders was discussed, and after deliberating a day, the venerable Hi-a-wat-ha arose and said:

"Friends and Brothers—You are members of many tribes and nations. You have come here, many of you, a great distance from your homes. We have met for one common purpose—to promote one common interest, and that is, to provide for our mutual safety, and how it shall best be accomplished. To oppose these foes from the north by tribes, singly and alone, would prove our certain destruction. We can make no progress in that way. We must unite ourselves into one common band of brothers; thus united, we may drive the invaders back; this must be done, and we shall be safe.

"You, the MOHAWKS, sitting under the shadow of the 'Great Tree,' whose roots sink deep into the earth, and whose branches spread over a vast country, shall be the first nation, because you are warlike and mighty.

"And you, ONEIDAS, a people who recline your bodies against the 'Everlasting Stone,' that can not be moved, shall be the second nation, because you give wise counsel.

"And you, ONONDAGAS, who have your habitation at the 'Great Mountain,' and are overshadowed by its crags, shall be the third nation, because you are greatly gifted in speech, and mighty in war.

"And you, CAYUGAS, a people whose habitation is the 'Dark Forest,' and whose home is everywhere, shall be the fourth nation, because of your superior cunning in hunting.

"And you, SENECAS, a people who live in the 'Open Country,' and possess much wisdom, shall be the fifth nation, because you understand better the art of raising corn and beans, and making cabins.

"You, five great and powerful nations, must unite and have but one common interest, and no foe shall be able to disturb or subdue you. If we unite, the Great Spirit will smile upon us. Brothers, these are the words of Hi-a-wat-ha—let them sink deep into your hearts. I have said it."

They reflected for a day, and then the people of the "Great Tree," the "Everlasting Stone," the "Great Mountain," the "Dark Forest," and the "Open Country," formed a league like that of the Amphyctioni of Greece. The enemy was repulsed, and the FIVE NATIONS became the terror of the Continent. Then Hi-a-watha said,

"The Great Master of Breath calls me to go. I have patiently waited his summons. I am ready—farewell!"

Myriads of singing voices burst upon the ears of the multitude, and the whole air seemed filled with music. Hi-a-wat-ha, seated in his white canoe, rose majestically above the throng, and as all eyes gazed in rapture upon the ascending wise man, he disappeared forever in the blue vault of heaven. The music melted into low whispers, like the soft summer breeze; and there were pleasant dreams in every cabin of the FIVE NATIONS on that blessed night.

[1] Page 17. [2] Page 374. [3] Page 22.

Miamies in the West,[1] and penetrated to the domains of the Catawbas[2] and Cherokees[3] in the South. They subjugated the Eries in 1655, and after a contest of twenty years, brought the Andastes into vassalage. They conquered the Miamies[4] and Ottawas[5] in 1657, and made incursions as far as the Roanoke and Cape Fear Rivers to the land of their kindred in dialect, the Tuscaroras, in 1701.[6] Thirty years afterward, having been joined by the Tuscaroras, and the name of the confederacy changed to that of the SIX NATIONS, they made war upon the Cherokees and Catawbas.[7] They were led on by Hi-o-ka-too, a Seneca chief. The Catawbas were almost annihilated by them, after a battle of two days. So determined were the FIVE NATIONS to subdue the southern tribes, that when, in 1744, they ceded a part of their lands to Virginia, they reserved a perpetual privilege of a war-path through the territory.

In the year 1712, the Tuscaroras having been signally defeated by the Carolinians,[8] came northward, and in 1714 joined the FIVE NATIONS. From that time the confederacy was known as the SIX NATIONS. They were generally the sure friends of the English and inveterate foes of the French.[9]

They were all friends of the British during the Revolution, except a part of the Oneidas, among whom the influence of the Rev. Samuel Kirkland[10] was

1 Page 17. 2 Page 26. 3 Page 27. 4 Page 17. 5 Page 17
6 Page 168. 7 Page 17. 8 Page 168. 9 Page 192.

10 Samuel Kirkland was one of the most laborious and self-sacrificing of the earlier missionaries, who labored among the tribes of the SIX NATIONS. He was born at Norwich, Connecticut, in December, 1741. He was educated at Dr. Wheelock's school, at Lebanon, where he prepared for that missionary work in which he labored forty years. His efforts were put forth chiefly among

very powerful, in favor of the Republicans. The Mohawks were the most active enemies of the Americans; and they were obliged to leave the State and take refuge in Canada at the close of the Revolution. The others were allowed to remain, and now [1856] mere fragments of that great confederation exist, and, in habits and character, they are radically changed. The confederacy was forever extinguished by the sale of the residue of the Seneca lands in 1838. In 1715, the confederacy numbered more than forty thousand souls; now [1856] they are probably less than four thousand, most of whom are upon lands beyond the Mississippi.[1]

CHAPTER IV.

THE CATAWBAS.

In that beautiful, hilly region, between the Yadkin and Catawba Rivers, on each side of the boundary line between North and South Carolina, dwelt the CATAWBA nation. They were south-westward of the Tuscaroras, and were generally on good terms with them. They were brave, but not warlike, and their conflicts were usually in defense of their own territory. They expelled the fugitive Shawnees in 1672,[2] but were overmatched and desolated by the warriors of the FIVE NATIONS[3] in 1701. They assisted the white people of South Carolina against the Tuscaroras and their confederates in 1712;[4] but when, three years afterward, the southern tribes, from the Neuse region to that of the St. Mary's, in Florida, and westward to the Alabama, seven thousand

---

the Oneidas; and, during the Revolution, he was active in restraining them from an alliance with the rest of the confederacy against the Patriots. He was exceedingly useful in treaty-making; for he had the entire confidence of the Indians. He died at Paris, in Oneida county, in February, 1808, in the 67th year of his age. See Lossing's "Eminent Americans" for a more elaborate sketch.

[1] The chief men of the FIVE NATIONS, known to the white people, are Garangula, who was distinguished toward the close of the seventeenth century for his wisdom and sagacity in council, and was of the Onondaga tribe. Logan, whose celebrated reply to a white messenger has been preserved by Mr. Jefferson, was of the Cayuga tribe. To the messenger he said: "I appeal to any white man to say if he ever entered Logan's cabin hungry, and he gave him no meat; if ever he came cold and naked and he clothed him not." Then speaking of the cruelty of the white people, who, in cold blood had murdered his family, he said: "They have murdered all the relations of Logan—not even sparing my women and children. This called on me for revenge; I have sought it. I have killed many. I have fully glutted my vengeance. For my country, I rejoice at the beams of peace. But do not harbor the thought that mine is the joy of fear. Logan never felt fear. He will not turn on his heel to save his life. Who is there to mourn for Logan? Not one!" Joseph Brant (Thayendanega), was the most celebrated of the Mohawk tribe; and Red Jacket (Sagoyewatha), was a very renowned Seneca, greatly distinguished for his eloquence. Cornplanter, who lived till past a century in age, was also a distinguished Seneca chief. Red Jacket was very intemperate toward the latter part of his life. On one occasion a lady inquired after his children. He had lost fourteen by consumption. Bowing his head, he said: "Red Jacket was once a great man, and in favor with the Great Spirit. He was a lofty pine among the smaller trees of the forest. But after years of glory, he degraded himself by drinking the fire-water of the white man. The Great Spirit has looked upon him in anger, and His lightning has stripped the pine of its branches!"

[2] Page 19.

[3] Page 23.

[4] Page 168.

strong, confederated in an attempt to exterminate the Carolinians,[1] the Catawbas were among them.

They were again the active allies of the Carolinians in 1760, when the Cherokees made war upon them,[2] and they remained true friends of the white people afterward. They joined the Americans during the Revolution, and have ever since experienced the fostering care of the State, in some degree.[3] Their chief village was upon the Catawba River, near the mouth of the Fishing Creek, in Yorkville district, South Carolina; and there the remnant of the nation, numbering less than a hundred souls, are now [1856] living upon a reservation, a few miles square. Their ancient language is almost extinct.

CHAPTER V.

THE CHERO'KEES.

Of all the Indian tribes, the Cherokees, who dwelt westward and adjoining the Tuscaroras[4] and Catawbas,[5] among the high hills and fertile valleys, have ever been the most susceptible to the influences of civilization. They have been properly called the mountaineers of the South. Their beautiful land extended from the Carolina Broad River on the east, to the Alabama on the west, including the whole of the upper portion of Georgia from the head waters of the Alatamaha, to those of the Tennessee. It is one of the most delightful regions of the United States.

These mountaineers were the determined foes of the Shawnees,[6] and after many conflicts, they finally drove them from the country south of the Ohio River. They joined with the Catawbas and the white people against the Tuscaroras in 1712,[7] but were members of the great confederation against the Carolinians in 1715,[8] which we shall consider hereafter.

The Five Nations and the Cherokees had bloody contests for a long time. A reconciliation was finally effected by the English about the year 1750, and the Cherokees became the allies of the peace-makers, against the French. They assisted in the capture of Fort Du Quesne in 1758,[9] but their irregularities, on their return along the border settlements of Virginia, gave the white people an apparent excuse for killing two or three warriors. Hatred was engendered, and the Cherokees soon afterward retaliated by spreading destruction

---

1 Page 170. 2 Page 204.

3 In 1822, a Catawba warrior made an eloquent appeal to the legislature of South Carolina for aid. "I pursued the deer for subsistence," he said, "but the deer are disappearing, and I must starve. God ordained me for the forests, and my ambition is the shade. But the strength of my arm decays, and my feet fail me in the chase. The hand that fought for your liberties is now open to you for relief." A pension was granted.

4 Page 25. 5 Page 204. 6 Page 19.
7 Page 168. 8 Page 170. 9 Page 186.

along the frontiers.[1] Hostilities continued a greater portion of three years, when peace was established in 1761, and no more trouble ensued.

During the Revolution the Cherokees adhered to the British; and for eight years afterward they continued to annoy the people of the upper country of the Carolinas. They were reconciled by treaty in 1791. They were friends of the United States in 1812, and assisted in the subjugation of the Creeks.[2] Civilization was rapidly elevating them from the condition of roving savages, to agriculturists and artisans, when their removal west of the Mississippi was required. They had established schools, a printing press, and other means for improvement and culture, when they were obliged to leave their farms and the graves of their fathers, for a new home in the wilderness.[3] They are now in a fertile country, watered by the Arkansas and its tributaries, and are in a prosperous condition. They now [1856] number about fourteen thousand souls.[4]

CHAPTER VI.

THE UCHEES.

In the pleasant country extending from the Savannah River, at Augusta, westward to Milledgeville, and along the banks of the Oconee and the head waters of the Ogeechee and Chattahooche, the Europeans found a remnant of the once powerful nation of the Uchees. Their language was exceedingly harsh, and totally unlike that of any other people on the continent. They claimed to be descendants of the most ancient inhabitants of the country, and took great pride in the fact; and they had no tradition of their ever occupying any other territory than the domain on which they were found. They, too, have been driven beyond the Mississippi by the pressure of civilization, and have become partially absorbed by the Creeks, with whom less than a thousand souls yet [1856] remain. They are, in fact, an extinct nation, and their language is almost forgotten.

---

[1] Page 204.

[2] Page 428.

[3] A native Cherokee, named by the white people, George Guess (Sequoyah), who was ignorant of every language but his own, seeing books in the missionary schools, and being told that the characters represented the words of the spoken English language, conceived the idea of forming a written language for his people. He first made a separate character for each word, but this made the whole matter too voluminous, and he formed a syllabic alphabet of eighty-five characters. It was soon ascertained that this was sufficient, even for the copious language of the Cherokees, and this syllabic alphabet was soon adopted, in the preparation of books for the missionary schools. In 1826, a newspaper, called the *Cherokee Phœnix*, printed in the new characters, was established. Many of the native Cherokees are now well educated, but the great body of the natives are in ignorance.

[4] Note 4, page 32.

CHAPTER VII.

THE NATCHEZ.

Of this once considerable nation, who inhabited the borders of the Mississippi, where a modern city now perpetuates their name, very little is known. When first discovered by the French, they occupied a territory about as large as that inhabited by the Uchees. It extended north-easterly from the Mississippi along the valley of the Pearl River, to the upper waters of the Chickasahaw. For a long time they were supposed to belong to the nation of Mobilian tribes, by whom they were surrounded, but their language proved them to be a distinct people. They were sun-worshippers; and from this circumstance, some had supposed that they had once been in intimate communication with the adorers of the great luminary in Central and South America. In many things they were much superior to their neighbors, and displayed signs of the refinement of a former more civilized condition. They became jealous of the French on their first appearance upon the Mississippi, and finally they conspired, with others, to drive the intruders from the country. The French fell upon, and almost annihilated the nation, in 1730. They never recovered from the shock, and after maintaining a feeble nationality for almost a century, they have become merged into the Creek confederacy. They now [1856] number less than three hundred souls, and their language, in its purity, is unknown.

CHAPTER VIII.

THE MOBILIAN TRIBES.

Like the Algonquins and Iroquois nations, the Mobilian was composed of a great number of tribes, speaking different dialects of the same language. Their territory was next in extent to that of the Algonquins.[1] It stretched along the Gulf of Mexico, from the Atlantic to the Mississippi, more than six hundred miles; up the Mississippi as far as the mouth of the Ohio; and along the Atlantic to Cape Fear. It comprised a greater portion of the present State of Georgia, the whole of Florida, Alabama, and Mississippi, and parts of South Carolina, Tennessee, and Kentucky. The nation was divided into three grand confederacies of tribes, namely, Muscogees or Creeks Choctaws, and Chickasaws.

---

[1] Page 17.

SOUTHERN INDIANS.

The Creek Confederacy extended from the Atlantic westward to the high lands which separate the waters of the Alabama and Tombigbee Rivers, including a great portion of the States of Alabama and Georgia, and the whole of Florida. Oglethorpe's first interviews[1] with the natives at Savannah, were with people of this confederacy.

The Yamassees, or Savannahs of Georgia and South Carolina, and the Seminoles of Florida, were of the Creek confederacy. The latter were strong and warlike. They were at the head of the Indian confederacy, to destroy the white people, in 1715.[2] When the general dispersion followed that abortive attempt, the Yamassees took refuge with the Spaniards of Florida. Small bands often annoyed the white frontier settlements of Georgia, but they were not engaged in general hostilities until the Revolution, when the whole Creek confederacy[3] took part with the British.

The most inveterate and treacherous enemy of the white people, have ever been the Seminoles. Bands of them often went out upon the war-path, with the Yamassees, to slay the pale-faces. They joined the British in 1812–14; and in 1817 they renewed hostilities.[4] They were subdued by General Jackson, and afterward remained comparatively quiet until 1835, when they again attacked the white settlements.[5] They were subjugated in 1842, after many lives and much treasure had been sacrificed.[6] A few of them yet [1856] remain in the everglades of Florida, but a greater portion of the tribe have gone west of the Mississippi, with the other members of the Creek confederacy. The Creeks proper now [1856] number about twenty-four thousand souls. The number of the whole confederacy is about thirty thousand. They occupy lands upon the Arkansas and its tributaries, and are among the most peaceable and order-loving of the banished tribes.

In the beautiful country bordering upon the Gulf of Mexico, and extending west of the Creeks to the Mississippi, lived the Choctaws. They were an agricultural people when the Europeans discovered them; and, attached to home and quiet pursuits, they have ever been a peaceful people. Their wars have always been on the defensive, and they never had public feuds with either their Spanish, French, or English neighbors. They, too, have been compelled to abandon their native country for the uncultivated wilderness west of Arkansas, between the Arkansas and Red Rivers. They now [1856] number about twenty-three thousand souls. They retain their peaceable character in their new homes.

The Chickasaw tribe inhabited the country along the Mississippi, from the borders of the Choctaw domain to the Ohio River, and eastward beyond the Tennessee to the lands of the Cherokees[7] and Shawnees.[8] This warlike people were the early friends of the English, and the most inveterate foes of the French,

---

[1] Page 102. [2] Page 170.
[3] This confederacy now [1856] consists of the Creeks proper, Seminoles, Natchez, Hichitties, and Alabamas. The Creeks, like many other tribes, claim to be the Original People.
[4] Page 448. [5] Page 466. [6] Page 468. [7] Page 27. [8] Page 19.

who had twice [1736–1740] invaded their country. They adhered to the British during the Revolution, but since that time they have held friendly relations with the Government of the United States. The remnant, about six thousand in number, are upon lands almost a hundred leagues westward of the Mississippi.

Thus, with almost chronological brevity, we have given an outline sketch of the history of the Aboriginal nations with whom the first European settlers in the United States became acquainted. They have now no legal habitation eastward of the Mississippi; and the fragments of those powerful tribes who once claimed sovereignty over twenty-four degrees of longitude and twenty degrees of latitude, are now [1856] compressed within a quadrangle of about nine degrees, between the Red and Missouri Rivers.[1] Whether the grave of the last of those great tribes shall be within their present domain, or in some valley among the crags of the Rocky Mountains, expediency will hereafter determine.

CHAPTER IX.

THE DAHCOTAH OR SIOUX TRIBES.

THE French were the earliest explorers of the regions of the Middle and Upper Mississippi, and they found a great number of tribes west of that river who spoke dialects of the same language. They occupied the vast domain from the Arkansas on the south, to the western tributary of Lake Winnipeg on the north, and westward to the eastern slopes of the Rocky Mountains. These have been classed into four grand divisions, namely, the WINNEBAGOES, who inhabited the country between Lake Michigan and the Mississippi, among the Algonquins;[2] the ASSINNIBOINS and SIOUX proper, the most northerly nation; the MINETAREE GROUP in the Minnesota Territory, and the SOUTHERN SIOUX, who dwelt in the country between the Arkansas and Platte Rivers, and whose hunting-ground extended to the Rocky Mountains.

The most uneasy of these tribes were the Winnebagoes, who often attacked the Sioux west of the Mississippi. They generally lived on friendly terms with the Algonquins, after their martial spirit was somewhat subdued by the Illinois, who, in 1640, almost exterminated them. They were enemies to the

[1] Mr. Bancroft [II., 253] after consulting the most reliable authorities on the subject, makes the following estimate of the entire Aboriginal population in 1650: Algonquins, 90,000; Eastern Sioux, less than 3,000; Iroquois, including their southern kindred, about 17,000; Catawbas, 3,000, Cherokees (now more numerous than ever), 12,000; Mobilian tribes, 50,000; Uchees, 1,000; Natchez, 4,000—in all, 180,000. These were the only nations and tribes then known. With the expansion of our territory westward and southward, we have embraced numerous Indian nations, some of them quite populous, until the number of the estimate above given has been more than doubled, according to the late census.

[2] Page 17.

United States during the second war with Great Britain,[1] and they confederated with the Sacs and Foxes in hostilities against the white people, under Black Hawk, in 1832.[2] The tribe, now [1856] less than four thousand strong, are seated upon the Mississippi, about eighty miles above St. Paul, the capital of Minnesota. Fear of the white people keeps them quiet.

In the cold, wet country of the North, the Assiniboins yet inhabit their native land. Having separated from the nation, they are called "rebels." Their neighbors, the Sioux proper, were first visited by the French in 1660, and have ever been regarded as the most fierce and warlike people on the continent. They also occupy their ancient domain, and are now [1856] about eighteen thousand strong.

Further westward are the Minetarees, Mandans, and Crows, who form the MINETAREE GROUP. They are classed with the Dahcotahs or Sioux, although the languages have only a slight affinity. The Minetarees and Mandans number about three thousand souls each. They cultivate the soil, and live in villages. The Crows number about fifteen hundred, and are wanderers and hunters. The Mandans are very light-colored. Some suppose them to be descendants of a colony from Wales, who, it is believed, came to America under Madoc, the son of a Welsh prince, in the twelfth century.[3]

There are eight in number of the SOUTHERN SIOUX tribes, namely, the Arkansas, Osages, Kansas, Iowas, Missouries, Otoes, Omahas, and Puncahs. They are cultivators and hunters. They live in villages a part of the year, and are abroad upon their hunting-grounds during the remainder. Of these tribes, the Osages are the most warlike and powerful. All of the Southern Sioux tribes are upon lands watered by the Missouri and the Platte, and their tributaries.

CHAPTER X.

THE EXTREME WESTERN TRIBES.

WITHIN a few years, our domain has been widely expanded, and in our newly-acquired possessions on the borders of Mexico and the Pacific coast, and the recently organized Territories in the interior of the continent, are numerous powerful and warlike tribes,[4] of whom little is known, and whose history

---

[1] Page 260. [2] Page 287.

[3] It is said that Madoc, son of Prince Owen Gwignedd, sailed from Wales, with ten ships and three hundred men, at about the year 1170, on an exploring voyage, and never returned. Many learned conjectures have been expressed, and among them the belief that the expedition reached the American continent, and became the progenitors of the Mandans, or White Indians, of our western plains.

[4] The whole number of Indians within the present limits of the United States, in 1853, is reported in the census to be a little more than 400,000. There are about 17,000 in the States eastward of the Mississippi, principally in New York, Michigan, and Wisconsin; the remainder, consisting of Cherokees, Choctaws, and Seminoles, being in North Carolina, Mississippi, and Florida. The

has no connection with that of the people of the United States, except the fact that they were original occupants of the soil, and that some of them, especially the California and Oregon Indians, yet [1856] dispute our right to sovereignty. Of these, the Comanches and Apaches of California are the most warlike. The Pawnees upon the Great Plains toward the Rocky Mountains are very numerous, but not so warlike; and the Utahs, among the Wasatch and neighboring ranges, are strong in numbers. Further northward and westward are the Blackfeet, Crow, Snake, Nezperces, and Flathead Indians, and smaller clans, with petty chiefs, whose domains stretch away toward the Knisteneaux and Esquimaux on the extreme north.

These tribes are rapidly fading in the light of modern civilization, and are destined to total annihilation. The scythe of human progress is steadily cutting its swathes over all their lands; and the time is not far distant when the foot-prints of the Indians will be no more known within the domain of our Republic. In future years, the dusky son of an exile, coming from the far-off borders of the Slave Lake, will be gazed at in the streets of a city at the mouth of the Yellow Stone, with as much wonder as the Oneida woman, with her blue cloth blanket and bead-work merchandize is now [1856] in the city of New York. So the Aboriginals of our land are passing away, and even now they may chant in sorrow:

"We, the rightful lords of yore,
Are the rightful lords no more;
Like the silver mist, we fail,
Like the red leaves on the gale—
Fail, like shadows, when the dawning
Waves the bright flag of the morning."

J. McLellan, Jr.

"I will weep for a season, in bitterness fed,
For my kindred are gone to the hills of the dead;
But they died not of hunger, or lingering decay—
The hand of the white man hath swept them away."

Henry Rowe Schoolcraft.

---

number in Minnesota and along the frontiers of the Western States and Texas (most of them emigrants from the country eastward of the Mississippi), is estimated at 110,000. Those on the Plains and among the Rocky Mountains, not within any organized Territory, at 63,000; in Texas, at 29,000; in New Mexico, at 45,000; in California, at 100,000; in Utah, at 12,000; in Oregon and Washington Territories, at 23,000. For more minute accounts of the Indians, see Heckewelder's "History of the Indian Nations;" Schoolcraft's "Algic Researches;" M'Kinney's "History of the Indian Tribes;" Drake's "Book of the Indians;" Catlin's "Letters and Notes."

COLUMBUS BEFORE THE COUNCIL OF SALAMANCA.

AMERIGO VESPUCCI.

SECOND PERIOD.

DISCOVERIES.

CHAPTER I.

SCANDINAVIAN VOYAGES AND DISCOVERIES.

ONE of the most interesting of the unsolved problems of history, is that which relates to the alleged discovery of America by mariners of northern Europe, almost five hundred years before Columbus left Palos, in Spain, to accomplish that great event. The tales and poetry of Iceland abound with intimations of such discoveries; and records of early voyages from Iceland to a continent southwestward of Greenland, have been found. These, and the results of recent investigations, appear to prove, by the strongest circumstantial evidence, that the New England[1] coast was visited, and that settlements thereon were attempted by Scandinavian navigators,[2] almost five centuries before the great Genoese undertook his first voyage in quest of a western passage to India.

NORTHMAN.

[1] The States of our Union eastward of New York are collectively called New England. P. 74.

[2] The ancients called the territory which contains modern Norway, Sweden, Denmark, Lapland, Iceland, Finland, etc., by the general name of Scandinavia.

The navigators of northern Europe were remarkable for their boldness and perseverance. They discovered Iceland in the year 860, and colonized it. In 890 they colonized Greenland, and planted colonies there also. There was traffic, friendly and lucrative, between the colonists of Iceland and Greenland, and the parent Norwegians and Danes, as early as the year 950, and no mariners were so adventurous as these Northmen. In the year 1002, according to an Icelandic chronicle, a Norwegian vessel, commanded by Captain Lief, sailed from Iceland for Greenland. A gale drove the voyagers to the coast of Labrador. They explored the shores southward to the region of a genial climate, where they found noble forests and abundance of grapes. This, it is supposed, was the vicinity of Boston. Other voyages to the new-found land were afterward made by the adventurous Scandinavians, and they appear to have extended their explorations as far as Rhode Island—perhaps as far south as Cape May.

NORMAN SHIP.

It is further asserted that settlements in that pleasant climate were attempted, and that the child of a Scandinavian mother was born upon the shore of Mount Hope Bay, in Rhode Island.[1] In the absence of actual charts and maps, to fix these localities of latitude and longitude, of course they must be subjects of conjecture only, for these explorers left no traces of their presence here, unless it shall be conceded that the round tower at Newport,[2] about the origin of which history and tradition are silent, was built by the Northmen.

TOWER AT NEWPORT.

The period of this alleged discovery was that of the dark ages, when ignorance brooded over Europe, like thick night. Information of these voyages seems not to have spread, and no records of intercourse with a western continent later than 1120, have been found. The great discovery, if made, was forgotten, or remembered only in dim traditionary tales of the exploits of the old "Sea-Kings"[3] of the North. For centuries afterward, America was an un-

[1] The old chronicle referred to says that Gudrida, wife of a Scandinavian navigator, gave birth to a child in America, to whom she gave the name of Snorre; and it is further asserted that Bertel Thorwalsden, the great Danish sculptor, was a descendant of this early white American. The records of these voyages were compiled by Bishop Thorlack, of Iceland, who was also a descendant of Snorre.

[2] This structure is of unhewn stone, laid in mortar made of the gravel of the soil around, and oyster-shell lime. It is a cylinder resting upon eight round columns, twenty-three feet in diameter, and twenty-four feet in height It was originally covered with stucco. It seems to have stood there when the white people first visited Rhode Island, and the Narraganset Indians, it is asserted, had no tradition of its origin. There can be little doubt, all things considered, of its having been constructed by those northern navigators, who made attempts at settlement in that vicinity.

[3] This name was given to bold adventurers of Norway, Sweden, and Denmark, who rebelled against Gorm the Old of Norway, and Harold Fairhair of Denmark, their conquerors, forsook their country, settled upon the islands of the North Sea, and Greenland, and from thence went forth upon piratical expeditions, even as far south as the pleasant coasts of France. They trafficked, as well as plundered; and finally sweeping over Denmark and Germany, obtained possession of some

known region. It had no place upon maps, unless as an imaginary island without a name, nor in the most acute geographical theories of the learned. When Columbus conceived the grand idea of reaching Asia by sailing westward, no whisper of those Scandinavian voyages was heard in Europe.

CHAPTER II.

SPANISH VOYAGES AND DISCOVERIES.

THE first half of the fifteenth century was distinguished for great commercial activity. Sluggish Europe was just awaking from its slumber of centuries, and maritime discoveries were prosecuted with untiring zeal by the people inhabiting the great south-western peninsula covered by Spain, Portugal, and France. The incentives to make these discoveries grew out of the political condition of Europe, and the promises of great commercial advantages. The rich commerce of the East centered in Rome, when that empire overshadowed the known world. When it fell into fragments, the Italian cities continued their monopoly of the rich trade of the Indies. Provinces which had arisen into independent kingdoms, became jealous of these cities, so rapidly outstripping them in power and opulence; and Castile and Portugal, in particular, engaged in efforts to open a direct trade with the East. The ocean was the only highway for such commerce, toward which the rivals could look with a hope of success. The errors of geographical science interposed great obstacles. Popular belief pictured an impassable region of fire beyond Cape Bajador, on the coast of Africa; but bold navigators, under the auspices of Prince Henry of Portugal, soon penetrated that dreaded latitude, crossed the torrid zone, and, going around the southern extremity of Africa, opened a pathway to the East, through the Indian Ocean.

COLUMBUS.

The Portuguese court at Lisbon soon became a point of great attraction to the learned and adventurous. Among others came Christopher Columbus, the son of a wool-carder of Genoa, a mariner of great experience and considerable repute, and then in the prime of life. In person he was tall and commanding, and, in manners, exceedingly winning and graceful, for one unaccustomed to the polish of courts, or the higher orders in society. The rudiments of geometry, which he had learned in the

of the best portions of Gaul. They finally invaded the British Islands, and placed Canute upon the throne of Alfred. It was among these people that chivalry, as an institution, originated; and back to those "Sea-Kings" we may look for the hardiest elements of progress among the people of the United States.

university of Pavia, had been for years working out a magnificent theory in his mind, and he came to Lisbon to seek an opportunity to test its truth.

Fortune appeared to smile beneficently upon Columbus, during his early residence in Lisbon. He soon loved and married the daughter of Palestrello, a deceased navigator of eminence, and he became possessed of nautical papers of great value. They poured new light upon his mind. His convictions respecting the rotundity of the earth, and the necessity of a continent in the Atlantic Ocean, to balance the land in the eastern hemisphere; or at least a nearer approach of eastern Asia to the shores of western Europe, than geographical science had yet revealed, assumed the character of demonstrated realities. He was disposed to credit the narratives of Plato and other ancient writers, respecting the existence of a continent beyond the glorious, but long-lost, island of Atlantis, in the waste of waters westward of Europe. He was convinced that Asia could be reached much sooner by sailing westward, than by going around the Cape of Good Hope.[1] He based his whole theory upon the fundamental belief that the earth was a terraqueous globe, which might be traveled round from east to west, and that men stood foot to foot at opposite points. This, it should be remembered, was seventy years before Copernicus announced his theory of the form and motion of the planets [1543], and one hundred and sixty years [1633] before Galileo was compelled, before the court of the Inquisition at Rome, to renounce his belief in the diurnal revolution of the earth.

A deep religious sentiment imbued the whole being of Columbus, and he became strongly impressed with the idea that there were people beyond the waste of waters westward, unto whom he was commissioned by heaven to carry the Gospel.[2] With the lofty aspirations which his theory and his faith gave him, he prosecuted his plans with great ardor. He made a voyage to Iceland, and sailed a hundred leagues beyond, to the ice-fields of the polar circle. He probably heard, there, vague traditions of early voyages to a western continent,[3] which gave strength to his own convictions; and on his return, he laid his plans first before his countrymen, the Genoese (who rejected them), and then before the monarchs of England[4] and Portugal.

The Portuguese monarch appeared to comprehend the grand idea of Columbus, but it was too lofty for the conceptions of his council and the pedantic wise men of Lisbon. For a long time Columbus was annoyed by delays on the part of those to whose judgment the king deferred; and attempts were meanly and clandestinely made to get from Columbus the information which he possessed. While awaiting a decision, his wife died. The last link that bound him to Portugal was broken, and, taking his little son Diego by the hand, he

---

1 This point was first discovered by Diaz, a Portuguese navigator, who named it Stormy Cape. But King John, believing it to be that remote extremity of Africa so long sought, named it *Cape of Good Hope*. Vasco de Gama passed it in 1497, and made his way to the East Indies beyond.

2 His name was suggestive of a mission. Christo or Christ, and Colombo, a pigeon—carrier-pigeon. By this combination of significant words in his name, he believed himself to be a *Christ*, or *Gospel-bearer*, to the heathen, and he often signed his name Christo-ferens, or Christ-bearer.

3 Page 34.

4 Page 46.

departed on foot to lay his proposition before Ferdinand and Isabella,[1] the monarchs of Spain—occupants of the united thrones of Arragon and Castile.

Very poor, and greatly dispirited, Columbus arrived at the gate of the monastery of Rabida, near the little port from whence he afterward sailed, and begged food and shelter for himself and child. The good Father Marchena received him kindly, entered warmly into his plans, and was of essential service to him afterward. Through him Columbus obtained access to the court; but the war with the Moors, then raging, delayed an opportunity for an audience with the monarchs for a long time. Yet he was not idle. He employed himself in the alternate pursuits of science, and engagements in some of the military campaigns. He was continually treated with great deference by the court and nobility, and at length his importunities were heeded. A council of the learned men of the nation was convened at Salamanca, to consider his plans and propositions.[2] The majority pronounced his scheme vain and impracticable, and unworthy of the support of the government. But a minority of the council, wiser than the rest, did not acquiesce in this decision, and, with Cardinal Mendoza and other officers of government, they encouraged the navigator by promises of their continual support. But he became disgusted by procrastination, and abandoning the hope of royal aid, he applied to two wealthy dukes for assistance. They refused, and he left with a determination to lay his plans before the King of France.

ISABELLA.

Columbus had been encouraged by Father Marchena (who had been Isabella's confessor),[3] and through his intercession, the navigator was recalled before he had entered France. He sought and obtained a personal interview with the queen. To her he revealed all his plans; told her of the immense treasures that lay hidden in that far distant India[4] which might be easily reached by a shorter way, and pleaded eloquently for aid in his pious design of carrying the Gospel to the heathen of unknown lands. The last appeal aroused the religious zeal of Isabella, and with the spirit of the Crusaders,[5] she dismissed Columbus with the assurance

1 Isabella was a sister of the profligate Henry the Fourth of Castile and Leon. She was a pious, virtuous, and high-minded woman, then almost a phenomenon in courts. She was of middle size, and well formed, with a fair complexion, auburn hair, and clear, blue eyes.

2 See the picture at the head of this chapter. The Council was composed of the professors of the university, various dignitaries of the Church, and learned friars. They were nearly all prejudiced against the poor navigator, and he soon discovered that ignorance and bigotry would defeat his purposes.

3 All Roman Catholics are obliged to confess their sins to a priest. Rich and titled persons often had a priest confessor for themselves and their families exclusively.

4 Marco Polo and other travelers had related wonderful stories of the beauty and wealth of a country beyond the limits of geographical knowledge, and had thus inflamed the avarice and ambition of the rich and powerful. The country was called *Zipangi*, and also *Cathay*. It included China and adjacent islands.

5 About 700 years ago, the Christian powers of Europe fitted out expeditions to conquer Palestine, with the avowed object of rescuing the sepulcher of Jesus, at Jerusalem, from the hands of the Turks. These were called *crusades—holy wars*. The lives of two millions of people were lost in them.

that he should have her aid in fitting out an exploring expedition, even if it should require the pawning of her crown jewels to obtain the money. And Isabella was faithful to her promise. She fitted out two *caravels* (light coasting ships), and Columbus, by the aid of friends, equipped a third and larger one. With this little fleet, bearing one hundred and twenty persons, he left Palos, on the Tinto River, in Andalusia, on Friday, the 3d of August, 1492, to explore the stormy Atlantic.[1]

Columbus started on that perilous voyage without a reliable chart for his guidance, and no director in his course but the sun and stars, and the imperfect mariner's compass, then used only by a few in navigating the pleasant seas of the Old World. After various delays at the Canary Islands, they left them in the dim distance behind, on Sunday, the 9th of September. The broad Atlantic, mysterious and unknown, was before them. A voyage of great trial for the navigator was now fairly entered upon. His theory taught him to believe that he would reach Asia in the course of a few days. But weeks wore away; the needle[2] became unfaithful; alarm and discontent prevailed, and several times his followers were on the point of compelling him to turn back.

One pleasant evening (the 11th of October), the perfumes of flowers came upon the night breeze, as tokens of approach to land. The vesper hymn to the Virgin was sung, and Columbus, after recounting the blessings of God thus far manifested in the voyage, assured the crews that he confidently expected to see land in the morning. Yet they hesitated to believe, for twice before they had been mocked by other indications of land being near.[3] On the high poop of his vessel the great navigator sat watching until midnight, when he saw the glimmer of moving lights upon the verge of the horizon. He called others to confirm his vision, for he was fearful of mistake. They, too, perceived blazing torches, and at dawn the next morning their delighted eyes saw green forests stretching along the horizon; and as they approached, they were greeted by the songs of birds and the murmur of human voices.

THE FLEET OF COLUMBUS.

1 Columbus was appointed high-admiral of all seas which he might discover, with the attendant honors. Also viceroy of all lands discovered. He was to have one-tenth of all profits of the first voyage, and by contributing an eighth of the expense of future voyages, was to have an eighth of all the profits. Although Isabella paid the whole expense, the contract was signed, also, by her husband.

2 Needle, or pointer, of the mariner's compass. This instrument was first known in Europe, at Amalfi, about 1302. The Chinese claim to have possessed a knowledge of it more than 1100 years before the birth of Christ. The needle was supposed to point toward the north star at all times. There is a continual variation from this line, now easily calculated, but unknown until discovered by Columbus. It perplexed, but did not dismay him.

3 They had seen birds, but they proved to be the petrel, an ocean fowl. Bits of wood and sea-weeds had also been seen. These had undoubtedly been seen on the outer verge of the Gulf Stream, north-east of the Bahamas, where, according to Lieutenant Maury [Physical Geography of the Sea], there may always be found a drift of sea-weed, and sometimes objects that have floated from the land.

BANNER OF THE EXPEDITION.

Arrayed in scarlet, and bearing his sword in one hand, and the banner of the expedition in the other, Columbus landed, with his followers, and in the midst of the gorgeous scenery and the incense of myriads of flowers, they all knelt down and chaunted a hymn of thanksgiving to God. The natives had gathered in wonder and awe, in the grove near by, regarding the Europeans as children of their great deity, the Sun.[1] Little did they comprehend the fatal significance to them, of the act of Columbus, when, rising from the ground, he displayed the royal standard, drew his sword, set up a rude cross upon the spot where he landed, and took formal possession of the beautiful country in the name of Ferdinand and Isabella.[2] The land first discovered by Columbus was one of the Bahamas, called by the natives Guanahama, but since named by the English, Cat Island. The navigator named it San Salvador (Holy Saviour); and believing it to be near the coast of further India, he called the natives Indians. This name was afterward applied to all the natives of the adjacent continent,[3] and is still retained.

The triumph of Columbus was now complete. After spending some time in examining the island, becoming acquainted with the simple habits of the natives, and unsuccessfully searching for "the gold, and pearls, and spices of Zipangi,"[4] he sailed southward, and discovered several other small islands. He finally discovered Cuba and St. Domingo, where he was told of immense gold-bearing regions in the interior. Impressed with the belief that he had discovered the *Ophir* of the ancients, he returned to Spain, where he arrived in March, 1493. He was received with great honors,[5] but considerations of State policy induced the Spanish government to conceal the importance of his discovery from other nations. This policy, and the jealousy which the sudden elevation of a foreigner inspired in the Spaniards, deprived him of the honor of having the New World called by his name. Americus Vespucius,[6] a Florentine, unfairly won the prize. In company with Ojeda, a companion of Colum-

---

[1] Almost all the natives of the torrid zone of America worshiped the sun as the chief visible deity. The great temples of the sun in Mexico and Peru were among the most magnificent structures of the Americans, when Europeans came.

[2] It was a common practice then, as now, for the discoverer of new lands to erect some monument, and to proclaim the title of his sovereign to the territories so discovered. The banner of the expedition, borne on shore by Columbus, was a white one, with a green cross. Over the initials F. and Y. (Ferdinand and Ysabella) were golden mural crowns.

[3] Chapter I, page 9.

[4] Note 4, page 38.

[5] Columbus carried back with him several of the natives, and a variety of the animals, birds, and plants of the New World. They excited the greatest astonishment. His journey from Palos to Barcelona, to meet the sovereigns, was like the march of a king. His reception was still more magnificent. The throne of the monarch was placed in a public square, and the great of the kingdom were there to do homage to the navigator. The highest honors were bestowed upon Columbus; and the sovereigns granted him a coat of arms bearing royal devices, and the motto, "To Castile and Leon Columbus gave a new world."

[6] See the protrait of Vespucius at the head of this Chapter. The Italians spell his name Amerigo Vespucci [Am-e-ree-go Ves-pute-se]. He died while in the service of the king of Spain, in 1514. He had made several voyages to South America, and explored the eastern coast as far southward as the harbor of Rio Janeiro.

bus during his first voyage, Americus visited the West Indies, and discovered and explored the eastern coast of South America, north of the Oronoco, in 1499. In 1504, he published a glowing account of the lands he had visited,[1] and that being the first formal announcement to the world of the great discovery, and as he claimed to have first set foot upon the *Continent* of the West, it was called AMERICA, in honor of the Florentine. This claim was not founded on truth, for Columbus had anticipated him; and two years earlier, Cabot, in command of an expedition from England, discovered Labrador, Newfoundland, and portions of the New England coast.

Columbus made three other voyages to the West Indies,[2] established settlements, and in August, 1498, he discovered the continent at the mouth of the Oronoco. This, too, he supposed to be an island near the coast of Asia, and he lived and died in ignorance of the real grandeur of his discoveries. Before departing on his third voyage, he was appointed Viceroy and High Admiral of the New World. During his absence, jealous and unscrupulous men poisoned the minds of the king and queen with false statements concerning the ambitious designs of Columbus, and he was sent back to Spain in chains. The navigator was guilty of serious wrongs, but not against his sovereign. He made slaves of the natives, and this offended the conscientious Isabella. But she was soon undeceived concerning his alleged political crimes, and he was allowed to depart on a fourth voyage. When he returned, the queen was dead, his enemies were in power, and he who had shed such luster upon the Spanish name, and added a new hemisphere to the Spanish realm, was allowed to sink into the grave in obscurity and neglect. He died at Valladolid on the 20th of May, 1506. His body was buried in a convent, from whence it was afterward carried to St. Domingo, and subsequently to Havana, in Cuba, where it now remains.

It was an unlucky hour for the nations of the New World when the eyes of Europeans were first opened upon it. The larger islands of the West India group were soon colonized by the Spaniards; and the peaceful, friendly, gentle, and happy natives, were speedily reduced to slavery. Their Paradise was made a Pandemonium for them. Bending beneath the weight of Spanish cruelty and wrong, they soon sunk into degradation. The women were compelled to intermarry with their oppressors, and from this union came many of the present race of Creoles, who form the numerical strength of Cuba and other West India Islands.

The wonderful stories of gold-bearing regions, told by the natives, and exaggerated by the adventurers, inflamed the avarice and cupidity of the Spaniards, and exploring voyages from Cuba, St. Domingo, and Porto Rico, were undertaken. The eastern coast of Yucatan was discovered in 1506; and in 1510, Vasco Nunez de Balboa, with a colony, settled upon the Isthmus

---

[1] First in a letter to Lorenzo de Medici, and then [1507] in a volume, dedicated to the Duke of Lorraine. These publications revealed what the Spanish Government wished to conceal. Note 4, page 47.

[2] In his second voyage [1493], Columbus took with him several horses, a bull, and some cows. These were the first animals of the kind taken from Europe to America.

of Darien. This was the first colony planted on the continent of America. Crossing the Isthmus in search of gold in 1513, Balboa saw the Pacific Ocean in a southerly direction from the top of a high mountain, and he called it the "South Sea." In full costume, and bearing the Spanish flag, he entered its waters and took possession of the "seas, lands," etc., "of the South," in the name of his sovereign.

BALBOA.[1]

In the year 1512 Florida was discovered by Juan Ponce de Leon, an old visionary, who had been governor of Porto Rico. With three ships he sailed for the Bahamas in search of a fountain which unlettered natives and wise men of Spain believed to exist there, and whose waters possessed the quality of restoring old age to the bloom of youth, and of making the recipient immortal.

It was on Easter Sunday,[2] March 27, 1512, the Pasquas de Flores[3] of the Spaniards, when the adventurer approached the shores of the great southern peninsula of the United States and landed near the site of St. Augustine.[4] The forests and the green banks were laden with flowers; and when, soon after landing, Ponce de Leon took possession of the country in the name of his sovereign, this fact and the holy day were regarded, and he called the beautiful domain, FLORIDA. He continued his searches for the Fountain of Youth all along the coast of the newly-discovered country, and among the Tortugas (Tortoise) Islands, a hundred miles from its southern cape, but without success; and he returned to Porto Rico, an older if not a wiser man. He soon afterward went to Spain, where he remained several years.

While Ponce de Leon was absent in Europe, some wealthy owners of plantations and mines in St. Domingo, sent Lucas Vasquez d'Ayllon, one of their number, with two vessels, to seize natives of the Bermudas, and bring them home for laborers. It was an unholy mission, and God's displeasure was made manifest. A storm drove the voyagers into St. Helen's Sound, on the coast of South Carolina, and after much tribulation, they anchored [1520] at the mouth of the Combahee River. The natives were kind and generous; and, judging their visitors by their own simple standard of honor, they unsuspectingly went upon the ship in crowds, to gratify their curiosity. While below, the hatches were closed, the sails were immediately spread, and those free children of the forest were borne away to work as bond-slaves in the mines of St. Domingo. But the perpetrators of the outrage did not accomplish their designs. One of the vessels was destroyed by a storm; and almost every prisoner in the other refused to take food, and died. The fruit of this perfidy was a feeling of hostility to white people, which spread throughout the whole of the Mobilian tribes,[5] and was a source of much trouble afterward.

---

1 This little picture gives a correct representation of those armed Spaniards who attempted conquests in the New World. Balboa's fellow-adventurers became jealous of his fame, and on their accusations he was put to death by the Governor of Darien, in 1517.

2 The day in which is commemorated in the Christian Church the resurrection of Jesus Christ.

3 Feast of flowers. 4 Page 51. 5 Chapter VIII., page 29.

Ponce de Leon returned to the West Indies soon after D'Ayllon's voyage, bearing the commission of Governor of Florida, with instructions to plant settlements there. In his attempts to do so, the angry natives, who had heard of the treachery of the Spaniards, attacked him furiously. He was mortally wounded, and almost all of his followers were killed. D'Ayllon was then appointed governor of the country which he had discovered and named Chicora. He went thither to conquer it, and was received with apparent friendship by the natives on the banks of the Combahee,[1] near the spot where his great crime of man-stealing had been perpetrated. Many of his men were induced to visit a village in the interior, when the natives practiced the lesson of treachery which D'Ayllon had taught them, and massacred the whole party. The commander himself was attacked upon his own ship, and it was with difficulty that he escaped. He died of his wounds at St. Domingo.

Another important discovery was made in 1517, by Francisco Fernandez de Cordova, who commanded an expedition from Cuba: the rich and populous domain of Mexico was revealed to the avaricious Spaniards. Cordova's report of a people half civilized, and possessing treasures in cities, awakened the keenest cupidity of his countrymen; and the following year Velasquez, the governor of Cuba, sent another expedition to Mexico, under Juan de Grijalva. That captain returned with much treasure, obtained by trafficking with the Mexicans. The avarice, cupidity, and ambition of Velasquez were powerfully aroused, and he determined to conquer the Mexicans, and possess himself of their sources of wealth. An expedition, consisting of eleven vessels, and more than six hundred armed men, was placed under the command of Fernando Cortez, a brave but treacherous and cruel leader. He landed first at Tobasco, and then at San Juan de Ulloa,[2] near Vera Cruz [April 12, 1519], where he received a friendly deputation from Montezuma, the emperor of the nation.[3] By falsehood and duplicity, Cortez and his armed companions were allowed to march to Mexico, the capital. By stratagem and boldness, and the aid of native tribes who were hostile to the Mexican dynasty, Cortez[4] succeeded, after many bloody contests during almost two years, in subduing the people. The city of Mexico surrendered to him on the 23d of August, 1521, and the vast and populous empire of Montezuma became a Spanish province.

Florida continued to command the attention of the Spaniards, in whose minds floated magnificent dreams of immense wealth in cities and mines within its deep forests; and seven years after the conquest of Mexico [1528], Pamphilo

---

[1] D'Ayllon named this river, Jordan, for he regarded the country as the new Land of Promise.

[2] Pronounced San-whahn-da-Ooloo-ah.

[3] The Mexicans at that time were making rapid advances in the march of civilization. They were acquainted with many of the useful arts of enlightened nations, and appear to have been as far advanced in science, law, religion, and domestic and public social organization, as were the Romans at the close of the Republic.

[4] Born at Medellon, in Estramadura, Spain, in 1485. He went to St. Domingo in 1504, and in 1511 accompanied Velasquez to Cuba. He committed many horrid crimes in Mexico. Yet he had the good fortune, unlike the more noble Columbus, to retain the favor of the Spanish monarch until his death. When, on his return to Spain, he urged an audience with the emperor, and was asked who he was, the bold adventurer replied, "I am the man who has given you more provinces than your father left you towns." He died in Estramadura, in 1554, at the age of 69 years.

de Narvaez having been appointed governor of that region, went from Cuba, with three hundred men,[1] to conquer it. Hoping to find a wealthy empire, like Mexico, he penetrated the unknown interior as far as the southern borders of Georgia. Instead of cities filled with treasures, he found villages of huts, and the monarch of the country living in a wigwam.[2] Disappointed, and continually annoyed by hostile savages, who had heard of the treachery at the Combahee,[3] he turned southward, and reaching the shores of Apallachee Bay, near St. Marks, he constructed rude boats and embarked for Cuba. The commander and most of his followers perished; only four escaped, and these wandered from tribe to tribe for several years before reaching a Spanish settlement in Mexico. Yet the misfortunes of Narvaez did not suppress the spirit of adventure, and Florida (the name then applied to all North America) was still regarded by the Spaniards as the new Land of Promise. All believed that in the vast interior were mines as rich, and people as wealthy as those of Mexico and Yucatan. Among the most sanguine of the possessors of such an opinion, was Ferdinand de Soto, a brave and wealthy cavalier, who had gained riches and military honors, with Pizarro, in Peru.[4] He obtained permission of the Spanish emperor to conquer Florida at his own expense, and for that purpose, was appointed governor of Cuba, and also of Florida. With ten vessels and six hundred men, all clad in armor, he sailed for the New World early in 1539. Leaving his wife to govern Cuba, he proceeded to Florida, and on the 10th of June landed on the shores of Tampa Bay. He then sent most of his vessels back, and made his way, among hostile savages, toward the interior of the fancied land of gold.[5] He wintered on the banks of the Flint River, in Georgia, and in the spring crossed the Appallachian Mountains, and penetrated the beautiful country of the Cherokees.[6]

DE SOTO.

This, all things considered, was one of the most remarkable expeditions on record. For several months, De Soto and his followers wandered over the hills and valleys of Alabama, in vain searches for treasure, fighting the fierce Mobilian tribes,[7] and becoming continually diminished in number by battle and disease. They passed the winter of 1541 on the banks of the Yazoo River, in the land of the Chickasaws.[8] In May of that year, they discovered and crossed the Mississippi River, probably not far below Memphis; and there, in the presence of almost twenty thousand Indians, De Soto erected a cross made of a huge pine tree, and around it imposing religious ceremonies were performed.

[1] They took with them about forty horses, the first ever landed upon the soil of the present United States. These all perished by starvation, or the weapons of the Indians.

[2] Page 13.

[3] Page 42.

[4] Pizarro was a follower of Balboa. He discovered Peru in 1524, and in connection with Almagro and Lucque, he conquered it in 1532, after much bloodshed. He was born, out of wedlock, in Estramadura, Spain, in 1475. He could neither read nor write, but seemed eminently fitted for the field of effort in which he was engaged. He quarreled with Almagro, civil war ensued, and he was murdered at Lima, in Peru, in 1541.

[5] De Soto had a large number of horses. He also landed some swine. These rapidly increased in the forests. They were the first of their species seen in America.

[6] Page 27.

[7] Chapter VIII., p. 29.

[8] Page 30.

To De Soto belongs the honor of first discovering that mighty river of our wide continent. After resting two days, the adventurers went up the western shore of the Mississippi as far as New Madrid. The ensuing summer and winter were spent by them in the wilderness watered by the Arkansas and its tributaries, and in the spring of 1542 they returned to the Mississippi, at the mouth of the Wachita, where De Soto sickened and died, after appointing his successor.[1] In these painful and perilous journeyings, they had marched full three thousand miles.

The death of their leader was a terrible blow to the followers of De Soto. They were now reduced to half their original number; and, abandoning all hopes of finding gold, or a wealthy people, they sought for Spanish settlements in Mexico. For many months they wandered over the prairies, and among the tributary streams of the Red River, as far as the land of the Comanches,[2] when impassable mountain ranges compelled them to retrace their steps to the Mississippi. At a little below Natchez they remained until the following July [1543], engaged in constructing several large boats, in which they embarked. Reaching the Gulf of Mexico, they crept cautiously along its coast; and, on the 20th of September, the little remnant of De Soto's proud army, half naked and starving, arrived at a Spanish settlement near the mouth of the Panuco, thirty miles north of Tampico. This was the last attempt of the Spanish cotemporaries of Columbus to explore, or to make settlements within the present territory of the United States, previous to the appearance of the English[3] in the same field. They were impelled by no higher motive than the acquisition of gold, and treachery and violence were the instruments employed to obtain it. They were not worthy to possess the magnificent country which they coveted only for its supposed wealth in precious metals; and it was reserved for others, who came afterward, with loftier aims, better hearts, and stronger hands, to cultivate the soil, and to establish an empire founded upon truth and justice. The Spaniards *did* finally become possessors of the southern portion of the Continent; and to this day the curse of moral, religious, and political despotism rests upon those regions.

CHAPTER III.

ENGLISH AND FRENCH DISCOVERIES.

WITH all its zealous vigilance, the Spanish court could not conceal the fact that a New World had been discovered,[4] and over Continental Europe and the

[1] De Soto's followers sunk the body of their leader deep in the Mississippi, so that the Indians should not find it.

[2] Page 33.

[3] Page 46. While De Soto was engaged in this expedition, another, no less adventurous, was undertaken by Coronada, at the command of Mendoza, Viceroy of Mexico. He took with him, from the south-eastern shore of the Gulf of California, three hundred and fifty Spaniards, and eight hundred Indians. He penetrated the country to the head waters of the Rio del Norte, and onward into the great interior desert, as far as the fortieth degree of north latitude. It was a perilous, but fruitless expedition.

[4] Page 40.

British Isles, were spread the most extravagant tales of gold-bearing regions beyond the Atlantic Ocean. By means of a papal *bull*,[1] Portugal and Spain vainly attempted to secure to themselves a monopoly of oceanic navigation. But in all maritime countries, cupidity and curiosity urged men to brave both the perils of the sea and the thunders of the Vatican, in search of the western paradise and the regions of gold. Monarchs and wealthy subjects projected new expeditions. Among those whose zeal in the cause of maritime discovery was newly awakened, was Henry the Seventh of England, who had turned a deaf ear to the appeals of Columbus before his great first voyage.[2]

SEBASTIAN CABOT.

The town of Bristol, in the west of England, was then one of the most important sea-ports in the realm; and among its adventurous mariners who had penetrated the polar waters, probably as far as Greenland, was Sebastian Cabot, son of a wealthy Venetian merchant of Bristol, whose father sought the aid of the king in making a voyage of discovery. Willing to secure a portion of the prize he had lost, Henry readily yielded to the solicitations of Cabot, and gave him and his sons a commission of discovery, dated March 16, 1496, which was similar, in some respects, to that which Columbus had received from Ferdinand and Isabella;[3] but unlike his Spanish cotemporaries, the English monarch did not bear the expenses of the voyage. The navigators were permitted to go, at their own expense, "to search for islands or regions inhabited by infidels, and hitherto unknown to Christendom," and take possession of them in the name of the King of England. They were to enjoy the sole right of trading thither—paying to the King, "in lieu of all customs and imposts," a fifth of all net profits, and the same proportion of the products of all mines.

According to recent discoveries made in searching the ancient records of England, it appears to be doubtful whether the elder Cabot, who was a merchant and a scientific man, ever voyaged to America. It is certain, however, that his son, Sebastian, accompanied, and, doubtless, commanded, the first expedition, which consisted of two vessels freighted by his father and others of Bristol and of London, and which sailed from the former port in May, 1497. They steered north-westerly until they encountered immense fields of ice westward of Cape Farewell, when they turned to the south-west, and on the 3d of July, of that year, discovered the rugged coast of Labrador. Passing Cape Charles, they saw Newfoundland; and, after touching at several points, probably as far southward as the coast of Maine, they hastened to England to announce the fact that they had first discovered a great western continent.

---

[1] This is the name of special edicts issued by the Pope of Rome. They are written on parchment, and have a great seal attached, made of wax, lead, silver, or gold. The name is derived from the seal, *bulla*. On one side, are the heads of Peter and Paul, and on the other, the name of the Pope and the year of his pontificate. The seal of the celebrated *golden bull* of the Emperor Charles IV., was made of gold. That bull became the fundamental law of the German Empire, at the Diet of Nuremburg, A. D. 1536.

[2] Page 37.

[3] Note 1, page 39.

The skill and energy of young Cabot secured the confidence of his father and friends in his ability to command successfully; and the following year, although he was only twenty-one years of age, he was placed in charge of another expedition, fitted out by his family and some Bristol merchants, for the purpose of traffic, and of discovering a north-west passage to India, a desire for which had now taken hold upon the minds of the commercial world. Ice in the polar seas presented an impassable barrier, and he was compelled to go southward. He explored the coast from the frozen regions of Labrador to the sunny land of the Carolinas. Nineteen years afterward [1517] he navigated the northern waters, as far as the entrance to Hudson's Bay; and nine years later [1526], while in the service of the monarch of Spain,[1] he explored the coast of Brazil, discovered and named the great *Rio de la Plata*, and penetrated the southern continent, in boats, upon the bosom of that river, almost four hundred miles. To the Cabots, father and son, belong the imperishable honor of first discovering the coast of the United States, through at least ten degrees of latitude. Italy may claim the glory of having given birth to the two great discoverers, Columbus and Americus Vespucius, whose name our continent now bears; while Sebastian Cabot drew his first breath in England.[2]

The immense numbers and commercial importance of the cod fishes in the vicinity of Newfoundland, were first discovered and made known by the Cabots; and within five or six years after their first voyages, many fishermen went thither from England, Brittany, and Normandy, for those treasures of the deep. Every French vessel that went to America, was on a commercial errand only, until 1523, when Francis the first fitted out four ships, for the purpose of exploring the coasts of the New World. He gave the command to John Verrazani, an eminent Florentine navigator. Verrazani sailed in December, 1523, but a tempest disabled three of his ships, and he was compelled to go with only one. He proceeded due west from the Madeiras on the 27th of January, 1524, and first touched the American Continent, in March following, near the mouth of the Cape Fear River, in North Carolina. After seeking a good harbor for fifty leagues further south, he sailed northward, and

VERRAZANI.

1 Sebastian Cabot was born at Bristol, in 1467. He was invested with the honorable title of Chief Pilot of both England and Spain: and to him England is indebted for her first maritime connection with Russia, by the establishment of the Russian Trading Company, of which he was appointed governor for life. He published a map of the world, and also an account of his southern voyages. He died in 1557, at the age of 90 years.

2 King John of Portugal, like Henry of England, had refused to aid Columbus, and lost the great prize. After the return of the navigator, he felt a desire to fit out an expedition for discoveries in the New World, but the Pope having given to Spain the whole region westward, beyond an imaginary line three hundred leagues west from the Azores, he dared not interfere with the Spanish mariners. But when the northern voyages of the Cabots became known, King John dispatched an expedition in that direction, under Gasper Cortoreal, toward the close of the year 1500, for the ostensible purpose of seeking a north-west passage to India. Cortoreal coasted along the shores of Labrador several hundred miles, and then freighting his ship with fifty natives whom he had caught, he returned to Portugal, and sold his living cargo, for slaves. Finding the adventure profitable, he sailed for another cargo, but he was never heard of afterward. Almost sixty years later some Portuguese settled in Newfoundland and Nova Scotia, and first imported cattle and swine there.

explored the coast from the Carolinas to Newfoundland. He anchored in the Bays of Delaware and New York,[1] the harbor of Newport, and probably that of Boston, and held intercourse with the natives, who were sometimes friendly and sometimes hostile. Verrazani gave the name of NEW FRANCE to the vast regions within the latitudes of the coasts which he had discovered. But at that time the French King was too much engrossed and impoverished by war with the Spanish monarch, to pay much attention to the important discoveries of Verrazani, or to listen to plans for future expeditions. Ten years elapsed before Admiral Chabon induced Francis to encourage another exploring enterprise, when a plan for making settlements in NEW FRANCE was arranged [1534], and James Cartier, a mariner of St. Malo, was appointed to the command of an expedition. He reached Newfoundland early in June, 1534. After exploring its coasts, he passed through the Straits of Belleisle, into the Gulf beyond, planted a cross with the arms of France upon it, on the shore of Gaspé inlet, and took possession of the whole country in the name of his king. After discovering the mouth of the great river of Canada, he sailed for France, in time to avoid the autumn storms on the American coast.

CARTIER'S SHIP.

ARMS OF FRANCE.

There was great joy at the French court, in the capital, and throughout the whole kingdom, because of the success of Cartier. He was commissioned for another voyage; and in May following [1535] he sailed for Newfoundland with three ships, accompanied by several young noblemen of France. They passed the Straits of Belleisle, and entered the Gulf on the day dedicated to St. Lawrence; and, on that account, Cartier gave the name of the martyr to the broad sheet of water over which they were sailing. They passed up the river which afterward received the same name, and mooring their ships at Quebec,[2] proceeded in a pinnace and boats to Hochelaga, where Montreal now stands, then the capital of the Huron king.[3] The natives were everywhere friendly and hospitable.

The land in all that region was very level, except a high mountain in the rear of the Indian town. Cartier ascended to its summit, and was so impressed with the glorious view that he called it Mont-Real (royal mountain), which name the fine city at its base yet retains. After exchanging presents and friendly salutations with the Indians, they returned to Quebec, and passed the severe winter on board their ships. In the spring, after setting up a cross, and

---

[1] Some authors say that Verrazani landed where the lower extremity of New York city is, and giving the natives some spirituous liquors, made many of them drunk. The Indians called the place *Manna-ha-ta*, or "place of drunkenness," and they were afterward called *Manna-ha-tans*. But this scene of intoxication probably occurred on board the *Half-Moon* the exploring ship of Hendrick Hudson. See page 59. [2] Pronounced *Ke-bec*. [3] Page 23.

taking formal possession of the country, they returned to France, having lost twenty-five seamen with the scurvy, a disease until then unknown. Their departure was disgraced by an act of treachery, which planted the seeds of hatred of the white people among the natives of the St. Lawrence. Cartier, under pretense of friendship, decoyed the hospitable Huron king on board one of his vessels and carried him off to France.

FRENCH NOBLEMAN IN 1540.

The results of this voyage were little else than a series of disappointments. Cartier's report of the rigors of the winter and the barrenness of the land in precious stones and metals, was discouraging, and four years elapsed before another expedition was planned. At length, Francis de la Roque, better known as lord of Robertval, in Picardy, obtained permission of the king to make further discoveries, and to plant settlements in NEW FRANCE.[1] The king invested him with the empty title of Viceroy of the whole country. Cartier's services being indispensable, he, too, was commissioned, but for subordinate command. He was ready long before Robertval's extensive preparations were completed, and being unwilling to bow to the new Viceroy's authority, he sailed, with five ships, in June, 1541, some months before the departure of his official superior. He had intended to take the Huron king back with him, but the broken-hearted monarch had died in France. It was an unfortunate occurrence. The natives received Cartier first with coldness, and then showed open hostility. Fearing the Indians, the French built a fort upon the island of Orleans, a little below Quebec. There they passed the winter without accomplishing any important achievement, and in June following [1542], departed for France, just as Robertval arrived at Newfoundland, with two hundred persons. Robertval passed up the St. Lawrence, built two more forts near Quebec, endured a winter of great distress, and, abandoning the idea of settlement, returned to France in the spring of 1543. Six years afterward, he again sailed for the St. Lawrence, and was never heard of again. The discoveries of Verrazani and Cartier, and also of French fishermen, served as the foundation for a claim by France to the northern portion of the American continent.

France was now convulsed by the conflicts of religious opinions. It was the era of the Reformation there.[2] The doctrines and the teachings of Calvin and others, in opposition to the faith and practice of the Roman Catholic Church, had already arrayed great masses of the people in violent hostility to each other. The religious war was an absorbing idea, and for fifty years the French government made no further attempts at discovery or colonization. But private enterprise sought to plant a French settlement in the land discovered by D'Ayllon.[3] The Huguenots, or French Protestants, who maintained the faith of early Christianity, were the weaker party in number, and felt the heavy heel of oppression. They had a powerful friend in Jasper Coligny, admiral of France, but a weak protector in the reigning monarch, Charles the Ninth.

[1] Page 48. [2] Note 14, page 62. [3] Page 42.

The fires of persecution were continually burning, and at length Coligny conceived the noble idea of providing a place of refuge for his Protestant brethren, beyond the Atlantic. The king granted him a commission for that purpose; and early in 1562 [Feb. 28], a squadron, under John Ribault, sailed for America. The little Huguenot fleet touched first near the harbor of St. Augustine, in Florida.[1] Sailing northward, they saw the mouth of the beautiful St. John's River [May, 1562], and, it being the fifth month of the year, they named it the "River of May." Making their way along the coast, they discovered Port Royal entrance, were charmed with the beauty of the scene, chose the spot for their future home, and built a small fort, which they named Carolina, in honor of the king. Leaving a garrison of twenty-six men to defend it, Ribault went back to France with the ships, for reinforcements. Bitter disappointment ensued. Civil war was raging in France, and Coligny was almost powerless. The reinforcements were not supplied, and the little garrison, though treated with hospitality by the Indians, became very discontented. Despairing of relief, they built a frail vessel, and, with insufficient stores, they embarked for France. Tempests assailed them, and famine was menacing them with death, when they were picked up by an English bark, and conveyed to Great Britain. Thus perished the first seeds of religious freedom which the storms of persecution bore to the New World.

The noble Coligny was not discouraged; and, during a lull in the tempest of civil commotion, another expedition was sent to America, under the command of Laudonniere, who had accompanied Ribault on his first voyage. They arrived in July, 1564, pitched their tents on the banks of the St. John's River (River of May), and built another Fort Carolina. But there were elements of dissolution among these immigrants. Many were idle, vicious, and improvident; and provisions soon became scarce. Under pretext of returning to France, to escape famine, quite a large party sailed, in December, in one of the vessels. They turned pirates, and depredated extensively upon Spanish property in the West Indies. The remainder became discontented, and were about to embark for France, when Ribault arrived with immigrants and supplies, and took command.[2]

Spanish jealousy and bigotry were now aroused, and when the monarch of Spain, the narrow Philip the Second, heard of the settlement of the French Protestants within his claimed territory, and of the piracies of some of the party, he adopted measures for their expulsion and punishment. Pedro Melendez, a brave but cruel military chief, was appointed Governor of Florida, on condition that he would expel the Frenchmen from the soil, conquer the natives, and plant a colony there within three years. That was an enterprise exactly suited to the character of Melendez. He came with a strong force, consisting of three hundred soldiers furnished by the king, and twenty-two hundred vol-

---

[1] Page 42.

[2] James Le Moyne, a skillful painter, was sent with this expedition, with instructions to make colored drawings of every object worthy of preservation. His illustrations of the costume and customs of the natives are very interesting, because authentic.

unteers—priests, sailors, mechanics, laborers, women, and children. The fleet was scattered by storms, and with only one third of his original number, Melendez landed in a fine harbor on the coast of Florida. There he laid the foundations of a city, which he named St. Augustine [Sept. 17, 1565], and formally proclaimed the king of Spain to be monarch of all North America. On hearing of the arrival of the Spaniards, a large party of the French, under Ribault, proceeded from the St. John's, by water, to attack them. A tempest wrecked every vessel; and most of the survivors, who fell into the hands of the Spaniards, were put to death. In the mean while, Melendez made his way through the swamps and forests with a strong force, to the defenseless French settlement, where he massacred about nine hundred men, women, and children, and over their dead bodies placed an inscription, avowing that he slew them, not "because they were Frenchmen, but Lutherans."[1] Upon that field of blood the monster erected a cross, and laid the foundation of a Christian church to commemorate the deed!

Charles the Ninth of France was not only a weak monarch, but an enemy to the Huguenots. He therefore took no steps to avenge the outrage, perpetrated under the sanction of the bigot of Spain. But one of his subjects, a fiery soldier of Gascony, named Dominic de Gourges, obtained permission to inflict retribution. He had suffered Spanish bondage and Spanish cruelty, and panted for revenge. He fitted out three ships at his own expense, and with one hundred and fifty men, sailed for Florida. He attacked the Spaniards upon the St. John's, surprised and captured Fort Carolina, which they occupied, made two hundred prisoners, and hanging his captives upon the trees almost upon the spot where his countrymen had been murdered, he placed over them the inscription—"I do not this as unto Spaniards or mariners, but unto traitors, robbers, and murderers." Too weak to brave the vengeance of Melendez, who was at St. Augustine, De Gourges immediately left the coast, and returned to France. The natives were delighted at seeing their common enemies thus destroying each other. The Spaniards, however, held possession, and a Spanish settlement was ever afterward maintained at St. Augustine, except during a few years.

It was now more than three quarters of a century since Columbus discovered the West India Islands, and yet no real progress toward a permanent European settlement, within the domain of the United States, had been made. Although the English seem not to have wholly relinquished the idea of planting settlements in America, it was not until the twentieth year of the brilliant reign of Queen Elizabeth, and almost eighty years after the discovery of the continent by Cabot,[2] that healthy efforts to found colonies in the New World, were made. Sir Martin Frobisher[3] (an eminent navigator) and others had

---

[1] The Protestants were often called by the general name of *Lutherans*, because the later Reformation was commenced by the bold opposition of Martin Luther to the corrupt practices of the Romish Church. Note 14, page 62.

[2] Page 46.

[3] Born in Yorkshire, England; was trained in the navigator's art; made several voyages for discovery; and died of wounds received in a naval battle near Brest, on the French coast, in 1594.

explored the north-western coast of North America, to the dreary region north of Hudson's Bay,[1] in search of precious metals and a north-west passage to India,[2] but without beneficial results. Newfoundland was visited every year by numerous English and French fishing-vessels, and the neighboring continent was frequently touched by the hardy mariners. Yet no feasible plans for colonization were matured. Finally, when the public mind of England was turned from the cold regions of Labrador and the fancied mineral wealth in its rugged mountains, to the milder South, and the more solid benefits to be derived from *plantations* than *min s*, a new and brilliant era in the history of civilization began. This change was produced incidentally by the Huguenot adventurers.[3] The remnant of Coligny's first colony, who were picked up at sea and taken to England, informed the queen of the glory of the climate, and the fertility of the soil of Carolina. When De Gourges returned from his foray upon the Spaniards,[4] Walter Raleigh, then a young man of much promise, was learning the art of war with Coligny, in France, and he communicated to his friends in England that chevalier's account of Florida, which was yet a wilderness free for the sons of toil. Enterprise was powerfully aroused by the promises of that warm and beautiful land, and the Protestant[5] feeling of England was strongly stirred by the cruelties of Melendez. These dissimilar, but auxiliary causes, produced great effects, and soon many minds were employed in planning schemes for colonizing the pleasant middle regions of North America. The first healthy plan for settlement there was proposed by the learned Sir Humphrey Gilbert, a step-brother of Walter Raleigh. He had served with honor in the wars of Ireland, France, and the Low Countries, and then was not only practically engaged in maritime affairs, but had written and published a treatise on the north-west passage to India. Having lost money in a vain endeavor to transmute baser metals into gold, he resolved to attempt to retrieve his fortune by planting a colony in the New World. In June, 1578, he obtained a liberal patent or grant from the queen. Raleigh gave him the aid of his hand and fortune; and early in 1579, Gilbert sailed for America, with a small squadron, accompanied by his step-brother. Heavy storms and Spanish war-vessels compelled them to return, and the scheme was abandoned for a time. Four years afterward [1583] Gilbert sailed with another squadron; and after a series of disasters, he reached the harbor of St. John's, Newfoundland. There he set up a pillar with the English arms upon it,[6] proclaimed the sovereignty of his queen, and then proceeded to explore the coast southward. After being terribly beaten by tempests off the shores of Nova Scotia and Maine, and losing his largest ship, he turned his vessel toward England. At midnight, in September, during a gale, his own little bark of ten tons went down, with all on board, and only one vessel of the expedition returned to England to relate the dreadful narrative.

The melancholy fate of the second expedition did not dismay the heart of

---

[1] Note 8, page 59. [2] Page 47. [3] Page 50.
[4] Page 51. [5] Note 14, page 62. [6] Note 2, page 40.

RALEIGH'S EXPEDITION AT ROANOKE.

Raleigh. He was a young man of great spirit, "the most restless, and ambitious, as he was the most versatile and accomplished, of all Elizabeth's courtiers." He now obtained a patent for himself [April, 1584], which made him lord proprietor of all lands that might be discovered by him in America, between the Santee and Delaware Rivers. He dispatched Philip Amidas and Arthur Barlow, with two well-furnished ships, to explore the American coast. They approached the shores of Carolina[1] in July, and landing upon the islands of Wocoken and Roanoke, which separate the waters of Pamlico and Albemarle Sounds from the Atlantic, they took possession of the country in the name of Elizabeth. They remained a few weeks, exploring the Sounds and trafficking with the natives, and then returned to England with two sons of the forest.[2] The glowing accounts of the newly-discovered country filled Raleigh's[3] heart with joy; and the queen declared the event to be (what it really was) one of the most glorious of her reign. In memorial of her unmarried state, she gave the name of VIRGINIA to the enchanting region. Raleigh was knighted, his patent was confirmed by act of Parliament, and the queen gave him a monopoly in the sale of sweet wines, as a means for enriching him.

RALEIGH.

The ardent and ever hopeful Raleigh now indulged in brilliant dreams of wealth and power to be derived from the New World, and he made immediate preparations for planting settlements on his trans-Atlantic domains. He dispatched a fleet of seven vessels on the 19th of April, 1585, under the command of Sir Richard Grenville. He was accompanied by Ralph Lane, the appointed governor of the colony, with learned companions; and also by Manteo, the native chief. They narrowly escaped shipwreck on the Carolina coast, in June, and in consequence of that danger, they named the land where their peril was greatest, Cape Fear. Entering Ocracock Inlet, they landed upon the island of Roanoke, in Albemarle Sound, and there prepared for a permanent residence.[4]

RALEIGH'S SHIPS.

---

1 The French Protestants had given the name of Carolina to the region where they attempted settlement, and it has ever since retained it. See page 50.

2 *Manteo* and *Wanchese*, natives of the adjacent continent: probably of the Hatteras tribe.

3 Born in Devonshire, England, 1552. He was one of the most illustrious men of the reign of Queen Elizabeth, which was remarkable for brilliant minds. His efforts to plant colonies in America, were evidences of a great genius and indomitable courage and perseverance. He was also a fine scholar, as well as a statesman, mariner, and soldier. His name will ever be held in reverence by all who can appreciate true greatness. He wrote a History of the World, while in prison under a false charge of high treason, and was beheaded in London, October 29, 1628.

4 The picture of the meeting of the English and natives of Roanoke, on page 53, exhibits truthful delineations of the persons and costumes of the Indians found there. They were copied and grouped from Harriot's "Brief and True Report of the new found land of Virginia," which was published in 1590. Harriot accompanied the expedition as historian and naturalist, remained a

The English made some fatal mistakes at the outset. Instead of looking to the fruition of seed-time for true riches, they turned from the wealthy soil upon which they stood, and went upon vain searches for gold in the forests of the adjoining continent. Instead of reciprocating the hospitable friendship of the natives, they returned harshness for kindness, and treachery for confidence, until a flame of revenge was kindled among the Indians which nothing but the blood of Englishmen could quench. Schemes for the destruction of the white intruders were speedily planned, and tribes in the interior stood ready to aid their brethren upon the seaboard. As soon as Grenville departed with the ships, for England, the natives withheld supplies of food, drew the English into perilous positions by tales of gold-bearing shores along the Roanoke River, and finally reduced the colony to the verge of ruin. At that moment, Sir Francis Drake arrived from the West Indies, with his fleet, and afforded them relief. But misfortune and fear made them anxious to leave the country, and the emigrants were all conveyed to England, in June, 1586, by Drake. A few days after their departure, a well-furnished vessel, sent by Raleigh, arrived; and a fortnight later, Grenville entered the inlet with three ships well provisioned. After searching for the departed colony, Grenville sailed for England, leaving fifteen men upon Roanoke.

The intrepid Raleigh was still undismayed by misfortune. He adopted a wise policy, and instead of sending out mere fortune-hunters,[1] he collected a band of agriculturists and artisans, with their families, and dispatched them [April 26, 1587], to found an industrial State in Virginia. He gave them a charter of incorporation for the settlement; and John White, who accompanied them, was appointed governor of the colony. They reached Roanoke in July: but instead of the expected greetings of the men left by Grenville, they encountered utter desolation. The bones of the fifteen lay bleaching on the ground. Their rude tenements were in ruins, and wild deer were feeding in their little gardens. They had been murdered by the Indians, and not one was left. Manteo[2] did not share in the Indian hatred of the white people, and like Massasoit of New England,[3] he remained their friend. By command of Raleigh, he received Christian baptism, and was invested, by White, with the title of *Lord of Roanoke*, the first and last peerage ever created in America. Yet Manteo could not avert nor control the storm that lowered among the Indian tribes, and menaced the English with destruction. The colonists were conscious that fearful perils were gathering, and White hastened to England toward the close of the year for reinforcements and provisions, leaving behind him his daughter, Eleanor Dare (wife of one of his lieutenants), who had just given birth to a child [August 18, 1587], whom they named *Virginia*. VIRGINIA DARE was the first offspring of English parents born within the territory of the United States.[4]

---

year in Virginia, and had correct drawings made of the inhabitants, their dwellings, their gardens, and every thing of interest pertaining to their costumes, customs, and general characteristics. The picture may be accepted as historically correct.

[1] Page 52. [2] Note 2, page 55. [3] Page 114. [4] Note 6, page 78.

The great Spanish Armada[1] was preparing for an invasion of Great Britain, when White reached England; and Raleigh, Grenville, and others, were deeply engaged in public affairs. It was not until the following May [1589], that White departed, with two ships, for Virginia. According to custom, he went by the way of the West Indies, and depredated upon Spanish property found afloat. He was beaten in an engagement, lost one of his vessels, and was obliged to return to England. Raleigh's fortune being materially impaired by his munificence in efforts at colonization, he assigned his proprietary rights to others; and it was not until 1590 that White was allowed to return to Roanoke in search of his daughter and the colony he had left. Both had then disappeared. Roanoke was a desolation; and, though Raleigh, who had abandoned all thoughts of colonization, had five times sent mariners, good and true, to search for the emigrants, they were never found.[2] Eighty years later, the Corees[3] told the English settlers upon the Cape Fear River, that their lost kindred had been adopted by the once powerful Hatteras tribe,[4] and became amalgamated with the children of the wilderness. The English made no further attempts at colonization at that time; and so, a century after Columbus sailed for America, there was no European settlement upon the North American Continent. Sir Francis Drake had broken up the military post at St. Augustine [1585], and the Red Men were again sole masters of the vast domain.

ENGLISH GENTLEMAN, 1580.

A dozen years after the failure of Raleigh's colonization efforts, Bartholomew Gosnold, who had been to America, and was a friend of the late proprietor of Virginia, sailed in a small bark [March 26, 1602] directly across the Atlantic for the American coast. After a voyage of seven weeks, he discovered the Continent near Nahant [May 14, 1602], and sailing southward, he landed upon a sandy point which he named Cape Cod, on account of the great number of those fishes in that vicinity. Continuing southward, he discovered Nantucket, Martha's Vineyard, and the group known as Elizabeth Islands. Upon one of them, which he named Elizabeth, in honor of his sovereign, Gosnold and his company prepared to found a settlement. Upon an islet, in a tiny lake, they built a fort and store-house.[5] Becoming alarmed at the menaces of the Indians and the want of supplies, they freighted their vessel with sassafras

[1] This was a great naval armament, fitted out by Spain, for the invasion of England, in the summer of 1588. It consisted of one hundred and fifty ships, two thousand six hundred and fifty great guns, and thirty thousand soldiers and sailors. It was defeated [July 20] by Admirals Drake and Howard.

[2] While Raleigh was making these fruitless searches, the Marquis de la Roche, a wealthy French nobleman, attempted to plant a French colony in America. He was commissioned by the King of France for the purpose, and in 1598 sailed for America with a colony, chiefly drawn from the prisons of Paris. Upon the almost desert island of Sable, near the coast of Nova Scotia, La Roche left forty men, while he returned to France for supplies. He died soon afterward, and for seven years the poor emigrants were neglected. When a vessel was finally sent for them, only twelve survived. They were taken to France, their crimes were pardoned by the knig, and their immediate wants were supplied.

[3] Page 20.

[4] Note 5, page 20.

[5] Dr. Jeremy Belknap, the historian of New Hampshire, discovered the cellar of this storehouse, in 1797.

roots, and returned to England in June, 1602. The glowing accounts of the country which Gosnold gave, awakened the enterprise of some Bristol merchants,[1] and the following year [1603] they fitted out two vessels for the purpose of exploration and traffic with the natives. The command was given to Martin Pring, a friend of both Raleigh and Gosnold. Following the track of the latter, he discovered the shores of Maine, near the mouth of the Penobscot [June], and coasting westward, he entered and explored several of the larger rivers of that State. He continued sailing along the coast as far as Martha's Vineyard, trading with the natives; and from that island he returned to England, after an absence of only six months. Pring made another voyage to Maine, in 1606, and more thoroughly explored the country. Maine was also visited in 1605, by Captain George Weymouth, who had explored the coast of Labrador, in search of a north-west passage to India.[2] He entered the Sagadahock, and took formal possession of the country in the name of King James. There he decoyed five natives on board his vessel, and then sailed for England. These forest children excited much curiosity; and the narratives of other mariners of the west of England, who visited these regions at about the same time, gave a new stimulus to colonizing efforts.

The French now began to turn their attention toward the New World again. In 1603, De Monts, a wealthy French Huguenot,[3] obtained a commission of viceroyalty over six degrees of latitude in New France,[4] extending from Cape May to Quebec. He prepared an expedition for settlement, and arrived at Nova Scotia,[5] with two vessels, in May, 1604.[6] He passed the summer there, trafficking with the natives; and in the autumn he crossed over to the mouth of the St. Croix (the eastern boundary of Maine), and erected a fort there. He had left a few settlers at Port Royal (now Annapolis), under Poutrincourt. These De Monts joined the following spring [1605], and organized a permanent colony. He named the place Port Royal; and the territory now included in Nova Scotia, New Brunswick, and the adjacent islands, he called ACADIE.[7] His efforts promised much success; but he was thwarted by jealous men. In 1608, he was deprived of his vice-royal commission, when he obtained a grant of the monopoly of the fur trade upon the St. Lawrence, for one year, and another commission, to plant a colony elsewhere in New France. The new expedition was placed under the command of Samuel Champlain (who accompanied the viceroy on his first voyage), and on the 3d of June, 1608, he arrived, with two vessels, at the mouth of the Saguenay, on the St. Lawrence. They ascended the great river, and on the site of Quebec, near where Cartier built his fort almost seventy years before,[8] they planted the first permanent

---

[1] Page 46. [2] Page 510. [3] Page 49. [4] Page 48. [5] Note 2. page 80.

[6] De Monts first brought swine, and other domestic animals, into this portion of America. Some were also taken from thence to French settlements planted in Canada a few years later. The company of which he was chief, fitted out four vessels. De Monts commanded the two here mentioned, assisted by Champlain and Poutrincourt.

[7] In 1613, Samuel Argall made a piratical visit to these coasts, under the direction of the governor of the Virginia colony. He destroyed the remnant of De Monts' settlement at St. Croix, broke up the peaceful colony at Port Royal, and plundered the people of every thing of value. See page 72.

[8] Page 49.

French settlement in the New World. The following summer, Champlain ascended the Richelieu or Sorel River, the outlet of Lake Champlain, with a war party of Huron[1] and Algonquin[2] Indians, and discovered the beautiful lake which bears his name, in the north-eastern part of the State of New York.[3]

The English were not idle while the French were exploring, and making efforts at settlement in the direction of the St. Lawrence. Several private enterprises were in progress, among the most important of which was that of a company of London merchants who sent Henry Hudson, an intimate friend of Captain Smith,[4] to search for a supposed north-eastern ocean passage to India. He made two unsuccessful voyages to the regions of polar ice [1607–8], when the attempt was abandoned. Anxious to win the honor of first reaching India by the northern seas, Hudson applied to the Dutch East India Company[5] for aid. The Amsterdam directors afforded it, and on the 4th of April, 1609, Hudson departed from Amsterdam, in command of the *Half-Moon*, a yacht of eighty tons. He sought a north-eastern passage; but after doubling the capes of Norway, the ice was impassable. Turning his prow, he steered across the Atlantic, and first touching the continent on the shores of Penobscot Bay, he arrived in sight of the capes of Virginia in August, 1609. Proceeding northward, he entered the mouths of several large rivers, and finally passed the Narrows[6] and anchored in New York Bay. He proceeded almost sixty leagues up the river that bears his name, and according to the formula of the age, took possession of the country in the name of the States General of Holland.[7] He returned to Europe[8] in November

HENRY HUDSON.

THE HALF-MOON.

1 Page 22. 2 Page 17.

3 Champlain penetrated southward as far as Crown Point; perhaps south of Ticonderoga. It was at about the same time that Hudson went up the river that bears his name, as far as Waterford, so that these eminent navigators, exploring at different points, came very near meeting in the wilderness. Six years afterward Champlain discovered Lake Huron, and there he joined some Huron Indians in an expedition against one of the Five Nations in Western New York. They had a severe battle in the neighborhood of the present village of Canandaigua. Champlain published an account of his first voyage, in 1613, and a continuation in 1620. He published a new edition of these in 1632, which contains a history of New France, from the discovery of Verrazani to the year 1631. Champlain died in 1634. 4 Page 65.

5 Dutch mariners, following the track of the Portuguese, opened a successful traffic with Eastern Asia, about the year 1594. The various Dutch adventurers, in the India trade, were united in one corporate body in 1602, with a capital of over a million of dollars, to whom were given the exclusive privilege of trading in the seas east of the Cape of Good Hope. This was the Dutch East India Company.

6 Entrance to New York Bay between Long and Staten Islands.

7 This was the title of the Government of Holland, answering, in a degree, to our *Congress*.

8 Hudson, while on another voyage in search of a north-west passage, discovered the great Bay in the northern regions, which bears his name. He was there frozen in the ice during the winter of 1610–11. While endeavoring to make his way homeward in the spring, his crew became mutinous. They finally seized Hudson, bound his arms, and placing him and his son, and seven sick companions, in an open boat, set them adrift upon the cold waters. They were never heard of afterward

1609, and his report of the goodly land he had discovered set in motion those commercial measures which resulted in the founding of a Dutch empire in the New World.

With these discoveries commenced the epoch of settlements. The whole Atlantic coast of North America had been thoroughly or partially explored, the general character and resources of the soil had become known, and henceforth the leading commercial nations of Western Europe—England, France, Spain, and Holland—regarded the transatlantic continent, not as merely a rich garden without a wall, where depredators from every shore might come, and, without hinderance, bear away its choicest fruit, but as a land where the permanent foundations of vast colonial empires might be laid, from which parent states would receive almost unlimited tribute to national wealth and national glory.

When we contemplate these voyages across the stormy Atlantic, and consider the limited geographical knowledge of the navigators, the frailty of their vessels[1] and equipments, the vast labors and constant privations endured by them, and the dangers to which they were continually exposed, we can not but feel the highest respect and reverence for all who were thus engaged in opening the treasures of the New World to the advancing nations of Europe. Although acquisitiveness, or the desire for worldly possessions, was the chief incentive to action, and gave strength to resolution, yet it could not inspire courage to encounter the great dangers of the deep and the wilderness, nor fill the heart with faith in prophecies of success. These sentiments must have been innate; and those who braved the multitude of perils were men of true courage, and their faith came from the teachings of the science of their day. History and Song, Painting and Sculpture, have all commemorated their deeds. If Alexander the Great was thought worthy of having the granite body of Mount Athos hewn into a colossal image of himself,[2] might not Europe and America appropriately join in the labor of fashioning some lofty summit of the Alleghanies[3] into a huge monument to the memory of the NAVIGATORS who lifted the vail of forgetfulness from the face of the New World?[4]

---

1 The first ships were generally of less than one hundred tons burden. Two of the vessels of Columbus were without decks; and the one in which Frobisher sailed was only twenty-five tons burden.

2 Dinocrates, a celebrated architect, offered to cut Mount Athos into a statue of Alexander the Great, so large, that it might hold a city in its right hand, and in its left a basin of sufficient capacity to hold all the waters that poured from the mountain.

3 Note 3, page 19.

4 Page 47. There has been much discussion concerning the claims of certain navigators, to the honor of first discovering the *Continent* of America. A "Memoir of Sebastian Cabot," illustrated by documents from the Rolls, published in London in 1832, appears to prove conclusively that he, *and not his father*, was the navigator who discovered North America. John Cabot was a man of science, and a merchant, and may have accompanied his son, in his first voyage in 1497. Yet, in the patent of February, 1498, in which the first voyage is referred to, are the words, "the land and isles of late found by the said John, in our name, and by our commandment." The first commission being issued in the name of John Cabot, the discoveries made by those employed by him, would of course be in his name. A little work, entitled "Researches respecting Americus Vespucius, and his Voyages," prepared by Viscount Santarem, ex-prime minister of Portugal, casts just doubts upon the statements of Vespucius, concerning his command on a voyage of discovery when, he claims, he discovered South America [page 41] in 1499. He was doubtless an officer under Ojeda; and it is quite certain that he got possession of the narratives of Ojeda and published them as his own. The most accessible works on American discoveries, are Irving's "Life of Columbus;" Prescott's "Ferdinand and Isabella;" Lives of Cabot and Hudson, in Sparks's "American Biography," and Histories of the United States by Bancroft and Hildreth.

BUILDING JAMESTOWN.

JOHN SMITH.

THIRD PERIOD.

SETTLEMENTS.

CHAPTER I.

THERE is a distinction to be observed in considering settlements and colonies. The act of forming a settlement is not equivalent to the establishment of a colony or the founding of a State. It is the initiatory step toward such an end, and may or may not exhibit permanent results. A colony becomes such only when settlements assume permanency, and organic laws, subservient to those of a parent government, are framed for the guidance of the people. It seems proper, therefore, to consider the era of *settlements* as distinct from that of *colonial organization.*

The period of settlements within the bounds of the thirteen original colonies which formed the Confederacy in the War for Independence,[1] extends from 1607 to 1733. For fifty years previous to the debarkation [1607] at Jamestown,[2] fishing stations had been established at various points on the Atlantic coast: and at St. Augustine,[3] the Spaniards had kept a sort of military post alive. Yet the time of the appearance of the English in the James River, is the true point from which to date the inception or beginning of our great confederacy of

[1] Page 229. [2] Page 64. [3] Page 51.

free States. Twelve years [1607 to 1619] were spent by English adventurers in efforts to plant a permanent settlement in Virginia.[1] For seventeen years [1609 to 1623] Dutch traders were trafficking on the Hudson River, before a permanent settlement was established in New York.[2] Fourteen years [1606 to 1620] were necessary to effect a permanent settlement in Massachusetts;[3] and for nine years [1622 to 1631] adventurers struggled for a foothold in New Hampshire.[4] The Roman Catholics were only one year [1634–5] in laying the foundation of the Maryland colony.[5] Seven years [1632 to 1639] were employed in effecting permanent settlements in Connecticut;[6] eight years [1636 to 1643] in organizing colonial government in Rhode Island;[7] and about fifty years [1631 to 1682] elapsed from the landing of the Swedes on South River,[8] before Delaware, New Jersey, and Pennsylvania (whose several histories of settlements are interwoven), presented colonial features.[9] Almost sixty years [1622 to 1680] passed by before the first settlements in the Carolinas became fully developed colonies;[10] but Georgia, the youngest of the thirteen States, had the foundation of its colonial government laid when Oglethorpe, with the first company of settlers, began to build Savannah in the winter of 1733.[11] The first permanent settlement within the bounds of the original colonies, was in

VIRGINIA. [1607—1619].

A century had not elapsed after the discoveries of Columbus [1492],[12] before a great social and political revolution had been effected in Europe. Commerce, hitherto confined to inland seas and along the coasts, was sending its ships across oceans. The art of printing had begun its wonderful work:[13] and, through its instrumentality, intelligence had become generally diffused. Mind thus acting upon mind, in vastly multiplied opportunities, had awakened a great moral and intellectual power, whose presence and strength had not been suspected. The Protestant Reformation[14] had weakened the bonds of spiritual dominion, and allowed the moral faculties fuller play; and the shadows of feudal institutions,[15] so chilling to individual effort, were rapidly disappearing before

[1] Page 71. [2] Page 73. [3] Page 79. [4] Page 80.
[5] Page 82. [6] Page 89. [7] Page 91. [8] Page 92.
[9] Page 97. [10] Page 99. [11] Page 103 [12] Page 40.

[13] About the year 1450. Rude printing from engraved blocks was done before that time; but when Peter Schœffer cast the first metal types, each letter separately, at about 1450, the art of printing truly had birth. John Faust established a printing-office at Mentz, in 1442. John Guttenberg invented cut metal types, and used them in printing a Bible which was commenced in 1445, and finished in 1460. The names of these three men are usually associated as the inventors of printing.

[14] Commenced by Wickliffe, in England, in 1360; by Huss, in Bohemia, in 1405; by Luther, in Germany, in 1517. From this period until 1562, the movement was general throughout Europe. It was an effort to purge the Christian Church of great impurities, by reforming its doctrine and ritual. The Reformers protested against the practices of the Roman Catholic Church, and the title of the movement was, therefore, the Protestant Reformation. The name of Protestants was first given to Luther and others, in 1529.

[15] The nature of feudal laws may be illustrated by a single example: William, the Norman conqueror of England, divided the land of that country into parts called *baronies*, and gave them to certain of his favorites, who became masters of the conquered people on their respective estates. For these gifts, and certain privileges, the *barons*, or masters, were to furnish the king with a stipu-

the rising sun of the new era in the history of the world. Freedom of thought and action expanded the area of ideas, and gave birth to those tolerant principles which lead to brotherhood of feeling. The new impulse developed nobler motives for human action than the acquisition of wealth and power, and these soon engendered healthy schemes for founding industrial empires in the New World. Aspirations for civil freedom, awakened by greater religious liberty, had begun the work, especially in England, where the Protestants were already divided into two distinct parties, called, respectively, Churchmen and Puritans. The former supported the throne and all monarchic ideas.; the latter were more republican; and from their pulpits went forth doctrines inimical to kingly power. These religious differences had begun to form a basis of political parties, and finally became prime elements of colonization.

Another event, favorable to the new impulse, now exerted a powerful influence. A long contest between England and France ceased in 1604. Soldiers, an active, restless class in England, were deprived of employment, and would soon become dangerous to the public peace. While population and general prosperity had greatly increased, there was another large class, who, by idleness and dissipation, had squandered fortunes, and had become desperate men. The soldiers needed employment, either in their own art, or in equally exciting adventures; and the impoverished spendthrifts were ready for any thing which promised gain. Such were the men who stood ready to brave ocean perils and the greater dangers of the Western World, when such minds as those of Fernando Gorges, Bartholomew Gosnold, Chief Justice Popham, Richard Hakluyt, Captain John Smith, and others, devised new schemes for colonization. The weak and timid James the First,[1] who desired and maintained peace with other nations during his reign, was glad to perceive a new field for restless and adventurous men to go to, and he readily granted a liberal patent [April 20, 1606] to the first company formed after his accession to the throne, for planting settlements in Virginia. The English then claimed dominion over a belt of territory extending from Cape Fear, in North Carolina, to Halifax, in Nova Scotia, and indefinitely westward. This was divided into two districts. One extended from the vicinity of New York city northward to the present southern boundary of Canada, including the whole of New England, and westward of it, and was called NORTH VIRGINIA. This territory was granted to a company of "knights, gentlemen, and merchants" in the west of England, called the *Plymouth Company*.[2] The other district extended from the mouth of the Potomac southward to Cape Fear, and was called SOUTH VIRGINIA. It was

lated amount of money, and a stated number of men for soldiers, when required. The *people* had no voice in this matter, nor in any public affairs, and were made essentially slaves to the barons. Out of this state of things originated the exclusive privileges yet enjoyed by the nobility of Europe. Except in Russia, the people have been emancipated from this vassalage, and the ancient forms of feudal power have disappeared.

[1] He was the Sixth James of Scotland, of the house of Stuart, and son of Mary, Queen of Scotland, by Lord Darnley. The crowns of England and Scotland were united by his accession to the throne of the former kingdom, in March, 1603.

[2] The chief members of the company were Thomas Hanham, Sir John and Raleigh Gilbert (sons of Sir Humphrey Gilbert), William Parker, George Popham, Sir John Popham (Lord Chief Justice of England), and Sir Fernando Gorges, Governor of Plymouth Fort.

granted to a company of "noblemen, gentlemen and merchants," chiefly residents of London, called the *London Company.*[1] The intermediate domain of almost two hundred miles, was a dividing line, so broad that disputes about territory could not occur, as neither company was allowed to make settlements more than fifty miles beyond its own boundary.

The idea of popular freedom was as yet the heritage of a favored few, and the political character of the first colonial charter, under which a permanent settlement was made within the territory of the United States, was unfavorable to the best interests of all. The king reserved to himself the right of appointing all officers, and of exercising all executive and legislative power. The colonists were to pay homage to the sovereign, and a tribute of one fifth of the net products of gold and silver found in Virginia; yet they possessed no rights of self-government. They were to be governed by a council of seven appointed by the king, who were allowed to choose a president from among themselves. There was also a Supreme Council in England, appointed by the king, who had the general supervision of the colonies, under the direction of the monarch. That charter was the conception of a narrow mind, and despotic temper, and proved totally inadequate as a constitution of government for a free people.

The North Virginia, or Plymouth Company, made the first attempt at settlement, and failed.[2] The South Virginia, or London Company, sent Captain Christopher Newport, with three vessels and one hundred and five emigrants [Dec., 1606], to make a settlement upon Roanoke Island,[3] where Raleigh's colony had perished almost twenty years before. Among them was Bartholomew Gosnold, the projector of the expedition. They possessed very poor materials for a colony. There was no *family* among them, and only "twelve laborers and a few mechanics." The remainder were "gentlemen,"[4] many of whom were vicious, dissolute men, totally unfit for such an enterprise, and quite unworthy to be actors in the glorious events anticipated by Gosnold and his enlightened associates at home. The voyage was a long and tedious one. Newport pursued the old route by the Canaries and the West Indies, and did not arrive upon the American coast until April, 1607, when a storm drove his vessels into Chesapeake Bay, where he found a good harbor. He named the capes at the entrance, *Charles* and *Henry*, in honor of the king's sons. A pleasant point of the Virginia peninsula, between the York and James Rivers, which they next landed upon and enjoyed repose, he named Point Comfort; and the noble Powhatan River which he soon afterward entered he called *James.* Sailing up the broad stream about fifty miles, the immigrants landed upon a beautiful, shaded peninsula,[5] where they chose a site for the capital of the new empire, and called it JAMESTOWN.

---

[1] The chief members of the company were Sir Thomas Gates, Sir George Somers, Richard Hakluyt (the historian), and Edward Maria Wingfield, who was the first governor of Virginia.

[2] Page 73.

[3] Page 55.

[4] This name was given to wealthy men, who were not engaged in any industrial pursuit, and often spent their lives in idleness and dissipation; a class which, in our day and country, number, happily, very few. Labor is worthily honored as more noble than idleness.

[5] This may be called an island, for the marsh which connects it with the mainland is often overflowed. The currents of the river have washed away large portions of the original island.

Ill feelings had been engendered before they reached the Canary Islands, and violent disputes had arisen during the long voyage. As the silly king had placed the names of the colonial council in a sealed box, with instructions not to open it until their arrival in Virginia, there was no competent authority on board to restore harmony. Captain Smith,[1] who was the most able man among them, excited the envy of his companions; and being charged with a design to murder the council, usurp government, and proclaim himself king, he was placed in confinement. On opening the sealed box, it was discovered that Smith was one of the council. He was released from confinement; but, through the influence of Wingfield, an avaricious, unprincipled, but talented man, he was excluded from office. Smith demanded a trial upon the absurd charges. The accusation was withdrawn, and he took his seat in the council, over which Wingfield was chosen to preside.

Soon after landing, Newport, Smith, and twenty others, ascended the James River to the Falls at Richmond, and visited the emperor of the Powhatans,[2] whose residence was a mile below the foot of the rapids. The title of the emperor was Powhatan, which signified supreme ruler, as did *Pharaoh* in the antient Egyptian language—the chief man in Egypt. He was a man of great ability, and commanded the reverence of the whole confederation. He appeared friendly to the English, notwithstanding his people murmured at their presence; and the visitors returned to Jamestown much gratified.

Early in June, 1607, Newport sailed for England, to obtain more settlers and provisions. The little band of emigrants soon perceived the perils of their situation. A large portion of their provisions had been spoiled during the voyage. They had not planted, therefore they could not reap. The neighboring tribes evinced hostility, and withheld supplies. Poisonous vapor arose from the marshes; and before the close of summer, one half of the adventurers perished by disease and famine. Among the victims was Gosnold. The settlers, in their despair, reproached themselves and the leaders of the expedition, and longed to depart for the Old World. In the midst of their despondency, the survivors discovered that president Wingfield was living on choice stores, and was preparing to abandon the colony and escape to the West Indies in the pinnace[3] left by Newport. Their indignation was thoroughly aroused, and he was deposed. Ratcliffe, a man as weak and wicked as Wingfield, was chosen his successor. He, too, was speedily dismissed; and the settlers, with one consent, wisely turned to Smith as ruler.

It was a happy hour for the Virginia settlers when Captain Smith took the reins of government. All was confusion; but he soon restored order; and by his courage and energy, inspired the Indians with awe, and compelled them to bring him supplies of food. In October, wild game became plentiful; and at the beginning of November, the abundant harvest of Indian corn was gathered

[1] See portrait at the head of this Chapter. Smith was one of the most remarkable men of his time. He was born in Lincolnshire, England; and after many adventures in Europe, went to America. He died in 1631. He wrote a History of Virginia, and several other works.

[2] Page 20.

[3] A small, light vessel, with sails and oars.

by the natives, and they supplied the settlers with all they needed. Having established a degree of comfort and prosperity, Smith started, with some companions, to explore the surrounding country. He ascended the Chickahomminy River fifty miles from its mouth, and then, with two companions, penetrated the vast forest that covered the land. His companions were slain by the natives, and he was made a captive. After being exhibited in several villages, he was taken to Opechancanough,[1] the eldest brother of Powhatan, who, regarding Smith as a superior being, spared his life, and conducted him to the emperor, then at Weroworomoco, on the York River.[2] A solemn council decided that the captive must die, and Smith was prepared for execution. His head was placed upon a stone, and the heavy clubs of the executioners were raised to crush it, when Pocahontas, a child of "ten or twelve years,"[3] the favorite

POCAHONTAS.

daughter of Powhatan, rushed from her father's side, and casting herself upon the captive, besought the king to spare his life. Powhatan consented, and Smith was conducted in safety to Jamestown by a guard of twelve men, after an absence of seven weeks.

God, in his providence, overrules every thing for good. It is seen in this event, for Smith's captivity was a public benefit. He had acquired a knowledge of the Indian character, and of the country and its resources, and also had formed friendly relations with the sachems and chiefs. Had his companions

---

[1] Note 5, page 106.
[2] At Shelly, nearly opposite the mouth of Queen's Creek, Gloucester County, Virginia.
[3] Page 70.

possessed half as much energy and honesty as Smith, all would have been well. But they were idle, improvident, and dissolute. As usual, he found every thing in disorder on his return from the forest. Only forty men were living, and a greater portion of them were on the point of escaping to the West Indies in the pinnace; but the courage and energy of Smith compelled them to remain. Conscious of the purity of their ruler and the wickedness of themselves, they hated him intensely, and from that time they plotted for his destruction, or the overthrow of his power.

Captain Newport arrived with supplies and one hundred and twenty immigrants, early in 1608. These were no better than the first adventurers. Instead of agriculturalists and mechanics, with families, they were idle "gentlemen," "packed hither," as Smith said, "by their friends, to escape ill destinies." There were also several unskillful goldsmiths, the very men least needed in the colony. Some glittering earth in the vicinity of Jamestown, was by them mistaken for gold; and in spite of the remonstrances of Smith, the whole industry of the colony was directed to the supposed treasure. "There was no talk, no hope, no work, but dig gold, work gold, refine gold, load gold." Newport loaded his vessel with the worthless earth, and returned to England, believing himself exceedingly rich; but science soon pronounced him miserably poor in useful knowledge and well-earned reputation.

The gold-fever had taken strong hold upon the indolent dreamers, and Smith remonstrated against idleness and pleaded for industry, in vain. He implored the settlers to plow and sow, that they might reap and be happy. They refused to listen, and he turned from Jamestown with disgust. With a few sensible men, he went to explore the Chesapeake in an open boat, and every bay, inlet, and creek, received his attention. He went up the Potomac to the falls above Washington city; and then, after exploring the shores of the Rappahannock to the site of Fredericsburg, he returned to Jamestown. A few days afterward he returned again to the Chesapeake, carefully explored each shore above the mouth of the Potomac, and entered the Patapsco, and ate Indian corn on the site of Baltimore. He also went up the Susquehannah to the beautiful vale of Wyoming,[1] and penetrated the forests even to the territory of the Five Nations,[2] and established friendly relations with the dusky tribes. Within three months he traveled full three thousand miles. It was one of the most wonderful of exploring expeditions, considered in all its aspects, ever recorded by the pen of history; and the map of the country, which Smith constructed on his return, is yet in existence in England, and is remarkable for its general accuracy.

Captain Smith returned to Jamestown on the 7th of September, 1608, and three days afterward he was formally made president of the settlement. Newport arrived soon afterward with seventy immigrants, among whom were two females, the first English women ever seen upon the James River.[3] To the soil they were compelled to look, chiefly, for their food, and Smith exerted all

[1] Page 290. [2] Page 23. [3] Page 105.

his energies to turn the little industry of the settlers to agriculture. He succeeded, in a degree, but he had poor materials out of which to form a healthy, self-sustaining commonwealth. He wrote to the Supreme Council[1] to send over a different class of men. "I entreat you," he said, "rather send but thirty carpenters, husbandmen, gardeners, fishermen, blacksmiths, masons, and diggers of trees' roots, well provided, than a thousand such as we have." Yet, with all his exertions, idleness and improvidence prevailed. At the end of two years from the first landing at Jamestown, and when the settlement numbered two hundred strong men, not more than forty acres were under cultivation. To the Indians the white people were compelled to look for their chief supply of food.

The London Company were disappointed, for the anticipations of sudden wealth, in which they had indulged, were not realized, and they sought and obtained a new charter [June 2, 1609], which gave them more ample privileges. The territory of SOUTH VIRGINIA[2] was extended northward to the head of the Chesapeake. The Supreme Council was vested with power to fill vacancies in its own body, and to appoint a governor for Virginia, whose rule was made absolute. The lives, liberties, and property of the settlers were at his disposal. and they were compelled to contribute a certain share of their earnings to the proprietors. Thus they were mere vassals at will, under a petty despotism, without any inherent power, then recognized, to cast off the yoke.

Under that charter, Lord De la Warr (Delaware), an enlightened peer, was appointed governor of Virginia, for life, and soon afterward Newport sailed for America [June 12, 1609], with nine ships, and more than five hundred emigrants.[3] Sir Thomas Gates, the governor's deputy, embarked with Newport, accompanied by Sir George Somers. Gates, Newport, and Somers, were commissioned to administer the government until the arrival of Delaware. When near the coast, a hurricane dispersed the fleet, and the vessel bearing the commissioners was wrecked on one of the Bermuda Islands. Seven vessels of the squadron reached the James River in safety. The colony would have been the gainer had these never arrived, for a greater portion of the new immigrants were more profligate, if possible, than the first. They were dissolute scions of wealthy families, and many of them came to avoid punishment for crimes at home. They regarded Virginia as a paradise for libertines, and believed the colony to be without a head until the arrival of the governor or his deputy. Smith, on the contrary, boldly asserted his authority as president, and maintained it until an accident in autumn compelled him to go to England for surgical aid,[4] when he delegated his authority to George Percy, brother of the duke of Northumberland.

When the idle and profligate settlers were released from the control of

---

[1] Page 64. [2] Page 63.

[3] Domestic animals were now first taken to Virginia. They consisted of six mares, one horse, six hundred swine, a few sheep and goats, and five hundred domestic fowls. Two years later one hundred cows and some other cattle were brought over.

[4] While passing down the James River, in a boat, from the Falls, Smith's bag of powder ignited, and the explosion almost killed him. His wounds were so severe as to require the most skillful surgery.

Smith, they gave themselves up to every irregularity of life. Their ample stock of provisions was rapidly consumed. The Indians had great respect for Smith, and were friendly while he remained, but after his departure, they openly showed their contempt for the English, withheld supplies of provisions, and conceived a plan for the total extermination of the white intruders. Famine ensued, and the winter and spring of 1610 were long remembered as "the starving time." Those who went to the cabins of the Indians, for food, were treacherously murdered; and finally a plan was matured by the natives for striking a blow of utter extermination. Again Pocahontas performed the part of a guardian angel.[1] On a dark and stormy night she hastened to Jamestown, revealed the plot, and was back to her couch before the dawn. Thus, she saved the colonists by placing them on their guard. Yet death hovered over them. The horrors of destitution increased, and the settlement which numbered five hundred persons when Smith left, was reduced to sixty within six months after his departure. The commissioners[2] finally arrived. They constructed a rude vessel upon the barren island where they were wrecked, and in it reached Virginia, in June, 1610. Instead of being greeted by a flourishing people, they were met by a mere remnant, almost famished. There appeared no way to obtain food, and Gates determined to sail immediately for Newfoundland,[3] and distribute the immigrants among the English fishing vessels there. Jamestown was utterly abandoned, and toward Hampton Roads[4] the dejected settlers sailed in four pinnaces. Early the next morning white sails greeted their vision. Lord Delaware had arrived with provisions and immigrants; and that very night, Jamestown, abandoned to pagans in the morning, was made vocal with hymns of thanksgiving to the true God, by the returned settlers.

Governor Delaware was a virtuous and prudent man, and under his administration the colony began to prosper. Failing health compelled him to return to England the following spring [March, 1611]; and he left the government in the hands of Percy, Smith's successor, who managed with prudence until the arrival of Sir Thomas Dale, with supplies.[5] Dale was an experienced soldier. and, assuming the government, he ruled by martial law. Early in September following, Sir Thomas Gates arrived with six well-furnished ships, and three hundred immigrants. With this arrival came hope for the colony. A large portion of the new settlers were sober, industrious men, and their arrival gave great joy to the four hundred colonists at Jamestown. Gates assumed the functions of governor, and Dale went up the river to plant new settlements at the mouth of the Appomattox and near the Falls.[6] And now a wise change in the domestic policy of the colony was made. Hitherto the land had been worked in common, and the product of labor was deposited in public storehouses. for the good of the community. The industrious created food for the indolent, and an incentive to effort was wanting. That incentive was necessary; and it was found in the plan of making an assignment of a few acres of land to each

[1] Page 66. [2] Page 68. [3] Page 47. [4] Note 3, page 297.
[5] Delaware afterward sailed for Virginia, to resume the reins of government, but died on the voyage. [6] Near the present City Point, and Richmond.

man, to be cultivated for his own private benefit. This regulation gave a powerful impulse to industry. Larger assignments were made, and soon the community system was abandoned, and industry on private account created an ample supply of food for all.[1]

A third charter was obtained by the London Company, on the 22d of March, 1612, by which the control of the king was annulled. The Supreme Council was abolished, and the whole company, sitting as a democratic assembly, elected the officers, and ordained the laws, for the colony. Yet no political privilege was granted to the settlers. Their very existence as a body politic, was completely ignored. They had no voice in the choice of rulers and the enactment of laws. Yet they were contented; and at the beginning of 1613 there were a thousand Englishmen in Virginia. At about this time an event occurred, which proved of permanent benefit to the settlement. Powhatan had continued to manifest hostile feelings ever since the departure of Smith. For the purpose of extorting advantageous terms of peace from the Indian king, Captain Argall (a sort of buccaneer),[2] bribed an Indian chief, with a copper kettle, to betray the trusting Pocahontas into his hands. She was induced to go on board his vessel, where she was detained as a prisoner for several months, until Powhatan ransomed her. In the mean while, a mutual attachment had grown up between the maiden and John Rolfe, a young Englishman of good family. He had instructed her in letters and religion: and, with the consent of Powhatan, she received the rite of Christian baptism, and became the wife of Rolfe, in April, 1613. This union brought peace, and Powhatan was ever afterward the friend of the English.

Prosperity now smiled upon the settlement, yet the elements of a permanent State were wanting. There were no families in Virginia, and all the settlers indulged in anticipations of returning to England, which they regarded as home. Gates went thither in March, 1614, leaving the administration of government with Sir Thomas Dale, who ruled with wisdom and energy for about two years, and then departed, after appointing George Yeardley deputy-governor. During Yeardley's administration, the culture of the tobacco plant[3] was promoted, and so rapidly did it gain in favor, that it soon became, not only the principal article of export, but the *currency* of the colony. And now [1617] Argall, the buccaneer, was appointed deputy-governor. He was a despot in feelings and practice, and soon disgusted the people. He was succeeded by Yeardley, who was appointed governor in 1619; and then dawned the natal morning of Virginia as a Republican State. Yeardley abolished martial law,

---

[1] A similar result was seen in the operations of the Plymouth colony. See page 116.

[2] Note 7, page 58.

[3] This plant, yet very extensively cultivated in Virginia and the adjoining States, was first discovered by Sir Francis Drake, near Tabaco, in Yucatan: hence its name. Drake and Raleigh first introduced it into England. King James conceived a great hatred of it, and wrote a treatise against its use. He forbade its cultivation in England, but could not prevent its importation from Virginia. It became a very profitable article of commerce, and the streets of Jamestown were planted with it. Other agricultural productions were neglected, and while cargoes of tobacco were preparing for England, the necessaries of life were wanting. The money value of tobacco was about sixty-six cents a pound.

released the planters from feudal service to the colony,[1] and established representative government.[2] The settlement was divided into eleven boroughs, and two representatives, called burgesses, were chosen by the people for each. These, with the governor and council, constituted the colonial government. The burgesses were allowed to debate all matters pertaining to the good of the colony; but their enactments were not legal until sanctioned by the company in England. The most important event of that year occurred on the 28th of June. On that day, the first representative assembly ever convened in America, met at Jamestown. Then and there, the foundations of the VIRGINIA commonwealth were laid. The people now began to regard Virginia as their home, and "fell to building houses and planting corn." Within two years afterward, one hundred and fifty reputable young women were sent over to become wives to the planters,[3] the tribe of gold-seekers and "gentlemen" was extinct, for "it was not the will of God that the new State should be formed of such material; that such men should be the fathers of a progeny born on the American soil, who were one day to assert American liberty by their eloquence, and defend it by their valor."[4]

CHAPTER II.

NEW YORK [1609—1623].

IN a preceding chapter,[5] we have considered the discovery and exploration of the river, bearing his name, by Henry Hudson, then in the service of the Dutch East India Company. On his return to England [Nov. 1609], he forwarded to his employers in Amsterdam,[6] a brilliant account of his discoveries in America. Jealous of the maritime enterprise and growing power of the Dutch, the British king would not allow Hudson to go to Holland, fearing he might be employed in making further discoveries, or in planting settlements in America. This narrow and selfish policy of James was of no avail, for the ocean pathway to new and fertile regions, once opened, could easily be traversed by inferior navigators. This fact was soon demonstrated. In 1610, some wealthy merchants of Amsterdam, directors of the Dutch East India Company,[7] sent a ship from the Texel, laden with merchandise, to traffic with the Indians upon the Mauritius,[8] as the present Hudson River was then called. Hudson's ship (the *Half-Moon*[9]) was also sent hither the same year on a like errand; and for three

---

[1] Page 68.

[2] Yeardley found the people possessed with an intense desire for that freedom which the English constitution gave to every subject of the realm, and it was impossible to reconcile that feeling with the exercise of the arbitrary power which had hitherto prevailed. He, therefore, formed a plan for a popular assembly as similar to the English parliament as circumstances would allow.

[3] Page 105.

[4] Bancroft.

[5] Page 59.

[6] Page 59.

[7] Note 5, page 59.

[8] So named, in honor of Prince Maurice, of Nassau.

[9] Page 59.

years afterward, private enterprise dispatched many vessels from Holland, to traffic for furs and peltries. Among other commanders came the bold Adrian Block, the first navigator of the dangerous strait in the East River, called Hell-Gate. Block's vessel was accidentally burned in the autumn of 1613, when he and his companions erected some rude huts for shelter, near the site of the Bowling Green, at the foot of Broadway, New York. These huts formed the germ of our great commercial metropolis. During the ensuing winter they constructed a vessel from the fine timber which grew upon Manhattan Island, and early in the spring they sailed up Long Island Sound on a voyage of discovery which extended to Nahant. Block first discovered the Connecticut and Thames Rivers, and penetrated Narraganset Bay to the site of Providence.

Intent upon gain, Dutch trading vessels now frequently ascended the Mauritius, and a brisk trade in furs and peltries was opened with the Indian tribes, almost two hundred miles from the ocean. The traders built a fort and storehouse upon a little island just below Albany, in 1614, which they called Fort Nassau; and nine years later, Fort Orange was erected near the river, a little south of the foot of the present State-street, in Albany, on the site of Albany. There is a doubt about a fort being erected on the southern extremity of Manhattan Island, at this time, as some chroniclers have asserted. It is probable the trading-house erected there was palisaded, as a precautionary measure, for they could not well determine the disposition of the Indians.

On the 11th of October, 1614, a special charter was granted to a company of Amsterdam merchants, giving them the monopoly of trade in the New World, from the latitude of Cape May to that of Nova Scotia, for three years. The territory was named New Netherland, in the charter, which title it held until it became an English province in 1664.[1] Notwithstanding it was included in the grant of James to the Plymouth company,[2] no territorial jurisdiction being claimed, and no English settlements having been made northward of Richmond, in Virginia, the Dutch were not disturbed in their traffic. The popular story, that Argall entered the Bay of New York on his return from Acadie in 1613, and made the Dutch traders promptly surrender the place to the English crown, seems unsusceptible of proof.[3]

Success attended the Dutch from the beginning. The trade in furs and peltries became very lucrative, and the company made an unsuccessful application for a renewal of their charter. More extensive operations were in contemplation; and on the 3d of June, 1621, the States General of Holland[4] incorporated the *Dutch West India Company*, and invested it with almost regal powers, for planting settlements in America from Cape Horn to Newfoundland; and in Africa, between the Cape of Good Hope and the Tropic of Cancer. The special object of its enterprise was New Netherland, and especially the region of the Mauritius.[5] The company was not completely organized

---

[1] Page 144. [2] Page 63.
[3] See Brodhead's "History of the State of New York," Appendix E, where the matter is discussed at some length. [4] Note 7, page 59. [5] Page 71.

until the spring of 1623, when it commenced operations with vigor. Its first efforts were to plant a permanent colony, and thus establish a plausible pretext for territorial jurisdiction, for now the English had built rude cabins on the shores of Massachusetts Bay.[1] In April, 1623, thirty families, chiefly Walloons (French Protestants who had fled to Holland), arrived at Manhattan, under the charge of Cornelius Jacobsen May, who was sent to reside in New Netherland, as first director, or governor. Eight of the families went up the Mauritius or Hudson River, and settled at Albany; the remainder chose their place of abode across the channel of the East River, and settled upon lands now covered by the eastern portions of Brooklyn, and the Navy Yard.[2] Then were planted the fruitful seeds of a Dutch colony—then were laid the foundations of the future commonwealth of NEW YORK.[3] The territory was erected into a province and the armorial distinction of a *count* was granted.[4]

SEAL OF NEW NETHERLAND.

CHAPTER III.

MASSACHUSETTS [1606—1620].

SOON after obtaining their charter, in 1606, the PLYMOUTH COMPANY[5] dispatched an agent in a small vessel, with two captive Indians, to examine North Virginia. This vessel was captured by a Spanish cruiser. Another vessel, fitted out at the sole expense of Sir John Popham, and commanded by Martin Pring, was sent, and reached America. Pring confirmed the accounts of Gosnold and others,[6] concerning the beauty and fertility of the New England region. The following year [1607], George Popham[7] came, with one hundred immigrants, and landing at the mouth of the Sagadahoc or Kennebec [August 21], they erected there a small stockade, a storehouse, and a few huts. All but forty-five returned to England in the vessels; those remained, and named their settlement *St. George*. A terrible winter ensued. Fire consumed their store-house and some of their provisions, and the keen frosts and deep snows

[1] Page 78.

[2] The first white child born in New Netherland was Sarah Rapelje, daughter of one of the Walloon settlers. Her birth occurred on the 7th of June, 1625. She has a number of descendants on Long Island.

[3] Page 144.

[4] Several hundred years ago, there were large districts of country in England, and on the continent, governed by Earls, who were subject to the crown, however. These districts were called counties, and the name is still retained, even in the United States, and indicates certain judicial and other jurisdiction. New Netherland was constituted a county of Holland, having all the individual privileges appertaining to an earldom, or separate government. The armorial distinction of an earl, or count, was a kind of cap, called coronet, seen over the shield in the above engraved representation of the seal of New Netherland. The figure of a beaver, on the shield, is emblematic of the Hudson River regions (where that animal then abounded), and of one of the grand objects of settlement there, the trade in furs.

[5] Page 63.

[6] Page 58.

[7] Note 2, page 63.

locked the waters and the forests against the fisherman and hunter. Famine menaced them, but relief came before any were made victims. Of all the company, only Popham, their president, died. Lacking courage to brave the perils of the wilderness, the settlement was abandoned, and the immigrants went back to England [1608] at the very time when the Frenchmen, who were to build Quebec,[1] were upon the ocean. Traffic with the Indian tribes was continued, but settlements were not again attempted for several years.[2]

Only the coast of the extensive country was seen by the several navigators who visited it. The vast interior, now called NEW ENGLAND, was an unknown land, until Captain John Smith, with the mind of a philosopher and the courage of a hero, came, in 1614, and explored, not only the shores but the rivers which penetrated the wilderness. Only himself and four London merchants had an interest in the expedition, which proved highly successful, not only in discoveries, but in trade. With only eight men, Smith examined the region between Cape Cod and the Penobscot, constructed a map of the country, and after an absence of less than seven months, he returned to England, and laid a report before Prince Charles (afterward the unfortunate king who lost his head), the heir apparent to the throne. The prince, delighted with the whole account, confirmed the title which Smith had given to the territory delineated on the map, and it was named NEW ENGLAND. Crime, as usual, dimmed the luster of the discovery. Hunt, commander of one of the vessels of the expedition, kidnapped twenty-seven of the Indians, with Squanto,[3] their chief, as soon as Smith had departed, took them to Spain and sold some of them into slavery.[4] And now, at various points from Florida to Newfoundland, men-stealers of different nations, had planted the seeds of hatred and distrust,[5] whose fruits, in after years were wars, and complicated troubles.

At the close of 1614, the Plymouth company employed Smith to make further explorations in America and to plant a colony. He sailed in the spring of 1615, but was driven back by a tempest. He sailed again on the 4th of July following. His crew became mutinous, and finally his vessel was captured by a French pirate, and they were all taken to France. Smith escaped to England, in an open boat, and arousing the sluggish energies of the Plymouth company and others, they planned vast schemes of colonization, and he was made admiral for life. Eager for gains, some of the members, joining with others, applied for a new charter. It was withheld for a long time. Finally, the king granted a charter [November 3, 1620] to forty of the wealthiest and most powerful men in the realm, who assumed the corporate title of THE COUNCIL OF PLYMOUTH, and superseded the original PLYMOUTH COMPANY.[6] The vast domain of more than a million of square miles, lying between the fortieth and forty-eighth degree of north latitude, and westward to the South Sea,[7]

---

[1] Page 49.

[2] The celebrated Lord Bacon, and others, fitted out an expedition to Newfoundland in 1610, but it was unsuccessful.

[3] Page 114.

[4] When some benevolent friars heard of Hunt's intentions, they took all of the Indians not yet sold, to instruct them as missionaries. Among them was Squanto.

[5] See pages 42 and 49.

[6] Page 63.

[7] Page 42.

was conveyed to them, as absolute owners of the soil. It was the finest portion of the Continent, and now embraces the most flourishing States and Territories of our confederacy. This vast monopoly was unpropitious, in all its elements, to the founding of an empire. It was not the will of God that mere speculators and mercenary adventurers like these should people this broad land. The same year when that great commercial monopoly was formed [1620], a company of devout men and women in Holland, who had been driven from England by a persecuting government, came to the wilderness of the New World, not to seek gold and return, but to erect a tabernacle, where they might worship the Great God in honest simplicity and freedom, and to plant in the wilderness the foundation of a commonwealth, based upon truth and justice. Who were they? Let History answer.

Because the pope of Rome would not sanction one of the most flagrant of his social crimes, Henry the Eighth of England defied the authority of the head of the Church,[1] and by the *Act of Supremacy*,[2] Parliament also cast off the papal yoke. The *people* were not benefited, for the king was pope of Great Britain, and they were his slaves. They enjoyed no religious freedom. Heresy was a high crime; and expressions of freedom of thought and opinion were not tolerated. The doctrines and rituals of the Romish church were enforced, while the *authority* of the pope was denied. The people discovered that in exchanging spiritual masters, they had gained nothing, except that the thunders of excommunication[3] had lost their effect upon the public mind, and thus one step toward emancipation was gained. Henry's son, Edward, established a more liberal Protestantism in England [1574], and soon the followers of Luther and Calvin[4] drew the tangible line of doctrinal difference which existed between them. The former retained or allowed many of the ceremonials of the church of Rome; the latter were more austere, and demanded extreme simplicity in worship, and great purity of life. For this they were called PURITANS, in derision; a name which soon became honorable. When Parliament established a liturgy for the church, the Puritans refused conformity, for they acknowledged no authority but the Bible in matters of religion. They became a distinct and influential party in the State [1550], and were specially commended by the continental reformers.

A PURITAN.

[1] The vicious king asked Pope Julius III. to divorce him from his queen, Catherine of Arragon, in order that he might marry the beautiful Anne Boleyn. The Pope properly refused to give his sanction to the crime; and the licentious monarch, who had been so much of a friend with the Roman Pontiff as to receive the title of "Defender of the Faith," quarreled with the Pontiff, and professed Protestantism. See Note 14, page 62.

[2] An Act of Parliament, adopted in 1534, which declared the king of England the superior head of the Church in that realm, and made Protestantism the established religion of England.

[3] The Pope of Rome assumes the right to excommunicate, or expel from Christian communion, whomsoever he pleases. In former times, even kings were not exempt. An excommunicated person lost social caste; and for centuries this was an iron rod in the hand of ecclesiastics to keep the people in submission to spiritual authority. Happily for mankind, this species of despotism has lost its power, and commands the obedience of only the ignorant and enslaved.

[4] See note 14, page 62. Calvin was the leading French Reformer.

Romanism was re-established in England in 1553, by Mary, the daughter and successor of Henry the Eighth, who was a bigoted persecutor of Protestants of every name. Lutherans and Calvinists were equally in peril. The fires of persecution were lighted, and the first Protestant martyrs were consumed at the stake.[1] Her reign was short, and she is known in history as *the bloody Mary.* She was succeeded by her half-sister, Elizabeth, in 1558, who was a professed Protestant, and the flames were extinguished. Elizabeth was no Puritan. She endeavored to reconcile the magnificent rituals of the Romish Church with the simple requisitions of the gospel. There was no affinity, and trouble ensued. The Puritans, struggling for power, asserted, in all its grandeur, the doctrine of private judgment in religious matters, and of untrammeled religious liberty. From this high position, it was but a step to the broad rock of civil freedom. The Puritan pulpits became the pulpits of the common people, and the preachers often promulgated the doctrine, *that the sovereign was amenable to public opinion when fairly expressed.* This was the very essence of democratic doctrine, and evinced a boldness hitherto unparalleled. The jealousy and the fears of the queen were aroused; and after several years of effort, the *Thirty-nine Articles* of belief, which constitute the rule of faith in the Church of England, were confirmed [1571] by an Act of Parliament.

And now bigotry in power began its wicked work. In 1583, a court of high commission was established, for the detection and punishment of Non-Conformists,[2] with powers almost as absolute as the Roman Inquisition. Persecution began its work in earnest, and continued active for twenty years. The Puritans looked to the accession of James of Scotland, which took place in 1604,[3] with hope, but were disappointed. He was the most contemptible monarch that ever disgraced the chair of supreme government in England. A brilliant English writer[4] says, "He was cunning, covetous, wasteful, idle, drunken, greedy, dirty, cowardly, a great swearer, and the most conceited man on earth." The pure in heart could expect no consideration from such a man. When he was fairly seated on the English throne, he said of the Puritans, "I will make them conform or I will harrie them out of the land." There were then more than thirty thousand of them in England. During the first year of James's reign, three hundred of their ministers were silenced, imprisoned, or exiled. The long struggle of the established church with the Roman Catholics on one hand, and the Puritans on the other, was now decided. It had been a struggle of three quarters of a century, not so much for *toleration* as for *supremacy;* and the Church of England was the final victor. During these trials, England lost some of her best men. Among the devout ones who fled

---

[1] John Rogers, a pious minister, and John Hooper, Bishop of Gloucester, were the first who suffered.

[2] This was the title of all those Protestants in England who refused to conform to the doctrines and ceremonials of the Established Church. This name was first given in 1572. Ninety years afterward [1662], 2,000 ministers of the Established Church, unwilling to subscribe to the Thirty-nine Articles, seceded, and were called Dissenters; a name yet applied to all British Protestants who are not attached to the Church of England.

[3] See note 1, page 63.

[4] Charles Dickens.

from persecution, was the Reverend John Robinson, pastor of a flock gathered in the northern counties. Informed that there was "freedom of religion for all men in Holland," he fled thither, with his people, in 1608, and established a church at Leyden. They were soon joined by others from their native country. Their purity of life and lofty independence commanded the admiration of the Dutch; and their loyalty to the country from which they had been driven, was respected as a noble virtue. There they learned many of those sound political maxims which lie at the foundation of our own government; for there those principles of civil liberty, which lay almost dormant in theory, in England, were found in daily practice.

At Leyden, the English exiles were charmed by the narratives of the Dutch voyagers to America. They felt that they had now no home, no abiding place—that they were only PILGRIMS—and they resolved to go to the New World, far away from persecutions, where they might establish a colony, with religious freedom for its basis. A deputation went to England in 1617,[1] and through the influence of powerful friends,[2] obtained the consent of the Plymouth Company to settle in North Virginia,[3] and also a promise from the king that he would wink at their heresy, and let them alone in their new home. They asked no more! Some London merchants formed a partnership with them, and furnished capital for the expedition.[4] Captain John Smith, the founder of Virginia and explorer of New England, offered his services, but on account of his aristocratic notions, they were declined. Two ships (*Speedwell* and *May-Flower*) were purchased and furnished,[5] and in the summer of 1620, a portion of the *Pilgrims* in Holland—"the youngest and strongest"—embarked from Delft-Haven for England.[6] Robinson and the larger portion of his flock remained at Leyden till a more convenient season,[7] and elder Brewster accompanied the voyagers as their spiritual guide. The two ships left Southampton, in England, on the 5th of August, 1620. The courage of the captain and company of the *Speedwell* failed, and the vessels put back to port. The sails of the *May-Flower* were again spread, in the harbor of Plymouth, on the 6th

MAY-FLOWER.

[1] John Carver and Robert Cushman.

[2] Sir Edward Sandys [page 105] was one of their chief advocates in England. [3] Page 63.

[4] The services of each emigrant were valued as a capital of ten pounds, and belonged to the company. All profits were to be reserved till the end of seven years, when all the lands, houses, and every production of their joint industry, were to be valued, and the amount divided among the shareholders, according to their respective interests. This was a community of interest, similar, in character, to those which have been proposed and attempted in our day, under the respective titles of Communism, Fourierism, and Socialism. It failed to accomplish its intended purpose, and was abandoned.

[5] The *Speedwell* was a vessel of 60 tons; the *May-Flower* of 180 tons.

[6] See engraving on page 104. This is a copy of a picture of *The Embarkation of the Pilgrims*, in the Rotunda of the Federal Capitol, painted by Professor Robert W. Weir, of the Military Academy, at West Point, New York.

[7] Mr. Robinson was never permitted to see America. Notes 3, and 5, page 116.

of September, and forty-one men, most of them with families[1] (one hundred and one in all)—the winnowed remnant of the PILGRIMS who left Delft-Haven—crossed the stormy Atlantic. These were they who came to the New World to enjoy liberty of conscience and freedom of action, and to lay, broad and deep, a portion of the foundations of our happy Republic. After a boisterous passage of sixty-three days, thee *May-Flower* anchored within Cape Cod.[2] Before proceeding to the shore, the PILGRIMS agreed upon a form of government, and committed it to writing.[3] To that *first constitution of government* ever subscribed by a whole people, the forty-one men affixed their names, and then elected John Carver to be their governor.[4] In the cabin of the *May-Flower* the first republican government in America was solemnly inaugurated. That vessel thus became truly the cradle of liberty in America, rocked on the free waves of the ocean.

The *May-Flower* was tossed about on the ocean for two long months, and the approach to land was a joyful event for the settlers. Exploring parties were sent out,[5] and after many hardships, they selected a place for landing. It was on the 22d day of December, 1620, that the PILGRIM FATHERS first set foot upon a bare rock on the bleak coast of Massachusetts Bay, while all around, the earth was covered with deep snow.[6] They called the landing-place

---

[1] The following are their names: John Carver, William Bradford, Edward Winslow, William Brewster, Isaac Allerton, Captain Miles Standish, John Alden, Samuel Fuller, Christopher Martin, William Mullins, William White, Richard Warren, John Howland, Stephen Hopkins, Edward Tilly, John Tilly, Peter Brown, Richard Britteridge, George Soule, Richard Clark, Richard Gardiner, Francis Cook, Thomas Rogers, Thomas Tinker, John Ridgdale, Edward Fuller, John Turner, Francis Eaton, James Chilton, John Crackston, John Billington, Moses Fletcher, John Goodman, Degory Priest, Thomas Williams, Gilbert Winslow, Edward Margeson, John Allerton, Thomas English, Edward Dotey, Edward Leister. Howland was Carver's servant; Soule was Winslow's servant; and Dotey and Leister were servants of Hopkins.

[2] The foolish statement has often been made, that the PILGRIMS intended to land at Manhattan Island (New York), but the commander of the *May-Flower*, having been bribed by the Dutch to do so, landed them further east beyond the Dutch possessions. The story is a fable. Coppin, the pilot, had been on the coast of New England before, and, in navigating the *May-Flower*, he only followed his old track.

[3] The following is a copy of the instrument: "In the name of God, Amen. We, whose names are underwritten, the loyal subjects of our dread sovereign lord, king James, by the grace of God, of Great Britain, France, and Ireland, king, defender of the faith, etc., having undertaken, for the glory of God and the advancement of the Christian faith, and honor of our king and country, a voyage to plant the first colony in the northern parts of Virginia, do, by these presents, solemnly and mutually, in the presence of God and of one another, covenant and combine ourselves together into a civil body politic, for our better ordering and preservation, and furtherance of the ends aforesaid; and by virtue hereof, to enact, constitute, and frame just and equal laws, ordinances, acts, constitutions, and offices from time to time, as shall be thought most meet and convenient for the general good of the colony; unto which we promise all due submission and obedience. In witness whereof we have hereto subscribed our names, at Cape Cod, the 11th of November, in the year of the reign of our sovereign Lord, King James of England, France, and Ireland, the Eighteenth, and of Scotland the Fifty-fourth. Anno Domini, 1620."

[4] John Carver was born in England, went with Robinson to Holland, and on the 3d of April, 1621, while governor of the Plymouth colony, he died.

[5] Their leader was Miles Standish, a brave soldier, who had served in the Netherlands. He was very active in the colony as military commander-in-chief, in both fighting and treating with the Indians, and is called "The Hero of New England." He was a magistrate many years, and died at Duxbury, Massachusetts, in 1656.

[6] While the explorers were searching for a landing-place, the wife of William White, a bride but a short time before leaving Holland, gave birth to a son, "the first Englishman born in New England." They named him Peregrine, and the cradle in which he was rocked is yet preserved. He died in Marshfield in 1704.

New Plymouth, and there a flourishing village is now spread out.[1] Dreary, indeed, was the prospect before them. Exposure and privations had prostrated one half of the men before the first blow of the axe had been struck to erect a habitation. Faith and hope nerved the arms of the healthy, and they began to build. One by one perished. The governor and his wife died on the 3d of April, 1621; and on the first of that month, forty-six of the one hundred immigrants were in their graves. Nineteen of these were signers to the Constitution. At one time only seven men were capable of assisting the sick. Fortunately, the neighboring tribes, weakened by a pestilence,[3] did not molest them. Spring and summer came. Game became plenty in the forest, and they caught many fishes from the waters. They sowed and reaped, and soon friends from England joined them.[4] The settlement, begun with so much sorrow and suffering, became permanent, and then and there the foundations of the commonwealth of MASSACHUSETTS were laid.

GOV. CARVER'S CHAIR.[2]

CHAPTER IV.

NEW HAMPSHIRE. [1622–1680.]

THE enterprising Sir Fernando Gorges, who, for many years, had been engaged in traffic with the Indians on the New England coast, projected a settlement further eastward than Plymouth, and for that purpose became associated with John Mason, a merchant, afterward a naval commander, and always "a man of action." Mason was secretary to the Plymouth Council, for New England,[5] and was well acquainted with all matters pertaining to settlements in the New World. Gorges and Mason obtained a grant of land in 1622, extending from the Merrimac to the Kennebec, and inland to the St. Lawrence. They named the territory LACONIA. Mason had obtained a grant the previous year, extending from Salem to the mouth of the Merrimac, which he had named MARIANA. The same year, a colony of fishermen, under David Thompson, seated themselves at Little Harbor, on the Piscataqua River, just below Portsmouth. Another party, under two brothers named Hilton, London fishmongers, commenced a settlement, in 1623, a few miles above, at Dover; but these were only fishing stations, and did not flourish.

---

[1] "Plymouth Rock" is famous. It is now [1856] in two pieces. One part remains in its original position at Hedge's Wharf, Plymouth; the other is in the center of the town, surrounded by an iron railing. It was dragged thither, in 1774, by twenty yoke of oxen, and over it the Whigs [note 4, page 226] erected a liberty-pole.

[2] This was the *throne* upon which sat the first Christian monarch of New England. Governor Carver was at the head of a new State, and, as chief magistrate, held the same relative position as king James of England, whose seat was richly ornamented and covered with a canopy of silk and gold.

[3] Page 114.

[4] Page 115.

[5] Page 74.

In the year 1629, the Rev. Mr. Wheelwright (a brother-in-law of the celebrated Anne Hutchinson, who was banished from the Massachusetts colony on a charge of sedition, in 1637) purchased from the Indians the wilderness between the Merrimac and the Piscataqua, and founded Exeter. The same year Mason obtained from Gorges exclusive ownership of that same portion of LACONIA. He named the domain NEW HAMPSHIRE, and in 1631 built a house upon the site of Portsmouth, the name which he gave to the spot.[1] Other settlements upon the Piscataqua, and along the present coast of Maine, as far as Portland, were attempted. At the latter place a company had a grant of land forty miles square, and formed an agricultural settlement in 1631, called LIGONIA.[2] Pemaquid Point was another settlement, which remained an independent community for almost forty years. Trading houses were established as far east as Machias, but they were broken up by the French, and the western limits of Acadie were fixed at Pemaquid Point, about half way from the Penobscot to the Kennebec. The several feeble and scattered settlements in New Hampshire formed a coalition with the flourishing Massachusetts colony in 1641, and remained dependencies of that province until 1680, when they were separated by order of the king, and New Hampshire became a royal province. Its first government consisted of a governor and council appointed by the king, and a house of representatives elected by the people. Then was founded the commonwealth of NEW HAMPSHIRE.

CHAPTER V.

MARYLAND. [1634.]

A LARGE portion of the American colonies were the fruitful growth of the seeds of civil liberty, wafted hither by the fierce gales of oppression in some

[1] Mason had been governor of Portsmouth, in Hampshire County, England, and these names were given in memory of his former residence.

[2] The people of these eastern settlements, which formed the basis of the present commonwealth of MAINE, did not like the government attempted to be established by the proprietor, and, taking political power into their own hands, placed themselves under the jurisdiction of Massachusetts in 1652. The territory was erected into a county, and called Yorkshire. In 1621, king James, as sovereign of Scotland, placed the Scottish seal to a charter granting to Sir William Alexander, afterward [1633] earl of Stirling, the whole territory eastward of the State of Maine, under the title of *Nova Scotia*, or New Scotland. The French had already occupied places along the coast, and called the country *Acadie*. The Scotch proprietor never attempted settlements, either in this territory or in Canada which Charles the First had granted to him, and the whole country had passed into the hands of the French, by treaty. The earl died in 1640, and all connection of his family with Nova Scotia ceased. His title was held afterward by four successors, the last of whom died in 1739. In 1759, William Alexander (General Lord Stirling during our War for Independence) made an unsuccessful claim to the title. The next claimant was Alexander Humphrey, who commenced operations in the Scottish courts in 1815, and by forgeries and frauds was partially successful. The whole was exposed in 1833. Humphrey was in this country in 1852, pressing his claims to the monopoly of the Eastern Fisheries, by virtue of the grants of kings James and Charles more than two hundred years ago!

form. Maryland, occupying a space between North and South Virginia,[1] was first settled by persecuted Roman Catholics from England and Ireland. While king James worried the Puritans on one hand, for non-conformity,[2] the Roman Catholics, at the other end of the religious scale, were subjected to even more severe penalties. As the Puritans increased in numbers and influence, their cry against the Roman Catholics grew louder and fiercer; and, while defending themselves from persecution with one hand, they were inflicting as severe a lash upon the Romanists with the other. Thus subjected to twofold oppŏsition, the condition of the Roman Catholics became deplorable, and, in common with other sufferers for opinion's sake, their eyes were turned toward free America. Among the most influential professors of Catholicism was George Calvert, an active member of the London Company,[3] and Secretary of State at the time when the PILGRIMS[4] were preparing to emigrate to America. He was so much more loyal in action to his sovereign than to his faith, that he did not lose the king's favor, although frankly professing to be a Roman Catholic; and for his services he was created an Irish peer in 1621, with the title of Lord Baltimore. He also obtained from James, a grant [1622] to plant a Roman Catholic colony on a portion of Newfoundland. He called the territory AVALON, but his scheme was not successful. The barren soil, and French aggressors from Acadie, were too much for the industry and courage of his colonists, and the settlement was abandoned.

Foiled in his projects in the east, Lord Baltimore went to Virginia in 1628, with a view of establishing a colony of his brethren there. But he found the Virginians as intolerant as the crown or the Puritans, and he turned his back upon their narrow prejudices, and went to examine the beautiful, unoccupied region beyond the Potomac. He was pleased with the country, and applied for a charter to establish a colony there. The London Company was now dissolved,[5] and the soil had become the property of the monarch. King Charles the First, then on the throne, readily granted a charter, but before it was completed, Lord Baltimore died. This event occurred on the 25th of April, 1632, and on the 20th of June following, the patent was issued to Cecil, his son and heir. In honor of the queen, Henrietta Maria,[6] the province was called MARYLAND. The territory defined in the charter extended along each side of Chesapeake Bay, from the 30th to the 45th degree of north latitude, its western line being the waters of the Potomac.

CECIL, SECOND LORD BALTIMORE.

It is believed that the Maryland charter was drawn by the first Lord Baltimore's own hand. It was the most liberal one yet granted by an English monarch, both in respect of the proprietor and the settlers. The government of the province was inde-

[1] Page 63. [2] Note 2, page 76. [3] Page 63. [4] Page 77. [5] Page 107.
[6] She was a Roman Catholic, and sister of Louis the Thirteenth of France.

pendent of the crown, and equality in religious rights and civil freedom was secured to every Christian sect. Unitarians, or those who denied the doctrine of the Trinity, as well as all unbelievers in Divine revelation, were not covered by this mantle of toleration. The king had no power to levy the smallest tax upon the colonists, and all laws were invalid until sanctioned by a majority of the freemen, or their deputies. Under such a wise and liberal charter the colony, when planted, flourished remarkably, for those persecuted by the Puritans in New England, and the Churchmen in Virginia, there sought refuge, and found peace.

Emigration to Maryland commenced in 1633. The first company, mostly Roman Catholics, sailed for America on the 2d of December of that year, under Leonard Calvert, brother of the proprietor, and appointed governor of the province. They arrived in March, 1634, and after sailing up the Potomac, as far as Mount Vernon, they descended the stream, almost to its mouth. They landed upon an estuary of the Chesapeake, purchased an Indian village, and laid the foundation of a town [April, 1634], which they named St. Mary.[1] The honesty of Calvert, in paying for the land, secured the good will of the Indians; and, unlike the first settlers of most of the other colonies, they experienced no sufferings from want, or the hostilities of the Aboriginals.

Popular government was first organized in Maryland on the 8th of March, 1635, when the first legislative assembly was convened at St. Mary. Every freeman being allowed to vote, it was a purely democratic legislature. As the number of colonists increased, this method of making laws was found to be inconvenient, and in 1639, a representative government was established, the people being allowed to send as many delegates as they pleased. The first representative assembly made a declaration of rights, defined the powers of the proprietor, and took measures to secure to the colonists all the civil liberties enjoyed by the people of Old England. Then was founded the commonwealth of MARYLAND.

CHAPTER VI.

CONNECTICUT. [1632—1639.]

ADRIAN BLOCK,[2] the Dutch navigator, discovered and explored the Connecticut River, as far as the site of Hartford, in 1614, and named it *Versche*,

[1] Trading posts were established a little earlier than this, within the Maryland province. In 1631, William Clayborne obtained a license from the king to traffic with the Indians; and when Calvert and his company came, he had two settlements, one on Kent Island, nearly opposite Annapolis, and another at the present Havre de Grace, at the mouth of the Susquehannah. He refused to acknowledge the authority of Baltimore, and trouble ensued. He collected his people on the eastern shore of Maryland in 1635, with a determination to defend his claims by force of arms; and in May quite a severe skirmish ensued between his forces and those of the colonists. Clayborne's men were taken prisoners, and he fled to Virginia. He was declared guilty of treason, and sent to England for trial. His estates were forfeited; but, being acquitted of the charge, he returned to Maryland and incited a rebellion. See page 151.

[2] Page 72.

HOOKER'S EMIGRATION TO CONNECTICUT.

or *Fresh* Water River.[1] Soon afterward Dutch traders were upon its banks, and might have carried on a peaceful and profitable traffic with the Indians, had honor and honesty marked their course. But the avaricious agent of the Dutch, imprisoned an Indian chief on board his vessel, and would not release him until one hundred and forty fathoms of wampum[2] had been paid. The exasperated Indians menaced the traders, and near the site of Hartford, at a place yet known as Dutch Point, the latter commenced the erection of a fort. The Indians were finally conciliated, and, at their request, the fort was abandoned for awhile.

A friendly intercourse was opened between the Dutch of New Netherland and the Puritans in 1627.[3] With the guise of friendship, but really for the purpose of strengthening the claims of the Dutch to the Connecticut valley, by having an English settlement there under the jurisdiction of New Netherland, Governor Minuit[4] advised the Puritans to leave the barren land of Massachusetts Bay, and settle in the fertile region of the Fresh Water River. In 1631, a Mohegan chief, then at war with the powerful Pequods,[5] desirous of having a strong barrier between himself and his foes, urged the English to come and settle in the Connecticut valley. The Puritans clearly perceived the selfish policy of both parties, and hesitated to leave. The following year [1632], however, Governor Winslow, of the Plymouth colony,[6] visited that fertile region, and, delighted with its appearance, resolved to promote emigration thither. In the mean while, the Council of Plymouth[7] had granted the soil of Connecticut [1630] to the Earl of Warwicke, who, in 1631, transferred his interest to Lord Say-and-Seal, Lord Brooke, John Hampden, and others. The eastern boundary of the territory was "Narraganset River," and the western (like all other charters at that time) was the South Sea, or Pacific Ocean.[8] The Dutch became apprised of these movements of the English; and perceiving no advantage (but detriment) to themselves, they purchased of the Indians the land at Hartford and vicinity, completed their fort, and placed two cannons upon it, in 1633, with the intention of preventing the English ascending the river.

Although the Plymouth people were aware of the preparations made by the Dutch, to defend their claim, they did not hesitate, and in October, 1633, Captain William Holmes and a chosen company arrived in the Connecticut River, in a sloop. Holmes bore a commission from Governor Winslow to make a settlement, and brought with him the frame of a house. When he approached the Dutch fort, the commander menaced him with destruction if he attempted to pass it. Holmes was not intimidated, and sailing by unhurt, he landed at the site of Windsor, and there erected his house. Seventy men were sent by the Dutch the following year, to drive him from the country. They were kept at bay, and finally a parley resulted in peaceful relations.[9] Holmes's colony flourished, and in the autumn of 1635, a party of sixty men, women, and children, from the Puritan settlements, commenced a journey through the wilder-

---

[1] *Connecticut* is the English orthography of the Indian word Quon-eh-ta-cut, which signifies "the long river." [2] Probably about four hundred dollars. See note 2, page 13.
[3] Page 75. [4] Page 139. [5] Page 21. [6] Page 79.
[7] Page 74. [8] Page 42. [9] See note 2, page 142.

ness [Oct. 25] to join him. With their cattle,[1] they made their slow and dreary way a hundred miles through dark forests and dismal swamps; and when they arrived upon the banks of the Connecticut [Nov. 25], the ground was covered with deep snow, and the river was frozen. It was a winter of great trial for them. Many cattle perished.[2] A vessel bearing food for the colony was lost on the coast, and the settlers were compelled to subsist upon acorns, and scanty supplies of Indian corn from the natives. Many of them made their way to the fort, then just erected at Saybrook, near the mouth of the river, and returned to Boston by water. Spring opened, and the necessities of those who remained were supplied. They erected a small house for worship on the site of Hartford, and in April, 1636, the first court, or organized government was held there. At about the time when this company departed, a son of Governor Winthrop,[3] of Massachusetts, Hugh Peters, and Henry Vane, arrived at Boston from England, as commissioners for the proprietors of Connecticut, with instructions to build a fort at the mouth of the river of that name, and to plant a colony there. The fort was speedily built, and the settlement was named Saybrook, in honor of the two peers named in the charter.[4]

FIRST MEETING-HOUSE.

Another migration of Puritans to the Connecticut valley, more important, and with better results, now took place. In June, 1636, Rev. Thomas Hooker, the "light of the western churches,"[5] with other ministers, their families, and flocks, in all about one hundred, left the vicinity of Boston for the new land of promise. It was a toilsome journey through the swamps and forests. They subsisted upon berries and the milk of their cows which they took with them, and on the 4th of July, they stood upon the beautiful banks of the Connecticut. On the 9th, Mr. Hooker preached and administered the communion in the little meeting-house at Hartford, and there a great portion of the company settled. Some chose Wethersfield for a residence; and others, from Roxbury, went up the river twenty miles, and settled at Springfield. There were now five distinct English settlements upon the Connecticut River, yet they were scattered and weak.

Clouds soon appeared in the morning sky, and the settlers in the Connecticut valley perceived the gathering of a fearful storm. The powerful Pequod Indians[6] became jealous of the white people, because they appeared to be the friends of their enemies, the Mohegans on the west, and of their more powerful foes, the Narragansetts, on the east. They first commenced petty annoyances; then kidnapped children, murdered men in the forests, and attacked families on

---

[1] This was the first introduction of cattle into Connecticut.

[2] The loss in cattle was estimated at about one thousand dollars.

[3] Page 117. [4] Page 85.

[5] Thomas Hooker was a native of Leicestershire, England, where he was born in 1586. He was silenced, because of his non-conformity, in 1630, when he left the ministry, and founded a grammar school at Cambridge. He was compelled to flee to Holland, from whence he came to America with Mr. Cotton, in 1633. He was a man of great benevolence, and was eminently useful. He died in July, 1647, at the age of sixty-one years. [6] Page 21.

the outskirts of the settlement at Saybrook. Their allies of Block Island[1] captured a Massachusetts trading vessel, killed the captain[2] [July, 1636], and plundered her. The Puritans in the east were alarmed and indignant, and an inefficient expedition from Boston and vicinity penetrated the Pequod country. It did more harm than good, for it resulted only in increasing the hatred and hostility of the savages. The Pequods became bolder, and finally sought an alliánce with their enemies, the Narragansetts, in an effort to exterminate the white people. At this critical moment a deliverer appeared when least expected. Roger Williams, who for his tolerant opinions had been banished from Massachusetts,[3] was now a friendly resident in the country of the Narragansetts, and heard of the proposed alliance. Forgetting the many injuries he had received, he warned the doomed people of the Bay colony, of impending danger. At the risk of his own life, he descended Narragansct Bay in an open canoe, on a stormy day, and visited Miantonomoh, the renowned sachem, at his seat near Newport, while the Pequod embassadors were there in council. The latter menaced Williams with death; yet that good man remained there three days, and effectually prevented the alliance.[4] And more—he induced the Narragansetts to renew hostilities with the Pequods. By this generous service the infant settlements were saved from destruction.

Although foiled in their attempt at alliance, the Pequods were not disheartened. During the ensuing winter they continued their murderous depredations. In the spring, the authorities of the English settlements on the Connecticut declared war against the Pequods [May, 1637], and the Massachusetts and Plymouth colonies agreed to aid them. Soon, Captain Mason, who was in command of the fort at Saybrook,[5] and Captain John Underhill, a brave and restless man, sailed in some pinnaces, with about eighty white men and seventy Mohegan Indians under Uncas,[6] for Narraganset Bay. There Miantonomoh, with two hundred warriors, joined them, and they marched for the Pequod country. Their ranks were swollen by the brave Niantics and others, until five hundred "bowmen and spearmen" were in the train of Captains Mason and Underhill.

The chief sachem of the Pequods, was Sassacus, a fierce warrior, and the terror of the New England tribes.[7] He could summon almost two thousand warriors to the field; and feeling confident in his strength, he was not properly vigilant. His chief fort and village on the Mystic River, eight miles north-east of New London, was surprised at dawn the 5th of June, 1637, and before sun-rise, more than six hundred men, women, and children, perished by fire and sword. Only seven escaped to spread the dreadful intelligence abroad. and arouse the surviving warriors. The Narragansetts turned homeward, and the English, aware of great peril, pressed forward to Groton on the Thames,

[1] This island, which lies nearly south from the eastern border of Connecticut, was visited by Adrian Block, the Dutch navigator, and was called by his name. At the time in question, it was thickly populated with fierce Indians.

[2] John Oldham, the first overland explorer of the Connecticut River. [3] Page 89.

[4] Page 91. [5] Page 85. [6] Page 21. [7] Page 22.

and there embarked for Saybrook. They had lost only two killed, and less than twenty wounded.

The brave Sassacus had hardly recovered from this shock, when almost a hundred armed settlers, from Massachusetts, under Captain Stoughton, arrived at Saybrook. The terrified Pequods made no resistance, but fled in dismay toward the wilderness westward, hotly pursued by the English. Terrible was the destruction in the path of the pursuers. Throughout the beautiful country on Long Island Sound, from Saybrook to New Haven, wigwams and cornfields were destroyed, and helpless women and children were slain. With Sassacus at their head, the Indians flew like deer before the hounds, and finally took shelter in Sasco swamp, near Fairfield, where, after a severe battle, they all surrendered, except Sassacus and a few followers. These fled to the Mohawks,[1] where the sachem was treacherously murdered, and his people were sold into slavery, or incorporated with other tribes. The blow was one of extermination, relentless and cruel. "There did not remain a sannup or squaw, a warrior or child of the Pequod name. A nation had disappeared in a day." The New England tribes[2] were filled with awe, and for forty years the colonists were unmolested by them.

With the return of peace, the spirit of adventure revived. In the summer of 1637, John Davenport, an eminent non-conformist[3] minister of London, with Theophilus Eaton and Edward Hopkins, rich merchants who represented a wealthy company, arrived at Boston. They were cordially received, and urgently solicited to settle in that colony. The Hutchinson controversy[4] was then at its height; and perceiving the religious agitations of the people, they resolved to found a settlement in the wilderness. The sagacious Puritans, while pursuing the Pequods, had discovered the beauty and fertility of the country along the Sound from the Connecticut to Fairfield, and Davenport and his companions heard their report with joy. Eaton and a few others explored the coast in autumn, and erecting a hut[5] near the Quinipiac Creek (the site of New Haven), they passed the winter there, and selected it for a settlement. In the spring [April 13, 1638] Davenport and others followed, and under a wide-spreading oak,[6] the good minister preached his first sermon. They purchased the lands at Quinipiac of the Indians, and, taking the Bible for their guide, they formed an independent government, or "plantation covenant," upon strictly religious principles. Prosperity blessed them, and they laid the foundations of a city, and called it NEW HAVEN. The following year, the settlers at Windsor, Hartford, and Wethersfield, met in convention at Hartford [January 24, 1639], and adopted a written constitution, which contained very liberal provisions. It ordained that the governor and legislature should be elected annually, by the people, and they were required to take an oath of allegiance to the commonwealth, and not to the king. The General Assembly, alone,

---

[1] Page 23. [2] Page 22. [3] Note 2, page 76. [4] Page 120.
[5] On the corner of Church and George-streets, New Haven.
[6] At the intersection of George and College-streets, New Haven.

could make or repeal laws; and in every matter the voice of the people was heard. This was termed the CONNECTICUT COLONY; and, notwithstanding it and the New Haven colony were not united until 1665, now was laid the foundation of the commonwealth of CONNECTICUT, which was governed by the Hartford Constitution for more than a century and a half.

CHAPTER VII.

RHODE ISLAND. [1636—1643.]

THE seed of the Rhode Island commonwealth was planted by brave hands, made strong by persecution. The first settler in Rhode Island was William Blackstone, a non-conformist minister,[1] who was also the first resident upon the peninsula of Shawmut, where Boston now stands.[2] Not liking the "lords brethren" in Massachusetts any more than the "lords bishops" of England, from whose frowns he had fled, he withdrew to the wilderness, and dwelt high up on the Seekonk or Pawtucket River, which portion of the stream still bears his name. There he planted, and called the place Rehoboth.[3] Although he was the first *settler*, Blackstone was not the *founder* of Rhode Island. He always held allegiance to Massachusetts, and did not aspire to a higher dignity than that of an exile for conscience' sake.

Roger Williams, an ardent young minister at Salem,[4] became the instrument of establishing the foundations of a new commonwealth in the wilderness. When he was banished from Massachusetts, toward the close of 1635,[5] he crossed the borders of civilization, and found liberty and toleration among the heathen. After his sentence,[6] his bigoted persecutors began to dread the influence of his enlightened principles, if he should plant a settlement beyond the limits of existing colonies, and they resolved to detain him. Informed of their scheme, he withdrew from Salem in the dead of winter [Jan., 1636], and through deep snows he traversed the forests alone, for fourteen weeks, sheltered only by the rude wigwam of the Indian, until he found the hospitable cabin[7] of

[1] Note 2, page 76. [2] Page 118.
[3] Room. The name was significant of his aim—he wanted *room* outside of the narrow confines of what he deemed Puritan intolerance.
[4] Roger Williams was born in Wales, in 1599, and was educated at Oxford. Persecution drove him to America in 1631, when he was chosen assistant minister at Salem. His extreme toleration did not find there a genial atmosphere, and he went to Plymouth. There, too, he was regarded with suspicion. He returned to Salem in 1634, formed a separate congregation, and in 1635, the general court of Massachusetts passed sentence of banishment against him. He labored zealously in founding the colony of Rhode Island, and had no difficulty with any people who came there, except the Quakers. He died at Providence, in April, 1683, at the age of eighty-four years.
[5] Page 119.
[6] Williams was allowed six weeks after the pronunciation of his sentence to prepare for his departure.
[7] Massasoit had become acquainted with the manner of building cabins adopted by the settlers at fishing-stations on the coast, and had constructed one for himself. They were much more comfortable than wigwams. See page 13.

Massasoit, the chief sachem of the Wampanoags,[1] at Mount Hope. There he was entertained until the buds appeared, when, being joined by five friends from Boston, he seated himself upon the Seekonk, some distance below Blackstone's plantation. He found himself within the territory of the Plymouth Company.[2] Governor Winslow[3] advised him to cross into the Narraganset country, where he could not be molested. With his companions he embarked in a light canoe, paddled around to the head of Narraganset Bay, and upon a green slope, near a spring,[4] they prayed, and chose the spot for a settlement. Williams obtained

Roger Williams

a grant of land from Canonicus, chief sachem of the Narragansetts, and in commemoration of "God's merciful providence to him in his distress," he called the place PROVIDENCE.

The freedom enjoyed there was soon spoken of at Boston, and persecuted men fled thither for refuge. Persons of every creed were allowed full liberty of conscience, and lived together happily. The same liberty was allowed in politics as in religion; and a pure democracy was established there. Each settler was required to subscribe to an agreement, that he would submit to such rules, "not affecting the conscience," as a majority of the inhabitants should adopt for the public good. Williams reserved no political power to himself, and the leader and follower had equal dignity and privileges. The government was

[1] Page 22. [2] Page 63. [3] Page 85.
[4] This spring is now [1856] beneath some fine sycamores on the west side of Benefit street, in Providence.

entirely in the hands of the people. Canonicus, the powerful Narragansett chief, became much attached to Williams, and his influence among them, as we have seen,[1] was very great. He saved his persecutors from destruction, yet they had not the Christian manliness to remove the sentence of banishment, and receive him to their bosoms as a brother. He could not compress his enlarged views into the narrow compass of their creed; and so, while they rejoiced in their deliverance, they anathematized their deliverer as a heretic and an outcast. But he enjoyed the favor of God. His settlement was entirely unmolested during the Pequod war,[2] and it prospered wonderfully.

Roger Williams opened his arms wide to the persecuted. Early in 1638, while Mrs. Hutchinson was yet in prison in Boston,[3] her husband, with William Coddington, Dr. John Clarke, and sixteen others, of concurrent religious views,[4] accepted the invitation of Williams to settle in his vicinity. Miantonomoh gave them the beautiful island of Aquiday[5] for forty fathoms of white wampum.[6] They called it Isle of Rhodes, because of its fancied resemblance to the island of that name in the Levant, and upon its northern verge they planted a settlement, and named it Portsmouth. A covenant, similar to the one used by Williams,[7] was signed by the settlers; and, in imitation of the Jewish form of government under the judges, Coddington was chosen judge, or chief ruler, with three assistants. Others soon came from Boston; and in 1639, Newport, toward the lower extremity of the island, was founded. Liberty of conscience was absolute; love was the social and political bond, and upon the seal which they adopted was the motto, *Amor vincit omnia*—"Love is all-powerful." Although the Rhode Island and the Providence plantations were separate in government, they were united in interest and aim. Unwilling to acknowledge allegiance to either Massachusetts or Plymouth,[8] they sought an independent charter. For that purpose Roger Williams went to England in 1643. The whole parent country was then convulsed with civil war.[9] After much delay, he obtained from Parliament (which was then contending fiercely with the king) a free charter of incorporation, dated March 24, 1644, and all the settlements were united under the general title of ***Rhode Island and Providence Plantations.*** Then was founded the commonwealth of RHODE ISLAND.

---

[1] Page 87. [2] Page 87. [3] Page 120. [4] Note 2, page 120.

[5] This was the Indian name of Rhode Island. It is a Narragansett word, signifying *Peaceable Isle.* It is sometimes spelled Aquitneck, and Aquitnet.

[6] Note 2, page 13. They also gave the Indians ten coats and twenty hoes, on condition that they should leave the island before the next winter.

[7] Page 90. The following is a copy of the government compact: "We, whose names are underwritten, do swear solemnly, in the presence of Jehovah, to incorporate ourselves into a body politic, and, as He shall help us, will submit our persons, lives, and estates, unto our Lord Jesus Christ, the King of kings, and Lord of Hosts, and to all those most perfect and absolute laws of His, given us in His holy Word of truth, to be guided and judged thereby."

[8] This unwillingness caused the other New England colonies to refuse the application of Rhode Island to become one of the Confederacy, in 1643. See page 121.

[9] Note 3, page 108.

CHAPTER VIII.

DELAWARE, NEW JERSEY, AND PENNSYLVANIA. [1631—1682.]

It is difficult to draw the line of demarcation between the first permanent settlements in the provinces of Delaware, New Jersey, and Pennsylvania, for they bore such intimate relations to each other that they may be appropriately considered as parts of one episode in the history of American colonization. We shall, therefore, consider these settlements, in close connection, in one chapter, commencing with

DELAWARE.

It was claimed by the Dutch, that the territory of New Netherland[1] extended southward to Cape Henlopen. In June, 1629, Samuel Godyn and others purchased of the natives the territory between the Cape and the mouth of the Delaware River. The following year, two ships, fitted out by Captain De Vries and others, and placed under the command of Peter Heyes, sailed from the Texel [Dec. 12, 1630] for America. One vessel was captured; the other arrived in April, 1631; and near the present town of Lewiston, in Delaware, thirty immigrants, with implements and cattle, seated themselves. Heyes returned to Holland, and reported to Captain De Vries.[2] That mariner visited America early the following year [1632], but the little colony left by Heyes was not to be found. Difficulties with the Indians had provoked savage vengeance, and they had exterminated the white people.

Information respecting the fine country along the Delaware had spread northward, and soon a competitor for a place on the South River, as it was called, appeared. Usselincx, an original projector of the Dutch West India Company,[3] becoming dissatisfied with his associates, visited Sweden, and laid before the enlightened monarch, Gustavus Adolphus, well-arranged plans for a Swedish colony in the New World. The king was delighted, for his attention had already been turned toward America; and his benevolent heart was full of desires to plant a free colony there, which should become an asylum for all persecuted Christians. While his scheme was ripening, the danger which menaced Protestantism in Germany, called him to the field, to contend for the principles of the Reformation.[4] He marched from his kingdom with a strong army to oppose the Imperial hosts marshaled under the banner of the Pope on the fields of Germany. Yet the care and tumults of the camp and field did not make him forget his benevolent designs; and only a few days before his death,

---

[1] Page 72.

[2] De Vries was an eminent navigator, and one of Godyn's friends. To secure his valuable services, the purchasers made him a partner in their enterprise, with patroon [page 139] privileges, and the first expedition was arranged by him. He afterward came to America, and was one of the most active men in the Dutch colonies. On his return to Holland, he published an account of his voyages.

[3] Page 72.

[4] Note 14, page 62.

at the battle of Lutzen [Nov. 6, 1632], Gustavus recommended the enterprise as "the jewel of his kingdom."

The successor of Gustavus was his daughter Christina, then only six years of age. The government was administered by a regency,[1] at the head of which was Axel, count of Oxenstierna. He was the earliest and most ardent supporter of the proposed great enterprise of Gustavus; and in 1634 he issued a charter for the Swedish West India Company. Peter Minuit,[2] who had been recalled from the governorship of New Netherland, and was also dissatisfied with the Dutch West India Company, went to Stockholm, and offered his services to the new corporation. They were accepted, and toward the close of 1637 he sailed from Gottenburg with fifty emigrants, to plant a colony on the west side of the Delaware. He landed on the site of New Castle, in April, 1638, and purchased from the Indians[3] the territory between Cape Henlopen and the Falls of the Delaware, at Trenton. They built a church and fort on the site of Wilmington, called the place Christina, and gave the name of New Sweden to the territory. The jealousy of the Dutch was aroused by this "intrusion," and they hurled protests and menaces against the Swedes.[4] The latter continued to increase by immigration; new settlements were planted; and upon Tinicum Island, a little below Philadelphia, they laid the foundations of a capital for a Swedish province.[5] The Dutch West India Company[6] finally resolved to expel or subdue the Swedes. The latter made hostile demonstrations, and defied the power of the Dutch. The challenge was acted upon; and toward the close of the summer of 1655, governor Stuyvesant, with a squadron of seven vessels, entered Delaware Bay.[7] In September every Swedish fort and settlement was brought under his rule, and the capital on Tinicum Island was destroyed. The Swedes obtained honorable terms of capitulation; and for twenty-five years they prospered under the rule of the Dutch and English proprietors of New Netherland.

NEW JERSEY.

All the territory of NOVA CÆSAREA, as New Jersey was called by the English, was included in the New Netherland charter,[8] and transient trading settlements were made [1622], first at Bergen, by a few Danes, and then on the Delaware. Early in 1623, the Dutch built a log fort near the mouth of Timber Creek, a few miles below Camden, and called it Nassau.[9] In June,

[1] A regent is one who exercises the power of king or emperor, during the absence, incapacity, or childhood of the latter. For many years, George the Third of England was incapable of ruling on account of his insanity, and his son who was to be his successor at his death, was called the Prince Regent, because Parliament had given him power to act as king, in the place of his father. In the case of Christina, three persons were appointed regents, or rulers.

[2] Page 139. [3] The Delawares. See page 20. [4] Page 143.

[5] This was done about forty years before William Penn became proprietor of Pennsylvania.

[6] Page 72. [7] Page 143. [8] Page 72.

[9] It was built under the direction of Captain Jacobus May, who had observed attempts made by a French sea-captain to set up the arms of France there. The fort was built of logs, and was little else than a rude block-house, with palissades. [See note 1, page 127.] A little garrison, left to protect it, was soon scattered, and the fort was abandoned.

1623, four couples, who had been married on the voyage from Amsterdam, were sent to plant a colony on the Delaware. They seated themselves upon the site of Gloucester, a little below Fort Nassau, and this was the commencement of settlements in West Jersey.

Seven years later [1630] Michael Pauw bought from the Indians the lands extending from Hoboken to the Raritan, and also the whole of Staten Island, and named the territory *Pavonia.*[1] In this purchase, Bergen was included. Other settlements were attempted, but none were permanent. In 1631, Captain Heyes, after establishing the Swedish colony at Lewiston,[2] crossed the Delaware, and purchased Cape May[3] from the Indians; and from that point to Burlington, traders' huts were often seen. The English became possessors of New Netherland in 1664, and the Duke of York, to whom the province had been given,[4] conveyed to Lord Berkeley and Sir George Carteret [June 24, 1664], all the territory between the *North* and *South* (Hudson and Delaware) *Rivers*, and northward to the line of forty-one degrees and forty minutes, under the title of *Nova Cæsarea* or NEW JERSEY. Soon afterward several families from Long Island settled at Elizabethtown,[5] and there planted the first fruitful seed of the New Jersey colony, for the one at Gloucester withered and died. The following year, Philip Carteret, who had been appointed governor of the new province, arrived with a charter, fair and liberal in all its provisions. It provided for a government to be composed of a representative assembly[6] chosen by the people, and a governor and council. The legislative powers resided in the assembly; the executive powers were intrusted to the governor and his council. Then [1665] was laid the foundation of the commonwealth of NEW JERSEY.

PENNSYLVANIA.

A new religious sect, called Quakers,[7] arose in England at about the commencement of the civil wars [1642—1651] which resulted in the death of Charles the First. Their preachers were the boldest, and yet the meekest of all non-conformists.[8] Purer than all other sects, they were hated and persecuted by all. Those who came to America for "conscience' sake" were persecuted by the Puritans of New England,[9] the Churchmen of Virginia and Maryland, and in a degree by the Dutch of New Amsterdam; and only in Rhode Island did they enjoy freedom, and even there they did not always dwell in peace. In 1673, George Fox, the founder of the Quaker sect, visited all his brethren in America. He found them a despised people everywhere, and his

---

1 Until the period of our War for Independence, the point of land in *Pavonia*, on which Jersey City, opposite New York, now stands, was called Paulus' Hook. Here was the scene of a bold exploit by Americans, under Major Henry Lee, in 1779. See page 298.

2 Page 92. 3 Named in honor of Captain Jacobus Mey, or May. 4 Page 159.

5 Page 159. 6 Note 3, page 159.

7 This name was given by Justice Burnet, of Derby, in 1650, who was admonished by George Fox, when he was cited before the magistrate, to *tremble and quake at the Word of the Lord*, at the same time Fox quaked, as if stirred by mighty emotions. See page 90.

8 Note 2, page 76. 9 Page 75.

heart yearned for an asylum for his brethren. Among the most influential of his converts was William Penn,[1] son of the renowned admiral of that name. Through him the sect gained access to the ears of the nobility, and soon the Quakers possessed the western half of New Jersey, by purchase from Lord Berkeley.[2] The first company of immigrants landed in the autumn of 1675, and named the place of debarkation *Salem*.[3] They established a democratic form of government; and, in November, 1681, the first legislative assembly of Quakers ever convened, met at Salem.

While these events were progressing, Penn, who had been chief peace-maker when disputes arose among the proprietors and the people, took measures to plant a new colony beyond the Delaware. He applied to Charles the Second for a charter. The king remembered the services of Admiral Penn,[4] and gave his son a grant [March 14, 1681] of "three degrees of latitude by five degrees

[1] William Penn was born in London, in October, 1644, and was educated at Oxford. He was remarkable, in his youth, for brilliant talents; and while a student, having heard the preaching of Quakers, he was drawn to them, and suffered expulsion from his father's roof, in consequence. He went abroad, obtained courtly manners, studied law after his return, and was again driven from home for associating with Quakers. He then became a preacher among them, and remained in that connection until his death. After a life of great activity and considerable suffering, he died in England, in 1718, at the age of seventy-four years.

[2] Page 119.

[3] Now the capital of Salem county, New Jersey.

[4] He was a very efficient naval commander, and by his skill contributed to the defeat of the Dutch in 1664. The king gave him the title of *Baron* for his services. Note 15, page 62.

of longitude west of the Delaware," and named the province ***Pennsylvania***, in honor of the proprietor. It included the principal settlements of the Swedes. To these people, and others within the domain, Penn sent a proclamation, filled with the loftiest sentiments of republicanism. William Markham, who bore the proclamation, was appointed deputy-governor of the province, and with him sailed [May, 1681] quite a large company of immigrants, who were members or employees of the *Company of Free Traders*,[1] who had purchased lands of the proprietor. In May, the following year, Penn published a frame of government, and sent it to the settlers for their approval. It was not a constitution, but a code of wholesome regulations for the people of the colony.[2] He soon afterward obtained by grant and purchase [Aug. 1682] the domain of the present State of Delaware, which the Duke of York claimed, notwithstanding it was clearly not his own. It comprised three counties, Newcastle, Kent, and Sussex, called *The Territories.*

Penn had been anxious, for some time, to visit his colony, and toward the close of August, 1682, he sailed in the *Welcome* for America, with about one hundred emigrants. The voyage was long and tedious; and when he arrived at Newcastle, in Delaware [Nov. 6], he found almost a thousand new comers there, some of whom had sailed before, and some after his departure from England. He was joyfully received by the old settlers, who then numbered almost three thousand. The Swedes said, "It is the best day we have ever seen;" and they all gathered like children around a father. A few days afterward, he proceeded to Shackamaxon (now Kensington suburbs of Philadelphia), where, under a wide-spreading elm, he entered into an honorable treaty with the Indians, for their lands, and established with them an everlasting covenant of peace and friendship. "We meet," said Penn, "on the broad pathway of good faith and good will; no advantage shall be taken on either side; but all shall be openness and love." And so it was.

"Thou'lt find," said the Quaker, "in me and in mine,
But friends and brothers to thee and thine,
Who abuse no power and admit no line
'Twixt the red man and the white.

And bright was the spot where the Quaker came,
To leave his hat, his drab, and his name,
That will sweetly sound from the trump of Fame,
Till its final blast shall die."

On the day after his arrival, Penn received from the agents of the Duke of York,[3] in the presence of the people, a formal surrender of *The Territories;*

---

[1] Lands in the new province were offered for about ten cents an acre. Quite a number of purchasers united, and called themselves *The Company of Free Traders*, with whom Penn entered into an agreement concerning the occupation of the soil, laying out of a city, &c.

[2] It ordained a General Assembly or court, to consist of a governor, a council of seventy, chosen by the freemen of the colony, and a house of delegates, to consist of not less than two hundred members, nor more than five hundred. These were also to be chosen by the people. The proprietor, or his deputy (the governor), was to preside, and to have a three-fold voice in the council; that is, on all questions, he was to have three votes for every one of the councillors.

[3] Page 144.

THE ASSEMBLY HOUSE.

and after resting a few days, he proceeded to visit his brethren in New Jersey, and the authorities at New York. On his return, he met the General Assembly of the province at Chester,[1] when he declared the union of *The Territories* with Pennsylvania. He made a more judicious organization of the local government, and then were permanently laid the foundations of the commonwealth of PENNSYLVANIA.

CHAPTER IX.

THE CAROLINAS. [1622—1680.]

UNSUCCESSFUL efforts at settlement on the coast of Carolina, were made during a portion of the sixteenth century. These we have already considered.[2] As early as 1609, some dissatisfied people from Jamestown settled on the Nansemond; and in 1622, Porey, then Secretary of Virginia, with a few friends, penetrated the country beyond the Roanoke. In 1630, Charles the First granted to Sir Robert Heath, his attorney-general, a domain south of Virginia, six degrees of latitude in width, extending from Albemarle Sound to the St. John's River, in Florida, and, as usual, westward to the Pacific Ocean. No settlements were made, and the charter was forfeited. At that time, Dissenters or Nonconformists[3] suffered many disabilities in Virginia, and looked to the wilderness for freedom. In 1653, Roger Green and a few Presbyterians left that colony and settled upon the Chowan River, near the present village of Edenton. Other dissenters followed, and the colony flourished. Governor Berkeley, of Virginia,[4] wisely organized them into a separate political community [1663], and William Drummond,[5] a Scotch Presbyterian minister, was appointed their governor. They received the name of *Albemarle County Colony*, in honor of the Duke of Albemarle, who, that year, became a proprietor of the territory. Two years previously [1661], some New England[6] adventurers settled in the vicinity of Wilmington, on the Cape Fear River, but many of them soon abandoned the country because of its poverty.

Charles the Second was famous for his distribution of the lands in the New World, among his friends and favorites, regardless of any other claims, Abo-

[1] The picture is a correct representation of the building at Chester, in Pennsylvania, wherein the Assembly met. It was yet standing in 1850. Not far from the spot, on the shore of the Delaware, at the mouth of Chester Creek, was also a solitary pine-tree, which marked the place where Penn landed.

[2] Pages 55 to 57 inclusive. [3] Note 2, page 76. [4] Page 78.

[5] Drummond was afterward executed on account of his participation in Bacon's revolutionary acts. See note 5, page 112. [6] Page 108.

riginal or European. In 1663, he granted the whole territory named in Sir Robert Heath's charter, to eight of his principal friends,[1] and called it CAROLINA.[2] As the Chowan settlement was not within the limits of the charter, the boundary was extended northward to the present line between Virginia and North Carolina, and also southward, so as to include the whole of Florida, except its peninsula. The Bahama Islands were granted to the same proprietors in 1667.[3] Two years earlier [1665], a company of Barbadoes planters settled upon the lands first occupied by the New England people, near the present Wilmington, and founded a permanent settlement there. The few settlers yet remaining were treated kindly, and soon an independent colony, with Sir John Yeamans[4] as governor, was established. It was called the *Clarendon County Colony*, in honor of one of the proprietors. Yeamans managed prudently, but the poverty of the soil prevented a rapid increase in the population. The settlers applied themselves to the manufacture of boards, shingles, and staves, which they shipped to the West Indies; and that business is yet the staple trade of that region of pine forests and sandy levels. Although the settlement did not flourish, it continued to exist; and then was founded the commonwealth of NORTH CAROLINA.

The special attention of the proprietors was soon turned toward the more southerly and fertile portion of their domain, and in January, 1670, they sent three ships with emigrants, under the direction of William Sayle[5] and Joseph West, to plant a colony below Cape Fear. They entered Port Royal, landed on Beaufort Island at the spot where the Huguenots built Fort Carolina in 1564,[6] and there Sayle died early in 1671. The immigrants soon afterward abandoned Beaufort, and sailing into the Ashley River,[7] seated themselves on its western bank, at a place a few miles above Charleston, now known as Old Town. There they planted the first seeds of a South Carolina colony. West exercised authority as chief magistrate, until the arrival of Sir John Yeamans, in December, 1671, who was appointed governor. He came with fifty families, and a large number of slaves.[8] Representative government was instituted in 1672[9] under the title of the *Carteret County Colony*. It was so called in honor of one of the proprietors.[10] Ten years afterward they abandoned the spot;

---

[1] Lord Clarendon, his prime minister; General Monk, just created Duke of Albemarle; Lord Ashley Cooper, afterward Earl of Shaftesbury; Sir George Carteret, a proprietor of New Jersey; Sir William Berkeley, Governor of Virginia; Lord Berkeley, Lord Craven, and Sir John Colleton.

[2] It will be perceived [note 1, page 55] that the name of Carolina, given to territory south of Virginia, was bestowed in honor of two kings named Charles, one of France, the other of England.

[3] Samuel Stephens succeeded Drummond as governor, in 1667; and in 1668, the first popular Assembly in North Carolina convened at Edenton.

[4] Yeamans was an impoverished English baronet, who had become a planter in Barbadoes, to mend his fortune. He was successful, and became wealthy.

[5] Sayle had previously explored the Carolina coast. Twenty years before, he had attempted to plant an "Eleutharia," or place dedicated to the genius of Liberty [see *Eleutheria*, Anthon's Classical Dictionary], in the isles near the coast of Florida.

[6] Page 50.

[7] Page 166.

[8] This was the commencement of negro slavery in South Carolina. Yeamans brought almost two hundred of them from Barbadoes. From the commencement, South Carolina has been a planting State.

[9] Note 5, page 165.

[10] He was also one of the proprietors of New Jersey. See page 119.

and upon Oyster Point, at the junction of Ashley and Cooper Rivers,[1] nearer the sea, they founded the present city of Charleston.[2] Immigrants came from various parts of Europe; and many Dutch families, dissatisfied with the English rule at New York,[3] went to South Carolina, where lands were freely given them; and soon, along the Santee and the Edisto, the wilderness began to blossom under the hand of culture. The people would have nothing to do with a government scheme prepared by Shaftesbury and Locke,[4] but preferred simple organic laws of their own making. Then were laid the foundations of the commonwealth of SOUTH CAROLINA, although the history of the two States, under the same proprietors, is inseparable, until the period of their dismemberment, in 1729.[5]

CHAPTER X.

GEORGIA. [1733.]

GEORGIA was the latest settled of the thirteen original English colonies in America. When the proprietors of the Carolinas surrendered their charter[6] to the crown in 1729, the whole country southward of the Savannah River, to the vicinity of St. Augustine, was a wilderness peopled by native tribes,[7] and claimed by the Spaniards as part of their territory of Florida.[8] The English disputed this claim, and South Carolina townships were ordered to be marked out as far south as the Alatamaha. The dispute grew warm and warlike, and the Indians, instigated by the Spaniards, depredated upon the frontier English settlements.[9] But, while the clouds of hostility were gathering in the firmament, and grew darker every hour, it was lighted up by a bright beam of benevolence, which proved the harbinger of a glorious day. It came from England, where, at that time, poverty was often considered a crime, and at least four thousand unfortunate debtors were yearly consigned to loathsome prisons. The honest and true, the noble and the educated, as well as the ignorant and the vile, groaned within prison walls. Their wailings at length reached the ears of benevolent men. Foremost among these was James Edward Oglethorpe,[10] a brave soldier and stanch loyalist, whose voice had been heard often in Parliament against imprisonment for debt.

A committee of inquiry into the subject of such imprisonments, was ap-

[1] These were so called in honor of Ashley Cooper, Earl of Shaftesbury. The Indian name of the former was *Ke-a-wah*, and of the latter *E-ti-wan*.

[2] Charleston was laid out in 1680 by John Culpepper, who had been surveyor-general for North Carolina. See page 166. [3] Page 164. [4] Page 144. [5] Page 171.

[6] Page 171. [7] Page 29. [8] Page 42. [9] Page 170.

[10] See portrait, page 104. General Oglethorpe was born in Surrey, England, on the 21st of December, 1698. He was a soldier by profession. In 1745, he was made a brigadier-general, and fought against Charles Edward, the Pretender, who was a grandson of James the Second, and claimed rightful heirship to the throne of England. Oglethorpe refused the supreme command of the British army destined for America in 1775. He died, June 30, 1785, aged eighty-seven years.

pointed by Parliament, and General Oglethorpe was made chairman of it. His report, embodying a noble scheme of benevolence, attracted attention and admiration. He proposed to open the prison doors to all virtuous men within, who would accept the conditions, and with these and other sufferers from poverty and oppression, to go to the wilderness of America, and there establish a colony of freemen, and open an asylum for persecuted Protestants[1] of all lands. The plan met warm responses in Parliament, and received the hearty approval of George the Second, then [1730] on the English throne. A royal charter for twenty-one years was granted [June 9, 1732] to a corporation "in trust for the poor," to establish a colony within the disputed territory south of the Savannah, to be called Georgia, in honor of the king.[2] Individuals subscribed large sums to defray the expenses of emigrants hither; and within two years after the issuing of the patent, Parliament had appropriated one hundred and eighty thousand dollars for the same purpose.[3]

The sagacious and brave Oglethorpe was a practical philanthropist. He offered to accompany the first settlers to the wilderness, and to act as governor of the new province. With one hundred and twenty emigrants he left England [Nov., 1732], and after a passage of fifty-seven days, touched at Charleston [Jan., 1733], where he was received with great joy by the inhabitants, as one who was about to plant a barrier between them and the hostile Indians and Spaniards.[4] Proceeding to Port Royal, Oglethorpe landed a large portion of his followers there, and with a few others, he coasted to the Savannah River. Sailing up that stream as far as Yamacraw Bluff, he landed, and chose the spot whereon to lay the foundation of the capital of a future State.[5]

On the 12th of February, 1733, the remainder of the immigrants arrived from Port Royal. The winter air was genial, and with cheerful hearts and willing hands they constructed a rude fortification, and commenced the erection of a town, which they called Savannah, the Indian name of the river.[6] For almost a year the governor dwelt under a tent, and there he often held friendly intercourse with the chiefs of neighboring tribes. At length, when he had mounted cannons upon the fort, and safety was thus secured, Oglethorpe met

---

[1] Note 14, page 62.

[2] The domain granted by the charter extended along the coast from the Savannah to the Alatamaha, and westward to the Pacific Ocean. The trustees appointed by the crown, possessed all legislative and executive power; and, therefore, while one side of the seal of the new province expressed the benevolent character of the scheme, by the device of a group of toiling silkworms, and the motto, *Non sibi, sed aliis;* the other side, bearing, between two urns the genius of "Georgia Augusta," with a *cap of liberty* on her head, a spear, and a horn of plenty, was a false emblem. There was no political liberty for the people.

[3] Brilliant visions of vast vintages, immense productions of silk for British looms, and all the wealth of a fertile tropical region, were presented for the contemplation of the commercial acumen of the business men of England. These considerations, as well as the promptings of pure benevolence, made donations liberal and numerous.

[4] Page 99.

[5] Some historians believe that Sir Walter Raleigh, while on his way to South America, in 1595, went up the Savannah River, and held a conference with the Indians on this very spot. This, probably, is an error, for nothing appears in the writings of Raleigh or his cotemporaries to warrant the inference that he ever saw the North American continent.

[6] The streets were laid out with great regularity; public squares were reserved; and the houses were all built on one model—twenty-four by sixteen feet, on the ground.

OGLETHORPE'S FIRST INTERVIEW WITH THE INDIANS.

fifty chiefs in council [May, 1733], with *To-mo-chi-chi*,[1] the principal sachem of the lower Creek confederacy,[2] at their head, to treat for the purchase of lands. Satisfactory arrangements were made, and the English obtained sovereignty over the whole domain [June 1, 1733] along the Atlantic from the Savannah to the St. John's, and westward to the Flint and the head waters of the Chattahoochee. The provisions of the charter formed the constitution of government for the people; and there, upon Yamacraw Bluff, where the flourishing city of Savannah now stands, was laid the foundation of the commonwealth of GEORGIA, in the summer of 1733. Immigration flowed thither in a strong and continuous stream, for all were free in religious matters; yet for many years the colony did not flourish.[3]

Wonderful, indeed, were the events connected with the permanent settlements in the New World. Never in the history of the race was greater heroism displayed than the seaboard of the domain of the United States exhibited during the period of settlements, and the development of colonies. Hardihood, faith, courage, indomitable perseverance, and untiring energy, were requisite to accomplish all that was done in so short a time, and under such unfavorable circumstances. While many of the early immigrants were mere adventurers, and sleep in deserved oblivion, because they were recreant to the great duty which they had self-imposed, there are thousands whose names ought to be perpetuated in brass and marble, because of their faithful performance of the mighty task assigned them. They came here as sowers of the prolific seed of human liberty; and during the colonizing period, many of them carefully nurtured the tender plant, while it was bursting into vigorous life. We, who are the reapers, ought to reverence the sowers and the cultivators with grateful hearts.

---

[1] To-mo-chi-chi was then an aged man, and at his first interview with Oglethorpe, he presented him with a buffalo skin, ornamented with the picture of an eagle. "Here," said the chief, "is a little present: I give you a buffalo's skin, adorned on the inside with the head and feathers of an eagle, which I desire you to accept, because the eagle is an emblem of speed, and the buffalo of strength. The English are swift as the bird, and strong as the beast, since, like the former, they flew over vast seas to the uttermost parts of the earth; and like the latter, they are so strong that nothing can withstand them. The feathers of an eagle are soft, and signify love; the buffalo's skin is warm, and signifies protection;—therefore I hope the English will protect and love our little families." Alas! the wishes of the venerable To-mo-chi-chi were never realized, for the white people more often plundered and destroyed, than loved and protected the Indians.

[2] Page 30.

[3] Pages 171 and 173.

EMBARKATION OF THE PILGRIMS.

JAMES EDWARD OGLETHORPE.

FOURTH PERIOD.

THE COLONIES.

CHAPTER I.

HAVING briefly traced the interesting events which resulted in the founding of several colonies by settlements we will now consider the more important acts of establishing permanent commonwealths, all of which still exist and flourish. The colonial history of the United States is comprised within the period commencing when the several settlements along the Atlantic coasts became organized into political communities, and ending when representatives of these colonies met in general congress in 1774,[1] and confederated for mutual welfare. There was an earlier union of interests and efforts. It was when the several English colonies aided the mother country in a long war against the combined hostilities of the French and Indians. As the local histories of the several colonies after the commencement of that war have but little interest for the general reader, we shall trace the progress of each colony only to that period, and devote a chapter to the narrative of the French and Indian war.[2]

---

[1] Page 228. [2] Page 179.

As we have already observed, a *settlement* acquires the character of a *colony* only when it has become permanent, and the people, acknowledging allegiance to a parent State, are governed by organic laws.[1] According to these conditions, the earliest of the thirteen colonies represented in the Congress of 1774, was

VIRGINIA. [1619.]

That was an auspicious day for the six hundred settlers in Virginia when the gold-seekers disappeared,[2] and the enlightened George Yeardley became governor, and established a representative assembly [June 28, 1619]—the first in all America.[3] And yet a prime element of happiness and prosperity was wanting. *There were no white women in the colony.* The wise Sandys, the friend of the *Pilgrim Fathers*,[4] was then treasurer of the London Company,[5] and one of the most influential and zealous promoters of emigration. During the same year when the Puritans sailed for America [1620], he sent more than twelve hundred emigrants to Virginia, among whom were ninety young women, "pure and uncorrupt," who were disposed of for the cost of their passage, as wives for the planters.[6] The following year sixty more were sent. The family relation was soon established; the gentle influence of woman gave refinement to social life on the banks of the Powhatan;[7] new and powerful incentives to industry and thrift were created; and the mated planters no longer cherished the prevailing idea of returning to England.[8] Vessel after vessel, laden with immigrants, continued to arrive in the James River, and new settlements were planted, even so remote as at the Falls,[9] and on the distant banks of the Potomac. The germ of an empire was rapidly expanding with the active elements of national organization. Verbal instructions would no longer serve the purposes of government, and in August, 1621, the Company granted the colonists a *written Constitution*,[10] which ratified most of the acts of Yeardley.[11] Provision was made for the appointment of a governor and council by the Company, and a popular Assembly, to consist of two burgesses or representatives from each borough, chosen by the people. This body, and the council, composed the General Assembly, which was to meet once a year, and pass laws for the

---

[1] Page 61. [2] Page 71. [3] Page 71. [4] Page 77. [5] Page 64.

[6] Tobacco had already become a circulating medium, or currency, in Virginia. The price of a wife varied from 120 to 150 pounds of this product, equivalent, in money value, to about $90 and $112 each. The second "cargo" were sold at a still higher price. By the king's special order, one hundred dissolute vagabonds, called "jail-birds" by the colonists, were sent over the same year, and sold as bond-servants for a specified time. In August, the same year, a Dutch trading vessel entered the James River with negro slaves. Twenty of them were sold into perpetual slavery to the planters. This was the commencement of negro slavery in the English colonies [note 4, page 177]. The slave population of the United States in 1850, according to the census, was 3,204,313.

[7] Page 64.

[8] Most of the immigrants hitherto were possessed of the spirit of mere adventurers. They came to America to repair shattered fortunes, or to gain wealth, with the ultimate object of returning to England to enjoy it. The creation of families made the planters more attached to the soil of Virginia.

[9] Near the site of the city of Richmond. The falls, or rapids, extend about six miles.

[10] The people of the *May-flower* formed a *written Constitution* for themselves [page 78]. That of Virginia was modeled after the Constitution of England.

[11] Page 70.

general good.[1] Such laws were not valid until approved by the Company, neither were any orders of the Company binding upon the colonists until ratified by the General Assembly. Trial by jury was established, and courts of law conformable to those of England were organized. Ever afterward claiming these *privileges* as *rights*, the Virginians look back to the summer of 1621 as the era of their civil freedom.

The excellent Sir Francis Wyatt, who had been appointed governor under the *Constitution*, and brought the instrument with him, was delighted with the aspect of affairs in Virginia. But a dark cloud soon arose in the summer sky. The neighboring Indian tribes[2] gathered in solemn council. Powhatan, the friend of the English after the marriage of his daughter,[3] was dead, and an enemy of the white people ruled the dusky nation.[4] They had watched the increasing strength of the English, with alarm. The white people were now four thousand in number, and rapidly increasing. The Indians read their destiny—annihilation—upon the face of every new comer; and, prompted by the first great law of his nature, self-preservation, the red man resolved to strike a blow for life. A conspiracy was accordingly formed, in the spring of 1622, to exterminate the white people. At mid-day, on the 1st of April, the hatchet fell upon all of the more remote settlements; and within an hour, three hundred and fifty men, women, and children, were slain.[5] Jamestown[6] and neighboring plantations were saved by the timely warning of a converted Indian.[7] The people were on their guard and escaped. Those far away in the forests defended themselves bravely, and when they had beaten back the foe, they fled to Jamestown. Within a few days, eighty plantations were reduced to eight.

The people, thus concentrated at Jamestown by a terrible necessity, prepared for vengeance. A vindictive war ensued, and a terrible blow of retaliation was given. The Indians upon the James and York Rivers were slaughtered by scores, or were driven far back into the wilderness. Yet a blight was upon the colony. Sickness and famine followed close upon the massacre. Within three months, the colony of four thousand souls was reduced to twenty-five hundred; and at the beginning of 1624, of the nine thousand persons who had been sent to Virginia from England, only eighteen hundred remained.

These disheartening events, and the selfish action of the king, discouraged the London Company.[8] The holders of the stock had now become very numerous, and their meetings, composed of men of all respectable classes, assumed a

---

[1] This was the beginning of the Virginia House of Burgesses, of which we shall often speak in future chapters [2] The Powhatans. See page 20. [3] Page 70.

[4] Powhatan died in 1618, and was succeeded in office by his younger brother, Opechancanough [see page 66]. This chief hated the English. He was the one who made Captain Smith a prisoner.

[5] Opechancanough was wily and exceedingly treacherous. Only a few days before the massacre, he declared that "sooner the skies would fall than his friendship with the English would be dissolved." Even on the day of the massacre, the Indians entered the houses of the planters with usual tokens of friendship. [6] Page 64.

[7] This was Chanco, who was informed of the bloody design the evening previous. He desired to save a white friend in Jamestown, and gave him the information. It was too late to send word to the more remote settlements. Among those who fell on this occasion, were six members of the council, and several of the wealthiest inhabitants. [8] Page 64.

political character, in which two distinct parties were represented, namely, the advocates of liberty, and the supporters of the royal prerogatives. The king was offended by the freedom of debates at these meetings, and regarded them as inimical to royalty, and dangerous to the stability of his throne.[1] He determined to regain what he had lost by granting the liberal third charter[2] to the company. He endeavored first to control the elections. Failing in this, he sought a pretense for dissolving the Company. A commission was appointed in May, 1623, to inquire into their affairs. It was composed of the king's pliant instruments, who, having reported in favor of a dissolution of the Company, an equally pliant judiciary accomplished his designs in October following, and a *quo warranto*[3] was issued. The Company made but little opposition, for the settlement of Virginia had been an unprofitable speculation from the beginning; and in July, 1624, the patents were cancelled.[4] Virginia became a royal province again,[5] but no material change was made in the domestic affairs of the colonists.

King James, with his usual egotism, boasted of the beneficent results to the colonists which would flow from this usurpation, by which they were placed under his special care. He appointed Yeardley,[6] with twelve councillors, to administer the government, but wisely refrained from interfering with the House of Burgesses.[7] The king lived but a few months longer, and at his death, which occurred on the 6th of April, 1625, he was succeeded by his son, Charles the First. That monarch was as selfish as he was weak. He sought to promote the welfare of the Virginia planters, because he also sought to reap the profits of a monopoly, by becoming himself their sole factor in the management of their exports. He also allowed them political privileges, not because he wished to benefit his subjects, but because he had learned to respect the power of those far-off colonists; and he sought their sanction for his commercial agency.[8]

Governor Yeardley died in November, 1627, and was succeeded, two years later [1629], by Sir John Harvey, a haughty and unpopular royalist. He was a member of the commission appointed by James; and the colonists so despised him, that they refused the coveted monopoly to the king. After many and violent disputes about land titles, the Virginians deposed him [1635] and appointed commissioners to proceed to England, with an impeachment. Harvey accompanied the commission. The king refused to hear complaints against the

[1] These meetings were quite frequent; and so important were the members, in political affairs, that they could influence the elections of members of Parliament. In 1623, the accomplished Nicholas Ferrar, an active opponent of the court party, was elected to Parliament, by the influence of the London Company. This fact, doubtless, caused the king to dissolve the Company that year.

[2] Page 70.

[3] A writ of *quo warranto* is issued to compel a person or corporation to appear before the king, and show by what authority certain privileges are held.

[4] The Company had expended almost $700,000 in establishing the colony, and this great sum was almost a dead loss to the stockholders.

[5] Page 63.

[6] Page 70.

[7] Note 1, page 106.

[8] In June, 1628, the king, in a letter to the governor and council, asked them to convene an assembly to consider his proposal to contract for the whole crop of tobacco. He thus tacitly acknowledged the legality of the republican assembly of Virginia, hitherto not *sanctioned*, but only *permitted*.

accused, and he was sent back clothed with full powers to administer the government, independent of the people. He ruled almost four years longer, and was succeeded, in November, 1639, by Sir Francis Wyatt, who administered government well for about two years, when he was succeeded [1641] by Sir William Berkeley,[1] an able and elegant courtier. For ten years Berkeley ruled with vigor, and the colony prospered wonderfully.[2] But, as in later years, commotions in Europe now disturbed the American settlements. The democratic revolution in England,[3] which brought Charles the First to the block, and placed Oliver Cromwell in power, now [1642] began, and religious sects in England and America assumed political importance. Puritans[4] had hitherto been tolerated in Virginia, but now the Throne and the Church were united in interest, and the Virginians being loyal to both, it was decreed that no minister should preach except in conformity to the constitution of the Church of England.[5] Many non-conformists[6] were banished from the colony. This was a dark cloud upon the otherwise clear skies of Virginia, but a darker cloud was gathering. The Indians were again incited to hostilities by the restless and vengeful Opechancanough,[7] and a terrible storm burst upon the English, in April, 1644. For two years a bloody border warfare was carried on. The king of the Powhatans[8] was finally made captive, and died while in prison at Jamestown, and his people were thoroughly subdued. The power of the confederation was completely broken, and after ceding large tracts of land to the English, the chiefs acknowledged allegiance to the authorities of Virginia, and so the political life of the Powhatans passed away forever.[9]

During the civil war in England [1641—1649], the Virginians remained loyal; and when republican government was proclaimed, they boldly recognized the son of the late king, although in exile, as their sovereign.[10] The republican parliament was highly incensed, and took immediate measures to coerce Virginia into submission to its authority. For that purpose Sir George Ayscue was sent with a powerful fleet, bearing commissioners of parliament, as representatives of the sovereignty of the commonwealth, and anchored in Hampton Roads in March, 1652.

---

[1] William Berkeley was born near London; was educated at Oxford; became, by travel and education, a polished gentleman; was governor of Virginia almost 40 years, and died in July, 1677.

[2] In 1648, the number of colonists was 20,000. "The cottages were filled with children, as the ports were with ships and immigrants."

[3] For a long time the exactions of the king fostered a bitter feeling toward him, in the hearts of the people. In 1641 they took up arms against their sovereign. One of the chief leaders of the popular party was Oliver Cromwell. The war continued until 1649, when the royalists were subdued, and the king was beheaded. Parliament assumed all the functions of government, and ruled until 1653, when Cromwell, the insurgent leader, dissolved that body, and was proclaimed supreme ruler, with the title of *Protector* of the Commonwealth of England. Cromwell was a son of a wealthy brewer of Huntingdon, England, where he was born in 1599. He died in September, 1658.

[4] Page 75.

[5] Page 75.

[6] Note 2, page 76.

[7] Note 5, page 106.

[8] Page 20.

[9] They relinquished all claim to the beautiful country between the York and James Rivers, from the Falls of the latter, at Richmond, to the sea, forever. It was a legacy of a dying nation to their conquerors. After that, their utter destruction was swift and thorough.

[10] Afterward the profligate Charles the Second. His mother was sister to the French king, and to that court she fled, with her children. It was a sad day for the moral character of England when Charles was enthroned. He was less bigoted, but more licentious than any of the Stuarts who governed Great Britain for more than eighty years.

The Virginians had resolved to submit rather than fight, yet they made a show of resistance. They declared their willingness to compromise with the invaders, to which the commissioners, surprised and intimidated by the bold attitude of the colonists, readily consented. Instead of opening their cannons upon the Virginians, they courteously proposed to them submission to the authority of parliament upon terms quite satisfactory to the colonists. Liberal political concessions to the people were secured, and they were allowed nearly all those civil rights which the Declaration of Independence,[1] a century and a quarter later, charged George the Third with violating.

Virginia was, virtually, an independent State, until Charles the Second was restored to the throne of his father [May 29, 1660], for Cromwell made no appointments except that of governor. In the same year [1652] when the parliamentary commissioners came, the people had *elected* Richard Bennet to fill Berkeley's place. He was succeeded by Edward Digges, and in 1656, Cromwell appointed Samuel Mathews governor. On the death of the Protector [1658], the Virginians were not disposed to acknowledge the authority of his son Richard,[2] and they *elected* Mathews their chief magistrate, as a token of their independence. Universal suffrage prevailed; all freemen, without exception, were allowed to vote; and white servants, when their terms of bondage ended, had the same privilege, and might become burgesses.

But a serious change came to the Virginians, after the restoration of Charles the Second. When intelligence of that event reached Virginia, Berkeley, whom the people had elected governor in 1660, repudiated the popular sovereignty, and proclaimed the exiled monarch "King of England, Scotland, Ireland, and *Virginia.*" This happened before he was proclaimed in England.[3] The Virginia republicans were offended, but being in the minority, could do nothing. A new Assembly was elected and convened, and high hopes of favor from the monarch were entertained by the court party. But these were speedily blasted, and in place of great privileges, came commercial restrictions to cripple the industry of the colony. The navigation act of 1651 was re-enacted in 1660, and its provisions were rigorously enforced.[4] The people murmured,

---

[1] See Supplement.

[2] Cromwell appointed his son Richard to succeed him in office. Lacking the vigor and ambition of his father, he gladly resigned the troublesome legacy into the hands of the people, and, a little more than a year afterward, Charles the Second was enthroned.

[3] When informed that Parliament was about to send a fleet to bring them to submission, the Virginians sent a message to Charles, then in Flanders, inviting him to come over and be king of Virginia. He had resolved to come, when matters took a turn in England favorable to his restoration. In gratitude to the colonists, he caused the arms of Virginia to be quartered with those of England, Scotland, and Ireland, as an independent member of the empire. From this circumstance Virginia received the name of *The Old Dominion.* Coins, with these quarterings, were made as late as 1773.

[4] The first Navigation Act, by the Republican Parliament, prohibited foreign vessels trading to the English colonies. This was partly to punish the sugar-producing islands of the West Indies, because the people were chiefly loyalists. The act of 1660 provided that no goods should be carried to or from any English colonies, but in vessels built within the English dominions, whose masters and at least three fourths of the crews were Englishmen; and that sugar, tobacco, and other colonial commodities should be imported into no part of Europe, except England and her dominions. The trade between the colonies, now struggling for prosperous life, was also taxed for the benefit of England.

but in vain. The profligate monarch, who seems never to have had a clear perception of right and wrong, but was governed by caprice and passion, gave away, to his special favorites, large tracts of the finest portions of the Virginia soil, some of it already well cultivated.[1]

Week after week, and month after month, the Royalist party continued to show more and more of the foul hand of despotism. The pliant Assembly abridged the liberties of the people. Although elected for only two years, the members assumed to themselves the right of holding office indefinitely, and the representative system was thus virtually abolished. The doctrines and rituals of the Church of England having been made the religion of the State, intolerance began to grow. Baptists and Quakers[2] were compelled to pay heavy fines. The salaries of the royal officers being paid from duties upon exported tobacco, these officials were made independent of the people.[3] Oppressive and unequal taxes were levied, and the idle aristocracy formed a distinct and ruling class. The "common people"—the men of toil and substantial worth—formed a republican party, and rebellious murmurs were heard on every side. They desired a sufficient reason for strengthening their power, and it soon appeared. The menaces of the Susquehannah Indians,[4] a fierce tribe of Lower Pennsylvania, gave the people a plausible pretense for arming during the summer of 1675. The Indians had been driven from their hunting-grounds at the head of the Chesapeake Bay by the Senecas,[5] and coming down the Potomac, they made war upon the Maryland settlements.[6] They finally committed murders upon Virginia soil, and retaliation[7] caused the breaking out of a fierce border war. The inhabitants, exasperated and alarmed, called loudly upon Governor Berkeley to take immediate and energetic measures for the defense of the colony. His slow and indecisive movements were very unsatisfactory, and loud murmurs were heard on every side. At length Nathaniel Bacon,[8] an energetic and highly esteemed republican, acting in behalf of his party, demanded permission for the people to arm and protect themselves.[9] Berkeley's sagacity perceived the danger of allowing discontented men to have arms, and he refused. The Indians came nearer and nearer, until laborers on Bacon's plantation, near Richmond, were murdered. That leader then yielded to the popular will, and placed himself at the head of four or five hundred men, to drive back the enemy. Berkeley, jealous of Bacon's popularity, proclaimed him a traitor

---

[1] In 1673, the king gave to Lord Culpepper and the Earl of Arlington, two of his profligate favorites, "all the dominion of land and water called Virginia," for the term of thirty years.

[2] Note 7, page 94.

[3] One of the charges made against the King of England in the Declaration of Independence, more than a hundred years later, was that he had "made judges dependent on his will alone for the tenure of their offices and the amount and payment of their salaries."

[4] Page 17.

[5] Page 23.

[6] Page 82.

[7] John Washington, an ancestor of the commander-in-chief of the American armies a century later, commanded some troops against an Indian fort on the Potomac. Some chiefs, who were sent to his camp to treat for peace, were treacherously slain, and this excited the fierce resentment of the Susquehannahs.

[8] He was born in England, was educated a lawyer, and in Virginia was a member of the council. He was about thirty years of age at that time.

[9] King Philip's war was then raging in Massachusetts, and the white people, everywhere, were alarmed. See page 124.

[May, 1676], and sent troops to arrest him. Some of his more timid followers returned, but sterner patriots adhered to his fortunes. The people generally sympathized with him, and in the lower counties they arose in open rebellion. Berkeley was obliged to recall his troops to suppress the insurrection, and in the mean while Bacon drove the Indians[1] back toward the Rappahannock. He was soon after elected a burgess,[2] but on approaching Jamestown, to take his seat in the Assembly, he was arrested. For fear of the people, who made hostile demonstrations, the governor soon pardoned him and all his followers, and hypocritically professed a personal regard for the bold republican leader.

Popular opinion had now manifestly become a power in Virginia; and the pressure of that opinion compelled Berkeley to yield at all points. The long aristocratic Assembly was dissolved; many abuses were corrected, and all the privileges formerly enjoyed by the people were restored.[3] Fearing treachery in the capital, Bacon withdrew to the Middle Plantation,[4] where he was joined by three or four hundred armed men from the upper counties, and was proclaimed commander-in-chief of the Virginia troops. The governor regarded the movement as rebellious, and refused to sign Bacon's commission. The patriot marched to Jamestown, and demanded it without delay. The frightened governor speedily complied [July 4, 1676], and, concealing his anger, he also, on compulsion, signed a letter to the king, highly commending the acts and motives of the "traitor." This was exactly one hundred years, to a day, before the English colonies in America declared themselves free and independent, the logic of which the King of Great Britain was compelled, reluctantly, to acknowledge, a few years later. The Virginia Assembly was as pliant before the successful leader as the governor, and gave him the commission of a general of a thousand men. On receiving it, Bacon marched against the Pamunkey Indians.[5] When he had gone, Berkeley, faithless to his professions, crossed the York River, and at Gloucester summoned a convention of royalists. All the proceedings of the Republican Assembly were reversed, and, contrary to the advice of his friends, the governor again proclaimed Bacon a traitor, on the 29th of July. The indignation of the patriot leader was fiercely kindled, and, marching back to Jamestown, he lighted up a civil war. The property of royalists was confiscated, their wives were seized as hostages, and their plantations were desolated. Berkeley fled to the eastern shore of the Chesapeake. Bacon proclaimed his abdication, and, dismissing the republican troops, called an Assembly in his own name, and was about to cast off all allegiance to the English Crown, when

---

[1] Page 40.

[2] The chief leaders of the republican party at the capital, were William Drummond, who had been governor of North Carolina [page 97], and Colonel Richard Lawrence.

[3] This event was the planting of one of the most vigorous and fruitful germs of American nationality. It was the first bending of power to the boldly-expressed will of the people.

[4] Williamsburg, four miles from Jamestown, and midway between the York and James Rivers, was then called the *Middle Plantation*. After the accession of William and Mary [see page 113], a town was laid out in the form of the ciphers WM., and was named Williamsburg. Governor Nicholson made it the capital of the province in 1698.

[5] This was a small tribe on the Pamunkey River, one of the chief tributaries of the York River.

intelligence was received of the arrival of imperial troops to quell the rebellion.[1] Great was the joy of the governor, when informed of the arrival of the hoped-for succor, for his danger was imminent. With some royalists and English sailors under Major Robert Beverley, he now [Sept. 7] returned to Jamestown. Bacon collected hastily his troops, and drove the governor and his friends down the James River. Informed that a large body of royalists and imperial troops were approaching, the republicans, unable to maintain their position at Jamestown, applied the torch [Sept. 30] just as the night shadows came over the village.[2] When the sun arose on the following morning, the first town built by Englishmen in America,[3] was a heap of smoking ruins. Nothing remained standing but a few chimneys, and that old church tower, which now attracts the eye and heart of the voyager upon the bosom of the James River. This work accomplished, Bacon pressed forward with his little army toward the York, determined to drive the royalists from Virginia. But he was smitten by a deadlier foe than armed men. The malaria of the marshes at Jamestown had poisoned his veins, and he died [Oct. 11, 1676] of malignant fever, on the north bank of the York. There was no man to receive the mantle of his ability and influence, and his departure was a death-blow to the cause he had espoused. His friends and followers made but feeble resistance, and before the first of November, Berkeley returned to the Middle Plantation[4] in triumph.

CHURCH TOWER.

The dangers and vexations to which the governor had been exposed during these commotions, rendered the haughty temper of the baron irascible, and he signalized his restoration to power by acts of wanton cruelty. Twenty-two of the insurgent leaders had been hanged,[5] when the more merciful Assembly implored him to shed no more blood. But he continued fines, imprisonments, and confiscations, and ruled with an iron hand and a stony heart until recalled by the king in April, 1677, who had become disgusted with his cruel conduct.[6] There was no printing press in Virginia to record current history,[7] and for a

[1] This was an error. The fleet sent with troops to quell the insurrection, did not arrive until April the following year, when all was over. Colonel Jeffreys, the successor of Berkeley, came with the fleet.

[2] Besides the church and court-house, Jamestown contained sixteen or eighteen houses, built of brick, and quite commodious, and a large number of humble log cabins.

[3] The church, of which the brick tower alone remains, was built about 1620. It was probably the third church erected in Jamestown. The ruin is now [1856] a few rods from the encroaching bank of the river, and is about thirty feet in height. The engraving is a correct representation of its present appearance. In the grave-yard adjoining are fragments of several monuments.

[4] Note 4, page 111.

[5] The first man executed was Colonel Hansford. He has been justly termed the first martyr in the cause of liberty in America. Drummond and Lawrence were also executed. They were considered ringleaders and the prime instigators of the rebellion.

[6] Charles said, "The old fool has taken more lives in that naked country than I have taken for the murder of my father."

[7] Berkeley was an enemy to popular enlightenment. He said to commissioners sent from England in 1671, "Thank God there are no free schools nor printing press; and I hope we shall not have these hundred years; for learning has brought disobedience, and heresy, and sects into the world, and printing has divulged these, and libels against the best government." Despots are always afraid of the printing press, for it is the most destructive foe of tyranny.

hundred years the narratives of the royalists gave hue to the whole affair. Bacon was always regarded as a *traitor*, and the effort to establish a free government is known in history as BACON'S REBELLION. Such, also, would have been the verdict of history, had Washington and his compatriots been unsuccessful. Too often *success* is accounted a virtue, but *failure*, a crime.

Long years elapsed before the effects of these civil commotions were effaced. The people were borne down by the petty tyranny of royal rulers, yet the principles of Republicanism grew apace. The popular Assembly became winnowed of its aristocratic elements; and, notwithstanding royal troops were quartered in Virginia,[1] to overawe the people, the burgesses were always firm in the maintenance of popular rights.[2] In reply to Governor Jeffreys, when he appealed to the authority of the Great Seal of England, in defense of his arbitrary act in seizing the books and papers of the Assembly, the burgesses said, "that such a breach of privilege could not be commanded under the Great Seal, because they could not find that any king of England had ever done so in former times." The king commanded the governor to "signify his majesty's indignation at language so seditious;" but the burgesses were as indifferent to royal frowns as they were to the governor's menaces.

A libertine from the purlieus of the licentious court now came to rule the liberty-loving Virginians. It was Lord Culpepper, who, under the grant of 1673,[3] had been appointed governor for life in 1677. He arrived in 1680. His profligacy and rapacity disgusted the people. Discontents ripened into insurrections, and the blood of patriots again flowed.[4] At length the king himself became incensed against Culpepper, revoked his grant[5] in 1684, and deprived him of office. Effingham, his successor, was equally rapacious, and the people were on the eve of a general rebellion, when king Charles died, and his brother James[6] was proclaimed [Feb. 1685] his successor, with the title of James the Second. The people hoped for benefit by the change of rulers, but their burdens were increased. Again the wave of rebellion was rising high, when the revolution of 1688 placed William of Orange and his wife Mary upon the throne.[7] Then a real change for the better took place. The detested and detestable Stuarts were forever driven from the seat of power in Great Britain. That event, wrought out by the people, infused a conservative principle into the workings of the English constitution. The popular will, expressed by Par-

[1] These troops were under the command of a wise veteran, Sir Henry Chicheley, who managed with prudence. They proved a source of much discontent, because their subsistence was drawn from the planters For the same cause, disturbances occurred in New York ninety years afterward. See page 218.

[2] Page 71.

[3] Note 1, page 110.

[4] By the king's order, Culpepper caused several of the insurgents, who were men of influence, to be hanged, and a "reign of terror," miscalled *tranquillity*, followed.

[5] Arlington [note 1, page 110] had already disposed of his interest in the grant to Culpepper.

[6] James, Duke of York, to whom Charles gave the New Netherlands in 1664. See page 144.

[7] James the Second, by his bigotry (he was a Roman Catholic), tyranny, and oppression, rendered himself hateful to his subjects. William, Prince of Orange, Stadtholder of Holland, who had married Mary, a Protestant daughter of James, and his eldest child, was invited by the incensed people to come to the English throne. He came with Dutch troops, and landed at Torbay on the 5th of November, 1688. James was deserted by his soldiers, and he and his family sought safety in flight. William and Mary were proclaimed joint monarchs of England on the 13th of February, 1689. This act consummated that revolution which Voltaire styled "the era of English liberty."

liament, became potential; and the personal character, or caprices of the monarch, had comparatively little influence upon legislation. The potency of the National Assembly was extended to similar colonial organizations. The powers of governors were defined, and the rights of the people were understood. Bad men often exercised authority in the colonies, but it was in subordination to the English Constitution; and, notwithstanding commercial restrictions bore heavily upon the enterprise of the colonies, the diffusion of just political ideas, and the growth of free institutions in America, were rapid and healthful.

From the revolution of 1688, down to the commencement of the French and Indian war, the history of Virginia is the history of the steady, quiet progress of an industrious people, and presents no prominent events of interest to the general reader.[1]

CHAPTER II.

MASSACHUSETTS. [1620.]

"Welcome, Englishmen! welcome, Englishmen!" were the first words which the *Pilgrim Fathers*[2] heard from the lips of a son of the American forest. It was the voice of Samoset, a Wampanoag chief, who had learned a few English words of fishermen at Penobscot. His brethren had hovered around the little community of sufferers at New Plymouth[3] for a hundred days, when he boldly approached [March 26, 1621], and gave the friendly salutation. He told them to possess the land, for the occupants had nearly all been swept away by a pestilence. The *Pilgrims* thanked God for thus making their seat more secure, for they feared the hostility of the Aborigines. When Samoset again appeared, he was accompanied by Squanto,[4] a chief who had recently returned from captivity in Spain; and they told the white people about Massasoit, the grand sachem of the Wampanoags, then residing at Mount Hope. An interview was planned. The old sachem came with barbaric pomp,[5] and he and Governor Carver[6] smoked the calumet[7] together. A preliminary treaty of friendship and alliance was formed [April 1, 1621], which remained unbroken

---

[1] The population at that time was about 50,000, of whom one half were slaves. The tobacco trade had become very important, the exports to England and Ireland being about 30,000 hogsheads that year. Almost a hundred vessels annually came from those countries to Virginia for tobacco. A powerful militia of almost 9,000 men was organized, and they no longer feared their dusky neighbors. The militia became expert in the use of fire-arms in the woods, and back to this period the Virginia rifleman may look for the foundation of his fame as a marksman. The province contained twenty-two counties, and forty-eight parishes, with a church and a clergyman in each, and a great deal of glebe land. But there was no printing press nor book-store in the colony. A press was first established in Virginia in 1729.

[2] Page 77. [3] Page 78. [4] Page 74.

[5] Massasoit approached, with a guard of sixty warriors, and took post upon a neighboring hill. There he sat in state, and received Edward Winslow as embassador from the English. Leaving Winslow with his warriors as security for his own safety, the sachem went into New Plymouth and treated with Governor Carver. Note 5, page 14. [6] Page 78. [7] Page 14.

for fifty years.[1] Massasoit rejoiced at his good fortune, for Canonicus, the head of the powerful Narragansetts,[2] was his enemy, and he needed strength.

Three days after the interview with the Wampanoag sachem [April 8], Governor Carver suddenly died. William Bradford,[3] the earliest historian of the colony, was appointed his successor. He was a wise and prudent man, and for thirty years he managed the public affairs of the colony with great sagacity. He was a man just fitted for such a station, and he fostered the colony with parental care. The settlers endured great trials during the first four years of their sojourn. They were barely saved from starvation in the autumn of 1621, by a scanty crop of Indian corn.[4] In November of that year, thirty-five immigrants (some of them their weak brethren of the *Speedwell*)[5] joined them, and increased their destitution. The winter was severe, and produced great suffering; and the colonists were kept in continual fear by the menaces of Canonicus, the great chief of the Narragansetts, who regarded the English as intruders. Bradford acted wisely with the chief, and soon made him sue for peace.[6] The power, but not the hatred, of the wily Indian was subdued, yet he was compelled to be a passive friend of the English.

Sixty-three more immigrants arrived at Plymouth in July, 1622. They had been sent by Weston, a wealthy, dissatisfied member of the Plymouth Company,[7] to plant a new colony. Many of them were idle and dissolute;[8] and after living upon the slender means of the Plymouth people for several weeks, they went to Wissagusset (now Weymouth), to commence a settlement. Their improvidence produced a famine; and they exasperated the Indians by begging and stealing supplies for their wants. A plot was devised by the savages for their destruction, but through the agency of Massasoit,[9] it was revealed [March, 1623] to the Plymouth people; and Captain Miles Standish, with eight men, hastened to Wissagusset in time to avert the blow. A chief and several warriors were killed in a battle;[10] and so terrified were the surrounding tribes by

---

[1] Page 124. [2] Page 22.

[3] William Bradford was born at Ansterfield, in the north of England, in 1588. He followed Robinson to Holland; came to America in the *Mayflower* [see page 77]; and was annually elected governor of the colony from 1621 until his death in 1657.

[4] While Captain Miles Standish and others were seeking a place to land [see page 78], they found some *maize*, or Indian corn, in one of the deserted huts of the savages. Afterward, Samoset and others taught them how to cultivate the grain (then unknown in Europe), and this supply serving for seed, providentially saved them from starvation. The grain now first received the name of *Indian corn*. Early in September [1621], an exploring party, under Standish, coasted northward to Shawmut, the site of Boston, where they found a few Indians. The place was delightful, and for a while, the Pilgrims thought of removing thither. [5] Page 77.

[6] Canonicus dwelt upon Connanicut Island, opposite Newport. In token of his contempt and defiance of the English, he sent [Feb., 1622] a bundle of arrows, wrapped in a rattlesnake's skin, to Governor Bradford. The governor accepted the hostile challenge, and then returned the skin, filled with powder and shot. These substances were new to the savages. They regarded them with superstitious awe, as possessing some evil influence. They were sent from village to village, and excited general alarm. The pride of Canonicus was humbled, and he sued for peace. The example of Canonicus was followed by several chiefs, who were equally alarmed. [7] Page 63.

[8] There was quite a number of indentured servants, and men of no character; a population wholly unfit to found an independent State.

[9] In gratitude for attentions and medicine during a severe illness, Massasoit revealed the plot to Edward Winslow a few days before the time appointed to strike the blow.

[10] Standish carried the chief's head in triumph to Plymouth. It was borne upon a pole, and was placed upon the palissades [note 1, page 127] of the little fort which had just been erected. The

the event, that several chiefs soon appeared at Plymouth to crave the friendship of the English. The settlement at Wissagusset was broken up, however, and most of the immigrants returned to England.

Social perils soon menaced the stability of the colony. The partnership of merchants and colonists[1] was an unprofitable speculation for all. The community system[2] operated unfavorably upon the industry and thrift of the colony, and the merchants had few or no returns for their investments. Ill feelings were created by mutual criminations, and the capitalists commenced a series of annoyances to force the workers into a dissolution of the league.[3] The partnership continued, however, during the prescribed term of seven years, and then [1627] the colonists purchased the interest of the London merchants for nine thousand dollars. Becoming sole proprietors of the soil, they divided the whole property equally, and to each man was assigned twenty acres of land in fee. New incentives to industry followed, and the blessings of plenty, even upon that unfruitful soil, rewarded them all.[4] At about the same time, the government of the colony became slightly changed. The only officers, at first, were a governor and an assistant. In 1624, five assistants were chosen; and in 1630, when the colony numbered almost five hundred souls, seven assistants were elected. This pure democracy prevailed, both in Church and State, for almost nineteen years, when a representative government was instituted [1639], and a pastor was chosen as spiritual guide.[5]

James the First died in the spring of 1625; and his son and successor, Charles the First, inherited his father's hatred of the Nonconformists.[6] Many of their ministers were silenced during the first years of his reign, and the uneasiness of the great body of Nonconformists daily increased. Already, White, a Puritan minister of Dorchester, in the west of England, had persuaded several influential men of that city to attempt the establishment of a new asylum for the oppressed, in America. They chose the rocky promontory of Cape Anne for the purpose [1624], intending to connect the settlement with the fishing business; but the enterprise proved to be more expensive than profitable,

good Robinson [page 77], when he heard of it, wrote, "Oh, how happy a thing it would have been, that you had converted some before you killed any."

[1] Page 77.

[2] Note 1, page 70.

[3] The merchants refused Mr. Robinson a passage to America; attempted to force a minister upon the colonists who was friendly to the Established Church; and even sent vessels to interfere with the infant commerce of the settlers.

[4] The colonists unsuccessfully tried the cultivation of tobacco. They raised enough grain and vegetables for their own consumption, and relied upon traffic in furs with the Indians, for obtaining the means of paying for cloths, implements, etc., procured from England. In 1627, they made the first step toward the establishment of the cod fishery, since become so important, by constructing a salt work, and curing some fish. In 1624, Edward Winslow imported three cows and a bull, and soon those invaluable animals became numerous in the colony.

[5] The colonists considered Robinson (who was yet in Leyden), as their pastor; and religious exercises, in the way of prayer and exhortation, were conducted by Elder Brewster and others. On Sunday afternoons a question would be propounded, to which all had a right to speak. Even after they adopted the plan of having a pastor, the people were so democratic in religious matters, that a minister did not remain long at Plymouth. The doctrine of "private judgment" was put in full practice; and the religious meetings were often the arena of intemperate debate and confusion. In 1629, thirty-five persons, the remainder of Robinson's congregation at Leyden, joined the Pilgrims at Plymouth, among whom was Robinson's family; but the good man never saw New England himself.

[6] Note 2, page 76.

and it was abandoned. A few years afterward, a company purchased a tract of land [March 29, 1628] defined as being "three miles north of any and every part of the Merrimac River," and "three miles south of any and every part of the Charles River," and westward to the Pacific Ocean.[1] In the summer of 1628, John Endicot, and a hundred emigrants came over, and at Naumkeag (now Salem) they laid the foundations of the Colony of Massachusetts Bay. The proprietors received a charter from the king the following year [March 14, 1629], and they were incorporated by the name of "The Governor and Company of the Massachusetts Bay in New England"[2]

FIRST COLONY SEAL.

The colony at Salem increased rapidly, and soon began to spread. In July, 1629, "three godly ministers" (Skelton, Higginson, and Bright) came with

two hundred settlers, and a part of them laid the foundations of Charlestown, at Mishawam. A new stimulus was now given to emigration by salutary arrange-

[1] This was purchased from the Council of Plymouth. The chief men of the company were John Humphrey (brother-in-law to the earl of Lincoln), John Endicot, Sir Henry Roswell, Sir John Young, Thomas Southcote, Simon Whitcomb, John Winthrop, Thomas Dudley, Sir Richard Saltonstall, and others. Eminent men in New England afterward became interested in the enterprise.

[2] The administration of affairs was intrusted to a governor, deputy, and eighteen assistants, who were to be elected annually by the stockholders of the corporation. A general assembly of the freemen of the colony was to be held at least four times a year, to legislate for the colony. The king claimed no jurisdiction, for he regarded the whole matter as a trading operation, not as the founding of an empire. The instrument conferred on the colonists all the rights of English subjects, and afterward became the text for many powerful discourses against the usurpation of royalty.

ments. On the 1st of September, the members of the company, at a meeting in Cambridge, England, signed an agreement to transfer the charter and government to the colonists. It was a wise and benevolent conclusion, for men of fortune and intelligence immediately prepared to emigrate when such a democracy should be established. John Winthrop[1] and others, with about three hundred families, arrived at Salem in July [1630] following. Winthrop had been chosen governor before his departure, with Thomas Dudley for deputy, and a council of eighteen. The new immigrants located at, and named Dorchester, Roxbury, Watertown, and Cambridge; and during the summer, the governor and some of the leading men, hearing of a spring of excellent water on the peninsula of Shawmut, went there, erected a few cottages, and founded Boston, the future metropolis of New England.[2] The peninsula was composed of three hills, and for a long time it was called TRI-MOUNTAIN.[3]

As usual, the ravens of sickness and death followed these first settlers. Many of them, accustomed to ease and luxury in England, suffered much, and before December, two hundred were in their graves.[4] Yet the survivors were not disheartened, and during the winter of intense suffering which followed, they applied themselves diligently to the business of founding a State. In May, 1631, it was agreed at a general assembly of the people, that all the officers of government should thereafter be chosen by the freemen[5] of the colony; and in 1634, the pure democracy was changed to a representative government, the second in America.[6] The colony flourished. Chiefs from the Indian tribes dined at Governor Winthrop's table, and made covenants of peace and friendship with the English. Winthrop journeyed on foot to exchange courtesies with Bradford at Plymouth,[7] a friendly salutation came from the Dutch in New Netherland,[8] and a ship from Virginia, laden with corn [May, 1632], sailed into Boston harbor. A bright future was dawning.

The character of the Puritans[9] who founded the colony of Massachusetts Bay, presents a strange problem to the scrutiny of the moral philosopher. Victims of intolerance, they were themselves equally intolerant when clothed with power.[10] Their ideas of civil and religious freedom were narrow, and their prac-

---

[1] He was born in England in 1558, and was one of the most active men in New England from 1630 until his death in 1649. His journal, giving an interesting account of the colony, has been published.

[2] The whole company under Winthrop intended to join the settlers at Charlestown, but a prevailing sickness there, attributed to unwholesome water, caused them to locate elsewhere. The fine spring of water which gushed from one of the three hills of Shawmut, was regarded with great favor.

[3] From this is derived the word *Tremont.*

[4] Among these was Higginson, Isaac Johnston (a principal leader in the enterprise, and the wealthiest of the founders of Boston), and his wife the "Lady Arabella," a daughter of the earl of Lincoln. She died at Salem, and her husband did not long survive her.

[5] None were considered freemen unless they were members of some church within the colony. From the beginning, the closest intimacy existed between the Church and State in Massachusetts, and that intimacy gave rise to a great many disorders. This provision was repealed in 1665.

[6] Page 71.

[7] Page 115.

[8] Page 72.

[9] Page 75.

[10] Sir Richard Saltonstall, who did not remain long in America, severely rebuked the people of Massachusetts, in a letter to the two Boston ministers, Wilson and Cotton. "It doth a little grieve my spirit," he said, "to hear what sad things are reported daily of your tyranny and persecutions in New England, as that you fine, whip, and imprison men for their consciences." Thirty years later [1665], the king's commissioner at Picataqua, in a manuscript letter before me, addressed to

tical interpretation of the Golden Rule, was contrary to the intentions of HIM who uttered it. Yet they were honest and true men; and out of their love of freedom, and jealousy of their inherent rights, grew their intolerance. They regarded Churchmen and Roman Catholics as their deadly enemies, to be kept at a distance.[1] A wise caution dictated this course. A consideration of the prevailing spirit of the age, when bigotry assumed the seat of justice, and superstition was the counselor and guide of leading men, should cause us to

> "Be to their faults a little blind,
> And to their virtues, very kind."

Roger Williams, himself a Puritan minister, and victim of persecution in England, was among those who first felt the power of Puritan intolerance. He was chosen minister at Salem, in 1634, and his more enlightened views, freely expressed, soon aroused the civil authorities against him. He denied the right of civil magistrates to control the consciences of the people, or to withhold their protection from any religious sect whatever. He denied the right of the king to require an oath of allegiance from the colonists; and even contended that obedience to magistrates ought not to be enforced. He denounced the charter from the king as invalid, because he had given to the white people the lands of other owners, the Indians.[2] These doctrines, and others more theological,[3] he maintained with vehemence, and soon the colony became a scene of great commotion on that account. He was remonstrated with by the elders, warned by the magistrates, and finally, refusing to cease what was deemed seditious preaching, he was banished [November, 1635] from the colony. In the dead of winter he departed [January, 1636] for the wilderness, and became the founder of Rhode Island.[4]

Political events in England caused men who loved quiet to turn their thoughts more and more toward the New World; and the year 1635 was remarkable for an immense immigration to New England. During that year full three thousand new settlers came, among whom were men of wealth and influence. The most distinguished were Hugh Peters[5] (an eloquent preacher),

---

the magistrates of Massachusetts, say, "It is possible that the charter which you so much idolize may be forfeited until you have cleared yourselves of those many injustices, oppressions, violences, and blood for which you are complained against."

[1] Lyford, who was sent out to the *Pilgrims*, by the London partners, as their minister, was refused and expelled, because he was friendly to the Church of England. John and Samuel Browne, residents at Salem, and members of Endicot's council, were arrested by that ruler, and sent to England as "factious and evil-conditioned persons," because they insisted upon the use of the Liturgy, or printed forms of the English Church, in their worship.

[2] See page 22. This was not strictly true, for, until King Philip's war [page 124], in 1675, not a foot of ground was occupied by the New England colonists, on any other score but that of fair purchase.

[3] He maintained that an oath should not be tendered to an unconverted person, and that no Christian could lawfully pray with such an one, though it were a wife or child! In the intemperance of his zeal, Williams often exhibited intolerance himself, and at this day would be called a bigot. Yet his tolerant teachings in general had a most salutary effect upon Puritan exclusiveness.

[4] Page 89.

[5] Peters afterward returned to England, was very active in public affairs during the civil war, and on the accession of Charles the Second, was found guilty of favoring the death of the king's father, and was executed in October, 1660.

and Henry Vane, an enthusiastic young man of twenty-five. In 1636, Vane was elected governor, an event which indirectly proved disastrous to the peace of the colony. The banishment of Roger Williams had awakened bitter religous dissensions, and the minds of the people were prepared to listen to any new teacher. As at Plymouth, so in the Massachusetts Bay colony, religious questions were debated at the stated meetings.[1] Women were not allowed to engage in these debates, and some deemed this an abridgment of their rights. Among these was Anne Hutchinson, an able and eloquent woman, who established meetings at her own house, for her sex, and there she promulgated peculiar views, which some of the magistrates and ministers pronounced seditious and heretical.[2] These views were embraced by Governor Vane, several magistrates, and a majority of the leading men of Boston.[3] Winthrop and others opposed them, and in the midst of great excitement, a synod was called, the doctrines of Mrs. Hutchinson were condemned, and she and her family were first imprisoned in Boston, and then banished [August, 1637] from the colony.[4] Vane lost his popularity, and failing to be elected the following year, he returned to England.[5] Some of Mrs. Hutchinson's followers left the colony, and established settlements in Rhode Island.[6]

The great abatement of danger to be apprehended from the Indians, caused by the result of the Pequod war,[7] was favorable to the security of the colony, and it flourished amazingly. Persecution also gave it sustenance. The nonconformists in the mother country suffered more and more, and hundreds fled to New England. The church and the government became alarmed at the rapid growth of a colony, so opposed, in its feelings and laws, to the character of both. Efforts were put forth to stay the tide of emigration. As early as 1633, a proclamation for that purpose had been published, but not enforced; and a fleet of eight vessels, bearing some of the purest patriots of the realm, was detained in the Thames [Feb. 1634], by order of the privy council.[8] Believing that the colonists "aimed not at new discipline, but at sovereignty," a demand was made for a surrender of the patent to the king.[9] The people were silent,

---

[1] Note 5, page 116.

[2] She taught that, as the Holy Spirit dwells in every believer, its revelations are superior to the teachings of men. It was the doctrine of "private judgment" in its fullest extent. She taught that every person had the right to judge of the soundness of a minister's teaching, and this was considered "rebellion against the clergy." She taught the doctrine of *Election*, and averred that the elect saints were sure of their salvation, however vicious their lives might be.

[3] Her brother, Rev. John Wheelwright, was an eloquent expounder of her views. The theological question assumed a political phase, and for a long time influenced the public affairs of the colony.

[4] Mrs. Hutchinson and her family took refuge within the Dutch domain, near the present village of New Rochelle, in New York. There she and all her family, except a daughter, were murdered by the Indians. Note 2, page 141.

[5] Vane was a son of the Secretary of State of Charles the First. He was a republican during the civil war [note 3, page 108], and for this, Charles the Second had him beheaded in June, 1662.

[6] Page 91.

[7] Page 87.

[8] [Note 1, page 400.] It was asserted, and is believed, that Oliver Cromwell and John Hampden were among the passengers. There is no positive evidence that such was the fact.

[9] The general patent for New England was surrendered by the Council of Plymouth, in June, 1635, without consulting the colonists. The inflexible courage of the latter prevented the evil that might have ensued by this faithless act of a company which had made extensive grants; and they firmly held the charter given to them by the king.

but firm. When a rumor reached them [September 18, 1634] that an arbitrary commission,[1] and a general governor was appointed for all the English colonies in America, the Massachusetts people, poor as they were, raised three thousand dollars to build fortifications for resistance. Even a *quo warranto* [April, 1638][2] did not affect either their resolution or their condition. Strong in their integrity, they continued to strengthen their new State by fostering education,[3] the "cheap defense of nations," and by other wise appliances of vigorous efforts. The civil war[4] which speedily involved the church and the throne in disaster, withdrew the attention of the persecutors from the persecuted. The hope of better times at home checked immigration, and thereafter the colony received but small accessions to its population, from the mother country.

The ties of interest and warmest sympathy united the struggling colonists of New England. Natives of the same country, the offspring of persecution—alike exposed to the weapons of hostile Indians and the depredations of the Dutch and French,[5] and alike menaced with punishment by the parent government—they were as one people. They were now [1643] more than twenty thousand in number, and fifty villages had been planted by them. The civil war in England[6] threatened a total subversion of the government, and the Puritans began to reflect on the establishment of an independent nation eastward of the Dutch dominions.[7] With this view, a union of the New England colonies was proposed in 1637, at the close of the Pequod war. It was favorably received by all, but the union was not consummated until 1643, when the colonies of Plymouth,[8] Massachusetts,[9] Connecticut and New Haven[10] confederated for mutual welfare. Rhode Island asked for admittance into the Union [1643], but was refused,[11] unless it would acknowledge the authority of Plymouth. Local jurisdiction was jealously reserved by each colony, and the doctrine of State Rights was thus early practically developed. It was a confederacy of independent States like our Union. The general affairs of the confederacy were managed by a board of commissioners, consisting of two church-members from each colony, who were to meet annually, or oftener if required. Their duty was to consider circumstances, and recommend measures for the general good. They had no executive power. Their propositions were considered and acted upon by the several colonies, each assuming an independent sovereignty. This confed-

---

[1] The Archbishop of Canterbury and associates received full power to establish governments and laws over the American settlements; to regulate religious matters; inflict punishments, and even to revoke charters. [2] Note 3, page 107.

[3] In 1636, the General Court at Boston appropriated two thousand dollars for the establishment of a college. In 1638, Rev. John Harvard bequeathed more than three thousand dollars to the institution which was then located at Cambridge, and it received the name of "Harvard College," now one of the first seminaries of learning in the United States. In 1647, a law was passed, requiring every township, which contained fifty householders, to have a school-house, and employ a teacher; and each town containing one thousand freeholders to have a grammar-school.

[4] Note 3, page 108.

[5] The Dutch of New Netherland [page 72], still claimed jurisdiction upon the Connecticut River, and the French settlers in Acadie, eastward of New England, were becoming troublesome to the Puritans.

[6] Note 3, page 108. [7] Page 72. [8] Page 78.
[9] Page 117. [10] Page 89. [11] Page 91.

eracy remained unmolested more than forty years[1] [1643—1686], during which time the government of England was changed three times.

The colony of Massachusetts Bay was always the leading one of New England, and assumed to be a "perfect republic." After the Union, a legislative change took place. The representatives had hitherto held their sessions in the same room with the governor and council; now they convened in a separate apartment; and the distinct *House of Representatives*, or democratic branch of the legislature, still existing in our Federal and State Governments, was established in 1644. Unlike Virginia,[2] the colonists of New England sympathized with the English republicans, in their efforts to abolish royalty. Ardently attached to the Parliament, they found in Cromwell,[3] when he assumed supreme authority, a sincere friend and protector of their liberties. No longer annoyed by the frowns and menaces of royalty, the energies of the people were rapidly developed, and profitable commerce was created between Massachusetts and the West Indies. This trade brought bullion, or uncoined gold and silver, into the colony; and in 1652, the authorities exercised a prerogative of independent sovereignty, by establishing a mint, and coining silver money,[4] the first within the territory of the United States. During the same year, settlements in the present State of Maine, imitating the act of those of New Hampshire,[5] eleven years earlier [1641], came under the jurisdiction of Massachusetts.

FIRST MONEY COINED IN THE UNITED STATES.

And now an important element of trouble and perplexity was introduced. There arrived in Boston, in July, 1656, two zealous religious women, named Mary Fisher and Ann Austin, who were called Quakers. This was a sect recently evolved from the heaving masses of English society,[6] claiming to be more rigid Puritans than all who had preceded them. Letters unfavorable to the sect had been received in the colony, and the two women were cast into prison, and confined for several weeks.[7] With eight others who arrived during

---

[1] When James the Second came to the throne, the charters of all the colonies were taken away or suspended. When local governments were re-established after the Revolution of 1688, there no longer existed a necessity for the Union, and the confederacy was dissolved.

[2] Page 108.

[3] Note 3, page 108.

[4] In October, 1651, the general court or legislature of Massachusetts ordered silver coins of the values of threepence, sixpence, and a shilling sterling, to be made. The mint-master was allowed fifteen pence out of every twenty shillings, for his trouble. He made a large fortune by the business. From the circumstance that the effigy of a *pine-tree* was stamped on one side, these coins, now very rare, are called *pine-tree money*. The date [1652] was not altered for thirty years. Massachusetts was also the first to issue paper money in the shape of treasury notes. See page 132.

[5] Page 80.

[6] The founder of the sect was George Fox, who promulgated his peculiar tenets about 1650. He was a man of education and exalted purity of character, and soon, learned and influential men became his co-workers. They still maintain the highest character for morality and practical Christianity. See note 7, page 94.

[7] Their trunks were searched, and the religious books found in them were burned by the hangman, on Boston Common. Suspected of being witches [note 7, page 132], their persons were examined in order to discover certain marks which would indicate their connection with the Evil One.

the year, they were sent back to England.[1] Others came, and a special act against the Quakers was put in force [1657], but to no purpose. Opposition increased their zeal, and, as usual with enthusiasts, precisely because they were not wanted, they came. They suffered stripes, imprisonments, and general contempt; and finally, in 1658, on the recommendation of the Federal Commissioners,[2] Massachusetts, by a majority of one vote, banished them, on pain of death. The excuse pleaded in extenuation of this barbarous law was, that the Quakers preached doctrines dangerous to good government.[3] But the death penalty did not deter the exiles from returning; and many others came because they courted the martyr's reward. Some were hanged, others were publicly whipped, and the prisons were soon filled with the persecuted sect. The severity of the law finally caused a strong expression of public sentiment against it. The Quakers were regarded as true martyrs, and the people demanded of the magistrates a cessation of the bloody and barbarous punishments. The death penalty was abolished, in 1661; the fanaticism of the magistrates and the Quakers subsided, and a more Christian spirit of toleration prevailed. No longer sufferers for opinion's sake, the Quakers turned their attention to the Indian tribes, and nobly seconded the efforts of Mahew and Eliot in the propagation of the gospel among the pagans of the forest.[4]

On the restoration of monarchy in 1660, the judges who condemned Charles the First to the block, were outlawed. Two of them (William Goffe and Edward Whalley) fled to America, and were the first to announce at Boston the accession of Charles the Second. Orders were sent to the colonial authorities for their arrest, and officers were dispatched from England for the same purpose. The colonists effectually concealed them, and for this act, and the general sympathy manifested by New England for the republican party, the king resolved to show them no favor. They had been exempt from commercial restrictions during Cromwell's administration; now these were revived, and the stringent provisions of a new Navigation Act[5] were rigorously enforced. The people vainly petitioned for relief; and finally, commissioners were sent [August, 1644] "to hear and determine all complaints that might exist in New England, and take such measures as they might deem expedient for settling the peace and security of the country on a solid foundation."[6] This was an unwise

[1] Mary Fisher went all the way from London to Adrianople, to carry a divine message to the Sultan. She was regarded as insane; and as the Moslems respect such people as special favorites of God, Mary Fisher was unharmed in the Sultan's dominions.

[2] Page 121.

[3] The Quakers denied all human authority, and regarded the power of magistrates as delegated tyranny. They preached purity of life, charity in its broadest sense, and denied the right of any man to control the opinions of another. Conscience, or "the light within," was considered a sufficient guide, and they deemed it their special mission to denounce "hireling ministers" and "persecuting magistrates," in person. It was this offensive boldness which engendered the violent hatred toward the sect in England and America.

[4] John Eliot has been truly called the Apostle to the Indians. He began his labors soon after his arrival in America, and founded the first church among the savages, at Natic, in 1660, at which time there were ten towns of converted Indians in Massachusetts. Thirty-five years later, it was estimated that there were not less than three thousand adult Christian Indians in the Islands of Martha's Vineyard and Nantucket, alone.

[5] Note 4, page 109.

[6] These were Colonel Richard Nicolls, Sir Robert Carr, George Cartwright and Richard Maverick. They came with a royal fleet, commanded by Colonel Nicolls, which had been sent to assert English authority over the possessions of the Dutch, in New Netherland. See page 144.

movement on the part of the mother country. The colonists regarded the measure with indignation, not only as a violation of their charters, but as an incipient step toward establishing a system of domination, destructive to their liberties. Massachusetts boldly protested against the exercise of the authority of the commissioners within her limits, but at the same time asserted her loyalty to the sovereign. The commissioners experienced the opposition of the other New England colonies, except Rhode Island. Their acts were generally disregarded, and after producing a great deal of irritation, they were recalled in 1666. The people of Massachusetts, triumphant in their opposition to royal oppression, ever afterward took a front rank in the march toward complete freedom. The licentious king and his ministers were too much in love with voluptuous ease, to trouble themselves with far-off colonies; and while Old England was suffering from bad government, and the puissance of the throne was lessening in the estimation of the nations, the colonies flourished in purity, peace, and strength, until *Metacomet*, the son of the good *Massasoit*,[1] kindled a most disastrous Indian war, known in history as

KING PHILIP'S WAR.

KING PHILIP.

Massasoit kept his treaty with the Plymouth colony[2] faithfully while he lived. *Metacomet*, or *Philip*,[3] resumed the covenants of friendship, and kept them inviolate for a dozen years. But as spreading settlements were reducing his domains acre by acre, breaking up his hunting grounds, diminishing his fisheries, and menacing his nation with servitude or annihilation, his patriotism was aroused, and he willingly listened to the hot young warriors of his tribe, who counseled a war of extermination against the English. At Mount Hope[4] the seat of the chief sachems of the Wampanoags, in the solitudes of the primeval forests, he planned, with consummate skill, an alliance of all the New England tribes,[5] against the European intruders.

At this time, there were four hundred "praying Indians," as the converts to Christianity were called, firmly attached to the white people. One of them, named John Sassamon, who had been educated at Cambridge, and was a sort of secretary to Philip, after becoming acquainted with the plans of the sachem,

---

[1] Page 114. [2] Page 114.

[3] Massasoit had two sons, whom Governor Price named Alexander and Philip, in compliment to their bravery as warriors. Alexander died soon after the decease of his father; and Philip became chief sachem of the Wampanoags.

[4] Mount Hope is a conical hill, 300 feet in height, and situated on the west side of Mount Hope Bay, about two miles from Bristol, Rhode Island. It was called Pokanoket by the Indians.

[5] The tribes which became involved in this war numbered, probably, about twenty-five thousand souls. Those along the coast of Massachusetts Bay, who had suffered terribly by a pestilence just before the PILGRIMS came [page 77], had materially increased in numbers; and other tribes, besides the New England Indians proper [page 22], became parties to the conflict.

revealed them to the authorities at Plymouth. For this he was slain by his countrymen, and three Wampanoags were convicted of his murder, on slender testimony, and hanged. The ire of the tribe was fiercely kindled, and they thirsted for vengeance. The cautious Philip was overruled by his fiery young men, and remembering the wrongs and humiliations he had personally received from the English,[1] he trampled upon solemn treaties, sent his women and children to the Narragansetts for protection, and kindled the flame of war. Messengers were sent to other tribes, to arouse them to co-operation, and with all the power of Indian eloquence, *Metacomet* exhorted his followers to curse the white men, and swear eternal hostility to the pale faces. He said, in effect:

"Away! away! I will not hear
Of aught but death or vengeance now;
By the eternal skies I swear
My knee shall never learn to bow!
I will not hear a word of peace,
Nor clasp in friendly grasp a hand
Linked to that pale-browed stranger race,
That works the ruin of our land.
* * * * * *
And till your last white foe shall kneel,
And in his coward pangs expire,
Sleep—but to dream of brand and steel:
Wake—but to deal in blood and fire!"

Although fierce and determined when once aroused, no doubt Philip commenced hostilities contrary to the teachings of his better judgment, for he was sagacious enough to foresee failure. "Frenzy prompted their rising. It was but the storm in which the ancient inhabitants of the land were to vanish away. They rose without hope, and therefore they fought without mercy. To them, as a nation, there was no to-morrow."

The bold Philip struck the first blow at Swanzey, thirty-five miles southwest from Plymouth. The people were just returning from their houses of worship, for it was a day of fasting and humiliation [July 4, 1675], in anticipation of hostilities. Many were slain and captured, and others fled to the surrounding settlements, and aroused the people. The men of Plymouth, joined by those of Boston and vicinity, pressed toward Mount Hope. Philip was besieged in a swamp for many days, but escaped with most of his warriors, and became a fugitive with the Nipmucs,[2] an interior tribe of Massachusetts. These espoused his cause, and with full fifteen hundred warriors, he hastened toward the white settlements in the far-off valley of the Connecticut. In the mean while the little army of white people penetrated the country of the Narragansetts,[3] and extorted a treaty of friendship from Canonchet,[4] chief sachem of

[1] In 1671, Philip and his tribe being suspected of secretly plotting the destruction of the English, were deprived of their fire-arms. He never forgot the injury, and long meditated revenge.

[2] Page 22. [3] Page 22.

[4] Son of Miantonomoh, whose residence was upon a hill a little north of the city of Newport, R. I. That hill still bears the name of Miantonomoh, abbreviated to "Tonomy Hill." Page 91.

that powerful tribe. Hearing of this, Philip was dismayed for a moment. But there was no hope for him, except in energetic action, and he and his followers aroused other tribes, to a war of extermination, by the secret and efficient methods of treachery, ambush, and surprise. Men in the fields, families in their beds at midnight, and congregations in houses of worship, were attacked and massacred. The Indians hung like the scythe of death upon the borders of the English settlements, and for several months a gloomy apprehension of the extermination of the whole European population in New England, prevailed.[1]

Dreadful were the scenes in the path of the Wampanoag chief. From Springfield northward to the present Vermont line, the valley of the Connecticut was a theater of confusion, desolation, and death, wherever white settlements existed. Almost the whole of a party of twenty Englishmen[2] sent to treat with the Nipmucs, were treacherously slain by the savages in ambush [Aug. 12, 1675], near Quaboag, now Brookfield. That place was set on fire, when a shower of rain put out the flames, and the Indians were driven away by a relief party of white people.[3] The village was partially saved, but immediately abandoned. Soon afterward a hot battle was fought near Deerfield[4] [Sept 5], and a week later [Sept. 12] that settlement also was laid in ashes. On the same day (it was the Sabbath), Hadley, further down the river, was attacked while the people were worshiping In the midst of the alarm and confusion, a tall and venerable-looking man, with white, flowing hair and beard, suddenly appeared, and brandishing a glittering sword, he placed himself at the head of the affrighted people, and led them to a charge which dispersed and defeated the foe. He as suddenly disappeared, and the inhabitants believed that an angel from heaven had been sent to their rescue. It was Goffe, the fugitive English judge,[5] who was then concealed in that settlement.

The scourge, stayed for a moment at Hadley, swept mercilessly over other settlements. On the 23d of September, the paths of Northfield were wet with the blood of many valiant young men under Captain Beers; and on the 28th, "a company of young men, the very flower of Essex," under Captain Lathrop, were butchered by almost a thousand Indians on the banks of a little stream near Deerfield, which still bears the name of Bloody Brook. Others, who came to their rescue, were engaged many hours in combat with the Indians until crowned with victory. Yet the Indians still prevailed. Philip, encouraged by success, now resolved to attack Hatfield, the chief settlement of the

---

[1] The white population in New England, at this time, has been estimated at fifty-five thousand. Haverhill, on the Merrimac, was the frontier town in the direction of Maine; and Northfield, on the borders of Vermont, was the highest settlement in the Connecticut valley. Westfield, one hundred miles west of Boston, was the most remote settlement in that direction.

[2] Captains Wheeler and Hutchinson were sent from Boston to endeavor to reclaim the Nipmucs. Apprised of their coming, the Indians lay in ambush, and fired upon them from the deep thickets of a swamp.

[3] Under Major Willard. The Indians set fire to every house except a strong one into which the people had secured themselves, and were besieged there two days. The Indians set fire to this last refuge, when rain extinguished the flames.

[4] Between 180 white people and 700 Indians. [See, also, page 135.]

[5] Page 123.

white people above Springfield. The Springfield Indians joined him,[1] and with almost a thousand warriors, he fell upon the settlement, on the 29th of October, 1675. The English were prepared for his reception, and he was repulsed with such loss, that, gathering his broken forces on the eastern bank of the Connecticut,[2] he marched toward Rhode Island. The Narragansetts, in violation of the recent treaty,[3] received him, became his allies, and went out upon the war path late in autumn. A terrible, retributive blow soon fell upon the savages, when fifteen hundred men of Massachusetts, Plymouth, and Connecticut, marched to punish Canonchet and his tribe, for their perfidy. The snows of early winter had fallen, and at least three thousand Indians had collected in their chief fort in an immense swamp,[4] where they were supplied with provisions for the winter. It was a stormy day in December [Dec. 29], when the English stood before the feeble palissades of the savages. These offered but little opposition to the besiegers; and within a few hours, five hundred wigwams, with the winter provisions, were in flames. Hundreds of men, women, and children, perished in the fire. A thousand warriors were slain or wounded, and several hundreds were made prisoners. The English lost eighty killed, and one hundred and fifty wounded. Canonchet was made prisoner, and slain; but Philip escaped, and with the remnant of the Narragansetts, he took refuge again with the Nipmucs.

The fugitive Wampanoag was busy during the winter. He vainly solicited the Mohawks[5] to join him, but he was seconded by the tribes eastward of Massachusetts,[6] who also had wrongs to redress. The work of desolation began early in the spring of 1676, and within a few weeks the war extended over a space of almost three hundred miles. Weymouth, Groton, Medfield, Lancaster, and Marlborough, in Massachusetts, were laid in ashes; Warwick and Providence, in Rhode Island, were burned; and everywhere, the isolated dwellings of settlers were laid waste. But internal feuds weakened the power of the savages; and both the Nipmucs[7] and the Narragansetts[8] charged their misfortunes to the ambition of Philip. The cords of alliance were severed. Some surrendered to avoid starvation; other tribes wandered off and joined those in Canada;[9] while Captain Benjamin Church,[10] the most famous of the partisan

[1] They had been friendly until now. They plotted the entire destruction of the Springfield settlement; but the people defended themselves bravely within their palisaded houses. Many of the strong houses of frontier settlements were thus fortified. Trunks of trees, eight or ten inches in diameter, were cut in uniform lengths, and stuck in the ground close together. The upper ends were sharpened, and the whole were fastened together with green withes or other contrivances.

PALISADED BUILDINGS.

[2] Page 82. [3] Page 125.

[4] This swamp is a small distance south-west of the village of Kingston, in Washington County, Rhode Island. The fort was on an island which contains about five acres of tillable land, in the north-west part of the swamp. The Stonington and Providence railway passes along the northern verge of the swamp.

[5] Page 23.

[6] Page 22. The tribes of Maine were then about four thousand strong.

[7] Page 22. [8] Page 22. [9] Page 22.

[10] Benjamin Church was born at Plymouth, Massachusetts, in 1639. He continued hostilities against the eastern Indians until 1704. He fell from his horse, and died soon afterward, at Little Compton, Jan. 17, 1718, aged 77 years.

officers of the English colonies, went out to hunt and to destroy the fugitives. During the year, between two and three thousand Indians were slain or had submitted. Philip was chased from one hiding-place to another, but for a long time he would not yield. He once cleft the head of a warrior who proposed submission. But at length, the "last of the Wampanoags" bowed to the pressure of circumstances. He returned to the land of his fathers[1] [August, 1676], and soon his wife and son were made prisoners. This calamity crushed him, and he said, "Now my heart breaks; I am ready to die." A few days after-

ward, a faithless Indian shot him, and Captain Church cut off the dead sachem's head.[2] His body was quartered; and his little son was sold to be a bond-slave in Bermuda.[3] So perished the last of the princes of the Wampanoags, and thus ended, in the total destruction of the power of the New England Indians, the famous KING PHILIP'S WAR.[4]

The terrible menaces of the Indian war, and the hourly alarm which it occasioned, did not make the English settlers unmindful of their political posi-

---

[1] Note 4, page 124.

[2] The rude sword, made by a blacksmith of the colony, with which Captain Church cut off Philip's head, is in the possession of the Massachusetts Historical Society.

[3] The disposal of the boy was a subject of serious deliberation. Some of the elders proposed putting him to death; others, professing more *mercy*, suggested selling him as a slave. The most *profitable* measure appeared the most *merciful*, and the child was sold into bondage. The head of Philip was carried in triumph to Plymouth, and placed upon a pole

[4] The result of this war was vastly beneficial to the colonists, for the fear of savages, which prevented a rapid spread of settlements, was removed. From this period may be dated the real, unimpeded growth of New England.

tion, nor hopeless respecting the future. While the Massachusetts colony was yet weak in resources, from the effects of the war,[1] and the people were yet engaged in hostilities with the eastern tribes,[2] it made territorial accessions by purchase, and at the same time boldly asserted its chartered rights. For many years there had been a controversy between the heirs of Sir F. Gorges[3] and John Mason, and the Massachusetts colony, concerning a portion of the present territory of Maine and New Hampshire, which, by acts of the inhabitants, had been placed [1641 and 1652] under the jurisdiction of the authorities at Boston.[4] The judicial decision [1677] was in favor of the heirs, and Massachusetts immediately purchased [May 1, 1677] their interest for six thousand dollars.[5] New Hampshire was detached three years afterward [1680], and made a royal province—the first in New England; but Maine, which was incorporated with Massachusetts in 1692, continued a part of that commonwealth until 1820.

Now rapidly budded that governmental tyranny which finally drove all the American colonies into open rebellion. The profligate king continued to draw the lines of absolute rule closer and closer in England, and he both feared and hated the growing republics in America, especially those in the East. They were ostensibly loyal portions of his realm, but were really independent sovereignties, continually reacting upon the mother country, to the damage of the "divine right" of kings. Charles had long cherished a desire to take their governments into his own hands, and he employed the occasion of the rejection of Edward Randolph (a custom-house officer, who had been sent to Boston [1679] to collect the revenues, and otherwise to exercise authority[6]), to declare the Massachusetts charter void. He issued a *quo warranto* in 1683,[7] and procured a decision in his favor in the High Court of Chancery, on the 28th of June, 1684, but he died on the 26th of February following, before his object was effected.

Charles's successor, James the Second,[8] continued the oppressive measures of his brother toward the New England colonies. The people petitioned and remonstrated, and were treated with contempt. Their hardships in conquering a wilderness, and their devotion to the English constitution, had no weight with the royal bigot.[9] He also declared the charter of Massachusetts forfeited, and appointed Joseph Dudley president of the country from Rhode Island to Nova Scotia. Sir Edmund Andros arrived at Boston soon afterward [Dec.

[1] During the war, New England lost six hundred men; a dozen towns were destroyed; six hundred dwellings were burned; every twentieth family was houseless; and every twentieth man, who had served as a soldier, had perished. The cost of the war equaled five hundred thousand dollars—a very large sum at that time.

[2] Page 22. [3] Page 79. [4] Page 80, and note 2, page 80.

[5] The portion of Maine then purchased, was the tract between the Piscataqua and the Kennebec. That between the Kennebec and the Penobscot belonged to the Duke of York, and the territory between the Penobscot and the St. Croix, was held by the French, pursuant to a treaty.

[6] Randolph appears to have been a greedy adventurer, and was, consequently, a faithful servant of his royal master in oppressing the colonists. He exaggerated the number and resources of the people of New England, and thus excited the king's fears and cupidity. Previous to Randolph's appointment, the colonies had dispatched agents to England, to settle impending difficulties amicably. They failed, and Randolph came in the same vessel in which they returned.

[7] Note 3, page 107. [8] Page 113. [9] Note 7, page 113.

30, 1686], clothed with authority to govern all New England. He came with a smiling face, and deceitful lips. He appears to have been a tyrant by nature, and came to execute a despot's will. He soon made bare the rod of oppression, and began to rule with a tyrant's rigor.[1] The people were about to practice the doctrine that "*resistance to tyrants is obedience to God*,"[2] when intelligence reached Boston [April 14, 1689], that James was driven from the throne [1688] and was succeeded by William and Mary, of Orange.[3] The inhabitants of Boston seized and imprisoned Andros and fifty of his political associates [April 28, 1689], sent them to England under a just charge of maladministration of public affairs, and re-established their constitutional government. Again republicanism was triumphant in Massachusetts.

The effects of the revolution in England were also sorrowful to the American colonies. That revolution became a cause of war between England and France. James (who was a Roman Catholic) fled to the court of Louis the Fourteenth, king of France, and that monarch espoused the cause of the fugitive. Hostilities between the two nations commenced the same year, and the quarrel extended to their respective colonies in America. The conflict then commenced, and which was continued more than seven years, is known in history as

KING WILLIAM'S WAR.

The colonists suffered terribly in that contest. The French Jesuits,[4] who had acquired great influence over the eastern tribes,[5] easily excited them to renew their fierce warfare with the English. They also made the savages their allies; and all along the frontier settlements, the pathway of murder and desolation was seen. Dover, a frontier town, was first attacked by a party of French and Indians, on the 7th of July, 1689, when the venerable Major Waldron[6] and twenty others of the little garrison were killed. Twenty-nine of the inhabitants were made captive, and sold as servants to the French in Canada. In August following, an Indian war party, instigated by Thury, a Jesuit, fell [August 12] upon an English stockade[7] at Pemaquid (built by Andros), and captured the garrison. A few months later, Frontenac sent a

---

[1] Among other arbitrary acts, Andros laid restraints upon the freedom of the press, and marriage contracts; and, to use a modern term, he "levied black mail;" that is, extorted money, by menaces, whenever opportunity offered. He advanced the fees of all officers of the government to an exorbitant degree; and finally threatened to make the Church of England the established religion in all America.

[2] This was Cromwell's motto; and Thomas Jefferson had it engraved upon his private seal.

[3] Note 7, page 113.

[4] This was a Roman Catholic religious order, founded by Ignatius Loyola, a Spaniard, in 1539. They have ever been remarkable for their great devotion to their cause, their self-denial, and masterly sagacity in the acquirement and maintenance of power. Their missionaries preached Christianity in every part of the habitable globe. They came with the first French adventurers to America, and under their influence, whole tribes of Indians eastward of Massachusetts and in Canada were made nominal Christians. This was one of the ties which made the savages such faithful allies to the French in the contests between them and the English, previous to 1763.

[5] Page 22.

[6] Waldron was eighty years of age. He had played false with the New Hampshire Indians during King Philip's war, and they now sought revenge. They tortured him to death.

[7] Note 2, page 183.

party of three hundred French and Indians from Montreal, to penetrate the country toward Albany. On a gloomy night in winter, when the snow was twenty inches in depth, they fell upon Schenectada [Feb. 18, 1690], a frontier town on the Mohawk, massacred many of the people, and burnt the village. Early in the spring, Salmon Falls [March 28], Casco [May 27], and other eastern villages, were attacked by another party of the same mongrel foe, the natural ferocity of the Indians being quickened by the teachings of the Jesuits concerning the proper fate of heretics.[1]

All the colonies were aroused, by these atrocities, to a sense of their danger in having such foes intent upon their destruction; and the New England people resolved on speedy retaliation. In May, Massachusetts fitted out an expedition, under Sir William Phipps, a native of Pemaquid, consisting of eight or nine vessels, with about eight hundred men. Phipps seized Port Royal,[2] in Acadie, and obtained sufficient plunder from the inhabitants to pay the expenses of the expedition. In June, Port Royal was again plundered by English privateers from the West Indies. Encouraged by these successes, the colonies of New England and New York coalesced in efforts to conquer Canada.[3] It was arranged to send a land expedition from New York, by way of Lake Champlain, against Montreal,[4] and a naval expedition against Quebec.[5] The command of the former was intrusted to the son of Governor Winthrop of Connecticut,[6] and the expenses were borne jointly by that colony and New York.[7] Sir William Phipps commanded the latter, which Massachusetts alone fitted out. It consisted of thirty-four vessels, with two thousand men. Both were unsuccessful. Some of Winthrop's troops, with Indians of the FIVE NATIONS,[8] under Colonel Schuyler, pushed toward the St. Lawrence, and were repulsed [Aug., 1690] by Frontenac, the governor of Canada. The remainder did not go beyond Wood Creek (now Whitehall), at the head of Lake Champlain, and all returned to Albany.[9] Phipps reached Quebec about the middle of October, and landed the troops; but the city was too strongly fortified[10] to promise a successful siege, and he returned to Boston before the winter set in.[11] Massa-

---

[1] In these massacres, instigated by the Jesuits, we may find a reason for the seeming intolerance of the Protestant majority in Maryland [page 152], the disabilities of Roman Catholics in Virginia, New York, and New England, and their exclusion from the privileges of freemen in tolerant Rhode Island. The most potent operations of the Jesuits were in secret, and the colonists were compelled to regard every Roman Catholic as the natural enemy of Protestants, and as laboring to destroy every measure tending to human freedom.

[2] Page 58. [3] Page 204. [4] Page 48.

[5] Page 48. [6] Page 86.

[7] Milborne, son-in-law of Jacob Leisler, the democratic governor of New York [page 148], undertook to provide subsistence for the army, which marched from Albany early in July.

[8] Page 23.

[9] Leisler was so much incensed at this failure, that he caused the arrest of Winthrop, at Albany. There had ever been a jealous rivalry between the people of New York and Connecticut; and the feud which continually prevailed among the mixed troops, was the chief cause of the miscarriage of the enterprise.

[10] Phipps, having no chart to guide him, was nine weeks cautiously making his way around Acadie and up the St. Lawrence. In the mean while, a swift Indian runner, from Pemaquid, sped across the country, and informed the French, at Quebec, of the approach of Phipps, in time for them to well prepare for defense.

[11] This repulse was considered so important by the French, that king Louis had a commemorative medal struck, with the legend—"FRANCE VICTORIOUS IN THE NEW WORLD."

chusetts was obliged to issue bills of credit, or paper money, to defray the expenses of this expedition.[1]

Sir William Phipps was sent to England soon after his return, to solicit aid in further warfare upon the French and Indians, and also to assist in efforts to procure a restoration of the charter of Massachusetts, taken away by King James.[2] Material assistance in prosecuting the war was refused; and King William instead of restoring the old charter, granted a new one, and united under it the colonies of Plymouth, Massachusetts, Maine, and Nova Scotia,[3] by the old name of *Massachusetts Bay Colony*, and made it a royal province. Phipps was appointed governor by the king, and returned to Boston with the charter, in May, 1692. But the new constitution was offensive to the people, for they were allowed scarcely any other political privileges than they already possessed, except the right to choose representatives. The king reserved the right to appoint the governor, his deputy, and the secretary of the colony, and of repealing the laws within three years after their passage. This abridgment of their liberties produced general dissatisfaction, and alienated the affections of the people from the mother country. It was one of a series of fatal steps taken by the English government, which tended toward the final dismemberment of the empire in 1776.[4] Yet one good resulted from the change. The theocratic or religious element in the government, which fostered bigotry and intolerance, lost its power, for toleration was guarantied to all Christian sects, except Roman Catholics; and the right of suffrage was extended to others than members of Congregational churches.[5]

A very strange episode in the history of Massachusetts now occurred. A belief in witchcraft[6] destroyed the peace of society in many communities, and shrouded the whole colony in a cloud of gloom. This belief had a strong hold upon the minds of the people of old England, and of their brethren in America. Excitement upon the subject suddenly broke out at Danvers (then a part of Salem), in March, 1692, and spread like an epidemic. A niece and daughter of the parish minister exhibited strange conduct; and under the influence of their own superstitious belief, they accused an old Indian servant-woman in the family of bewitching them. Fasting and prayer, to break the "spell," were of no avail, for the malady increased. The alarm of the family spread to the

---

[1] Note 4, page 122. The total amount of the issue was $133,338. [2] Page 129.

[3] New Scotland, the name given to the country which the French called Acadie. See note 2, page 80. [4] Page 251. [5] Note 5, page 118.

[6] A belief in witchcraft, or the exercise of supernatural power, by men and women, has been prevalent for ages. Punishment of persons accused of it, was first sanctioned by the Church of Rome a little more than three hundred years ago. Certain tests were instituted, and thousands of innocent persons were burned alive, drowned, or hanged, in Europe. Within three months, in 1515, five hundred persons were burned in Geneva, in Switzerland. In the diocese of Como, one thousand were burned in one year. In 1520, an incredible number, from among all classes, suffered death in France. And within fifty or sixty years, during the sixteenth century, more than one hundred thousand persons perished in the flames in Germany alone. Henry the Eighth of England made the practice of witchcraft a capital offense; and a hundred years later, "witch-detectors" traversed the country, and brought many to the stake. Enlightened men embraced the belief; and even Sir Matthew Hale, the most distinguished of England's judges, repeatedly tried and condemned persons accused of witchcraft. The English laws against witchcraft were adopted in New England; and as early as 1648, four persons had suffered death for the alleged offense, in the vicinity of Boston.

community; and soon a belief prevailed throughout the colony, that evil spirits, having ministering servants among men, overshadowed the land. Old and ill-favored women were first accused of practising the art of witchcraft; but at length neither age, sex, nor condition afforded protection from the accuser's tongue. Even the lady of Governor Phipps did not escape suspicion. Magistrates were condemned, many pious persons were imprisoned, and Mr. Burroughs, a worthy minister, was executed. Men of strong minds and scholarly attainments were thoroughly deluded. Among these was the eminent Cotton Mather, whose father before him had yielded to the superstition, and published

Cotton Mather.

an account of all the supposed cases of witchcraft in New England. Cotton Mather, on account of his position as a leading divine, and his talents, probably did more than any other man to promote the spread of that fearful delusion, which prevailed for more than six months. During that time, twenty persons suffered death, fifty-five were tortured or frightened into a confession of witchcraft, and when a special court, or legislature, was convened in October, 1692, one hundred and fifty accused persons were in prison. A reaction, almost as sudden as the beginning of the excitement, now took place in the public mind. The prison doors were opened to the accused, and soon many of the accusers shrunk abashed from the public gaze.[1] Standing in the light of the present century, we look back to "Salem witchcraft," as it is called, with amazement.

[1] The belief in witchcraft did not cease with the strange excitement; and Cotton Mather and other popular men, wrote in its defense. Calef, a citizen of Boston, exposed Mather's credulity, which greatly irritated the minister. He first called his opponent "a weaver turned minister;" but as his tormentor's blows fell thick and fast, in a series of letters, Mather called him "a coal from

"King William's war"[1] continued until 1697, when a treaty of peace, made at Ryswick, in the west of Holland, on the 20th of September of that year, terminated hostilities.[2] Up to that time, and later, the New England people suffered greatly from their mongrel foe. Remote settlements in the direction of Canada and Nova Scotia continued to be harassed. Almost a hundred persons were killed or made captive [July 28, 1694] at Oyster River (now Durham), ten miles from Portsmouth, in New Hampshire. Two years later [July 25, 1696], Baron St. Castine, and a large force of French and Indians, captured the garrison at Pemaquid, and exchanged the prisoners for French soldiers in the hands of the English.[3] In March, 1697, Haverhill, thirty miles from Boston, was attacked, and forty persons were killed or carried into captivity;[4] and during the following summer, more remote settlers were great sufferers. A respite now came. The treaty at Ryswick produced a lull in the storm of cruel warfare, which had so long hung upon the English frontiers, continually menacing the colonists with wide-spread destruction.[5] It was very brief, however, for pretexts for another war were not long wanting. James the Second died in September, 1701, and Louis the Fourteenth, who had sheltered the exile,[6] acknowledged his son, Charles Edward (commonly known as the Pretender), to be the lawful heir to the English throne. This offended the English, because the crown had been settled upon Anne, second daughter of James, who was a Protestant. Louis had also offended the English, by placing his grandson, Philip of Anjou, upon the throne of Spain, and thus

---

hell," and prosecuted him for slander. The credulous clergyman was glad to withdraw the suit. Cotton Mather was born in Boston, in February, 1633, and was educated at Harvard College. He was very expert in the acquirement of knowledge, and at the age of nineteen years, he received the degree of Master of Arts. He became a gospel minister at twenty-two, and holding a ready pen, he wrote much. Few of his writings have survived him. With all his learning, he was but a child in that which constitutes true manhood, and he is now regarded more as a pedant than as a scholar. He died in February, 1728. For the benefit of young men, we will here introduce an anecdote connected with him. It was thus related by Dr. Franklin, to Samuel, a son of Cotton Mather: "The last time I saw your father was in the beginning of 1724, when I visited him after my first trip to Pennsylvania. He received me in his library; and on my taking leave, showed me a shorter way out of the house through a narrow passage, which was crossed by a beam overhead. We were still talking as I withdrew, he accompanying me behind, and I turning partly toward him, when he said hastily, 'Stoop! stoop!' I did not understand until I felt my head hit against the beam. He was a man that never missed an occasion of giving instruction, and upon this he said to me, 'You are young, and have the world before you; stoop as you go through, and you will escape many hard thumps.' This advice, thus beat into my head, has frequently been of use to me; and I often think of it when I see pride mortified, and misfortunes brought upon people by carrying their heads too high."

[1] Page 130.

[2] This war cost England one hundred and fifty millions of dollars, in cash, besides a loan of one hundred millions more. This loan was the commencement of the enormous national debt of England, now [1856] amounting to about four thousand millions of dollars.

[3] They also took the English fort of St. John's, Newfoundland, and several other posts on that island.

[4] Among their captives was a Mrs. Dustan, her child, and nurse. Her infant was soon killed, and she and her nurse were taken to Canada. A little more than a month afterward, Mrs. D., her companion, and another prisoner, killed ten of twelve sleeping Indians, who had them in custody, and made their way back to Haverhill.

[5] Just before the conclusion of this treaty, a *Board of Trade and Plantations* was established by the English government, whose duty it was to have a general oversight of the American colonies. This was a permanent commission, consisting of a president and seven members, called *Lords of Trade.* This commission was always an instrument of oppression in the hands of royalty, and, as will be seen, was a powerful promoter of that discontent which led to the rebellion of the colonies in 1775.

[6] Page 130.

extended the influence of France among the dynasties of Europe. These, and some minor causes, impelled England again to declare war against France.[1] Hostilities commenced in 1702, and continued until a treaty of peace was concluded at Utrecht, in Holland, on the 11th of April, 1713. As usual, the French and English in America were involved in this war; and the latter suffered much from the cruelties of the Indians who were under the influence of the former. This is known in America as

QUEEN ANNE'S WAR.

It was a fortunate circumstance for the people of New York that the FIVE NATIONS had made a treaty of neutrality with the French in Canada [Aug. 4, 1701], and thus became an impassable barrier against the savage hordes from the St. Lawrence. The tribes from the Merrimac to the Penobscot had made a treaty of peace with New England, in July, 1703, but the French induced them to violate it; and before the close of summer, the hatchet fell upon the people of the whole frontier from Casco to Wells. Blood flowed in almost every valley; and early the next spring [March, 1704], a large party of French and Indians, under Major Hertel de Rouville, attacked Deerfield, on the Connecticut River, applied the torch,[2] killed forty of the inhabitants, and carried one hundred and twelve away to the wilderness. Among these was Rev. John Williams, the minister, whose little daughter, after a long residence with the Indians, became attached to them, and married a Mohawk chief.[3]

WILLIAMS'S HOUSE.

Similar scenes occurred at intervals during the whole progress of the war. Remote settlements were abandoned, and the people on the frontier collected in fortified houses,[4] and cultivated their fields in armed parties of half a dozen or more. This state of things became insupportable to the English colonists, and in the spring of 1707, Massachusetts, Rhode Island, and New Hampshire, determined to chastise the French on their eastern borders. Connecticut refused to join in the enterprise, and the three colonies alone prepared an armament. Early in June, a thousand men under Colonel Marsh, sailed from Nantucket for Port Royal,[5] in Acadie, convoyed by an English man-of-war. The French were prepared for them, and nothing was effected except the destruction of considerable property outside the fort. Three years later, an armament left

---

[1] It is known in European history as the *War of the Spanish Succession.*

[2] The only house that escaped the flames was that of the Rev. John Williams, represented in the engraving. It stood near the centre of the village, until within a few years.

[3] Mrs. Williams and other captives, who were unable to travel as rapidly as the Indians, were murdered. On his arrival in Canada, Mr. Williams was treated with respect by the French, and after two years of captivity, was ransomed, and returned to Massachusetts. The chief object of the expedition to Deerfield, appears to have been to carry off the bell that hung in Williams's church. That bell was purchased the year previous for the church of Saut St. Louis, at Caughnawaga, near Montreal. The vessel in which it was brought from Havre was captured by a New England privateer, and the bell was purchased for the Deerfield meeting-house. Father Nicolas, of the church at Caughnawaga, accompanied the expedition, and the bell was carried in triumph to its original destination, where it still remains.

[4] Note 1, page 127.

[5] Page 58.

Boston [September, 1710], and, in connection with a fleet from England, under Colonel Nicholson, demanded and obtained a surrender of the fort and garrison [Oct. 13], at Port Royal. The name of the place was then changed to Annapolis, in honor of the Queen, Anne, and Acadie was annexed to the English realm under the title of Nova Scotia, or New Scotland.

In July, the following year [1711], Sir Hovendon Walker arrived at Boston, with an English fleet and army, designed for the conquest of Canada. New England promptly raised additional forces, and on the 10th of August, fifteen men-of-war and forty transports, bearing almost seven thousand troops, departed for the St. Lawrence to attack Quebec. Walker, like Braddock,[2] haughtily refused to listen to experienced subordinates, and lost eight of his ships, and almost a thousand men, on the rocks at the mouth of the river, on the night of the 2d of September. Disheartened by this calamity, Walker returned to England with the remainder of his fleet, and the colonial troops went back to Boston. On hearing of this failure of the naval expedition, a body of troops marching from Albany to attack Montreal, retraced their steps.[3] Hostilities were now suspended, and in the spring of 1713, a treaty of peace was concluded [April 11] at Utrecht. The eastern Indians sent a flag to Boston, and sued for peace; and at Portsmouth the Governor of Massachusetts and New Hampshire entered into a pacific compact [July 24] with the chiefs of the tribes.

A long peace now ensued, and for thirty years succeeding the close of *Queen Anne's War*, the colonists enjoyed comparative repose. Then, again, the selfish strifes of European monarchs awakened the demon of discord, and its bloody footsteps were soon apparent along the northern frontiers of the English colonies in America. The interim had been a period of much political agitation in Massachusetts, during which a great stimulus had been given to the growth of republican principles. Disputes, sometimes violent, and sometimes in a conciliatory spirit, had been carried on between the royal governors and the representatives of the people; the former contending for prerogatives and salaries which the people deemed inadmissible.[4] These internal disputes were arrested when they heard that France had declared hostility to England [March 15, 1744], and the colonists cheerfully prepared to commence the contest known in America as

KING GEORGE'S WAR.[5]

This war was not productive of many stirring events in America. The principal and very important one was the capture of the strong fortress of

[1] King William had no children; and Anne, the daughter of James the Second (who was married to Prince George of Denmark), succeeded him as sovereign of England in 1702. [2] Page 186.

[3] These were four thousand in number, under the command of General Nicholson. They were furnished by New York and Connecticut.

[4] The chief topic of controversy was the payment of salaries. Governors Shute, Burnet and Belcher, all contended for a permanent salary, but the people claimed the right to vote such salary, each year, as the services of the governor appeared justly to demand. A compromise was finally effected by an agreement to vote a certain sum each year. The subject of salaries was a cause of contention with the royal governors, until the Revolution.

[5] The husband of Queen Anne died several years previous to her death, which occurred in August, 1704. George, Elector of Hanover, in Germany, was immediately proclaimed King of

Louisburg, on the island of Cape Breton. It had been constructed by the French after the treaty of Utrecht, at an expense of five and a half millions of dollars, and because of its strength, was called *The Gibraltar of America.* William Shirley,[1] a soldier and energetic statesman, was Governor of Massachusetts when hostilities were proclaimed. He immediately perceived the importance of Louisburg in the coming contest, and plans for its capture were speedily perfected by the Legislature of Massachusetts.[2] Rhode Island, New Hampshire, and Connecticut furnished their proper quota of troops. New York sent artillery, and Pennsylvania provisions. Thus common danger was extending the idea of a necessity for a union of the Anglo-American colonies, long before it assumed a practical form in 1754.[3]

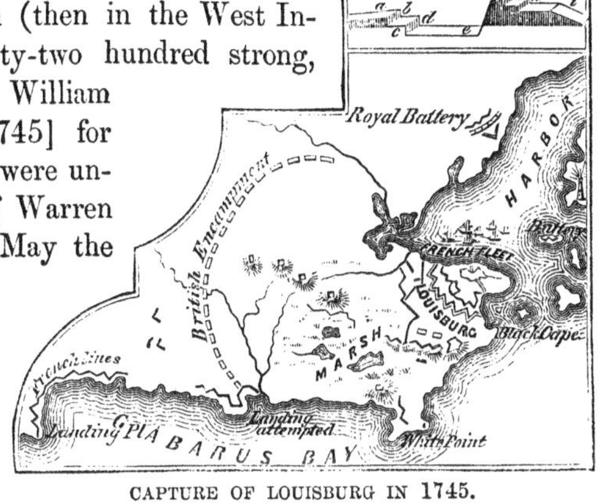

CAPTURE OF LOUISBURG IN 1745.

After vainly waiting for some time in the expectation of aid from Commodore Warren (then in the West Indies), the colonial forces, thirty-two hundred strong, under the general command of William Pepperell,[4] sailed [April 4, 1745] for Louisburg.[5] At Canseau they were unexpectedly joined by the fleet of Warren [May 9], and on the 11th of May the combined forces, four thousand strong, landed at Gabarus Bay, a short distance from their destination. The sudden appearance of this formidable armament, was the first intimation to the French, that an attack was meditated, and great consternation prevailed in the fortress and town. A

England, by the title of George the First. His son George succeeded him in 1727, and also retained the title and privileges of Elector of Hanover. A contest arose between Maria Theresa, Empress of Austria, and the Elector of Bavaria, for the throne of Austria. The King of England espoused the cause of the empress, in 1743, and the King of France took part with her opponent. This led France to declare war against England—a contest known in America as *King George's War*, but in Europe, the *War of the Austrian Succession.*

[1] William Shirley was born in England; made governor of Massachusetts in 1741; was afterward made governor of one of the Bahama Islands, and died at Roxbury, near Boston, in 1771. He appears conspicuous in history during a portion of the contest known in America as *The French and Indian War.*

[2] Shirley proposed an expedition, but the Legislature hesitated. The measure was finally agreed upon by a majority of only one vote.

[3] Page 183.

[4] Pepperell was a native of Maine, and a wealthy merchant. He was afterward made a baronet. He died in 1759.

[5] Louisburg is on the east side of the island of Cape Breton, with a fine, deep harbor. The landing-place of the British, position of the camp, etc., will be seen by reference to the map. The *Royal Battery* was taken by four hundred men. When they approached, the French thought the whole English army was upon them. They immediately spiked their guns (that is, drove iron spikes into the touch-holes of the cannons, so as to make them useless), and fled In the upper part of the map is a profile of the fortifications at Louisburg. It is given here so as to illustrate certain terms which may be used hereafter: *a*, the *glacis*, is the extreme outside slope of the works; *b*, the *banquet*, or step upon which the soldiers stand to fire over the parapet; *c*, a *covered way* into the fort, under the *banquet; d, counterscarp*, a bank or wall, outside the *ditch, e; f*, the *parapet*, a protection for the men and guns from balls from without; *g*, the inner *banquet; h*, ramparts—the most solid embankment of the fortress; *i* the last slope in the interior of the fort, called *talus.*

direct approach was difficult on account of a morass, and a combined attack by sea and land was carefully arranged. The land forces encamped in a curve in rear of the town, and detachments secured the French outposts, one after another. Cannons were dragged on sledges over the morass,[1] trenches were dug, batteries were erected, and a regular siege was commenced, on the 31st of May. In the mean while, Commodore Warren captured a French ship of seventy-four guns, and secured, as prisoners, over five hundred men, with a large quantity of military stores. While the siege was in progress, other English vessels of war arrived, and the fleet and army agreed to make a combined attack on the 29th of June. Despairing of successful resistance, the French surrendered the fortress, the city of Louisburg, and the island of Cape Breton, on the 28th of June, 1745.[2]

The pride of France was greatly mortified by this daring and successful expedition, and the following year [1746] the Duke D'Anville was sent with a powerful naval armament[3] to recover the lost fortress, and to desolate the English settlements along the seaboard. Storms wrecked many of his vessels, and disease soon wasted hundreds of his men; and D'Anville, thoroughly dispirited, abandoned the enterprise without striking a blow.[4] Two years afterward a treaty of peace was concluded at Aix-la-Chapelle, in western Germany, when it was agreed that all prisoners should be released, and all acquisitions of property or territory, made by either party, were to be restored. Both of the principal parties were heavy losers by the contest;[5] while the strength of the colonists, yet to be called forth in a more important struggle, was revealed and noted.

Old national animosities, religious differences, and recent causes for irritation, had inspired the English and French with intense mutual hatred, when the treaty of Aix-la-Chapelle was signed on the 18th of October, 1748. The allegiance of Massachusetts and its sister colonies to the British crown, and the acknowledged duty of obedience, restrained the resentment of the American people, while England and France were at peace. Soon, disputes about local boundaries began,[6] and it was not long before preparations for war between the two races, were visible in America. Then came that final bloody struggle between the English and French, for dominion in the New World, known as the *French and Indian War.*[7] This we shall consider hereafter.

---

[1] The artillery was commanded by Richard Gridley, who was the engineer of the continental army at Boston in 1775 and 1776. See page 234.

[2] The prizes and stores obtained by the English amounted, in value, to little less than five millions of dollars.

[3] It consisted of forty ships of war, fifty-six transports, thirty-five hundred men, and forty thousand muskets for the use of the French and Indians in Canada.

[4] D'Anville, with two or three vessels, anchored at Chebucto (now Halifax, Nova Scotia), where he died, it is believed, by poison. His lieutenant also committed suicide, in consequence of mortified pride. These disasters to the French fleet were regarded by the people of New England as special manifestations of Providence in their favor. Public thanksgivings were offered; and no one doubted the right of the English to the whole of Acadie.

[5] Parliament afterward reimbursed to the colonies the cost of their preparations against Canada, amounting to more than a million of dollars. See page 199.

[6] Page 180.

[7] Page 179.

CHAPTER III.

NEW YORK. [1623.]

THE State of New York commenced its political career when Peter Minuit,[1] recently appointed Governor of New Netherland,[2] arrived at New Amsterdam (as the germ of the present city of New York was called), in May, 1626. He immediately purchased of the Indians, for about twenty-four dollars, the whole of the island of Manhattan,[3] on which the city of New York now stands, and began vigorously to perfect the founding of a State similar to those of Holland. He erected a strong fortification near the site of the present *Battery*, and called it *Fort Amsterdam*.[4] By conciliatory measures, he gained the confidence of the Indians; and he also opened a friendly correspondence with the Puritans at Plymouth.[5] The English reciprocated the friendly expressions of the Dutch; at the same time, they requested the latter not to send their trappers quite as far eastward as Narraganset Bay, to catch otters and beavers.[6]

For the purpose of encouraging emigration to New Netherland, the Dutch West India Company[7] offered, in 1629, large tracts of land, and certain privileges, to those persons who should lead or send a given number of emigrants to occupy and till the soil.[8] Directors of the company[9] availed themselves of the privilege, and sent Wouter (Walter) Van Twiller to examine the country and select the lands. Immigrants came; and then were laid the foundations of the most noted of the manorial estates of New York.[10] The proprietors were called *patroons* (patrons), and held a high political and social station in the New World.

The agent of the *Patroons* seems to have performed his duty well, and he was appointed governor of the colony, in 1633. The beginning of Van Twiller's administration was marked by difficulties with the English on the Con-

---

[1] Page 93. [2] Page 72. [3] Note 1, page 48. [4] See picture on page 144. [5] Page 78.

[6] Trade in furs was the chief occupation of the Dutch of New Netherland at this time. They became expert trappers, and were seen as far east as Nantucket, and even Cape Cod. The trade soon became profitable to the Company. The first year's remittance of furs to Amsterdam was valued at $11,000. This trade greatly increased; and before the troubles with the Indians in 1640, the value of furs sent to Holland, annually, was more than $60,000. [7] Page 72.

[8] The land was to be fairly purchased of the Indians, and then the title was to be confirmed by the Dutch government. The privileges granted to the purchasers made them, in a degree, feudal lords [note 15, page 62], yet they were exempted from paying tribute to supreme authority.

[9] Killian Van Rensselaer, who purchased a tract at Fort Orange (Albany); Samuel Godyn and Samuel Bloemart, who selected lands in West Jersey, on the Delaware; and Michael Pauw, whose domain included Jersey City and vicinity. See page 94.

[10] Van Rensselaer. Immense tracts of land in Albany and Rensselaer counties, portions of the first Patroon's estates, are yet [1856] in possession of the family. Since 1840, many scenes of violence and bloodshed have been witnesssd on those lands, growing out of disputes with tenants, when they have been called upon to pay even the almost nominal rent which is demanded. Social and political questions have arisen, and produced two strong parties. The defense of the tenantry is termed *Anti-Rentism.* Conciliatory measures have been proposed by a purchaser of a large portion of the ancient manor, in Albany county, by which the tenants are allowed to buy the land, and obtain a title in fee simple. In time, the whole estate will thus pass into the hands of numerous new owners, and these angry disputes will become items of past history.

necticut River.[1] He was more distinguished for his marriage connection with Van Rensselaer, one of the *Patroons*, than for any administrative qualities. Yet circumstances favored the advancement of the colony, and he ruled quite satisfactorily, especially to the company, whose interests he faithfully served. He was succeeded in office, in May, 1638, by Sir William Keift, at the moment when the Swedish colony[2] were seating themselves upon the banks of the Delaware. Keift was a bold, rapacious, and unscrupulous man, and soon brought serious trouble upon the people. He began a tyrannous rule by concentrating executive power in his own hands; and his administration was a stormy and unfortunate one. The sum of its record is a tale of continual strife with the Swedes on the Delaware,[3] the English on the Connecticut,[4] the Indians all around him, and the colonists at his door. His difficulties with the Indians proved the most disastrous of all, and finally wrought his own downfall. Previous to his arrival, the intercourse of the Dutch with the natives had been quite friendly.[5] The fur trade was extending, and trappers and traders were all abroad among the native tribes. These carried a demon of discord with them. They furnished the Indians with *rum*, and quarrels and murders ensued. The avaricious Keift also demanded tribute of wampum[6] and beaver-skins from the River tribes; and in a short time their friendship for the Dutch became weakened.

A crisis came. Some Raritan[7] Indians in New Jersey were accused of robbery. Keift sent an armed force to punish them [July, 1640], and blood flowed. Several Indians were killed, and their crops were destroyed. Savage vengeance did not slumber long. The Raritans murdered four planters on Staten Island [June, 1641], and destroyed considerable property.[8] An expedition sent to punish the offenders was unsuccessful. Soon afterward, a young Westchester Indian, whose uncle had been murdered by a Hollander, near where the Halls of Justice now stand,[9] revenged the murder, according to the customs of his people,[10] by killing an inoffensive Dutchman living at Turtle Bay.[11] His tribe refused to surrender him on the demand of Keift, and the governor determined to make war upon all the offending savages.

The people of New Netherland had already begun to murmur at Keift's course, and they charged the troubles with the Indians directly upon him. Unwilling to assume the entire responsibility of a war, himself, the governor called a meeting [Aug. 23, 1641] of the heads of families in New Amsterdam for consultation. They promptly chose "twelve select men" [August 29], with De

---

[1] Page 85. [2] Page 93. [3] Page 93. [4] Page 85.

[5] The Dutch had made a settlement, and built a fort at Albany [page 72], and made a treaty of friendship with the Mohawks [page 23]. This the River Indians, in the vicinity of New Amsterdam, did not like, for the Mohawks were their oppressors.

[6] Note 2, page 13.

[7] A tribe of the Lenni-Lenapes. Page 16.

[8] This plantation belonged to De Vries [note 2, page 92], who was a friend of the Indians.

[9] On Center street, New York city. There was once a fresh-water pond there, surrounded by the forest.

[10] The Indians had a custom concerning an *avenger of blood*, similar to that of the Jews. It was the duty and the privilege for the next of kin to the murdered man, to avenge his blood by killing the murderer. The Indians took the life of any of the tribe of the offender.

[11] At the foot of Forty-fifth street, on the East River.

Vries[1] at their head, to act for them; and this was the first representative assembly ever formed among Europeans on Manhattan Island. They did not agree with the governor's hostile views; and Keift finding them not only opposed to his war designs, but that they were also taking cognizance of alleged grievances of the people, dissolved them, in February, 1642. Finally, the commission of other murders by Indians, and the presence of a body of Mohawks, who had come down to exact tribute from the River tribes, concurred with the changed opinions of some leading citizens of New Amsterdam, to make Keift resolve to embrace this opportunity to chastise the savages. A large number of them had fled before the Mohawks, and sought shelter with the Hackensacks, near Hoboken, and there craved the protection of the Dutch. Now was offered an opportunity for a wise and humane governor to make a covenant of peace and friendship; but Keift could not be satisfied without a flow of blood. At midnight, in February, 1643, a body of Hollanders and Mohawks crossed the Hudson, fell upon the unsuspecting fugitives, and before the dawn, they massacred almost a hundred men, women, and children. Many were driven from the cliffs at Hoboken into the freezing flood; and at sunrise the bloody marauders returned to New Amsterdam with thirty prisoners, and the heads of several Indians.

The fiery hatred and vengeance of all the surrounding tribes were aroused by this massacre, and a fierce war was soon kindled. Villages and farms were desolated, and white people were butchered wherever they were found by the incensed Indians.[2] The Long Island tribes,[3] hitherto friendly, joined their kindred, and the very existence of the Dutch colony was menaced. Fortunately for the settlers, that eminent peace-maker, Roger Williams,[4] arrived [1643], to embark for England,[5] and he pacified the savages, and secured a brief repose for the colony. But the war was soon renewed, and for two years the colony suffered dreadfully. Having no competent leader, they employed Captain John Underhill,[6] who successfully beat back and defeated the Indians, and hostilities ceased. The Mohawks came and claimed sovereignty over the River Indians, made a treaty of peace with the Dutch, and the hatchet was buried.

The conduct of Governor Keift was so offensive to the colonists and the Company, that he was recalled, and he sailed for Europe in 1647, in a richly laden-vessel. It was wrecked on the coast of Wales, and there he perished. He had already been succeeded in office [May, 27, 1647], by Peter Stuyvesant, lately governor of Curaçoa, a soldier of eminence, and possessed of every requisite for an efficient administration of government. His treatment of the Indians was very kind and just, and they soon exhibited such friendship for the Dutch, that Stuyvesant was falsely charged with a design to employ them in murdering the English in New England.[7] Long accustomed, as a military leader, to

---

[1] Note 2, page 92.

[2] It was during this frenzy of revenge that Mrs. Hutchinson, who had been banished from Massachusetts, and had taken up her residence near the present New Rochelle, Westchester County, New York, was murdered, with all her family. The stream upon which she lived is yet known as Hutchinson's River. [3] Page 21. [4] Page 87. [5] Page 91. [6] Page 87.

[7] See page 121. This idea prevailed, because during almost the entire winter of 1652–3, *Ninigret*

arbitrary rule, he was stern and inflexible, but he had the reputation of an honest man. He immediately commenced much needed reforms; and during his whole administration, which was ended by the subjugation of the Dutch by the English,[1] in 1664, he was the faithful and energetic defender of the integ-

rity of the province against its foes. By prudent management he avoided collisions with the English, and peaceably ended boundary disputes[2] with them in the autumn of 1650. This cause for irritation on his eastern frontier being removed, Stuyvesant turned his attention to the growing power of the Swedes, on the Delaware.

Governor Stuyvesant built Fort Casimir, on the site of the present New

---

and two other Narragansett sachems had been in New Amsterdam, and on very friendly terms with Stuyvesant. These sachems, who were true friends of the English, positively disclaimed all bad intentions on the part of Stuyvesant, and yet historians of the present day repeat the slander.

[1] Page 144.

[2] See page 85. He went to Hartford, and there made a treaty which fixed the eastern boundary of New Netherland nearly on the line of the present division between New York and Connecticut, and across Long Island, at Oyster Bay, thirty miles eastward of New York. The Dutch claims to lands on the Connecticut River were extinguished by this treaty. From the beginning of difficulties, the Dutch were clearly in the right. This was acknowledged by impartial and just New Englanders. In a manuscript letter before me, from Edward Winslow to Governor Winthrop, dated at "Marshfield, 2d of 6th month, 1644," in which he replies to a charge of being favorable to the Dutch, in some respects, he says that he had asserted in substance, that he "would not defend the Hartford men's cause, for they had hitherto (or thus long) wronged the Dutch."

Castle, in Delaware, in 1651. This was soon seized by the Swedes, and the garrison made prisoners. The States-General[1] resolved to prevent further trouble with these enterprising neighbors of the Dutch, and for this purpose, gave Stuyvesant full liberty to subjugate the Swedes. At the head of six hundred men, he sailed for the Delaware, in August, 1655, and by the middle of October, he had captured all the Swedish fortresses, and sent the governor (Risingh) and several other influential men, to Europe. Some of the settlers withdrew to Maryland and Virginia, but the great body of them quietly submitted, took an oath of allegiance to the States-General of Holland, and continued in peaceable possession of their property. Thus, after an existence of about seventeen years [1638—1655], NEW SWEDEN[2] disappeared by absorption into NEW NETHERLAND.

New trouble now appeared, but it was soon removed. While Stuyvesant and his soldiery were absent on the Delaware, some Indians, who were not yet reconciled to the Dutch, menaced New Amsterdam.[3] The return of the governor produced quiet, for they feared and respected him, and, for eight years, the colony was very little disturbed by external causes. Then the Esopus Indians suddenly fell upon the Dutch settlements [June, 1663] at Wiltwyck (now Kingston, in Ulster County),[4] and killed and captured sixty-five of the inhabitants. Stuyvesant promptly sent a sufficient force to chastise them; and so thoroughly was the errand performed, that the Indians sued for peace in May, 1664, and made a treaty of friendship.

External difficulties gave Stuyvesant little more trouble than a spirit opposed to his aristocratic views, which he saw manifested daily around him. While he had been judiciously removing all cause for ill-feeling with his neighbors, there was a power at work within his own domain which gave him great uneasiness. The democratic seed planted by the Twelve, in Keift's time,[5] had begun to grow vigorously under the fostering care of a few enlightened Hollanders, and some Puritans who had settled in New Netherland. The latter, by their applause of English institutions, had diffused a desire among the people to partake of the blessings of English liberty, as they understood it, and as it appeared in New England. Stuyvesant was an aristocrat by birth, education, and pursuit, and vehemently opposed every semblance of democracy. At the beginning he found himself at variance with the people. At length an assembly of two deputies from each village in New Netherland, chosen by the inhabitants, convened at New Amsterdam [December, 1653], without the approbation of the governor. It was a spontaneous, and, in the eyes of the governor, a revolutionary movement. Their proceedings displeased him; and finding argument of no avail, he exercised his official prerogative, and commanded obedience to his will. The people grew bolder at every rebuff, and finally they not only resisted taxation, but openly expressed a willingness to bear English rule for the sake of enjoying English liberty.

The opportunity for a change of rulers was not long delayed. A crisis in

---

[1] Note 7, page 59. [2] Page 93. [3] Page 139. [4] Page 283. [5] Page 140.

the affairs of New Netherland now approached. Charles the Second, of England, without any fair pretense to title, gave the whole territory of New Netherland [March 22, 1664] to his brother James, Duke of York.[1] The duke sent an English squadron, under the command of Colonel Richard Nicolls,[2] to secure the gift; and on the 3d of September, 1664, the red cross of St. George[3] floated in triumph over the fort, and the name of New Amsterdam was changed to New York.[4] It was an easy conquest, for, while the fortifications and other means of defense were very weak, the people were not unwilling to try English rule. Stuyvesant began to make concessions to the people, when it was too late, and when his real strength, the popular will, had departed from him. He hesitated long before he would sign the articles of capitulation; and thus, until the end, he was faithful to his employers, the *Dutch West India Company*.[5] With the capital, the remainder of the province passed into the hands of the English; and early in October, 1664, New Netherland was acknowledged a part of the British realm, and Nicolls, the conqueror became governor.[6] Let us now consider

NEW YORK UNDER THE ENGLISH.

CITY OF NEW YORK IN 1664.

Very soon after the conquest the people of New York[7] perceived that a change of masters did not enhance their prosperity and happiness. They were disappointed in their hopes of a representative government; and their taxes, to support a government in which they had no voice, were increased. Lovelace, the vile successor of Nicolls, in 1667, increased their burdens; and when they sent a respectful protest to him, he ordered the paper to be burned by the common hangman. He was a petty tyrant, and declared that the people should have "liberty for no thought but how to pay their taxes." But the people *did* think of something else, and were on the eve of open rebellion when

---

1 Page 94. 2 Note 6, page 123.

3 The royal standard of England is sometimes so named because it bears a red cross, which is called the "cross of St. George," the patron saint of Great Britain. After the union with Scotland [note 1, page 63], the cross of St. Andrew (in the form of an X), was added, and is now seen on the British flag. In the centre are the royal arms. This *Union*, as the figure is called, was borne upon the American flags, sometimes, until after the Declaration of Independence, in 1776. It was upon the flag of thirteen stripes, alternate red and white, which Washington caused to be unfurled at Cambridge, on the first day of that year. See page 245.

4 The name of Fort Orange settlement [note 9, page 139], was changed to Albany, one of the duke's titles. 5 Page 72.

6 We have elsewhere noticed the fact, that before Nicolls was dispatched, the duke, being certain of victory, sold that part of New Netherland now included in New Jersey, to other parties. [See page 94.] Long Island, which had been previously granted to the Earl of Stirling, was purchased by the Dutch, in total disregard of the claims of Connecticut. The colonies on the Delaware remained under the jurisdiction of New York, and were governed by deputies.

7 The above picture is a correct view of the city of New York two hundred years ago It is now [1856] the largest city on the American continent. On the left of the picture is seen Fort Amsterdam, with the church and governor's house within it, and a windmill. The point of Manhattan Island, from the present Battery Place to the foot of Wall-street, is here seen.

STUYVESANT SURRENDERING THE FORT TO THE ENGLISH.

the clouds of national war overshadowed local difficulties. War again commenced between England and Holland in 1672, and in July the following year, a Dutch squadron sailed up the Bay of New York, and, in the absence of the governor, took possession of the fort and town [August 9th, 1673] without giving a shot. The easy conquest was the work of treason; yet, as the royal libertine (Charles the Second) on the throne of England doubtless shared in the bribe, the traitor went unpunished.[1] New Jersey and the Territories of Delaware[2] yielded, and for sixteen months [from July, 1673, to November, 1674] New York was again New Netherlands. When the two nations made a treaty of peace, the province was restored to the English, and remained in their possession until our Independence was declared in 1776.[3] These changes raised some doubts concerning the validity of the duke's title, and the king gave him another grant in July, 1674. Sir Edmond Andros[4] was appointed governor under the new charter, and continued arbitrary rule with increased rigor.[5]

At the close of 1683, Governor Andros returned to England, when the duke (who was a Roman Catholic) appointed Thomas Dongan, of the same faith, to succeed him. In the mean while, the duke had listened to the judicious advice of William Penn, and instructed Dongan to call an assembly of representatives. They met [October 17, 1683], and with the hearty concurrence of the governor, a CHARTER OF LIBERTIES was established,[6] and the permanent foundation of a representative government was laid. The people rejoiced in the change, and were heartily engaged in the efforts to perfect a wise and liberal government, when the duke was elevated to the throne, as James the Second, on the death of Charles, in February, 1685. As king, he refused to confirm the privileges which, as duke, he had granted; and having determined to introduce the Roman Catholic religion into the province as the established church, he commenced by efforts to enslave the people. A direct tax was ordered; the printing press—the right arm of knowledge and freedom—was forbidden a place in the colony; and the provincial offices were filled by Roman Catholics. These proceedings gave pain to the liberal-minded Dongan; and when the king, in his religious zeal, instructed the governor to introduce French priests among the FIVE NATIONS,[7] he resisted the measure as highly inexpedient.[8] His firm-

---

[1] The traitor was Captain John Manning, the commandant of the fort. He was, doubtless, bribed by the Dutch commander; and the fact that the king screened him from punishment, gave the color of truth to the charge that the monarch shared in the bribe. [2] Page 96.

[3] Page 251. [4] Page 129.

[5] The duke claimed the country from the Connecticut River to Cape Henlopen. Andros attempted to exercise authority eastward of the line agreed upon by the Dutch and the Connecticut people [note 2, page 142], and went to Saybrook in the summer of 1676, with an armed party, to enforce the claim. He met with such resistance, that he was compelled to return to New York without accomplishing his design. See page 116.

[6] The Assembly consisted of the governor and ten councillors, and seventeen deputies elected by the freeholders. They adopted a *Declaration of Rights*, and asserted the principle, so nobly fought for a hundred years later, that *taxation* and *representation* are inseparable; in other words—that taxes can not be levied without the consent of the people, expressed by their representatives. At this time the colony was divided into twelve counties. [7] Page 23.

[8] This measure would have given the French, in Canada, an influence over the Indians that might have proved fatal to English power on the Continent. The FIVE NATIONS remained the fast friends of the English, and stood as a powerful barrier against the French, when the latter twice invaded the Iroquois territory, in endeavors to reach the English, at Albany.

ness gave the people confidence, and they were again on the eve of open rebellion, when the intelligence of the flight of James, and the accession of William and Mary[1] reached them. They immediately appointed a committee of safety, and with almost unanimous voice, sanctioned the conduct of Jacob Leisler (an influential merchant and commander of the militia), who had taken possession of the fort in the name of the new sovereigns, and by order of the inhabitants. Afraid of the people, Nicholson, the successor of Dongan, fled on board a vessel and departed, and the people consented to Leisler's assuming the functions of governor until a new one should be appointed. The aristocracy and the magistrates were offended, and denouncing Leisler as a usurper, they accused him of treason, when Governor Sloughter arrived, in 1691.

Leisler, in the mean while, conducted affairs with prudence and energy. Having the sanction of the people, he needed no further authority; and when a letter from the British ministers arrived [December, 1689], directed to Governor Nicholson, "or, in his absence, to such as, for the time being," conducted affairs, he considered it as fairly addressed to himself. Milborne, his son-in-law, acted as his deputy, and was included in the accusations of the magistrates, who had now retired to Albany. They held Fort Orange[2] until the invasion of the French, in February, 1690,[3] when they felt the necessity of claiming the protection of the government at New York. They then yielded, and remained comparatively quiet until the arrival of Richard Ingoldsby, Sloughter's lieutenant, early in 1691. That officer announced the appointment of Henry Sloughter as governor; and without producing any credentials of authority, he haughtily demanded of Leisler [February 9, 1691] the surrender of the fort. Of course Leisler refused compliance; but as soon as Sloughter arrived [March 29], he sent a messenger to announce his desire to surrender all authority into his hands. Leisler's enemies had resolved on his destruction; and when he came forward to deliver the fort, in person, he and his son-in-law were seized and cast into prison. They were tried on a charge of treason, found guilty, and condemned to suffer death. Sloughter withheld his signature to their death warrant; but, when made drunk at a dinner party prepared for the purpose, he put his name to the fatal instrument. Before he became sober, Leisler and Milborne were suspended upon a gallows on the verge of Beekman's swamp [May 26, 1691], where Tammany Hall—fronting on the City Hall Park, New York—now stands. These were the proto-martyrs of popular liberty in America.[4]

Henry Sloughter was a weak and dissolute man, yet he came with an earnest desire to promote the welfare of the colonists. He convened a popular assembly, and formed a constitution, which provided for trial by jury, and an exemption from taxes, except by the consent of the representatives of the people. Light was thus dawning hopefully upon the province, when *delirium*

---

[1] Note 7, page 113. [2] Note 9, page 139.

[3] At this time, Schenectada was desolated. See page 131.

[4] Their estates were confiscated; but after a lapse of several years, and when the violence of party spirit had subsided, the property was restored to their families.

tremens, at the close of a drunken revel, ended the administration and the life of the governor [August 2, 1691], in less than three months after the murder of Leisler and Milborne. He was succeeded by Benjamin Fletcher, a man of violent passions, and quite as weak and dissolute, who became the tool of the aristocracy, and was hated by the people. Party spirit, engendered by the death of Leisler, burned intensely during the whole administration of Fletcher; and at the same time the French and Indians, under the guidance of Frontenac, the able Governor of Canada,[1] were traversing the northern frontiers of the province. Fletcher prudently listened to the advice of Major Schuyler,[2] of Albany, respecting the Indians; and under his leadership, the English, and their unwavering allies, the FIVE NATIONS, successfully beat back the foe to the St. Lawrence, and so desolated the French settlements in 1692, in the vicinity of Lake Champlain,[3] that Frontenac was glad to remain quiet at Montreal.

A better ruler for New York now appeared. The Earl of Bellomont, an honest and energetic Irish peer, succeeded Fletcher in 1698; and the following year, New Hampshire[4] and Massachusetts[5] were placed under his jurisdiction. He commenced reform with great earnestness, and made vigorous efforts to suppress piracy,[6] which had become a fearful scourge to the infant commerce of the colonists. With Robert Livingston[7] and others, he fitted out an expedition under the famous Captain Kidd, to destroy the buccaneers. Kidd, himself, was afterward hung for piracy [1701], and the governor and his sons were charged with a participation in his guilt. At any rate, there can be little doubt that wealthy men in the colony expected a share in the plunder, and that Kidd, as a scape-goat for the sins of the others, was the victim of a political conspiracy.[8]

Unfortunately for the colony, death removed Bellomont, on the 16th of March, 1701, when his liberal policy was about to bear fruit. He was succeeded by Edward Hyde (afterward Lord Cornbury),[9] a libertine and a knave, who cursed the province with misrule for seven years. He was a bigot, too, and persecuted all denominations of Christians, except those of the Church of England. He embezzled the public moneys, involved himself in heavy debts, and on all occasions was the practical enemy of popular freedom. The people

---

[1] From 1678 to 1682, and again from 1689 to 1698, when he died, at the age of 77.

[2] Peter Schuyler. He was mayor of Albany, and acquired unbounded influence over the FIVE NATIONS of Indians. See page 23.

[3] Schuyler's force was about three hundred Mohawks, and as many English. They slew about three hundred of the French and Indians, at the north end of the lake. [4] Page 79. [5] Page 117.

[6] Because Spain claimed the exclusive right to the West India seas, her commerce in that region was regarded as fair plunder. Privateer commissions were readily granted by the English, French, and Dutch governments; and daring spirits from all countries were found under their flags. The buccaneers, as they were called, became very numerous and powerful, and at length depredated upon English commerce as well as Spanish. *Privateers*, or those legally authorized to seize the property of an enemy, became *pirates*, or sea robbers. Privateering is only legalized piracy.

[7] An immigrant from Scotland, and ancestor of the Livingston family in this country. He was connected, by marriage, with the Van Rensselaer and Schuyler families; and in 1685, he received from governor Dongan a grant of a feudal principality (see *patroon*, page 139) on the Hudson, yet known as Livingston's Manor.

[8] King William himself was a shareholder in the enterprise for which Kidd was fitted out. Kidd appeared publicly in Boston, where he was arrested, then sent to England, tried, and executed.

[9] Page 161.

finally demanded and obtained his recall, and the moment his official career ceased, in 1708, his creditors cast him into prison, where he remained until his accession to the peerage, on the death of his father.[1] From this period until the arrival of William Cosby, as governor [1732], the royal representatives,[2] unable to resist the will of the people, as expressed by the Assembly, allowed democratic principles to grow and bear fruit.[3]

The popular will and voice now began to be potential in the administration of public affairs. Rip Van Dam, "a man of the people," was acting governor when Cosby came. They soon quarreled, and two violent parties arose—the democratic, which sided with Van Dam, and the aristocratic, which supported the governor. Each party had the control of a newspaper,[4] and the war of words raged violently for a long time. The governor, unable to compete with his opponent, finally ordered the arrest of Zenger [November, 1734], the publisher of the democratic paper, on a charge of libel. After an imprisonment of thirty-five weeks, Zenger was tried by a jury, and acquitted, in July, 1735. He was defended by Andrew Hamilton, of Philadelphia, who was presented by the magistrates of the city of New York with a gold box, as a token of their esteem for his noble advocacy of popular rights. Then was distinctly drawn the line of demarcation between republicans and royalists (Whigs and Tories),[5] which continued prominent until the war of the revolution was ended in 1783.

From the arrival of Cosby until the commencement of the French and Indian war,[6] the history of New York is composed chiefly of the records of party strife, and presents very little matter of interest to the general reader. Only one episode demands special attention, namely, the excitement and results incident to a supposed conspiracy of the negroes, in 1741, to burn and plunder the city, murder the inhabitants, and set up a government under a man of their own color. Several incendiary fires had occurred in rapid succession, and a house had been robbed by some slaves. The idea of a regular and horrid conspiracy at once prevailed, and, as in the case of the Salem Witchcraft,[7] an intense panic pervaded all classes, and many innocent persons suffered.[8] This is known in history as *The Negro Plot.*

---

[1] According to an unjust law of England, a peer of the realm (who is consequently a member of the House of Lords [note 2, page 218]) can not be arrested for debt. This law, enacted in the reign of Henry the Eighth, still prevails.

[2] Lord Lovelace, Ingoldsby, Hunter, Schuyler, Burnet, and Montgomerie.

[3] We have already noticed (page 135) the breaking out of *Queen Anne's War*, in 1702, and the successful expeditions fitted out and sent in the direction of Montreal in 1709 and 1711. The debt which these expeditions laid upon New York, was felt for many years.

[4] *The New York Weekly Journal* (democratic), by John Peter Zenger; *The New York Gazette* (aristocratic), by William Bradford. The latter owned the first press ever set up in the province. He commenced printing in New York in 1696. See note 3, page 179.

[5] Note 4, page 226. [6] Page 179. [7] Page 132.

[8] Before the panic was allayed, four white people were hanged, and eleven negroes were burned, eighteen were hanged, and fifty were sent to the West Indies and sold.

CHAPTER IV.

MARYLAND. [1639.]

WHEN the first popular assembly convened at St. Mary, for legislative purposes, on the 8th of March, 1635,[1] Maryland had then its colonial birth. Its sturdy growth began when, in 1639, the more convenient form of representative government was established. It was crude, but it possessed the elements of republicanism. The freemen chose as many representatives as they pleased, and others were appointed by the proprietor. These, with the governor and secretary, composed the legislature. At this first session a Declaration of Rights was adopted, the powers of the governor were defined, and all the privileges enjoyed by English subjects were guarantied to the colonists.[2]

Very soon the Indians in the vicinity, becoming jealous of the increasing strength of the white people, began to evince hostility. Frequent collisions occurred; and in 1642, a general Indian war commenced in the region between the Potomac and the Chesapeake. It was terminated in 1645, but the quiet of the province was soon disturbed again. Clayborne had returned from England[3] [1645], and speedily fanned the embers of discontent into a flame of open rebellion. He became too powerful for the local authorities, and Governor Calvert[4] was obliged to flee to Virginia. During a year and a half, the insurgents held the reins of government, and the horrors of civil war brooded over the colony. The rebellion was suppressed in the summer of 1646, and in August, Calvert resumed his office.

In the year 1649, a very important law, known as The Toleration Act, was passed by the Assembly. Religious freedom was guarantied by the charter,[5] yet, as much animosity existed between the Protestants[6] and Roman Catholics, the Assembly[7] thought proper to give the principle the solemn sanction of law. By that act every professed believer in Jesus Christ and the Trinity, was allowed free exercise of his religious opinions, and no man was permitted to reproach another on account of his peculiar doctrines, except under the penalty of a fine, to be paid to the person so insulted. Thither persecuted Churchmen of New England, and oppressed Puritans of Virginia, fled and found an asylum. This act, short of full toleration as it was (for it placed Unitarians beyond the pale of its defense), is the pride and glory of the early legislature of Maryland; yet it was not the first instance in America, as is often alleged, when religious toleration received the sanction of law.[8] Rhode Island has that honor.

---

[1] Page 82. [2] Page 82. [3] Note 1, page 82.
[4] Page 81. [5] Page 81. [6] Note 14, page 62.

[7] Bozman, in his *History of Maryland* (II. 350—356), maintains that the majority of the members of the Assembly of 1649, were Protestants.

[8] In May, 1647, the General Assembly of Rhode Island, convened at Portsmouth, adopted a code of laws which closed with the declaration that "all men might walk as their consciences persuaded them, without molestation—every one in the name of his God." This was broader toleration than the Maryland act contemplated, for it did not restrict men to a belief in Jesus Christ.

Being favored by events in the mother country, republicanism grew steadily in the new State. Royalty was abolished in England [1649], and for more than ten years the democratic idea was prevalent throughout the realm. Lord Baltimore, the proprietor of Maryland, professed republicanism on the death of the king, but he had been too recently a royalist to secure the confidence of Parliament. Stone, his lieutenant, was removed from office [April 16, 1651] by commissioners (of whom Clayborne was one), who were sent to administer the government of the colony. He was soon afterward [July 8] restored. On the dissolution of the Long Parliament [1653][1] Cromwell restored full power to the proprietor, but the commissioners, who withdrew to Virginia, returned soon afterward, and compelled Stone to surrender the government into their hands.

The colonial government had been re-organized in the mean while. The legislative body was divided into an Upper and Lower House in 1650; the former consisting of the governor and his council, appointed by the proprietor, and the latter of representatives chosen by the people. At the same session a law was passed prohibiting all taxes, unless levied with the consent of the freemen. Political questions were freely discussed by the people; and soon the two chief religious sects were marshaled in opposition, as prime elements of political parties. So great had been the influx of Protestants, that they now [1654] outnumbered the Roman Catholics as voters and in the Assembly. They acknowledged the authority of Cromwell, and boldly questioned the rights and privileges of an hereditary proprietor.[2] The Roman Catholics adhered to Lord Baltimore, and bitter religious hatred was fostered. The Protestants finally disfranchised their opponents, excluded them from the Assembly, and in November, 1654, passed an act declaring Roman Catholics not entitled to the protection of the laws of Maryland.

This unchristian and unwise act of the Protestant party, was a great wrong as well as a great mistake. Civil war ensued. Stone returned to St. Mary,[3] organized an armed force composed chiefly of Roman Catholics, seized the colonial records, and assumed the office of governor. Skirmishes followed, and finally a severe battle was fought [April 4, 1655] not far from the site of Annapolis, in which Stone's party was defeated, with a loss of about fifty men, killed and wounded. Stone was made prisoner, but his life was spared. Four other leading supporters of the proprietor were tried for treason and executed. Anarchy prevailed in the province for many months, when the discordant elements were brought into comparative order by the appointment of Josiah Fendall [July 20, 1656] as governor. He was suspected of favoring the Roman Catholics, and was soon arrested by order of the Protestant Assembly. For two years bitter strife continued between the people and the agents of the

---

[1] When Charles the First was beheaded [note 3, page 108], the Parliament assumed supreme authority, and remained in permanent session. Cromwell, with an army at his back, entered that assembly in the autumn of 1653, ordered them to disperse, and assumed supreme power himself, under the title of Lord Protector. That British legislature is known in history as the Long Parliament.

[2] According to the original charter, the heirs and successors of Lord Baltimore were to be proprietors forever.

[3] Page 82.

proprietor, when, after concessions by the latter, Fendall was acknowledged governor, on the 3d of April, 1658. His prudence secured the confidence of the people, but the death of Cromwell, in September, 1658, presaging a change in the English government, gave them uneasiness. After long deliberation, the Assembly determined to avoid all further trouble with the proprietor, by asserting the supreme authority of the people. They accordingly dissolved the Upper House [March 24, 1660],[1] and assumed the whole legislative power of the State. They then gave Fendall a commission as governor for the people.

The restoration of monarchy in England took place in June, 1660,[2] and the original order of things was re-established in Maryland. Lord Baltimore, having assured the new king that his republican professions[3] were only temporary expedients, was restored to all his proprietary rights, by Charles. Fendall was tried, and found guilty of treason, because he accepted a commission from the rebellious Assembly. Baltimore, however, wisely proclaimed a general pardon for all political offenders in Maryland; and for almost thirty years afterward, the province enjoyed repose. A law, which established absolute political equality among professed Christians, was enacted; and after the death of the second Lord Baltimore [Dec. 10, 1675], his son and successor confirmed it. Under that new proprietor, Charles Calvert, Maryland was governed mildly and prudently, and the people were prospering in their political quietude, when the Revolution in England[4] shook the colonies. The deputy governor of Maryland hesitated to proclaim William and Mary,[5] and this was made a pretense, by a restless spirit, named Coode,[6] for exciting the people. He gave currency to the absurd report that the local magistrates and the Roman Catholics had leagued with the Indians[7] for the destruction of all the Protestants in the colony. A similar actual coalition of Jesuits[8] and savages on the New England frontiers[9] gave a coloring of truth to the story, and the old religious feud instantly burned again intensely. The Protestants formed an armed association [Sept., 1689], and led on by Coode, they took forcible possession of St. Mary, and by capitulation, received the provincial records and assumed the government. They called a Convention, and invested it with legislative powers. Its first acts were to depose the third Lord Baltimore, and to re-assert the sovereign majesty of the people.

Public affairs were managed by the Convention until 1691, when the king unjustly deprived Baltimore of all his political privileges as proprietor [June 11], and made Maryland a royal province.[10] Lionel Copley was appointed the first royal governor, in 1692. New laws were instituted—religious toleration,

---

[1] Page 152. [2] Note 2, page 109. [3] Page 152. [4] Note 7, page 113. [5] Page 113.

[6] Coode had been a confederate in a former insurrection, but escaped conviction.

[7] A treaty with the Indians had just been renewed, and the customary presents distributed among them. These things Coode falsely adduced as evidences of a coalition with the savages.

[8] Note 5, page 130. [9] Page 130.

[10] King William had an exalted idea of royal prerogatives, and was as much disposed as the Stuarts (the kings of England from James the First to James the Second) to suppress democracy in the colonies. He repeatedly vetoed (refused his assent) to Bills of Rights enacted by the colonial Assemblies; refused his assent to local laws of the deepest interest to the colonists; and instructed his governors to prohibit printing in the colonies. Note 7, page 112.

was abolished—the Church of England was made the established religion, to be supported by a tax on the people; and in the State founded by Roman Catholics, the members of that denomination were cruelly disfranchised, with the consent of their sovereign. A few years later [1716], the proprietary rights of Lord Baltimore (now deceased) were restored to his infant heir, and the original form of government was re-established. Such continued to be the political complexion of the colony, until the storm of the Revolution in 1776, swept away every remnant of royalty and feudalism, and the State of Maryland was established.

CHAPTER V.

CONNECTICUT. [1639.]

THE CONNECTICUT COLONY[1] formed a political Constitution on the 24th of January, 1639, and in June following, the NEW HAVEN COLONY performed the same important act.[2] The religious element was supreme in the new organization; and, in imitation of the Constitution of the Plymouth settlers, none but church members were allowed the privileges of freemen[3] at New Haven. They first appointed a committee of twelve men, who selected seven of their members to be "pillars" in the new State. These had power to admit as many others, as confederate legislators, as they pleased. Theophilus Eaton was chosen governor,[4] and the Bible was made the grand statute-book of the colony. Many of the New Haven settlers being merchants, they sought to found a commercial colony, but heavy losses by the wreck of vessels[5] discouraged them, and they turned their special attention to agriculture. Prudence marked the course of the magistrates of the several colonies in the Connecticut valley,[6] and they were blessed with prosperity. But difficulties with the Dutch respecting territorial boundaries,[7] and menaces of the neighboring Indians, gave them uneasiness, and made them readily join the New England confederation in 1643.[8] The following year the little independent colony at Saybrook[9] purchased the land of one of the proprietors of Connecticut,[10] and became permanently annexed to that at Hartford.[11]

The future appeared serene and promising. The treaty made with Governor Stuyvesant, at Hartford, in 1650,[12] gave token of future tranquillity. But the repose was soon broken by international war. England and Holland drew the sword against each other in 1652; and because it was reported that Ninigret, the wily sachem of the Narragansetts,[13] had spent several weeks at New

---

[1] Page 89. [2] Page 89. The people assembled in a barn to form a new Constitution.
[3] Note 5, page 118.
[4] He was annually chosen to fill the office, until his death, which occurred in 1657.
[5] In 1647, a new ship belonging to the colony foundered at sea. It was laden with a valuable cargo, and the passengers belonged to some of the leading families in the colony.
[6] Page 86. [7] Page 85, and note 2, page 142. [8] Page 121. [9] Page 86.
[10] Page 85. [11] Page 88. [12] Note 2, page 142. [13] Note 7, page 141.

Amsterdam in the winter of 1652–3[1] the belief prevailed in New England, as we have already observed, that Stuyvesant was leaguing with the Indians for the destruction of the English.[2] Great excitement ensued, and a majority of the commissioners decided,[3] in 1653, upon war with the Dutch. Immediate hostilities were prevented by the refusal of Massachusetts to furnish its quota of supplies. The Connecticut colonies (who were more exposed to blows from the Dutch than any other) applied to Cromwell for aid, and he sent four ships of war for the purpose. Before their arrival,[4] a treaty of peace was concluded between the two nations, and blood and treasure were saved. The Assembly at Hartford took possession of all property then claimed by the Dutch; and after that the latter abandoned all claims to possessions in the Connecticut valley.

On the restoration of Charles the Second, in 1660, the *Connecticut colony* expressed its loyalty, and obtained a charter. At first, Charles was disposed to refuse the application of Winthrop,[5] the agent of the colony, for he had heard of the sturdy republicanism of the petitioners. But when Winthrop presented his majesty with a ring which Charles the First had given to his father, the heart of the king was touched, and he granted a charter [May 30, 1662] which not only confirmed the popular Constitution of the colony, but contained more liberal provisions than any yet issued from the royal hand.[6] It defined the eastern boundary of the province to be Narraganset Bay, and the western, the Pacific Ocean. It thus included a portion of Rhode Island, and the whole *New Haven Colony*.[7] The latter gave a reluctant consent to the union in 1665, but Rhode Island positively refused the alliance. A charter given to the latter the year after one was given to Connecticut [1663],[8] covered a portion of the Connecticut grant in Narraganset Bay. Concerning this boundary the two colonies disputed for more than sixty years.

The colony of Connecticut suffered but little during King Philip's War,[9] which broke out in 1675, with the exception of some settlements high up on the fresh water river.[10] Yet it furnished its full quota of men and supplies, and its soldiers bore a conspicuous part in giving the vigorous blows which broke the power of the New England Indians.[11] At the same time, the colonists were obliged to defend their liberties against the attempted usurpations of Edmund Andros, then governor of New York.[12] He claimed jurisdiction to the

---

[1] This report was set afloat by Uncas, the mischievous Mohegan sachem [page 87], who hated the Narragansetts. It had no foundation in truth. See, also, page 21.

[2] Page 141. [3] Page 121.

[4] Roger Williams, then in England, managed to delay the sailing of the fleet, and thus, again, that eminent peace-maker prevented bloodshed. Page 87.

[5] John Winthrop, son of Governor Winthrop, of Massachusetts. He was chosen governor of Connecticut in 1657, and held the office several years. Such was his station when he appeared in England to ask a charter of the king. Hopkins (who was one of the founders of the New Haven colony) was chosen the first governor of the Connecticut colony, and for several years he and Haynes were alternately chosen chief magistrates.

[6] This original charter is now [1856] in the office of the Secretary of the State of Connecticut. It contains a portrait of Charles the Second, handsomely drawn in India ink, and forming part of an initial letter. This was the instrument afterward hidden in the great oak mentioned on the next page.

[7] Page 88. Thus the several settlements were united under the general name of Connecticut.

[8] Page 156. [9] Page 124. [10] Page 85. [11] Page 22. [12] Page 147.

mouth of the Connecticut River, and in July, 1675, he proceeded to Saybrook with a small naval force, to assert his authority. He was permitted to land; but when he ordered the garrison in the fort to surrender, and began to read his commission to the people, Captain Bull, the commander, ordered him to be silent. Perceiving the strength and determination of his adversary, Andros wisely withdrew, and greatly irritated, returned to New York.

During the next dozen years, very little occurred to disturb the quiet and prosperity of Connecticut. Then a most exciting scene took place at Hartford, in which the liberties of the colony were periled. Edmund Andros again appeared as a usurper of authority. He had been appointed governor of New England in 1686,[1] and on his arrival he demanded a surrender of the charters of all the provinces. They all complied, except Connecticut. She steadily refused to give up the guaranty of her political rights; and finally Andros proceeded to Hartford with sixty armed men, to enforce obedience. The Assembly were in session when he arrived [Nov. 10, 1687], and received him courteously. He demanded the surrender of the charter, and declared the colonial government dissolved. Already a plan had been arranged for securing the safety of that precious instrument, and at the same time to preserve an appearance of loyalty. The debates were purposely protracted until the candles were lighted, at evening, when the charter was brought in and laid upon the table. Just as Andros stepped forward to take it, the candles were suddenly extinguished. The charter was seized by Captain Wadsworth, of the militia, and under cover of the night it was effectually concealed in the hollow trunk of a huge oak, standing not far from the Assembly chamber.[2] When the candles were relighted, the members were in perfect order, but the charter could not be found. Andros was highly incensed at being thus foiled, but he wisely restrained his passion, assumed the government, and with his own hand wrote the word FINIS after the last record of the Charter Assembly. The government was administered in his own name until he was driven from Boston in 1689,[3] when the charter was taken from the oak [May 19, 1689], a popular Assembly was convened, Robert Treat was chosen governor, and Connecticut again assumed her position as an independent colony.

THE CHARTER OAK.

Petty tyrants continued to molest. A little more than four years later, the Connecticut people were again compelled to assert their chartered liberties. Colonel Fletcher, then governor of New York,[4] held a commission which gave him command of the militia of Connecticut.[5] As that power was reserved to

[1] Page 129.

[2] That tree remained vigorous until ten minutes before one o'clock in the morning, August 21, 1856, when it was prostrated during a heavy storm, and nothing but a stump remains. It stood on the south side of Charter-street, a few rods from Main-street, in the city of Hartford. The cavity in which the charter was concealed, had become partially closed.

[3] Page 130.

[4] Page 147.

[5] The declared object of this commission was to enable Fletcher to call forth the Connecticut militia when proper, to repel an expected invasion of Northern New York, by the French and Indians.

the colony by the charter, the Legislature refused to acknowledge Fletcher's authority. In November, 1693, he repaired to Hartford, and, notwithstanding the Legislature was in session, and again promptly denied his jurisdiction, he ordered the militia to assemble. The Hartford companies, under Captain Wadsworth,[1] were drawn up in line; but the moment Fletcher attempted to read his commission, the drums were beaten. His angry order of "Silence!" was obeyed for a moment; but when he repeated it, Wadsworth boldly stepped in front of him, and said, "Sir, if they are again interrupted, I'll make the sun shine through you in a moment." Fletcher perceived the futility of a parley, or further assumption of authority; and, pocketing his commission, he and his attendants returned to New York, greatly chagrined and irritated. The matter was compromised when referred to the king, who gave the governor of Connecticut militia jurisdiction in time of peace, but in the event of war, Colonel Fletcher should have the command of a certain portion of the troops of that colony.

And now, in the year 1700, Connecticut had a population of about thirty thousand, which rapidly increased during the remainder of her colonial career. During *Queen Anne's War*,[2] and the stirring events in America from that time until the commencement of the French and Indian War,[3] when her people numbered one hundred thousand, Connecticut went hand in hand with her sister colonies for mutual welfare; and her history is too closely interwoven with theirs to require further separate notice.

CHAPTER VI.

RHODE ISLAND. [1644.]

When the *Providence* and *Rhode Island* plantations were united under the same government in 1644, the colony of Rhode Island commenced its independent career.[4] That charter was confirmed by the Long Parliament[5] in October, 1652, and this put an end to the persevering efforts of Massachusetts to absorb "Williams's Narraganset Plantation." That colony had always coveted the beautiful Aquiday,[6] and feared the reaction of Williams's tolerant principles upon the people from whose bosom he had been cruelly expelled.[7] A dispute concerning the eastern boundary of Rhode Island was productive of much ill feeling during the progress of a century, when, in 1741, commissioners decided the present line to be the proper division, and wrangling ceased.

[1] Page 156. [2] Page 135. [3] Page 179.

[4] Page 91. A general assembly of deputies from the several towns, met at Portsmouth on the 29th of May, 1647, and organized the new government by the election of a president and other officers. At that time a code of laws was adopted, which declared the government to be a democracy, and that "all men might walk as their conscience persuaded them." Page 151.

[5] Note 1, page 150. [6] Note 5, page 91. [7] Page 91.

Nor was Rhode Island free from those internal commotions, growing out of religious disputes and personal ambition, which disturbed the repose of other colonies. These were quieted toward the close of 1653, when Roger Williams was chosen president. Cromwell confirmed the royal charter on the 22d of May, 1655, and during his administration the colony prospered. On the accession of Charles the Second,[1] Rhode Island applied for and obtained a new charter [July 8, 1663], highly democratic in its general features, and similar, in every respect, to the one granted to Connecticut.[2] The first governor elected under this instrument, was Benedict Arnold;[3] and by a colonial law, enacted during his first administration, the privileges of freemen were granted only to freeholders and their eldest sons.

Bowing to the mandates of royal authority, Rhode Island yielded to Andros, in January, 1687; but the moment intelligence reached the people of the accession of William and Mary[4] [May 11, 1689], and the imprisonment of the petty tyrant at Boston,[5] they assembled at Newport, resumed their old charter, and re-adopted their seal—an *anchor*, with *Hope* for a motto. Under this charter, Rhode Island continued to be governed for one hundred and fifty-seven years, when the people, in representative convention, in 1842, adopted a constitution.[6] Newport soon became a thriving commercial town; and when, in 1732, John Franklin established there the first newspaper in the colony, it contained five thousand inhabitants, and the whole province about eighteen thousand.[7] Near Newport the celebrated Dean Berkeley purchased lands in 1729; and with him came John Smibert, an artist, who introduced portrait painting into America.[8] Notwithstanding Rhode Island was excluded from the New England confederacy,[9] it always bore its share in defensive efforts; and its history is identified with that of New England in general, from the commencement of King William's War.[10]

---

[1] Page 109.

[2] Page 154. This charter guarantied free toleration in religious matters, and the legislature of the colony re-asserted the principle, so as to give it the popular force of law. The assertion, made by some, that Roman Catholics were excluded from voting, and that Quakers were outlawed, is erroneous.

[3] He was governor several times, serving in that office, altogether, about eleven years. He was chief magistrate of the colony when he died, in 1678.

[4] Page 130.

[5] Page 130.

[6] Page 477.

[7] Of these, about one thousand were Indians, and more than sixteen hundred were negroes.

[8] Berkeley preached occasionally in a small Episcopal church at Newport, and presented the congregation with an organ, the first ever heard in America. Smibert was a Scotchman, and married and settled at Boston. His picture of Berkeley and his family is still preserved at Yale College [page 178], in New Haven. Berkeley (afterward made bishop of a diocese in Ireland) made great efforts toward the establishment of the Arts and Learning, in America. Failing in his project of founding a new University, he became one of the most liberal benefactors of Yale College. In view of the future progress of the colonies, he wrote that prophetic poem, the last verse of which contains the oft-quoted line—

"Westward the course of Empire takes its way."

[9] Page 121.

[10] Page 130.

CHAPTER VII.

NEW JERSEY. [1664.]

THE *settlements* in New Jersey, Pennsylvania, and Delaware, we have considered together in the same chapter,[1] as constituting a series of events having intimate relations with each other. The history of the colonial organization of the first two, is separate and distinct. Delaware was never an independent colony or State, until after the Declaration of Independence, in 1776. The founding of the New Jersey colony occurred when, in 1664, the Duke of York sold the territory to Lord Berkeley and Sir George Carteret,[2] and the new proprietors began the work of erecting a State. They published a form of agreement which they called "Concessions,"[3] in which liberal offers were made to emigrants who might settle within the territory. Among other provisions, the people were to be exempt from the payment of quit-rents and other burdens, for the space of five years. Allured by the liberality of the "Concessions," as well as by the salubrity of the climate and the fertility of the soil, many families came from Long Island in 1664, and settled at Elizabethtown;[4] and in August, the following year, Philip Carteret (brother of one of the proprietors) was appointed governor, and arrived at Elizabethtown with a number of settlers.

At first all was peaceable. Nothing disturbed the repose of the colony during the five years' exemption from rents; but when, in 1670, the specified halfpenny, for the use of each acre of land, was required, murmurs of discontent were loud and universal. Those who had purchased land from the Indians, denied the right of the proprietors to demand rent from them; and some of the towns had even denied the authority of the Assembly, at its first sitting, in 1668. The whole people combined in resisting the payment of quit-rents; and after disputing with the proprietors almost two years, they revolted, called a new Assembly, appointed a dissolute, illegitimate son of Sir George Carteret, governor, in May, 1672, and in July following, compelled Philip Carteret to leave the province. Preparations were in progress to coerce the people into submission, when New Jersey, and all other portions of the territory claimed by the Duke of York, fell into the hands of the Dutch,[5] in August, 1673. On the restoration of the territory to the English,[6] in November, 1674, the Duke of York procured a new charter,[7] and then, regardless of the rights of Berkeley and Carteret, he appointed Edmund Andros, "the tyrant of New England,"[8]

---

[1] Page 92.

[2] Page 94. The province was called New Jersey, in honor of Carteret, who was governor of the island of Jersey, in the British Channel, during the civil war. He was a staunch royalist, and was the last commander to lower the royal flag, when the Parliament had triumphed.

[3] This was a sort of *constitution*, which provided for a government to be composed of a governor and council appointed by the proprietors, and an Assembly chosen by the freeholders of the province. The legislative power resided in the Assembly; the executive in the governor. The Council and the Assembly were each restricted to twelve members.

[4] So called, in honor of Elizabeth, wife of Sir George Carteret.

[5] Page 147. [6] Page 147. [7] Page 147. [8] Page 130.

governor of the whole domain. Carteret demurred, and the duke partially restored his rights; not, however, without leaving Andros a sufficient pretense for asserting his authority, and producing annoyances. Berkeley had become disgusted, and sold his interest in the province [March 28, 1674] to Edward Byllinge, an English Quaker. Pecuniary embarrassment caused Byllinge to assign his interest to William Penn, and two others,[1] in 1675. These purchasers, unwilling to maintain a political union with other parties, successfully negotiated with Carteret for a division of the province, which took place on the 11th of July, 1676. Carteret received the eastern portion as his share, and the Quakers the western part. From that time the divisions were known as EAST and WEST JERSEY.

The WEST JERSEY proprietors gave the people a remarkably liberal constitution of government [March 13, 1677]; and in 1677, more than four hundred Quakers came from England and settled below the Raritan. Andros required them to acknowledge the authority of the Duke of York. They refused; and the matter was referred to the eminent Sir William Jones (the oriental scholar) for adjudication, who decided against the claims of the duke. The latter submitted to the decision, released both provinces from allegiance to him, and the JERSEYS became independent of foreign control. The first popular assembly in West Jersey met at Salem, in November, 1681, and adopted a code of laws for the government of the people.[2]

Soon after the death of Carteret, in December, 1679, the trustees of his estate offered East Jersey for sale. It was purchased by William Penn and eleven of his brethren, on the 11th of February, 1682, who obtained a new charter, and on the 27th of July, 1683, appointed Robert Barclay,[3] a very eminent Quaker preacher, from Aberdeen, governor for life. A large number of his sect came from Scotland and England; and others from New England and Long Island settled in East Jersey to enjoy prosperity and repose. But repose, as well as the administration of Barclay, was of short duration; for when James succeeded Charles,[4] he appeared to consider his contracts made while *duke*, not binding upon his honor as *king*. He sought to annul the American charters, and succeeded, as we have seen, in subverting the governments of several,[5] through the instrumentality of Andros. The JERSEYS were sufferers in this respect, and were obliged to bow to the tyrant. When he was driven from the country in 1689,[6] the provinces were left without regular governments, and for more than twelve years anarchy prevailed there. The claims of the proprietors to jurisdiction, were repudiated by the people; and in 1702, they gladly relinquished the government by surrendering it, on the 25th of

---

[1] These purchasers immediately sold one half of their interest to the Earl of Perth, from whom the present town of Perth Amboy derives a part of its name. Amboy, or *Ambo*, is an Indian name.

[2] A remarkable law was enacted at that session. It provided that in all criminal cases, except treason, murder, and theft, the aggrieved party should have power to pardon the offender.

[3] He was the author of "An Apology for Quakers," a work highly esteemed by his sect. It was written in Latin, and translated into several continental languages. Barclay and Penn were intimate personal friends, and travelled much together. He died in Ury, in 1690, aged 42 years.

[4] Page 113. [5] Pages 129, 156, and 158. [6] Page 130.

April, to the crown.[1] The two provinces were united as a royal domain, and placed under the government of Lord Cornbury, the licentious ruler of New York,[2] in July following.

The province of New Jersey remained a dependency of New York, with a distinct legislative assembly of its own, until 1738, when, through the efforts of Lewis Morris,[3] the connection was for ever severed. Morris was appointed the first royal governor of New Jersey, and managed public affairs with ability and general satisfaction. From that period until the independence of the colonies was declared, in 1776, the history of the colony presents but few events of interest to the general reader.

CHAPTER VIII.

PENNSYLVANIA. [1682.]

THE colonial career of Pennsylvania began when, in the autumn of 1682, William Penn arrived,[4] and by a surrender by the agents of the Duke of York, and a proclamation in the presence of the popular Assembly, the *Territories* which now constitute the State of Delaware were united with his province.[5] Already, Penn had proclaimed his intention of being governed by the law of kindness in his treatment of the Indians; and when he came, he proceeded to lay the foundation of his new State upon Truth and Justice.[6] Where the Kensington portion of the city of Philadelphia now stands, as we have elsewhere mentioned, he met the Delaware chiefs in council, under the leafless branches of a wide-spreading elm,[7] on the 4th of November, 1682, and there made with them a solemn covenant of peace and friendship, and paid them the stipulated price for their lands. The Indians were delighted, and their hearts melted with good feeling. Such treatment was an anomaly in the history of the intercourse of their race with the white people. Even then the fires of a disastrous war were smouldering on the New England frontiers.[8] It was wonderful how the savage heart, so lately the dwelling of deepest hatred toward the white man, became the shrine of the holiest attribute of our nature. "We will live in love

[1] The proprietors retained their property in the soil, and their claims to quit-rents. Their organization has never ceased; and unsold, barren tracts of land in West Jersey are still held by that ancient tenure.

[2] Page 149.

[3] Son of an officer in Cromwell's army, who purchased an estate near New York, known as Morrisiana. He died in 1746. A part of that estate yet [1856] remains in possession of the Morris family.

[4] Page 96.

[5] Page 96.

[6] By his direction, his agent, William Markham, had opened a friendly correspondence with the Indians, and Penn himself had addressed a letter to them, assuring them of his love and brotherly feelings toward them.

[7] The Penn Society of Philadelphia erected a monument upon the spot where the venerable elm stood, near the intersection of Hanover and Beach-streets, Kensington district. The tree was blown down in 1810, and was found to be 283 years old. The monument is upon the site of the tree, and bears suitable inscriptions.

[8] King Philip's War, page 92.

with William Penn and his children," they said, "as long as the moon and the sun shall endure." They were true to their promise—not a drop of Quaker blood was ever shed by an Indian.

Having secured the lands, Penn's next care was to found a capital city. This he proceeded to do, immediately after the treaty with the Indians, upon lands purchased from the Swedes, lying between the Delaware and the Schuylkill Rivers. The boundaries of streets were marked upon the trunks of the chestnut, walnut, pine, and other forest trees which covered the land,[1] and the city was named Philadelphia, which signifies *brotherly love.* Within twelve months almost a hundred houses were erected,[2] and the Indians came daily with wild fowl and venison, as presents for their "good Father Penn." Never was a State blessed with a more propitious beginning, and internal peace and prosperity marked its course while the Quakers controlled its councils.

PENN'S HOUSE.

The proprietor convened a second Assembly at Philadelphia, in March, 1683, and then gave the people a "Charter of Liberties," signed and sealed by his own hand. It was so ample and just, that the government was really a representative democracy. Free religious toleration was ordained, and laws for the promotion of public and private morality were framed.[3] Unlike other proprietors, Penn surrendered to the people his rights in the appointment of officers; and until his death, his honest and highest ambition appeared to be to promote the happiness of the colonists. Because of this happy relation between the people and the proprietor, and the security against Indian hostilities, Pennsylvania outstripped all of its sister colonies in rapidity of settlement and permanent prosperity.

In August, 1684, Penn returned to England, leaving five members of the Council with Thomas Lloyd, as president, to administer the government during his absence. Soon afterward, the English Revolution occurred [1688] and king James was driven into exile.[4] Penn's personal regard for James continued after his fall; and for that loyalty, which had a deeper spring than mere political considerations, he was accused of dissaffection to the new government, and suffered imprisonments. In the mean while, discontents had sprung up in

---

[1] This fact was the origin of the names of Chestnut, Walnut, Pine, Spruce, and other streets in Philadelphia. For many years after the city was laid out, these living street-marks remained, and afforded shade to the inhabitants.

[2] Markham, Penn's agent, erected a house for the proprietor's use, in 1682. It is yet [1856] standing in Letitia court, the entrance to which is from Market-street, between Front and Second-streets. Another, and finer house, was occupied by Penn in 1700. It yet remains on the corner of Norris's alley and Second-street. It was the residence of General Arnold in 1778. Note 3, page 287.

[3] It was ordained "that to prevent lawsuits, three arbitrators, to be called Peace Makers, should be appointed by the county courts, to hear and determine small differences between man and man; that children should be taught some useful trade; that factors wronging their employers should make satisfaction, and one third over; that all causes for irreligion and vulgarity should be repressed; and that no man should be molested for his religious opinions.

[4] Note 7, page 113.

Pennsylvania, and the "three lower counties on the Delaware,"[1] offended at the action of some of the Council, withdrew from the Union[2] in April, 1691. Penn yielded to their wishes so far as to appoint a separate deputy governor for them.

An important political change now occurred in the colony. Penn's provincial government was taken from him in 1692 [Oct. 31], and Pennsylvania was placed under the authority of Governor Fletcher, of New York, who reunited the Delaware counties [May, 1693], to the parent province. All suspicions of Penn's disloyalty having been removed in 1694, his chartered rights were restored to him [Aug. 30], and he appointed his original agent, William Markham, deputy governor. He returned to America in December, 1699, and was pained to find his people discontented, and clamorous for greater political privileges. Considering their demands reasonable, he gave them a new charter, or frame of government [Nov. 6, 1701], more liberal in its concessions than the former. It was cheerfully accepted by the Pennsylvania people, but those of the Delaware territories, whose delegates had already withdrawn from the Assembly [Oct. 20], evidently aiming at independence, declined it. Penn acquiesced in their decision, and allowed them a distinct Assembly. This satisfied them, and their first independent legislature was convened at Newcastle in 1703. Although Pennsylvania and Delaware ever afterward continued to have separate legislatures, they were under the same governor until the Revolution in 1776.

A few weeks after adjusting difficulties, and granting the new charter, Penn returned to England [Dec., 1701], and never visited America again. His departure was hastened by the ripening of a ministerial project for abolishing all the proprietary governments in America. His health soon afterward declined, and at his death he left his American possessions to his three sons (Thomas, John, and Richard), then minors, who continued to administer the government, chiefly through deputies, until the War for Independence in 1776. Then it became a free and independent State, and the commonwealth purchased all the claims of Penn's heirs in the province, for about five hundred and eighty thousand dollars.[3]

CHAPTER IX.

THE CAROLINAS. [1665—1680.]

NOTWITHSTANDING the many failures which had dampened the ardor of English speculators, who had engaged in planting settlements in America, hope still remained buoyant. Success finally crowned the efforts in New England

[1] Page 96. [2] Page 96.

[3] On account of the expenses incurred in Pennsylvania, Penn was compelled to borrow $30,000, and mortgage his province as security. This was the commencement of the State debt of Pennsylvania, now [1856] amounting to about $40,000,000.

and further south, and the proprietors of the Carolinas, when settlements within that domain became permanent,[1] and tides of emigration from various sources flowed thitherward, began to have gorgeous visions of an empire in America, that should outshine those of the Old World. It then became their first care to frame a constitution of government, with functions adequate to the grand design, and to this task, the earl of Shaftesbury, one of the ablest statesmen of his time, and John Locke, the eminent philosopher, were called. They completed their labors in March, 1669, and the instrument was called the *Fundamental Constitutions.*[2] It was in the highest degree monarchical in its character and tendency, and contemplated the transplantation, in America, of all the ranks and aristocratic distinctions of European society.[3] The spirit of the whole thing was adverse to the feelings of the people, and its practical development was an impossibility; so, after a contest between proprietors and colonists, for twenty years, the magnificent scheme was abandoned, and the people were allowed to govern themselves, in their own more simple way.[4] The disorders which prevailed when the first attempts were made to impose this scheme of government upon the people, soon ripened into rebellion, especially in the *Albemarle*, or northern colony.[5] Excessive taxation and commercial restrictions bore heavily upon the industry of the people, and engendered wide-spread discontent. This was fostered by refugees from Virginia, after Bacon's rebellion, in 1676,[6] who sought shelter among the people below the Roanoke. They scattered, broad-cast, over a generous soil, vigorous ideas of popular freedom, and a year after Bacon's death,[7] the people of the *Albemarle County Colony*[8] revolted. The immediate cause of this movement was the attempt of the acting governor to enforce the revenue laws against a New England vessel. Led on by John Culpepper, a refugee from the CARTERET *County Colony* of South Carolina,[9] the people seized the chief magistrate [Dec. 10, 1677] and the public funds, imprisoned him and six of his council, called a new Assembly, appointed a new magistrate and judges, and for two years conducted the affairs of government independent of foreign control. Culpepper went to England to plead the cause of the people, and was arrested and tried on a charge of treason.

---

[1] Pages 97 and 98.

[2] It consists of one hundred and twenty articles, and is supposed to have been the production, chiefly, of the mind of Shaftesbury.

[3] There were to be two orders of nobility: the higher to consist of landgraves, or *earls*, the lower of caciques, or *barons*. The territory was to be divided into counties, each containing 480,000 acres, with one landgrave, and two caciques. There were also to be lords of manors, who, like the nobles, might hold courts and exercise judicial functions. Persons holding fifty acres were to be freeholders; the tenants held no political franchise, and could never attain to a higher rank. The four estates of proprietors, earls, barons, and commons, were to sit in one legislative chamber. The proprietors were always to be eight in number, to possess the whole judicial power, and have the supreme control of all tribunals. The commons were to have four members in the legislature to every three of the nobility. Thus an aristocratic majority was always secured, and the real representatives of the *people* had no power. Every religion was professedly tolerated, but the Church of England, only, was declared to be orthodox. Such is an outline of the absurd scheme proposed for governing the free colonies of the Carolinas.

[4] A governor, with a council of twelve—six chosen by the proprietors, and six by the Assembly—and a House of Delegates chosen by the freeholders.

[5] Page 97. [6] Page 110. [7] Page 112.

[8] Page 97. [9] Page 98.

Shaftesbury procured his acquittal, and he returned to the Carolinas.[1] Quiet was restored to the colony, and until the arrival of the unprincipled Seth Sothel (one of the proprietors), as governor, the people enjoyed repose. Thus early the inhabitants of that feeble colony practically asserted the grand political maxim, that *taxation without representation is tyranny*,[2] for the defense of which our Revolutionary fathers fought, a century afterward.

Governor Sothel arrived in North Carolina in 1683. Martin says that "the dark shades of his character were not relieved by a single ray of virtue;" and Chalmers asserts that "the annals of delegated authority included no name so infamous as Sothel." He plundered the people, cheated the proprietors, and on all occasions prostituted his office to purposes of private gain. After enduring his oppression almost six years, the people seized him [1689], and were about sending him to England to answer their accusations before the proprietors, when he asked to be tried by the colonial Assembly. The favor was granted, and he was sentenced to banishment for one year, and a perpetual disqualification for the office of governor. He withdrew to the southern colony, where we shall meet him again.[3] His successor, Philip Ludwell, an energetic, incorruptible man, soon redressed the wrongs of the people, and restored order and good feelings. Governors Harvey and Walker also maintained quiet and good will among the people. And the good Quaker, John Archdale, who came to govern both Carolinas in 1695, placed the colony in a position for attaining future prosperity, hitherto unknown.

While these events were transpiring in the northern colony, the people of the *Carteret*,[4] or southern colony, were steadily advancing in wealth and numbers. Their first popular legislature of which we have records, was convened in 1674,[5] but it exhibited an unfavorable specimen of republican government. Jarring interests and conflicting creeds produced violent debates and irreconcilable discord. For a long time the colony was distracted by quarrels, and anarchy prevailed. At length the Stono Indians gathered in bands, and plundered the plantations of grain and cattle, and even menaced the settlers with destruction. The appearance of this common enemy healed their dissensions, and the people went out as brothers to chastise the plunderers. They completely subdued the Indians, in 1680. Many of them were made prisoners, and sold for slaves in the West Indies, and the Stonos never afterward had a tribal existence.

Wearied by the continual annoyance of the Indians, many English families

---

[1] Culpepper afterward became surveyor-general of the province, and in 1680, he was employed in laying out the new city of Charleston. [See next page.] His previous expulsion from the southern colony, was on account of his connection with a rebellious movement in 1672.

[2] Page 211. [3] Page 167. [4] Page 98.

[5] The settlers brought with them an unfinished copy of the "*Fundamental Constitutions*," but they at once perceived the impossibility of conformity to that scheme of government. They held a "parliamentary convention" in 1672, and twenty delegates were elected by the people to act with the governor and the council, as a legislature. Thus early, representative government was established, but its operations seem not to have been very successful, and a legislature proper, of which we have any record, was not organized until 1674, when an upper and a lower House was established, and laws for the province were enacted.

crossed the Ashley, and seated themselves upon the more eligible locality of Oyster Point, where they founded the present city of Charleston,[1] in 1680. There a flourishing village soon appeared; and after the subjugation of the savages,[2] the old settlement was abandoned, and now not a vestige of it remains upon the cultivated plantation at Old Town, where it stood. The Dutch settlers[3] spread over the country along the Edisto and Santee, and planted the seeds of future flourishing communities, while immigrants from different parts of Europe and from New England swelled the population of Charleston and vicinity. Nor did they neglect political affairs. While they were vigilant in all that pertained to their material interests, they were also aspirants, even at that early day, for political independence.

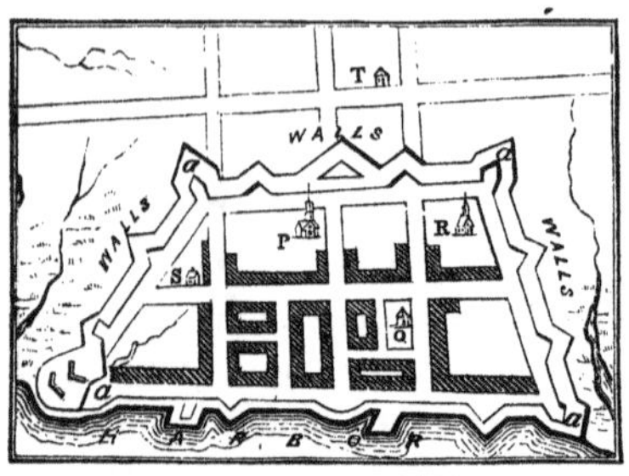

CHARLESTON IN 1680.

Another popular legislature was convened at Charleston in 1682. It exhibited more harmony than the first,[4] and several useful laws were framed. Emigration was now pouring in a tide of population more rapid than any of the colonies below New England had yet experienced. Ireland, Scotland,[5] Holland, and France, contributed largely to the flowing stream. In 1686–7, quite a large number of Huguenots, who had escaped from the fiery persecutions which were revived in France by the revocation of the Edict of Nantes,[6] landed at Charleston. English hatred of the French[7] caused the settlers to look with jealousy upon these refugees, and for more than ten years [1686 to 1697] the latter were denied the rights of citizenship.

Shaftesbury's scheme of government was as distasteful to the people of South Carolina, as to those of the northern colony,[8] and they refused to accept it. They became very restive, and seemed disposed to cast off all allegiance to the proprietors and the mother country. At this crisis, James Colleton, a brother of one of the proprietors, was appointed governor [1686], and was vested with full powers to bring the colonists into submission. His administration of about four years was a very turbulent one. He was in continual colli-

[1] Note 1, page 165. The above engraving illustrates the manner of fortifying towns, as a defense against foes. It exhibits the walls of Charleston in 1680, and the location of churches in 1704. The points marked *a a a*, etc., are bastions for cannons. P, English church; Q, French church; R, Independent church; S, Anabaptist church; and T, Quaker meeting-house.

[2] Page 165.

[3] They had founded the village of Jamestown several miles up the Ashley River.

[4] Page 164.

[5] In 1684, Lord Cardon, and ten Scotch families, who had suffered persecution, came to South Carolina, and settled at Port Royal. The Spaniards at St. Augustine claimed jurisdiction over Port Royal; and during the absence of Cardon [1686], they attacked and dispersed the settlers, and desolated their plantations.

[6] In the city of Nantes, Henry the Fourth of France issued an edict, in 1598, in favor of the Huguenots, or Protestants, allowing them free toleration. The profligate Louis the Fourteenth, stung with remorse in his old age, sought to gain the favor of Heaven by bringing his whole people into the bosom of the Roman Catholic Church. He revoked the famous edict in 1686, and instantly the fires of persecution were kindled throughout the empire. Many thousands of the Protestants left France, and found refuge in other countries.

[7] Page 180.

[8] Page 97.

sion with the people, and at length drove them to open rebellion. They seized the public records, imprisoned the secretary of the province, and called a new Assembly. Pleading the danger of an Indian or Spanish invasion,[1] the governor called out the militia, and proclaimed the province to be under martial law.[2] This measure only increased the exasperation of the people, and he was impeached, and banished from the province by the Assembly, in 1690.

While this turbulence and misrule was at its height, Sothel arrived from North Carolina, pursuant to his sentence of banishment,[3] and the people unwisely consented to his assumption of the office of governor.[4] They soon repented their want of judgment. For two years he plundered and oppressed them, and then [1692] the Assembly impeached and banished him also. Then came Philip Ludlow to re-establish the authority of the proprietors, but the people, thoroughly aroused, resolved not to tolerate even so good a man as he, if his mission was to enforce obedience to the absurd *Fundamental Constitutions.*[5] After a brief and turbulent administration, he gladly withdrew to Virginia, and soon afterward [1693], the proprietors abandoned Shaftesbury's scheme, and the good Quaker, John Archdale, was sent, in 1695, to administer a more simple and republican form of government, for both the Carolinas. His administration was short, but highly beneficial;[6] and the people of South Carolina always looked back to the efforts of that good man, with gratitude. He healed dissensions, established equitable laws, and so nearly effected an entire reconciliation of the English to the French settlers, that in the year succeeding his departure from the province, the Assembly admitted the latter [1697] to all the privileges of citizens and freemen. From the close of Archdale's administration, the progress of the two Carolina colonies should be considered as separate and distinct, although they were not politically separated until 1729.[7]

NORTH CAROLINA.

We may properly date the permanent prosperity of North Carolina from the adminstration of Archdale,[8] when the colonists began to turn their attention to the interior of the country, where richer soil invited the agriculturist, and the fur of the beaver and otter allured the adventurous hunter. The Indians along the sea-coast were melting away like frost in the sunbeams. The powerful Hatteras tribe,[9] which numbered three thousand in Raleigh's time, were reduced to fifteen bowmen; another tribe had entirely disappeared; and the remnants of some others had sold their lands or lost them by fraud, and were driven back to the deep wilderness. Indulgence in strong drinks, and other vices of civiliz-

[1] The Spaniards at St. Augustine had menaced the English settlements in South Carolina, and, as we have seen [note 5, page 166], had actually broken up a little Scotch colony at Port Royal.

[2] Note 8, page 170.

[3] Page 165.

[4] On his arrival, Sothel took sides with the people against Colleton, and thus, in the moment of their anger, he unfortunately gained their good will and confidence.

[5] Page 164.

[6] The culture of rice was introduced into South Carolina during Archdale's administration. Some seed was given to the governor by the captain of a vessel from Madagascar. It was distributed among several planters, and thus its cultivation began.

[7] Page 171.

[8] Page 165.

[9] Note 5, page 20.

ation, had decimated them, and their beautiful land, all the way to the Yadkin and Catawba, was speedily opened to the sway of the white man.

At the commencement of the eighteenth century, religion began to exert an influence in North Carolina. The first Anglican[1] church edifice was then built in Chowan county, in 1705. The Quakers[2] multiplied; and in 1707, a company of Huguenots,[3] who had settled in Virginia, came and sat down upon the beautiful banks of the Trent, a tributary of the Neuse River. Two years later [1709], a hundred German families, driven from their homes on the Rhine, by persecution, penetrated the interior of North Carolina, and under Count Graffenried, founded settlements along the head waters of the Neuse, and upon the Roanoke. While settlements were thus spreading and strengthening, and general prosperity blessed the province, a fearful calamity fell upon the inhabitants of the interior. The broken Indian tribes made a last effort, in 1711, to regain the beautiful country they had lost. The leaders in the conspiracy to crush the white people, were the Tuscaroras[4] of the inland region, and the Corees[5] further south and near the sea-board. They fell like lightning from the clouds upon the scattered German settlements along the Roanoke and Pamlico Sound. In one night [Oct. 2, 1711], one hundred and thirty persons perished by the hatchet. Along Albemarle Sound, the savages swept with the knife of murder in one hand, and the torch of desolation in the other, and for three days they scourged the white people, until disabled by fatigue and drunkenness. Those who escaped the massacre called upon their brethren of the southern colony for aid, and Colonel Barnwell, with a party of Carolinians and friendly Indians of the southern nations,[6] marched to their relief. He drove the Tuscaroras to their fortified town in the present Craven county, and there made a treaty of peace with them. His troops violated the treaty on their way back, by outrages upon the Indians, and soon hostilities were renewed. Late in the year [Dec., 1712], Colonel Moore[7] arrived from South Carolina with a few white men and a large body of Indians, and drove the Tuscaroras to their fort in the present Greene county, wherein [March, 1713] he made eight hundred of them prisoners. The remainder of the Tuscaroras fled northward in June, and joining their kindred on the southern borders of Lake Ontario, they formed the sixth nation of the celebrated IROQUOIS confederacy in the province of New York.[8] A treaty of peace was made with the Corees in 1715, and North Carolina never afterward suffered from Indian hostilities.[9]

SOUTH CAROLINA.

Although really united, the two colonies acted independently of each other from the close of the seventeenth century. Soon after the commencement of

---

[1] The established Church of England was so called, to distinguish it from the Romish Church.
[2] Page 122. [3] Page 49. [4] Page 25. [5] Page 20.
[6] They consisted of Creeks, Catawbas, Cherokees, and Yamassees. See pages 26 to 30, inclusive.
[7] A son of James Moore, who was governor of South Carolina in 1700. [8] Page 23.
[9] The province issued bills of credit (for the first time) to the amount of about forty thousand dollars, to defray the expenses of the war.

Queen Anne's War[1] [May, 1702], Governor Moore of South Carolina, proposed an expedition against the Spaniards at St. Augustine.[2] The Assembly assented, and appropriated almost ten thousand dollars for the service. Twelve hundred men (one half Indians) were raised, and proceeded, in two divisions, to the attack. The main division, under the governor, went by sea, to blockade the harbor, and the remainder proceeded along the coast, under the command of Colonel Daniels. The latter arrived first, and attacked and plundered the town. The Spaniards retired within their fortress with provisions for four months; and as the Carolinians had no artillery, their position was impregnable. Daniels was then sent to Jamaica, in the West Indies, to procure battery cannon, but before his return, two Spanish vessels had appeared, and so frightened Governor Moore that he raised the blockade, and fled. Daniels barely escaped capture, on his return, but he reached Charleston in safety. This ill-advised expedition burdened the colony with a debt of more than twenty-six thousand dollars, for the payment of which, bills of credit were issued. This was the first emission of paper money in the Carolinas.

A more successful expedition was undertaken by Governor Moore, in December, 1703, against the Apalachian[3] Indians, who were in league with the Spaniards. Their chief villages were between the Alatamaha and Savannah Rivers. These were desolated. Almost eight hundred Indians were taken prisoners, and the whole territory of the Apalachians was made tributary to the English. The province had scarcely become tranquil after this chastisement of the Indians, when a new cause for disquietude appeared. Some of the proprietors had long cherished a scheme for establishing the Anglican Church,[4] as the State religion, in the Carolinas. When Nathaniel Johnson succeeded Governor Moore, he found a majority of churchmen in the Assembly, and by their aid, the wishes of the proprietors were gratified. The Anglican Church was made the established religion, and Dissenters[5] were excluded from all public offices. This was an usurpation of chartered rights; and the aggrieved party laid the matter before the imperial ministry. Their cause was sustained; and by order of Parliament, the colonial Assembly, in November, 1706, repealed the law of disfranchisement, but the Church maintained its dominant position until the Revolution.

The ire of the Spaniards was greatly excited by the attack upon St. Augustine,[6] and an expedition, composed of five French and Spanish vessels,[7] with a large body of troops, was sent from Havana to assail Charleston, take possession of the province, and annex it to the Spanish domain of Florida.[8] The squadron crossed Charleston bar in May, 1706, and about eight hundred troops were landed at different points. The people seized their arms, and, led by the governor and Colonel Rhett, they drove the invaders back to their vessels, after

---

[1] Page 135. [2] Page 51.
[3] A tribe of the Mobilian family [page 29] situated south of the Savannah River.
[4] Note 1, page 168. [5] Note 2, page 76. [6] Page 51.
[7] It will be remembered [see page 135] that in 1702, England declared war against France, and that Spain was a party to the quarrel. [8] Page 42.

killing or capturing almost three hundred men. They also captured a French vessel, with its crew. It was a complete victory. So the storm which appeared so suddenly and threatening, was dissipated in a day, and the sunshine of peace and prosperity again gladdened the colony.

A few years later, a more formidable tempest brooded over the colony, when a general Indian confederacy was secretly formed, to exterminate the white people by a single blow. Within forty days, in the spring of 1715, the Indian tribes from the Cape Fear to the St. Mary's, and back to the mountains, had coalesced in the conspiracy; and before the people of Charleston had any intimation of danger, one hundred white victims had been sacrificed in the remote settlements. The Creeks,[1] Yamasees,[2] and Apalachians[3] on the south, confederated with the Cherokees,[4] Catawbas,[5] and Congarees[6] on the west, in all six thousand strong; while more than a thousand warriors issued from the Neuse region, to avenge their misfortunes in the wars of 1712–13.[7] It was a cloud of fearful portent that hung in the sky; and the people were filled with terror, for they knew not at what moment the consuming lightning might leap forth. At this fearful crisis, Governor Craven acted with the utmost wisdom and energy. He took measures to prevent men from leaving the colony; to secure all the arms and ammunition that could be found, and to arm faithful negroes to assist the white people. He declared the province to be under martial law,[8] and then, at the head of twelve hundred men, black and white, he marched to meet the foe who were advancing with the knife, hatchet, and torch, in fearful activity. The Indians were at first victorious, but after several bloody encounters, the Yamassees and their southern neighbors were driven across the Savannah [May, 1715], and halted not until they found refuge under Spanish guns at St. Augustine. The Cherokees and their northern neighbors had not yet engaged in the war, and they returned to their hunting grounds, deeply impressed with the strength and greatness of the white people.

And now the proprietary government of South Carolina was drawing to a close. The governors being independent of the people, were often haughty and exacting, and the inhabitants had borne the yoke of their rule for many years, with great impatience. While their labor was building up a prosperous State, the proprietors refused to assist them in times of danger, or to re-imburse their expenses in the protection of the province from invasion. The whole burden of debt incurred in the war with the Yamassees, was left upon the shoulders of the people. The proprietors not only refused to pay any portion of it, but enforced their claims for quit-rents with great severity. The people saw no hope in the future, but in royal rule and protection. So they met in convention; resolved to forswear all allegiance to the proprietors; and on Governor Johnson's refusal to act as chief magistrate, under the king, they

---

[1] Page 30. [2] Page 30. [3] Note 3, page 168. [4] Page 27. [5] Page 26.

[6] This was a small tribe that inhabited the country in the vicinity of the present city of Columbia, in South Carolina. [7] Page 168.

[8] Martial law may be proclaimed by rulers, in an emergency, and the civil law, for the time being, is made subservient to the military. The object is to allow immediate and energetic action for repelling invasions, or for other purposes.

appointed [December 21, 1719] Colonel Moore[1] governor of the colony. The matter was laid before the imperial government, when the colonists were sustained, and South Carolina became a royal province.[2]

The people of North Carolina[3] also resolved on a change of government; and after a continued controversy for ten years, the proprietors, in 1729, sold to the king, for about eighty thousand dollars, all their claims to the soil and incomes in both provinces. North and South Carolina were then separated. George Burrington was appointed the first royal governor over the former, and Robert Johnson over the latter. From that period until the commencement of the French and Indian war,[4] the general history of the CAROLINAS presents but few features of interest, except the efforts made for defending the colony against the Spaniards and the Indians. The people gained very little by a change of owners; and during forty-five years, until the revolution made the people independent, there was a succession of disputes with the royal governors.

CHAPTER X.

GEORGIA. [1732.]

THE colony founded by Oglethorpe on the Savannah River rapidly increased in numbers, and within eight years, twenty-five hundred immigrants were sent over, at an expense to the trustees[5] of four hundred thousand dollars. Yet prosperity did not bless the enterprise. Many of the settlers were unaccustomed to habits of industry, and were mere drones; and as the use of slave labor was prohibited, tillage was neglected. Even the industrious Scotch, German, and Swiss families who came over previous to 1740, could not give that vitality to industrial pursuits, which was necessary to a development of the resources of the country. Anxious for the permanent growth of the colony, Oglethorpe went to England in 1734, and returned in 1736, with about three hundred immigrants. Among them were one hundred and fifty Highlanders, well skilled in military affairs. These constituted the first army of the colony during its early struggles. John Wesley, founder of the Methodist denomination, also came with Oglethorpe, to make Georgia a religious colony, and to spread the gospel among the Indians. He was unsuccessful; for his strict moral doctrines, his fearless denunciations of vice, and his rigid exercise of ecclesiastical authority made him quite unpopular among the great mass of the colonists, who winced at restraint. The eminent George Whitefield also visited Georgia in 1738, when only twenty-three years of age, and succeeded in establishing an orphan asylum near Savannah, which flourished many years, and

---

[1] Note 7, page 168.
[2] The first governor, by royal appointment, was Francis Nicholson, who had been successively governor of New York [page 144], Maryland, Virginia, and Nova Scotia.
[3] Page 167. [4] Page 179. [5] Page 100.

was a real blessing. The Christian efforts of those men, prosecuted with the most sincere desire for the good of their fellow-mortals, were not appreciated. Their seed fell upon stony ground, and after the death of Whitefield, in 1770, his "House of Mercy" in Georgia, deprived of his sustaining influence, became a desolation.

A cloud of trouble appeared in the Southern horizon. The rapid increase of the new colony excited the jealousy of the Spaniards at St. Augustine, and the vigilant Oglethorpe, expecting such a result, prepared to oppose any hostile movements against his settlement. He established a fort on the site of Augusta, as a defence against the Indians, and he erected fortifications at Darien, on Cumberland Island, at Frederica (St. Simon's Island), and on the north bank of the St. John, the southern boundary of the English claims. Spanish commissioners came from St. Augustine to protest against these preparations, and to demand the immediate evacuation of the whole of Georgia, and of all South Carolina below Port Royal.[1] Oglethorpe, of course, refused compliance, and the Spaniards threatened him with war. In the winter of 1736–7, Oglethorpe went to England to make preparations to meet the exigency. He returned in October following, bearing the commission of a brigadier, and leading a regiment of six hundred well-disciplined troops, for the defense of the whole southern frontier of the English possessions.[2] But for two years their services were not much needed; then war broke out between England and Spain [November, 1739], and Oglethorpe prepared an expedition against St. Augustine. In May, 1740, he entered Florida with four hundred of his best troops, some volunteers from South Carolina, and a large body of friendly Creek Indians;[3] in all more than two thousand men. His first conquest was Fort *Diego*, twenty miles from St. Augustine. Then Fort *Moosa*, within two miles of the city, surrendered; but when he appeared before the town and fortress, and demanded instant submission, he was answered by a defiant refusal. A small fleet under Captain Price blockaded the harbor, and for a time cut off supplies from the Spaniards, but swift-winged galleys[4] passed through the blockading fleet, and supplied the garrison with several weeks' provisions. Oglethorpe had no artillery with which to attack the fortress, and being warned by the increasing heats of summer, and sickness in his camp, not to wait for their supplies to become exhausted, he raised the siege and returned to Savannah.

The ire of the Spaniards was aroused, and they, in turn, prepared to invade Georgia in the summer of 1742. An armament, fitted out at Havana and St. Augustine, and consisting of thirty-six vessels, with more than three thousand troops, entered the harbor of St. Simon's, and landed a little above the town of the same name, on the 16th of July, 1742, and erected a battery of twenty guns. Oglethorpe had been apprised of the intentions of the Spaniards, and

---

[1] Note 5, page 166.

[2] His commission gave him the command of the militia of South Carolina also, and he stood as a guard between the English and Spanish possessions of the southern country.

[3] Page 30.

[4] A low built vessel propelled by both sails and oars. The war vessels of the ancients were all galleys. See Norman vessel, page 35.

after unsuccessfully applying to the governor of South Carolina for troops and supplies, he marched to St. Simon's, and made his head-quarters at his princi- fortress at Frederica.[1] He was at Fort Simon, near the landing place of the invaders, with less than eight hundred men, exclusive of Indians, when the enemy appeared. He immediately spiked the guns of the fort, destroyed his stores, and retreated to Frederica. There he anxiously awaited hoped-for reinforcements and supplies from Carolina, and then he successfully repulsed several detachments of the Spaniards, who attacked him. He finally resolved to make a night assault upon the enemy's battery, at St. Simon's. A deserter (a French soldier) defeated his plan; but the sagacity of Oglethorpe caused the miscreant to be instrumental in driving the invaders from the coast. He bribed a Spanish prisoner to carry a letter to the deserter, which contained information respecting a British fleet that was about to attack St. Augustine.[2] Of course the letter was handed to the Spanish commander, and the Frenchman was arrested as a spy. The intelligence in Oglethorpe's letter alarmed the enemy; and while the officers were holding a council, some Carolina vessels, with supplies for the garrison at Frederica, appeared in the distance. Believing them to be part of the British fleet alluded to, the Spaniards determined to attack the Georgians immediately, and then hasten to St. Augustine. On their march to assail Frederica, they were ambuscaded in a swamp. Great slaughter of the invaders ensued, and the place is still called *Bloody Marsh.* The survivors retreated in confusion to their vessels, and sailed immediately to St. Augustine.[3] On their way, they attacked the English fort at the southern extremity of Cumberland Island,[4] on the 19th of July, but were repulsed with the loss of two galleys. The whole expedition was so disastrous to the Spaniards, that the commander (Don Manuel de Monteano) was dismissed from the service. Oglethorpe's stratagem saved Georgia, and, perhaps, South Carolina, from utter ruin.

Having fairly established his colony, Oglethorpe went to England in 1743, and never returned to Georgia, where, for ten years, he had nobly labored to secure an attractive asylum for the oppressed.[5] He left the province in a tranquil state. The mild military rule under which the people had lived, was changed to civil government in 1743, administered by a president and council, under the direction of the trustees,[6] yet the colony continued to languish. Several causes combined to produce this condition. We have already alluded to the inefficiency of most of the earlier settlers, and the prohibition of slave labor.[7] They were also deprived of the privileges of commerce and of traffic

[1] The remains of Fort Frederica yet [1856] form a very picturesque ruin on the plantation of W. W. Hazzard, Esq., of St. Simon's Island.

[2] Oglethorpe addressed the Frenchman as if he was a spy of the English. He directed the deserter to represent the Georgians as in a weak condition, to advise the Spaniards to attack them immediately, and to persuade the Spaniards to remain three days longer, within which time six British men-of-war, and two thousand men, from Carolina, would probably enter the harbor of St. Augustine.

[3] They first burned Fort Simon, but in their haste they left several of their cannons and a quantity of provisions behind them.

[4] Fort William. There was another small fort on the northern end of the island, called Fort Andrew.

[5] Page 100.

[6] Page 100.

[7] Page 171.

with the Indians; and were not allowed the ownership, in fee, of the lands which they cultivated.[1] In consequence of these restrictions, there were no incentives to labor, except to supply daily wants. General discontent prevailed. They saw the Carolinians growing rich by the use of slaves, and by commerce with the West Indies. Gradually the restrictive laws were evaded. Slaves were brought from Carolina, and hired, first for a short period, and then for a hundred years, or for life. The price paid for life-service was the money value of the slave, and the transaction was, practically, a sale and purchase. Then slave-ships came to Savannah directly from Africa; slave labor was generally used in 1750, and Georgia became a planting State. In 1752, at the expiration of the twenty-one years named in the patent,[2] the trustees gladly resigned the charter into the hands of the king, and from that time until the Revolution, Georgia remained a royal province.

CHAPTER XI.

A RETROSPECT. [1492—1756.]

In the preceding pages we have considered the principal events which occurred within the domain of our Republic from the time of first discoveries, in 1492, to the commencement of the last inter-colonial war between the English and French settlers, a period of about two hundred and sixty years. During that time, fifteen colonies were planted,[3] thirteen of which were commenced within the space of about fifty-six years—from 1607 to 1673. By the union of Plymouth and Massachusetts,[4] and Connecticut and New Haven,[5] the number of colonies was reduced to thirteen, and these were they which went into the revolutionary contest in 1775. The provinces of Canada and Nova Scotia, conquered by the English, remained loyal, and to this day they continue to be portions of the British empire.

In the establishment of the several colonies, which eventually formed the thirteen United States of America, several European nations contributed vigorous materials; and people of opposite habits, tastes, and religious faith, became commingled, after making impressions of their distinctive characters where their influence was first felt. England furnished the largest proportion of colonists, and her children always maintained sway in the government and industry of the whole country; while Scotland, Ireland, Germany, Holland, France, Sweden, Denmark, and the Baltic region, contributed large quotas of people and other colonial instrumentalities. Churchmen and Dissenters,[6] Roman Catholics and

---

[1] Page 116. [2] Page 100.
[3] Virginia, Plymouth, Massachusetts Bay, New Hampshire, Connecticut, New Haven, Rhode Island, New York, New Jersey, Delaware, Maryland, Pennsylvania, North and South Carolina, and Georgia. [4] Page 132. [5] Page 89. [6] Note 2, page 76.

Quakers,[1] came and sat down by the side of each other. For a while, the dissonance of nations and creeds prevented entire harmony; but the freedom enjoyed, the perils and hardships encountered, and endured, the conflicts with pagan savages on one hand, and of hierarchical[2] and governmental oppression on the other, which they maintained for generations, shoulder to shoulder, diffused a brotherhood of feeling throughout the whole social body of the colonists, and resulted in harmony, sympathy, and love. And when, as children of one family, they loyally defended the integrity of Great Britain (then become the "mother country" of nearly all) against the aggressions of the French and Indians[3] [1756 to 1763], and yet were compelled, by the unkindness of that mother, to sever the filial bond[4] [1776], their hearts beat as with one pulsation, and they struck the dismembering blow as with one hand.

There was a great diversity of character exhibited by the people of the several colonies, differing according to their origin and the influence of climate and pursuits. The Virginians and their southern neighbors, enjoying a mild climate, productive of tendencies to voluptuousness and ease, were from those classes of English society where a lack of rigid moral discipline allowed free living and its attendant vices. They generally exhibited less moral restraint, more hospitality, and greater frankness, and social refinement, than the people of New England. The latter were from among the middle classes, and included a great many religious enthusiasts, possessing more zeal than knowledge. They were extremely strict in their notions; very rigid in manners, and jealous of strangers. Their early legislation, recognizing, as it did, the most minute regulations of social life, often presented food for merriment.[5] Yet their intentions were pure; their designs were noble; and, in a great degree, their virtuous purposes were accomplished. They aimed to make every member of society a Christian, according to their own pattern; and if they did not fully accomplish their object, they erected strong bulwarks against those

---

[1] Note 6, page 122, and note 3, page 123.

[2] Hierarchy is, in a general sense, a priestly or ecclesiastical government. Such was the original form of government of the ancient Jews, when the priesthood held absolute rule.

[3] Period IV., chapter xii., page 179.

[4] Page 251.

[5] They assumed the right to regulate the expenditures of the people, even for wearing-apparel, according to their several incomes. The general court of Massachusetts, on one occasion, required the proper officers to notice the "apparel" of the people, especially their "ribands and great boots." Drinking of healths, wearing funeral badges, and many other things that seemed improper, were forbidden. At Hartford, the general court kept a constant eye upon the morals of the people. Freemen were compelled to vote under penalty of a fine of sixpence; the use of tobacco was prohibited to persons under twenty years of age, without the certificate of a physician; and no others were allowed to use it more than once a day, and then they must be ten miles from any house. The people of Hartford were all obliged to rise in the morning when the watchman rang his bell. These are but a few of the hundreds of similar enactments found on the records of the New England courts. In 1646, the Legislature of Massachusetts passed a law, which imposed the penalty of a flogging upon any one who should kiss a woman in the streets. More than a hundred years afterward, this law was enforced in Boston. The captain of a British man-of-war happened to return from a cruise, on Sunday. His overjoyed wife met him on the wharf, and he kissed her several times. The magistrates ordered him to be flogged. The punishment incurred no ignominy, and he associated freely with the best citizens. When about to depart, the captain invited the magistrates and others on board his vessel, to dine. When dinner was over, he caused all the magistrates to be flogged, on deck, in sight of the town. Then assuring them that he considered accounts settled between him and them, he dismissed them, and set sail.

EARLY N. E. HOUSE.[1]

little vices which compose great private and public evils. Dwelling upon a parsimonious soil, and possessing neither the means nor the inclination for sumptuous living, indulged in by their southern brethren, their dwellings were simple, and their habits frugal.

DUTCHMAN. [1660.]

In New York, and portions of Pennsylvania and New Jersey, the manners, customs, and pursuits of the Dutch prevailed even a century after the English conquest of New Netherland[2] [1664], and society had become permeated by English ideas and customs. They were plodding money-getters; abhorred change and innovation, and loved ease. They possessed few of the elements of progress, but many of the substantial social virtues necessary to the stability of a State, and the health of society. From these the Swedes and Finns upon the Delaware[3] did not differ much; but the habits of the Quakers, who finally predominated in West Jersey[4] and Pennsylvania,[5] were quite different. They always exhibited a refined simplicity and equanimity, without ostentatious displays of piety, that won esteem; and they were governed by a religious sentiment without fanaticism, which formed a powerful safeguard against vice and immorality.

In Maryland,[6] the earlier settlers were also less rigid moralists than the New Englanders, and greater formalists in religion. They were more refined, equally industrious, but lacked the stability of character and perseverance in pursuits, of the people of the East. But at the close of the period we have been considering [1756], the peculiarities of the inhabitants of each section were greatly modified by inter-migration, and a general conformity to the necessities of their several conditions, as founders of new States in a wilderness. The tooth of religious bigotry and intolerance had lost its keenness and its poison, and when the representatives of the several colonies met in a general Congress[7] [Sept., 1774], for the public good, they stood as brethren before one altar, while the eloquent Duché laid the fervent petitions of their hearts before the throne of Omnipotence.[8]

The chief pursuit of the colonists was, necessarily, agriculture; yet, during the time we have considered, manufactures and commerce were not wholly neglected. Necessity compelled the people to make many things which their poverty would not allow them to buy; and manual labor, especially in the New England provinces, was dignified from the beginning. The settlers came where a throne and its corrupting influences were unknown, and where the idleness and privileges of aristocracy had no abiding-place. In the magnificent forests

---

[1] This is a picture of one of the oldest houses in New England, and is a favorable specimen of the best class of frame dwellings at that time. It is yet standing [1856], we believe, near Medfield, in Massachusetts. [2] Page 144. [3] Page 93. [4] Page 160. [5] Page 161. [6] Page 81. [7] Page 228. [8] Page 228.

of the New World, where a feudal lord[1] had never stood, they began a life full of youth, vigor, and labor, such as the atmosphere of the elder governments of the earth could not then sustain. They were compelled to be self-reliant, and what they could not buy from the workshops of England for their simple apparel and furniture, and implements of culture, they rudely manufactured,[2] and were content.

The commerce of the colonies had but a feeble infancy; and never, until they were politically separated from Great Britain [1776], could their interchange of commodities be properly dignified with the name of *Commerce.* England early became jealous of the independent career of the colonists in respect to manufactured articles, and navigation acts,[3] and other unwise and unjust restraints upon the expanding industry of the Americans, were brought to bear upon them. As early as 1636, a Massachusetts vessel of thirty tons made a trading voyage to the West Indies; and two years later [1638], another vessel went from Salem to New Providence, and returned with a cargo of salt, cotton, tobacco, and negroes.[4] This was the dawning of commerce in America. The eastern people also engaged quite extensively in fishing; and all were looking forward to wealth from ocean traffic, as well as that of the land, when the passage of the second Navigation Act,[5] in 1660, evinced the strange jealousy of Great Britain. From that period, the attention of Parliament was often directed to the trade and commerce of the colonies, and in 1719, the House of Commons declared "that erecting any manufactories in the colonies, tended to lessen their dependence upon Great Britain." Woolen goods, paper, hemp, and iron were manufactured in Massachusetts and other parts of New England, as early as 1732; and almost every family made coarse cloth for domestic use. Heavy duties had been imposed upon colonial iron sent to England; and the colonists, thus deprived of their market for pig iron, were induced to attempt the manufacture of steel and bar iron for their own use. It was not until almost a century [1750] afterward that the mother country perceived the folly of her policy in this respect, and admitted colonial pig iron, duty free, first into London, and soon afterward into the rest of the kingdom. Hats were manufac-

[1] Note 15, page 62.

[2] From the beginning of colonization there were shoemakers, tailors, and blacksmiths in the several colonies. Chalmers says of New England in 1673: "There be fine iron works which cast no guns; no house in New England has above twenty rooms; not twenty in Boston have ten rooms each; a dancing-school was set up here, but put down; a fencing-school is allowed. There be no musicians by trade. All cordage, sail-cloth, and mats, come from England; no cloth made there worth four shillings per yard; no alum, no copperas, no salt, made by their sun."

[3] The first Navigation Act [1651] forbade all importations into England, except in English ships, or those belonging to English colonies. In 1660, this act was confirmed, and unjust additions were made to it. The colonies were forbidden to export their chief productions to any country except to England or its dependencies. Similar acts, all bearing heavily upon colonial commerce, were made law, from time to time. See note 4, page 109.

[4] This was the first introduction of slaves into New England. The first slaves introduced into the English colonies, were those landed and sold in Virginia in 1620. [See note 6, page 105.] They were first recognized as such, by law, in Massachusetts, in 1641; in Connecticut and Rhode Island, about 1650; in New York, in 1656; in Maryland, in 1663; and in New Jersey, in 1665. There were but few slaves in Pennsylvania, and those were chiefly in Philadelphia. There were some there as early as 1690. The people of Delaware held some at about the same time. The introduction of slaves into the Carolinas was coeval with their settlement, and into Georgia about the year 1750, when the people generally evaded the prohibitory law. Page 174.

[5] Note 4, page 109.

tured and carried from one colony to the other in exchange; and at about the same time, brigantines and small sloops were built in Massachusetts and Pennsylvania, and exchanged with West India merchants for rum, sugar, wines, and silks. These movements were regarded with disfavor by the British Government, and unwisely considering the increase of manufactures in the colonies to be detrimental to English interests, greater restrictions were ordained. It was enacted that all manufactories of iron and steel in the colonies, should be considered a "common nuisance," to be abated within thirty days after notice being given, or the owner should suffer a fine of a thousand dollars.[1] The exportation of hats even from one colony to another was prohibited, and no hatter was allowed to have more than two apprentices at one time. The importation of sugar, rum, and molasses was burdened with exorbitant duties; and the Carolinians were forbidden to cut down the pine-trees of their vast forests, and convert their wood into staves, and their juice into turpentine and tar, for commercial purposes.[2] These unjust and oppressive enactments formed a part of that "bill of particulars" which the American colonies presented in their account with Great Britain, when they gave to the world their reasons for declaring themselves "free and independent States."

From the beginning, education received special attention in the colonies, particularly in New England. Schools for the education of both white and Indian children were formed in Virginia as early as 1621; and in 1692, William and Mary College was established at Williamsburg.[3] Harvard College, at Cambridge, Massachusetts, was founded in 1637. Yale College, in Connecticut, was established at Saybrook in 1701,[4] and was removed to its present location, in New Haven, in 1717. It was named in honor of Elihu Yale, president of the East India Company, and one of its most liberal benefactors. The college of New Jersey, at Princeton, called *Nassau Hall*, was incorporated in 1738;[5] and King's (now Columbia) College, in the city of New York, was foudned in 1750. The college of Philadelphia was incorporated in 1760. The college of Rhode Island (now Brown University) was established at Warren in 1764. Queen's (now Rutger's) College, in New Jersey, was founded in 1770; and Dartmouth College, at Hanover, New Hamshire, was opened in

---

[1] A law was enacted in 1750, which prohibited the "erection or contrivance of any mill or other engine for slitting or rolling iron, or any plating forge to work with a tilt hammer, or any furnace for making steel in the colonies." Such was the condition of manufactures in the United States one hundred years ago. Notwithstanding we are eminently an agricultural people, the census of 1850 shows that we have, in round numbers, $530,000,000 invested in manufactures. The value of raw material is estimated at $550,000,000. The amount paid for labor during that year, was $240,000,000, distributed among 1,050,000 operatives. The value of manufactured articles is estimated at more than a thousand millions of dollars!

[2] For a hundred years the British government attempted to confine the commerce of the colonies to the interchange of their agricultural products for English manufactures only. The trade of the growing colonies was certainly worth securing. From 1738 to 1748, the average value of exports from Great Britain to the American colonies, was almost three and a quarter millions of dollars annually.

[3] The schools previously established did not flourish, and the funds appropriated for their support were given to the college.

[4] In 1700, ten ministers of the colony met at Saybrook, and each contributed books for the establishment of a college. It was incorporated in 1701. See note 8, page 158.

[5] It was a feeble institution at first. In 1747, Governor Belcher became its patron.

1771. It will be seen that the colonies could boast of no less than nine colleges when the War for Independence commenced—three of them under the supervision of Episcopalians, three under Congregationalists, one each under Presbyterians, the Reformed Dutch Church, and the Baptists. But the pride and glory of New England have ever been its common schools. Those received the earliest and most earnest attention. In 1636, the Connecticut Legislature enacted a law which required every town that contained fifty families, to maintain a good school, and every town containing one hundred householders, to have a grammar school.[1] Similar provisions for general education soon prevailed throughout New England; and the people became remarkable for their intelligence. The rigid laws which discouraged all frivolous amusements, induced active minds, during leisure hours, to engage in reading. The subjects contained in books then in general circulation, were chiefly History and Theology, and of these a great many were sold. A traveler mentions the fact, that, as early as 1686, several booksellers in Boston had "made fortunes by their business."[2] But newspapers, the great vehicle of general intelligence to the popular mind of our day, were very few and of little worth, before the era of the Revolution.[3]

Such, in brief and general outline, were the American people, and such their political and social condition, at the commencement of the last inter-colonial war, which we are now to consider, during which they discovered their strength, the importance of a continental union, and their real independence of Great Britain.

CHAPTER XII.

THE FRENCH AND INDIAN WAR. [1756—1763.]

WE are now to consider one of the most important episodes in the history of the United States, known in Europe as the SEVEN YEARS' WAR, and in

---

[1] These townships were, in general, organized religious communities, and had many interests in common.

[2] Previous to 1753, there had been seventy booksellers in Massachusetts, two in New Hampshire, two in Connecticut, one in Rhode Island, two in New York, and seventeen in Pennsylvania.

[3] The first newspaper ever printed in America was the Boston *News Letter*, printed in 1704. The next was established in Philadelphia, in 1719. The first in New York was in 1725; in Maryland, in 1728; in South Carolina, in 1731; in Rhode Island, in 1732; in Virginia, in 1736; in New Hampshire, in 1753; in Connecticut, in 1755; in Delaware, in 1761; in North Carolina, in 1763; in Georgia, in 1763; and in New Jersey, in 1777. In 1850, there were published in the United States, 2,800 newspapers and magazines, having a circulation of 5,000,000 of copies. The number of copies printed during that whole year was about 423,000,000.

[4] We have no exact enumeration of the inhabitants of the colonies; but Mr. Bancroft, after a careful examination of many official returns and private computations, estimates the number of white people in the colonies, at the commencement of the French and Indian War, to have been about 1,165,000, distributed as follows: In New England (N. H., Mass., R. I., and Conn.), 425,000; in the middle colonies (N. Y., N. J., Penn., Del., and Md.), 457,000; and in the southern colonies (Va., N. and S. Carolina, and Geo.), 283,000. The estimated number of slaves, 260,000, of whom about 11,000 were in New England; middle colonies, 71,000; and the southern colonies, 178,000. Of the 1,165,000 white people, Dr. Franklin estimated that only about 80,000 were of foreign birth, showing the fact that emigration to America had almost ceased. At the beginning of the Revolution, in 1775, the estimated population of the thirteen colonies was 2,803,000. The documents of Congress, in 1775, gives the round number of 3,000,000.

America as the FRENCH AND INDIAN WAR. It may with propriety be considered introductory to the War for Independence, which resulted in the birth of our Republic. The first three inter-colonial wars, or the conflicts in America between the English and French colonies, already noticed,[1] originated in hostilities first declared by the two governments, and commenced in Europe. The fourth and last, which resulted in establishing the supremacy of the English in America, originated here in disputes concerning territorial claims. For a hundred years, the colonies of the two nations had been gradually expanding and increasing in importance. The English, more than a million in number, occupied the seaboard from the Penobscot to the St. Mary, a thousand miles in extent, all eastward of the great ranges of the Alleghanies, and far northward toward the St. Lawrence. The French, not more than a hundred thousand strong, made settlements along the St. Lawrence, the shores of the great lakes, on the Mississippi and its tributaries, and upon the borders of the Gulf of Mexico. They early founded Detroit [1683], Kaskaskia [1684], Vincennes [1690], and New Orleans [1717]. The English planted agricultural colonies; the French were chiefly engaged in traffic with the Indians. This trade, and the operations of the Jesuit[2] missionaries, who were usually the self-denying pioneers of commerce in its penetration of the wilderness, gave the French great influence over the tribes of a vast extent of country lying in the rear of the English settlements.[3]

France and England at that time were heirs to an ancient quarrel. Originating far back in feudal ages, and kept alive by subsequent collisions, it burned vigorously in the bosoms of the respective colonists in America, where it was continually fed by frequent hostilities on frontier ground. They had ever regarded each other with extreme jealousy, for the prize before them was supreme rule in the New World. The trading posts and missionary stations of the French, in the far north-west, and in the bosom of a dark wilderness, several hundred miles distant from the most remote settlement on the English frontier, attracted very little attention, until they formed a part of more extensive operations. But when, after the capture of Louisburg,[4] in 1745, the French adopted vigorous measures for opposing the extension of British power in America: when they built strong vessels at the foot of Lake Ontario[5]—made treaties of friendship with the Delaware[6] and Shawnee[7] tribes; strengthened Fort Niagara;[8] and erected a cordon of fortifications, more than sixty in number, between Montreal and New Orleans—the English were aroused to immediate and effective action in defense of the territorial claims given them in their ancient charters. By virtue of these, they claimed dominion westward to the Pacific Ocean, south of the latitude of the north shore of Lake Erie; while the French claimed a title to all the territory watered by the Mississippi and its tributaries, under the more plausible plea, that they had made the first explorations and settlements

---

[1] *King William's War* (page 130); *Queen Anne's War* (page 135); and *King George's War* (page 136).
[2] Note 4, page 130.
[3] Chiefly of the Algonquin nation. Page 17.
[4] Page 138.
[5] At Fort Frontenac, now Kingston, Upper Canada.
[6] Page 20.
[7] Page 19.
[8] Page 200.

in that region.[1] The claims of the real owner, the Indian, were lost sight of in the discussion.[2]

These disputes soon ended in action. The territorial question was speedily brought to an issue. In 1749, George the Second granted six hundred thousand acres of land, on the south-east bank of the Ohio River, to a company composed of London merchants and Virginia land speculators, with the exclusive privilege of traffic with the Indians. It was called *The Ohio Company.* Surveyors were soon sent to explore, and make boundaries, and prepare for settlements; and English traders went even as far as the country of the Miamies[3] to traffic with the natives. The French regarded them as intruders, and, in 1753, seized and imprisoned some of them. Apprehending the loss of traffic and influence among the Indians, and the ultimate destruction of their line of communication between Canada and Louisiana, the French commenced the erection of forts between the Alleghany River and Lake Erie, near the present western line of Pennsylvania.[4] *The Ohio Company* complained of these hostile movements; and as their grant lay within the chartered limits of Virginia, the authorities of that colony considered it their duty to interfere. Robert Dinwiddie, the lieutenant-governor, sent a letter of remonstrance to M. De St. Pierre, the French commander.[5] George Washington was chosen to be the bearer of the dispatch. He was a young man, less than twenty-two years of age, but possessed much experience of forest life. He already held the commission of adjutant-general of one of the four militia districts of Virginia. From early youth he had been engaged in land surveying, had become accustomed to the dangers and hardships of the wilderness, and was acquainted with the character of the Indians, and of the country he was called upon to traverse.

Young Washington, as events proved, was precisely the instrument needed for such a service. His mission involved much personal peril and hardship. It required the courage of the soldier, and the sagacity of the statesman, to perform the duty properly. The savage tribes through which he had to pass, were hostile to the English, and the French he was sent to meet were national enemies, wily and suspicious. With only two or three attendants,[6] Washington started from Williamsburg late in autumn [Oct. 31, 1753], and after journeying full four hundred miles (more than half the distance through a dark wilderness), encountering almost incredible hardships, amid snow, and icy floods, and hostile Indians, he reached the French outpost at Venango on the 4th of De-

---

[1] Page 180.

[2] When the agent of the Ohio Company went into the Indian country, on the borders of the Ohio River, a messenger was sent by two Indian sachems, to make the significant inquiry, "Where is the Indian's land? The English claim it all on one side of the river, the French on the other; where does the Indian's land lay?"

[3] Page 19.

[4] Twelve hundred men erected a fort on the south shore of Lake Erie, at Presque Isle, now Erie; soon afterward, another was built at Le Bœuf, on the Venango (French Creek), now the village of Waterford; and a third was erected at Venango, at the junction of French Creek and the Alleghany River, now the village of Franklin.

[5] Already the governors of Virginia and Pennsylvania had received orders from the imperial government, to repel the French by force, whenever they were "found within the undoubted limits of their province."

[6] He was afterward joined by two others at Willis Creek (now Cumberland), in Maryland.

cember. He was politely received, and his visit was made the occasion of great conviviality by the officers of the garrison. The free use of wine made the Frenchmen incautious, and they revealed to the sober Washington their hostile designs against the English, which the latter had suspected. He perceived the necessity of dispatching business, and returning to Williamsburg, as speedily as possible; so, after tarrying a day at Venango, he pushed forward to the head-quarters of St. Pierre, at Le Bœuf. That officer entertained him politely during four days, and then gave him a written answer to Dinwiddie's remonstrance, enveloped and sealed. Washington retraced his perilous pathway through the wilderness, and after an absence of eleven weeks, he again stood in the presence of Governor Dinwiddie, on the 16th of January, 1754, his mission fulfilled to the satisfaction of all. His judgment, sagacity, courage, and executive force—qualities which eminently fitted him for the more important duties as chief of the Revolutionary armies, more than twenty years afterward [1775] —were nobly developed in the performance of his mission. They were publicly acknowledged, and were never forgotten.

Already the Virginians were restive under royal rule, and at that time were complaining seriously of an obnoxious fee allowed by the Board of Trade, in the issue of patents for lands. The House of Burgesses refused, at first, to pay any attention to Dinwiddie's complaints against the French; but at length they voted fifty thousand dollars for the support of troops which had been enlisted to march into the Ohio country. The revelations made to Washington, and the tenor of St. Pierre's reply, confirmed the suspicions of Dinwiddie, and showed the wisdom of the legislative co-operation. St. Pierre said he was acting in obedience to the orders of his superior, the Marquis Du Quesne,[1] at Montreal, and refused to withdraw his troops from the disputed territory. Dinwiddie immediately prepared an expedition against the French, and solicited the co-operation of the other colonies. It was the first call for a general colonial union against a common enemy. All hesitated except North Carolina. The legislature of that colony promptly voted four hundred men, and they were soon on the march for Winchester, in Virginia. They eventually proved of little use, for becoming doubtful as to their pay, a greater part of them had disbanded before reaching Winchester. Some volunteers from South Carolina and New York, also hastened toward the seat of future war. The Virginians responded to the call, and a regiment of six hundred men was soon organized, with Colonel Joshua Fry as its commander, and Major Washington as his lieutenant. The troops rendezvoused at Alexandria, and from that city, Washington, at the head of the advanced corps, marched [April 2, 1754] toward the Ohio.

Private and public interest went hand in hand. While these military preparations were in progress, the *Ohio Company* had sent thirty men to construct a fort at the confluence of the Alleghany and Monongahela Rivers, now the site of Pittsburg. They had just commenced operations [April 18], when a party of French and Indians, under Contrecœur, attacked and expelled them, completed

[1] Pronounced Du Kane.

the fortification, and named it Du Quesne, in honor of the governor-general of Canada.[1] When intelligence of this event reached Washington on his march, he hastened forward with one hundred and fifty men, to a point on the Monongahela, less than forty miles from Fort Du Quesne. There he was informed that a strong force was marching to intercept him, and he cautiously fled back to the Great Meadows, where he erected a stockade,[2] and called it Fort Necessity.[3] Before completing it, a few of his troops attacked an advanced party of the French, under Jumonville. They were surprised at the dead of night [May 28], and the commander and nine of his men were slain. Of the fifty who formed the French detachment, only about fifteen escaped. This was the first blood-shedding of that long and eventful conflict known as the *French and Indian War*. Two days afterward [May 30], Colonel Fry died, and the whole command devolved on Washington. Troops hastened forward to join the young leader at Fort Necessity, and with about four hundred men, he proceeded toward Fort Du Quesne. M. de Villiers, brother of the slain Jumonville, had marched at about the same time, at the head of more than a thousand Indians and some Frenchmen, to avenge the death of his kinsman. Advised of his approach, Washington fell back to Fort Necessity, and there, on the 3d of July, he was attacked by almost fifteen hundred foes. After a conflict of about ten hours, de Villiers proposed an honorable capitulation.[4] Washington signed it on the morning of the 4th, and marching out of the stockade with the honors of war, departed, with his troops, for Virginia.

It was during this military campaign, that a civil movement of great importance was in progress. The English and French governments had listened to the disputes in America with interest. At length the British ministry, perceiving war to be inevitable, advised the colonies to secure the continued friendship of the SIX NATIONS,[5] and to unite in a plan for general defense. All the colonies were invited to appoint delegates to meet in convention at Albany, in the summer of 1754. Only seven responded by sending delegates.[6] The convention was organized on the 19th of June.[7] Having renewed a treaty with the Indians, the subject of colonial union was brought forward. A plan of confederation, similar to our Federal Constitution, drawn up by Dr. Franklin, was submitted.[8] It was adopted on the 4th of July, 1754, and was ordered to be laid before the several colonial Assemblies, and the imperial Board of Trade,[9]

[1] Page 182.

[2] Stockade is a general name of structures for defense, formed by driving strong posts in the ground, so as to make a safe inclosure. It is the same as a palisade. See picture on page 127.

[3] Near the national road from Cumberland to Wheeling, in the south-eastern part of Fayette county, Pennsylvania. The Great Meadows are on a fertile bottom about four miles from the foot of Laurel Hill, and fifty from Cumberland.

[4] A mutual restoration of prisoners was to take place, and the English were not to erect any establishment beyond the mountains, for the space of a year. The English troops were to march, unmolested, back to Virginia.

[5] Page 25.

[6] New Hampshire, Massachusetts, Rhode Island, Connecticut, New York, Pennsylvania, and Maryland.

[7] James Delancy, of New York was elected president. There were twenty-five delegates in all.

[8] Franklin was a delegate from Pennsylvania. The idea of union was not a new one. William Penn suggested the advantage of a union of all the English colonies as early as 1700; and Coxe, Speaker of the New Jersey Assembly, advocated it in 1722. Now it first found tangible expression under the sanction of authority.

[9] Note 5, page 134.

for ratification.[1] Its fate was singular. The Assemblies considering it too *aristocratic*—giving the royal governor too much power—refused their assent; and the Board of Trade rejected it because it was too *democratic.*[2] Although a legal union was not consummated, the grand idea of political fraternization then began to bud. It blossomed in the midst of the heat of the Stamp Act excitement eleven years later [1765], and its fruit appeared in the memorable Congress of 1774.

The convention at Albany had just closed its labors, when the Indians commenced murderous depredations upon the New England frontiers [August and September, 1754]; and among the tribes west of the Alleghanies, French emissaries were busy arousing them to engage in a war of extermination against the English. Even in full view of these menaces, some of the colonies were tardy in preparations to avert the evil. Shirley was putting forth energetic efforts in Massachusetts; New York voted twenty-five thousand dollars for military service, and Maryland thirty thousand dollars for the same. The English government sent over fifty thousand dollars for the use of the colonists, and with it a commission to Governor Sharpe of Maryland, appointing him commander-in-chief of all the colonial forces. Disputes about military rank and precedence soon ran high between the Virginia regimental officers, and the captains of independent companies. To silence these, Dinwiddie unwisely dispensed with all field officers, and broke the Virginia regiments into separate companies. This arrangement displeased Washington; he resigned his commission, and the year 1754 drew to a close without any efficient preparations for a conflict with the French.[3]

CAMPAIGN OF 1755.

Yet war had not been declared by the two nations; and for more than a year and a half longer the colonies were in conflict, before England and France formally announced hostility to each other. In the mean while the British government, perceiving that a contest, more severe than had yet been seen, must soon take place in America, extended its aid to its colonies. Edward Braddock, an Irish officer of distinction, arrived in Chesapeake Bay, with two regiments of his countrymen, on the 20th of February, 1755. He had been

---

[1] It proposed a general government to be administered by one chief magistrate, to be appointed by the crown, and a council of forty-eight members, chosen by the several legislatures. This council, answering to our Senate, was to have power to declare war, levy troops, raise money, regulate trade, conclude peace, and many other things necessary for the general good. The delegates from Connecticut alone, objected to the plan, because it gave the governor-general veto power, or the right to refuse his signature to laws ordained by the Senate, and thus prevent them becoming statutes.

[2] The Board of Trade had proposed a plan which contained all the elements of a system for the utter enslavement and dependence of the Americans. They proposed a general government, composed of the governors of the several colonies, and certain select members of the several councils. These were to have power to draw on the British Treasury for money to carry on the impending war: the sum to be reimbursed by taxes imposed upon the colonists by Parliament. The colonists preferred to do their own fighting, and levy their own taxes, independent of Great Britain.

[3] According to a return made to the Board of Trade at about this time, the population of the colonies amounted to one million four hundred and eighty-five thousand, six hundred and thirty-four. Of these, two hundred and ninety-two thousand seven hundred and thirty-eight were negroes.

appointed commander-in-chief of all the British and provincial forces in America; and at his request, six colonial governors[1] met in convention at Alexandria, in April following, to assist in making arrangements for a vigorous campaign. Three separate expeditions were planned; one against Fort du Quesne, to be led by Braddock; a second against Niagara and Frontenac (Kingston), to be commanded by Governor Shirley; and a third against Crown Point, on Lake Champlain, under General William Johnson,[2] then an influential resident among the Mohawk nation of the IROQUOIS confederacy.[3] Already a fourth expedition had been arranged by Shirley and Governor Lawrence of Nova Scotia, designed to drive the French out of that province, and other portions of ancient Acadie.[4] These extensive arrangements, sanctioned by the imperial government, awakened the most zealous patriotism of all the colonists, and the legislatures of the several provinces, except Pennsylvania and Georgia, voted men and supplies for the impending war. The Quaker Assembly of Pennsylvania was opposed to military movements; the people of Georgia were too poor to contribute.

There was much enthusiasm in New England, and the eastern expedition first proceeded to action. Three thousand men, under General John Winslow,[5] sailed from Boston on the 20th of May, 1755, and landed at the head of the Bay of Fundy. There they were joined by Colonel Monckton with three hundred British regulars[6] from the neighboring garrison, and that officer, having official precedence of Winslow, took the command. They captured the forts in possession of the French there, in June, without difficulty, and placed the whole region under martial rule.[7] This was the legitimate result of war. But the cruel sequel deserves universal reprobation. The total destruction of the French settlements was decided upon. Under the plea that the Acadians would aid their French brethren in Canada, the innocent and happy people were seized in their houses, fields, and churches, and conveyed on board the English vessels. Families were broken, never to be united; and to compel the surrender of those who fled to the woods, their starvation was insured by a total destruction of their growing crops. The Acadians were stripped of every thing, and those who were carried away, were scattered among the English colonies, helpless beggars, to die heart-broken in a strange land. In one short month, their paradise had become a desolation, and a happy people were crushed into the dust.

The western expedition, under Braddock, was long delayed on account of difficulties in obtaining provisions and wagons. The patience of the commander was sorely tried, and in moments of petulance he used expressions against the colonists, which they long remembered with bitterness. He finally commenced his march from Will's Creek (Cumberland) on the 10th of June, 1755, with about two thousand men, British and provincials. Anxious to reach Fort du

---

[1] Shirley, of *Massachusetts;* Dinwiddie, of *Virginia;* Delancey, of *New York;* Sharpe, of *Maryland;* Morris, of *Pennsylvania;* and Dobbs, of *North Carolina.* Admiral Keppel, commander of the British fleet, was also present. [2] Page 190. [3] Page 25. [4] Page 58.

[5] He was a great grandson of Edward Winslow, the third governor of Plymouth. He was a major-general in the Massachusetts militia, but on this occasion held the office of lieutenant-colonel.

[6] This term is used to denote soldiers who are attached to the regular army, and as distinguished from *volunteers* and *militia.* The latter term applies to the great body of citizens who are liable to do perpetual military duty only in time of war. [7] Note 8, page 170.

Quesne before the garrison should receive re-inforcements, he made forced marches with twelve hundred men, leaving Colonel Dunbar, his second in command, to follow with the remainder, and the wagons. Colonel Washington[1] had consented to act as Braddock's aid, and to him was given the command of the provincials. Knowing, far better than Braddock, the perils of their march and the kind of warfare they might expect, he ventured, modestly, to give advice, founded upon his experience. But the haughty general would listen to no suggestions, especially from a provincial subordinate. This obstinacy resulted in his ruin. When within ten miles of Fort du Quesne, and while marching at noon-day, on the 9th of July, in fancied security, on the south side of the Monongahela, a volley of bullets and a cloud of arrows assailed the advanced guard, under Lieutenant-Colonel Gage.[2] They came from a thicket and ravine close by, where a thousand dusky warriors lay in ambush. Again Washington asked permission to fight according to the provincial custom, but was refused. Braddock must maneuver according to European tactics, or not at all. For three hours, deadly volley after volley fell upon the British columns, while Braddock attempted to maintain order, where all was confusion. The slain soon covered the ground. Every mounted officer but Washington was killed or maimed, and finally, the really brave Braddock himself, after having several horses shot under him, was mortally wounded.[3] Washington remained unhurt.[4] Under his direction the provincials rallied, while the regulars, seeing their general fall, were fleeing in great confusion. The provincials covered their retreat so gallantly, that the enemy did not follow. A week afterward, Washington read the impressive funeral service of the Anglican Church,[5] over the corpse of Braddock, by torchlight [July 15, 1755]; and he was buried, where his grave may now [1856] be seen, near the National road, between the fifty-third and fifty-fourth mile from Cumberland, in Maryland. Colonel Dunbar received the flying troops, and marched to Philadelphia in August, with the broken companies. Washington, with the southern provincials, went back to Virginia. Thus ended the second expedition of the campaign of 1755.

FORT DU QUESNE.

GEN. BRADDOCK.

[1] Page 181.

[2] Afterward *General* Gage, commander-in-chief of the British troops at Boston, at the beginning of the Revolution. Page 226.

[3] Braddock was shot by Thomas Faucett, one of the provincial soldiers. His plea was self-preservation. Braddock had issued a positive order, that none of the English should protect themselves behind trees, as the French and Indians did. Faucett's brother had taken such position, and when Braddock perceived it, he struck him to the earth with his sword. Thomas, on seeing his brother fall, shot Braddock in the back, and then the provincials, fighting as they pleased, were saved from utter destruction.

[4] Dr. Craik, who was with Washington at this time, and also attended him in his last illness, says, that while in the Ohio country with him, fifteen years afterward, an old Indian chief came, as he said, "a long way" to see the Virginia colonel at whom he fired his rifle fifteen times during the battle on the Monongahela, without hitting him. Washington was never wounded in battle. On this occasion he had two horses shot under him, and four bullets passed through his coat. Writing of this to his brother, he remarked, "By the all-powerful dispensations of Providence, I have been protected beyond all human probability or expectation, * * * although death was leveling my companions on every side."

[5] Note 1, page 168. See picture on page 187.

BURIAL OF BRADDOCK.

The third expedition, under Governor Shirley, designed to operate against the French posts at Niagara and Frontenac, experienced less disasters, but was quite as unsuccessful. It was late in August before Shirley had collected the main body of his troops at Oswego, from whence he intended to go to Niagara by water. His force was twenty-five hundred strong on the 1st of September, yet circumstances compelled him to hesitate. The prevalence of storms, and of sickness in his camp, and, finally, the desertion of the greater part of his Indian allies,[1] made it perilous to proceed, and he relinquished the design. Leaving sufficient men to garrison the forts which he had commenced at Oswego,[2] he marched the remainder to Albany [Oct. 24], and returned to Massachusetts.

The fourth expedition, under General Johnson, prepared for attacking Crown Point,[3] accomplished more than that of Braddock[4] or Shirley, but failed to achieve its main object. In July [1755], about six thousand troops, drawn from New England, New York, and New Jersey, had assembled at the head of boat navigation on the Hudson (now the village of Fort Edward), fifty miles north of Albany. They were under the command of General Lyman,[5] of Connecticut; and before the arrival of General Johnson, in August, with cannons and stores, they had erected a strong fortification, which was afterward called Fort Edward.[6] On his arrival, Johnson took command, and with the main body of the troops, marched to the head of Lake George, about fifteen miles distant, where he established a camp, protected on both sides by an impassable swamp.

While the provincial troops were making these preparations, General the Baron Dieskau (a French officer of much repute), with about two thousand men, chiefly Canadian militia and Indians, was approaching from Montreal, by way of Lake Champlain, to meet the English.[7] When Johnson arrived at Lake George, on the 7th of September, Indian scouts informed him that Dieskau was disembarking at the head of Lake Champlain (now the village of

---

[1] Tribes of the SIX NATIONS [page 25], and some Stockbridge Indians. The latter were called Housatonics, from the river on which they were found. They were a division of the Mohegan [page 21] tribe.

[2] Fort Ontario on the east, and Fort Pepperell on the west of Oswego River. Fort Pepperell was afterward called Fort Oswego. See map, page 192. The house was built of stone, and the walls were three feet thick. It was within a square inclosure composed of a thick wall, and two strong square towers.

[3] Upon this tongue of land on Lake Champlain, the French erected a fortification, which they called Fort St. Frederick. On the Vermont side of the lake, opposite, there was a French settlement as early as 1731. In allusion to the chimnies of their houses, which remained long after the settlement was destroyed, it is still known as Chimney Point.

[4] Page 185.

[5] Born in Durham, Connecticut, in the year 1716. He was a graduate of Yale College, and became a lawyer. He was a member of the colonial Assembly in 1750, and performed important services during the whole war that soon afterward ensued. He commanded the expedition that captured Havana in 1762; and at the peace, in 1763, he became concerned in lands in the Mississippi region. He died in Florida in 1775.

[6] It was first called Fort Lyman. Johnson, meanly jealous of General Lyman, changed the name to Fort Edward.

[7] Dieskau and his French troops, on their way from France, narrowly escaped capture by Admiral Boscawen, who was cruising, with an English fleet, off Newfoundland. They eluded his fleet during a fog, and went in safety up the St. Lawrence.

Whitehall), preparatory to marching against Fort Edward. The next scouts brought Johnson the intelligence that Dieskau's Indians, terrified by the English cannons when they approached Fort Edward, had induced him to change his plans, and that he was marching to attack his camp. Colonel Ephraim Williams, of Deerfield, Massachusetts, was immediately sent [Sept. 8], with a thousand troops from that colony, and two hundred Mohawks,[1] under the famous chief, Hendrick, to intercept the enemy. They met in a narrow defile, four miles from Lake George. The English suddenly fell into an ambuscade. Williams and Hendrick were both killed,[2] and their followers fell back in great confusion, upon Johnson's camp, hotly pursued by the victors. One of the Massachusetts regiments, which fought bravely in this action, was commanded by Timothy Ruggles, who was president of the Stamp Act Congress,[3] held at New York in 1765, but who, when the Revolution broke out, was active on the side of the Crown.

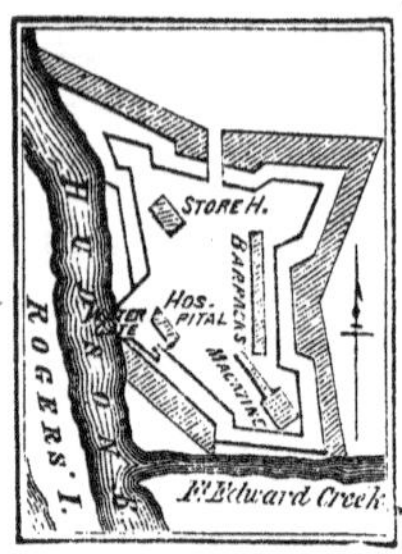

FORT EDWARD.

The commander-in-chief was assured of the disaster before the flying fugitives made their appearance. He immediately cast up a breastwork of logs and limbs, placed upon it two cannons which he had received from Fort Edward two days before, and when the enemy came rushing on, close upon the heels of the English, he was prepared to receive them. The fugitives had just reached Johnson's camp when Dieskau and his flushed victors appeared. Unsuspicious of heavy guns upon so rude a pile as Johnson's battery exhibited, they rushed forward, with sword, pike, and tomahawk, and made a spirited attack. One volley from the English cannons made the Indians flee in terror to the shelter of the deep forests around. The Canadian militia also fled, as General Lyman and a body of troops approached from Fort Edward; and, finally, the French troops, after continuing the conflict several hours, and losing their commander,[4] withdrew, and hastened to Crown Point. Their baggage was captured by some New Hampshire troops from Fort Edward, and the defeat was complete.

SIR WILLIAM JOHNSON.

General Johnson erected a fortification on the site of his camp, at the head of the lake, and called it Fort William Henry. It was constructed under the direction of Richard Gridley, who commanded the artillery in the siege of Louisburg, ten years before.[5] Being informed that the French were strength-

---

[1] Page 23.

[2] While on his way north, Williams stopped at Albany, made his will, and bequeathed certain property to found a free school for western Massachusetts. That was the foundation of "Williams' College"—his best monument. The rock near which his body was found, on the right side of the road from Glenn's Falls to Lake George, still bears his name; and a collection of water on the battle-ground, is called *Bloody Pond.*

[3] Page 215.

[4] Dieskau was found mortally wounded, carried into the English camp, and there tenderly treated. He was afterward conveyed to New York, from whence he sailed to England, where he died.

[5] Note 1, page 137.

ening their works at Crown Point, and were fortifying Ticonderoga,[1] he thought it prudent to cease offensive operations. He garrisoned Fort Edward and Fort William Henry, returned to Albany, and as the season was advanced [October, 1755], he dispersed the remainder of his troops. For his services in this campaign, the king conferred the honor of knighthood upon him, and gave him twenty-five thousand dollars with which to support the dignity. This honor and emolument properly belonged to General Lyman, the real hero of the campaign.[2] Johnson had Sir Peter Warren and other friends at court, and so won the unmerited prize.

FORT WILLIAM HENRY.

CAMPAIGN OF 1756.

The home governments now took up the quarrel. The campaign of 1755, having assumed all the essential features of regular war, and there appearing no prospect of reconciliation of the belligerents, England formally proclaimed hostilities against France, on the 17th of May, 1756, and the latter soon afterward [June 9] reciprocrated the action. Governor Shirley, who had become commander-in chief, after the death of Braddock, was superseded by General Abercrombie[3] in the spring of 1756. He came as the lieutenant of Lord Loudon, whom the king had appointed to the chief command in America, and also governor of Virginia. Loudon was an indolent man, and a remarkable procrastinater, and the active general-in-chief was Abercrombie, who, also, was not remarkable for his skill and forethought as a commander. He arrived with several British regiments early in June. The plan of the campaign for that year had already been arranged by a convention of colonial governors held at Albany early in the season. Ten thousand men were to attack Crown Point;[4] six thousand were to proceed against Niagara;[5] three thousand against Fort du Quesne;[6] and two thousand were to cross the country from the Kennebec, to attack the French settlements on the Chaudiere River.

ABERCROMBIE.

The command of the expedition against Crown Point was intrusted to General Winslow,[7] who had collected seven thousand men at Albany, when Aber-

[1] Page 196.

[2] Lyman urged Johnson to pursue the French, and assail Crown Point. The Mohawks burned for an opportunity to avenge the death of Hendrick. But Johnson preferred ease and safety, and spent the autumn in constructing Fort William Henry. He meanly withheld all praise from Lyman, in his dispatches to government. Johnson was born in Ireland, in 1714. He came to America to take charge of the lands of his uncle, Admiral Warren [page 137], on the Mohawk River, and gained great influence over the Indians of New York. He died at his seat (now the village of Johnstown) in the Mohawk valley, in 1774.

[3] A strong party in England, irritated by the failures of the campaign of 1755, cast the blame of Braddock's defeat and other disasters, upon the Americans, and finally procured the recall of Shirley. He completely vindicated his character, and was afterward appointed governor of the Bahama Islands.

[4] Page 200.

[5] Page 200.

[6] Page 186.

[7] Page 185.

crombie arrived. Difficulties immediately occurred, respecting military rank, and caused delay. They were not adjusted when the tardy Loudon arrived, at midsummer; and his arrogant assumption of superior rank for the royal officers, increased the irritation and discontent of the provincial troops. When these matters were finally adjusted, in August, the French had gained such positive advantages, that the whole plan of the campaign was disconcerted.

Baron Dieskau[1] was succeeded by the Marquis de Montcalm, in the command of the French troops in Canada. Perceiving the delay of the English, and knowing that a large number of their troops was at Albany, short of provisions, and suffering from small-pox, and counting wisely upon the inefficiency of their commander-in-chief, he collected about five thousand Frenchmen, Canadians, and Indians, at Frontenac,[2] and crossing Lake Ontario, landed, with thirty pieces of cannon, a few miles east of Oswego. Two days afterward, he appeared before Fort Ontario [Aug. 11, 1756], on the east side of the river, then in command of Colonel Mercer. After a short but brave resistance, the garrison abandoned the fort [Aug. 12], and withdrew to an older fortification, on the west side of the river.[3] Their commander was killed, and they were soon obliged to surrender themselves [Aug. 14] prisoners of war. The spoils of victory for Montcalm, were fourteen hundred prisoners, a large amount of military stores, consisting of small arms, ammunition, and provisions; one hundred and thirty-four pieces of cannon, and several vessels, large and small, in the harbor. After securing them, he demolished the forts,[4] and returned to Canada. The whole country of the SIX NATIONS was now laid open to the incursions of the French.

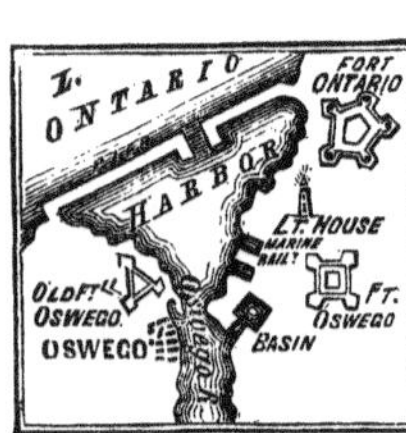

FORTS AT OSWEGO.

The loss of Oswego was a severe blow to the English. When intelligence of that event reached Loudon, he recalled the troops then on their way toward Lake Champlain; and all the other expeditions were abandoned. Forts William Henry[5] and Edward[6] were strengthened; fifteen hundred volunteers and drafted militia, under Washington, were placed in stockades[7] for the defense of the Pennsylvania and Virginia frontiers; and on the western borders of the Carolinas several military posts were established as a protection against the

BLOCK HOUSE.

[1] Page 189. [2] Note 5, page 180.

[3] A palisaded block-house, built by order of Governor Burnet in 1727, near the spot where Fort Pepperell was erected. A redoubt or block-house is a fortified building, of peculiar construction, well calculated for defense. They were generally built of logs, in the form represented in the engraving. They were usually two stories, with narrow openings through which to fire muskets from within. They were sometimes prepared with openings for cannons.

[4] This was to please the SIX NATIONS, who had never felt contented with this supporter of power in their midst. The demolition of these forts, induced the Indians to assume an attitude of neutrality, by a solemn treaty.

[5] Page 191. It commanded a view of the lake from its head to the Narrows, fifteen miles.

[6] Page 190. The Hudson is divided at Fort Edward, into two channels, by Roger's Island, upon which the provincial troops out of the fort, usually encamped. [7] Note 2, page 183.

Cherokees[1] and Creeks,[2] whom French emissaries were exciting to hostilities against the English. Hitherto, since the commencement of hostilities, some of the colonial Assemblies had been slow to make appropriations for the support of the war. Pennsylvania and South Carolina, actuated by different motives, had held back, but now the former made an appropriation of thirty thousand pounds, to be issued in paper, and the latter granted four thousand pounds toward enlisting two companies for the public service.

The most important achievement of the provincials during that year, was the chastisement of the Indians at Kittaning, their chief town, situated on the Alleghany River. During several months they had spread terror and desolation along the western frontiers of Pennsylvania and Virginia, and almost a thousand white people had been murdered or carried into captivity. These acts aroused the people of Pennsylvania, and Dr. Franklin undertook the military command of the frontier, with the rank of colonel. His troops were voluntary militia. Under his directions, a chain of forts and blockhouses was erected along the base of the Kittaning mountains, from the Delaware to the Maryland line. Franklin soon perceived that he was not in his right place, and he abandoned military life forever. The Indians continuing their depredations, Colonel John Armstrong of Pennsylvania,[3] accompanied by Captain Mercer[4] of Virginia, with about three hundred men, attacked them on the night of the 8th of September [1756], killed their principal chiefs, destroyed their town, and completely humbled them. Thus ended the campaign of 1756. The French still held in possession almost all of the territory in dispute, and of the most important of their military posts. They had also expelled the English from Oswego and Lake George, and had compelled the powerful SIX NATIONS to make a treaty of neutrality. On the whole, the campaign of 1756 closed with advantages on the part of the French.

CAMPAIGN OF 1757.

A military council was held at Boston on the 19th of January, 1757, when Lord Loudon proposed to confine the operations of that year to an expedition against Louisburg,[5] and to the defense of the frontiers. Because he was commander-in-chief, wiser and better men acquiesced in his plans, but deplored his want of judgment and executive force. The people of New England, in particular, were greatly disappointed when they ascertained that the execution of their favorite scheme of driving the French from Lake Champlain was to be deferred. However, the general ardor of the colonists was not abated, and the call for troops was so promptly responded to, that Loudon found himself at the head of six thousand provincials on the first of June. The capture of Louisburg was Loudon's first care. He sailed from New York on the 20th of that month, and on arriving at Halifax ten days afterward [June 30], he was joined

[1] Page 27. [2] Page 30.
[3] He was a general in the war for Independence, twenty years later. See note 1, page 249.
[4] Page 269. [5] Page 137.

by Admiral Holborne, with a powerful naval armament and five thousand land troops, from England. They were about to proceed to Cape Breton,[1] when they were informed that six thousand troops were in the fortress at Louisburg,[2] and that a French fleet, larger than Holborne's, was lying in that harbor. The latter had arrived and taken position while Loudon was moving slowly, with his characteristic indecision. The enterprise was abandoned, and Loudon returned to New York [Aug. 31], to hear of defeat and disgrace on the northern frontier, the result of his ignorance and utter unskillfulness.

Montcalm had again borne away important trophies of victory. Toward the close of July, he left Ticonderoga with about nine thousand men (of whom two thousand were Indians), and proceeded to besiege Fort William Henry, at the head of Lake George.[3] The garrison of three thousand men was commanded by Colonel Monro, a brave English officer, who felt strengthened in his position by the close proximity of his chief, General Webb, who was at the head of four thousand troops at Fort Edward,[4] only fifteen miles distant. But his confidence in his commanding general was sadly misplaced. When Montcalm demanded a surrender of the fort and garrison [August 3, 1757], Monro boldly refused, and sent an express to General Webb, for aid. It was not furnished. For six days Montcalm continued the siege, and expresses were sent daily to Webb for reinforcements, but in vain. Even when General Johnson,[5] with a corps of provincials and Putnam's Rangers,[6] had, on reluctant permission, marched several miles in the direction of the beleaguered fort, Webb recalled them, and sent a letter to Monro, advising him to surrender. That letter was intercepted by Montcalm,[7] and with a peremptory demand for capitulation, he sent it to Monro. Perceiving further resistance to be useless, Monro yielded. Montcalm was so pleased with the bravery displayed by the garrison, that he agreed upon very honorable terms of surrender, and promised the troops a safe escort to Fort Edward. His Indians, expecting blood and booty, were enraged by the merciful terms, and at the moment when the English entered the forests, a mile from Fort William Henry, the savages fell upon them with great fury, slaughtered a large number, plundered their baggage, and pursued them to within cannon shot of Fort Edward. Montcalm declared his inability to restrain the Indians, and expressed his deep sorrow. The fort and all its appendages were burned or otherwise destroyed.[8] It was never rebuilt; and until 1854, nothing marked

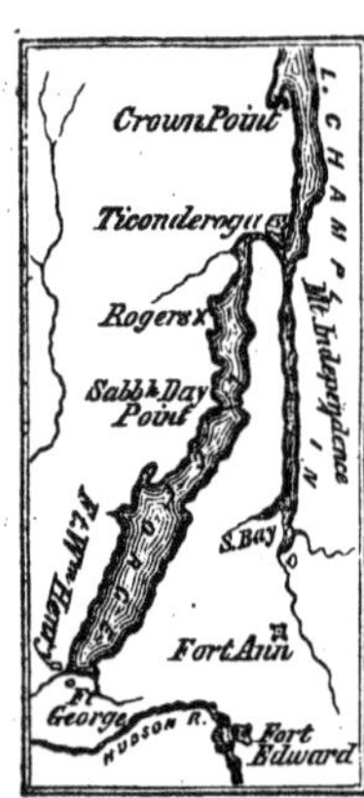

LAKE GEORGE AND VICINITY.

[1] Note 5, page 137. [2] Page 137. [3] Page 191. [4] Page 190. [5] Page 190.

[6] Israel Putnam, afterward a major-general in the army of the Revolution. He now held the commission of major, and with Major Rogers and his rangers, performed important services during the whole French and Indian War.

[7] It is said that Montcalm was just on the point of raising the siege and returning to Ticonderoga, when Webb's cowardly letter fell into his hands. The number and strength of Johnson's troops had been greatly exaggerated, and Montcalm was preparing to flee.

[8] Major Putnam visited the ruins while the fires were yet burning, and he described the scene as very appalling. The bodies of murdered Englishmen were scattered in every direction, some of

its site but an irregular line of low mounds on the border of the lake, a short distance from the village of Caldwell. Since then a hotel has been erected upon the spot, for the accommodation of summer tourists. Thus ended the military operations of the inefficient Earl of Loudon, for the year 1757.

The position of affairs in America now alarmed the English people. The result of the war, thus far, was humiliating to British pride, while it incited the French to greater efforts in the maintenance of their power in the West. In the Anglo-American[1] colonies there was much irritation. Thoroughly imbued with democratic ideas, and knowing their competency, unaided by royal troops, to assert and maintain their rights, they regarded the interferences of the home government as clogs upon their operations. Some of the royal governors were incompetent and rapacious, and all were marked by a haughty deportment, offensive to the sturdy democracy of the colonists. Their *demands* for men and money, did not always meet with cheerful and ample responses; and the arrogant assumption of the English officers, disgusted the commanders of the provincial troops, and often cooled the zeal of whole battalions of brave Americans. Untrammeled by the orders, exactions, and control of imperial power, the Americans would probably have settled the whole matter in a single campaign; but at the close of the second year of the war [1756] the result appeared more uncertain and remote than ever. The people of England had perceived this clearly, and clamored for the dismissal of the weak and corrupt ministry then in power. The popular will prevailed, and William Pitt, by far the ablest statesman England had yet produced, was called to the control of public affairs in June, 1757. Energy and good judgment marked every movement of his administration, especially in measures for prosecuting the war in America. Lord Loudon was recalled,[2] and General Abercrombie[3] was appointed to succeed him. A strong naval armament was prepared and placed under the command of Admiral Boscawen; and twelve thousand additional English troops were allotted to the service in America.[4] Pitt addressed a letter to the several colonies, asking them to raise and clothe twenty thousand men. He promised, in the name of Parliament, to furnish arms, tents, and provisions for them; and also to reimburse the several colonies all the money they should expend in raising and clothing the levies. These liberal offers had a magical effect, and an excess of levies soon appeared. New England alone raised fifteen thousand men;[5] New York furnished almost twenty-seven hundred, New Jersey one

---

them half consumed among the embers of the conflagration. Among the dead were more than one hundred women, many of whom had been scalped [note 4, page 14] by the Indians.

[1] This is the title given to Americans who are of English descent. Those who are descendants of the Saxons who settled in England, are called Anglo-Saxons.

[2] Pitt gave as a chief reason for recalling Loudon, that he could never hear from him, and did not know what he was about. Loudon was always arranging great plans, but executed nothing. It was remarked to Dr. Franklin, when he made inquiries concerning him, that he was "like St. George on the signs—always on horseback, but never rides forward."

[3] Page 191.

[4] Pitt had arranged such an admirable militia system for home defense, that a large number of the troops of the standing army could be spared for foreign service.

[5] Public and private advances during 1758, in Massachusetts alone, amounted to more than a million of dollars. The taxes on real estate, in order to raise money, were enormous; in many instances equal to two thirds of the income of the tax-payers. Yet it was levied *by their own representatives*, and they did not murmur. A few years later, an almost nominal tax in the form of duty

thousand, Pennsylvania almost three thousand, and Virginia over two thousand. Some came from other colonies. Royal American troops (as they were called) organized in the Carolinas, were ordered to the North ; and when Abercrombie took command of the army in the month of May, 1758, he found fifty thousand men at his disposal; a number greater than the whole male population of the French dominions in America, at that time.[1]

CAMPAIGN OF 1758.

The plan of the campaign of 1758, was comprehensive. Louisburg,[2] Ticonderoga, and Fort du Quesne,[3] were the principal points of operations pecified in it. This was a renewal of Shirley's scheme, and ample preparations were made to carry it out. The first blow was directed against Louisburg. Admiral Boscawen arrived at Halifax early in May, with about forty armed vessels bearing a land force of over twelve thousand men, under General Amherst[4] as chief, and General Wolfe[5] as his lieutenant. They left Halifax on the 28th of May, and on the 8th of June, the troops landed, without much opposition, on the shore of Gabarus Bay, near the city of Louisburg.[6] The French, alarmed by this demonstration of power, almost immediately deserted their outposts, and retired within the town and fortress. After a vigorous resistance of almost fifty days, and when all their shipping in the harbor was destroyed, the French surrendered the town and fort, together with the island of Cape Breton and that of St. John (now Prince Edward), and their dependencies, by capitulation, on the 26th of July, 1758. The spoils of victory were more than five thousand prisoners, and a large quantity of munitions of war. By this victory, the English became masters of the coast almost to the mouth of the St. Lawrence. When Louisburg fell, the power of France in America began to wane, and from that time its decline was continual and rapid.

LORD AMHERST.

Activity now prevailed everywhere. While Amherst and Wolfe were conquering in the East, Abercrombie and young Howe were leading seven thousand regulars, nine thousand provincials, and a heavy train of artillery, against Ticonderoga, then occupied by Montcalm with about four thousand men. Abercrombie's army had rendezvoused at the head of Lake George, and at the close of a calm Sabbath evening [July, 1758] they went down that beautiful sheet of water in flat-boats, and at dawn

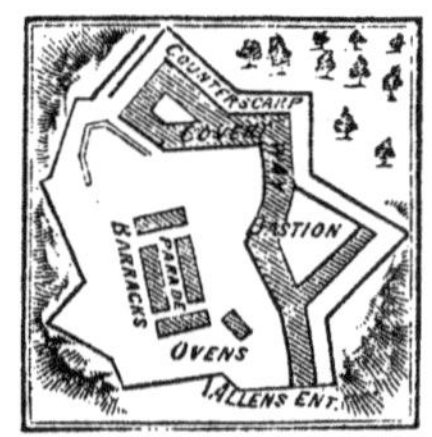

TICONDEROGA.

upon an article of luxury, levied *without their consent*, excited the people of that colony to rebellion. See page 169.

[1] The total number of inhabitants in Canada, then capable of bearing arms, did not exceed twenty thousand. Of them, between four and five thousand were regular troops.

[2] Page 229.

[3] Page 186.

[4] Lord Jeffrey Amherst was born in Kent, England, in 1717. He was commander-in-chief of the army in England, during a part of our war for independence, and afterward He died in 1797, aged eighty years.

[5] Note 8, page 200.

[6] Note 5, page 137.

LORD HOWE.

[July 6] landed at its northern extremity. The whole country from there to Ticonderoga was then covered with a dense forest, and tangled morasses lay in the pathway of the English army. Led by incompetent guides, they were soon bewildered, and while in this condition, they were suddenly attacked by a French scouting party. The enemy was repulsed, but the victory was at the expense of the life of Lord Howe.[1] He fell at the head of the advanced guard, and a greater part of the troops, who considered him the soul of the expedition, retreated in confusion to the landing-place.

In the midst of the temporary confusion incident to the death of Howe, intelligence reached Abercrombie that a reinforcement for Montcalm was approaching. Deceived concerning the strength of the French lines across the neck of the peninsula on which the fortress stood,[2] he pressed forward to the attack without his artillery, and ordered his troops to scale the breastworks [July 8], in the face of the enemy's fire. These proved much stronger than he anticipated,[3] and after a bloody conflict of four hours, Abercrombie fell back to Lake George, leaving almost two thousand of his men dead or wounded, in the deep forest.[4] He hastened to his former camp at the head of the lake, and then, on the urgent solicitation of Colonel Bradstreet, he detached three thousand men under that officer, to attack the French post at Frontenac.[5] They went by way of Oswego

RUINS OF TICONDEROGA.

---

[1] Lord Howe was brother of Admiral Lord Howe, who commanded the British fleet on the American coast, in 1776–77, and of Sir William Howe, the commander of the land forces. He was greatly beloved by the troops; and Mante, who was in the service, remarks: "With him the soul of the expedition seemed to expire." He was only thirty-four years of age when he fell. The legislature of Massachusetts Bay appropriated one thousand two hundred and fifty dollars for a monument to his memory, in Westminster Abbey. His remains were conveyed to Albany by Captain (afterward General) Philip Schuyler, and there placed in a vault belonging to the family of that officer. They were afterward removed to a place under the chancel of St. Peter's Church, on State-street, Albany, where they remain. At the time of their removal, it was found that Lord Howe's hair, which was very short when he was killed, had grown several inches, and exhibited beautiful smooth and glossy locks.

[2] The diagram (p. 196) shows the general form of the principal works. The ground on which Ticonderoga stood is about one hundred feet above the level of the lake. Water is upon three sides, and a deep morass extends almost across the fourth, forming a narrow neck, where the French had erected a strong line of breastworks with batteries. This line was about a mile north-west of the fortress, which occupied the point of the peninsula. The ruins of the fort, delineated in the above sketch, are yet [1856] quite picturesque.

[3] The breastworks were nine feet in height, covered in front by sharpened branches of felled trees, pointing outward like a mass of bayonets.

[4] Among the wounded was Captain Charles Lee, afterward a general in the army of the Revolution. See note 4, page 248.

[5] Page 180.

and Lake Ontario, and two days after landing [August 27, 1758], they captured the fort, garrison, and shipping, without much resistance.[1] Bradstreet lost only three or four men in the conflict, but a fearful sickness broke out in his camp, and destroyed about five hundred of them. With the remainder, he slowly retraced his steps, and at the carrying-place on the Mohawk, where the village of Rome now stands, his troops assisted in building Fort Stanwix.[2] Abercrombie, in the mean while, after garrisoning Fort George,[3] returned with the remainder of his troops to Albany.

The expedition against Fort du Quesne,[4] in the West, was commanded by General John Forbes, who, in July, had about nine thousand men at his disposal, at Fort Cumberland and Raystown, including the Virginia troops under Colonel Washington, the Carolina Royal Americans, and an auxiliary force of Cherokee Indians. Protracted sickness, and perversity of will and judgment on the part of Forbes, caused delays almost fatal to the expedition. Contrary to the advice of Washington, he insisted, under the advice of some Pennsylvania land speculators, in constructing a new road, further north, over the mountains, instead of following the one made by Braddock. His progress was so slow, that in September, when it was known that not more than eight hundred men were at Fort du Quesne,[5] Forbes, with six thousand troops, was yet east of the Alleghanies. Major Grant, at the head of a scouting party of Colonel Boquet's advanced corps, was attacked [Sept. 21], defeated, and made prisoner. Still Forbes moved slowly and methodically, and it was November [Nov. 8] before he joined Boquet with the main body, fifty miles from the point of destination. The approach of winter, and discontent of the troops, caused a council of war to decide upon abandoning the enterprise, when three prisoners gave information of the extreme weakness of the French garrison. Washington was immediately sent forward, and the whole army prepared to follow. Indian scouts discovered the Virginians when they were within a day's march of the fort, and their fear greatly magnified the number of the provincials. The French garrison, reduced to five hundred men, set fire to the fort [Nov. 24], and fled down the Ohio in boats, in great confusion, leaving every thing behind them. The Virginians took possession the following day. Forbes left a detachment of four hundred and fifty men, to repair and garrison the fort, and then hastened back to go into winter quarters. The name of Fort *du Quesne* was changed to Fort *Pitt*, in honor of the great English statesman.[6]

---

[1] They made eight hundred prisoners, and seized nine armed vessels, sixty cannons, sixteen mortars, a large quantity of ammunition and stores, and goods designed for traffic with the Indians. Among Bradstreet's subalterns, was Nathaniel Woodhull, afterward a general at the commencement of the war for Independence. [See note 3, page 252.] Stark, Ward, Pomeroy, Gridley, Putnam, Schuyler, and many others who were distinguished in the Revolutionary struggle, were active participants in the scenes of the French and Indian War.

[2] Page 278.

[3] Fort George was erected about a mile south-east of the ruins of Fort William Henry, at the head of Lake George. The ruins of the main work, or citadel, are still [1856] quite prominent.

[4] Page 186.

[5] The capture of Fort Frontenac spread alarm among the French west of that important post, because their supplies from Canada were cut off. It so affected the Indians with fear, that a greater part of those who were allied to the French, deserted them, and Fort du Quesne was feebly garrisoned.

[6] Page 195.

With this event, closed the campaign of 1758, which resulted in great gain to the English. They had effectually humbled the French, by capturing three of their most important posts,[1] and by weakening the attachment of their Indian allies. Many of the Indians had not only deserted the French, but at a great council held at Easton, on the Delaware, during the summer of that year they had, with the SIX NATIONS,[2] made treaties of friendship or neutrality with the English.[3] The right arm of French success was thus paralyzed, and peace was restored to the frontiers of Pennsylvania and Virginia.

CAMPAIGN OF 1759.

Four years had elapsed since the commencement of this inter-colonial war. The final struggle was now at hand. Encouraged by the success of the campaigns just closed, Pitt conceived the magnificent scheme of conquering all Canada, and destroying, at one blow, the French dominion in America. That dominion was now confined to the region of the St. Lawrence, for more distant settlements in the west and south, were like weak colonies cut off from the parent country. Pitt had the rare fortune to possess the entire confidence and esteem of the Parliament and the colonists. The former was dazzled by his greatness; the latter were deeply impressed with his justice. He had promptly reimbursed all the expenses incurred by the provincial Assemblies during the campaign,[4] amounting to almost a million of dollars, and they as promptly seconded his scheme of conquest, which had been communicated to them under an oath of secresy. The unsuccessful Abercrombie[5] was succeeded by the successful Amherst,[6] and early in the spring of 1759, the new commander-in-chief found twenty thousand provincial troops at his disposal. A competent land and naval force was also sent from England to co-operate with the Americans, and the campaign opened with brilliant prospects for the colonies. The general plan of operations against Canada was similar to that of Phipps and Winthrop in 1690.[7] A strong land and naval force, under General Wolfe, was to ascend the St. Lawrence, and attack Quebec. Another force, under Amherst, was to drive the French from Lake Champlain, seize Montreal, and join Wolfe at Quebec; and a third expedition, commanded by General Prideaux, was to capture Fort Niagara, and then hasten down Lake Ontario to Montreal.

On the 22d of July, 1759, General Amherst appeared before Ticonderoga with eleven thousand men. The French commander had just heard of the arrival of Wolfe at Quebec [June 27], and offered no resistance. The garrison left the lines on the 23d of July, and retired within the fort, and three days afterward [July 26] they abandoned that also, partially demolished it, and fled to Crown Point. Amherst pursued them, and on his approach, they took to their boats [Aug. 1], and went down the lake to Isle Aux Noix,[8] in the Sorel

---

[1] Louisburg, Frontenac, and Du Quesne. Others, except Quebec, were stockades. Note 2, page 183.

[2] Page 25.

[3] The chief tribes represented, were the Delawares, Shawnees, Nanticokes, Mohegans, Conoys, and Monseys. The Twightwees, on the Ohio [page 19], had always remained the friends of the English.

[4] Page 195.

[5] Page 191.

[6] Page 196.

[7] Page 131.

[8] Pronounced *O Noo-ah.*

River. Amherst remained at Crown Point long enough to construct a sufficient number of rude boats to convey his troops, artillery, and baggage, and then started to drive his enemy before him, across the St. Lawrence. It was now mid-autumn [Oct. 11], and heavy storms compelled him to return to Crown Point, and place his troops in winter quarters.[1] While there, they constructed that strong fortress, whose picturesque ruins, after the lapse of almost a hundred years, yet [1856] attest its strength.

CROWN POINT.[2]

Accompanied by Sir William Johnson, as his lieutenant, Prideaux collected his forces (chiefly provincials)[3] at Oswego, and sailed from thence to Niagara. He landed without opposition, on the 17th of July, and immediately commenced the siege. On the same day he was killed, by the bursting of a gun, and was succeeded in command by General Johnson. The beleaguered garrison, in daily expectation of reinforcements which had been ordered from the southern and western forts, held out bravely for three weeks, when, on the 24th of July, the expected troops appeared. They were almost three thousand strong, one half being French regulars, and the remainder Indians, many of them from the Creek[4] and Cherokee[5] nations. A severe conflict ensued. The relief forces were completely routed, and on the following day [July 25], Fort Niagara and its dependencies, and the garrison of seven hundred men, were surrendered to Johnson. The connecting link of French military posts between Canada and Louisiana[6] was effectually broken, never again to be united. Encumbered with his prisoners, and unable to procure a sufficient number of vessels for the purpose, Johnson could not proceed to Montreal, to co-operate with Amherst and Wolfe on the St. Lawrence, according to the original plan.[7] He garrisoned Fort Niagara, and returned home.

FORT NIAGARA.

Animated with high hopes, Wolfe[8] left Louisburg, with eight thousand troops, under a convoy of twenty-two line-of-battle ships, and as many frigates

[1] While at Crown Point, Major Rogers, at the head of his celebrated Rangers, went on an expedition against the St. Francis Indians, who had long been a terror to the frontier settlements of New England. The village was destroyed, a large number of Indians were slain, and the Rangers were completely victorious. They suffered from cold and hunger while on their return, and many were left dead in the forest before the party reached the nearest settlement at Bellows Falls. Rogers went to England after the war, returned in 1775, joined the British army at New York, and soon went to England again, where he died.

[2] The above diagram shows the general form of the military works at Crown Point. These, like the ruins at Ticonderoga, are quite picturesque remains of the past. A A A shows the position of the strong stone barracks, portions of which are yet standing. W shows the place of a very deep well, dug through the solid rock. It was filled up, and so remained until a few years ago, when some money-diggers, foolishly believing there was treasure at the bottom, cleaned it out. They found nothing but a few scraps of iron and other rubbish.

[3] Johnson's influence over the Six Nations, made many of them disregard the treaty of neutrality made with Montcalm [note 4, page 192], and a considerable number accompanied him to Niagara. [4] Page 30. [5] Page 27. [6] Page 180. [7] Page 199.

[8] James Wolfe was the son of a British general, and was born in Kent, England, in 1726. Before he was twenty years of age, he was distinguished in battle. He was now only thirty-three years old.

and smaller armed vessels, commanded by Admirals Holmes and Saunders, and, on the 27th of June, landed upon Orleans Island, a few miles below Quebec. That city then, as now, consisted of an Upper and Lower Town, the former within fortified walls, upon the top and declivities of a high peninsula; the latter lying upon a narrow beach at the edge of the water. Upon the heights, three hundred feet above the water, was a level plateau called the *Plains of Abraham*. At the mouth of the St. Charles, which here enters the St. Lawrence, the French had moored several floating batteries.[1] The town was strongly garrisoned by French regulars, and along the north bank of the St. Lawrence, from the St. Charles to the Montmorenci River, was the main French army, under Montcalm,[2] in a fortified camp. It was composed chiefly of Canadian militia and Indians.

GENERAL WOLFE.

On the 30th of July, the English, after a slight skirmish, took possession of Point Levi, opposite Quebec, and throwing hot shot from a battery, they almost destroyed the Lower Town. They could not damage the strong fortifications of the city from that distance, and Wolfe resolved to attack the French camp. He had already landed a large force, under Generals Townshend and Murray, and formed a camp [July 10, 1759], below the River Montmorenci. General Monckton, with grenadiers[3] and other troops, crossed from Point Levi, and landed upon the beach [July 31], at the base of the high river bank, just above that stream. Murray and Townshend were ordered to force a passage across the Montmorenci, and co-operate with him, but Monckton was too eager for attack to await their coming. He unwisely rushed forward, but was soon repulsed, and compelled to take shelter behind a block-house[4] near the beach, just as a heavy thunder-storm, which had been gathering for several hours, burst upon the combatants. Night came on before it ceased, and the roar of the rising tide warned the English to take to their boats. Five hundred of their number had perished.

MILITARY OPERATIONS AT QUEBEC.

Two months elapsed, and yet the English had gained no important advantages. Wolfe had received no intelligence from Amherst, and the future ap-

---

[1] These were a kind of flat-boats, with proper breastworks or other defenses, and armed with cannons.

[2] He was descended from a noble family. He was appointed governor of Canada in 1756. His remains are beneath the Ursuline convent at Quebec.

[3] Grenadiers are companies of the regular army, distinguished from the rest by some peculiarity of dress and accoutrements, and always composed of the tallest and most muscular men in the service. They are generally employed in bayonet charges, and sometimes carry grenades, a kind of small bomb-shell.

[4] Note 3, page 192.

peared gloomy. The exposure, fatigue, and anxiety which he had endured produced a violent fever, and at the beginning of September [1759], he lay prostrate in his tent. He called a council of war at his bedside, and, on the suggestion of Townshend, it was resolved to scale the heights of Abraham,[1] and assail the town on its weakest side. Wolfe heartily approved of the design. A plan was speedily matured, and feeble as he was, the commander-in-chief determined to lead the assault in person. The camp at the Montmorenci was broken up [Sept. 8], and the attention of Montcalm was diverted from the real designs of the English, by seeming preparations to again attack his lines. The affair was managed so secretly and skillfully, that even De Bourgainville, who had been sent up the St. Lawrence by Montcalm, with fifteen hundred men, to watch the movements of the English, had no suspicion of their designs.

All preparations having been completed, the English ascended the river, in several vessels of the fleet, on the evening of the 12th of September. They went several miles above the intended landing-place. Leaving the ships at midnight, they embarked in flat boats, with muffled oars, and moved silently down to the mouth of a ravine, a mile and a half from the city, and landed.[2] At dawn [Sept. 13], Lieutenant-Colonel Howe[3] led the van up the tangled ravine, in the face of a sharp fire from a guard above. He was followed by the generals and the remainder of the troops, with artillery; and at sunrise the whole army stood in battle array upon the Plains of Abraham. It was an apparition little anticipated by the vigilant Montcalm. He perceived the peril of the city; and marching his whole army immediately from his encampment, crossed the St. Charles, and between nine and ten o'clock in the morning, confronted the English. A general, fierce, and bloody battle now ensued. Although twice severely wounded, Wolfe kept his feet; and as the two armies closed upon each other, he placed himself at the head of his grenadiers, and led them to a charge. At that moment a bullet entered his breast. He was carried to the rear, and a few moments afterward, Monckton, who took the command, also fell, severely wounded. Townshend continued the battle. Montcalm soon received a fatal wound;[4] and the French, terribly pierced by English bayonets, and smitten by Highland broadswords, broke and fled. Wolfe died just as the battle ended, with a smile upon his lips, because his ears heard the victory-shouts of his army. Five hundred French-

MONUMENT TO WOLFE AND MONTCALM.

[1] The declivity from Cape Diamond, on which the chief fortress stands, along the St. Lawrence to the cove below Sillery, was called by the general name of the Heights of Abraham, the plains of that name being on the top. See map on page 201.

[2] This place is known as *Wolfe's Cove;* and the ravine, which here breaks the steepness of the rocky shore, and up which the English clambered, is called *Wolfe's Ravine.*

[3] Afterward General Sir William Howe, the commander-in-chief of the English forces in America, when the Revolution had fairly commenced. Page 247.

[4] He was carried into the city, and when told that he must die, he said, "So much the better; I shall then be spared the mortification of seeing the surrender of Quebec." His remains are yet in Quebec; those of Wolfe were conveyed to England. People of the two nations have long dwelt peaceably together in that ancient city, and they have united in erecting a tall granite obelisk, dedicated to the linked memory of Wolfe and Montcalm.

men were killed, and (including the wounded) a thousand were taken prisoners. The English lost six hundred, in killed and wounded.

General Townshend now prepared to besiege the city. Threatened famine within aided him; and five days after the death of Wolfe [Sept. 18, 1759], Quebec, with its fortifications, shipping, stores, and people, was surrendered to the English, and five thousand troops, under General Murray, immediately took possession. The fleet, with the sick and the French prisoners, sailed for Halifax. The campaign now ended, yet Canada was not conquered. The French yet held Montreal, and had a considerable land and naval force above Quebec.

CAMPAIGN OF 1760.

Notwithstanding these terrible disasters, the French were not dismayed, and early in the spring of 1760, Vaudreuil, then governor-general of Canada, sent M. Levi, the successor of Montcalm, to recover Quebec. He went down the St. Lawrence, with six frigates and a strong land force. General Murray marched out, and met him at Sillery, about three miles above Quebec, and there, on the 4th of April, was fought one of the most sanguinary battles of the war. Murray was defeated. He lost all his artillery, and about a thousand men, but succeeded in retreating to the city with the remainder. Levi now laid siege to Quebec, and Murray's condition was becoming perilous, from the want of supplies, when an English squadron, with reinforcements and provisions, appeared [May 9] in the St. Lawrence. Levi supposed it to be the whole British fleet, and at once raised the siege [May 10], and fled to Montreal, after losing most of his shipping.

Now came the final struggle. The last stronghold of the French was now to be assailed; and Vandreuil gathered all his forces at Montreal for the conflict. Amherst had made extensive preparations during the summer; and early in September [Sept. 6–7], three English armies met before the doomed city. Amherst, at the head of ten thousand troops, and a thousand warriors of the SIX NATIONS, under General Johnson,[1] arrived on the 6th, and was joined, the same day, by General Murray, and four thousand troops, from Quebec. The next day, Colonel Haviland arrived, with three thousand troops, from Crown Point,[2] having taken possession of Isle Aux-Noix[3] on the way. Against such a crushing force, resistance would be vain; and Vandreuil immediately signed a capitulation [Sept. 8, 1760], surrendering Montreal, and all other French posts in Canada, into the hands of the English.[4] The regular troops, made prisoners at Montreal, were to be sent to France; and the Canadians were guarantied perfect security, in person, property, and religion.[5] General Gage[6] was appointed governor at Montreal; and Murray, with four thousand men, garrisoned Quebec.

---

[1] Page 190. [2] Page 198. [3] Note 8, page 197.

[4] The chief posts surrendered were Presque Isle (now Erie, Pennsylvania), Detroit, and Mackinaw.

[5] They were chiefly Roman Catholics, and that is yet the prevailing religion in Lower Canada.

[6] Pages 186 and 226.

The conquest of Canada produced great joy in the Anglo-American colonies,[1] and in none was it more intense than in that of New York, because its whole northern frontier lay exposed to the enemy. The exultation was very great in New England, too, for its eastern frontiers were now relieved from the terrible scourge of Indian warfare, by which they had been desolated six times within a little more than eighty years. In these wars, too, the Indians had become almost annihilated. The subjugation of the French seemed to be a guaranty of peace in the future, and the people everywhere assembled to utter public thanksgiving to HIM who rules the nations.

Although the war had ceased in America, the French and English continued it upon the ocean, and among the West India Islands, with almost continual success for the latter, until 1763, when a definitive treaty of peace,[2] agreed upon the year before, was signed at Paris [February 10, 1763], by which France ceded to Great Britain all her claimed possessions in America, eastward of the Mississippi, north of the latitude of Iberville River.[3] At the same time, Spain, with whom the English had been at war for a year previously, ceded [February 10, 1763] East and West Florida to the British crown. And now, England held undisputed possession (except by the Indians) of the whole Continent, from the shores of the Gulf of Mexico to the frozen North, and from ocean to ocean.[4]

The storm of war still lowered in the southern horizon, when the French dominion ceased in Canada. While the English were crushing the Gallic power in the north, the frontier settlements of the Carolinas were suffering dreadfully from frequent incursions of Indian war parties. French emissaries were busy among the Cherokees, hitherto the treaty friends of the English; and their influence, and some wrongs inflicted upon the Indians by some frontier Virginia Rangers, produced hostilities, and a fierce war was kindled in March, 1760.[5] The whole western frontier of the Carolinas was desolated in the course of a few weeks. The people called aloud for help, and Amherst heeded their supplications. Early in April, Colonel Montgomery, with some British regulars and provincial troops, marched from Charleston, South Carolina, and laid waste a portion of the Cherokee country.[6] Those bold aboriginal highlanders were not subdued; but when, the following year, Colonel Grant led a stronger force against them,[7] burned their towns, desolated their fields, and killed many of their warriors, they humbly sued for peace [June, 1761], and ever afterward remained comparatively quiet.

The storm in the South had scarcely ceased, when another, more portentous and alarming, gathered in the North-west. Pontiac, a sagacious chief of

---

[1] Note 1. page 193. [2] France and England, Spain and Portugal, were parties to this treaty.
[3] New Orleans, and the whole of Louisiana, was ceded by France to Spain at the same time. and she relinquished her entire possessions in North America. In 1800, Spain, by a secret treaty, retroceded Louisiana to France; and in 1803, Napoleon sold it to the United States for fifteen millions of dollars. See page 390.
[4] The cost, to England, of this *Seven Years' War*, as the conflict was called in Europe, was five hundred and sixty millions of dollars. [5] Page 27. [6] Page 27.
[7] Marion, Moultrie, and several other men, afterward distinguished in the war for Independence, accompanied Grant on this occasion.

the Ottawas,[1] who had been an early ally of the French, secretly confederated several of the ALGONQUIN tribes, in 1763, for the purpose of expelling the English from the country west of the Alleghanies.[2] After the fall of Montreal,[3] Pontiac had professed an attachment to the English; and as there seemed safety for settlers west of the mountains, immigration began to pour its living stream over those barriers. Like Philip of Mount Hope,[4] Pontiac saw, in the future, visions of the displacement, perhaps destruction, of his race, by the pale-faces; and he determined to strike a blow for life and country. So adroitly were his plans matured, that the commanders of the western forts had no suspicions of his conspiracy until it was ripe, and the first blow had been struck, in the month of June. Within a fortnight, all the posts in possession of the English, west of Oswego, fell into his hands, except Niagara,[5] Fort Pitt,[6] and Detroit. Colonel Bouquet saved Pittsburg;[7] Niagara was not attacked; and Detroit, after sustaining a siege of almost twelve months, was relieved by Colonel Bradstreet,[8] who arrived there with reinforcements, in May, 1764. The Indians were now speedily subdued, their power was broken, and the hostile tribes sent their chiefs to ask for pardon and peace. The haughty Pontiac refused to bow to the white people, and took refuge in the country of the Illinois, where he was treacherously murdered[9] in 1769. This was the last act in the dramaof the FRENCH AND INDIAN WAR.[10]

In our consideration of the history of the United States, we have now arrived at a point of great interest and importance. We have traced the growth of the colonies through infancy and youth, as their interests and destinies gradually commingled, until they really formed one people,[11] strong and lusty, like

---

[1] Page 18.

[2] The confederation consisted of the Ottawas, Miamies, Wyandots, Chippewas, Pottawatomies, Mississaguies, Shawnees, Outagamies or Foxes, and Winnebagoes. The Senecas, the most westerly clan of the SIX NATIONS, also joined in the conspiracy.

[3] Page 203.

[4] Page 124.

[5] Page 200.

[6] Page 198.

[7] Henry Bouquet was a brave English officer. He was appointed lieutenant-colonel in 1756, and was in the expedition against Fort du Quesne (page 198). In 1763, Amherst sent him from Montreal, with provisions and military stores for Fort Pitt. His arrival was timely, and he saved the garrison from destruction. The following year he commanded an expedition against the Indians in Ohio, and was successful. His journal was published after the war.

[8] Page 198.

[9] An English trader bribed a Peoria Indian to murder him, for which he gave him a barrel of rum. The place of his death was Cahokia, a small village on the east side of the Mississippi, a little below St. Louis. Pontiac was one of the greatest of all the Indian chiefs known to the white people, and deserved a better fate. It is said, that during the war of 1763, he appointed a commissary, and issued bills of credit. So highly was he esteemed by the French inhabitants, that these were received by them. Montcalm thought much of him; and at the time of his death, Pontiac was dressed in a French uniform, presented to him by that commander. See page 202. Pontiac was buried where the city of St. Louis now stands, and that busy mart is his monument, though not his memorial.

[10] The work most accessible to the general reader, in which the details of colonial events may be found, is Graham's *Colonial History of the United States*, in two volumes octavo, published by Blanchard and Lea, Philadelphia.

[11] It must not be understood, that there was yet a perfect unity of feeling among the various colonists. Sectional interests produced sectional jealousies, and these worked much mischief, even while soldiers from almost every colony were fighting shoulder to shoulder [page 190] in the continental army. Burnaby, who traveled in America at this period, expressed the opinion, that sectional jealousy and dissimilarity would prevent a permanent union; yet he avers that the people were imbued with ideas of independence, and that it was frequently remarked among them, that "the tide of dominion was running westward, and that America was destined to be the mistress of the world." The colonists themselves were not unmindful of the importance of their position, and

the mature man, prepared to vindicate natural rights, and to fashion political and social systems adapted to their position and wants. We view them now, conscious of their physical and moral strength, possessing clear views of right and justice, and prepared to demand and defend both. This is the point in the progress of the new and growing nation to which our observation is now directed, when the great question was to be decided, whether independent self-control should be enjoyed, or continued vassalage to an ungenerous parent should be endured. Our next topic will be the events connected with the settlement of that question. It is a topic of highest significance. It looms up in the panorama of national histories like some giant Alp, far above its fellows, isolated in grandeur, yet assimilated in sympathy with all others.

---

they gave freely of their substance to carry on the contest for the mastery. Probably, the "Seven Years' War" cost the colonies, in the aggregate, full twenty millions of dollars, besides the flower of their youth; and, in return, Parliament granted them, during the contest, at different periods, about five millions and a half of dollars. Parliament subsequently voted one million of dollars to the colonies, but, on account of the troubles arising from the Stamp Act and kindred measures, ministers withheld the sum.

The following is a list, taken from official records, of "The grants in Parliament for Rewards, Encouragement, and Indemnification to the Provinces in North America, for their Services and Expenses during the last [seven years'] War:

"On the 3d of February, 1756, as a free gift and reward to the colonies of New England, New York, and Jersey, for their past services, and as an encouragement to continue to exert themselves with vigor, $575,000.

"May 19th, 1757. For the use and relief of the provinces of North and South Carolina, and Virginia, in recompense for services performed and to be performed, $250,000.

"June 1st, 1758. To reimburse the province of Massachusetts Bay their expenses in furnishing provisions and stores to the troops raised by them in 1756, $136,900. To reimburse the province of Connecticut their expenses for ditto, $68,680.

"April 30th, 1759. As a compensation to the respective colonies for the expenses of clothing, pay of troops, etc., $1,000,000.

"March 31st, 1760. For the same, $1,000,000. For the colony of New York, to reimburse their expenses in furnishing provisions and stores to the troops in 1756, $14,885.

"Jan. 20th, 1761. As a compensation to the respective colonies for clothing, pay of the troops, etc., $1,000,000.

"Jan. 26th, 1762. Ditto, $666,666.

"March 15th, 1763. Ditto, $666,666.

"April 22d, 1770. To reimburse the province of New Hampshire their expenses in furnishing provisions and stores to the troops in the campaign of 1756, $30,045. Total, $5,408,842."

In a pamphlet, entitled *Rights of* BRITAIN *and Claims of* AMERICA, an answer to the Declaration of the Continental Congress, setting forth the causes and the necessity of their taking up arms, printed in 1776, is a table showing the annual expenditures of the British government in support of the civil and military powers of the American colonies, from the accession of the family of Hanover, in 1714, until 1775. The expression of the writer is, "Employed in the defense of America." This is incorrect; for the wars with the French on this continent, which cost the greatest amount of money, were wars for conquest and territory, though ostensibly for the defense of the Anglo-American colonies against the encroachments of their Gallic neighbors. During the period alluded to (sixty years), the sums granted for the army amounted to $43,899,625; for the navy, $50,000,000; money laid out in Indian presents, in holding Congresses, and purchasing cessions of land, $30,500,000; making a total of $123,899,625. Within that period the following bounties on American commodities were paid: On indigo, $725,110; on hemp and flax, $27,800; on naval stores imported into Great Britain from America, $7,293,810; making the total sum paid on account of bounties, $8,047,320. The total amount of money expended in sixty years on account of America, $131,946,945.

PATRICK HENRY BEFORE THE VIRGINIA ASSEMBLY.

JAMES OTIS

FIFTH PERIOD.

THE REVOLUTION. PRELIMINARY EVENTS.
1761—1775.

CHAPTER I.

PRINCIPLES, like the ultimate particles of matter, and the laws of God, are eternal, indestructible, and unchangeable. They have existed in the moral realm of our world since the advent of man; and devious as may be their manifestations, according to circumstances, they remain the same, inherently, and always exhibit the same tendencies. When God gave to man an intelligent soul, and invested him with the prerogatives of moral free agency, then was born that instinctive love of liberty which, through all past time, has manifested itself in individuals and in societies; and in every age, the consciences of men have boldly and indignantly asked, in the presence of oppression,

> "If I'm design'd yon lordling's slave,
> By Nature's laws designed;
> Why was an independent wish
> E'er planted in my mind?
> If not, why am I subject to
> His cruelty or scorn?
> Or why has man the will and pow'r
> To make his fellow mourn?" [1]

[1] Burns.

Nations, like men, have thus spoken. The principles of civil and religious liberty, and the inalienable rights of man which they involve, were recognized and asserted long before Columbus left Palos for the New World.[1] Their maintenance had shaken thrones and overturned dynasties before Charles the First was brought to the block;[2] and they had lighted the torch of revolution long before the trumpet-tones of James Otis[3] and Patrick Henry[4] aroused the Anglo-Americans[5] to resist British aggression. From the earliest steps in the progress of the American colonies, we have seen the democratic theories of all past reformers developed into sturdy democratic practice; and a love of liberty which had germinated beneath the heat of persecution in the Old World, budded and blossomed all over the New, wherever English hearts beat, or English tongues gave utterance. Nor did English hearts alone cherish the precious seedling, nor English tongues alone utter the noble doctrines of popular sovereignty; but in the homes of all in this beautiful land, whatever country gave the inmates birth, there was a shrine of freedom, and a refuge for the oppressed. Here king-craft and priest-craft never had an abiding-place, and their ministers were always weak in the majestic presence of the popular will.

Upon the bleak shores of Massachusetts Bay; upon the banks of the Hudson, the Delaware, the Potomac, and the James; and amid the pine-forests or beneath the palmettos of the Carolinas, and the further South, the colonists, from the very beginning, had evinced an impatience of arbitrary rule; and every manifestation of undue control by local magistrates or distant monarchs—every effort to abridge their liberties or absorb their gains, stimulated the growth of democratic principles. These permeated the whole social and political life in America, and finally evolved from the crude materials of royal charters, religious covenants, and popular axioms, that galaxy of representative governments which, having the justice of the English Constitution, the truth of Christian ethics, and the wisdom of past experience for their foundation, were united in "the fullness of time," in that symmetrical combination of free institutions known as the REPUBLIC OF THE UNITED STATES OF AMERICA.

It is a common error to regard the Revolution which attended the birth of this Republic, as an isolated episode in the history of nations, having its causes in events immediately preceding the convulsion. It was not the violent result of recent discontents, but the culmination of a long series of causes tending to such a climax. The parliamentary enactments which kindled the rebellion in 1775, were not oppressive measures entirely novel. They had their counterparts in the British statute books, even as early as the restoration of monarchy [1660][6] a hundred years before, when navigation laws,[7] intended to crush the growing commerce of the colonies were enacted. They were only re-assertions of tyrannical legislative power and royal prerogatives, to which the colonies, in the weakness of their infancy and early youth, were compelled to submit. Now they had grown to maturity, and dared to insist upon receiving exact justice.

---

[1] Page 39. [2] Note 3, page 103. [3] Page 212. [4] Note 1, page 214. [5] Note 1, page 193. [6] Page 100. [7] Note 4, page 109.

They had recently emerged from an exhausting war, which, instead of weakening them, had taught them their real moral, political, and physical strength. They had also learned the important lesson of power in union, and profited by its teachings. Having acquired a mastery over the savages of the wilderness, and assisted in breaking the French power on their frontiers, into atoms,[1] they felt their manhood stirring within them, and they tacitly agreed no longer to submit to the narrow and oppressive policy of Great Britain. Their industry and commerce were too expansive to be confined within the narrow limits of those restrictions which the Board of Trade,[2] from time to time, had imposed, and they determined to regard them as mere ropes of sand. For long and gloomy years they had struggled up, unaided and alone, from feebleness to strength. They had built fortifications, raised armies, and fought battles, for England's glory and their own preservation, without England's aid, and often without her sympathy.[3] And it was not until the growing importance of the French settlements excited the jealousy of Great Britain, that her ministers perceived the expediency of justice and liberality toward her colonies, in order to secure their loyalty and efficient co-operation.[4] Compelled to be self-reliant from the beginning, the colonists were made strong by the mother's neglect; and when to that neglect she added oppression and scorn, they felt justified in using their developed strength in defense of their rights.

The colonists had grown strong, not only in material prosperity, perceptions of inalienable rights, and a will to be free, but in many things in which the strength and beauty of a State consist, they exhibited all the most prominent developments of a great nation. A love for the fine arts had been growing apace for many years; and when the Revolution broke out, West[5] and Copley,[6] natives of America, were wearing, in Europe, the laurel-crowns of supreme excellence as painters. Literature and science were beginning to be highly appreciated, and the six colonial colleges[7] were full of students. Godfrey, the glazier, who invented the quadrant, had flourished and passed away;[8]

---

[1] Page 203. [2] Note 5, page 134.

[3] Georgia, alone, received parliamentary aid [page 100], in the establishment of settlements. In all the other colonies, where vast sums were expended in fitting out expeditions, purchasing the soil of the Indians, and sustaining the settlers, neither the crown nor parliament ever contributed a farthing of pecuniary aid. The settling of Massachusetts alone, cost a million of dollars. Lord Baltimore spent two hundred thousand dollars in colonizing Maryland; and William Penn became deeply involved in debt, in his efforts to settle and improve Pennsylvania. [4] Page 197.

[5] Benjamin West was born in Chester county, Pennsylvania, in 1738. His parents were Quakers. He commenced art-life as a portrait-painter, when wealthy men furnished him with means to go to Italy. He soon triumphed, went to England, was patronized by the king, and became the most eminent historical painter of his age. He died in London in 1820, in the eighty-second year of his age.

[6] John Singleton Copley was also born in 1738, in the city of Boston. He became a pupil of Smibert [note 8, page 158], and became an eminent portrait-painter. His family relations identified him with the Royalists at the commencement of the Revolution, and he went to England to seek employment, where he was patronized by West. There he painted two memorable pictures; one for the House of Lords, the other for the House of Commons. These established his fame, and led to fortune. His son became lord chancellor of England, and was made a peer, with the title of Lord Lyndhurst. Copley died in England, in 1815, at the age of seventy-seven years.

[7] Page 178.

[8] Thomas Godfrey was a native of Pennsylvania, and was born in 1704. He was the real inventor of the quadrant known as Hadley's. See Lossing's *Eminent Americans.*

Bartram, the farmer, had become "American Botanist to his Majesty;"[1] Franklin, the printer, was known, wherever civilization had planted her banners, as the lightning-tamer and profound moral philosopher; and Rittenhouse, the clock-maker, had calculated and observed the transit of Venus, and con-

structed that Planetarium which is yet a wonder in the world of mechanism.[2] Theology and the legal profession, had taken high ground. Edwards[3] had written his great work on *The Freedom of the Will*, and was among the dead; and already Otis,[4] Henry,[5] Dickenson,[6] Rutledge,[7] and other lawyers, had made their brilliant marks, and were prepared to engage in the great struggle at hand. All classes of men had noble representatives in the colonies, when the conflict commenced.

There was no cause for complaint on the part of the colonists, of the willful exercise of tyrannical power, for purposes of oppression, by Great Britain.

---

[1] See Lossing's *Eminent Americans.*

[2] David Rittenhouse was born in Roxborough, Pennsylvania, in 1732. As he exhibited great mechanical genius, his father apprenticed him to a clock-maker, and he became one of the most eminent mechanicians and mathematicians of his time. He discovered that remarkable feature in algebraic analysis, called *fluxions*, and applied it to the mechanic arts. He constructed a machine which represented the motions of the solar system. That Planetarium is now in the possession of the College of New Jersey, at Princeton. Rittenhouse succeeded Franklin as president of the American Philosophical Society. He died in 1793, at the age of sixty-four years.

[3] Jonathan Edwards was one of the most eminent of American divines. He was born in East Windsor, Connecticut, in 1703, and died at Princeton, New Jersey, while president of the college, in 1758. [4] Page 212. [5] Page 214. [6] Page 219. [7] Page 310.

There was no motive for such a course. But they reasonably complained of an unjust and illiberal policy, which accomplished all the purposes of absolute tyranny. The rod of iron was often covered with velvet, and was wielded as often by ignorant, rather than by wicked, hands. Yet the ignorant hand, with

the concealed rod, smote as lustily and offensively, as if it had been a wicked one, and the rod bare. The first form of governmental and proprietary oppression[1] was in the appointment of local rulers. The people were not *represented* in the appointing power. Then came commercial restrictions,[2] prohibitions to manufacture,[3] imposts upon exchanges,[4] and direct taxation, by enactments of parliament, in which the colonists were not *represented.* At the beginning, they had asserted, and during their whole progress they had maintained, that important political maxim, that TAXATION *without* REPRESENTATION, *is tyranny.* This was the fundamental doctrine of their political creed—this was the test of all parliamentary measures—this was the strong rock upon which the patriots of the Revolution anchored their faith and hope.

When the French and Indian War was closed by the treaty of Paris,

---

[1] Three forms of government had existed, namely, *charter*, *proprietary*, and *royal*. The New England governments were based upon royal charters; New Jersey, Pennsylvania, Maryland, and the Carolinas, were owned and governed by individuals or companies, and the remainder were immediately subject to the crown. Notwithstanding this diversity in the source of government, the anti-monarchical spirit pervaded the people of all, from the beginning, and gave birth to popular legislative assemblies.

[2] Note 3, page 177. [3] Pages 177 and 178. [4] Page 178.

in 1763, the colonists looked forward to long years of prosperity and repose. A young monarch,[1] virtuous and of upright intentions, had been recently [1761] seated upon the British throne. Having confidence in his integrity, and having lately felt the justice of the government, under the direction of Pitt,[2] they were disposed to forget past grievances; and being identified with the glory of England, now become one of the first powers on the earth, they were fond of their connection. But the serenity of the political sky soon disappeared, and it was not long before violent tempests were raging there. Even before the treaty at Paris, a cloud had arisen which portended future trouble. The war had exhausted the British treasury,[3] and ministers devised various schemes for replenishing it. They had observed the resources of the colonists, as manifested by their efforts during the recent struggle,[4] and as they were relieved from further hostilities by the subjugation of Canada[5] [1759], the government looked to them for aid. Instead of asking it as a *favor*, it was demanded as a *right;* instead of inviting the colonial Assemblies to levy taxes and make appropriations, government assumed the right to tax their expanding commerce; and then commenced a vigorous enforcement of existing revenue laws, which had hitherto been only nominally oppressive.[6]

One of the first acts which revealed the intentions of Parliament to tax the colonies by enforcing the revenue laws, was the authorization, in 1761, of *Writs of Assistance.* These were general search-warrants, which not only allowed the king's officers who held them, to break open any citizen's store or dwelling, to search for and seize foreign merchandise, on which a duty had not been paid, but compelled sheriffs and others to assist in the work. The people could not brook such a system of petty oppression. The sanctities of private life might be invaded, at any time, by hirelings, and the assertion, based upon the guaranties of the British Constitution, that "every Englishman's house is his castle," would not be true. These writs were first issued in Massachusetts, and immediately great excitement prevailed. Their legality was questioned, and the matter was brought before a court held in the old town hall in Boston. The advocate for the Crown (Mr. Gridley) argued, that as Parliament was the supreme legislature for the whole British nation, and had authorized these writs, no subject had a right to complain. He was answered by James Otis,[7]

---

[1] George the Third. He was crowned in 1761, at the age of twenty years. He reigned almost sixty years, and died in 1820. [2] Page 195. [3] Note 4. page 204.
[4] French and Indian War. [5] Page 204.

[6] Commercial restrictions were imposed upon the colonies as early as 1651 [note 4, page 109]. In 1660, 1672, 1676, 1691, and 1692, attempts were made by parliament to derive a revenue by a tariff-taxation upon the colonies. In 1696 a proposition was made to levy a direct tax upon the colonies. Then, not only in Britain, but in America, the power of parliament (wherein the colonists were not represented), to tax those colonies, was strenuously denied.

[7] James Otis was born in Barnstable, Massachusetts, in 1725, and became the leader of the Revolutionary party in that province, at the beginning. He was wounded by a blow from a cudgel, in the hands of a British official in 1769, and never fairly recovered. For years he was afflicted with occasional lunacy, and presented but a wreck of the orator and scholar. The following anecdote is related of Mr. Otis, as illustrative of his ready use of Latin, even during moments of mental aberration. Men and boys, heartless or thoughtless, would sometimes make themselves merry at his expense, when he was seen in the streets afflicted with lunacy. On one occasion he was passing a crockery store, when a young man, who had a knowledge of Latin, sprinkled some water

the younger, then advocate-general of the province. On that occasion, the intense fire of his patriotism beamed forth with inexpressible brilliancy, and his eloquence was like lightning, far-felt and consuming. On that day the trumpet of the Revolution was sounded. John Adams afterward said, "The seeds of patriots and heroes were then and there sown;" and when the orator exclaimed, "To my dying day I will oppose, with all the power and faculties God has given me, all such instruments of slavery on one hand, and villany on the other," the independence of the colonies was proclaimed.[1] From that day began the triumphs of the popular will. Very few writs were issued, and these were ineffectual.

Young King George unwisely turned his back upon Pitt,[2] and listened to the councils of Bute,[3] an unprincipled Scotch adventurer, who had been his tutor. Disastrous consequences ensued. Weak and corrupt men controlled his cabinet, and the pliant Parliament approved of illiberal and unjust measures toward the colonists. The Sugar bill,[4] which had produced a great deal of ill-feeling in the colonies, was re-enacted; and at the same time, George Grenville, then prime minister, proposed "certain stamp duties on the colonies." The subject was left open for consideration almost a year, when, in the spring of 1765, in defiance of the universal opposition of the Americans, the famous Stamp Act, which declared that no legal instrument of writing should be valid, unless it bore a government stamp, became a law.[5] Now was executed, without hesitation, a measure which no former ministry had possessed courage or recklessness enough to attempt.[6]

---

upon him from a sprinkling-pot with which he was wetting the floor of the second story, at the same time saying, *Pluit tantum, nescio quantum. Scis ne tu?* "It rains so much, I know not how much. Do you know?" Otis immediately picked up a missile, and, hurling it through the window of the crockery store, it smashing every thing in its way, exclaimed, *Fregi tot, nescio quot. Scis ne tu?* "I have broken so many, I know not how many. Do you know?" Mr. Otis, according to his expressed desire, was killed by lightning in 1782. See portrait at the head of this chapter.

[1] Later than this [1708], Otis wrote to a friend in London, and said: "Our fathers were a *good* people; we have been a *free* people, and if you will not let us remain so any longer, we shall be a *great* people, and the present measures can have no tendency but to hasten with great rapidity, events which every good and honest man would wish delayed for ages." He evidently alluded to the future independence of the colonies.

[2] Pitt, disgusted by the ignorance and assurance of Bute and the misplaced confidence of the king, resigned his office, and retired to his country seat at Hayes. The king esteemed him highly, but was too much controlled by Bute to follow his own inclinations. It was not long, however, before public affairs became so complicated, that the king was compelled to call upon the great commoner to untangle them.

[3] Bute was a gay Scotch earl, poor and proud. He became a favorite with the mother of George the Third, was appointed his tutor, and acquired such influence over the mind of the prince, that on his accession to the throne, he made him his chief minister and adviser. The English people were much incensed; and the unwise measures of the early years of George's reign, were properly laid to the charge of Bute. A placard was put up in London, with the words, "No Scotch minister—no petticoat government." The last clause referred to the influence of the queen mother.

[4] A bill which imposed a duty upon sugar, coffee, indigo, &c., imported into the colonies from the West Indies.

[5] The stamps were upon blue paper, in the form seen in the engraving on page 213, and were to be attached to every piece of paper or parchment, on which a legal instrument was written. For these stamps government charged specific prices: for example, for a common property deed, one shilling and sixpence; for a diploma or certificate of a college degree, two pounds, &c., &c.

[6] During Robert Walpole's administration [1732], a stamp duty was proposed. He said, "I will leave the taxation of America to some of my successors, who have more courage than I have." Sir William Keith, governor of Pennsylvania, proposed such a tax in 1739. Franklin thought it just, when a delegate in the Colonial Congress at Albany, in 1754 [page 183]. But when it was proposed to Pitt in 1759, he said, "I will never burn my fingers with an American Stamp Act."

The colonists had watched with anxiety the growth of this new germ of oppression; and the intelligence of the passage of the Act produced general and intense indignation in America. The hearts of the people were yet thrilled by the eloquent denunciations of Otis; and soon Patrick Henry sent forth a

response equally eloquent from the heaving bosom of the Virginia Assembly.[1] The people, in cities and villages, gathered in excited groups, and boldly expressed their indignation. The pulpit denounced the wicked scheme, and

---

[1] Patrick Henry was a very Boanerges at the opening of the Revolution. He was born in Hanover County, Virginia, in 1736. In youth and manhood he was exceedingly indolent and dull. At the age of twenty-seven, his eloquence suddenly beamed forth in a speech in court, in his native county, and he soon became a leading man in Virginia. He was elected the first Republican governor of his State, in 1776, and held that office again in 1784. He died in 1799, at the age of almost sixty-three years. At the time alluded to in the text, Henry introduced a series of resolutions, highly tinctured with rebellious doctrines. He asserted the general rights of all the colonies; then the exclusive right of the Virginia Assembly to tax the people of that province, and boldly declared that the people were not bound to obey any law relative to taxation, which did not proceed from their representatives. The last resolution declared that whoever should dissent from the doctrines inculcated in the others, should be considered an "enemy of the colonies." The introduction of these resolutions produced great excitement and alarm. Henry supported them with all the power of his wonderful eloquence. Some rose from their seats, and others sat in breathless silence. At length, when alluding to tyrants, he exclaimed, "Cæsar had his Brutus, Charles the First his Cromwell, and George the Third"—there was a cry of "Treason! Treason!" He paused a moment, and said—"may profit by their example. If that be treason, make the most of it." [See picture at the head of this chapter.] A part of his resolutions were adopted, and these formed the first gauntlet of defiance cast at the feet of the British monarch. Their power was felt throughout the land.

associations of *Sons of Liberty*[1] in every colony put forth their energies in defense of popular freedom. The press, then assuming great power, spoke out like an oracle of Truth. In several cities popular excitement created mobs, and violence ensued. The Stamps were seized on their arrival, and secreted or burned. Stamp distributors[2] were insulted and despised; and on the first of November, 1765, when the law was to take effect, there were no officials courageous enough to enforce it.

A STAMP.

The people did not confine their opposition to expressions at indignation meetings, and acts of violence. The public sentiment took a more dignified form, and assumed an aspect of nationality. There was a prevailing desire for a general Congress, and several colonies, in the midst of the great excitement, appointed delegates for that purpose. They met in the city of New York, on the 7th of October, 1765,[3] continued in session fourteen days, and in three well-written documents,[4] they ably set forth the grievances and the rights of the colonists, and petitioned the king and parliament for a redress of the former, and acknowledgment of the latter. The proceedings of this *Second Colonial Congress*[5] were applauded by all the provincial Assemblies, and the people of America were as firmly united in heart and purpose then, as they were after the Declaration of Independence, more than ten years later.

At length the momentous day—the first of November—arrived. It was observed as a day of fasting and mourning. Funeral processions paraded the streets of cities, and bells tolled funeral knells. The colors of sailing vessels were placed at half-mast, and the newspapers exhibited the black-line tokens of public grief. The courts were now closed, legal marriages ceased, ships remained in port, and for some time all business was suspended. But the lull in the storm was of brief duration. The people were only gathering strength for more vigorous achievements in defense of their rights. The *Sons of Liberty* put forth new efforts; mobs began to assail the residences of officials, and burn distinguished royalists, in effigy.[6] Merchants entered into agreements

[1] These associations were composed of popular leaders and others, who leagued with the avowed determination to resist oppression to the uttermost. After their organization in the different colonies, they formed a sort of national league, and by continual correspondence, aided effectually in preparing the way for the Revolution.

[2] Men appointed by the crown to sell the government stamps, or stamped paper.

[3] Massachusetts, Connecticut, Rhode Island, New Jersey, Pennsylvania, Maryland, and South Carolina, were represented. The Assemblies of those not represented, declared their readiness to agree to whatever measures the Congress might adopt. Timothy Ruggles, of Massachusetts (who afterward commanded a corps of Tories) [note 4, page 224], presided.

[4] A *Declaration of Rights*, written by John Cruger, of New York; a *Memorial to both Houses of Parliament*, by Robert R. Livingston, of New York; and a *Petition to the king*, by James Otis, of Massachusetts.

[5] Page 183.

[6] Public indignation is thus sometimes manifested. A figure of a man intended to represent the obnoxious individual, is paraded, and then hung upon a scaffold, or burned at a stake, as an intimation of the deserved fate of the person thus represented. It was a common practice in England at the time in question, and has been often done in our own country since. Nowhere was popular indignation so warmly manifested as in New York. Cadwallader Colden, a venerable Scotchman of eighty years, was acting-governor of New York. He refused to deliver up the

not to import goods from Great Britain while the obnoxious Act remained a law; and domestic manufactures were commenced in almost every family.[1] The wealthiest vied with the middling classes in economy, and wore clothing of their own manufacture. That wool might not become scarce, the use of sheep

flesh for food, was discouraged. Soon, from all classes in America, there went to the ears of the British ministry, a respectful but firm protest. It was seconded by the merchants and manufacturers of London, whose American trade was prostrated,[2] and the voice, thus made potential, was heard and heeded in high places.

---

stamped paper on the demand of the people, when they proceeded to hang him in effigy, near the spot where Leisler was executed [page 148] seventy-five years before. They also burned his fine coach in front of the fort, near the present Bowling Green, and upon the smoking pile they cast his effigy. Colden was a man of great scientific attainments. He wrote a *History of the Five Nations* [page 23], and was in constant correspondence with some of the most eminent philosophers and scholars of Europe. A life of Colden, from the pen of John W. Francis, M.D., L.LD., may be found in the *American Medical and Philosophical Register*, 1811. He died in September, 1776.

[1] The newspapers of the day contain many laudatory notices of the conformity of wealthy people to these agreements. On one occasion, forty or fifty young ladies, who called themselves "Daughters of Liberty," met at the house of the Rev. Mr. Morehead, in Boston, with their spinning-wheels, and spun two hundred and thirty-two skeins of yarn, during the day, and presented them to the pastor. It is said "there were upward of one hundred spinners in Mr. Morehead's Society." "Within eighteen months," wrote a gentleman at Newport, R. I., "four hundred and eighty-seven yards of cloth, and thirty-six pairs of stockings, have been spun and knit in the family of James Nixon, of this town."

[2] Half a million of dollars were due them by the colonists, at that time, not a dime of which could be collected under the existing state of things.

While these events were in progress, Grenville had been succeeded in office by the Marquis of Rockingham, a friend of the colonies, and an enlightened statesman. William Pitt,[1] who had been called from his retirement by the voice of the people, hoping much from the new ministry, appeared in Parliament, and was there the earnest champion of the Americans. Justice and expediency demanded a repeal of the Stamp Act, and early in January, 1766, a bill for that purpose was introduced into the House of Commons, and was warmly supported by Pitt, Colonel Barrè, and others. Then Edmund Burke first appeared as the champion of right; and during the stormy debates on the subject, which ensued, he achieved some of those earliest and most wonderful triumphs of oratory, which established his fame, and endeared him to the American people.[2] The obnoxious act was repealed on the 18th of March, 1766, when London warehouses were illuminated, and flags decorated the shipping in the Thames. In America, public thanksgivings, bonfires, and illuminations, attested the general joy; and Pitt,[3] who had boldly declared his conviction that Parliament had no right to tax the colonies without their consent,[4] was lauded as a political Messiah. Non-importation associations were dissolved, business was resumed, and the Americans confidently expected justice from the mother country, and a speedy reconciliation. Alas! the scene soon changed.

WILLIAM PITT.

Another storm soon began to lower. Pitt, himself tenacious of British honor, and doubtful of the passage of the Repeal Bill without some concessions, had appended to it an act, which declared that Parliament possessed the power "to bind the colonies, in all cases whatsoever." The egg of tyranny which lay concealed in this "declaratory act," as it was called, was not perceived by the colonists, while their eyes were filled with tears of joy; but when calm reflection came, they saw clearly that germ of future oppressions, and were uneasy. They perceived the Repeal Bill to be only a truce in the war upon freedom in America, and they watched every movement of the government party with suspicion. Within a few months afterward, a brood of obnoxious measures were hatched from that egg, and aroused the fiercest indignation of the colonists.

The American people, conscious of rectitude, were neither slow nor cautious

---

[1] Note 2, page 213.

[2] Edmund Burke was born in Ireland, in 1730. He became a lawyer, and was a very popular writer, as well as a speaker. He was in public office about thirty years, and died in 1797.

[3] William Pitt was born in England in 1708, and held many high offices of trust and emolument. During an exciting debate in Parliament, on American affairs, in the spring of 1778, he swooned, and died within a month afterward.

[4] "Taxation," said Pitt, "is no part of the governing or legislative power. Taxes are the voluntary gift or grant of the commons alone." "I rejoice," he said, "that America has resisted. Three millions of people, so dead to all the feelings of liberty, as voluntarily to become slaves, would have been fit instruments to make slaves of the rest." And Colonel Barrè declared that the colonists were planted by English oppression, grew by neglect, and in all the essential elements of a free people, were perfectly independent of Great Britain. He then warned the government to act justly, or the colonies would be lost to Great Britain forever.

in exhibiting their indignation, and this boldness irritated their oppressors. A large portion of the House of Lords,[1] the whole bench of bishops,[2] and many of the Commons, were favorable to coercive measures toward the Americans. Not doubting the power of Parliament to tax them, they prevailed on the ministry to adopt new schemes for replenishing the exhausted treasury[3] from the coffers of the colonists, and urged the justice of employing arms, if necessary, to enforce obedience. Troops were accordingly sent to America, in June, 1766; and a Mutiny Act was passed, which provided for their partial subsistence by the colonies.[4] The appearance of these troops in New York, and the order for the people to feed and shelter the avowed instruments of their own enslavement, produced violent outbreaks in that city, and burning indignation all over the land. The Assembly of New York at once arrayed itself against the government, and refused compliance with the demands of the obnoxious act.

In the midst of the darkness, light seemed to dawn upon the Americans. Early in the month of July, Pitt was called to the head of the British ministry, and on the 30th of that month, he was created Earl of Chatham. He opposed the new measures as unwise and unjust, and the colonists hoped for reconciliation and repose. But Pitt could not always prevent mischief. During his absence from Parliament, on account of sickness, the Chancellor of the Exchequer (Charles Townshend) coalesced with Grenville in bringing new taxation schemes before that body.[5] A bill was passed in June, 1767, for levying duties upon tea, glass, paper, painters' colors, etc., which should be imported into the colonies. Another was passed, in July, for establishing a Board of Trade in the colonies, independent of colonial legislation, and for creating resident commissioners of customs to enforce the revenue laws.[6] Then another, a few days later, which forbade the New York Assembly to perform any legislative act whatever, until it should comply with the requisitions of the Mutiny Act. These taxation schemes, and blows at popular liberty, produced excitement throughout the colonies, almost as violent as those on account of the Stamp Act.[7] The colonial Assemblies boldly protested; new non-importation associations were formed; pamphlets and newspapers were filled with inflammatory appeals to the people, defining their rights, and urging them to a united resistance;[8] and early in 1768, almost every colonial Assembly had boldly ex-

[1] Every peer in the British realm is a legislator by virtue of his title; and when they are assembled for legislative duties, they constitute the House of Lords, or upper branch of the legislature, answering, in some degree, to our Senate.

[2] Two archbishops, and twenty-four bishops of England and Wales, have a right to sit and vote in the House of Lords, and have the same political importance as the peers. By the act of union between Ireland and England, four "lords spiritual" from among the archbishops and bishops of the former country, have a seat in the House of Lords. The "lords temporal and lords spiritual" constitute the *House of Lords*. The *House of Commons* is composed of men elected by the people, and answers to the *House of Representatives* of our Federal Congress.

[3] Page 212.

[4] This act also allowed military officers, possessing a warrant from a justice of the peace, to break into any house where he might suspect deserters were concealed. Like the *Writs of Assistance* [page 212], this power might be used for wicked purposes.

[5] In January, 1767, Grenville proposed a direct taxation of the colonies to the amount of twenty thousand dollars.

[6] Note 6, page 212, and note 5, page 134.

[7] Page 215.

[8] Among the most powerful of these appeals, were a series of letters, written by John Dickenson, of Philadelphia, and entitled *Letters of a Pennsylvania farmer.* Like Paine's *Crisis*, ten years

pressed its conviction, that Parliament had no right to tax the colonies. These expressions were in response to a circular issued by Massachusetts [Feb., 1768] to the several Assemblies, asking their co-operation in obtaining a redress of grievances. That circular greatly offended the Ministry; and the governor of

Massachusetts was instructed to command the Assembly, in the king's name, to rescind the resolution adopting it. The Assembly, on the 30th of June following, passed an almost unanimous vote *not* to rescind,[1] and made this very order an evidence of the intentions of government to enslave the colonists, by restraining the free speech and action of their representatives.

The British Ministry, ignorant and careless concerning the character and temper of the Americans, disregarded the portentous warnings which every vessel from the New World bore to their ears. Having resolved on employing physical force in the maintenance of obedience, and not doubting its potency,

later [note 4, page 250], these Letters produced a wide-spread and powerful effect on the public mind. James Otis asserted, in a pamphlet, that "taxes on trade [tariffs], if designed to raise a revenue, were as much a violation of their rights as any other tax." John Dickenson was born in Maryland, in November, 1732. He studied law in England for three years, and made his first appearance in public life, as a member of the Pennsylvania Assembly. He was a member of the Stamp Act Congress [page 215], and of the Continental Congress [page 226]. He was an eloquent speaker, and elegant writer. He was opposed to the independence of the colonies, but acquiesced, and was an able member of the convention that framed the Federal Constitution. He remained long in public life, and died in 1808, at the age of seventy-five years.

[1] James Otis and Samuel Adams were the principal speakers on this occasion. "When Lord Hillsborough [colonial secretary] knows," said the former, "that we will not rescind *our* acts, he should appeal to Parliament to rescind *theirs*. Let Britons rescind their measures, or the colonies are lost to them forever."

they became less regardless of even the forms of justice, and began to treat the colonists as rebellious subjects, rather than as free British brethren. Ministers sent orders to the colonial Assemblies, warning them not to imitate the factious disobedience of Massachusetts; and the royal governors were ordered to enforce submission by all means in their power. The effect of these circulars was to disgust and irritate the Assemblies, and to stimulate their sympathy for Massachusetts, now made the special object of displeasure.

It was in the midst of the general excitement, in May, 1768, that the new commissioners of customs arrived at Boston. They were regarded with as much contempt as were the tax-gatherers in Judea, in the time of our Saviour.[1] It was difficult to restrain the more ignorant and excitable portion of the population from committing personal violence. A crisis soon arrived. In June, 1768, the sloop *Liberty*, belonging to John Hancock, one of the leaders of the popular mind in Boston,[2] arrived at that port with a cargo of Madeira wine. The commissioners demanded the payment of duties, and when it was refused, they seized the vessel. The news spread over the town, and the people resolved on immediate and effectual resistance. An assemblage of citizens soon became a mob, who dragged a custom-house boat through the town, burned it upon the Common, assailed the commissioners, damaged their houses, and compelled them to seek safety in Castle William, a small fortress at the entrance to the harbor.[3] Alarmed by these demonstrations of the popular feeling, Governor Bernard unwisely invited General Gage,[4] then in command of British troops at Halifax, to bring soldiers to Boston to overawe the inhabitants.[5] They came in September [Sept. 27, 1768], seven hundred in number, and on a quiet Sabbath morning, landed under cover of the cannons of the British ships which brought them, and with drums beating, and colors flying, they marched to the Common,[6] with all the parade of a victorious army entering a conquered city. Religion, popular freedom, patriotism, were all outraged, and the cup of the people's indignation was full.[7] The colonists were taught the bitter, but necessary lesson, that armed resistance must oppose armed oppression.[8]

Like the Assembly of New York, that of Massachusetts refused to afford

---

[1] The *publicans*, or toll-gatherers of Judea, being a standing monument of the degradation of the Jews under the Roman yoke, were abhorred. One of the accusations against our Saviour was, that he did "eat with *publicans* and sinners."

[2] Page 231.

[3] About three miles south-east from Boston. The fortress was ceded to the United States in 1798; and the following year it was visited by President Adams, and named *Fort Independence*, its present title. In connection with Castle William, we find the first mention of the tune of "Yankee Doodle." In the Boston *Journal of the Times*, September 29, 1768, is the following: "The fleet was brought to anchor near Castle William; that night there was throwing of sky-rockets; and those passing in boats observed great rejoicings, and that the *Yankee Doodle Song* was the capital piece in the band of music."

[4] Page 186.

[5] The British ministry had already resolved to send troops to Boston to subdue the rebellious propensities of the people.

[6] A large public park on the southern slope of Beacon Hill.

[7] As the people refused to supply the troops with quarters, they were placed, some in the State House, some in Faneuil Hall [page 225], and others in tents on the Common. Cannons were planted at different points; sentinels challenged the citizens as they passed; and the whole town had the appearance of a camp.

[8] There were, at that time, full two hundred thousand men in the colonies capable of bearing arms.

food and shelter for the royal troops in that province, and for this offense, Parliament, now become the supple instrument of the crown, censured their disobedience, approved of coercive measures, and, by resolution, prayed the king to revive a long obsolete statute of Henry the Eighth, by which the governor of the refractory colony should be required to arrest, and send to England for trial, on a charge of treason, the ringleaders in the recent tumults. The colonial Assembly indignantly responded, by re-asserting the chartered privileges of the people, and denying the right of the king to take an offender from the country, for trial. And in the House of Commons a powerful minority battled manfully for the Americans. Burke pronounced the idea of reviving that old statute, as "horrible." "Can you not trust the juries of that country?" he asked. "If you have not a party among two millions of people, you must either change your plans of government, or renounce the colonies forever." Even Grenville, the author of the Stamp Act, opposed the measure, yet a majority voted in favor of the resolution, on the 26th of January, 1769.

The British troops continued to be a constant source of irritation, while, month after month, the colonies were agitated by disputes with the royal governors, the petty tyranny of lesser officials, and the interference of the imperial government with colonial legislation. The Assembly of Massachusetts, encouraged by the expressed sympathy of the other colonies, firmly refused to appropriate a single dollar for the support of the troops. They even demanded their withdrawal from the city, and refused to transact any legislative business while they remained. Daily occurrences exasperated the people against the troops, and finally, on the 2d of March, 1770, an event, apparently trifling in its character, led to bloodshed in the streets of Boston. A rope-maker quarreled with a soldier, and struck him. Out of this affray grew a fight between several soldiers and rope-makers. The latter were beaten, and the result aroused the vengeance of the more excitable portion of the inhabitants. A few evenings afterward [March 5], about seven hundred of them assembled in the streets, for the avowed purpose of attacking the troops.[1] A sentinel was assaulted near the custom-house, when Captain Preston, commander of the guard, went to his rescue with eight armed men. The mob dared the soldiers to fire, and attacked them with stones, pieces of ice, and other missiles. One of the soldiers who received a blow, fired, and his six companions also discharged their guns. Three of the citizens were killed, and five were dangerously wounded.[2] The mob instantly retreated, when all

SAMUEL ADAMS.

[1] These were addressed by a tall man, disguised by a white wig and a scarlet cloak, who closed his harangue by shouting, "To the main guard! to the main guard!" and then disappeared. It was always believed that the tall man was Samuel Adams, one of the most inflexible patriots of the Revolution, and at that time a popular leader. He was a descendant of one of the early Puritans [page 75], and was born in Boston in 1722. He was one of the signers of the Declaration of Independence; was afterward governor of Massachusetts; and died in 1803. A purer patriot than Samuel Adams, never lived.

[2] The leader of the mob was a powerful mulatto, named Crispus Attucks. He and Samuel Gray and James Caldwell, were killed instantly; two others received mortal wounds.

the bells of the city rang an alarum, and in less than an hour several thousands of exasperated citizens were in the streets. A terrible scene of blood would have ensued, had not Governor Hutchinson assured the people that justice should be vindicated in the morning. They retired, but with firm resolves not to endure the military despotism any longer.

The morning of the 6th of March was clear and frosty. At an early hour Governor Hutchinson was called upon to fulfill his promise. The people demanded the instant removal of the troops from Boston, and the trial of Captain Preston and his men, for murder. These demands were complied with. The troops were removed to Castle William [March 12, 1770], and Preston, ably defended by John Adams and Josiah Quincy, two of the popular leaders, was tried and acquitted, with six of his men, by a Boston jury. The other two soldiers were found guilty of manslaughter. This result was a comment on the enforcement of the statute of Henry the Eighth, highly favorable to the Americans. It was so regarded in England, and was used with good effect by the opposition in Parliament. It showed that in the midst of popular excitement, the strong conservative principles of justice bore rule. The victims of the riot were regarded as martyrs to liberty,[1] and for many years, the memory of the "Boston Massacre," as it was called, was kept alive by anniversary orations in the city and vicinity.

Perceiving the will and the power of the colonists in resisting taxation without their consent, the British ministry now wavered. On the very day of the bloody riot in Boston [March 5], Lord North, who was then the English prime minister, proposed to Parliament a repeal of all duties imposed by the act of 1767,[2] except that upon tea. An act to that effect was passed a month afterward [April 12]. This concession was wrung from the minister partly by the clamor of English merchants and manufacturers, who again felt severely the operations of the non-importation associations in America. As tea was a luxury, North supposed the colonists would not object to the small duty laid upon that article, and he retained it as a standing assertion of the *right* of Parliament to impose such duties. The minister entirely mistook the character of the people he was dealing with. It was not the petty *amount* of duties of which they complained, for all the taxes yet imposed were not in the least burdensome to them. They were contending for a great *principle*, which lay at the foundation of their liberties; and they regarded the imposition of a duty upon one article as much a violation of their sacred rights, as if ten were included. They accepted the ministerial concession, but, asserting their rights, continued their non-importation league against the purchase and use of tea.[3]

---

[1] They were buried with great parade. All the bells of Boston and vicinity tolled a funeral knell while the procession was moving; and as intended, the affair made a deep impression on the public mind.

[2] Page 218.

[3] Even before North's proposition was made to Parliament, special agreements concerning the disuse of tea, had been made. Already the popular feeling on this subject had been manifested toward a Boston merchant who continued to sell tea. A company of half-grown boys placed an effigy near his door, with a finger upon it pointing toward his store. While a man was attempting to pull it down, he was pelted with dirt and stones. He ran into the store, and seizing a gun, discharged its contents among the crowd. A boy named Snyder was killed, and Christopher Gore

The spirit of opposition was not confined to the more northern and eastern colonies. It was rife below the Roanoke, and was boldly made manifest when occasion required. In 1771, the Carolinas, hitherto exempted from violent outbursts of popular indignation, although never wanting in zeal in opposing the Stamp Act, and kindred measures, became the theater of great excitement. To satisfy the rapacity and pride of royal governors, the industry of the province of North Carolina, especially, was enormously taxed.[1] The oppression was real, not an abstract principle, as at the North. The people in the interior at length formed associations, designed to resist unjust taxation, and to control public affairs. They called themselves ***Regulators;*** and in 1771, they were too numerous to be overawed by local magistrates. Their operations assumed the character of open rebellion; and in the spring of that year, Governor Tryon[2] marched into that region with an armed force, to subdue them. They met him upon Alamance Creek, in Alamance county, on the 16th of May, and there a bloody skirmish ensued. The Regulators were subdued and dispersed, and Tryon marched back in triumph to the sea-board, after hanging six of the leaders, on the 19th of June following. These events aroused, throughout the South, the fiercest hatred of British power, and stimulated that earnest patriotism so early displayed by the people below the Roanoke, when the Revolution broke out.[3]

The upper part of Narraganset Bay exhibited a scene, in the month of June, 1772, which produced much excitement, and widened the breach between Great Britain and her colonies. The commander of the British armed schooner *Gaspè*, stationed there to assist the commissioners of customs[4] in enforcing the revenue laws, annoyed the American navigators by haughtily commanding them to lower their colors when they passed his vessel, in token of obedience. The William Tells of the bay refused to bow to the cap of this petty Gesler.[5] For such disobedience, a Providence sloop was chased by the schooner. The latter grounded upon a low sandy point; and on that night [June 9, 1772], sixty-four armed men went down from Providence in boats, captured the people on board the *Gaspè*, and burned the vessel. Although a large reward was offered for the perpetrators (who were well known in Providence[6]), they were never betrayed.

(afterward governor of Massachusetts) was wounded. The affair produced great excitement. At about the same time, three hundred "mistresses of families" in Boston signed a pledge of total abstinence from the use of tea, while the duty remained upon it. A few days afterward a large number of young ladies signed a similar pledge.

[1] Governor Tryon caused a palace to be erected for his residence, at Newbern, at a cost of $75,000, for the payment of which the province was taxed. This was in 1768, and was one of the principal causes of discontent, which produced the outbreak here mentioned.

[2] Page 248. [3] Page 237. [4] Page 220.

[5] Gesler was an Austrian governor of one of the cantons of Switzerland. He placed his cap on a pole, at a gate of the town, and ordered all to bow to it, when they should enter. William Tell, a brave leader of the people, refused. He was imprisoned for disobedience, escaped, aroused his countrymen to arms, who drove their Austrian masters out of the land, and achieved the independence of Switzerland.

[6] One of the leaders was Abraham Whipple, a naval commander during the Revolution [page 310]. Several others were afterward distinguished for bravery during that struggle. Four years afterward, when Sir James Wallace, a British commander, was in the vicinity of Newport, Whipple became known as the leader of the attack on the *Gaspè*. Wallace sent him the following letter: "You, Abraham Whipple, on the 9th of June, 1772, burned his majesty's vessel, the *Gaspè*, and I will hang you at the yard-arm." To this Whipple replied: "To Sir James Wallace. Sir: Always catch a man before you hang him.—JAMES WHIPPLE."

These rebellious acts, so significant of the temper of the Americans, greatly perplexed the British ministry. Lord North[1] would gladly have conciliated them, but he was pledged by words and acts to the maintenance of the asserted principle, that Parliament had the undoubted right to tax the colonies without their consent. He labored hard to perceive some method by which conciliation and parliamentary supremacy might be made to harmonize, and early in 1773, a new thought upon taxation entered his brain. The East India Company,[2] having lost their valuable tea customers in America, by the operation of the non-importation associations, and having more than seventeen millions of pounds of the article in their warehouses in England, petitioned Parliament to take off the duty of three pence a pound, levied upon its importation into America. The company agreed to pay the government more than an equal amount, in export duty, if the change should be made. Here was an excellent opportunity for the government to act justly and wisely, and to produce a perfect reconciliation; but the stupid ministry, fearing it might be considered a submission to "rebellious subjects," refused the olive branch of peace. Continuing to misapprehend the real question at issue, North introduced a bill into Parliament, allowing the company to export their teas to America on their own account, without paying an export duty. As this would make tea cheaper in America than in England, he concluded the Americans would not object to paying the three pence duty. This concession to a commercial monopoly, while spurning the appeals of a great principle, only created contempt and indignation throughout the colonies.

LORD NORTH.

Blind as the minister, the East India Company now regarded the American market as open for their tea, and soon after the passage of the bill [May 10, 1773], several large ships, heavily laden with the article, were on their way across the Atlantic. Intelligence of these movements reached America before the arrival of any of the ships, and the people in most of the sea-board towns, where consignments of tea had been made, resolved that it should not even be landed. The ships which arrived at New York and Philadelphia, returned to England with their cargoes. At Charleston it was landed, but was not allowed to be sold; while at Boston, the attempts of the governor and his friends,[3] who

[1] Frederick, Earl of Guilford (Lord North), was a man of talent, sincerely attached to English liberty, and conscientious in the performanance of his duties. Like many other statesmen of his time, he utterly misapprehended the character of the American people, and could not perceive the justice of their claims. He was prime minister during the whole of our War for Independence. He was afflicted with blindness during the last years of his life. He died in July, 1792, at the age of sixty years.

[2] The English East India Company was formed and chartered in 1600, for the purpose of carrying on a trade by sea, between England and the countries lying east of the Cape of Good Hope [note 1, page 37]. It continued prosperous; and about the middle of the last century, the governor of its stations in India, under the pretense of obtaining security for their trade, subdued small territories, and thus planted the foundation of that great British empire in the East, which now comprises the whole of Hindostan, from Cape Comorin to the Himalaya mountains, with a population of more than one hundred and twenty millions of people.

[3] The public mind in Massachusetts was greatly inflamed against Governor Hutchinson at this

were consignees, to land the tea in defiance of the public feeling, resulted in the destruction of a large quantity of it. On a cold moonlight night [December 16, 1773], at the close of the last of several spirited meetings of the citizens held at Faneuil Hall,[1] a party of about sixty persons, some disguised as Indians, rushed on board two vessels in the harbor, laden with tea, tore open the hatches, and in the course of two hours, three hundred and forty-two chests containing the proscribed article, were broken open, and their contents cast into the water. This event produced a powerful sensation throughout the British realm, and led to very important results.

FANEUIL HALL.

While the American colonies, and even Canada, Nova Scotia, and the British West Indies, sympathized with the Bostonians, and could not censure them, the exasperated government adopted retaliatory measures, notwithstanding payment for all damage to their property was promised to the East India Company. Parliament, by enactment [March 7, 1774], ordered the port of Boston to be closed against all commercial transactions whatever, and the removal of the custom-house, courts of justice, and other public offices, to Salem. The Salem people patriotically refused the proffered advantage at the expense of their neighbors; and the inhabitants of Marblehead, fifteen miles distant, offered the free use of their harbor and wharves, to the merchants of Boston. Soon after the passage of the Boston Port Bill, as it was called, another act, which leveled a blow at the charter of Massachusetts, was made a law [March 28, 1774]. It was equivalent to a total subversion of the charter, inasmuch as it deprived the people of many of the dearest privileges guarantied by that instrument.[2] A third retaliatory act was passed on the 21st of April, providing for the trial, in England, of all persons charged in the colonies with murders committed in support of government, giving, as Colonel Barrè said, "encouragement to military insolence already so insupportable." A fourth bill, providing for the quartering of troops in America, was also passed by large majorities in both Houses of Parliament; and in anticipation of rebellion in America, a fifth act was passed, making great concessions to the Roman Catholics in Canada, known as the Quebec Act. This excited the animosity of

---

time, whose letters to a member of Parliament, recommending stringent measures toward the colonies, had been procured in England, and sent to the speaker of the colonial Assembly, by Dr. Franklin. At about the same time, Parliament had passed a law, making the governor and judges of Massachusetts independent of the Assembly for their salaries, these being paid out of the revenues in the hands of the commissioners of customs. This removal of these officials beyond all dependence upon the people, constituted them fit instruments of the crown for oppressing the inhabitants, and in that aspect the colonists viewed the measure, and condemed it.

[1] Because the Revolutionary meetings in Boston were held in Faneuil Hall, it was (and still is) called *The Cradle of Liberty*. It was built, and presented to the town, by Peter Faneuil, in 1742. The picture shows its form during the Revolution. The vane on the steeple, in the form of a grasshopper (symbolical of devouring), yet holds its original place.

[2] It empowered sheriffs appointed by the crown, to select juries, instead of leaving that power with the selectmen of the towns, who were chosen by the people. It also prohibited all town meetings and other gatherings. It provided for the appointment of the council, judges, justices of the peace, etc., by the crown or its representative.

all Protestants. These measures created universal indignation toward the government, and sympathy for the people of Boston.

On the first of June, 1774, the Boston Port Bill went into operation. It was a heavy blow for the doomed town. Business was crushed, and great suffering ensued. The utter prostration of trade soon produced wide-spread distress. The rich, deprived of their rents, became straitened; and the poor, denied the privilege of laboring, were reduced to beggary. All classes felt the scourge of the oppressor, but bore it with remarkable fortitude. They were conscious of being right, and everywhere, tokens of the liveliest sympathy were manifested. Flour, rice, cereal grains, fuel, and money, were sent to the suffering people from the different colonies; and the city of London, in its corporate capacity, subscribed one hundred and fifty thousand dollars for the poor of Boston.

For the purpose of enforcing these oppressive laws, General Gage, the commander-in-chief of the British army in America,[1] was appointed governor of Massachusetts, and an additional military force was ordered to Boston. These coercive demonstrations greatly increased the public irritation, and diminished the hopes of reconciliation. Slavish submission or armed resistance, was now the alternative presented to the American people. Committees of correspondence which had been formed in every colony in 1773,[2] had been busy in the interchange of sentiments and opinions, and throughout the entire community of Anglo-Americans there was evidently a general consonance of feeling, favorable to united efforts in opposing the augmenting tyranny of Great Britain. Yet they hesitated, and resolved to deliberate in solemn council before they should appeal to "the last argument of kings."[3]

SNAKE DEVICE.

The patriots of Massachusetts stood not alone in their integrity. In all the colonies the WHIGS[4] were as inflexible and bold, and as valiantly defied the power of royal governors, when unduly exercised. But those of Massachusetts, being the special objects of ministerial vengeance, suffered more, and required more boldness to act among bristling bayonets and shotted cannons, prepared expressly for their bosoms. Yet they grew stronger every day under persecution, and bolder as the frowns of British power became darker.[5] Even while

---

[1] Page 220.

[2] At a consultation of leading members of the Virginia House of Assembly, in March, 1773, held in the old Raleigh tavern at Williamsburg, at which Patrick Henry, Thomas Jefferson, Richard Henry Lee, and others, were present, it was agreed to submit a resolution in the House the following day, appointing a committee of vigilance and correspondence, and recommending the same to the other colonies. The measure was carried, and these committees formed one of the most powerful engines in carrying on the work of the Revolution. Similar committees had already been formed in several towns in Massachusetts.

[3] These words, in Latin, were often placed upon cannons. There are several old French cannons, made of brass, in the State armory at Richmond, Virginia, on two of which these words appear. They also appear upon some French cannons at West Point.

[4] The terms, WHIG and TORY, had long been used in England as titles of political parties. The former denoted the opposers of royalty; the latter indicated its supporters. These terms were introduced into America two or three years before the Revolution broke out, and became the distinctive titles of the *patriots* and *loyalists*.

[5] Even the children seemed to lose their timidity, and became bolder. They nobly exhibited it

troops, to overawe them were parading the streets of Boston, sturdy representatives of the people assembled at Salem,[1] and sent forth an invitation to all the colonies to appoint delegates to meet in a general Congress at Philadelphia on the 5th of September following. It met with a hearty response from twelve of

the thirteen colonies, and the Press and the Pulpit seconded the measures with great emphasis. Some newspapers bore a significant device. It was a snake cut into thirteen parts, each part bearing the initials of a colony upon it, as seen in the engraving.[2] Under these were the significant words, *Unite or die.*

The delegates were all appointed before the close of August, and the First

---

on one occasion. They were in the habit of building mounds of snow in winter, on Boston Common. These the soldiers battered down, so as to annoy the boys. This being repeated, a meeting of larger boys was held, and a deputation was sent to General Gage, to remonstrate. "We come, sir," said the tallest boy, "to demand satisfaction." "What!" exclaimed Gage; "have your fathers been teaching you rebellion, and sent you here to exhibit it?" "Nobody sent us here, sir," said the boy, while his eyes flashed with indignation. "We have never insulted nor injured your troops, but they have trodden down our snow-hills, and broken the ice on our skating-grounds. We complained; and, calling us young rebels, told us to help ourselves if we could. We told the captain of this, and he laughed at us. Yesterday our works were destroyed for the third time, and we will bear it no longer." Gage admired the spirit of the boys, promised them redress, and turning to an officer, he said, "The very children here draw in a love of liberty with the air they breathe."

[1] At that meeting of the General Assembly of Massachusetts, the patriots matured a plan for a general Congress, provided for munitions of war to resist British power in their own province, and formed a general non-importation league for the whole country. In the midst of their proceedings, General Gage sent his secretary to dissolve them, but the doors of the Assembly chamber were locked, and the key was in Samuel Adams's pocket. Having finished their business, the Assembly adjourned, and thus ended the last session of that body, under a royal governor.

[2] Page 226.

CONTINENTAL CONGRESS[1] assembled in Carpenter's Hall, Philadelphia, on the 5th of September, 1774, the day named in the circular. All but Georgia were represented. Peyton Randolph, of Virginia, was appointed President, and Charles Thomson of Pennsylvania, Secretary.[2] The regular business of the Congress commenced on the morning of the 7th,[3] after an impressive prayer for Divine guidance, uttered by the Rev. Jacob Duché,[4] of Philadelphia. They remained in session until the 26th of October, during which time they matured measures for future action, which met with the general approbation of the American people.[5] They prepared and put forth several State papers,[6] marked by such signal ability and wisdom, as to draw from the Earl of Chatham these words in the House of Lords: "I must declare and avow, that in all my reading and study of history—(and it has been my favorite study—I have read Thucydides, and have studied and admired the master States of the world)—that for solidity of reasoning, force of sagacity, and wisdom of conclusion, under such a complication of circumstances, no nation or body of men can stand in preference to the general Congress at Philadelphia.[7]

CARPENTER'S HALL.

In all its proceedings Congress manifested decorum, firmness,[8] moderation,

---

[1] This name was given to distinguish it from the two colonial Congresses [pages 183 and 215] already held; one at Albany in 1754, the other at New York in 1765.

[2] Thomson was secretary of Congress, perpetually, from 1774, until the adoption of the Federal Constitution, and the organization of the new government, in 1789. Watson relates that Thomson had just come into Philadelphia, with his bride, and was alighting from his chaise, when a messenger from the delegates in Carpenter's Hall came to him, and said they wanted him to come and take minutes of their proceedings, as he was an expert at such business. For his first year's service, he received no pay. So Congress informed his wife that they wished to compensate *her* for the absence of her husband during that time, and wished her to name what kind of a piece of plate she would like to receive. She chose an *urn*, and that silver vessel is yet in the family. Thomson was born in Ireland in 1730, came to America when eleven years of age, and died in 1824, at the age of ninety-four years.

[3] When the delegates had assembled on the 5th, no one seemed inclined to break the silence, and deep anxiety was depicted in every countenance. Soon a grave-looking man, in a suit of "minister's gray," and unpowdered wig, arose, and, with a sweet, musical voice, he uttered a few eloquent words, that electrified the whole audience. "Who is he?" was a question that went from lip to lip. A few who knew him, answered, "It is Patrick Henry, of Virginia." There was no longer any hesitation. He who, nine years before, had cast the gauntlet of defiance at the feet of British power, now set in motion that august machinery of civil power, which assisted in working out the independence of the United States.

[4] Duché was a minister of the Church of England, and afterward became a Tory.

[5] They prepared a plan for a general commercial non-intercourse with Great Britain and her West India possessions, which was called *The American Association*, and was recommended for adoption throughout the country. It consisted of fourteen articles. In addition to the non-intercourse provisions, it was recommended to abandon the slave-trade, to improve the breed of sheep, to abstain from all extravagance in living and indulgence in horse-racing, etc., and the appointment of a committee in every town to promote conformity to the requirements of the *Association*. It was signed by the fifty-two members present.

[6] A Bill of Rights; an address to the people of Great Britain, written by John Jay; another to the several Anglo-American colonies, written by William Livingston; another to the inhabitants of Quebec, and a petition to the king. In these, the grievances and the rights of the colonies were ably set forth.

[7] He also said, in a letter to Stephen Sayre, on the 24th of December, 1774: "I have not words to express my satisfaction that the Congress has conducted this most arduous and delicate business, with such manly wisdom and calm resolution, as do the highest honor to their deliberation."

[8] On the 8th of October, they unanimously resolved, "That this Congress approve the opposition

and loyalty; and when the delegates resolved to adjourn, to meet again at the same place on the 10th of May following [1775], unless the desired redress of grievances should be obtained, they did so with an earnest hope that a reconciliation might speedily take place, and render another national council unnecessary. But they were doomed to bitter disappointment. Great Britain was blind and stubborn still.

CHAPTER II.

FIRST YEAR OF THE WAR FOR INDEPENDENCE. [1775.]

PERSUADED that war was inevitable, the colonists began to prepare for that event, during the summer and autumn of 1774. They practiced daily in military exercises; the manufacture of arms and gunpowder was encouraged; and throughout Massachusetts in particular, where the heel of the oppressor bore heaviest, the people were enrolled in companies. Fathers and sons, encouraged by the gentler sex, received lessons together in the art of war, and prepared to take arms at a moment's warning. From this circumstance, they were called *minute-men*. The Whig[1] journals grew bolder every hour. Epigrams, parables, sonnets, dialogues, and every form of literary expression, remarkable for point and terseness, filled their columns. We give a single specimen of some of the rhymes of the day:

"THE QUARREL WITH AMERICA FAIRLY STATED.

"Rudely forced to drink tea, Massachusetts in anger
Spills the tea on John Bull; John falls on to bang her;
Massachusetts, enraged, calls her neighbors to aid,
And give Master John a severe bastinade.
Now, good men of the law! pray, who is in fault,
The one who began or resents the assault?"

The Massachusetts leaders, in the mean while, were laboring, with intense zeal, to place the province in a condition to rise in open and united rebellion, when necessity should demand. And all over the land, the provincial assemblies, speakers at public gatherings, and from the pulpit, were boldly proclaiming the right of resistance. These demonstrations alarmed General Gage,[2] and he commenced fortifying Boston Neck.[3] He also seized and conveyed to

of the inhabitants of Massachusetts Bay, to the execution of the late acts of Parliament, and if the same shall be attempted to be carried into execution by force, in such case all America ought to support them in their opposition." This resolution, in letter and spirit, was the embodiment of the revolutionary sentiment.

[1] Note 4, page 226.

[2] Thomas Gage was a native of England. He was governor of Montreal [page 203] in 1760, and commander-in-chief of the British army in America, in 1763. He was appointed governor of Massachusetts, in 1774; left America in 1775; and died in 1787.

[3] The peninsula of Boston was originally connected with the main land by a narrow isthmus called the Neck. It has been greatly widened by filling in the marginal morasses; and over it now passes the fine avenue which connects the city with Roxbury, on the main.

the city large quantities of ammunition found in the neighboring villages, and employed stringent measures for preventing intercourse between the patriots in the city and in the country. The exasperated people needed but the electric spark of even a slight offense to kindle their suppressed indignation into a blaze. They were ready to sound the battle-cry, and evoke the sword of rebellion from its scabbard; and they were even anxious to attack the soldiers in Boston, but they were restrained by prudent conselors.[1]

A rumor went abroad on the third of September, that British ships were cannonading Boston. From the shores of Long Island Sound to the green hills of Berkshire, "To arms! to arms!" was the universal shout. Instantly, on every side, men of all ages were seen cleansing and burnishing their weapons; and within two days, full thirty thousand *minute-men* were under arms, and hastening toward that city. They were met by a contradiction of the rumor; but the event conveyed such a portentous lesson to Gage, that he pushed forward his military operations with as much vigor as the opposition of the people would allow.[2] He thought it expedient to be more conciliatory; and he summoned the colonial Assembly to meet at Salem on the 5th of October. Then dreading their presence, he revoked the order. Ninety delegates met, however, and organized by the appointment of John Hancock[3] president. They then went to Cambridge, where they formed a Provincial Congress, independent of royal authority (the first in America), and labored earnestly in preparations for that armed resistance, now become a stern necessity. They made provisions for an army of twelve thousand men; solicited other New England colonies to augment it to twenty thousand; and appointed Jedediah Preble and Artemas Ward[4] men of experience in the French and Indian war,[5] generals of all the troops that might be raised.

The Americans were now, fairly aroused to action. They had counted the cost of armed rebellion, and were fully resolved to meet it. The defiant position of the colonists arrested the attention of all Europe. When the British Parliament assembled early in 1775, that body presented a scene of great excitement. Dr. Franklin and others,[6] then in England, had given a wide circulation to the State papers put forth by the Continental Congress;[7] and the

---

[1] Many hundreds of armed men assembled at Cambridge. At Charlestown, the people took possession of the arsenal, after Gage had carried off the powder. At Portsmouth, N. H., they captured the fort, and carried off the ammunition. At Newport, R. I., the people seized the powder, and took possession of forty pieces of cannon at the entrance of the harbor. In New York, Philadelphia, Annapolis, Williamsburg, Charleston, and Savannah, the people took active defensive measures, and the whole country was in a blaze of indignation.

[2] Carpenters refused to work on the fortifications, and much of the material was destroyed by fire, at night, in spite of the vigilance of the guards. Gage sent to New York for timber and workmen; but the people there would not permit either to leave their port.

[3] John Hancock was one of the most popular of the New England patriots, throughout the whole war. He was born in Braintree, Massachusetts, in 1737, was educated at Harvard College; became a counting-room clerk to his uncle, and inherited that gentleman's great wealth. He entered public life early; was a representative in the Continental Congress, and was its president when the Declaration of Independence was adopted. He was afterward governor of Massachusetts. Mr. Hancock died in October, 1793, at the age of fifty-six years.

[4] Note 5, page 238.

[5] Page 179.

[6] Dr. Franklin had then been agent in England, for several of the colonies, for about ten years

[7] Note 6, page 228.

English mind was already favorably influenced in favor of the Americans. Pitt came on crutches[1] from his retirement, to cast the weight of his mighty influence into the scale of justice, by action in the House of Lords. He proposed [January 7, 1775] conciliatory measures. They were rejected, as well

as others offered by Burke, Conway, and Hartly; and in their stead, Parliament, in March, struck another severe blow at the industry of New England, by prohibiting fishing on the banks of Newfoundland.[2] Already Lord North had moved, in the House of Commons [February, 1775], for an address to the king, affirming that Massachusetts was in a state of rebellion. The Ministers also endeavored to promote dissensions in America, by crippling the trade of New England and other colonies, but exempting New York, Delaware, and North Carolina. The bait of favor for these three colonies was indignantly

[1] Pitt was greatly afflicted with the gout. Sometimes he was confined to his house for weeks by it; and he was sometimes seen on the floor of Parliament leaning upon crutches, and his legs swathed in flannels. In this condition he made two of his most eloquent speeches in favor of the Americans.

[2] At that time, there were employed by the Americans, in the British Newfoundland fisheries, four hundred ships, two thousand fishing shallops, and twenty thousand men. On account of this blow to the fishing trade, a great many inhabitants of Nantucket and vicinity, chiefly Quakers, went to North Carolina, and in Orange and Guilford counties, became planters. Their descendants are yet numerous there. The principal meeting-house is at New Garden.

spurned—the scheme of disunion signally failed. Common dangers and common interests drew the ligaments of fraternity closer than ever. When the trees budded, and the flowers bloomed in the spring of 1775, all hope of reconciliation had vanished. It was evident that

"King, Commons, and Lords, were uniting amain,"

to destroy the Liberty Tree, planted by faithful hands. The people of the colonies, though weak in military resources, were strong in purpose; and, relying upon the justice of their cause, and the assistance of the Lord God Omnipotent, they resolved to defy the fleets and armies of Great Britain.

There was great moral sublimity in the rising of the colonies against the parent country; for it was material weakness arrayed against great material strength. There were more than three thousand British troops in Boston, on the first of April, 1775. Confident in his power, Gage felt certain that he could repress insurrections, and keep the people quiet. Yet he felt uneasy concerning the gathering of ammunition and stores,[1] by the patriots, at Concord, sixteen miles from Boston. Toward midnight, on the 18th [April], he secretly dispatched eight hundred men, under lieutenant-colonel Smith and Major Pitcairn, to destroy them. So carefully had he arranged the expedition, that he believed it to be entirely unknown to the patriots. All his precautions were vain. The vigilant Dr. Warren,[2] who was secretly watching all the movements of Gage, became aware of the expedition early in the evening; and when it moved, Paul Revere,[3] one of the most active of the Sons of Liberty in Boston, had landed at Charlestown, and was on his way to Concord to arouse the inhabitants and minute-men. Soon afterward, church-bells, muskets, and cannons spread the alarm over the country; and when, at dawn, on the 19th of April. 1775—a day memorable in the annals of our Republic—Pitcairn, with the advanced guard, reached Lexington, a few miles from Concord, he found seventy determined men drawn up to oppose him. Pitcairn rode forward and shouted, "Disperse! disperse, you rebels! Down with your arms, and disperse!" They refused obedience, and he ordered his men to fire. That dreadful order was obeyed, and the FIRST BLOOD OF THE REVOLUTION flowed upon the tender grass on the Green at Lexington. Eight citizens were killed, several were wounded, and the remainder were dispersed. The last survivor of that noble band[4] died in March, 1854, at the age of almost ninety-six years.

---

[1] Early in the year, secret orders had been sent by the ministry to the royal governors, to remove all ammunition and stores out of the reach of the people, if they made any hostile demonstrations.

[2] Afterward killed in the battle on Breed's Hill. See page 235.

[3] Revere was an engraver, and previous to this time had executed some creditable specimens of his art. He engraved a picture of the naval investment of Boston, in 1768, and of the *Boston Massacre*, in 1770. As a Grand Master of the Masonic order, he was very influential; yet, like those of Isaac Sears, of New York, his eminent services in the cause of freedom have been overlooked. Their fame is eclipsed by men of greater minds, but of no sturdier patriotism.

[4] Jonathan Harrington, who played the fife for the *minute-men*, on the morning of the battle. The writer visited him in 1848, when he was ninety years of age. He then had a perfect recollection of the events of that morning. A portrait of him, as he appeared at that time, is published in Lossing's *Pictorial Field Book of the Revolution*, page 554, vol. i.

Confident of full success, the British now pressed forward to Concord, and destroyed the stores. They were terribly annoyed by the minute-men on their way, who fired upon them from behind walls, trees, and buildings. Having accomplished their purpose, and killed several more patriots in a skirmish there, the royal troops hastily retreated to Lexington. The country was now thoroughly aroused, and minute-men were gathering by scores. Nothing but the timely arrival of Lord Percy with reinforcements,[1] saved the eight hundred men from total destruction. The whole body now retreated. All the way back to Bunker's Hill,[2] in Charlestown, the troops were terribly assailed by the patriots; and when, the following morning, they crossed over to Boston, they ascertained their loss to be, in killed and wounded, two hundred and seventy-three. The loss of the Americans in killed, wounded, and missing, was one hundred and three.[3]

The initial blow for freedom had now been struck. It was appalling to friend and foe. The news of this tragedy spread over the country like a blaze of lightning from a midnight cloud, and like the attendant thunder-peal, it aroused all hearts. From the hills and valleys of New England, the patriots went forth by hundreds, armed and unarmed; and before the close of the month [April 1775], an army of twenty thousand men were forming camps and piling fortifications around Boston, from Roxbury to the river Mystic, determined to confine the fierce tiger of war, which had tasted their blood, upon that little peninsula. The provincial Congress,[4] sitting at Watertown, with Dr. Warren at its head, worked day and night in consonance with the gathering army. They appointed military officers, organized a commissariat for supplies, issued bills of credit for the payment of troops (for which the province was pledged), to the amount of three hundred and seventy-five dollars, and declared [May 5] General Gage to be an "inveterate enemy" of the people. And as the intelligence went from colony to colony, the people in each were equally aroused. Arms and ammunition were seized by the *Sons of Liberty*, provincial Congresses were formed, and before the close of summer, the power of every royal governor, from Massachusetts to Georgia, was utterly destroyed. Everywhere the inhabitants armed in defense of their liberties, and took vigorous measures for future security.

Some aggressive enterprises were undertaken by volunteers. The most important of these was the seizure of the strong fortresses of Ticonderoga[5] and Crown Point,[6] on Lake Champlain, chiefly by Connecticut and Vermont

---

[1] Earl Percy was a son of the Duke of Northumberland. When he was marching out of Boston, his band struck up the tune of Yankee Doodle, in derision. He saw a boy at Roxbury making himself very merry as he passed. Percy inquired why he was so merry. "To think," said the lad, "how you will dance by-and-by to *Chevy Chase*." Percy was often much influenced by presentiments, and the words of the boy made him moody. Percy was a lineal descendant of the Earl Percy who was slain in the battle of *Chevy Chase*, and he felt all day as if some great calamity might befall him.

[2] Page 235.

[3] Appropriate monuments have been erected to the memory of the slain, at Lexington, Concord, and Acton. Davis, the commander of the militia at Concord, was from Acton, and so were most of his men. The estimated value of the property destroyed by the invaders, was as follows: In Concord, one thousand three hundred and seventy-five dollars; in Lexington, eight thousand three hundred and five dollars; in Cambridge, six thousand and ten dollars.

[4] Page 230.

[5] Page 196.

[6] Page 200.

militia, under the command of Colonels Ethan Allen and Benedict Arnold. Ticonderoga and its garrison were taken possession of at dawn, on the 10th of May, 1775;[1] and two days afterward, Colonel Seth Warner, of the expedition, with a few men, captured Crown Point. The spoils of victory taken at these two posts, consisting of almost one hundred and fifty pieces of cannon, and a large quantity of ammunition and stores, were of vast consequence to the Americans. A few months later [March, 1776], some of these cannons were hurling death-shots into the midst of the British troops in Boston.[2]

Having repudiated royal authority, the people of Massachusetts were obedient to their chosen rulers, and efficient civil government was duly inaugurated. On the 19th of May [1775], the provincial Congress of Massachusetts clothed the Committee of Safety, sitting at Cambridge, with full powers to regulate the operations of the army. Artemas Ward was appointed commander-in-chief, Richard Gridley,[3] chief engineer, and Israel Putnam, John Stark, and other veterans, who had served bravely in the French and Indian war, were appointed to important commands. The military genius developed in that old conflict, was now brought into requisition. Day by day the position of the British army became more perilous. Fortunately for its safety, large reinforcements, under those three experienced commanders, Generals Howe, Clinton, and Burgoyne, arrived on the 25th of May. It was timely: and then the whole British force in Boston amounted to about twelve thousand men, besides several well-manned vessels of war, under Admiral Graves. Gage now resolved to attack the Americans and penetrate the country.

Preparatory to an invasion of the province, Gage issued a proclamation [June 10, 1775], declaring all Americans in arms to be rebels and traitors, and offering a free pardon to all who should return to their allegiance, except those arch-offenders, John Hancock and Samuel Adams.[4] These he intended to seize and send to England to be hanged. The vigilant patriots, aware of Gage's hostile intentions, strengthened their intrenchments on Boston Neck,[5] and on the evening of the 16th of June, General Ward sent Colonel Prescott[6] with a detachment of one thousand men, to take possession of, and fortify, Bunker's Hill, in Charlestown, which commanded an important part of Boston and the surrounding water. By mistake they ascended Breed's Hill, within cannon shot of the city, and laboring with pick and spade all that night, they had cast up a strong redoubt[7] of earth, on the summit of that eminence, before the Brit-

---

[1] Allen was in chief command. Having taken possession of the fort and garrison by surprise, he ascended to the door of the commandant's apartment, and awoke Captain De La Place, by heavy blows with the hilt of his sword. The astonished commander, followed by his wife, came to the door. He knew Allen. "What do you want?" he inquired. "I want you to surrender this fort," Allen answered. "By what authority do *you* demand it?" asked De La Place. "By the Great Jehovah and the Continental Congress!" said Allen, with the voice of a Stentor. The captain submitted, and the fortress became a possession of the patriots.

[2] Page 247.

[3] Note 1, page 138.

[4] Note 1, page 221.

[5] Note 3, page 229.

[6] William Prescott was born at Groton, Massachusetts, in 1726. He was at Louisburg [page 137] in 1745. After the battle of Bunker's Hill, he served under Gates, until the surrender of Burgoyne, when he left the army. He died in 1795.

[7] A redoubt is a small fortification generally composed of earth, and having very few features of a regular fort, except its arrangement for the use of cannons and muskets. They are often tem-

ish were aware of their presence. Gage and his officers were greatly astonished at the apparition of this military work, at the dawn of the 17th.

The British generals were not only astonished, but alarmed, and at once perceived the necessity for driving the Americans from this commanding position, before they should plant a heavy battery there, for in that event, Boston must be evacuated before sunrise. The drums beat to arms, and soon the city was in a great tumult. The imminent danger converted many Tories into professedly warm Whigs, for the days of British rule appeared to be closing. Every eminence and roof in Boston swarmed with people and at about sunrise [June 17, 1775], a heavy cannonade was opened upon the redoubt, from a battery on Copp's Hill, in Boston,[1] and from the shipping in the harbor, but with very little effect. Hour after hour the patriots toiled on in the completion of their work, and at noon-day, their task was finished, and they laid aside their implements of labor for knapsacks and muskets. General Howe, with General Pigot, and three thousand men, crossed the Charles River at the same time, to Morton's Point, at the foot of the eastern slope of Breed's Hill, formed his troops into two columns, and marched slowly to attack the redoubt. Although the British commenced firing cannons soon after they began to ascend the hill, and the great guns of the ships, and the battery on Copp's Hill, poured an incessant storm upon the redoubt, the Americans kept perfect silence until they had approached within close musket shot. Hardly an American could be seen by the slowly approaching enemy, yet behind those rude mounds of earth, lay fifteen hundred determined men,[2] ready to pour deadly volleys of musket-balls upon the foe, when their commanders should order them.

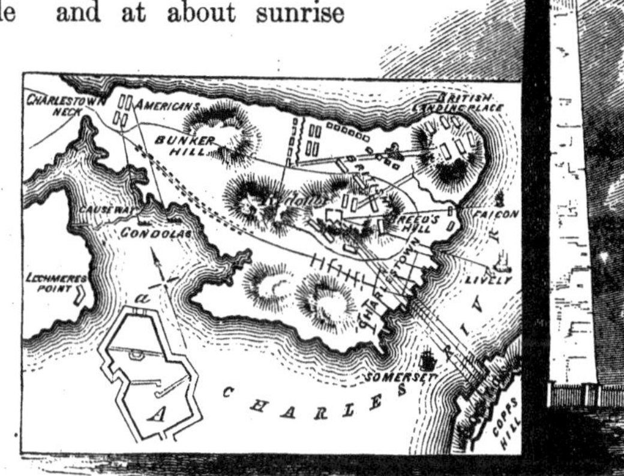

PLAN OF BUNKER'S HILL BATTLE. MONUMENT.

porary structures, cast up in the progress of a siege, or a protracted battle. The diagram *A*, on the map, shows the form of the redoubt, *a* is the entrance.

[1] That portion of Copp's Hill, where the British battery was constructed, is a burial-ground, in which lie many of the earlier residents of that city. Among them, the Mather family, distinguished in the early history of the Commonwealth. See page 133.

[2] During the forenoon, General Putnam had been busy in forwarding reinforcements for Prescott, and when the battle began, about five hundred had been added to the detachment. Yet he found it difficult to urge many of the raw recruits forward; and after the war, he felt it necessary to arise in the church of which he was a member, and in the presence of the congregation, acknowledge the sin of swearing on that occasion. He partially justified himself by saying, "It was almost enough to make an angel swear, to see the cowards refuse to secure a victory so nearly won."

It was now three o'clock in the afternoon. When the British column was within ten rods of the redoubt, Prescott shouted *Fire!* and instantly whole platoons of the assailants were prostrated by well-aimed bullets.[1] The survivors fell back in great confusion, but were soon rallied for a second attack. They were again repulsed, with heavy loss, and while scattering in all directions, General Clinton arrived with a few followers, and joined Howe, as a volunteer. The fugitives were again rallied, and they rushed up to the redoubt in the face of a galling fire. For ten minutes the battle raged fearfully, and, in the mean while, Charlestown, at the foot of the eminence, having been fired by a carcass[2] from Copp's Hill,[3] sent up dense columns of smoke, which completely enveloped the belligerents. The firing in the redoubt soon grew weaker, for the ammunition of the Americans had become exhausted. It ceased altogether, and then the British scaled the bank and compelled the Americans to retreat, while they fought fiercely with clubbed muskets.[4] Overpowered, they fled across Charlestown Neck,[5] gallantly covered by Putnam and a few brave men, and under that commander, they took position on Prospect Hill, and fortified it. The British took possession of Bunker's Hill,[6] and erected a fortification there. There was absolutely no victory in the case. Completely exhausted, both parties sought rest, and hostilities ceased for a time. The Americans had lost, in killed, wounded, and prisoners, about four hundred and fifty men. The loss of the British from like causes, was almost eleven hundred.[7] This was the first real *battle*[8] of the Revolution, and lasted almost two hours.

Terrible for the people of Boston and vicinity, were the events of that bright and cloudless, and truly beautiful June day. All the morning, as we have observed, and during the fierce conflict, roofs, steeples, and every high place, in and around the city, were filled with anxious spectators. Almost every family had a representative among the combatants; and in an agony of suspense, mothers, wives, sisters, and daughters, gazed upon the scene. Many a loved

---

[1] Prescott ordered his men to aim at the waistbands of the British, and to pick off their officers, whose fine clothes would distinguish them. It is said that men, at the first onset in battle, always fire too high, hence the order to aim at the waistbands.

[2] A *carcass* is a hollow case, formed of ribs of iron covered with cloth or metal, with holes in it. Being filled with combustibles and set on fire, it is thrown from a mortar, like a bomb-shell, upon the roofs of buildings, and ignites them. A bomb-shell is a hollow ball with an orifice, filled with powder (sometimes mixed with slugs of iron), which is ignited by a slow match when fired, explodes, and its fragments produce terrible destruction.

[3] See map on page 235.

[4] Most of the American muskets were destitute of bayonets, and they used the large end as clubs. This is a last resort.

[5] Charlestown, like Boston, is on a peninsula, almost surrounded by water and a marsh. The Neck was a narrow causeway, connecting it with the main. Charlestown was a flourishing rival of Boston, at the time of the battle. It was then completely destroyed. Six hundred buildings perished in the flames. Burgoyne, speaking of the battle and conflagration, said, it was the most awful and sublime sight he had ever witnessed.

[6] As the battle took place on *Breed's*, and not on *Bunker's* Hill, the former name should have been given to it; but the name of *Bunker's Hill* has become too sacred in the records of patriotism to be changed.

[7] The provincial Congress estimated the loss at about fifteen hundred; General Gage reported one thousand and fifty-four. Of the Americans, only one hundred and fifteen were killed; the remainder were wounded or made prisoners.

[8] A *battle* is a conflict carried on by large bodies of troops, according to the rules of military tactics; a *skirmish* is a sudden and irregular fight between a few troops.

one perished; and there the country lost one of its most promising children, and freedom a devoted champion. Dr. Warren, who had just been appointed major-general, had crossed Charlestown Neck in the midst of flying balls from the British shipping, and reached the redoubt on Breed's Hill, at the moment when the enemy scaled its banks. He was killed by a musket ball, while retreating. Buried where he fell, near the redoubt, the tall Bunker Hill monument of to-day, standing on that spot, commemorates his death, as well as the patriotism of his countrymen.

JOSEPH WARREN.

The storm was not confined to the east. While these events were occurring in New England, the Revolution was making rapid progress elsewhere. Even before the tragedy at Lexington and Concord, Patrick Henry[2] had again aroused his countrymen by his eloquence, and in the Virginia Assembly, convened at Richmond, on the 23d of March, 1775, he concluded a masterly speech with that noted sentiment, which became the war-cry of the patriots, "GIVE ME LIBERTY, OR GIVE ME DEATH!" When, twenty-six days later [April 20], Governor Dunmore, by ministerial command,[3] seized and conveyed on board a British vessel of war, a quantity of gunpowder belonging to the colony, that same inflexible patriot went at the head of armed citizens, and demanded and received from the royal representative, full restitution. And before the battle of Bunker's Hill, the exasperated people had driven Dunmore[4] from his palace at Williamsburg [June], and he was a refugee, shorn of political power, on board a British man-of-war in the York River.

Further south, still bolder steps had been taken. The people in the interior of North Carolina, where the Regulator Movement occurred four years earlier, asserted their dignity and their rights as freemen, in a way that astonished even the most sanguine and determined patriots elsewhere. A convention of delegates chosen by the people, assembled at Charlotte, in Mecklenberg county, in May, 1775, and by a series of resolutions, they virtually declared their constituents absolved from all allegiance to the British crown,[5] organized local government, and made provisions for military defense. In South Carolina and Georgia, also, arms and ammunition had been seized by the people, and all royal authority was repudiated.

While the whole country was excited by the rising rebellion, and on the

---

[1] Joseph Warren was born in Roxbury, in 1740. He was at the head of his profession as a physician, when the events of the approaching revolution brought him into public life. He was thirty-five years of age when he died. His remains rest in St. Paul's church, in Boston.

[2] Note 1, page 214.

[3] Note 1, page 232.

[4] Dunmore was strongly suspected of a desire to have the hostile Indians west of the Alleghanies annihilate the Virginia troops sent against them in the summer of 1774. They suffered terrible loss in a battle at Point Pleasant on the Ohio, in October of that year, in consequence of the failure of promised aid from Dunmore. They subdued the Indians, however.

[5] This "Declaration of Independence," as it is called, was made about thirteen months previous to the general Declaration put forth by the Continental Congress, and is one of the glories of the people of North Carolina. It consisted of a series of twenty resolutions, and was read, from time to time, to other gatherings of the people, after the convention at Charlotte.

very day [May 10] when Allen and Arnold took Ticonderoga,[1] the SECOND CONTINENTAL CONGRESS convened at Philadelphia. Notwithstanding New England was in a blaze of war, royal authority had virtually ceased in all the colonies, and the conflict for independence had actually begun,[2] that august body held out to Great Britain a loyal, open hand of reconciliation. Congress sent [July, 1775] a most loyal petition to the king, and conciliatory addresses to the people of Great Britain. At the same time they said firmly, "We have counted the cost of this contest, and find nothing so dreadful as voluntary slavery." They did not foolishly lose present advantages in waiting for a reply, but pressed forward in the work of public security. Having resolved on armed resistance, they voted to raise an army of twenty thousand men; and two days before the battle of Bunker's Hill [June 15, 1775], they elected GEORGE WASHINGTON commander-in-chief of all the forces raised, or to be raised, for the defense of the colonies.[3] That destined *Father of his Country*, was then forty-three years of age. They also adopted the incongruous mass of undisciplined troops at Boston,[4] as a CONTINENTAL ARMY, and appointed general officers[5] to assist Washington in its organization and future operations.

General Washington took command of the army at Cambridge, on the 3d of July, and with the efficient aid of General Gates, who was doubtless the best disciplined soldier then in the field, order was soon brought out of great confusion, and the Americans were prepared to commence a regular siege of the British army in Boston.[6] To the capture or expulsion of those troops, the efforts of Washington were mainly directed during the summer and autumn of 1775. Fortifications were built, a thorough organization of the army was effected, and all that industry and skill could do, with such material, in perfecting arrangements for a strong and fatal blow, was accomplished. The army,

---

[1] Page 234. [2] Page 232.

[3] Washington was a delegate in Congress from Virginia, and his appointment was wholly unexpected to him. When the time came to choose a commander-in-chief, John Adams arose, and after a brief speech, in which he delineated the qualities of the man whom he thought best fitted for the important service, he expressed his intenton to propose a member from Virginia for the office of generalissimo. All present understood the allusion, and the next day, Thomas Johnson, of Maryland, nominated Colonel Washington, and he was, by unanimous vote, elected commander-in-chief. At the same time Congress resolved that they would "maintain and assist him, and adhere to him, with their lives and fortunes, in the cause of American liberty." When President Hancock announced to Washington his appointment, he modestly, and with great dignity, signified his acceptance in the following terms: "Mr. President—Though I am truly sensible of the high honor done me, in this appointment, yet I feel great distress, from a consciousness that my abilities and military experience may not be equal to the extensive and important trust. However, as the Congress desire it, I will enter upon the momentous duty, and exert every power I possess in their service, and for the support of the glorious cause. I beg they will accept my most cordial thanks for this distinguished testimony of their approbation. But lest some unlucky event should happen, unfavorable to my reputation, I beg it may be remembered by every gentleman in this room, that I, this day, declare with the utmost sincerity, I do not think myself equal to the command I am honored with. As to pay, sir, I beg leave to assure the Congress that, as no pecuniary consideration could have tempted me to accept the arduous employment, at the expense of my domestic ease and happiness, I do not wish to make any profit from it. I will keep an exact account of my expenses. Those, I doubt not, they will discharge, and that is all I desire."

[4] Page 232.

[5] Artemas Ward, Charles Lee, Philip Schuyler, and Israel Putnam, were appointed *major-generals;* Horatio Gates, *adjutant-general;* and Seth Pomeroy, Richard Montgomery, David Wooster, William Heath, Joseph Spencer, John Thomas, John Sullivan, and Nathaniel Green (all New England men), *brigadier-generals.*

[6] Page 232.

fourteen thousand strong at the close of the year, extended from Roxbury on the right, to Prospect Hill, two miles north-west of Breed's Hill, on the left. The right was commanded by General Ward, the left by General Lee. The centre, at Cambridge, was under the immediate control of the commander-in-chief.

At the close of May, Congress sent an affectionate address to the people of Canada. They were cordially invited to join their Anglo-American[1] neighbors[2] in efforts to obtain redress of grievances, but having very little sympathy in language, religion, or social condition with them, they refused, and were necessarily considered positive supporters of the royal cause. The capture of the two fortresses on Lake Champlain[3] [May, 1775], having opened the way to the St. Lawrence, a well-devised plan to take possession of that province and prevent its becoming a place of rendezvous and supply of invading armies from Great Britain, was matured by Congress and the commander-in-chief.[4] To

[1] Note 1, page 193.
[2] The Congress of 1774, made an appeal *To the inhabitants of Quebec*, in which was clearly set forth the grievances of the colonists, and an invitation to fraternize with those already in union.
[3] Page 234.
[4] A committee of Congress, consisting of Dr. Franklin, Thomas Lynch, and Benjamin Harrison, went to Cambridge, in August, and there the plan of the campaign against Canada was arranged.

accomplish this, a body of New York and New England troops were placed under the command of Generals Schuyler[1] and Montgomery,[2] and ordered to proceed by way of Lake Champlain to Montreal and Quebec.

Had Congress listened to the earnest advice of Colonel Ethan Allen, to invade Canada immediately after the capture of Ticonderoga and Crown Point, the result of the expedition would doubtless have been very different, for at that time the British forces in the province were few, and they had made no preparations for hostilities. It was near the close of August before the invading army appeared before St. John on the Sorel, the first military post within the Canadian line. Deceived in regard to the strength of the garrison and the disposition of the Canadians and the neighboring Indians, Schuyler fell back to Isle Aux Noix,[3] and after making preparations to fortify it, he hastened to Ticonderoga to urge forward more troops. Sickness compelled him to return to Albany, and the whole command devolved upon Montgomery, his second in command. That energetic officer did not remain long within his island intrenchments, and toward the close of September, he laid siege to St. John. The garrison maintained an obstinate resistance for more than a month, and Montgomery twice resolved to abandon it. During the siege, small detachments of brave men went out upon daring enterprises. One, of eighty men, under Colonel Ethan Allen,[4] pushed across the St. Lawrence, and attacked Montreal [September 25, 1775], then garrisoned by quite a strong force under General Prescott.[5] This was done at the suggestion of Colonel John Brown, who was to cross the river with his party, a little above, and co-operate with Allen. He failed to do so, and disaster ensued. Allen and his party were defeated, and he was made prisoner and, with several of his men, was sent to England in irons. Another expedition under Colonel Bedell, of New Hampshire, was more successful. They captured the strong fort (but feeble garrison) at Chambly [October 30], a few miles north of St. John; and at about the same time, Sir Guy Carleton, governor of Canada, with a reinforcement for the garrison of St. John, was repulsed [November 1] by a party under Colonel Warner, at Longueil, nearly opposite Montreal. These events alarmed Preston, the commander of St. John, and he surrendered that post to Montgomery, on the 3d of November.

When the victory was complete, the Americans pressed on toward Mont-

---

[1] Philip Schuyler was born at Albany, New York, in 1733, and was one of the wisest and best men of his time. He was a captain under Sir William Johnson [page 190] in 1755, and was active in the public service, chiefly in civil affairs, from that time until the Revolution. During that struggle, he was very prominent, and after the war, was almost continually engaged in public life, until his death, which occurred in 1804.

[2] Richard Montgomery was born in Ireland, in 1737. He was with Wolfe, at Quebec [page 201], and afterward married a sister of Chancellor Livingston, and settled in the State of New York. He gave promise of great military ability, when death ended his career. See portrait on page 242.

[3] Note 8, page 197.

[4] Ethan Allen was born in Litchfield county, Connecticut. He went to Vermont at an early age, and in 1770 was one of the bold leaders there in the opposition of the settlers to the territorial claims of New York. He was never engaged in active military services after his capture. He died in Vermont in February, 1789, and his remains lie in a cemetery two miles from Burlington, near the Winooski.

[5] Page 271.

real. Governor Carleton, conscious of his weakness, immediately retreated on board one of the vessels of a small fleet lying in the river, and escaped to Quebec; and on the following day [November 13], Montgomery entered the city in triumph. He treated the people humanely, gained their respect, and with the woolen clothing found among the spoils, he commenced preparing his soldiers for the rigors of a Canadian winter. There was no time to be lost, by delays. Although all their important posts in Canada were in possession of the patriots, yet, Montgomery truly said, in a letter to Congress, "till Quebec is taken, Canada is unconquered." Impressed with this idea, he determined to push forward to the capital, notwithstanding the inclemency of the weather and the desertion of his troops. Winter frosts were binding the waters, and blinding snow was mantling the whole country.

The spectacle presented by this little army, in the midst of discouragements of every kind, was one of great moral grandeur. Yet it was not alone at that perilous hour; for while this expedition, so feeble in number and supplies, was on its way to achieve a great purpose, another, consisting of a thousand men, under Colonel Benedict Arnold,[1] had left Cambridge [Sept., 1775], and was making its way through the deep wilderness by the Kennebec and Chaudiere[2] Rivers, to join Montgomery before the walls of Quebec. That expedition was one of the most wonderful on record. For thirty-two days they traversed a gloomy wilderness, without meeting a human being. Frost and snow were upon the ground, and ice was upon the surface of the marshes and the streams, which they were compelled to traverse and ford, sometimes arm-pit deep in water and mud. Yet they murmured not; and even women followed in their train.[3] After enduring incredible toils and hardships, exposed to intense cold and biting hunger, they arrived at Point Levi,[4] opposite Quebec, on the 9th of November. Four days afterward [Nov. 13], and at about the same time when Montgomery entered Montreal, the intrepid Arnold, with only seven hundred and fifty half-naked men, not more than four hundred muskets, and no artillery, crossed the St. Lawrence to Wolfe's Cove,[5] ascended to the Plains of Abraham,[6] and boldly demanded a surrender of the city and garrison within the massive walls. Soon the icy winds, and intelligence of an intended sortie[7] from the garrison, drove Arnold from his bleak encampment, and he ascended the St. Lawrence to *Point au Trembles*, twenty miles above Quebec, and there

[1] Page 234. [2] Pronounced *Sho-de-are.*

[3] Judge Henry, of Pennsylvania, then a young man, accompanied the expedition. He wrote an account of the siege of Quebec, and in it he mentions the wives of Sergeant Grier and of a private soldier, who accompanied them. "Entering the ponds," he says, "and breaking the ice here and there with the butts of our guns, and our feet, we were soon waist-deep in mud and water. As is generally the case with youths, it came to my mind that a better path might be found than that of the more elderly guide. Attempting this, the water in a trice cooling my arm-pits, made me gladly return in the file. Now, Mrs. Grier had got before me. My mind was humbled, yet astonished, at the exertions of this good woman." Like the soldiers, she waded through the deep waters and the mud.

[4] Page 201. Several men who were afterward prominent actors in the Revolution, accompanied Arnold in this expedition. Among them, also, was Aaron Burr, then a youth of twenty, who was afterward Vice-President of the United States. [5] Page 202. [6] Page 202.

[7] This is a French term, significant of a sudden sally of troops from a besieged city or fortress, to attack the besiegers. See page 434.

awaited the arrival of Montgomery. These brave generals met on the 1st of December [1775], and woolen clothes which Montgomery brought from Montreal, were placed on the shivering limbs of Arnold's troops. The united forces, about nine hundred strong, then marched to Quebec.

It was on the evening of the 5th of December when the Americans reached Quebec, and the next morning early, Montgomery sent a letter to Carleton, by a flag,[1] demanding an immediate surrender. The flag was fired upon, and the invaders were defied. With a few light cannons and some mortars, and exposed to almost daily snow-storms in the open fields, the Americans besieged the city for three weeks. Success appearing only in assault, that measure was agreed upon, and before dawn, on the morning of the last day of the year [Dec. 31, 1775], while snow was falling thickly, the attempt was made. Montgomery had formed his little army into four columns, to assail the city at different points. One of these, under Arnold, was to attack the lower town, and march along the St. Charles to join another division, under Montgomery, who was to approach by way of Cape Diamond,[2] and the two were to attempt a forced passage into the city, through Prescott Gate.[3] At the same time, the other two columns, under Majors Livingston and Brown, were to make a feigned attack upon the upper town, from the Plains of Abraham. In accordance with this plan, Montgomery descended Wolfe's Ravine, and marched carefully along the ice-strewn beach, toward a pallisade and battery at Cape Diamond. At the head of his men, in the face of the driving snow, he had passed the pallisade unopposed, when a single discharge of a cannon from the battery, loaded with grape-shot,[4] killed him instantly, and slew several of his officers, among whom were his two aids, McPherson and Cheeseman. His followers instantly retreated. In the mean while, Arnold had been severely wounded, while attacking a barrier on the St. Charles,[5] and the command of his division devolved upon Captain Morgan,[6] whose expert riflemen, with Lamb's artillery, forced their way into the lower town. After a contest of several hours, the Americans, under Morgan, were obliged to surrender them-

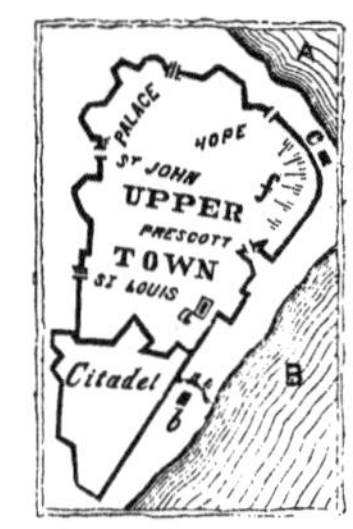

WALLS OF QUEBEC.

GENERAL MONTGOMERY.

---

[1] Messengers are sent from army to army with a white flag, indicating a desire for a peaceful interview. These flags, by common consent, are respected, and it is considered an outrage to fire on the bearer of one. The Americans were regarded as rebels, and undeserving the usual courtesy.

[2] The high rocky promontory on which the citadel stands.

[3] Prescott Gate is on the St. Lawrence side of the town, and there bars Mountain-street in its sinuous way from the water up into the walled city. The above diagram shows the plan of the city walls, and relative positions of the several gates mentioned. A is the St. Charles River, B the St. Lawrence, *a* Wolfe and Montcalm's monument [page 202], *b* the place where Montgomery fell, *c* the place where Arnold was wounded.

[4] These are small balls confined in a cluster, and then discharged at once from a cannon. They scatter, and do great execution.

[5] This was at the foot of the precipice, below the present *grand battery*, near St. Paul's-street.

[6] Afterward the famous General Morgan, whose rifle corps became so renowned, and who gained the victory at *The Cowpens*, in the winter of 1781. See page 331.

selves prisoners of war. The whole loss of the Americans, under Montgomery and Arnold, in this assault, was about one hundred and sixty. The British loss was only about twenty killed and wounded.

Colonel Arnold, with the remainder of the troops, retired to Sillery, where he formed a camp, and passed a rigorous Canadian winter. He was relieved from chief command by General Wooster,[1] on the 1st of April, who came down from Montreal with reinforcements, when another ineffectual attempt was made to capture Quebec. When, a month afterward, General Thomas took the chief command [May, 1776], Carleton was receiving strong reinforcements from England, and the patriots were compelled to abandon all hope of conquering Canada. They were obliged to retreat so hastily before the overwhelming forces of Carleton, that they left their stores and sick behind them.[2] Abandoning one post after another, the Americans were driven entirely out of Canada by the middle of June.

The Virginians were rolling on the car of the Revolution, with a firm and steady hand, while the patriots were suffering defeats and disappointments at the North. We have already alluded to the fact, that the people of Williamsburg, then the capital of Virginia, had driven Lord Dunmore, the royal governor, away from his palace, to take refuge on board a ship of war.[3] He was the first royal representative who "abdicated government," and he was greatly exasperated because he was compelled to do so in a very humiliating manner. From that vessel he sent letters, messages, and addresses to the Virginia House of Burgesses,[4] and received the same in return. Each exhibited much spirit. Finally, in the autumn, the governor proceeded to Norfolk, with the fleet, and collecting a force of Tories and negroes, commenced depredations in lower Virginia. With the aid of some British vessels, he attacked Hampton, near Old Point Comfort,[5] on the 24th of October, and was repulsed. He then declared open war. The Virginia militia flew to arms, and in a severe battle, fought on the 9th of December, at the Great Bridge, near the Dismal Swamp, twelve miles from Norfolk, Dunmore was defeated, and compelled to seek safety with the British shipping in Norfolk harbor. In that battle, the regiment of men, chiefly from Culpepper county, raised by Patrick Henry, and at the head of whom he demanded payment for the powder removed from Williamsburg,[6] did very important service.[7]

---

[1] Page 270.

[2] General Thomas was seized with the small-pox, which had been raging some time in the American camp, and died at Chambly on the 30th of May. He was a native of Plymouth, Mass., and was one of the first eight brigadiers appointed by Congress [note 5, page 238]. Carleton treated the prisoners and sick with great humanity. He afterward, on the death of his father, became Lord Dorchester. He died in 1808, aged eighty-three years.

[3] Page 237. [4] Page 71. [5] Page 64. [6] Page 237.

CULPEPPER FLAG.

[7] This regiment had adopted a flag with the significant device of a coiled rattle-snake, seen in the engraving. This device was upon many flags in the army and navy of the Revolution. The expression, "Don't tread on me," had a double signification. It might be said in a supplicating tone, "*Don't* tread on me;" or menacingly, "Don't tread on *me*." The soldiers were dressed in green hunting-shirts, with Henry's words, LIBERTY OR DEATH [page 237], in large white letters, on their bosoms. They had bucks' tails in their hats, and in their belts tomahawks and scalping-knives. Their fierce appearance alarmed the people, as they marched through the country.

Five days after the battle at the Great Bridge, the Virginians, under Colonel Woodford, entered Norfolk in triumph [Dec. 14, 1775], and the next morning they were joined by Colonel Robert Howe,[1] with a North Carolina regiment, when the latter assumed the general command. Dunmore was greatly exasperated by these reverses, and, in revenge, he caused Norfolk to be burned early on the morning of the 1st of January, 1776. The conflagration raged for fifty hours, and while the wretched people were witnessing the destruction of their property, the modern Nero caused a cannonade to be kept up.[2] When the destruction was complete, he proceeded to play the part of a marauder along the defenseless coast of Virginia. For a time he made his head quarters upon Gwyn's island, in Chesapeake Bay, near the mouth of the Piankatank River, from which he was driven, with his fleet, by a brigade of Virginia troops under General Andrew Lewis.[3] After committing other depredations, he went to the West Indies, carrying with him about a thousand negroes which he had collected during his marauding campaign, where he sold them, and in the following autumn returned to England. These atrocities kindled an intense flame of hatred to royal rule throughout the whole South, and a desire for political independence of Great Britain budded spontaneously in a thousand hearts where, a few months before, the plant of true loyalty was blooming.

CHAPTER III.

SECOND YEAR OF THE WAR FOR INDEPENDENCE. [1776.]

THERE was great anxiety in the public mind throughout the colonies at the opening of the year 1776. The events of the few preceding months appeared unpropitious for the republican cause, and many good and true men were disposed to pause and consider, before going another step in the path of rebellion. But the bolder leaders in the senate and in the camp were undismayed; and the hopeful mind of Washington, in the midst of the most appalling discouragements, faltered not for a moment. He found himself strong enough to be the effectual jailor of the British army in Boston, and now he was almost prepared to commence those blows which finally drove that army and its Tory abettors to the distant shores of Nova Scotia.[4] He had partially re-organized the conti-

---

[1] Page 292.

[2] When Dunmore destroyed Norfolk, its population was six thousand; and so rapidly was it increasing in business and wealth, that in two years, from 1773 to 1775, the rents in the city increased from forty thousand to fifty thousand dollars a year. The actual loss by the cannonade and conflagration was estimated at fifteen hundred thousand dollars. The personal suffering was inconceivable.

[3] General Lewis was a native of Virginia, and was in the battle when Braddock was killed. He was the commander of the Virginia troops in the battle at Point Pleasant [note 4, page 237], in the summer of 1774. He left the army, on account of illness, in 1780, and died not long afterward, while absent from home.

[4] Note 2, page 80.

nental forces under his command; and on the first of January, 1776, he unfurled the *Union Flag*, for the first time, over the American camp at Cambridge.[1] His army had then dwindled to less than ten thousand effective men, and these were scantily fed and clothed, and imperfectly disciplined. But the camp was well supplied with provisions, and about ten thousand minute-men,[2] chiefly in Massachusetts, were held in reserve, ready to march when called upon.

UNION FLAG.

During the summer and autumn of 1775, the Continental Congress had put forth all its energies in preparations for a severe struggle with British power, now evidently near at hand. Articles of war were agreed to on the 30th of June; a declaration of the causes for taking up arms was issued on the 6th of

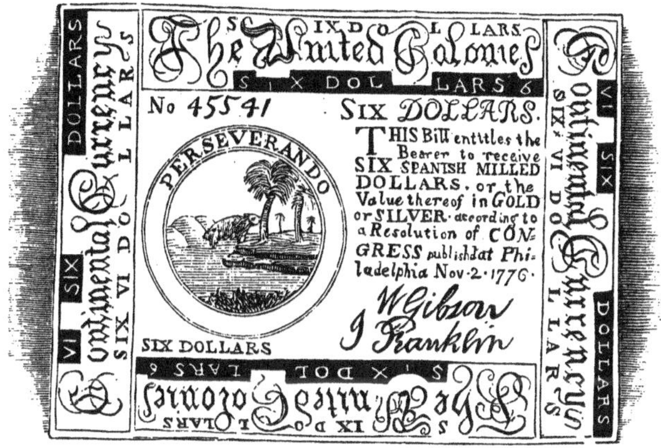

A BILL OF CREDIT, OR CONTINENTAL MONEY.

July; and before the close of the year, bills of credit, known as "continental money," representing the value of six millions of Spanish dollars, had been issued.[3] A naval establishment had also been commenced;[4] and at the opening

[1] The hoisting of that ensign was hailed by General Howe, the British commander in Boston, with great joy, for he regarded it as a token that a gracious speech of the king on American affairs, lately communicated to Parliament, was well received by the army, and that submission would speedily follow. That flag was composed of thirteen stripes, alternate red and white, symbolizing the thirteen revolted colonies. In one corner was the device of the British *Union Flag*, namely, the cross of St. George, composed of a horizontal and perpendicular bar, and the cross of St. Andrew (representing Scotland), which is in the form of ×. It was the appearance of that symbol of the British union that misled Howe. This flag is represented in the above little sketch. On the 14th of June, 1777, Congress ordered "thirteen stars, white, in a blue field," to be put in the place of the British union device. Such is the design of our flag at the present day. A star has been added for every new State admitted into the Union, while the original number of stripes is retained.

[2] Page 229.

[3] The resolution of the Continental Congress, providing for the emission of bills, was adopted on the 22d of June, 1775. The bills were printed and issued soon after, and other emissions were authorized, from time to time, during about four years. At the beginning of 1780, Congress had issued two hundred millions of dollars in paper money. After the second year, these bills began to depreciate; and in 1780, forty paper dollars were worth only one in specie. At the close of 1781, they were worthless. They had performed a temporary good, but were finally productive of great public evil, and much individual suffering. Some of these bills are yet in existence, and are considered great curiosities. They were rudely engraved, and printed on thick paper, which caused the British to call it "the paste-board money of the rebels."

[4] Note 1, page 307.

of 1776, many expert privateersmen[1] were hovering along our coasts, to the great terror and annoyance of British merchant vessels.

There had been, up to this time, a strange apathy concerning American affairs, in the British Parliament, owing, chiefly, to the confidence reposed in the puissance of the imperial government, and a want of knowledge relative to the real strength of the colonies. Events had now opened the eyes of British statesmen to a truer appreciation of the relative position of the contestants, and the importance of vigorous action; and at the close of 1775, Parliament had made extensive arrangements for crushing the rebellion. An act was passed [Nov., 1775], which declared the revolted colonists to be *rebels;* forbade all intercourse with them; authorized the seizure and destruction or confiscation of all American vessels; and placed the colonies under martial law.[2] An aggregate land and naval force of fifty-five thousand men was voted for the American service, and more than a million of dollars were appropriated for their pay and sustenance. In addition to these, seventeen thousand troops were hired by the British government from the Landgrave of Hesse-Cassel, and other petty German rulers,[3] to come hither to butcher loyal subjects who had petitioned for their rights for ten long years, and now, even with arms in their hands, were praying for justice, and begging for reconciliation. This last act filled the cup of government iniquity to the brim. It was denounced in Parliament by the true friends of England, as "disgraceful to the British name," and it extinguished the last hope of reconciliation. The sword was now drawn, and the scabbard was thrown away.

Intelligence of the proceedings in Parliament reached America in January, 1776, and Congress perceived the necessity of putting forth immediate and efficient efforts for the defense of the extensive sea-coast of the colonies. Washington was also urged to attack the British in Boston, immediately; and, by great efforts, the regular army was augmented to about fourteen thousand men toward the close of February. In the mean while, the provincial Congress of Massachusetts organized the militia of the province anew, and ten regiments, making about three thousand men, arrived in camp early in February. The entire army now numbered about seventeen thousand effective men, while the British force did not exceed five thousand fit for duty. Reinforcements were daily expected from Halifax, New York, and Ireland, and the present seemed a proper moment to strike. Bills of credit,[4] representing four millions of dollars more, were issued; Congress promised energetic co-operation; and on the

---

[1] Private individuals, having a license from government to arm and equip a vessel, and with it to depredate upon the commerce of a nation with which that people are then at war, are called *privateersmen*, and their vessels are known as *privateers*. During the Revolution, a vast number of English vessels were captured by American privateersmen. It is, after all, only legalized piracy, and enlightened nations begin to view it so.

[2] Note 8, page 170.

[3] The Landgrave (or petty prince) of Hesse-Cassel, having furnished the most considerable portion of these troops, they were called by the general name of *Hessians*. Ignorant, brutal, and bloodthirsty, they were hated by the patriots, and despised even by the regular English army. They were always employed in posts of greatest danger, or in expeditions least creditable. These troops cost the British government almost eight hundred thousand dollars, besides the necessity, according to the contract, of defending the little principalities thus stripped, against their foes.

[4] Page 245.

1st of March, Washington felt strong enough to attempt a dislodgment of the enemy from the crushed city.[1]

On the evening of the 2d of March [1776], a heavy cannonade was opened upon Boston, from all the American batteries, and was continued, with brief intermissions, until the 4th. On the evening of that day, General Thomas,[2] with twelve hundred men with intrenching tools, and a guard of eight hundred, proceeded secretly to a high hill, near Dorchester, on the south side of Boston, and before morning, they cast up a line of strong intrenchments, and planted heavy cannons there, which completely commanded the city and harbor. It was the anniversary of the memorable Boston Massacre,[3] and many patriots felt the blood coursing more swiftly through their veins, as the recollection of that event gave birth to vengeful feelings. It had nerved their arms while toiling all that long night, and they felt a great satisfaction in knowing that they had prepared works which not only greatly astonished and alarmed the British, but which would be instrumental in achieving a great victory. The enemy felt the danger, and tried to avert it.

Perceiving the imminent peril of both fleet and army, General Howe prepared an expedition to drive the Americans from their vantage-ground on Dorchester heights. A storm suddenly arose, and made the harbor impassable.[4] The delay allowed the patriots time to make their works almost impregnable, and the British were soon compelled to surrender as prisoners of war, or to evacuate the city immediately, to avoid destruction. As prisoners, they would have been excessively burdensome to the colonies; so, having formally agreed to allow them to depart without injury, Washington had the inexpressible pleasure of saying, in a letter written to the President of Congress, on Sunday, the 17th of March, "that this morning the ministerial troops evacuated the town of Boston, without destroying it, and that we are now in full possession." Seven thousand soldiers, four thousand seamen, and fifteen hundred families of loyalists,[5] sailed for Halifax on that day.

The gates on Boston Neck were now unbarred; and General Ward, with five thousand of the troops at Roxbury, entered the city, with drums beating, and banners waving, greeted on every side with demonstrations of joy by the redeemed people. General Putnam soon afterward [March 18] entered with another division, and, in command of the whole, he took possession of the city and all the forts, in the name of the *Thirteen United Colonies.*

---

[1] Page 226. [2] Page 243. [3] Page 221.

[4] A similar event occurred to frustrate the designs of the British at Yorktown, several years afterward. See page 341.

[5] It must be remembered that the Americans were by no means unanimous in their opposition to Great Britain. From the beginning there were many who supported the crown; and as the colonists became more and more rebellious, these increased. Some because they believed their brethren to be wrong; others through timidity; and a greater number because they thought it their *interest* to adhere to the king. The loyalists, or *Tories*, were the worst and most efficient enemies of the *Whigs* [note 4, page 226] during the whole war. Those who left Boston at this time, were afraid to encounter the exasperated patriots, when they should return to their desolated homes in the city, from which they had been driven by military persecution. The churches had been stripped of their pulpits and pews, for fuel, fine shade trees had been burned, and many houses had been pillaged and damaged by the soldiery.

GENERAL LEE.

Washington had been informed, early in January, that General Sir Henry Clinton had sailed from Boston, with a considerable body of troops, on a secret expedition. Apprehending that the city of New York was his destination, he immediately dispatched General Charles Lee to Connecticut to raise troops, and to proceed to that city to watch and oppose Clinton wherever he might attempt to land. Six weeks before the evacuation of Boston [March 17, 1776], Lee had encamped near New York with twelve hundred militia. Already the *Sons of Liberty*[1] had been busy, and overt acts of rebellion had been committed by them. They had seized the cannons at Fort George,[2] and driven Tryon,[3] the royal governor, on board the *Asia*, a British armed vessel in the harbor. In March, Clinton arrived at Sandy Hook, just outside New York harbor, and on the same day, the watchful Lee[4] providentially entered the city. The movement, although without a knowledge of Clinton's position, was timely, for it kept him at bay. Foiled in his attempt upon New York, that commander sailed southward, where we shall meet him presently.

The destination of Howe, when he left Boston, was also unknown to Washington. Supposing he, too, would proceed to New York, he put the main body of his army in motion toward that city, as soon as he had placed Boston in a state of security. He arrived in New York about the middle of April [April 14], and proceeded at once to fortify the town and vicinity, and also the passes of the Hudson Highlands, fifty miles above. In the mean while, General Lee, who had been appointed to command the American forces in the South, had left his troops in the charge of General Lord Stirling[5] [March 7], and was hastening toward the Carolinas to watch the movements of Clinton, arouse the Whigs, and gather an army there.

In the spring of 1776, a considerable fleet, under Admiral Sir Peter Parker, was sent from England, to operate against the sea-coast towns of the southern colonies. Parker was joined by Clinton, at Cape Fear, in May, when the latter took the chief command of all the land forces. The fleet arrived off Charleston bar on the 4th of June, and on the same day, Clinton, with several hundred men, landed on Long Island, which lies eastward of Sullivan's Island. Apprised of these hostile designs, and elated by a victory obtained by North Carolina militia, under Colonel Caswell, over fifteen hundred loyalists[6] [February 27,

[1] Note 1, page 215.

[2] This fort stood at the foot of Broadway, on a portion of the site of the present "Battery."

[3] Page 223.

[4] Charles Lee was born in Wales in 1731. He was a brave officer in the British army during the French and Indian War. He settled in Virginia in 1773, and was one of the first brigadiers of the Continental army appointed by Congress. His ambition and perversity of temper, finally caused his ruin. He died in Philadelphia in 1782. See page 288.

[5] Page 254.

[6] These were chiefly Scotch Highlanders, and were led by Donald McDonald, an influential Scotchman then residing at Cross Creek, now Fayetteville. The husband of Flora McDonald, so celebrated in connection with the flight of the young Pretender from Scotland, at the close of the rebellion in 1745, was in the battle. Flora was then living at Cross Creek.

1776], on Moore's Creek, in the present Hanover county, the southern patriots had cheerfully responded to the call of Governor Rutledge, and about six thousand armed men had collected in and near Charleston, when the enemy appeared.[1] The city and eligible posts near it, had been fortified, and quite a strong fort, composed of palmetto logs and sand, and armed with twenty-six mounted cannons, had been erected upon Sullivan's Island, to command the channel leading to the town. This fort was garrisoned by about five hundred men, chiefly militia, under Colonel William Moultrie.[2]

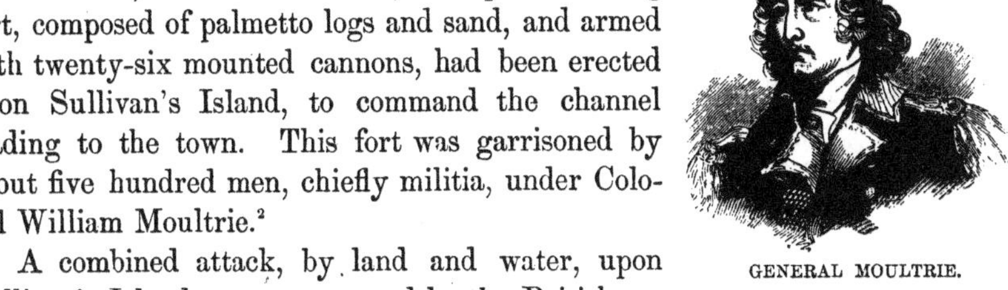

GENERAL MOULTRIE.

A combined attack, by land and water, upon Sullivan's Island, was commenced by the British, on the morning of the 28th of June, 1776. While the fleet was pouring a terrible storm of iron balls upon Fort Sullivan, Clinton endeavored, but in vain, to force a passage across a narrow creek which divided the two islands, in order to attack the yet unfinished fortress in the rear. But Colonel Thompson, with a small battery on the east end of Sullivan's Island, repelled every forward movement of Clinton, while the cannons of the fort were spreading havoc among the British vessels.[3] The conflict raged for almost ten hours, and only ceased when night fell upon the scene. Then the British fleet, almost shattered into fragments, withdrew, and abandoned the enterprise.[4] The slaughter of the British had been frightful. Two hundred and twenty-five had been killed or wounded, while only two of the garrison were killed, and twenty-two were wounded.[5] The British departed for New York three days afterward[6] [June 31, 1776], and for more than two years, the din of war was not heard below the Roanoke. This victory had a most inspiriting effect upon the patriots throughout the land.

---

[1] General Armstrong of Pennsylvania [page 193], had arrived in South Carolina in April, and took the general command. Lee arrived on the same day when the British, under Clinton, landed on Long Island.

[2] Born in South Carolina, in 1730. He was in the Cherokee war [page 204], in 1761. He was an active officer until made prisoner, in 1780, when for two years he was not allowed to bear arms. He died in 1805. General Moultrie wrote a very interesting memoir of the war in the South.

[3] At one time, every man but Admiral Parker was swept from the deck of his vessel. Among those who were badly wounded, was Lord William Campbell, the royal governor of South Carolina, who afterward died of his wounds.

[4] The *Acteon*, a large vessel, grounded on a shoal between Fort Sullivan and the city, where she was burned by the Americans.

[5] The strength of the fort consisted in the capacity of the spongy palmetto logs, upon which cannon-balls would make very little impression. It appeared to be a very insecure defense, and Lee advised Moultrie to abandon it when the British approached. But that brave officer would not desert it, and was rewarded with victory. The ladies of Charleston presented his regiment with a pair of elegant colors, and the "slaughter pen," as Lee ironically called Fort Sullivan, was named Fort Moultrie. During the action, the staff, bearing a large flag, was cut down by a cannon-ball from the fleet. The colors fell outside the fort. A sergeant named Jasper, leaped down from one of the bastions, and in the midst of the iron hail that was pouring from the fort, coolly picked up the flag, ascended to the bastion, and calling for a sponge-staff, tied the colors to it, stuck it in the sand, and then took his place among his companions in the fort. A few days afterward, Governor Rutledge took his own sword from his side, and presented it to the brave Jasper; he also offered him a lieutenant's commission, which the young man modestly declined, because he could neither read nor write, saying, "I am not fit to keep officers' company—I am but a sergeant."

[6] Page 252.

Important events in the progress of the war were now thickening. Rebellion had become revolution. While the stirring events at the South, just mentioned, were transpiring, and while Washington was augmenting and strengthening the continental army in New York, and British troops and German hirelings[1] were approaching by thousands, the Continental Congress, now in permanent session in the State House at Philadelphia, had a question of vast importance under consideration. A few men, looking beyond the storm-clouds of the present, beheld bright visions of glory for their country, when the people, now declared to be rebels,[2] and out of the protection of the British king, should organize themselves into a sovereign nation. "The lightning of the Crusades was in the people's hearts, and it needed but a single electric touch, to make it blaze forth upon the world," says James, in writing of an earlier disruption of political systems.[3] So it was now, in the American colonies. The noble figure of an independent nation stood forth with a beauty that almost demanded worship. The grand idea began to flash through the popular mind at the close of 1775; and when, early in 1776, it was tangibly spoken by Thomas Paine, in a pamphlet entitled *Common Sense*[4] (said to have been suggested by Dr. Rush),[5] and whose vigorous thoughts were borne by the press to every community, a desire for *independence* filled the hearts of the people. In less than eighty days after the evacuation of Boston [March 17, 1776], almost every provincial Assembly had spoken in favor of *independence;* and on the 7th of June, in the midst of the doubt, and dread, and hesitation, which for twenty days had brooded over the Continental Congress, Richard Henry Lee,[6]

STATE HOUSE.

---

[1] Page 246. [2] Page 246. [3] *History of the Crusades*, by G. P. R. James.

[4] The chief topic of this remarkable pamphlet, was the right and expediency of colonial independence. Paine also wrote a series of equally powerful papers, called *The Crisis:* The first number was written in Fort Lee, on the Hudson, in December, 1776, and published while Washington was on the banks of the Delaware. See page 192. These had a powerful effect in stimulating the people to efforts for independence. They were highly valued by the commander-in-chief, and he promoted their circulation. Writing to a friend soon after the appearance of *Common Sense*, Washington said, "By private letters which I have lately received from Virginia, I find that *Common Sense* is working a powerful change there in the minds of many men."

[5] Benjamin Rush was one of the most eminent men of his time, as a physician, a man of science, and an active patriot during the whole Revolution. He was born twelve miles from Philadelphia, in 1745. He was educated at Princeton, completed his scientific studies in Edinburg, and after his return, he soon rose to the highest eminence in his profession. He was the recipient of many honors, and as a member of the Continental Congress, in 1776, he advocated and signed the Declaration of Independence. His labors during the prevalence of yellow fever in Philadelphia, in 1793, gave him the imperishable crown of a true philanthropist. He founded the Philadelphia Dispensary in 1786; and he was also one of the principal founders of Dickinson College, at Carlisle, Pennsylvania. He was president of the American Society for the abolition of slavery; of the Philadelphia Medical Society; vice-president of the Philadelphia Bible Society; and one of the vice-presidents of the American Philosophical Society. He died in April, 1813, at the age of almost sixty-eight years. A portrait of Dr. Rush may be found on the next page.

[6] Richard Henry Lee was born in Westmoreland county, Virginia, in 1732. He was educated in England, and was in public life most of the time after reaching his majority. He was one of the earliest opposers of the Stamp Act; was a member of the first Continental Congress, and signed that Declaration of Independence which he so nobly advocated. He was afterward a member of the United States Senate; and soon after his retirement to private life, in 1794, he died, when in the

of Virginia, arose in his place, and with his clear, musical voice, read aloud the Resolution, "That these united colonies are, and, of right, ought to be, free and independent States; that they are absolved from all allegiance to the British crown, and that all political connection between them and the State of Great Britain, is, and ought to be totally dissolved."[1]

Benjamin Rush

This was an exceedingly bold step, and the resolution did not meet with general favor in Congress, at first. Many yet hoped, even against hope, for reconciliation, and thought it premature, and there were some timid ones who trembled while standing so near the borders of high treason. After debating the subject for three days, the further consideration of it was postponed until the first of July. A committee[2] was appointed [June 11], however, to draw

---

sixty-third year of his age. A characteristic anecdote is told of his son, who was at school, in England, at the time the Declaration of Independence was promulgated. One day a gentleman asked his tutor, "What boy is this?" "He is the son of Richard Henry Lee, of America," the tutor replied. The gentleman put his hand on the boy's head, and said, "We shall yet see your father's head upon Tower Hill." The boy instantly answered, "You may have it when you can get it." That boy was the late Ludwell Lee, Esq.

[1] On the 10th of May, Congress had, by resolution, recommended the establishment of independent State governments in all the colonies. This, however, was not sufficiently national to suit the bolder and wiser members of that body, and the people at large. Lee's resolution more fully expressed the popular will.

[2] Thomas Jefferson, of Virginia; John Adams, of Massachusetts; Benjamin Franklin, of Pennsylvania; Roger Sherman, of Connecticut; and Robert R. Livingston, of New York. Mr. Lee was summoned home to the bedside of a sick wife, on the day before the appointment of the committee, or he would doubtless have been its chairman.

up a declaration in accordance with the resolution, and were instructed to report on the same day when the latter should be called up. Thomas Jefferson, of Virginia, the youngest member of the committee, was chosen its chairman, and to him was assigned the task of preparing the Declaration. Adams and Franklin made a few alterations in his draft, and it was submitted to Congress at the same hour when Mr. Lee's resolution was taken up for consideration. On the following day [July 2], the resolution was adopted by a large majority. The Declaration was debated almost two days longer; and finally, at about mid-day, on the 4th of July, 1776, the representatives of thirteen colonies unanimously declared them free and independent States, under the name of THE UNITED STATES OF AMERICA. Only John Hancock, the president of Congress, signed it on that day, and thus it first went forth to the world. It was ordered to be written on parchment, and on the 2d of August following, the names of all but two of the fifty-six signers,[1] were placed upon it. These two were added afterward. It had then been read to the army;[2] at public meetings; from a hundred pulpits, and in all legislative halls in the land, and everywhere awakened the warmest responses of approval.

Pursuant to instructions, General Howe proceeded toward New York, to meet General Clinton and Parker's fleet. He left Halifax on the 11th of June, [1776], and arrived at Sandy Hook[3] on the 29th. On the 2d of July he took possession of Staten Island, where he was joined by Sir Henry Clinton [July 11], from the South,[4] and his brother, Admiral Lord Howe [July 12], with a fleet and a large land force, from England. Before the first of August, other vessels arrived with a part of the Hessian troops,[5] and on that day, almost thirty thousand soldiers, many of them tried veterans, stood ready to fall upon the republican army of seventeen thousand men,[6] mostly militia, which lay intrenched in New York and vicinity, less than a dozen miles distant.[7] The

---

[1] This document, containing the autographs of those venerated fathers of our republic, is carefully preserved in a glass case, in the rooms of the *National Institute* at Washington city. Not one of all that band of patriots now survives. Charles Carrol was the last to leave us. He departed in 1832, at the age of ninety years. See Supplement. It is worthy of remembrance that *not one* of all those signers of the Declaration of Independence, died with a tarnished reputation. The memory of *all*, is sweet.

[2] Washington caused it to be read at the head of each brigade of the army, then in New York city, on the 9th of July. That night, citizens and soldiers pulled down the leaden equestrian statue of George III., which stood in the Bowling Green, and it was soon afterward converted into bullets for the use of the Continental army. The statue was gilded. The head of the horse was toward the Hudson River. The Rev. Zachariah Greene, yet [1856] living at Hempstead, Long Island, heard the Declaration read to the soldiers. He was in the army.

[3] Sandy Hook is a low ridge of sand, extending several miles down the New Jersey shore, from the entrance to Raritan or Amboy Bay. Between it and the shore, the water is navigable; and near the mouth of Shrewsbury River, the ridge is broken by an inlet.

[4] Page 249.

[5] Page 246.

[6] There were about twenty-seven thousand men enrolled, but not more than seventeen thousand men were fit for duty. A great many were sick, and a large number were without arms.

[7] Many of the ships passed through the Narrows, and anchored in New York Bay. Howe's flag-ship, the *Eagle*, lay near Governor's Island. While in that position, a bold soldier went in a submarine vessel, with a machine for blowing up a ship, and endeavored to fasten it to the bottom of the *Eagle*, but failed. He was discovered, and barely escaped. An explosion of the machine took place near the *Eagle*, and the commander was so alarmed, that she was hastily moved further down the Bay. This machine was constructed by David Bushnell, of Connecticut, and was called a *torpedo*. See Note 2, page 285.

grand object in view was the seizure of New York and the country along the Hudson, so as to keep open a communication with Canada, separate the patriots of New England from those of the other States, and to overrun the most populous portion of the revolted colonies. This was the military plan, arranged by ministers. They had also prepared instructions to their commanding generals, to be pacific, if the Americans appeared disposed to submit. Lord Howe[1] and his brother, the general, were commissioned to "grant pardon to all who deserved mercy," and to treat for peace, but only on terms of absolute submission on the part of the colonies, to the will of the king and parliament. After making a foolish display of arrogance and weakness, in addressing General Washington as a private gentleman,[2] and being assured that the Americans had been guilty of no offense requiring a "pardon" at their hands, they prepared to strike an immediate and effective blow. The British army was accordingly put in motion on the morning of the 22d of August [1776], and during that day, ten thousand effective men, and forty pieces of cannon, were landed on the western end of Long Island, between the present Fort Hamilton and Gravesend village.

GENERAL PUTNAM.

Already detachments of Americans under General Sullivan, occupied a fortified camp at Brooklyn, opposite New York, and guarded seven passes on a range of hills which extend from the Narrows to the village of Jamaica.[3] When intelligence of the landing of the invading army reached Washington, he sent General Putnam,[4] with large reinforcements, to take the chief command on Long Island, and to prepare to meet the enemy. The American troops on the island now [August 26], numbered about five thousand. The British moved in three divisions. The left, under General Grant, marched along the shore toward Gowanus; the right, under Clinton and Cornwallis, toward the interior of the island; and the center, composed chiefly of Hessians,[5] under De Heister, marched up the Flatbush road, south of the hills.

Clinton moved under cover of night, and before dawn on the morning of

---

[1] Richard, Earl Howe, was brother of the young Lord Howe [page 197], killed at Ticonderoga. He was born in 1725, and died in 1799.

[2] The letters of Lord Howe to the American commander-in-chief, were addressed, "George Washington, Esq." As that did not express the public character of the chief, and as he would not confer with the enemies of his country in a private capacity, Washington refused to receive the letters. Howe was instructed not to acknowledge the authority of Congress in any way, and as Washington had received his commission from that body, to address him as "general," would have been a recognition of its authority. He meant no disrespect to Washington. Congress, by resolution, expressed its approbation of Washington's dignified course.

[3] General Nathaniel Green had been placed in command of this division, but having been prostrated by bilious fever, about a week before the landing of the British at the Narrows, Sullivan was placed at the head of the troops.

[4] Israel Putnam was born in Salem, Massachusetts, in 1718. He was a very useful officer during the French and Indian war, and was in active service in the continental army, until 1779, when bodily infirmity compelled him to retire. He died in 1790, at the age of seventy-two years.

[5] Page 246.

BATTLE OF LONG ISLAND.

the 27th, he had gained possession of the Jamaica pass, near the present East New York. At the same time, Grant was pressing forward along the shore of New York Bay, and at day-break, he encountered Lord Stirling,[1] where the monuments of Greenwood cemetery now dot the hills. De Heister advanced from Flatbush at the same hour, and attacked Sullivan, who, having no suspicions of the movements of Clinton, was watching the Flatbush Pass. A bloody conflict ensued, and while it was progressing, Clinton descended from the wooded hills, by the way of Bedford, to gain Sullivan's rear. As soon as the latter perceived his peril, he ordered a retreat to the American lines at Brooklyn. It was too late; Clinton drove him back upon the Hessian bayonets, and after fighting desperately, hand to hand, with the foe in front and rear, and losing a greater portion of his men, Sullivan was compelled to surrender.

As usual, misfortunes did not come single. While these disasters were occurring on the left, Cornwallis descended the port-road to Gowanus, and attacked Stirling. They fought desperately, until Stirling was made prisoner.[2] Many of his troops were drowned while endeavoring to escape across the Gowanus Creek, as the tide was rising; and a large number were captured. At noon the victory for the British was complete. About five hundred Americans were killed or wounded, and eleven hundred were made prisoners. These were soon suffering dreadful horrors in prisons and prison-ships, at New York.[3] The British loss in killed, wounded, and prisoners, was three hundred and sixty-seven.

It was with the deepest anguish that Washington had viewed, from New York, the destruction of his troops, yet he dared not weaken his power in the city, by sending reinforcements to aid them. He crossed over on the following morning [August 28], with Mifflin,[4] who had come down from the upper end of York island with a thousand troops, and was gratified to find the enemy encamped in front of Putnam's lines, and delaying an attack until the British fleet should co-operate with him. This delay allowed Washington time to form and execute a plan for the salvation of the remainder of the army, now too weak to resist an assault with any hope of success. Under cover of a heavy fog, which fell upon the hostile camps at midnight of the 29th, and continued until the morning of the 30th, he silently withdrew them from the camp,[5] and,

---

[1] William Alexander, Lord Stirling, was a descendant of the Scotch earl of Stirling, mentioned in note 2, page 80. He was born in the city of New York, in 1726. He became attached to the patriot cause, and was an active officer during the war. He died in 1783, aged fifty-seven years.

[2] Stirling was sent immediately on board of the *Eagle*, Lord Howe's flag-ship.

[3] Among the prisoners was General Nathaniel Woodhull [Note 1, page 198], late president of the provincial Congress of New York. He was taken prisoner on the 30th, and after being severely wounded at the time, he was so neglected, that his injuries proved fatal in the course of a few days. His age was fifty-three. See Onderdonk's *Revolutionary Incidents of Long Island.*

[4] Page 352.

[5] During the night, a woman living near the present Fulton Ferry, where the Americans embarked, having become offended at some of the patriots, sent her negro servant to inform the

Retreat of the Americans from Long Island.

unperceived by the British, they all crossed over to New York in safety, carrying every thing with them but their heavy cannons. When the fog rolled away, and the sunlight burst upon Brooklyn and New York, the last boat-load of patriots had reached the city shore. Mifflin, with his Pennsylvania battalion, and the remains of two broken Maryland regiments, formed the covering party. Washington and his staff, who had been in the saddle all night, remained until the last company had embarked. Surely, if "the stars in their courses fought against Sisera," in the time of Deborah,[1] the wings of the Cherubim of Mercy and Hope were over the Americans on this occasion. Howe, who felt sure of his prey, was greatly mortified, and prepared to make an immediate attack upon New York, before the Americans should become reinforced, or should escape from it.[2]

Unfortunately for the cause of freedom, at that time, the troops under Washington lacked that unity of feeling and moral stamina, so necessary for the accomplishment of success in any struggle. Had patriotism prevailed in every heart in the American army, it might have maintained its position in the city, and kept the British at bay. But there were a great many of merely selfish men in the camp. Sectional differences[3] weakened the bond of union, and immorality of every kind prevailed.[4] There was also a general spirit of insubordination, and the disasters on Long Island disheartened the timid. Hundreds deserted the cause, and went home. Never, during the long struggle of after years, was the hopeful mind of Washington more clouded by doubts, than during the month of September, 1776. In the midst of the gloom and perplexity, he called a council of war [Sept. 12th], and it was determined to send the military stores to Dobbs' Ferry, a secure place twenty-two miles up the Hudson, and to retreat to and fortify Harlem Heights,[5] near the upper end of York

---

British of the movement. The negro fell into the hands of the Hessians. They could not understand a word of his language, and detained him until so late in the morning that his information was of no avail.

[1] Judges, chapter v., verse 20.

[2] He ordered several vessels of war to sail around Long Island, and come down the Sound to Flushing Bay, so as to cover the intended landing of the troops upon the main [page 258], in Westchester county. In the mean while, Howe made an overture for peace, supposing the late disaster would dispose the Americans to listen eagerly to almost any proposition for reconciliation. He parolled General Sullivan, and by him sent a verbal communication to Congress, suggesting a committee for conference. It was appointed, and consisted of Dr Franklin, John Adams, and Edward Rutledge. On the 11th of September, they met Lord Howe at the house of Captain Billop, on Staten Island, opposite Perth Amboy. The committee would treat only for *independence*, and the conference had no practical result, except to widen the breach. When Howe spoke patronizingly of *protection* for the Americans, Dr. Franklin told him, courteously, that the Americans were not in need of British protection, for they were fully able to protect themselves.

[3] The army, which at first consisted chiefly of New England people, had been reinforced by others from New York, New Jersey, Pennsylvania, Delaware, Maryland, and Virginia, all of them jealous of their respective claims to precedence, and materially differing in their social habits.

[4] Cotemporary writers give a sad picture of the army at this time. Among many of the subordinate officers, greed usurped the place of patriotism. Officers were elected on condition that they should throw their pay and rations into a joint stock for the benefit of a company; surgeons sold recommendations for furloughs, for able-bodied men, at sixpence each; and a captain was cashiered for stealing blankets from his soldiers. Men went out in squads to plunder from friend and foe, to the disgrace of the army. Its appointments, too, were in a wretched condition. The surgeons' department lacked instruments. According to a general return of fifteen regiments, there were not more than sufficient instruments for one battalion. [See Washington's Letter to Congress, Sept. 24, 1776.]

[5] These extend from the plain on which the village of Harlem stands, about seven and a half

Island.[1] This was speedily accomplished; and when, on the 15th, a strong detachment of the British army crossed the East River from Long Island, and landed three miles above the town, at Kipps' Bay (now foot of Thirty-fourth-street, East River), without much opposition,[2] the greater portion of the Americans were busy in fortifying their new camp on Harlem Heights.

The invading Britons formed a line almost across the island to Bloomingdale, within two miles of the American intrenchments, just beyond the present Manhattanville, while the main army on Long Island was stationed at different points from Brooklyn to Flushing.[3] On the 16th, detachments of the belligerents met on Harlem plains, and a severe skirmish ensued. The Americans were victorious, but their triumph cost the lives of two brave officers—Colonel Knowlton of Connecticut, and Major Leitch of Virginia. Yet the effect of the victory was inspiriting; and so faithfully did the patriots ply muscle and implement, that before Howe could make ready to attack them, they had constructed double lines of intrenchments, and were prepared to defy him. At once perceiving the inutility of attacking the Americans in front, he next endeavored to gain their rear. Leaving quite a strong force to keep possession of the city[4] [Sept. 20], he sent three armed vessels up the Hudson to cut off the communications of the Americans with New Jersey, while the great bulk of his army (now reinforced by an arrival of fresh troops from England)[5] made their way [Oct. 12] to a point in Westchester county,[6] beyond the Harlem River. When Washington perceived the designs of his enemy, he placed a garrison of almost three thousand men, under Colonel Magaw, in Fort Washington,[7] and withdrew the remainder of his army[8] to a position on the Bronx River, in Westchester county, to oppose Howe, or retreat in safety to the Hudson Highlands, if necessary. He established his head-quarters at White Plains village, and there, on the 28th

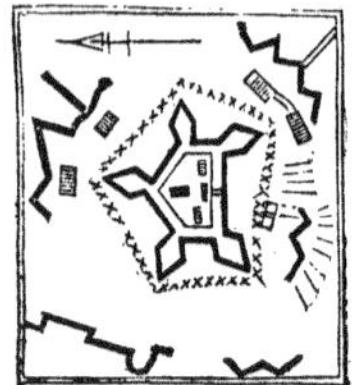
FORT WASHINGTON.

miles from the City Hall, New York to Two Hundred and Sixth-street, near King's Bridge, at the upper end of the island.

[1] Also called Manhattan. See note 1, page 48.

[2] Some Connecticut troops, frightened by the number and martial appearance of the British, fled at their approach. Washington, then at Harlem, heard the cannonade, leaped into his saddle, and approached Kipp's Bay in time to meet the flying fugitives. Mortified by this exhibition of cowardice before the enemy, the commander-in-chief tried to rally them, and in that effort, he was so unmindful of himself, that he came near being captured.

[3] Wishing to ascertain the exact condition of the British army, Washington engaged Captain Nathan Hale, of Knowlton's regiment, to secretly visit their camps on Long Island, and make observations. He was caught, taken to Howe's head-quarters, Turtle Bay, New York, and executed as a spy by the brutal provost-marshal, Cunningham. He was not allowed to have a Bible nor clergyman during his last hours, nor to send letters to his friends. His fate and Andre's [page 326] have been compared. For particulars of this affair, see Onderdonk's *Revolutionary Incidents of Long Island*, etc., and Lossing's *Pictorial Field-Book of the Revolution.*

[4] At one o'clock on the morning of the 21st, a fire broke out in a small groggery near the foot of Broad-street, and before it was extinguished, about five hundred buildings were destroyed. The British charged the fire upon the Americans. Although such incendiarism had been contemplated when the Americans found themselves compelled to evacuate the city, this was purely accidental.

[5] The whole British army now numbered about 35,000 men.

[6] Throg's Neck, sixteen miles from the city.

[7] Fort Washington was erected early in 1776, upon the highest ground on York Island, ten miles from the city, between One Hundred and Eighty-first-street and One Hundred and Eighty-sixth-streets, and overlooking both the Hudson and Harlem Rivers. There are a few traces of its embankments yet [1856] visible.

[8] Nominally, nineteen thousand men, but actually effective, not more than half that number.

of October, a severe engagement took place.[1] The Americans were driven from their position, and three days afterward [Nov. 1, 1776], formed a strong camp on the hills of North Castle, five miles further north. The British general was afraid to pursue them; and after strengthening the post at Peekskill, at the lower entrance to the Highlands, and securing the vantage-ground at North Castle,[2] Washington crossed the Hudson [Nov. 12] with the main body of his army, and joined General Greene at Fort Lee, on the Jersey shore, about two miles south of Fort Washington. This movement was made on account of an apparent preparation by the British to invade New Jersey and march upon Philadelphia, where the Congress was in session.[3]

General Knyphausan and a large body of Hessians[4] had arrived at New York, and joined the British army at Westchester, previous to the engagement at White Plains. After Washington had crossed the Hudson, these German troops and a part of the English army, five thousand strong, proceeded to attack Fort Washington. They were successful, but at a cost to the victors of full one thousand brave men.[5] More than two thousand Americans were made prisoners of war [Nov. 16], and like their fellow-captives on Long Island,[6] they were crowded into loathsome prisons and prison-ships.[7] Two days afterward [Nov. 18], Lord Cornwallis, with six thousand men, crossed the Hudson at Dobbs' Ferry, and took possession of Fort Lee, which the Americans had abandoned on his approach, leaving all the baggage and military stores behind them. During the siege, General Washington, with Putnam, Greene, and Mercer, ascended the heights, and from the abandoned mansion of Roger Morris,[8] surveyed the scene of operations. Within fifteen minutes after they had left that mansion, Colonel Stirling, of the British army, who had just repulsed an

---

[1] The combatants lost about an equal number of men—not more than three hundred each in killed, wounded, and prisoners.

[2] General Heath was left in command in the Highlands, and General Lee at North Castle.

[3] Page 250. That body afterward adjourned to Baltimore, in Maryland. See page 262.

[4] Page 246.

[5] The loss of the Americans, in killed and wounded, did not exceed one hundred.

[6] Page 254.

[7] Nothing could exceed the horrors of these crowded prisons, as described by an eye-witness. The sugar-houses of New York being large, were used for the purpose, and therein scores suffered and died. But the most terrible scenes occurred on board several old hulks, which were anchored in the waters around New York, and used for prisoners. Of them the *Jersey* was the most notorious for the sufferings it contained, and the brutality of its officers. From these vessels, anchored near the present Navy Yard, at Brooklyn, almost eleven thousand victims were carried ashore during the war, and buried in shallow graves in the sand. Their remains were gathered in 1808, and put in a vault situated near the termination of Front-street and Hudson-avenue, Brooklyn. See Onderdonk's *Revolutionary Incidents of Long Island.* Lossing's *Field Book*, supplement.

THE JERSEY PRISON-SHIP.

[8] That mansion, elegant even now [1856], is standing on the high bank of the Harlem River, at One Hundred and Sixty-ninth-street. Roger Morris was Washington's companion-in-arms on the field where Braddock was defeated, and he had married Mary Phillipse, a young lady whose charms had captivated the heart of Washington when he was a young Virginia colonel. It is now the property of Madame Jumel, widow of Aaron Burr, who was Vice-President of the United States, under Jefferson.

American party, came with his victorious troops, and took possession of it. It was a narrow escape for those chief commanders.

A melancholy and a brilliant chapter in the history of the war for Independence, was now opened. For three weeks Washington, with his shattered and daily diminishing army, was flying before an overwhelming force of Britons. Scarcely three thousand troops now remained in the American army. Newark, New Brunswick, Princeton, and Trenton, successively fell into the power of Cornwallis. So close were the British vanguards upon the rear of the Americans, sometimes, that each could hear the music of the other. Day after day, the militia left the army as their terms of enlistment expired, for late reverses had sadly dispirited them, and many of the regulars[1] deserted. Loyalists were swarming all over the country through which they passed,[2] and when, on the 7th of December, Washington reached the frozen banks of the Delaware, at Trenton, he had less than three thousand men, most of them wretchedly clad, half famished, and without tents to shelter them from the biting winter air. On the 8th that remnant of an army crossed the Delaware in boats, just as one division of Cornwallis's pursuing army marched into Trenton with all the pomp of victors, and sat down, almost in despair, upon the Pennsylvania shore.

Washington had hoped to make a stand at New Brunswick, but was disappointed. The services of the Jersey and Maryland brigades expired on the day when he left that place, and neither of them would remain any longer in the army. During his flight, Washington had sent repeated messages to General Lee,[3] urging him to leave North Castle,[4] and reinforce him. That officer, ambitious as he was impetuous and brave, hoping to strike a blow against the British that might give himself personal renown, was so tardy in his obedience, that he did not enter New Jersey until the Americans had crossed the Delaware. He had repeatedly, but in vain, importuned General Heath, who was left in command at Peekskill, to let him have a detachment of one or two thousand men, with which to operate. His tardiness in obedience, cost him his liberty. Soon after entering New Jersey, he was made a prisoner [December

---

[1] Note 6, page 185.

[2] General Howe had sent out proclamations through the country, offering pardon and protection to all who might ask for mercy. Perceiving the disasters to the American arms during the summer and autumn, great numbers took advantage of these promises, and signed petitions. They soon found that *protection* did not follow *pardon*, for the Hessian troops, in their march through New Jersey, committed great excesses, without inquiring whether their victims were *Whigs* or *Tories*. Note 4, page 226. Among the prominent men who espoused the republican cause, and now abandoned it, was Tucker, president of the New Jersey Convention, which had sanctioned the Declaration of Independence, and Joseph Galloway, a member of the first Continental Congress. These, and other prominent recusants, received some hard hits in the public prints. A writer in the *Pennsylvania Journal*, of February 5, 1777, thus castigated Galloway:

"Gall'way has fled, and join'd the venal Howe,
To prove his baseness, see him cringe and bow;
A traitor to his country and its laws,
A friend to tyrants and their cursed cause.
Unhappy wretch! thy interest must be sold
For Continental, not for polish'd gold.
To sink the money thou thyself cried down,
And stabb'd thy country to support the crown."

[3] Note 4, page 185.

[4] Page 259.

13, 1776], and his command devolved upon General Sullivan.[1] At about the same time intelligence reached the chief that a British squadron, under Sir Peter Parker (who, as we have seen [page 247], was defeated at Charleston), had sailed into Narraganset Bay [December 8th], taken possession of Rhode Island, and blockaded the little American fleet, under Commodore Hopkins,[2] then lying near Providence. This intelligence, and a knowledge of the failure of operations on Lake Champlain,[3] coupled with the sad condition of the main army of patriots, made the future appear gloomy indeed.[4]

It was fortunate for the patriot cause that General Howe was excessively cautious and indolent. Instead of allowing Cornwallis to construct boats,[5] cross the Delaware at once, overwhelm the patriots, and push on to Philadelphia, as he might have done, he ordered him to await the freezing of the waters, so as to cross on the ice. He was also directed to place four thousand German troops in cantonments along the Jersey shore of the river, from Trenton to Burlington, and to occupy Princeton and New Brunswick with strong British detachments. Both Congress and Washington profited by this delay. Measures for re-organizing the army, already planned, were put in operation. A loan of five millions of dollars, in hard money, with which to pay the troops, was authorized. By the offer of liberal bounties,[6] and the influence of a stirring appeal put forth by Congress, recruits immediately flocked to Washington's standard at Newtown.[7] Almost simultaneously, Lee's detachment under Sullivan, and another from Ticonderoga,[8] joined him; and on the 24th of December he found himself in command of almost five thousand effective troops, many of them fresh and hopeful.[9] And the increased pay of officers, the proffered bounties to the

---

[1] Both Sullivan and Stirling, who were made prisoners on Long Island [page 254], had been exchanged, and were now again with the army. Lee was captured at Baskingridge, where Lord Stirling resided, and remained a prisoner until May, 1778, when he was exchanged for General Prescott, who was captured on Rhode Island. See page 271. [2] Note 1, page 307.

[3] General Gates was appointed to the command of the army at the north, after the death of General Thomas [note 2, page 243]; and during the summer and autumn of 1776, Colonel Arnold became a sort of commodore, and commanded flotillas of small vessels in warfare with others prepared by General Carleton (the British commander in Canada), on Lake Champlain. He had two severe engagements (11th and 13th of October), in which he lost about ninety men; the British about forty. These operations were disastrous, yet they resulted in preventing the British forces in Canada uniting with those in New York, and were thus of vast importance.

[4] Although the Americans had generally suffered defeats, they had been quite successful in making captives. The number of Americans taken by the British, up to the close of 1776, was four thousand, eight hundred and fifty-four; the number of British taken by the Americans, was two thousand, eight hundred and sixty. In addition to men, the Americans had lost twelve brass cannons and mortars, and two hundred and thirty-five made of iron; twenty-three thousand, nine hundred and seventy-nine empty shells, and seventeen thousand, one hundred and twenty-two filled; two thousand six hundred and eighty-four double-headed shot; a large quantity of grape-shot; two thousand eight hundred muskets: four hundred thousand cartridges; sixteen barrels of powder; five hundred intrenching tools; two hundred barrows and other instruments, and a large quantity of provisions and stores.

[5] The Americans took every boat they could find at Trenton, and cautiously moved them out of the river after they had crossed.

[6] Each soldier was to have a bounty of twenty dollars, besides an allotment of land at the close of the war. A common soldier was to have one hundred acres, and a colonel five hundred. These were given to those only who enlisted to serve "during the war."

[7] A small village north of Bristol, about two miles from the Delaware. [8] Page 234.

[9] According to the adjutant's return to Washington on the 22d of December, the American army numbered ten thousand one hundred and six men, of whom five thousand three hundred and ninety-nine were sick, on command elsewhere, or on furlough, leaving an effective force of four thousand seven hundred and seven.

soldiers, and the great personal influence of the commander-in-chief, had the effect to retain in the service, for a few weeks at least, more than one half of the old soldiers.

There were about fifteen hundred Hessians,[1] and a troop of British light horse, at Trenton, and these Washington determined to surprise. The British commanders looked with such contempt upon the American troops—the mere ghost of an army—and were so certain of an easy victory beyond the Delaware, where, rumor affirmed, the people were almost unanimous in favor of the king, that vigilance was neglected. So confident were they that the contest would be ended by taking possession of Philadelphia, that Cornwallis actually returned to New York, to prepare to sail for England! And when Rall, the commander of the Hessians at Trenton, applied to General Grant for a reinforcement, that officer said to the messenger, "Tell the colonel he is very safe. I will undertake to keep the peace in New Jersey, with a corporal's guard." How they mistook the character of Washington! During all the gloom of the past month, hope had beamed brightly upon the heart of the commander-in-chief. Although Congress had adjourned to Baltimore[2] [December 12, 1776], and the public mind was filled with despondency, his reliance upon Providence in a cause so just, was never shaken; and his great soul conceived, and his ready hand planned a bold stroke for deliverance. The Christmas holiday was at hand—a day when Germans, especially, indulge in convivial pleasures. Not doubting the Hessians would pass the day in sports and drinking, he resolved to profit by their condition, by falling suddenly upon them while they were in deep slumber after a day and night of carousal. His plan was to cross the Delaware in three divisions, one a few miles above Trenton, another a few miles below, and a third at Bristol to attack Count Donop[3] at Burlington. Small parties were also to attack the British posts at Mount Holly, Black Horse, and Bordentown, at the same time.

On the evening of Christmas day [1776], Washington gathered twenty-four hundred men, with some heavy artillery, at McConkey's Ferry, eight or nine miles above Trenton.[4] They expected to cross, reach Trenton at midnight, and take the Hessians by surprise. But the river was filled with floating ice, and sleet and snow were falling fast. The passage was made in flat-boats; and so difficult was the navigation, that it was almost four o'clock in the morning [December 26] when the troops were mustered on the Jersey shore. They were arranged in two divisions, commanded respectively by Greene and Sullivan, and approached Trenton by separate roads. The enterprise was eminently successful. Colonel Rall, the Hessian commander, was yet indulging in wine at the end of a night spent in card-

---

[1] Page 246.

[2] Alarmed at the approach of the British, Congress thought it prudent to adjourn to Baltimore. A committee to represent that body was left in Philadelphia, to co-operate with the army. Congress assembled at Baltimore on the 20th.

[3] Page 275.

[4] Taylorsville is the name of the little village at that place. The river there, now spanned by a covered bridge, is about six hundred feet in width, and has a considerable current.

playing, when the Americans approached, a little after sunrise;[1] and while endeavoring to rally his affrighted troops, he fell, mortally wounded, in the streets of Trenton. Between forty and fifty of the Hessians were killed and fatally wounded, and more than a thousand were made prisoners, together with arms, ammunition, and stores. Five hundred British cavalry barely escaped, and fled to Bordentown. Generals Ewing and Cadwalader, who commanded the other two divisions, destined to attack the enemy below Trenton, were unable to cross the river on account of the ice, to co-operate with Washington. With a strong enemy so near as Burlington and Princeton, the commander-in-chief thought it imprudent to remain on the Jersey shore, so with his prisoners and booty he re-crossed the Delaware on the evening after his victory.

BATTLE AT TRENTON.

This was indeed a victory in more aspects than that of a skillful military operation. The Germans under Dunop, on the river below, thoroughly alarmed, fled into the interior. The Tories and pliant Whigs[2] were abashed; the friends of liberty, rising from the depths of despondency, stood erect in the pride and strength of their principles; the prestige of the Hessian name, lately so terrible, was broken, and the faltering militia, anxious for bounties and honors, flocked to the victorious standard of Washington. Fourteen hundred soldiers, chiefly of the eastern militia, whose terms of enlistment would expire with the year, agreed to remain six weeks longer, on a promise to each of a bounty of ten dollars. The military chest was not in a condition to permit him to fulfill his promise, and he wrote to Robert Morris, the eminent financier of the Revolution, for aid, and it was given. Fifty thousand dollars, in hard money, were sent to the banks of the Delaware, in time to allow Washington to fulfill his engagement.[3]

The victory was also productive of more vigilant efforts on the part of the

---

[1] Rall spent the night at the house of a loyalist, named Hunt. Just at dawn, a messenger, sent by a Tory on the line of march of the patriots, came in hot haste to the colonel. Excited by wine, and intent upon his game, that officer thrust the note into his pocket. Like the Athenian polemarch, who, when he received dispatches relative to a conspiracy, refused to open them, saying, "Business to-morrow," Rall did not look at the message, but continued his amusement until the roll of the American drum, and the crack of his rifle, fell upon his dull ears, and called him to duty.

[2] Note 4, page 226.

[3] Then it was that Robert Morris not only evinced his faith in the success of the patriot cause, and his own love of country, but he tested the strength of his credit and mercantile honor. The sum was large, and the requirement seemed almost impossible to meet. Government credit was low, but confidence in Robert Morris was unbounded. On leaving his office, musing upon how he should obtain the money, he met a wealthy Quaker, and said, "I want money for the use of the army." "Robert, what security canst thou give?" asked the Quaker. "My note and my honor," promptly replied Morris. "Thou shalt have it," as promptly responded the lender, who offered him a considerable sum, and the next morning it was on its way to the camp of Washington. Robert Morris was a native of England, where he was born in 1733. He came to America in 1744, and became a merchant's clerk in Philadelphia. By the force of industry, energy, and a good character, he arose to the station of one of the first merchants of his time. He was a signer of the Declaration of Independence, and was active as a public financier, throughout the war. Toward its close [1781], he was instrumental in establishing a national bank. After the war, he was a state legislator, and Washington wished him to be his first Secretary of the Treasury, but he declined it. By land speculations he lost his fortune, and died in comparative poverty, in May, 1806, when a little more than seventy years of age. See his portrait on next page.

invaders. Believing the rebellion to be at an end, and the American army hopelessly annihilated, when Washington, with his shivering, half-starved troops, fled across the Delaware, Cornwallis, as we have observed, had returned to New York to embark for England. The contempt of the British for the

"rebels," was changed to respect and fear, and when intelligence of the affair at Trenton reached Howe, he ordered Cornwallis back with reinforcements, to gain the advantage lost. Congress, in the mean while, perceiving the necessity of giving more power to the commander-in-chief, wisely clothed him [December 27] with all the puissance of a military dictator, for six months, and gave him absolute control of all the operations of war, for that period.[1] This act was accomplished before that body could possibly have heard of the victory at Trenton, for they were then in session in Baltimore.

Inspirited by his success at Trenton, the panic of the enemy, and their retirement from the Delaware, Washington determined to recross that river, and act on the offensive. He ordered General Heath, who was with quite a

[1] When Congress adjourned on the 12th, to meet at Baltimore, almost equal powers were given to Washington, but they were not then defined. Now they were so, by resolution. They wrote to Washington, when they forwarded the resolution, "Happy is it for this country, that the general of their forces can be safely intrusted with unlimited power, and neither personal security, liberty, nor property, be in the least degree endangered thereby." At that time, Congress had given General Putnam almost unlimited command in Philadelphia. All munitions of war there, were placed under his control. He was also authorized to employ all private armed vessels in the Delaware, in the defense of Philadelphia. See note 1, page 246.

large body of New England troops at Peekskill,[1] to move into New Jersey with his main force; and the new militia levies were directed to annoy the flank and rear of the British detachments, and make frequent attacks upon their outposts. In the mean while, he again crossed the Delaware [December 30th], with his whole army, and took post at Trenton, while the British and German troops were concentrating at Princeton, only ten miles distant. Such was the position and the condition of the two armies at the close of the second year of the War for Independence—the memorable year when this great Republic of the West was born.

CHAPTER IV.

THIRD YEAR OF THE WAR FOR INDEPENDENCE. [1777.]

THE strange apathy of nations, like individuals, in times of great danger, or when dearest interests depend upon the utmost vigilance and care, is a remarkable phase in human character, and the records thereof appear as monstrous anomalies upon the pages of history. Such was the case with the executive and legislative power of the British nation during the momentous year of 1776, when the eye of ordinary forecast could not fail to perceive that the integrity of the realm was in imminent danger, and that the American colonies, the fairest jewels in the British crown, were likely to be lost forever. Such an apathy, strange and profound, seemed to pervade the councils of the British Government, even while the public mind of England was filled with the subject of the American rebellion. Notwithstanding an army had been driven from one city[2] [March, 1776], a fleet expelled from another[3] [June], their colonies declared independent[4] [July 4], and almost thirty thousand of their choice troops and fierce hirelings had been defied and combatted[5] [August], Parliament did not assemble until the last day of October, to deliberate on these important matters. Then the king, in his speech, congratulated them upon the success of the royal troops in America, and assured them (but without the shadow of good reason for the belief) that most of the continental powers entertained friendly feelings toward Great Britain. During a dull session of six weeks, new supplies for the American service were voted, while every conciliatory proposition was rejected; and when Parliament adjourned, in December, to keep the Christmas holidays, the members appeared to feel that their *votes* had crushed the rebellion, and that, on their re-assembling in January, they would be invited to join in a *Te Deum*[6] at St. Paul's, because of submission and peace in

[1] On the east bank of the Hudson, at the entrance to the Highlands, forty-five miles from the city of New York. See page 270.

[2] Page 247. [3] Page 249. [4] Page 251. [5] Page 253.

[6] The *Te Deum Laudamus* (*We praise thee, O God*) is always chanted in churches in England, and on the continent, after a great victory, great deliverance, etc. There is something revolting in

America. At that very moment, Washington was planning his brilliant achievement on the banks of the Delaware.[1]

In contrast with this apathy of the British Government, was the vigilance and activity of the Continental Congress. Their perpetual session was one of perpetual labor. Early in the year [March, 1776], the Secret Committee of that body had appointed Silas Deane,[2] a delegate from Connecticut, to proceed to France, as their agent, with general powers to solicit the co-operation of other governments. Even these remote colonists knew that the claims of the king of England to the friendship of the continental powers, was fallacious, and that France, Spain, and Holland, the Prince of Orange, and even Catharine of Russia, and Pope Clement the Fourteenth (Ganganelli), all of whom feared and hated England, instead of being friendly to her, were anxious for a pretense to strike her fiercely, and humble her pride, because of her potency in arms, her commerce, her diplomacy, and her strong Protestantism. All of these spoke kindly to the American agent, and Deane was successful in his embassy. He talked confidently, and by skillful management, during the summer of 1776, he obtained fifteen thousand muskets from the French arsenals, and abundant promises of men and money. And when the Declaration of Independence had been made [July 4], Congress appointed a regular embassy[3] [Sept. 22, 1776], to the court of France, and finally sent agents to other foreign courts.[4] They also planned, and finally executed measures for strengthening the bond of union between the several colonies, already made powerfully cohesive by common dangers and common hopes. *Articles of Confederation*, which formed the organic laws of the nation until the adoption of

SILAS DEANE.

---

this to the true Christian mind and heart. War, except strictly defensive as a last extremity, is always a monstrous injustice; and for its success in soddening God's fair earth with human blood, men in epaulettes, their hands literally dripping with gore, will go into the temple dedicated to the Prince of Peace, and there sing a *Te Deum!*

[1] Page 261.

[2] Silas Deane was born at Groton, in Connecticut, and was educated at Yale College. He was elected to the first Congress [page 228] in 1774, and after being some time abroad, as agent for the Secret Committee, he was recalled, on account of alleged bad conduct. He published a defense of his character in 1778, but he failed to reinstate himself in the public opinion. He went to England toward the close of 1784, where he died in extreme poverty, in 1789.

[3] The embassy consisted of Dr. Franklin, Silas Deane, and Arthur Lee. Franklin and Lee joined Deane at Paris, at the middle of December, 1776. Lee had then been in Europe for some time, as a sort of private agent of the Secret Committee. He made an arrangement with the French king to send a large amount of arms, ammunition, and specie, to the colonists, but in such a way that it would appear as a commercial transaction. The agent on the part of the French was Beaumarchais, who assumed the commercial title of Roderique Hortales & Co., and Lee took the name of Mary Johnson. This arrangement with the false and avaricious Beaumarchais, was a source of great annoyance and actual loss to Congress in after years. What was a gratuity on the part of the French government, in the name of Hortales & Co., Beaumarchais afterward presented a claim for, and actually received from Congress four hundred thousand dollars. Benjamin Franklin was born in Boston, in 1706. He was a printer; worked at his trade in London; became eminent in his business in Philadelphia; obtained a high position as a philosopher and statesman; was agent in England for several colonies; was chief embassador for the United States in Europe during the Revolution, and filled various official stations in the scientific and political world. He was one of the most remarkable men that ever lived; and, next to Washington, is the best known and most revered of all Americans. He died in 1790, at the age of more than eighty-four years. Arthur Lee was a brother of Richard Henry Lee [page 250], and was born in Virginia, in 1740. He was a fine scholar, and elegant writer. He died in 1782.

[4] Holland, Spain, and Prussia.

the Federal Constitution, were, after more than two years' consideration, approved by Congress, and produced vastly beneficial results during the remainder of the struggle.[1]

Such, in brief, were the chief operations of the civil power of the revolted colonies. Let us now turn to the military operations at the opening of a new

[1] In July, 1775, Dr. Franklin submitted a plan of union to Congress. On the 11th of June, 1776, a committee was appointed to draw up a plan. Their report was laid aside, and not called up until April, 1777. From that time until the 15th of November following, the subject was debated two or three times a week, when thirteen *Articles of Confederation* were adopted. The substance was that the thirteen confederated States should be known as the *United States of America;* that all engage in a reciprocal treaty of alliance and friendship, for mutual advantage, each to assist the other when help should be needed; that each State should have the right to regulate its own internal affairs; that no State should separately send or receive embassies, begin any negotiations, contract engagements or alliances, or conclude treaties with any foreign power, without the consent of the general Congress; that no public officer should be allowed to accept any presents, emoluments, office, or title, from any foreign power, and that neither Congress nor State governments should possess the power to confer any title of nobility; that none of the States should have the right to form alliances among themselves, without the consent of Congress; that they should not have the power to levy duties contrary to the enactments of Congress; that no State should keep up a standing army or ships of war, in time of peace, beyond the amount stipulated by Congress; that when any of the States should raise troops for the common defense, all the officers of the rank of colonel and under, should be appointed by the legislature of the State, and the superior officers by Congress; that all expenses of the war should be paid out of the public treasury; that Congress alone should have the power to coin money; and that Canada might at any time be admitted into the confederacy when she felt disposed. The last clauses were explanatory of the power of certain governmental operations, and contained details of the same. Such was the form of government which existed as the basis of our Republic, for almost twelve years. See Supplement.

year. Congress, we have observed,[1] delegated all military power to Washington, and he used it with energy and discretion. We left him at Trenton, prepared to act offensively or defensively, as circumstances should require. There he was joined by some troops under Generals Mifflin and Cadwalader, who came from Bordentown and Crosswicks, on the night of the 1st of January. Yet with these, his effective force did not exceed five thousand men. Toward the evening of the 2d of January, 1777, Cornwallis, with a strong force, approached from Princeton, and after some skirmishing, the two armies encamped on either side of a small stream which runs through the town, within pistol-shot of each other. Washington commenced intrenching his camp, and Cornwallis, expecting reinforcements in the morning, felt sure of his prey, and deferred an attack for the night.

The situation of Washington and his little army was now perilous in the extreme. A conflict with such an overwhelming force as was gathering, appeared hopeless, and the Delaware becoming more obstructed by ice every hour, rendered a retreat across it, in the event of a surprise, almost impossible. A retreat down the stream was equally perilous. An escape under cover of the night, was the only chance of safety, but the ground was too soft to allow the patriots to drag their heavy cannons with them; and could they withdraw unobserved by the British sentinels, whose hourly cry could be heard from the camp? This was a question of deep moment, and there was no time for long deliberation. A higher will than man's determined the matter. The Protector of the righteous put forth his hand. While a council of war was in session, toward midnight, the wind changed, and the ground was soon so hard frozen, that there could be no difficulty in conveying away the cannons. Instantly all was in activity in the American camp, while Cornwallis and his army were soundly sleeping—perhaps dreaming of the expected sure victory in the morning. Leaving a few to keep watch and feed the camp-fires, to allay suspicion, Washington silently withdrew, with all his army, artillery, and baggage; and at dawn [January 3, 1777], he was in sight of Princeton, prepared to fall upon Cornwallis's reserve there.[2] The British general had scarcely recovered from his surprise and mortification, on seeing the deserted camp of the Americans, when the distant booming of cannons, borne upon the keen winter air, fell ominously upon his ears. Although it was mid-winter, he thought it was the rumbling of distant thunder. The quick ear of General Erskine decided otherwise, and he exclaimed, "To arms, general! Washington has out-generaled us. Let us fly to the rescue at Princeton!" Erskine was right, for, at that moment, Washington and the British reserve were combating.

Owing to the extreme roughness of the roads, Washington did not reach Princeton as early as he expected, and instead of surprising the British, and then pushing forward to capture or destroy the enemy's stores at New Brunswick, he found a portion of the troops already on their march to join Corn-

---

[1] Page 264.

[2] A brigade, under Lieutenant-colonel Mawhood, consisting of three regiments and three troops of dragoons, were quartered there.

wallis at Trenton. A severe encounter occurred, when the American militia giving way, the British, with a victorious shout, rushed forward, expecting to produce a general rout. At that moment Washington advanced with a select corps, brought order out of confusion, and leading on his troops with waving sword and cheering voice, turned the tide of battle and achieved a victory. The brave General Mercer,[1] while fighting at the head of his men, was killed, and many other beloved officers were lost on that snowy battle-field.[2] Nor was the conflict of that morning yet ended. When Cornwallis perceived the desertion of the American camp, and heard the firing at Princeton, he hastened with a greater portion of his troops, to the aid of his reserve, and to secure his stores at New Brunswick. The Americans, who had not slept, nor scarcely tasted food for thirty-six hours, were compelled, just as the heat of the first battle was over, to contest with fresh troops, or fly with the speed of strong men. Washington chose the latter alternative, and when Cornwallis entered Princeton, not a "rebel" was to be found.[3] History has no parallel to offer to these events of a few days. Frederic the Great of Prussia, one of the most renowned commanders of modern times, declared that the achievements of Washington and his little band of compatriots, between the 25th of December and the 4th of January following, were the most brilliant of any recorded in the annals of military performances.

BATTLE AT PRINCETON.

The Americans were too weak to attempt the capture of the British stores at New Brunswick, so, with his fatigued troops Washington retreated rapidly toward the hill country of East Jersey.[4] Allowing time only to refresh his little army at Pluckemin, he pressed forward to Morristown, and there established his winter quarters. But he did not sit down in idleness. After planting small cantonments[5] at different points from Princeton to the Hudson Highlands, he sent out detachments to harass the thoroughly perplexed British. These expeditions were conducted with so much skill and spirit, that on the first

---

[1] Mercer's horse had been shot under him, and he was on foot at the head of his men, when a British soldier felled him with a clubbed musket [note 4, page 236]. At first, the British believed it to be Washington, and, with a shout, they cried, "The rebel general is taken." Hugh Mercer was a native of Scotland. He was a surgeon on the field of Culloden, and was practicing medicine in Fredericksburg, Virginia, when the Revolution broke out. He was with Washington in the French and Indian War. He was made commander of the flying camp in 1776, and at the time of his death was about fifty-six years of age. The picture of a house in the corner of the map of the battle at Princeton, is a representation of the house in which General Mercer died. It is yet [1856] standing.

[2] The chief of these were Colonels Haslett and Potter, Major Morris, and Captains Shippen, Fleming and Neal. The loss of the Americans in this engagement, was about thirty, including the officers above named.

[3] We have mentioned, on page 210, the planetarium, at Princeton, constructed by David Rittenhouse. This excited the admiration of Cornwallis, and he intended to carry it away with him. It is also said that Silas Deane [page 264] proposed to present this work of art to the French government, as a bonus for its good will. Cornwallis was kept too busy in providing for his own safety, while in Princeton, to allow him to rob the college of so great a treasure.

[4] Page 160.

[5] Permanent stations for small bodies of troops.

of March, 1777, not a British nor a Hessian soldier could be found in New Jersey, except at New Brunswick and Amboy.[1] Those dreaded battalions which, sixty days before, were all-powerful in New Jersey, and had frightened the Continental Congress from Philadelphia, were now hemmed in upon the Raritan, and able to act only on the defensive. Considering the attending circumstances, this was a great triumph for the Americans. It revived the martial spirit of the people, and the hopes of all good patriots; and hundreds in New Jersey, who had been deceived by Howe's proclamation, and had suffered Hessian brutality, openly espoused the Whig cause. Congress had returned to Philadelphia,[2] and commenced its labors with renewed vigor.

It was almost the first of June before the main body of the two armies commenced the summer campaign. In the mean while, smaller detachments were in motion at various points. A strong armament was sent up the Hudson, in March, to destroy American stores at Peekskill, at the southern entrance to the Highlands. The Americans there, under the command of General McDougal, perceiving a defense of the property to be futile, set fire to the stores and retreated to the hills in the rear. The British returned to New York the same evening [March 23, 1777]. Almost a month afterward [April 13], Cornwallis went up the Raritan from New Brunswick, to surprise the Americans under General Lincoln, at Boundbrook. The latter escaped, with difficulty, after losing about sixty men and a part of his baggage. Toward the close of April [April 25], Governor Tryon,[3] at the head of two thousand British and Tories, went up Long Island Sound, landed at Compo [April 26], between Norwalk and Fairfield, marched to Danbury, destroyed a large quantity of stores belonging to the Americans, burned the town, and cruelly treated the inhabitants. Perceiving the militia to be gathering in great numbers, he retreated rapidly the next morning, by way of Ridgefield. Near that village, he had some severe skirmishing with the militia under Generals Wooster, Arnold,[4] and Silliman. Wooster was killed,[5] Arnold narrowly escaped, but Silliman, keeping the field, harassed the British all the way to the coast. At Compo, and while embarking, they were terribly galled by artillery under Lamb.[6] Tryon lost almost three hundred men during this expedition, and killed or wounded about half that number of Americans. His atrocities on that

---

[1] The Americans went out in small companies, made sudden attacks upon pickets, out-posts, and foraging parties, and in this way frightened the detachments of the enemy and drove them in to the main body on the Raritan. At Springfield, a few miles from Elizabethtown, they attacked a party of Hessians who were penetrating the country from Elizabethport [January 7, 1777], killed between forty and fifty of them, and drove the remainder in great confusion back to Staten Island. A larger foraging party was defeated near Somerset court house [January 20] by about five hundred New Jersey militia under General Dickinson; and Newark, Elizabethtown and Woodbridge, were taken possession of by the patriots.

[2] Page 262.

[3] Page 223.

[4] Page 234. For his gallantry at Ridgefield, Congress ordered a horse, richly caparisoned, to be presented to him.

[5] David Wooster was born in Stratford, Connecticut, in 1710. He was at Louisburg in 1745 [page 137], became a captain in the British army, and was in the French and Indian War. He was in Canada in the spring of 1776 [page 243], and gave promise of being one of the most efficient of the American officers in the war for Independence. His loss, at such a critical period of the conflict, was much deplored. The State of Connecticut erected a monument to his memory, in 1854.

[6] Page 240.

occasion were never forgotten nor forgiven. The name of Tryon will ever be held in detestation by all lovers of justice and humanity. He had already, while governor of North Carolina, been named by the Indians, *The Great Wolf*, and in his marauding expeditions during the earlier years of the war for Independence, his conduct confirmed the judgment of the Red Men. We shall meet him again.

The Americans did not always act upon the defensive: they were sometimes the aggressors. Toward the close of May [May 22, 1777], Colonel Meigs, with one hundred and seventy men, crossed Long Island Sound in whale-boats, from Guilford, Connecticut, and at two o'clock in the morning of the 23d of that month, attacked a British provision post at Sagg Harbor, near the eastern extremity of Long Island. They burned a dozen vessels, and the store-houses and contents, secured ninety prisoners, and reached Guilford at two o'clock the next day, without losing a man of their own party. For this exploit, Congress voted thanks to Colonel Meigs and his men, and a sword to the commander. A little later in the season, an equally bold exploit was performed on Rhode Island. On a dark night in July [July 10], Colonel William Barton, with a company of picked men, crossed Narraganset Bay in whale-boats, in the midst of the British fleet, stole cautiously to the quarters of General Prescott,[1] the British commander on Rhode Island, seized him while in bed, and carried him in triumph across the bay to Warwick. There a carriage was in waiting for him, and at sunrise he was under a strong guard at Providence. From thence he was sent to the headquarters of Washington, at Middlebrook, on the Raritan,[2] and was exchanged, in April, the next year, for General Charles Lee.[3] For Colonel Barton's bravery, on that occasion, Congress voted him an elegant sword, and he was promoted to the rank and pay of a colonel in the continental army.

The American commander-in-chief continued his head quarters at Morristown until near the last of May. During the spring he had inoculated a large portion of his troops for the small-pox;[4] and when the leaves put forth, a fair degree of health prevailed in his camp, and his army had increased by recruits, to almost ten thousand men. He was prepared for action, offensive and defensive; but the movements of the British perplexed him. Burgoyne was assembling an army at St. John, on the Sorel,[5] and vicinity, preparatory to an invasion of New York, by way of Lake Champlain, to achieve that darling object of the British ministry, the occupation of the country on the Hudson.[6]

---

[1] Page 240. Prescott's quarters were at a house yet [1856] standing, a short distance above Newport, and about a mile from the bay.

[2] While on his way, his escort stopped at Lebanon, Connecticut, to dine. Prescott was a morose, haughty, and violent-tempered man. At the table, a dish of succotash (beans and corn) was brought to him. Not being accustomed to such food, he regarded it as an insult, and taking the dish from the hands of the hostess, he strewed its contents upon the floor. Her husband being informed of it, flogged the general severely, with a horsewhip.

[3] Note 4, page 248; also page 288.

[4] The common practice of vaccination at the present day was then unknown in this country. Indeed, the attention of Jenner, the father of the practice, had then just been turned to the subject. It was practiced here a year after the close of the war.

[5] Page 240.

[6] Page 283.

But whether Howe was preparing to co-operate with Burgoyne, or to make another attempt to seize Philadelphia,[1] Washington could not determine. He prepared for both events by stationing Arnold with a strong detachment on the west side of the Delaware, concentrating a large force on the Hudson, and moving the main body of his army to Middlebrook, within ten miles of the British camp at New Brunswick.

Washington was not kept in suspense a great while. On the 12th of June [1777], Howe passed over from New York, where he made his head quarters during the winter, concentrated the main body of his army at New Brunswick, and tried to draw Washington into an engagement by a feigned movement [June 14] toward the Delaware. The chief, perceiving the meaning of this movement, and aware of his comparative strength, wisely remained in his strong position at Middlebrook until Howe suddenly retreated [June 19], sent some of his troops over to Staten Island [June 22], and appeared to be evacuating New Jersey. This movement perplexed Washington. He was fairly deceived; and ordering strong detachments in pursuit, he advanced several miles in the same direction, with his whole army. Howe suddenly changed front [June 25], and attempted to gain the rear of the Americans; but, after Stirling's brigade had maintained a severe skirmish with a corps under Cornwallis [June 26], the Americans regained their camp without much loss. Five days afterward [June 30], the whole British army crossed over to Staten Island, and left New Jersey in the complete possession of the patriots.

Washington now watched the movements of his enemy with great anxiety and the utmost vigilance. It was evident that some bold stroke was about to be attempted by the British. On the 12th of July, Burgoyne, who had been moving steadily up Lake Champlain, with a powerful army, consisting of about seven thousand British and German troops, and a large body of Canadians and Indians, took possession of Crown Point and Ticonderoga,[2] and spread terror over the whole North. At the same time the British fleet at New York took such a position as induced the belief that it was about to pass up the Hudson and co-operate with the victorious invader. Finally, Howe left General Clinton in command at New York, and embarking on board the fleet with eighteen thousand troops [July 23], he sailed for the Delaware. When Washington comprehended this movement, he left a strong force on the Hudson, and with the main body of his troops pushed forward to Philadelphia. There he was saluted by a powerful ally, in the person of a stripling, less than twenty years of age. He was a wealthy French nobleman, who, several months before, while at a dinner with the Duke of Gloucester,[3] first heard of the struggle of the Americans, their Declaration of Independence, and the preparations made to crush them. His young soul was fired with aspirations to give them his aid; and quitting the army, he hurried to Paris. Although he had just married a young and beautiful girl, and a bright career was opened for him in his own

[1] Page 261. [2] Page 234.
[3] The duke was the brother of the king of England, and at the time in question, was dining with some French officers, in the old town of Mentz, in Germany.

country, he left all, and hastened to America in a vessel fitted out at his own expense. He offered his services to the Continental Congress, and that body gave him the commission [July 31] of a major-general. Three days afterward [Aug. 3] he was introduced to Washington at a public dinner; and within less than forty days he was gallantly fighting [September 11], as a volunteer, for freedom in America, on the banks of the Brandywine. That young general was the Marquis de LA FAYETTE,[1] whose name is forever linked with that of Washington and Liberty.

GENERAL LA FAYETTE.

The British fleet, with the army under Sir William Howe,[2] did not go up the Delaware, as was anticipated, but ascended Chesapeake Bay, and at its head, near the village of Elkton, in Maryland, the land forces disembarked [Aug. 25], and marched toward Philadelphia. Washington had advanced beyond the Brandywine Creek, and took post a few miles from Wilmington. Howe's superior force compelled him to fall back to the east side of the Brandywine; and at Chad's Ford, several miles above Wilmington, he made a stand for the defense of Philadelphia. At that point, the Hessians under Knyphausen[3] attacked the left wing of the Americans [Sept. 11, 1777], commanded by Washington in person; while Howe and Cornwallis, crossing the stream several miles above, fell upon the American right, under General Sullivan, near the Birmingham meeting-house.[4] The contest raged fearfully during the whole day. At night the shattered and defeated battalions of patriots retreated to Chester, and the following day [Sept. 12] to Philadelphia. Many brave men were killed or disabled on that sanguinary field. La Fayette was severely wounded;[5] and the patriots lost full twelve hundred men, killed, wounded, and

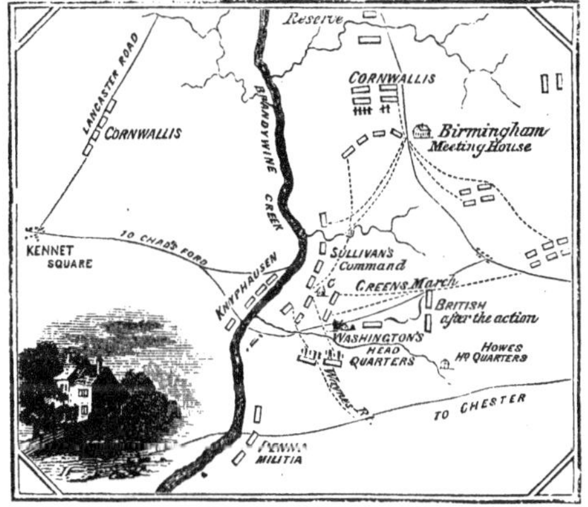

BATTLE AT THE BRANDYWINE.

[1] He was born on the 6th of September, 1757. He married the daughter of the Duke de Noailles, a beautiful heiress, at the age of eighteen years. He first landed on the coast of South Carolina, in Winyaw Bay, near Georgetown, and made a land journey to Philadelphia. His application was not received at first, by the Continental Congress; but when his true character and designs were known, they gave him a major-general's commission. He was afterward an active patriot in his own country in many perilous scenes. He visited America in 1824–5 [page 453], and died in 1834, at the age of seventy-seven years. The Baron de Kalb [page 316] and eleven other French and Polish officers, came to America in La Fayette's vessel.

[2] After the battle near Brooklyn [page 254], the king conferred the honor of knighthood upon General William Howe, the commander-in-chief of the British forces in America. The ceremony was performed by several of his officers, at his quarters in the Beekman House, Turtle Bay, East River.

[3] Page 259.

[4] This was (and is yet) a Quaker meeting-house, situated a few miles from Chad's Ford, on the road from Jefferis's Ford (where Howe and Cornwallis crossed) to Wilmington.

[5] A bullet passed through his leg. He was conveyed to Bethlehem, in Pennsylvania, where

made prisoners. The British lost almost eight hundred. Washington failed of success more on account of false intelligence, by which he was kept in ignorance of the approach of the British on his left, than by want of skill or force.[1]

Washington did not remain idle in the Federal capital, but as soon as the troops were rested, he crossed the Schuylkill, and proceeded to confront Howe, who was making slow marches toward Philadelphia. They met [Sept. 16] twenty miles west of that city, and some skirmishing ensued; but a heavy rain prevented a general battle, and the Americans withdrew toward Reading. General Wayne, in the mean while, was hanging upon the rear of the enemy with about fifteen hundred men. On the night of the 20th, he was surprised by a party of British and Hessians, under General Grey, near the Paoli Tavern, and lost about three hundred of his party.[2] With the remainder he joined Washington, then near Valley Forge, and vigilantly watching the movements of Howe. As these indicated the intention of the British commander to attempt the seizure of a large quantity of ammunition and military stores which the Americans had collected at Reading, Washington abandoned Philadelphia, and took position at Pottsgrove, thirty-five miles distant, to protect those indispensable materials for his army. Howe crossed the Schuylkill [Sept. 23, 1777], near Norristown, and marched to the Federal city[3] [Sept. 26], without opposition. Congress fled at his approach, first to Lancaster [Sept. 27], and then to York, where it assembled on the 30th, and continued its session until the following summer.' The main body of the British army was encamped at Germantown, four miles from Philadelphia, and Howe prepared to make the latter place his winter quarters.[4]

Upon opposite sides of the Delaware, a few miles below Philadelphia, were two forts of considerable strength (Mifflin and Mercer), garrisoned by the Americans. While the British army was marching from the Chesapeake[5] to Philadelphia, the fleet had sailed around to the Delaware, and had approached to the head of that bay. The forts commanded the river; and *chevaux-de-frise*[6] just below them, completely obstructed it, so that the army in Philadelphia could obtain no supplies from the fleet. The possession of these forts was

---

the Moravian sisters nursed him during his confinement. Count Pulaski began his military career in the American army, on the field of Brandywine, where he commanded a troop of horse, and after the battle he was appointed to the rank of Brigadier. He was slain at Savannah. See note 3, page 350.

[1] The building seen in the corner of the map, is a view of the head quarters of Washington, yet [1856] standing, a short distance from Chad's Ford.

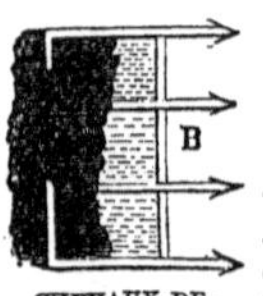

CHEVAUX-DE-FRISE.

[2] The bodies of fifty-three Americans, found on the field the next morning, were interred in one broad grave; and forty years afterward, the "Republican Artillerists" of Chester county, erected a neat marble monument over them. It stands in the center of an inclosure which contains the ground consecrated by the burial of these patriots.

[3] Philadelphia, New York, and Washington, have been, respectively, federal cities, or cities where the Federal Congress of the United States assembled.

[4] Note 2, page 285.

[5] Page 273.

[6] *Chevaux-de-frise* are obstructions placed in river channels to prevent the passage of vessels. They are generally made of a series of heavy timbers, pointed with iron, and secured at an angle in a strong frame filled with stones, as seen in the engraving. Figure A shows the position under water; figure B shows how the timbers are arranged and the stones placed in them.

important, and on the 22d of October, they were attached by detachments sent by Howe. Fort Mercer was assailed by two thousand Hessian grenadiers under Count Donop.[1] They were repulsed by the garrison of less than five hundred men, under Lieutenant-Colonel Christopher Greene, of Rhode Island, after losing their commander,[2] and almost four hundred soldiers. The garrison of Fort Mifflin, under Lieutenant-Colonel Samuel Smith, also made a gallant defense, but after a series of assaults by land and water, it was abandoned [Nov. 16, 1777]. Two days afterward, Fort Mercer was also abandoned, and several British ships sailed up to Philadelphia.[3]

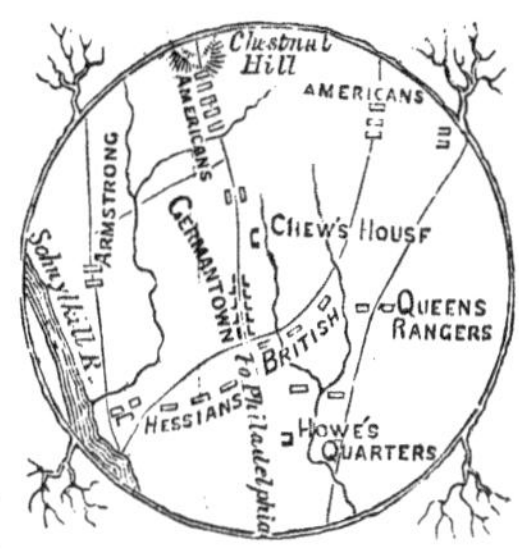

BATTLE AT GERMANTOWN.

When Washington was informed of the weakened condition of the British army, by the detachment of these forces to attack the Delaware forts, he resolved to assail the camp at Germantown. He had moved down the Schuylkill to Skippack Creek [Sept. 25], and from that point he marched, silently, on the evening of the 3d of October [1777], toward the camp of the enemy. He reached Chestnut Hill, beyond Germantown, at dawn the following morning, and the attack soon commenced near there. After a severe battle, which continued almost three hours, the patriots were repulsed, with a loss, in killed, wounded, and prisoners, about equal to that at Brandywine.[4] The British lost only about six hundred. On the 19th, Howe broke up his encampment at Germantown, and three weeks afterward, he proceeded to place his whole army in winter quarters in Philadelphia. Washington retired to his camp on Skippack Creek; and on the 29th of November, he prepared to go into winter quarters at White Marsh, fourteen miles from Philadelphia.

Let us now turn for a while from these scenes of conflict and disaster in which the beloved commander-in-chief was personally engaged, to the consideration of important events which were transpiring on the waters and banks of Lake Champlain and the Hudson River. Burgoyne, with more than ten thousand men, invested Ticonderoga on the 2d of July. The fortress was garrisoned by General St. Clair, with only about three thousand men. Upon

---

[1] Page 263.

[2] Donop was terribly wounded, and taken to the house of a Quaker near by, where he expired three days afterward. He was buried within the fort. A few years ago his bones were disinterred, and his skull was taken possession of by a New Jersey physician.

[3] In the defense of these forts, the Americans lost about three hundred men, and the enemy almost double that number.

[4] Washington felt certain of victory at the beginning of the battle. Just as it commenced, a dense fog overspread the country; and through the inexperience of his troops, great confusion, in their movements, was produced. A false rumor caused a panic among the Americans, just as the British were about to fall back, and a general retreat and loss of victory was the result. In Germantown, a strong stone house is yet [1856] standing, which belonged to Judge Chew. This a part of the enemy occupied, and from the windows fired with deadly effect, upon the Americans. No blame was attached to Washington for this defeat, when victory seemed easy and certain. On the contrary, Congress, on the receipt of Washington's letter, describing the battle, passed a vote of thanks to him for his "wise and well-concerted attack upon the enemy's army near Germantown;" and "to the officers and soldiers of the army, for their brave exertions on that occasion." A medal was also ordered to be struck, and presented to Washington.

Mount Independence, on the opposite side of the lake, was a small fortification and a weak garrison.[1] These composed the entire force, except some feeble detachments of militia, to oppose the invaders. On the approach of Burgoyne, St. Clair[2] left his outworks, gathered his forces near the fortress, and prepared for an assault; but when, on the evening of the 5th, he saw the scarlet uniforms of the British on the top of Mount Defiance,[3] and a battery of heavy guns planted there,[4] more than five hundred feet above the fort, he knew resistance would be vain. That evening he sent his ammunition and stores up the lake to Skenesborough,[5] and under cover of the darkness, silently crossed over to Mount Independence, and commenced a retreat to Fort Edward,[6] the head-quarters of General Schuyler, who was then in command of the northern army.

GENERAL ST. CLAIR.

The retreating army would have been beyond the reach of pursuers by dawn, had not their exit been discovered. Contrary to express orders, a building was fired on Mount Independence, and by its light their flight was discovered by the enemy, and a strong party, consisting of the brigade of General Fraser, and two Hessian corps under Riedesel, was immediately sent in pursuit. At dawn, the British flag was waving over Ticonderoga; and a little after sunrise [July 7, 1777], the rear division of the flying Americans, under Colonel Seth Warner,[7] were overtaken in Hubbardton, Vermont, and a severe engagement followed. The patriots were defeated and dispersed, and the victors returned to Ticonderoga.[8] Before sunset the same evening, a flotilla of British vessels had overtaken and destroyed the Americans' stores which St. Clair had sent up the lake, and also a large quantity at Skenesborough. The fragments of St. Clair's army reached Fort Edward on the 12th, thoroughly dispirited. Disaster had followed disaster in quick succession. Within a week, the Americans had lost almost two hundred pieces of artillery, and a large amount of provisions and military stores.

---

[1] During the previous years, the Americans constructed a picketed fort, or stockade [note 2, page 183], on that eminence, built about three hundred huts or barracks, dug several wells, and placed batteries at different points. The remains of these are now [1856] everywhere visible on Mount Independence. That eminence received this name because the troops took possession of it on the 4th of July, 1776. Page 250.

[2] Arthur St. Clair was a native of Scotland, and came to America with Admiral Boscawen, early in May, 1755. He served under Wolfe [page 201]; and when the Revolution broke out, he entered the American army. He served during the war, and afterward commanded an expedition against the Indians in Ohio, where he was unsuccessful. He died in 1818, at the age of eighty-four years.

[3] This is a hill about 750 feet in height, situated on the south-west side of the outlet of Lake George, opposite Ticonderoga.

[4] With immense labor, Burgoyne opened a road up the northern slope of Mount Defiance, and dragged heavy artillery to the summit. From that point, every ball might be hurled within the fort below without difficulty. The position of that road may yet [1856] be traced by the second growth of trees on its line up the mountain.

[5] Now Whitehall. It was named after Philip Skene, who settled there in 1764. The narrow part of Lake Champlain, from Ticonderoga to Whitehall, was formerly called *Wood Creek* (the name of the stream that enters the lake at Whitehall), and also *South River*. [6] Page 188. [7] Page 232.

[8] The Americans lost, in killed, wounded, and missing, a little more than three hundred; the British reported their loss at one hundred and eighty-three.

The force under General Schuyler was very small, and even with this reinforcement by the fugitives from the lake, he had only about four thousand effective men—a number totally inadequate to combat with those of Burgoyne. He therefore sent a strong party toward Skenesborough to fell huge trees across the roads, and to destroy all the bridges, so as to obstruct the march of the invaders, while he slowly retreated down the Hudson valley to the mouth of the Mohawk, and there established a fortified camp.[1] His call for aid was nobly responded to, for the whole country was thoroughly aroused to a sense of peril. Detachments were sent from the regular army to strengthen him; and soon General Lincoln came with a large body of New England militia. When General Gates arrived, to take the chief command,[2] he found an army of thirteen thousand men, ready to meet the invader.

The progress of Burgoyne was slow, and he did not reach Fort Edward until the 30th of July.[3] The obstructions ordered by Schuyler, and the destruction of the bridges, were great hinderances.[4] His army was also worn down by fatigue, and his provisions were almost exhausted. To replenish his stores, he sent five hundred Germans, Canadians, and Tories, and one hundred Indians, under Colonel Baume, to seize provisions and cattle which the Americans had collected at Bennington, thirty-five miles distant. Colonel John Stark had called out the New Hampshire militia; and near Hoosick, within five miles of Bennington, they met [Aug. 16] and defeated the marauders. And toward evening, when another German party, under Colonel Breyman, approached, they also were defeated by a continental force under Colonel Seth Warner.[5] Many of the enemy were killed, and a large number were made prisoners. Burgoyne's entire loss, in this expedition, was almost a thousand men. The Americans had one hundred killed, and as many wounded. This defeat was fatal to Burgoyne's future operations[6]—this victory was a day-star of hope to the

[1] Thaddeus Kosciuszko, a Polish refugee, who came with Lafayette [page 273], was now attached to Schuyler's army, as engineer. Under his direction, the intrenchments at the mouth of the Mohawk River, were constructed; also, those at Stillwater and Saratoga. The camp at the mouth of the Mohawk was upon islands just below the Great, or Cohoes' Falls.

KOSCIUSZKO.

[2] General Schuyler had superseded Gates in June, and had been skillfully confronting Burgoyne. But Gates, seeing a chance for gaining laurels, and having a strong party of friends in Congress, sought the chief command of the northern army. It was ungenerously taken from Schuyler at the moment when, by great exertions and through great hardships, he had a force prepared to confront Burgoyne, with some prospect of success.

[3] It was while Burgoyne was approaching that point, that Jane M'Crea, the betrothed of a young Tory in the British army, was shot, while being conveyed by a party of Indians from Fort Edward to the British camp. Her death was untruly charged upon the Indians, and it was made the subject of the most bitter denunciations of the British ministers, for employing such cruel instrumentalities. The place of her death is a short distance from the village of Fort Edward. The pine-tree which marked the spot, decayed a few years since, and in 1853, it was cut down, and converted into canes and boxes for the curious.

[4] Burgoyne was obliged to construct forty bridges on the way, and to remove the many trees which lay across the roads. To estimate the amount of fatigue which the troops must have endured during that hot month, it must be remembered that each soldier bore a weight of sixty pounds, in arms, accoutrements, and supplies.

[5] Pages 234 and 240.

[6] It dispirited his troops, who were worn down with the fatigue of the obstructed march from Skenesborough to Fort Edward. It also caused a delay of a month at that place, and in the mean

Americans. Applause of the New Hampshire militia rang through the land, and Stark was made a brigadier in the continental army.

JOSEPH BRANT.

During Burgoyne's approach, the Mohawk valley had become a scene of great confusion and alarm. Colonel St. Leger and his savages, joined by the Mohawk Indians, under Brant,[1] and a body of Tories, under Johnson[2] and Butler, had arrived from Oswego, and invested Fort Stanwix, on the 3d of August [1777]. The garrison was commanded by Colonel Gansevoort, and made a spirited defense. General Herkimer rallied the militia of his neighborhood; and while marching to the assistance of Gansevoort, he fell into an Indian ambuscade [Aug. 6] at Oriskany.[3] His party was totally defeated, after a bloody conflict, and himself was mortally wounded. On the same day, a corps of the garrison, under Colonel Willet, made a successful sortie,[4] and broke the power of the besiegers. Arnold, who had been sent by Schuyler to the relief of the fort, soon afterward approached, when the besiegers fled [Aug. 22], and quiet was restored to the Mohawk valley.

GENERAL BURGOYNE.

The disastrous events at Bennington and Fort Stanwix, and the straitened condition of his commissariat, greatly perplexed Burgoyne. To retreat, advance, or remain inactive, seemed equally perilous. With little hope of reaching Albany, where he had boasted he would eat his Christmas dinner, he crossed the Hudson and formed a fortified camp on the hills and plains of Saratoga, now the site of Schuylerville. General Gates advanced to Bemis's Heights, about four miles north of

---

while their provisions were rapidly diminishing. While at Fort Edward, Burgoyne received intelligence of the defeat of St. Leger at Fort Stanwix.

[1] Joseph Brant was a Mohawk Indian, and a great favorite of Sir William Johnson. He adhered to the British, and went to Canada after the war, where he died in 1807, aged sixty-five years.

A TREATY.

[2] Sir William Johnson [page 190] (then dead) had been a sort of autocrat among the Indians and Tories in the Mohawk valley. He flattered the chiefs in various ways, and through them he obtained almost unbounded influence over the tribes, especially that of the Mohawks. He was in the habit of giving those chiefs who pleased him, a diploma, certifying their good character, and faithfulness to his majesty. These contained a picture, representing a treaty council, of which the annexed engraving is a copy. His family were the worst enemies of the Americans during the war, in that region. His son, John, raised a regiment of Tories, called the *Johnson Greens* (those who joined St. Leger); and John Butler, a cruel leader, was at the head of another band, called *Butler's Rangers*. These co-operated with Brant, the great Mohawk sachem, and for years they made the Mohawk valley and vicinity truly a "dark and bloody ground." These men were the allies of St. Leger on the occasion in question.

[3] The place of the battle is about half way between Utica and Rome. The latter village is upon Fort Stanwix, built by Bradstreet and his troops in 1758 [page 197]. It was repaired and garrisoned in 1776, and its name was changed to Fort Schuyler. Another Fort Schuyler was built during the French and Indian War, where Utica now stands.

[4] Note 7, page 241.

Burgoyne Surrendering his Sword to Gates.

Stillwater (and twenty-five from Albany), and also formed a fortified camp.[1] Burgoyne perceived the necessity for immediate operations, and advancing toward the American camp, a severe but indecisive action ensued, on the 19th of September [1777]. Night terminated the conflict, and both parties claimed the victory.[2] Burgoyne fell back to his camp, where he resolved to await the arrival of expected detachments from General Clinton, who was to attack the posts on the Hudson Highlands, and force his way to Albany.[3] But after waiting a few days, and hearing nothing from Clinton, he prepared for another attempt upon the Americans, for the militia were flocking to Gates's camp, and Indian warriors of the SIX NATIONS[4] were gathering there. His own force, on the contrary, was hourly diminishing. As his star, which arose so brightly at Ticonderoga,[5] began to decline upon the Hudson, the Canadians and his Indian allies deserted him in great numbers.[6] He was compelled to fight or flee. Again he advanced; and after a severe battle of several hours, on the 7th of October, and almost on the same ground occupied on the 19th of September, he was compelled to fall back to the heights of Saratoga, and leave the patriots in the possession of the field. Ten days afterward [October 17], finding only three days' provisions in his camp, hearing nothing of Clinton, and perceiving retreat impossible, he was compelled to surrender his whole army prisoners of war.[7] Of necessity, the forts upon Lake Champlain now fell into the hands of the patriots.

BEMIS'S HEIGHTS.

---

[1] The remains of some of the intrenchments were yet visible in 1850, when the writer visited the locality.

[2] The number of Americans engaged in this action, was about two thousand five hundred; that of the British was about three thousand. The former lost, in killed, wounded, and missing, three hundred and nineteen; the British loss was rather less than five hundred.

[3] Page 283.

[4] Page 25.

[5] Page 276.

[6] The Indians had been disappointed in their expectations of blood and plunder; and now was their hunting season, when provisions must be secured for winter use. The Canadians saw nothing but defeat in the future, and left the army in whole companies.

[7] The whole number surrendered was five thousand seven hundred and ninety-one, of whom two thousand four hundred and twelve were Germans or *Hessians* [page 183], under the chief command of the Baron Riedesel, whose wife accompanied him, and afterward wrote a very interesting account of her experience in America. Burgoyne *did* dine at Albany, but as a prisoner, though a guest at the table of General Schuyler. That noble patriot, though smarting under the injustice of Congress and the pride of Gates, did not abate his zeal for the good cause when he had surrendered his command into the hands of his successor, but, as a private citizen, gave his time, his labor, and his money freely, until he saw the invader humbled; and then, notwithstanding Burgoyne, without the show of a just excuse, had destroyed Schuyler's fine mansion, his mills, and much other property, at Saratoga, he made the vanquished general a guest at his own table. When Burgoyne said, "You are very kind to one who has done you so much injury," the generous patriot replied, "That was the fate of war; let us say no more about it." Burgoyne's troops laid down their arms upon the plain in front of Schuylerville; and the meeting of the conqueror and the conquered, for the latter to surrender his sword, was a very significant scene. The two came out of Gates's marquee together. Without exchanging a word, Burgoyne, according to previous arrangement, stepped back, drew his sword, and, in the presence of the two armies, presented it to General Gates. The latter received it with a courteous inclination of the head, and instantly returned it to the vanquished general. They then returned to the marquee together. The British filed off, and took up their line of march for Boston; and thus ended this important act in the great drama, upon the heights of Saratoga. Burgoyne's troops were marched to Cambridge, Massachusetts, with the view of sending

Glorious, indeed, was this victory for the Americans. It gave them a fine train of brass artillery, five thousand muskets, and a vast amount of munitions of war. Its moral effect was of greater importance. All eyes had been anxiously turned to the army of the North, and Congress and the people listened eagerly for every breath of rumor from Saratoga. How electric was the effect when a shout of victory came from the camp of Gates![1] It rolled over the land, and was echoed from furrows, workshops, marts of commerce, the halls of legislation, and from the shattered army of Washington at Whitemarsh.[2] Toryism stood abashed; the bills of Congress rose twenty per cent. in value;[3] private capital came from its hiding-places for public employment; the militia flocked to the standards of leaders, and the great patriot heart of America beat with strong pulsations of hope. The effect in Europe was also favorable to the Americans. The highest hopes of the British ministry rested on this expedition, and the generalship of Burgoyne justified their expectations. It was a most severe blow, and gave the opposition in Parliament the keenest weapons. Pitt, leaning upon his crutches,[4] poured forth eloquent denunciations [December, 1777] of the mode of warfare pursued—the employment of German hirelings[5] and brutal savages.[6] "If I were an American, as I am an Englishman," he exclaimed, "while a foreign troop was landed in my country, I never would lay down my arms—never, never, never!" In the Lower House,[7] Burke, Fox, and Barré were equally severe upon the government. When, on the 3d of December, the news of Burgoyne's defeat reached London, the latter arose in his place in the Commons,[8] and with a serene and solemn countenance, asked Lord George Germain, the Secretary of War, what news he had received by his last expresses from Quebec, and to say, upon his word of honor, what had become of Burgoyne and his brave army. The haughty secretary was irritated by the cool irony of the question, but was compelled to acknowledge that the unhappy intelligence of Burgoyne's surrender had reached him. He added, "The intelligence needs confirmation." That confirmation was not slow in reaching the ministry.

Mightily did this victory weigh in favor of the Americans, at the French

---

them to Europe, but Congress thought it proper to retain them, and they were marched to the interior of Virginia. John Burgoyne was a natural son of Lord Bingley, and was quite eminent as a dramatic author. On his return to England, he resumed his seat as a member of Parliament, and opposed the war. He died in 1792.

[1] General Gates was so elated with the victory, which had been prepared for him by General Schuyler, and won chiefly by the valor of Arnold and Morgan [page 331], that he neglected the courtesy due to the commander-in-chief, and instead of sending his dispatches to him, he sent his aid, Colonel Wilkinson, with a verbal message to Congress. That body also forgot its dignity in the hour of its joy, and the young officer was allowed to announce the victory himself, on the floor of Congress. In his subsequent dispatches, Gates did not even mention the names of Arnold and Morgan. History has vindicated their claims to the honor of the victory, and placed a just estimate upon the ungenerous conduct of their commander. Congress voted a gold medal to Gates.

[2] Page 275. [3] Note 3, page 245. [4] Note 1, page 231. [5] Note 3, page 246.

[6] A member justified the employment of the Indians, by saying that the British had a right to use the means "which God and nature had given them." Pitt scornfully repeated the passage, and said, "These abominable principles, and this most abominable avowal of them, demands most decisive indignation. I call upon that right reverend bench (pointing to the bishops), those holy ministers of the gospel, and pious pastors of the church—I conjure them to join in the holy work, and to vindicate the religion of their God." [7] Note 2, page 218. [8] Note 2, page 218.

court. Unaided by any foreign power, the Americans had defeated and captured a well-trained army of about six thousand men, led by experienced commanders. "Surely such a people possess the elements of success, and will achieve it. We may now safely strike England a severe blow,[1] by acknowledging the independence, and forming an alliance with her revolted colonies," argued the French government. And so it did. Intelligence of the surrender of Burgoyne reached Paris on the 4th of December, 1777. King Louis then cast off all disguise, and informed the American commissioners that the treaty of alliance and commerce, already negotiated, would be ratified, and "that it was decided to acknowledge the independence of the United States." Within a little more than a hundred days after Burgoyne laid down his arms at Saratoga, France had formed an alliance with the confederated States [Feb. 6, 1778], and publicly avowed it. The French king, in the mean while, wrote to his uncle, the king of Spain, urging his co-operation; for, according to the family compact of the Bourbons, made in 1761, the king of Spain was to be consulted before such a treaty could be ratified.

While these events were in progress at Saratoga, General Clinton was making hostile demonstrations upon the banks of the lower Hudson. He attempted the concerted co-operation with Burgoyne, but he was too late for success. He ascended the Hudson with a strong force, captured Forts Clinton and Montgomery, in the Highlands[2] [October 6, 1777], and sent a marauding expedition above these mountain barriers, to devastate the country [October 13], and endeavor to draw off some of the patriot troops from Saratoga.[3] These marauders burned Kingston, and penetrated as far as Livingston's Manor, in Columbia county. Informed of the surrender of Burgoyne, they hastily retreated, and Clinton and his army returned to New York. Some of Gates' troops now joined Washington at White Marsh,[4] and Howe made several attempts to entice the chief from his encampment, but without success.[5] Finally

---

[1] France rejoiced at the embarrassments of England, on account of her revolted colonies, and from the beginning secretly favored the latter. She thought it inexpedient to aid the colonies openly, until there appeared some chance for their success, yet arms and money were secretly provided [note 3, page 266], for a long time previous to the alliance. Her motives were not the benevolent ones to aid the patriots, so much as a selfish desire to injure England for her own benefit. The French king, in a letter to his uncle, of Spain, avowed the objects to be to "prevent the union of the colonies with the mother country," and to "form a beneficial alliance with them." A Bourbon (the family of French kings) was never known to be an *honest* advocate of free principles.

[2] These forts were situated on opposite sides of a stream which forms the dividing line between Orange and Rockland counties. Fort Indpendence, near Peekskill, and Fort Constitution, opposite West Point, were abandoned on his approach. Fort Putnam, at West Point, was not yet erected.

[3] While the garrison of the two forts (who escaped) were re-gathering, back of New Windsor, a man from the British army was arrested on suspicion of being a spy. He was seen to swallow something. An emetic brought it up, and it was discovered to be a hollow silver bullet, containing a dispatch from Clinton to Burgoyne, written on thin paper. That bullet is yet in the family of George Clinton, who was the first republican governor of New York. The dispatch was as follows: "*Nous y voici* [Here we are], and nothing between us and Gates. I sincerely hope this little success of ours will facilitate your operations. In answer to your letter of the 28th of September, by C. C., I shall only say, I can not presume to order, or even advise, for reasons obvious. I heartily wish you success. Faithfully yours, H. CLINTON." The prisoner was taken to Kingston, and there hanged as a spy.

[4] Page 275.

[5] Howe marched out to attack Washington on the 4th of December, expecting to take him by surprise. A Quaker lady of Philadelphia, at whose house some British officers were quartered, had

Washington moved from that position [December 11], and went into winter quarters at Valley Forge, where he might easier afford protection to Congress at York, and his stores at Reading.[1] The events of that encampment at Valley Forge afford some of the gloomiest as well as some of the most brilliant scenes in the records of American patriotism.

CHAPTER V.

FOURTH YEAR OF THE WAR FOR INDEPENDENCE. [1778.]

If there is a spot on the face of our broad land wherein patriotism should delight to pile its highest and most venerated monument, it should be in the bosom of that rugged gorge on the bank of the Schuylkill, twenty miles north-

west from Philadelphia, known as Valley Forge, where the American army was encamped during the terrible winter of 1777–'78.[2] In all the world's his-

overheard them talking about this enterprise, gave Washington timely information, and he was too well prepared for Howe, to fear his menaces. After some skirmishes, in which several Americans were lost, Howe returned to Philadelphia.

[1] Page 274.

[2] That was a winter of severe and protracted cold. The waters of New York Bay were so firmly frozen, that the British took heavy cannons from the city to Staten Island, on the ice.

tory, we have no record of purer devotion, holier sincerity, or more pious self-immolation, than was then and there exhibited in the camp of Washington. Many of the soldiers had marched thither from Whitemarsh, bare-footed, and left bloody foot-prints in the snow on their dreary journey.[1] There, in the midst of frost and snow, half-clad and scantily fed, they shivered in rude huts, while the British army was indulging in comforts and luxuries within a large city.[2] Yet that freezing and starving army did not despair; nor did the commander-in-chief, who shared their privations and suffered injury at the hands of intriguing men,[3] lose confidence in the patriotism of the people or his troops, or doubt the wisdom of Providence.[4] The winter wore away, and when the buds began to burst, a cheering ray of glad tidings came from Europe. The intelligence of the treaty of alliance with France,[5] was a hopeful assurance of success, and when the news spread through the camp, on the 1st of May [1778], shouts loud and long shook the forests which shrouded the hills around Valley Forge.[6]

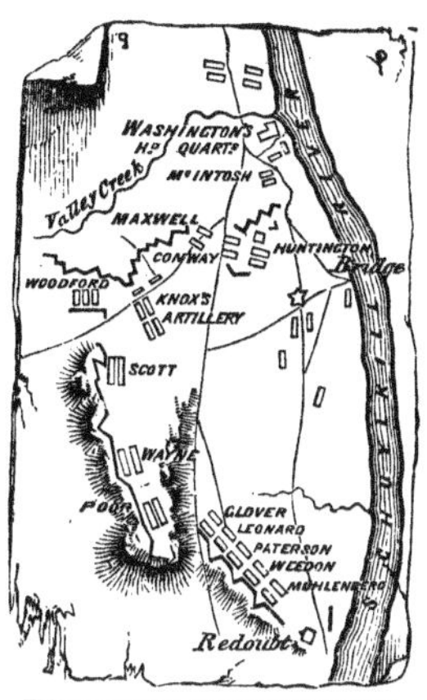

ENCAMPMENT AT VALLEY FORGE.

Nor was that a solitary gleam of hope. Light also emanated from the

[1] Gordon, the historian, says, that while at Washington's table in 1784, the chief informed him that bloody foot-prints were everywhere visible in the course of their march of nineteen miles, from Whitemarsh to Valley Forge.

[2] The power of the British army was much weakened by indulgence, during that winter. Profligacy begat disease, crime, and insubordination. The evil effects produced upon the army led Dr. Franklin to say, "Howe did not take Philadelphia—Philadelphia took Howe." General Howe took leave of the army in May, and the officers gave him a splendid farewell *fête*, which was called a *Mischianza*, signifying a medley. For a full description, see Lossing's *Field Book of the Revolution*. During their occupation of the city, the enemy were annoyed by the patriots in various ways. In January, some Whigs at Bordentown, where Francis Hopkinson, one of the signers of the Declaration of Independence, resided, sent a number of kegs down the Delaware, which were filled with powder, and furnished with machinery, in such a manner, that on rubbing against any object in the stream, they would explode. These were the torpedoes invented by Bushnell of Connecticut, already mentioned on page 252. The British vessels, hauled into the docks to keep clear of the ice, escaped receiving any injury from these missiles. One of them exploded near the city, and produced intense alarm. Not a stick or a chip was seen floating, for twenty-four hours afterward, but it was fired at by the British. This circumstance afforded the theme for that remarkable poem from the pen of Hopkinson, entitled *The Battle of the Kegs*. Hopkinson [see page 284] was a native of Philadelphia and married and settled in Bordentown, New Jersey. He was an elegant writer, a great wit, a good musician, and a thorough-bred gentleman. He was a warm and active patriot, became eminent as a jurist after the war, and died in 1791, at the age of forty-seven years. His brother, Joseph Hopkinson, was the author of our national song, *Hail Columbia*.

[3] During this season a scheme was formed among a few officers of the army, and members of Congress, for depriving Washington of his command, and giving it to Gates or Lee. Both of these ambitious men sought the honor, and the former was fully identified with the clandestine movements toward that end. One of the chief actors in the plot, who was more the instrument of others than a voluntary and independent schemer, was General Conway, an Irishman, who belonged to the continental army. The plot was discovered and defeated, and Conway was led to make a most humble apology to Washington, for his conduct.

[4] On one occasion, Isaac Potts, whose house was Washington's head-quarters at Valley Forge, discovered the chief in a retired place, pouring out his soul in prayer to his God. Potts went home to his wife, and said, with tears in his eyes, "If there is any one on this earth to whom the Lord will listen, it is George Washington."

[5] Page 283.

[6] On the 7th day of May the army fired salutes in honor of the event, and by direction of the chief, they all shouted, "*Huzza for the king of France!*"

British throne and Parliament. The capture of Burgoyne, and the general failure of the campaign of 1777, had made the English people, and a powerful minority in Parliament, clamorous for peace and reconciliation. Lord North, the prime-minister,[1] was compelled to listen. To the astonishment of every body, he proposed [Feb. 17] a repeal of all the acts of Parliament obnoxious to the Americans, which had been enacted since 1763; and in the course of his speech in favor of his conciliatory plan, he actually proposed to treat the Continental Congress as a legal body.[2] Two bills, expressing these conciliatory measures, were passed after much opposition,[3] and received the signature of the king, on the 11th of March. Commissioners[4] were appointed to proceed to America to negotiate for peace with Congress, and the British government seemed really anxious to offer the olive branch, without qualification. But the Americans had been too often deceived to accept any thing confidingly from that source, and as soon as these bills reached Congress [April 15], and it was found that they made no mention of the independence of the colonies, that body at once rejected them as deceptive. When the commissioners came [June 4], Congress refused to negotiate with them until Great Britain should withdraw her fleets and armies, or unequivocally acknowledge the independence of the United States. After unsuccessfully appealing to the American people, and one of them endeavoring to bribe members of Congress,[5] the commissioners returned to England, and the war went on.

The alliance with France gave the patriots greater confidence in their ultimate success. It was immediately productive of action. The first movement of the French government, in compliance with the requirements of that treaty, was to dispatch a squadron, consisting of twelve ships of the line, and four large frigates, under Count D'Estaing, to blockade the British fleet in the Delaware. When, a month before he sailed, the British ministry was officially informed [March 17, 1778] of the treaty, and it was considered equivalent to a declaration of war, a vessel was dispatched with a message to the British commanders, ordering them to evacuate Philadelphia and the Delaware, and to concentrate their forces at New York. Fortunately for Lord Howe, he had left

---

[1] Page 224. [2] Note 2, page 253.

[3] Pitt was favorable to these bills, but when a proposition was made to acknowledge the independence of the colonies, and thus dismember the British empire, he opposed the measure with all his might. He was in favor of *reconciliation*, not of *separation*. It was during his speech on this subject, that he was seized [April 7] with the illness which terminated his life a month afterward. Pitt was born in November, 1708, and died on the 11th of May, 1778, when almost seventy years of age.

[4] The Earl of Carlisle, George Johnstone, formerly governor of Florida, and William Eden, a brother of Sir Robert Eden, the last royal governor of Maryland. Adam Ferguson, the eminent professor of Moral Philosophy in the University of Edinburg, accompanied them as secretary.

[5] Among those who were approached was General Joseph Reed, a delegate from Pennsylvania. Mrs. Ferguson, wife of a relative to the secretary of the commissioners, then residing in Philadelphia, and who was intimate with Mr. Reed, was employed to sound him. Mr. Reed had been suspected by some of his compatriots of rather easy virtue as a republican, and the fact that he was approachable in this way, confirmed their suspicions. Mrs. Ferguson was authorized to offer him high official station and a large sum of money, if he would use his influence in favor of peace, according to the submissive terms offered by the commissioners. Her mission became known, and General Reed alleged that he said to her, "I am not worth purchasing; but such as I am, the king of England is not rich enough to do it."

the Delaware a few days before the arrival of D'Estaing[1] [July 8, 1778], and found safety in the waters of Amboy or Raritan Bay, into which the heavy French vessels could not enter over the bar that stretches northward from Sandy Hook toward the Narrows. A little earlier than this, there had been a change in the command of the British army. Sir Henry Clinton,[2] a more efficient officer than Howe, had succeeded him as general-in-chief, toward the close of May, and on the 18th of June, he withdrew his whole army from Philadelphia. With eleven thousand men, and an immense baggage and provision train, he started for New York, by the way of New Brunswick and Amboy. Washington, suspecting some important movement, was on the alert, and breaking up his encampment at Valley Forge, he pursued Clinton with more than equal force.[3] By adroit movements, detachments of the American army so intercepted Clinton's march, as to compel him to change his course in the direction of Sandy Hook, while New Jersey militia continually harassed his flanks and rear.[4] Finally, a general engagement took place [June 28, 1778] on the plains of Monmouth, in the present village of Freehold, in New Jersey.

GENERAL CLINTON.

The 28th of June, 1778, a day memorable in the annals of Freedom, was the Christian Sabbath. The sky was cloudless over the plains of Monmouth,[5] when the morning dawned, and the sun came up with all the fervor of the summer solstice. It was the sultriest day of the year—one of the warmest ever known. On that calm Sabbath morning, in the midst of paradisal beauty, twenty thousand men girded on the implements of hellish war, to maim and destroy each other—to sully the green grass and the fragrant flowers with human blood. Nature was smiling in her summer garments, and in earth and air there was fullness of love and harmony. Man, alone, was the discordant note in the universal melody. He, alone, the proud "lord of creation," disturbed the chaste worship of the hour, which ascended audibly from the groves, the streams, the meadows, and the woodlands.

The two armies began to prepare for action at about one o'clock in the morning, and at day-break they were in motion. Before nine, detachments met

---

[1] Silas Deane [page 266] returned to America in D'Estaing's flag-ship, and Gerard, the first French minister to the United States, came in the same vessel. Congress was now in session in Philadelphia, having returned from York [page 274] on the 30th of June, twelve days after the British had left for New York.

[2] Henry Clinton was a son of George Clinton, governor of the province of New York in 1743, and a grandson of the Earl of Lincoln. After the war he was made governor of Gibraltar [1795], and died there the same year.

[3] Arnold was yet quite lame from the effects of a severe wound in the leg, which he received in the battle on Bemis's Heights [page 278], and at his solicitation, Washington left him in command of a corps at Philadelphia, with the powers of a military governor. Washington crossed the Delaware in pursuit of Clinton, with a little more than 12,000 men.

[4] Washington was anxious to attack Clinton when he was in the vicinity of Allentown, but Lee and others overruled his opinions, in a council of war. Greene, La Fayette, and Wayne agreed with the chief, and supported by these able officers, he resolved on a general engagement.

[5] The battle of Monmouth was fought in the immediate vicinity of the present village of Freehold, New Jersey, chiefly within the space of two miles north-west of the town.

in deadly conflict, and from that hour until dark, on that long summer day, the terrible contest raged. It was commenced by the advanced division of the American army, under General Charles Lee.[1] His apparent want of skill or courage, and a misunderstanding of orders on the part of some of his officers, produced a general and tumultuous retreat of his division. The fugitives were met by the approaching main body, under Washington,[2] and being speedily checked and restored to order by the chief, they were led to action, and the battle became general. Many fell under the excessive heat of the day, and when night came, both parties were glad to rest. The Americans slept on their arms[3] during the night, with the intention of renewing the battle at dawn, but when light appeared, the British camp was deserted. Clinton had silently withdrawn [June 29], and was far on his way toward Sandy Hook.[4] Washington did not follow, but marching to New Brunswick, and thence to the Hudson River, he proceeded to White Plains,[5] where he remained until late in autumn. Then he crossed into New Jersey, and made his winter quarters at Middlebrook, on the Raritan, where he was

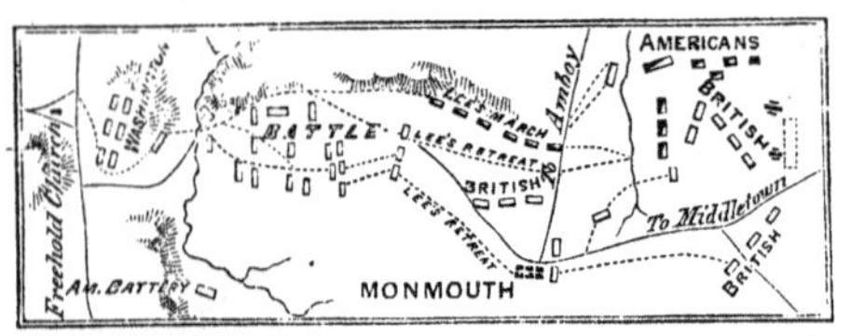

BATTLE AT MONMOUTH.

[1] Page 248. This command was first given to La Fayette, but when Lee, who had opposed the measure in council, signified his readiness to lead it, it was given to him, as he was the senior officer.

[2] Washington was greatly irritated when he met the fugitives, and riding up to Lee, he addressed him with much warmth of language, and directed him to assist in restoring order. Lee promptly obeyed, but the sting of Washington's words rankled in his bosom, and on that day, after the battle, he addressed an offensive letter to the chief. Lee was arrested and tried by a court-martial, on the charges of disobedience of orders, misbehavior before the enemy, and disrespect to the commander-in-chief. He was found guilty, and was suspended from command for one year. He never entered the army again, and died in obscurity, in Philadelphia, in October, 1782. He was brave, but bad in manners and morals, profane in language, and a contemner of religion. It is believed that he was willing to have Washington lose the battle of Monmouth, because he (Lee), was opposed to it, and at the same time was seeking to rise to the chief command upon the ruins of Washington's reputation. We have already alluded to the conspiracy toward that end, on page 285. The hottest of the battle occurred a short distance from the Freehold Presbyterian Church yet [1856] standing. Near it is a board, with an inscription, showing the burial-spot of Colonel Monckton, of the British army, who was killed in the battle.

[3] This expression is used respecting troops who sleep with all their accoutrements on, and their weapons by their side, ready for action in a moment. The British left about three hundred killed on the field of battle. They also left a large number of the sick and wounded to the mercy of the Americans. The Americans lost in killed, wounded, and missing, two hundred and twenty-eight. Many of the missing afterward rejoined the army. They had less than seventy killed.

[4] In his dispatch to the Secretary of War, General Clinton said, "I took advantage of the *moonlight* to rejoin General Knyphausen," &c. As, according to an almanac of that year, the moon was quite new, and set two hours before Clinton's march, this boast of leaving in the moonlight occasioned much merriment. Trumbull, in his *M'Fingal*, alluding to this, says,

"He forms his camp with great parade,
While evening spreads the world in shade,
Then still, like some endanger'd spark,
Steals off on tiptoe in the dark;
Yet writes his king, in boasting tone,
How grand he march'd by light of moon!

* * * * * * * * * * *

Go on, great general, nor regard
The scoffs of every scribbling bard,
"Who sings how gods, that fearful night,
Aided by miracle your flight;
As once they used, in Homer's day,
To help weak heroes run away;
Tells how the hours, at this sad trial,
Went back, as erst on Ahaz' dial,
While British Joshua stayed the moon
On Monmouth's plain for Ajalon.
Heed not their sneers or gibes so arch,
Because she set before your march."

[5] Page 305.

encamped in the spring and summer of the previous year.[1] Clinton's shattered forces went on board the British fleet at Sandy Hook, and proceeded to New York, where the head quarters of the royal army continued until the close of the war.[2] And when D'Estaing appeared off Sandy Hook, the British fleet was safe in Raritan Bay. As we have already mentioned, the bar from Sandy Hook to Staten Island would not allow the heavy French vessels to pass, and D'Estaing therefore relinquished his design of attacking Howe's fleet, and on the solicitation of Washington, he proceeded to Newport, to assist the Americans in an attempt to drive the British from Rhode Island.[3] General Sullivan had been sent to supersede General Spencer in command there; and Washington also dispatched La Fayette, with two continental regiments (accompanied by General Greene, then quartermaster general), to aid in the expedition. John Hancock[4] came at the head of Massachusetts militia, and similar troops gathered at Tiverton, from Connecticut and Rhode Island.[5] On the 9th of August, [1778], the whole American force crossed from Tiverton to the north end of Rhode Island, and the British guards fled to the camp of General Pigot, at Newport.

COUNT D'ESTAING.

Several ships of war came from England at about this time, to reinforce the British fleet at New York, and a few days after D'Estaing sailed for Newport, a large squadron under Howe, proceeded to the relief of Pigot. It appeared off Rhode Island on the same day [Aug. 9] when the Americans landed on the northern end of it. D'Estaing, who was then within the harbor, went out to meet Howe, but before they came to an engagement, a terrible storm arose [Aug. 12], and scattered and disabled both fleets.[6] The French squadron returned to Newport [August 20], and immediately sailed for Boston to be repaired. The Americans had then advanced almost to Newport, with every prospect of making a successful siege. They had been promised four thousand land troops from the French fleet. These were denied them; and refusing to listen to entreaties or remonstrances, D'Estaing sailed for Boston and abandoned the Americans.[7] The latter hastily withdrew to the north end of the island

[1] Page 272. [2] Page 350. [3] Page 261. [4] Page 231.

[5] The people of Rhode Island had suffered dreadfully from the brutality of the British troops. There had been some amelioration of their condition since the capture of Prescott [page 271], and under the rule of Pigot, the present commander. When success seemed possible, thousands of volunteers flocked to the standards of Sullivan and La Fayette. John Hancock was appointed a general of some of these volunteers. But his term of service was short. Like Dr. Franklin [page 193], Hancock was better fitted for a statesman than a soldier.

[6] Very old people on Rhode Island, who remembered this gale, spoke of it to the writer in 1850, as "the great storm." So violent was the wind, that it brought spray from the ocean a mile distant, and encrusted the windows of the town with salt.

[7] This conduct was warmly censured by the American commanders, because it had no valid excuse. It deprived them of a victory just within their grasp. Congress, however, afraid to offend the French, uttered not a word of blame. The matter was passed over, but not forgotten. Once again [page 305], the same admiral abandoned the Americans. D'Estaing was a native of Auvergne, France. He became involved in the French Revolution, in 1792, and in the spring of 1793, he was guillotined. The guillotine was an instrument for cutting off the head, invented by M. Guillotine, who was eventually beheaded by it himself.

[August 28], pursued by the British, and a severe engagement took place [August 29] at Quaker Hill. Sullivan repulsed the British, and on the night of the 30th, withdrew his whole army to the main, near Bristol, in time to avoid an interception by Sir Henry Clinton, who had just arrived with four thousand troops, in light vessels.[1] The Americans lost in this expedition, thirty killed, and one hundred and seventy-two wounded and missing. The British loss was about two hundred and twenty.

While these events were transpiring on the sea-board, a dreadful tragedy was enacted in the interior, when the Wyoming, Mohawk, Schoharie, and Cherry Valleys, were made the theaters of terrible scenes of blood and devastation. Tories from distant Niagara,[2] and savages upon the head waters of the Susquehanna, gathered at Tioga early in June; and at the beginning of July, eleven hundred of these white and dusky savages, under the general command of Colonel John Butler,[3] entered [July 2, 1778] the lovely valley of Wyoming, in northern Pennsylvania. Most of the strong men were then away on distant duty, and families and homes found defenders only in aged men, tender youths, resolute women, and a few trained soldiers. These, about four hundred strong, under Colonel Zebulon Butler,[4] marched up the valley [July 4], to drive back the invaders. But they were terribly smitten by the foe, and a large portion of them were slain or made prisoners. A few escaped to Forty Fort, near Wilkesbarre, wherein families, for miles around, had sought safety. Uncertain of their fate—for the invaders were sweeping like a dark storm down the Susquehanna—the night of the battle-day was a terrible one for the people in the fort. But their agony of suspense was ended the following morning, when the leader of the invaders, contrary to the expectations of those who knew him, agreed upon humane terms of surrender.[5] The gates of the fort were thrown open, and most of the families returned to their homes in fancied security. They were doomed to terrible disappointment and woe. Brant, the great Indian

[1] When Clinton was assured of the security of Rhode Island, he detached General Grey on a marauding expedition upon the southern shores of Massachusetts, and among the adjacent islands, and then returned to New York. Grey burned about seventy vessels in Buzzard's Bay, near New Bedford, and in that vicinity destroyed property valued at more than three hundred and twenty-three thousand dollars. He then went to Martha's Vineyard [page 57], and carried away, for the army in New York, about three hundred oxen, and ten thousand sheep. On the first of October, Clinton sent a successful expedition to capture American stores at Little Egg Harbor, on the New Jersey coast.

[2] Page 200.

[3] Note 2, page 278.

[4] Zebulon Butler was a native of Connecticut, and was born in 1731. He was in the French and Indian War, and was one of the earlier settlers in Wyoming. In 1778 he was appointed colonel, and was with Sullivan in his memorable expedition against the Senecas [page 304] the following year. He was in active service thoughout the war, and died in Wyoming in 1795, at the age of sixty-four years.

[5] All our histories contain horrible statements of the fiend-like character of John Butler, and his unmitigated wickedness on this occasion. They also speak of the "monster Brant" [page 278] as the leader of the Indians, and the instigator of the crimes of which they were guilty. Both of these men were bad enough; but recent investigations clearly demonstrate that Brant was not there at all; and the treaty for surrender, which is still in existance, granted most humane terms to the besieged, instead of the terrible one reported in our histories. The fugitives who fled over the mountains, and made their way back to their native Connecticut, crossed the Hudson, many of them at Poughkeepsie, where John Holt was publishing a weekly paper. Their fears had magnified events, and their tales of terror were published in Holt's journal, and thus became records for future historians. Among other things, it was related that when the question was asked, on what terms the fort might be surrendered, Colonel John Butler, with more than savage cruelty, replied, *The Hatchet!* This is wholly untrue, and yet the story is repeated in all our histories.

leader, was not there to restrain his savage bands,[1] and their thirst for blood and plunder soon overcame all their allegiance to their white commander. Before sunset they had scattered over the valley; and when night fell upon the scene, the blaze of more than twenty dwellings cast its lurid glare over the paradise of yesterday. The cries of the murdered went up from almost every house and field; and when the moon arose, the terrified inhabitants were fleeing to the Wilkesbarre mountains, and the dark morasses of the Pocono beyond. In that vast wilderness between the valley and the Delaware, appropriately called the *Shades of Death*, many women and children, who escaped the hatchet, perished by hunger and fatigue. That "Wyoming Massacre," as it has been appropriately called, stands out in bold relief as one of the darkest crimes perpetrated during the War for Independence.

In the mean while, Brant[2] was leading or sending war parties through the country south of the Mohawk River; and the Johnsons[3] and their Tory adherents were allies of the savages in the Mohawk valley. On the 11th and 12th of November [1778], a party of Tories, under Walter N. Butler,[4] accompanied by Indians, under Brant, fell like lightning upon the settlement of Cherry Valley. Many of the people were killed, or carried into captivity; and for months no eye was closed in security at night, within an area of a hundred miles and more, around this desolated village. Tryon county, as that region of New York was then called, was a "dark and bloody ground" for full four years, and the records of the woes of the people have filled volumes.[5] Our space allows us to mention only the most prominent events of that period.

And now, when the year 1778—the fourth year of the war—drew to a close, the British army had accomplished very little more in the way of conquest, than at the end of the second year. The belligerent forces occupied almost the same relative position which they did in the autumn of 1776, while the Americans had gained strength by a knowledge of military tactics,[6] naval operations,

---

[1] The Indians were led by Gi-en-gwa-tah (he who goes in the smoke), a celebrated Seneca chief. [2] Page 278. [3] Note 2, page 278.

[4] He was a son of Colonel John Butler, and one of the most brutal of the Tory leaders. In the attack upon the defenseless people at Cherry Valley, on the 10th of November, 1778, he was the most conspicuous for cruelty; in fact, he was the head and front of all the villainy perpetrated there. Thirty-two of the inhabitants, mostly women and children, and sixteen soldiers of the little garrison there, were killed. The whole settlement was then plundered, and every building in the village was fired. Among the prisoners carried into captivity, were the wife and children of Colonel Campbell, who was then absent. One of the children (Judge James S. Campbell of Cherry Valley), then six years of age, still [1856] survives, and during the summer of 1855, after an absence of seventy-five years, he visited the Indian village of Caughnawaga, twelve miles from Montreal, where he resided some time with his captors. Walter Butler was shot by an Oneida Indian, in West Canada Creek, and his body was left to be eaten by wild beasts.

[5] See Campbell's *Annals of Tryon County*, Simm's *History of Schoharie County*, Stone's *Life of Brant*, etc.

BARON STEUBEN.

[6] Among the foreign officers who came to America in 1777, was the Baron Steuben, who joined the Continental army at Valley Forge [page 285]. He was a veteran from the armies of Frederic the Great of Prussia, and a skillful disciplinarian. He was made Inspector-General of the army; and the vast advantages of his military instruction were seen on the field of Monmouth [page 287], and in subsequent conflicts. Steuben died at Steubenville, in the interior

and the art of civil government; and they had secured the alliance of France, the powerful European rival of Great Britain, and the sympathies of Spain and Holland. The British forces occupied the real position of prisoners, for they were hemmed in upon only two islands,[1] almost two hundred miles apart, and each about fourteen miles in length; while the Americans possessed every other stronghold of the country, and, unlike the invaders, were warring for the dearest rights of common humanity.

The scene of the most active military operations now changed. In the autumn [Nov. 3, 1778], D'Estaing sailed for the West Indies, to attack the British possessions there. To defend these, it was necessary for the British fleet on our coast to proceed to those waters.[2] This movement would prevent any co-operation between the fleet and army in aggressive movements against the populous and now well-defended North; they could only co-operate in active operations against the sparsely-settled South. These considerations caused a change in the plans of the enemy; and late in November [Nov. 27], Sir Henry Clinton dispatched Colonel Campbell, with about two thousand troops, to invade Georgia, then the weakest member of the Confederacy. They proceeded by water, and landed at Savannah, the capital of the State, on the morning of the 29th of December. General Robert Howe[3] was there, with only about a thousand men, and these were dispirited by the failure of a recent expedition against Florida in which they had been engaged.[4] They defended the city nobly, however, until an overwhelming force, by power and stratagem, compelled them to retire. They then fled, in confusion, up the Savannah River, and took shelter in the bosom of South Carolina. The capital of Georgia became the head-quarters of the British army at the South; and the enemy retained it until near the close of the contest [1782], even when every foot of soil in the State, outside the intrenchments around the city, was possessed by the patriots.

CHAPTER VI.

FIFTH YEAR OF THE WAR FOR INDEPENDENCE. [1779.]

THICKLY mottled with clouds of evil forebodings for the Republican cause, was the political firmament at the dawn of the year 1779. The finances of the

---

of New York, in 1795, and his remains rest beneath a slab in the town of Steuben, about seven miles north-west of Trenton Falls.

[1] Manhattan, or York Island, and Rhode Island.

[2] Admiral Hotham sailed for the West Indies on the 3d of November; and early in December, Admiral Byron, who had just succeeded Lord Howe in chief naval command, also sailed for that destination.

[3] Page 244.

[4] A great number of Tories were organized in Florida, and committed so many depredations upon the settlers on the Georgian frontiers, that Howe, during the summer of 1778, went thither to disperse them. He penetrated to the St. Mary's River, in June, where he awaited reinforcements, and supplies, by water. Want of co-operation on the part of the governor of Georgia and the naval commander, produced much disunion; and sickness soon reduced the number of effective men so much, that the enterprise was abandoned.

country were in a most wretched condition. Already, one hundred millions of dollars of continental money[1] were afloat without the security of even good public credit;[2] and their value was rapidly depreciating. While the amount of the issues was small, the credit of the bills was good; but when new emissions took place, and no adequate measures for redemption were exhibited, the people became suspicious of those frail representatives of money, and their value began to depreciate. This effect did not occur until eighteen months after the time of the first emission.[3] Twenty millions of the continental bills were then in circulation, besides a large amount of local issues by the several States. It was perceived that depreciation was inevitable, and Congress proposed, as a substitute for further issues, a loan of five millions, at an interest of four per cent. A lottery had been early authorized, and was now in operation, designed to raise a like sum, on loan, the prizes being payable in loan-office certificates.[4] Although these offices were opened in all the States, and the interest raised to six per cent., the loans came in slowly. The treasury became almost exhausted, the loan-offices were overdrawn upon by the commissioners' drafts, and the issue of bills was reluctantly recommenced.

The financial embarrassments were increased by the circulation of an immense amount of counterfeits of the continental bills, by the British and the loyalists, which rapidly depreciated the currency. They were sent out from New York, literally, by "cart-loads."[5] Congress felt the necessity of making some extraordinary efforts for redeeming the genuine bills, so as to sustain their credit. The several States were taxed, and on the 2d of January, 1779, it was, by Congress, "Resolved, That the United States be called on to pay in their respective quotas of fifteen millions of dollars, for the year 1779, and of six millions of dollars annually for eighteen years, from and after the year 1779, as a fund for sinking the emissions," &c.; yet all was in vain; prices rose as the bills sank in value, and every kind of trade was embarrassed and

[1] Page 245.

[2] At this time, when Congress could not borrow a dollar upon its own credit, Robert Morris [page 264] found no difficulty in raising millions upon his own. For a long time he, alone, furnished the "hard money" used by that body.

[3] Note 3, page 245.

[4] On the first of November, 1776, the Continental Congress "Resolved, That a sum of money be raised by way of lottery, for defraying the expenses of the next campaign, the lottery to be drawn in Philadelphia." A committee was appointed to arrange the same, and on the 18th, reported a scheme. The drawer of more than the minimum prize in each class, was to receive either a treasury bank note, payable in five years, with an annual interest at four per cent., or the preëmption of such billets in the next succeeding class; this was optional with the adventurers. Those who should not call for their prizes within six weeks after the end of the drawing, were considered adventurers in the next succeeding class. Seven managers were appointed, who were authorized to employ agents in different States to sell the tickets. The first drawing was decided to be made at Philadelphia, on the first of March, 1777; but purchasers were comparatively few and tardy, and the drawing was postponed from time to time. Various impediments continually presented themselves, and the plan, which promised such success at the beginning, appears to have been a failure. Many purchasers of tickets were losers; and this, like some other financial schemes of the Revolution, was productive of much hard feeling toward the Federal Government.

[5] It was no secret at the time, as appears by the following advertisement in Gaines' *New York Mercury:* "ADVERTISEMENT. Persons going into other colonies, may be supplied with any number of counterfeited Congress notes, for the price of the paper per ream. They are so neatly and exactly executed, that there is no risk in getting them off, it being almost impossible to discover that they are not genuine. This has been proven by bills to a very large amount, which have already been successfully circulated. Inquire of Q. E. D., at the Coffee-house, from 11 A. M., to 4 P. M., during the present month.

deranged. The federal government was thoroughly perplexed. Only about four millions of dollars had been obtained, by loan, from Europe, and present negotiations appeared futile. No French army was yet upon our soil, to aid us, nor had French coin yet gladdened the hearts of unpaid soldiers. A French fleet had indeed been upon our coasts,[1] but had now gone to fight battles for France in the West Indies, after mocking our hopes with broken promises of aid.[2] Gloomy, indeed, appeared the firmament at the dawn of 1779, the fifth year of the War for Independence.

In the autumn of 1778, a plan for invading Canada and the eastern British provinces, and for seizing the British posts on the western lakes, had been matured by Congress and the Board of War,[3] but when it was submitted to Washington, his sagacious mind perceived its folly, and the influence of his opinions, and the discovery, by true patriots, that it was a part of the secret plan, entered into by Gates and others, to deprive Washington of chief command, caused an abandonment of the scheme. Others, more feasible, occupied the attention of the Federal Legislature; and for several weeks the commander-in-chief co-operated with Congress [January, 1779], in person, in preparing a plan for the campaign of 1779. It was finally resolved to act on the defensive, except in retaliatory expeditions against the Indians and Tories in the interior.[4] This scheme promised the most beneficial results, for it would be safer and less expensive, than offensive warfare. During the entire year, the principal military operations were carried on in the two extreme sections of the confederacy. The chief efforts of the Americans were directed to the confinement of the British army to the seaboard, and chastising the Indian tribes. The winter campaign opened by Lieutenant-colonel Campbell[5] [December 29, 1778], continued until June, and resulted, as we have mentioned [page 292], in the complete subjugation of Georgia to British rule.

When Campbell had garrisoned Savannah, and arranged for its defense, he prepared to march against Sunbury, twenty-eight miles further south, the only post of any consequence now left to the Americans on the Georgia seaboard. He treated the people leniently, and, by proclamation, invited them to join the British standard. These measures had their desired effect, and timid hundreds, seeing the State under the heel of British power, proclaimed their loyalty, and rallied beneath the standard of King George. At the same time, General Prevost, who was in command of the British and Indians in east Florida, marched northward, captured Sunbury [January 9, 1779], and assumed the chief command of the British forces in the South. With this post fell the hopes of the Republicans in east Georgia. In the

GENERAL LINCOLN.

[1] Page 289.
[2] Page 289.
[3] On the 12th of June, 1776, Congress appointed a committee, to be styled the "Board of War and Ordnance," to have the general supervision of military affairs. John Adams was the chairman, and Richard Peters was secretary. Peters was the real "Secretary of War" under the old Confederation, until 1781, when he was succeeded by General Lincoln. General Gates was chairman in 1778.
[4] Page 291.
[5] Page 293

mean while, General Benjamin Lincoln, of Massachusetts, had been appointed [September, 1778], commander-in-chief of the southern army of patriots.[1] He made his head-quarters at Purysburg [January 6], twenty-five miles above Savannah, and there commenced the formation of an army, composed of some continental regiments, new recruits, and the broken forces of General Howe.[2] While Lincoln was collecting his army on the Carolina bank of the Savannah, Campbell marched up the Georgia side to Augusta,[3] for the purpose of encouraging the Tories, opening a communication with the Creek Indians[4] in the West (among whom the British had active emissaries), and to awe the Whigs. At the same time a band of Tories, under Colonel Boyd, was desolating the Carolina frontiers, while on their march to join the royal troops. When within two days' march of Augusta, they were attacked[5] [February 14, 1779] and utterly defeated by Colonel Pickens, at the head of the militia of Ninety-six.[6] Boyd and seventy of his men were killed, and seventy-five were made prisoners.[7] Pickens lost thirty-eight of his men.

This defeat of Boyd alarmed Campbell and encouraged Lincoln. The latter immediately sent General Ashe, of North Carolina, with about two thousand men,[8] to drive Campbell from Augusta, and to confine the invaders to the low, sickly sections near the sea, hoping for aid from the deadly malaria of the swamps, when the heats of summer should prevail. The British fled [February 13, 1779] at the approach of Ashe, and were pursued by him [February 16] as far as Brier Creek, about forty miles below Augusta, where he halted to establish a camp. There Ashe was surprised and defeated [March 3] by General Prevost, who, with quite a large force, was marching up the Savannah to the relief of Campbell. Ashe lost almost his entire army by death, captivity, and dispersion. Some were killed, others perished in the morasses, and many were drowned in attempting to escape across the Savannah.[9] This blow deprived Lincoln of one fourth of his army, and led to the temporary re-establishment of royal government in Georgia.[10]

---

[1] Benjamin Lincoln was born in Hingham, Massachusetts, in 1733. He was a farmer, yet took an active part in public affairs. He joined the continental army in 1777, and rose rapidly to the station of major-general. He commanded the militia against Shay's insurgents [See 5, page 353.] in 1786. He was also a useful public officer in civil affairs, and died in 1810. [2] Page 292.

[3] When Campbell departed for Augusta, Prevost sent Colonel Gardiner with some troops, to take possession of Port Royal Island, some sixty miles below Charleston, preparatory to a march upon that city. Gardiner was attacked by General Moultrie [page 249], with Charleston militia, on the morning of the 3d of February. Almost every British officer (except the commander), and many privates, were killed. Gardiner and a few men escaped in boats, and Moultrie, whose loss was trifling, joined Lincoln at Purysburg. [4] Page 30.

[5] The place of the skirmish was upon Kettle Creek, in Oglethorpe county, Georgia.

[6] Page 336.

[7] Seventy of them were tried and found guilty of treason, and sentenced to be hung. Only five were executed.

[8] Lincoln was joined by Generals Ashe and Rutherford, with North Carolina regiments, about the first of February, and his army now amounted to little more than three thousand men. John Ashe was born in England in 1721, and came to America when a child. He was engaged in the *Regulator War* [page 223], and was one of the most active of the North Carolina patriots. He died of small-pox in 1781.

[9] About one hundred and fifty were killed and drowned, eighty-nine were made prisoners, and a large number, who were dispersed, did not take up arms again for several months.

[10] At the beginning of 1776, the bold Whigs of Savannah had made the royal governor, Sir James Wright, a prisoner in his own house; and the provincial Assembly, assuming governmental

Prevost now prepared for an invasion of South Carolina. Toward the last of April, he crossed the Savannah [April 27] with two thousand regulars, and a large body of Tories and Creek Indians, and marched for Charleston. Lincoln had recruited, and was now in the field with about five thousand men, preparing to recover lost Georgia, by entering the State at Augusta, and sweeping the country to the sea. But when he discovered the progress of Prevost, and that even the danger of losing Savannah did not deter that active general from his attempts upon Charleston, Lincoln hastened to the relief of the menaced city. The people on the line of his march hailed him as a deliverer, for Prevost had marked his progress by plunder, conflagration, and cruelty. Fortunately for the Republicans, the invader's march was so slow, that when he arrived [May 11] before the city, the people were prepared for resistance.

Prevost, on the morning of the 11th of May, approached the American intrenchments thrown across Charleston Neck,[1] and demanded an immediate surrender of the city. He was answered by a prompt refusal, and the remainder of the day was spent by both parties, in preparations for an assault. That night was a fearful one for the citizens, for they expected to be greeted at dawn with bursting bomb-shells,[2] and red-hot cannon-balls. When morning came [May 12, 1779], the scarlet uniforms of the enemy were seen across the waters upon John's Island, and not a hostile foot was upon the Charleston peninsula. The cause of this was soon made manifest. Prevost had been informed of the approach of Lincoln, and fearing his connection with Savannah might be cut off, he commenced a retreat toward that city, at midnight, by way of the islands along the coast. For more than a month some British detachments lingered upon John's Island. Then they were attacked at Stono Ferry, ten miles below Charleston [June 20] by a party of Lincoln's army, but after a severe engagement, and the loss of almost three hundred men in killed and wounded, they repulsed the Americans whose loss was greater. Prevost soon afterward established a military post at Beaufort, on Port Royal Island,[3] and then retreated to Savannah. The hot season produced a suspension of hostilities in the South, and that region enjoyed comparative repose for several months.

Sir Henry Clinton was not idle while these events were in progress at the South. He was sending out marauding expeditions from New York, to plunder and harass the people on the sea-coast. Governor Tryon[4] went from Kingsbridge[5] on the 25th of March [1779], with fifteen hundred British regulars and

---

powers, made provisions for military defense [February, 1776], issued bills of credit, &c. Wright escaped, and went to England. He returned in July, 1779, and resumed his office as governor of the "colony."

[1] Charleston, like Boston [note 3, page 229], is situated upon a peninsula, the neck of which is made quite narrow by the Ashley and Cooper Rivers, and the marshes. Across this the Americans had hastily cast up embankments. They served a present purpose, and being strengthened, were of great value to the Americans the following year. See page 310.

[2] Hollow balls or shells of cast iron, filled with gunpowder, slugs, &c. In an orifice communicating with the powder, is a slow match. This is ignited, and the shell is hurled from a mortar (a short cannon) into the midst of a town or an army. When the powder ignites, the shell is bursted into fragments, and these with the slugs make terrible havoc. They are sometimes the size of a man's head.

[3] Note 5, page 166.

[4] Page 248.

[5] The passage across the Harlem River (or as it is sometimes there called, Spuyten Duyvil Creek), at the upper end of York or Manhattan Island.

Hessians,[1] to destroy some salt-works at Horseneck, and attack an American detachment under General Putnam, at Greenwich, in Connecticut. The Americans were dispersed [March 26], and Putnam barely escaped capture by some dragoons.[2] He rallied his troops at Stamford, pursued the British on their return toward New York the same evening, recaptured a quantity of plunder in their possession, and took thirty-eight of them prisoners.

On the 9th of May, Sir George Collier entered Hampton Roads,[3] with a small fleet, bearing General Mathews, with land troops, destined to ravage the country in that vicinity. They spread desolation on both sides of the Elizabeth River, from the Roads to Norfolk and Portsmouth. After destroying a vast amount of property, they withdrew; and at the close of the month, the same vessels and the same troops were up the Hudson River, assisting Sir Henry Clinton in the capture of the fortress at Stony Point, and also the small fort on Verplanck's Point, opposite. Both of these posts fell into the power of the British, after a spirited resistance; the first on the 31st of May, and the latter on the 1st of June. These achievements accomplished, Collier, with a band of twenty-five hundred marauders, under Governor Tryon, sailed on the night of the 4th of July [1779], for the shores of Connecticut, to plunder and destroy the towns on the coast. They plundered New Haven on the 5th, laid East Haven in ashes on the 6th, destroyed Fairfield in the same way on the 8th, and burned and plundered Norwalk on the 12th. Not content with this wanton destruction of property, the invaders insulted and cruelly abused the defenseless inhabitants. While Norwalk was burning, Tryon sat in a rocking-chair, upon an eminence near by, and viewed the scene with great complacency, and apparent pleasure—a puny imitation of Nero, who fiddled while Rome was blazing.[4] The Hessian mercenaries generally accompanied these expeditions, for, unlike the British soldiers, they were ever eager to apply the torch and abuse the inhabitants. They were the fit instruments for such a warfare. When Tryon (whom the English *people* abhorred for his wrong-doings in America), had completed the destruction of these pleasant villages, he boasted of his ex-

---

[1] Page 246.

[2] On this occasion he performed the feat, so often related, of descending a steep hill on horseback, making his way, as common history asserts, down a flight of stone steps, which had been constructed for the convenience of people who had to ascend this hill to a church on its summit. The whole matter is an exaggeration. An eye-witness of the event says that Putnam pursued a zig-zag course down the hill, and only descended four or five of the steps near the bottom. The feat was not at all extraordinary when we consider that a troop of dragoons, with loaded pistols, were at his heels. These, however, dared not follow the general. In 1825, when a company of horsemen were escorting La Fayette—the "Nation's Guest"—along the road at that place, some of them went down the same declivity on horseback. The stone steps are now [1856] visible in some places, among the shrubbery and overlying sod.

[3] Page 69. This is a body of water at the conjunction of the James and Elizabeth Rivers, and communicating with the sea. It is one of the most spacious harbors in the world. The village of Hampton lies upon its northern border. See page 243.

[4] Alluding to these outrages of Tryon, and the burning of Kingston [page 283] by Vaughan, Trumbull, in his *M'Fingal*, says:

"Behold, like whelps of British lion,
Our warriors, Clinton, Vaughan, and Tryon,
March forth, with patriotic joy,
To ravish, plunder, and destroy.
Great generals! Foremost in their nation—
The journeymen of desolation!"

treme clemency in leaving a single house standing on the New England coast.

While these marauding forays were in progress, the Americans were not idle. They were preparing to strike the enemy heavy and unexpected blows. Only three days after the destruction of Norwalk [July 15], General Anthony Wayne was marching secretly to attempt the re-capture of Stony Point, on the Hudson. The fort stood upon a rocky promontory, surrounded by water and a marsh, and was very strong in its position. So secretly was the whole movement conducted, that the British garrison were unsuspicious of danger. At midnight, the little army of patriots crossed the morass in the rear, and attacked the fort with ball and bayonet, at two separate points, in the face of a heavy cannonade from the aroused garrison. At two o'clock in the morning [July 16, 1779], Wayne, though so badly wounded in the head by a glancing blow of a bullet, as to fall senseless, wrote to Washington, "The fort and garrison, with Colonel Johnson, are ours. Our officers and men behaved like men who are determined to be free." This was considered one of the most brilliant events of the war.[1] The British lost, in killed, wounded, and prisoners, about six hundred men; the loss of the Americans was fifteen killed, and eighty-three wounded. The spoils were a large amount of military stores. The post was abandoned by the Americans, for, at that time, troops sufficient to garrison it could not be spared.[2]

STONY POINT.

GENERAL WAYNE.

The capture of Stony Point was followed by another brilliant achievement, three days later [July 19], when Major Henry Lee,[3] at three o'clock in the morning, surprised a British garrison at Paulus' Hook (now Jersey City),[4] opposite New York, killed thirty soldiers, and took one hundred and sixty pris-

[1] Wayne was highly complimented by all. General Charles Lee [page 248], who was not on the most friendly terms with Wayne, wrote to him, saying, "I do most seriously declare that your assault of Stony Point is not only the most brilliant, in my opinion, throughout the whole course of the war, on either side, but that it is the most brilliant I am acquainted with in history. The assault of Schiveidnitz, by Marshal Laudon, I think inferior to it." Dr. Rush wrote, saying, "Our streets rang for many days with nothing but the name of General Wayne. You are remembered constantly next to our good and great Washington, over our claret and Madeira. You have established the national character of our country; you have taught our enemies that bravery, humanity, and magnanimity are the national virtues of the Americans." Congress gave him thanks, and a gold medal; and silver medals were awarded to Colonels Stewart and De Fleury, for their gallantry on the occasion. Anthony Wayne was born in Pennsylvania in 1745. He was a professional surveyor, then a provincial legislator, and became a soldier in 1775. He was very active during the whole war; and was efficient in subduing the Indians in the Ohio country, in 1795 [see page 374]. He died at Erie, on his way home, near the close of 1796.

[2] After the Americans had captured Stony Point, they turned the cannons upon Fort La Fayette, upon Verplanck's Point, opposite. General Robert Howe [page 292] was directed to attack that post, but on account of some delays, he did not reach there before Sir Henry Clinton sent up relief for the garrison.

[3] Note 2, page 133.

[4] Note 1, page 94.

oners. This gallant act was greatly applauded in the camp, in Congress, and throughout the country, and made the enemy more cautious and circumspect. The hero was honored by Congress with thanks and a gold medal. These and some smaller successes at about this time, elated the Americans; but their joy was soon turned into sorrow, because of disasters in the extreme East. Massachusetts had fitted out almost forty vessels to attempt the seizure of a British post on the Penobscot River. The assailants delayed more than a fortnight after their arrival [July 25] before determining to carry the place by storm. Just as the troops were about to land for the purpose, a British fleet arrived, destroyed the flotilla, took many of the soldiers and sailors prisoners, and drove the remainder into the wilderness [Aug. 13]. These, after great hardships in the forests, reached Boston toward the close of September.

Daniel Boone

The storm of war was not confined to the Atlantic settlements. It burst over the lofty Alleghanies, and at an early period, even while it was gathering, a low, muttering peal of thunder came from clouds that brooded over the far-off wilderness of the great valleys of the West. Pioneers from the sea-board colonies were there, and they were compelled, almost at the moment of arrival, to wage war with the Indian, and hunt savage men as well as savage beasts. Among the earliest and most renowned of these pioneers, was Daniel Boone, the great "Hunter of Kentucky," of whom Byron wrote,

> "Of all men, saving Sylla, the man-slayer,
> Who passes for, in life and death, most lucky,

Of the great names which in our faces stare,
 The General Boone, backwoodsman of Kentucky,
Was happiest among mortals anywhere." [1]

He went west of the Blue Ridge as early as 1769, and in 1773, his own and a few other families accompanied him to the paradise lying among the rich valleys south of the Ohio River.[2] From that period until the power of the western Indians (who were continually incited to hostilities by the British and

Tories) was broken by George Rogers Clarke, Boone's life was one of almost continual warfare with the children of the forest.

Nor did Boone and his companions measure strength with the Indians alone;

---

[1] Don Juan, VIII., lxi.

[2] The wife and daughters of Boone were the first white females that set foot in the valleys west of the Alleghanies. Daniel Boone was born in Berks county, Pennsylvania, in 1734. While he was a small boy, his parents settled on the Yadkin, in North Carolina. When in the prime of life, he went over the mountains, and became a famous hunter. He planted the first settlement on the *Kain-tuck-ee* River, yet known as Boonsborough. During the Revolution he fought the Indians bravely, and was a prisoner among them for some time, but escaped. He was active in all matters pertaining to the settlement of Kentucky, until it became an independent State. Yet he was, by the technicalities of law, doomed to be disinherited of every foot of the soil he had helped to redeem from the wilderness, and, at almost eighty years of age, he was trapping beaver upon the Little Osage River, beyond the Mississippi. He died in Missouri, when almost ninety years of age, in September, 1820.

Clark's Expedition across the Drowned Lands.

but in time they confronted white leaders and white followers. These conflicts, however, were only a series of border forays, until 1778, when Major George Rogers Clarke[1] led a regular expedition against the frontier posts of the enemy, in the wilderness in the far north-west, now the States of Indiana and Illinois. His little army rendezvoused at the Falls of the Ohio, where Louisville now stands, where he was joined by Simon Kenton, and other pioneers. From thence they penetrated the country northward, and on the 4th of July [1778], they captured Kaskaskia.[2] On the 9th, they took the village of Cahokia, sixty miles further up the river; and finally, in August, the stronger British post of Vincennes, on the Wabash, fell into their hands.

Acting in the capacity of a peace-maker, Clarke was working successfully toward the pacification of the western tribes, when, in the month of January, 1779, the commander of the British fort at Detroit retook Vincennes. With one hundred and seventy-five men, Clarke penetrated the dreadful wilderness a hundred miles from the Ohio. For a whole week they traversed the "drowned lands" of Illinois, suffering every privation from wet, cold, and hunger. When they arrived at the Little Wabash, at a point where the forks of the stream are three miles apart, they found the intervening space covered with water to the depth of three feet. The points of dry land were five miles apart, and all that distance those hardy soldiers, in the month of February, waded the cold snow-flood[3] in the forest, sometimes arm-pit deep! They arrived in sight of Vincennes on the 18th [February, 1779], and the next morning at dawn, with their faces blackened with gunpowder, to make themselves appear hideous, they crossed the river in a boat, and pushed toward the town. On the 20th, the stripes and stars were again unfurled over the fort at Vincennes and a captured garrison. Had armed men dropped from the clouds, the people and soldiers at Vincennes could not have been more astonished, than at the apparition of these troops, for it seemed impossible for them to have traversed the deluged country.

The indignation of the people was fiercely aroused by the atrocities at Wyoming and upon the head waters of the Susquehanna; and in the summer of 1779, General Sullivan[4] was sent into the heart of the country of the SIX NATIONS,[5] to chastise and humble them. He collected troops in the Wyoming

---

[1] George Rogers Clarke, was born in Albemarle county, Virginia, in 1752, and first appears in history as an adventurer beyond the Alleghanies, twenty years afterward. He had been a land-surveyor, and first went to the Ohio region in 1772. He was a captain in Dunmore's army [note 4, page 237] in 1774, and in 1775, he accompanied some emigrants to Kentucky. Pleased with the country, he determined to make it his home; and during the war for Independence, he labored nobly to secure the vast region of the west and north-west, as a home for the free. Under his leadership, what afterward became the North-west Territory, was disenthralled, and he has been appropriately styled the Father of that region. He was promoted to the rank of brigadier, after serving under the Baron Steuben against Arnold, in Virginia, in 1781, and at the close of the war he remained in Kentucky. He died near Louisville, in February, 1818, at the age of sixty-six years.

[2] Page 180.

[3] Note 3, page 241.

[4] John Sullivan was born in Maine, in 1740. He was a delegate in the first Continental Congress [1774], and was one of the first eight brigadiers in the Continental Army. After being in active service about four years, he resigned his commission in 1779. He was afterward a member of Congress, and governor of New Hampshire, and died in 1795.

[5] Page 25. British emissaries had gained over to the royal interest the whole of the SIX NATIONS except the Oneidas. These were kept loyal to the republicans, chiefly through the instru-

Valley; and on the last day of July, marched up the Susquehanna, with about three thousand soldiers. At Tioga Point, he met General James Clinton,[1] on the 22d of August, who came from the Mohawk Valley, with about sixteen hundred men. On the 29th, they fell upon a body of Indian and Tory savages, strongly fortified, at Chemung (now Elmira), and dispersed them. Without waiting for them to rally, Sullivan moved forward, and penetrated the country to the Genesee River. In the course of three weeks, he destroyed forty Indian villages, and a vast amount of food growing in fields and gardens. One hundred and sixty thousand bushels of corn in the fields and in granaries were destroyed; a vast number of the finest fruit-trees, the product of years of tardy growth, were cut down; hundreds of gardens covered with edible vegetables, were desolated; the inhabitants were driven into the forests to starve, and were hunted like wild beasts; their altars were overturned, and their graves trampled upon by strangers; and a beautiful, well-watered country, teeming with a prosperous people, and just rising from a wilderness state, by the aid of cultivation, to a level with the productive regions of civilization, was desolated and cast back a century in the space of a fortnight.[2] To us, looking upon the scene from a point so remote, it is difficult to perceive the necessity that called for a chastisement so cruel and terrible. But that such necessity seemed to exist we should not doubt, for it was the judicious and benevolent mind of Washington that conceived and planned the campaign, and ordered its rigid execution in the manner in which it was accomplished. It awed the Indians for the moment, but it did not crush them. In the reaction they had greater strength. It kindled the fires of deep hatred, which spread far among the tribes upon the lakes and in the valley of the Ohio. Washington, like Demetrius, the son of Antigonus, received from the savages the name of An-na-ta-kau-les, which signifies *a taker of towns*, or Town Destroyer.[3]

GENERAL SULLIVAN.

---

mentality of one or two Christian missionaries. After the war, those of the Six Nations who joined the British, pleaded, as an excuse, the noble sentiment of loyalty. They were the friends of the English, and regarded the parent country as their ally. When they saw the children of their great father, the king, rebelling against him, they felt it to be their duty, in accordance with stipulations of solemn treaties, to aid him.

[1] General James Clinton was born in Ulster county, New York, in 1736. He was a captain in the French and Indian War, and an active officer during the Revolution. He died in 1812.

[2] The Seneca Indians were beginning to cultivate rich openings in the forests, known as the "Genesee Flats," quite extensively. They raised large quantities of corn, and cultivated gardens and orchards. Their dwellings, however, were of the rudest character, and their villages consisted of a small collection of these miserable huts, of no value except for winter shelter.

[3] At a council held in Philadelphia in 1792, Corn Planter, the distinguished Seneca chief, thus addressed Washington, then President of the United States: "Father—The voice of the Seneca nation speaks to you, the great counselor, in whose heart the wise men of all the thirteen fires have placed their wisdom. It may be very small in your ears, and, therefore, we entreat you to hearken with attention, for we are about to speak to you of things which to us are very great. When your army entered the country of the Six Nations, we called you *The Town Destroyer;* and to this day, when that name is heard, our women look behind them and turn pale, and our children cling close to the necks of their mothers. Our counselors and warriors are men, and can not be afraid; but their hearts are grieved with the fears of our women and children, and desire that it may be buried so deep that it may be heard no more."

While these events were in progress at the North, the Southern army, under Lincoln,[1] was preparing to attack Savannah, in concert with the French fleet, then in the West Indies. During that summer, Count D'Estaing had battled successfully with Admiral Byron there, and early in September, he appeared off the coast of Georgia with a powerful fleet, prepared to co-operate with Lincoln. D'Estaing landed troops and heavy battery cannon a few miles below Savannah; and on the 23d of September, the combined armies commenced the siege. It was soon perceived that the town must be taken by regular approaches, and to that end all energy was directed. On the morning of the 4th of October, a heavy cannonade and bombardment was opened upon the Britsh works. It continued for five days, but with very little effect upon the strong British intrenchments. D'Estaing became impatient of delay,[2] and proposed an attempt to take the place by storm. It was reluctantly agreed to, for there seemed a certainty of final victory if the siege should continue. D'Estaing would listen to no remonstrances, and the assault commenced on the morning of the 9th of October. After five hours of severe conflict, there was a truce for the purpose of burying the dead. Already, nearly a thousand of the French and Americans had been killed and wounded.[3] The standards of France and Carolina, which gallant men had planted upon the parapet, had been torn down. Yet important breaches were made, and another assault promised a sure triumph. But D'Estaing, strangely perverse, was unwilling to renew the assault, and made preparations to withdraw. Lincoln yielded a reluctant assent to the movement, and the enterprise was abandoned at the moment when the American commander felt certain of victory.[4] Ten days afterward, the French fleet had left the coast, and Lincoln was retreating toward Charleston. Thus closed the campaign for 1779, at the South. The repulse at Savannah was a severe blow to the hopes of the patriots of Georgia, and spread a gloom over the whole South. Toward the Georgia seaboard, every semblance of opposition to royal power was crushed, and only in the interior did armed resistance appear.

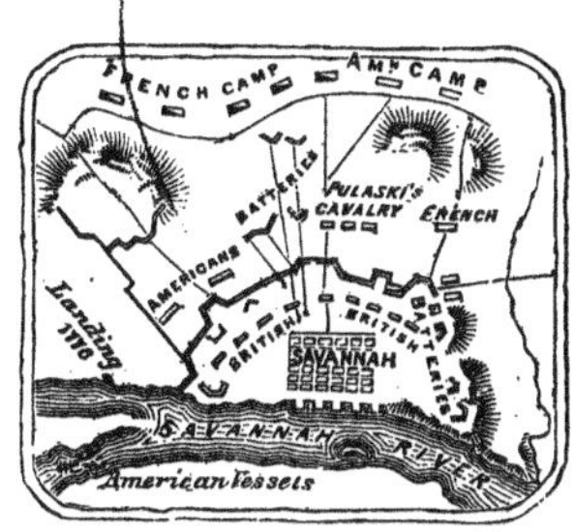

SIEGE OF SAVANNAH. 1779.

---

[1] Page 294.

[2] D'Estaing expressed his fears, not only of the arrival of a British fleet, to blockade his own in the Savannah River, but of the autumn storms, which might damage his vessels before he could get to sea.

COUNT PULASKI.

[3] Among the mortally wounded, was Count Pulaski, the brave Pole whom we first met in the battle on the Brandywine [note 5, page 273]. He died on board a vessel bound for Charleston, a few days after the siege. Serjeant Jasper, whose bravery at Fort Moultrie we have noticed [note 5, page 249], was also killed, while nobly holding aloft, upon a bastion of the British works which he had mounted, one of the beautiful colors [note 5, page 249] presented to Moultrie's regiment by ladies of Charleston. The colors were beautifully embroidered, and given to the regiment, in the name of the ladies of Charleston, by Mrs. Susanna Elliott. Just before he died, Jasper said, "Tell Mrs. Elliott I lost my life supporting the colors she presented to our regiment." These colors, captured during this siege, are among British trophies in the tower of London. Savannah honors both these heroes by having finely-shaded parks bearing their respective names.

[4] Page 289.

After the close of Sullivan's campaign against the Senecas, very little of general interest transpired at the North, except the withdrawal of the British troops from Rhode Island, on the 25th of October, 1779. La Fayette had been in France during the summer, and chiefly through his efforts, the French government had consented to send another powerful fleet,[1] and several thousand troops, to aid the Americans. When informed of this intended expedition, the British ministry ordered Clinton to cause the evacuation of Rhode Island, and to concentrate, at New York, all his troops at the North. This was accomplished with as little delay as possible, for rumors had reached Rhode Island that the new French armament was approaching the coast. So rapid was the retreat of the British, caused by their fears, that they left behind them all their heavy artillery, and a large quantity of stores. Clinton sailed for the South at the close of the year [December 25], with about five thousand troops, to open a vigorous campaign in the Carolinas. Washington, in the mean while, had gone into winter quarters at Morristown,[2] where his troops suffered terribly from the severity of the cold, and the lack of provisions, clothing, and shelter.[3] Strong detachments were also stationed among the Hudson Highlands, and the cavalry were cantoned in Connecticut.

During this fifth year [1779] of the war for Independence, difficulties had gathered thick and fast around Great Britain. Spain had declared war against her[4] on the 16th of June, and a powerful French and Spanish naval armament had attempted to effect an invasion of England in August. American and French cruisers now became numerous and quite powerful, and were hovering around her coasts; and in September, the intrepid John Paul Jones[5] had conquered two of her proud ships of war, after one of the most desperate

---

[1] Page 286. [2] Page 269.

[3] Dr. Thacher, in his *Military Journal*, says, "The sufferings of the poor soldiers can scarcely be described; while on duty they are unavoidably exposed to all the inclemency of storms and severe cold; at night, they now have a bed of straw upon the ground, and a single blanket to each man; they are badly clad, and some are destitute of shoes. We have contrived a kind of stone chimney outside, and an opening at one end of our tents gives us the benefit of the fire within. The snow is now [January 6th, 1780] from four to six feet deep, which so obstructs the roads as to prevent our receiving a supply of provisions. For the last ten days we have received but two pounds of meat a man, and we are frequently for six or eight days entirely destitute of meat, and then as long without bread. The consequence is, the soldiers are so enfeebled from hunger and cold as to be almost unable to perform their military duty, or labor in constructing their huts. It is well known that General Washington experiences the greatest solicitude for the suffering of his army, and is sensible that they, in general, conduct with heroic patience and fortitude." In a private letter to a friend, Washington said, "We have had the virtue and patience of the army put to the severest trial. Sometimes it has been five or six days together without bread, at other times as many without meat, and once for two or three days at a time without either. * * * At one time the soldiers ate every kind of horse food but hay. Buckwheat, common wheat, rye, and Indian corn composed the meal which made their bread. As an army, they bore it with the most heroic patience; but sufferings like these, accompanied by the want of clothes, blankets, &c., will produce frequent desertions in all armies; and so it happened with us, though it did not excite a single mutiny."

[4] Hoping to regain Gibraltar, Jamaica, and the two Floridas, which Great Britain had taken from her, Spain made a secret treaty of peace with France in April, 1779, and in June declared war against Great Britain. This event was regarded as highly favorable to the Americans, because any thing that should cripple England, would aid them.

[5] John Paul Jones was born in Scotland in 1747, and came to Virginia in boyhood. He entered the American naval service in 1775, and was active during the whole war. He was afterward very active in the Russian service, against the Turks, in the Black Sea, and was created rear-admiral in the Russian navy. He died in Paris in 1782.

naval fights ever known. These were the *Serapis* and *Countess of Scarborough.* The conflict occurred in the evening, off Flamborough Head, on the east coast of Scotland. Jones's ship was the *Bonhomme Richard,* which had been fitted out in France. After much maneuvering, the *Serapis* and

Richard came alongside of each other, their rigging intermingling, and in this position they poured heavy broadsides from their respective guns. Three times both ships were on fire, and their destruction appeared inevitable. A part of the time the belligerents were fighting hand to hand upon the decks. Finally, the commander of the *Serapis* was obliged to yield, and ten minutes afterward, the *Countess of Scarborough,* which had been fighting with another vessel of Jones's little fleet, struck her colors. The *Richard* was a perfect wreck, and was fast sinking when the conflict ended; and sixteen hours afterward, she went down into the deep waters of the North Sea, off Bridlington Bay. Jones, with his prizes, sailed for Holland, having, during that single cruise, captured property to the value of two hundred thousand dollars.[1]

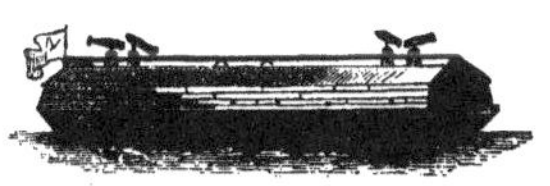

A GUN-BOAT AT BOSTON.

[1] The naval operations during the war for Independence, do not occupy a conspicuous place in history, yet they were by no means insignificant. The Continental Congress took action on the subject of an armed marine, in the autumn of 1775. Already Washington had fitted out some armed vessels at Boston, and constructed some gun-boats for use in the waters around that city. These were propelled by oars, and covered. In November, the government of Massachusetts established a *Board of Admiralty.* A committee on naval affairs, of which Silas Deane [page 266] was chairman, was appointed by the Continental Congress in Octo-

On the land, in America, there had been very little success for the British arms; and sympathy for the patriots was becoming more and more manifest in Europe. Even a great portion of the intelligent English people began to regard the war as not only useless, but unjust. Yet in the midst of all these difficulties, the government put forth mighty energies—energies which might have terminated the war during the first campaign, if they had been then executed. Parliament voted eighty-five thousand seamen and thirty-five thousand troops for general service, in 1780, and appropriated one hundred millions of dollars to defray the expenses. This formidable armament in prospective, was placed before the Americans, at this, the gloomiest period of the war, yet they neither quailed nor faltered. Relying upon the justice of their cause, and the favor of a righteous God, they felt prepared to meet any force that Great Britain might send to enslave them

---

ber, 1775. Before the close of the year, the construction of almost twenty vessels had been ordered by Congress; and the *Marine Committee* was so re-organized as to have in it a representative from each colony. In November, 1776, a *Continental Navy Board*, to assist the *Marine Committee*, was appointed; and in October, 1779, a *Board of Admiralty* was installed. Its Secretary (equivalent to our Secretary of the Navy) [page 382] was John Brown, until 1781, when he was succeeded by General McDougal. Robert Morris also acted as authorized *Agent of Marine;* and many privateers were fitted out by him on his own account. In November, 1776, Congress determined the relative rank of the naval commanders, such as *admiral* to be equal to a *major-general* on land: a *commodore* equal to a *brigadier-general*, &c. The first commander-in-chief of the navy, or high admiral, was Esek Hopkins, of Rhode Island, whom Congress commissioned as such in December, 1775. He first went against Dunmore [page 244] on the coast of Virginia. He also went to the Bahamas, and captured the town of New Providence and its governor. Sailing for home, he captured some British vessels off the east end of Long Island, and with these prizes, he went into Narraganset Bay. In the mean while, Paul Jones and Captain Barry were doing good service, and New England cruisers were greatly annoying English shipping on our coast. In 1777, Dr. Franklin, under the authority of Congress, issued commissions to naval officers in Europe. Expeditions were fitted out in French sea-ports, and these produced great alarm on the British coasts.

ADMIRAL HOPKINS.

While these things were occurring in European waters, Captains Biddle, Manly, M'Neil, Hinman, Barry, and others, were making many prizes on the American coasts. Finally, in the spring of 1779, an expedition was fitted out at L'Orient, under the auspices of the French and American governments. It consisted of five vessels under the command of John Paul Jones. They sailed first, in June, for the British waters, took a few prizes, and returned. They sailed again in August, and on the 23d of September, while off the coast of Scotland, not far above the mouth of the Humber, Jones, with his flag-ship (the *Bonhomme Richard*), and two others, fell in with and encountered a small British fleet, which was convoying a number of merchant vessels to the Baltic Sea, when the engagement took place which is described in the text. Congress gave Jones a gold medal for his bravery. Many other gallant acts were performed by American seamen, in the regular service and as privateers, during the remainder of the war. The "whale-boat warfare" on the coast, was also very interesting, and exhibited many a brave deed by those whose names are not recorded in history—men who belong to the great host of "unnamed demi-gods," who, in all ages, have given their services to swell the triumphs of leaders who, in real merit, have often been less deserving than themselves.

For a condensed account of the whole naval operations of the Revolution, on the coast, see supplement to Lossing's *Field Book of the Revolution.*

CHAPTER VII.

SIXTH YEAR OF THE WAR FOR INDEPENDENCE. [1780.]

WHEN, on Christmas day, 1779, Sir Henry Clinton sailed for the South, with the main body of his army, he left the Hessian general, Knyphausen,[1] in command at New York. To aid the southern patriots, Washington sent thither the Baron De Kalb[2] and others the following spring [1780], and thus the two armies were so much weakened at head-quarters, that military operations at the North almost ceased during that year. The Carolinas became the chief theater of war, and many and bloody were the acts upon that stage. Invasions from without, and the cruelties of Tories[3] in their midst, made 1780 a year of great woe for the patriots and their families below the Roanoke, for they also suffered all the horrors of civil war. At no time, during the whole conflict, were the Tories, or adherents of the crown, more active throughout the whole country, than in 1780. They were the most inveterate enemies of the patriots, and the leaders were in continual correspondence with each other, with the British government, and with the royal commanders in America. Their correspondence was carried on chiefly in cipher writing, understood only by themselves, so that in the event of their letters falling into the hands of the Whigs, their contents would remain a secret. These characters sometimes varied, and it was a frequent occurrence for two persons to invent a cipher alphabet, for their own exclusive use. The engraving shows the alphabet of the cipher writing of some New York Tories.

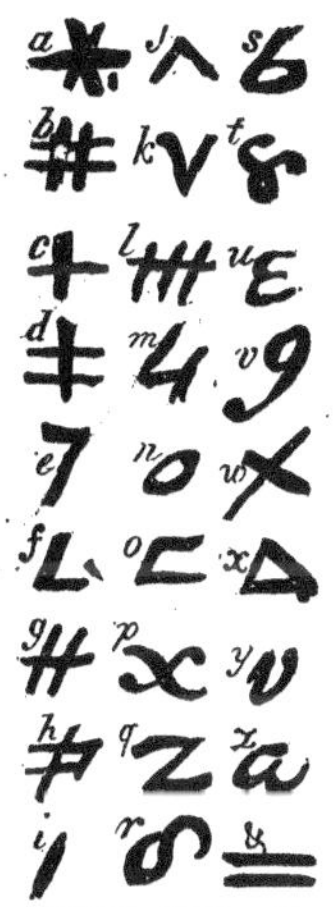

CIPHER ALPHABET.

A fleet, under Admiral Arbuthnot, with two thousand marines, bore the forces of Sir Henry Clinton to the southern waters. After encountering heavy storms,[4] they arrived on the coast of Georgia in January; and early in February [Feb. 10], turned northward, and proceeded to invest Charleston. Clinton's troops were landed [Feb. 11] upon the islands below the city, on the shores of the Edisto Inlet, thirty miles distant; but instead of marching at once to make an assault upon the town, the British commander prepared for a regular siege. General Lincoln was in Charleston with a feeble force[5] when Clinton landed; and he was about to evacuate the city and flee to the interior, when intelligence of the tardy plans of the British reached him. He then resolved to remain, and prepare for de-

[1] Page 259. [2] Page 316. [3] Note 4, page 226.

[4] During a severe storm off Cape Hatteras, one vessel, carrying heavy battery cannons, was lost, and almost all the cavalry horses of Tarleton's legion, perished at sea. Tarleton supplied himself with others, soon after landing, by plundering the plantations near the coast.

[5] During the preceding winter, Lincoln's army had dwindled to a mere handful. The repulse at Savannah had so disheartened the people, that very few recruits could be obtained, and when Clinton arrived, Lincoln's army did not exceed fourteen hundred men in number. The finances of the State were in a wretched condition, and the Tories were everywhere active and hopeful.

fense. John Rutledge,[1] the governor of South Carolina, was clothed with all the powers of an absolute dictator; and so nobly did the civil and military authorities labor for the public good, that when the invaders crossed the Ashley [March 29, 1780], and sat down before the American works on Charleston Neck,[2] the besieged felt strong enough to resist them. In the mean while, the intrenchments had been greatly strengthened, and works of defense had been cast up along the wharves, and at various points around the harbor. Fort Moultrie[3] was strongly garrisoned, and Commodore Whipple[4] was in command of a flotilla of small armed ships in the harbor.

GOVERNOR RUTLEDGE.

On the 25th of March, Admiral Arbuthnot crossed Charleston bar, drove Whipple's little fleet to the waters near the town, and cast anchor in Five

[1] John Rutledge was born in Ireland, and came to South Carolina when a child. He was one of the most active patriots of the South. After the war he was made a judge of the Supreme Court of the United States, and also chief justice of South Carolina. He died in the year 1800.

[2] Note 1, page 296. [3] Note 5, page 249.

[4] Abraham Whipple was born in Providence, Rhode Island, in 1733. His early life was spent chiefly upon the ocean, and, in later years, he was long engaged in the merchant service. At the age of twenty-seven, he was commander of a privateer, and during a single cruise, in 1760, he took twenty-three French prizes. He was engaged in the destruction of the *Gaspé*, in 1772 [page 223]. In 1775, he was appointed to the command of vessels to drive Sir James Wallace from Narragansett Bay. He was active in naval service until the fall of Charleston, when he was taken prisoner.

Fathom Hole, not far from St. John's Island. On the morning of the 9th of April, he sailed up the harbor, and sustaining but trifling damage from the guns of Fort Moultrie, anchored within cannon-shot of the city. As Whipple could not contend with the strong ships, he sunk several of his vessels near the mouth of the Cooper River, and formed a *chevaux-de-frise*[1] to prevent the enemy's ships passing beyond the town, so as to enfilade the American works on the Neck. Clinton, in the mean while, had erected batteries[2] in front of these works, and both commanders joined in a summons for the patriots to surrender. Expecting reinforcements from the interior, the people of the beleagured city refused compliance, and for more than a month the siege went on.[3] In the mean while, American detachments sent out between the Cooper and Santee Rivers to keep open a communication with the interior, were attacked and defeated by parties of British horsemen;[4] and at the close of the month [April, 1780], the city was completely environed by the foe Cornwallis had arrived [April 18], from New York, with three thousand fresh troops, and all hopes for the patriots faded.

The night of the 9th of May was a terrible one for Charleston. That day a third summons to surrender had been refused, and late in the evening a general cannonade commenced. Two hundred heavy guns shook the city with their thunders, and all night long destructive bombshells[5] were hailed upon it. At one time the city was on fire in five different places. Nor did morning bring relief. The enemy had determined to take the city by storm. The cannonade continued all the day, and the fleet moved toward the town to open a bombardment. Further resistance would have been sheer madness, for the destruction of the town and the people seemed inevitable. At two o'clock on the morning of the 12th, a proposition for surrender was made to Clinton, and his guns were all silenced before daylight. At about noon on the 12th [May, 1780], the continental troops marched out, and laid down their arms, after a gallant and desperate defense for forty days. Lincoln and his army, with a large number of citizens, were made prisoners of war. The citizens, and a great number of soldiers, were paroled.[6]

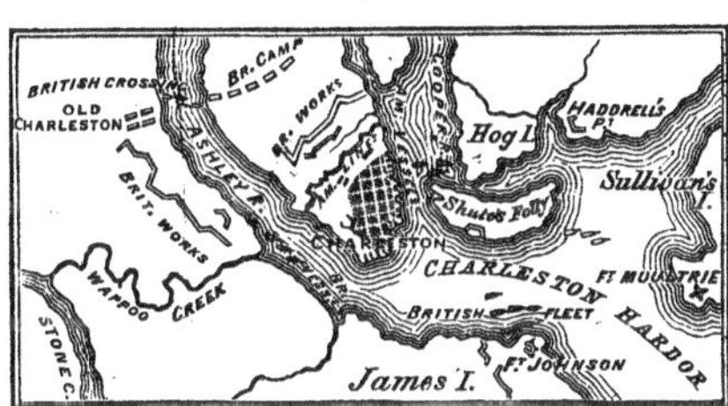

SIEGE OF CHARLESTON. 1780.

He was the first who unfurled the American flag in the Thames, at London, after the war. Accompanying settlers to Ohio, he became a resident of Marietta, from which he sailed, in 1800, down the Ohio, with pork and flour, for Havana. He died in 1819, at the age of eighty-five years.

[1] Note 6, page 274.

[2] On Saturday morning, the first of April, the British first broke ground in the face of eighty cannons and mortars on the American works.

[3] General Woodford had just arrived with seven hundred Virginians, and others from North Carolina were reported on their way.

[4] On the 14th of April, Tarleton defeated Colonel Huger on the head waters of the Cooper River, and killed twenty-five Americans. On the 6th of May, a party under Colonel White, of New Jersey, were routed at a ferry on the Santee, with a loss of about thirty in killed, wounded, and prisoners. These British detachments overran the whole country below the Cooper and Santee, in the course of a few days.

[5] Note 2, page 236.

[6] A prisoner on *parole* is one who is left free to go anywhere within a prescribed space of coun-

Altogether, the captives amounted to between five and six thousand;[1] and among the spoils of victory were four hundred pieces of cannon.

The fall of Charleston, and the loss of this southern army, was a severe

blow for the Republicans. It paralyzed their strength; and the British commanders confidently believed that the finishing stroke of the war had been given. It was followed by measures which, for a time prostrated South Caro-

---

try, or within a city, under certain restrictions relative to conduct. Prisoners taken in war are often paroled, and allowed to return to their friends, with an agreement not to take up arms. It is a point of honor, with a soldier, to "keep his parole," and when such a one is again taken in battle, during the period of his parole, he is treated not as a prisoner, but as a traitor.

[1] In violation of the solemn agreement for surrender, Clinton caused a great number of the leading men in Charleston to be seized, and carried on board prison-ships, where hundreds suffered terribly. Many were taken to St. Augustine, and immured in the fortress there. Among other prominent citizens thus treated, were Lieutenant-Governor Christopher Gadsden, and David Ramsay, the historian, who, with about twenty others, remained in prison at St. Augustine almost eleven months, before they were paroled. Both of these men were exceedingly active patriots. Ramsay was a native of Lancaster county, Pennsylvania, where he was born in 1749. He was educated at Princeton; studied medicine, and became an eminent physician at Charleston. He was an efficient member of the Council of Safety when the Revolution broke out, and was also an esteemed legislator. He was also a member of the Continental Congress. In 1790, he published his *History of the American Revolution.* He wrote and published a *Life of Washington*, in 1801; a *History of South Carolina*, in 1808; and when he died, from a shot by a maniac, in 1815, he had almost completed a *History of the United States.* Soon after the assembling of the first Federal Congress, under the new Constituion, in 1789, Dr. Ramsay sent in a petition, asking for the passage of a law for securing to him and his heirs the exclusive right to vend and dispose of his books, respectively entitled, *History of the Revolution in South Carolina*, and *A History of the American Revolution.* A bill for that purpose was framed and discussed. Finally, in August, it was "postponed until the next Congress." A similar bill was introduced in January, 1790, and on the 30th of April following, the first copyright law recorded on the statute books of Congress, was passed.

lina at the feet of royal power. With an activity hitherto unusual for the British officers, Clinton took steps to extend and secure his conquest, and to re-establish royal power in the South. He sent out three strong detachments of his army to overrun the country. One under Cornwallis marched up the Santee toward Camden; another under Lieutenant-colonel Cruger, was ordered to penetrate the country to Ninety-six,[1] and a third, under Lieutenant-colonel Brown, marched to Augusta,[2] in Georgia. A general truce was proclaimed, and a pardon to all who should accept British protection. The silence of fear overspread the whole country; and mistaking this lull in the storm of war for permanent tranquillity, Clinton and Arbuthnot, with a large body of troops, sailed, on the 5th of June [1780], for New York.

The last and most cruel blow struck by the British, was that which almost annihilated an American detachment under Colonel Abraham Buford. He had hastened toward Charleston for the relief of Lincoln; but when he heard of the disasters there, he commenced retreating toward North Carolina. His force consisted of nearly four hundred Continental infantry, a small detachment of Colonel Washington's cavalry, and two field-pieces. He had evacuated Camden, and, in fancied security, was retreating leisurely toward Charlotte, in North Carolina. Cornwallis resolved to strike Buford, if possible, and, for that purpose, he dispatched Tarleton, with seven hundred men, consisting of his cavalry and mounted infantry. That officer marched one hundred and five miles in fifty-four hours, and came up with Buford upon the Waxhaw. Impatient of delay, he had left his mounted infantry behind, and with only his cavalry, he almost surrounded Buford before that officer was aware of danger. Tarleton demanded an immediate surrender upon the terms granted to the Americans at Charleston. These terms were humiliating, and Buford refused compliance. While the flags for conference were passing and re-passing, Tarleton, contrary to military rules, was making preparations for an assault, and the instant he received Buford's reply, his cavalry made a furious charge upon the American ranks. Having received no orders to defend themselves, and supposing the negotiations were yet pending, the Continentals were utterly dismayed by this charge. All was confusion; and while some fired upon their assailants, others threw down their arms and begged for quarter. None was given; and men without arms were hewn in pieces by Tarleton's cavalry. One hundred and thirteen were slain; one hundred and fifty were so maimed as to be unable to travel; and fifty-three were made prisoners, to grace the triumphal entry of the conqueror into Camden. Only five of the British were killed, and fifteen wounded. The whole of Buford's artillery, ammunition, and baggage, fell into the hands of the enemy. For this savage feat, Cornwallis eulogized Tarleton, and commended him to the ministry as worthy of special favor. It was nothing less than a cold-blooded massacre; and *Tarleton's quarter* became proverbial as a synonym to cruelty.[3] The liberal press, and all right-minded

[1] Page 336. [2] Page 336.

[3] Stedman, one of Cornwallis's officers, and afterward an eminent English historian of the war, says, "On this occasion, the virtue of humanity was totally forgot."

men in England, cried Shame! After the battle, a large number of the wounded were taken to the log meeting-house of the Waxhaw Presbyterian Congregation, where they were tenderly cared for by those who had courage to remain. This blow, however, was so terrible, that fear seized the people, and women and children fled from their homes in dismay, to avoid falling in the track of the invader.[1]

Brief was the lull of the storm. De Kalb[2] did not reach the borders of South Carolina until midsummer, and then not an American was in arms in the lower country. Although Congress had confidence in the skill of De Kalb (who by the capture of Lincoln, became the commander-in-chief at the South), yet it was thought best to send General Gates[3] thither, because of the influence of his name. The prospect before him was far from flattering. An army without strength; a military chest without money; but little public spirit in the commissary department; a climate unfavorable to health; the spirit of the Republicans cast down; loyalists swarming in every direction; and a victorious enemy pressing to spread his legions over the territory he had come to defend, were grave obstacles in the way of success. Yet Gates did not despond; and, retaining De Kalb in command of his division, he prepared to march into South Carolina. When it was known that he was approaching, southern hearts beat high with hope, for they expected great things from the conqueror of Burgoyne.[4] Many patriots, who, in their extremity, had signed "paroles" and "protections,"[5] seeing how little solemn promises were esteemed by the conqueror, disregarded both, and flocked to the standard of those brave partisan leaders, Sumter, Marion, Pickens, and Clarke, who now called them to the field. While Gates and his army were approaching, these partisans were preparing the way for conquest. They swept over the country in small bands, striking a British

GENERAL GATES.

---

[1] Among those who fled, was the widowed mother of Andrew Jackson, the seventh President of the United States, who, with her two sons, Robert and Andrew, took refuge in the vicinity of Charlotte, North Carolina. The dreadful scenes of that massacre, was the first lesson that taught Andrew to hate tyranny. It fired his patriotism; and at the age of thirteen years, he entered the army, with his brother Robert, under Sumter. They were both made prisoners; but even while in the power of the British, the indomitable courage of the after man appeared in the boy. When ordered to clean the muddy boots of a British officer, he proudly refused, and for his temerity received a sword-cut. After their release, Andrew and his brother returned to the Waxhaw settlement with their mother. That patriotic matron and two sons perished during the war. Her son Hugh was slain in battle, and Robert died of a wound which he received from a British officer while he was prisoner, because, like Andrew, he refused to do menial service. The heroic mother, while on her way home from Charleston, whither she went to carry some necessaries to her friends and relations on board a prison-ship, was seized with prison-fever, and died. Her unknown grave is somewhere between what was then called the Quarter House and Charleston. Andrew was left the sole survivor of the family.

[2] Page 316.

[3] Horatio Gates was a native of England, and was educated for military life. He was the first adjutant-general of the Continental army [note 5, page 238], and was made major-general in 1776. He retired to his estate in Virginia at the close of the war, and finally took up his abode in New York, where he died in 1806, at the age of seventy-eight years.

[4] Page 281.

[5] Note 6, page 311.

detachment here, and a party of Tories there; and soon, they so effectually alarmed the enemy in the interior, as to check the onward progress of invasion.

GENERAL SUMTER.

General Sumter[1] first appeared in power on the Catawba River. Already Whigs, between that and the Broad River, led by local officers, had assailed the enemy at different points. In the mean-while Sumter had collected a considerable force, and on the 30th of July, he attacked a British post at Rocky Mount, on the Catawba. He was repulsed, but not disheartened. He immediately crossed the river, and at Hanging-rock, a few miles eastward, he fell upon and dispersed a large body of British and Tories, on the 6th of August. Through the folly of his men, he did not secure a victory. They commenced plundering, and drinking the liquors found in the camp, after they had secured it, and becoming intoxicated, were unable to complete the triumph. Yet the British dared not follow Sumter in his slow retreat. Marion, at the same time, was smiting the enemy, with sudden and fierce blows, among the swamps of the lower country, on the borders of the Pedee. Pickens was annoying Cruger in the neighborhood of the Saluda; and Clarke was calling for the patriots along the Savannah, Ogeechee, and Alatamaha, to drive Brown[2] from Augusta.

General Clinton left Earl Cornwallis in the chief command of the British army at the South, and his troops on the Santee were intrusted to Lord Rawdon, an active and meritorious officer. When that general heard of the approach of Gates, he gathered all his available forces at Camden, where he was soon joined by the earl. Rumor had greatly magnified the number of the army under Gates. The loyalists became alarmed, and the patriots took courage. He came down from the hill country, through Lancaster district, and took post at Clermont, a few miles north of Camden. Feeling certain of victory, he marched from his camp on the night of the 15th of August, to surprise the British at Camden. Without being aware of this movement, Cornwallis and Rawdon advanced at the same hour to surprise the Americans. A little after midnight the belligerents met [August 16, 1780], near Sanders's Creek, about seven miles north of Camden, on the Lancaster road. The sand was so deep that the footsteps of the approaching armies could not be heard by each other. They came together in the dark, almost noiselessly, and both were equally surprised. A slight skirmish between the vanguards ensued, and early in the morning a general battle began. After a desperate struggle with an overwhelming force, the Americans were compelled to yield to the British bayonets in

SANDERS'S CREEK.

[1] Thomas Sumter was a native of South Carolina, and was early in the field. Ill health compelled him to leave the army just before the close of the war, in 1781. He was afterward a member of the Federal Congress, and died on the High Hills of Santee [page 337], in 1832, at the age of ninety-eight years.

[2] Page 336.

front, and the sabres of Tarleton's dragoons on their flanks. The rout became general. The militia fell in great numbers, under the heavy blows from the British cavalry; and for more than two miles, along the line of their retreat, the open wood was strewn with the dead and dying. Arms, artillery, horses, and baggage, were scattered in every direction. More than a third of the continental troops were killed; and the entire loss of the Americans, in killed, wounded, and prisoners, was about a thousand men, besides all of their artillery and ammunition, and a greater portion of their baggage and stores.[1] The British loss was three hundred and twenty-five. Among the killed was the brave Baron de Kalb,[2] whose remains were buried at Camden, and there they yet lie, under a neat monument, the corner-stone of which was laid by La Fayette in 1825.[3]

BARON DE KALB.

Having vainly endeavored to rally his flying troops, Gates fled to Charlotte,[4] eighty miles distant. There he continued to be joined by officers and men, and he began to hope that another army might be speedily collected. But when, a few days after his own defeat, he received intelligence that Sumter's force had been nearly annihilated by Tarleton[5] near the Catawba, he almost despaired. That event was a sad one for the republicans. Sumter had been ordered, by Gates, to intercept a British detachment which was conveying stores for the main army, from Ninety-Six.[6] He was joined by other troops sent to assist him, and they captured forty-four wagons loaded with clothing, and made a number of prisoners. On hearing of the defeat of Gates, Sumter continued his march up the Catawba, and on the 18th [August, 1780] he encamped near the mouth of the Fishing Creek. There he was surprised by Tarleton, and his troops were routed with great slaughter. More than fifty were killed, and three hundred were made prisoners. All the booty captured by the Americans fell into the hands of Tarleton. Sumter escaped, but was stripped of power.

COLONEL TARLETON.

With the dispersion of Gates's army, and Sumter's brave band, the victory of the British was again complete; and at the close of summer, there were no

---

[1] General Gates had felt so certain of victory, that he had made no provisions for a retreat, or the salvation of his stores in the rear. His troops were scattered in all directions, and he, apparently panic-stricken by the terrible blow, fled, almost alone, to Charlotte. Even now [1856] bullets are found in the old pine-trees on the route of their retreat. Gates did indeed, as General Charles Lee predicted he would, when he heard of his appointment to the command of the southern army, "exchange his northern laurels for southern willows."

[2] De Kalb was a native of Alsace, a German province ceded to France. He had been in America as a secret French agent, about fifteen years before. He came to America with La Fayette in 1777, and Congress commissioned him a major-general. He died of his wounds at Camden, three days after the battle.

[3] Page 453.

[4] Page 237.

[5] Tarleton was one of the most active and unscrupulous officers of the British army. He was distinguished for his abilities and cruelties during the southern campaigns of 1780–'81. He was born in Liverpool, in 1754. He married a daughter of the Duke of Ancaster, in 1798, and was afterward made a major-general.

[6] Page 336.

republicans in arms in South Carolina, except Marion and his men. Within three months [May 12 to August 16], two American armies had been annihilated, and one of the most formidable partisan corps (Sumter's) scattered to the winds.

The exploits of Marion[1] and his men, form the materials of one of the most interesting chapters in the history of our War for Independence. He was in Charleston during the long siege, but having been disabled by an accident,[2] he had retired to the country, and was not among the prisoners when the city passed in the possession of the British.[3] He was therefore untrammeled by any parole, and as soon as he was able, he mounted his horse, and took the field. With a few ragged followers, equal in grotesque appearance to any Falstaff

---

[1] Francis Marion was a descendant of a Huguenot [page 49] settler, and was born near Georgetown, South Carolina, in 1732. His first military lessons were learned in the war with the Cherokees [page 204], in 1761. He entered the army at the commencement of the Revolution, and was one of the bravest and most useful of all the partisan officers at the South. He was also a member of the South Carolina Legislature, during, and after the war. He died at his home, near Eutaw Springs, on his beloved Santee, in 1795, in the sixty-third year of his age.

[2] Marion was dining with some friends at a house in Tradd-street, Charleston, when, on an attempt being made to cause him to drink wine, contrary to his practice and desire, he leaped from a window, and sprained his ankle. The Americans yet kept the country toward the Santee, open, and Marion was conveyed to his home.

[3] Page 311.

ever saw,[1] he was annoying the Tories in the neighborhood of the Pedee, when Gates was moving southward; and just before the battle at Camden, he appeared in Gates's camp. The proud general would have treated him with contempt, had not Governor Rutledge,[2] then in the camp, known the sterling worth of the man before them. While Marion was there, the people of the Williamsburg district, who had arisen in arms, sent for him to be their commander. Governor Rutledge gave him the commission of a brigadier on the spot; and soon afterward, Marion organized that noted *brigade*, which performed such wonderful exploits among the swamps, the broad savannahs, and by the water-courses of the South. It was this motley brigade, only, that appeared in the field, and defied British power, after the dispersion of Gates's army at Camden.

Had Cornwallis been governed by good judgment and humanity, the conquest of South Carolina might have been permanent, for the State swarmed with Tories, and the Republicans were wearied with the unequal contest. But he was governed by a foolish and wicked policy, and proceeded to establish royal authority by the most severe measures. Instead of winning the respect of the people by wisdom and clemency, he thought to subdue them by cruelty. Private rights were trampled under foot, and social organization was superseded by the iron rule of military despotism.[3] His measures created the most bitter hatred; and hundreds of patriots, who might have been conciliated, were goaded into active warfare by the lash of military power. Everywhere the people thirsted for vengeance, and only awaited the call of leaders, to rally and strike again for homes and freedom.

LORD CORNWALLIS.

Now, feeling confident of his power in South Carolina, Cornwallis[4] prepared to invade the North State. Early in September he proceeded with his army to Charlotte,[5] while detachments were sent out in various directions to awe the Republicans and encourage the loyalists. While Tarleton, with his legion,

---

[1] Colonel Otho H. Williams said of his appearance then, that his followers were "distinguished by small leathern caps, and the wretchedness of their attire. Their number did not exceed twenty men and boys, some white, some black, and all mounted, but most of them miserably equipped. Their appearance was, in fact, so burlesque, that it was with much difficulty the diversion of the regular soldiery was restrained by the officers; and the general himself [Gates] was glad of an opportunity of detaching Colonel Marion, at his own instance, toward the interior of South Carolina, with orders to watch the motions of the enemy, and furnish intelligence."

[2] Page 310.

[3] He issued cruel orders to his subalterns. They were directed to hang every militia-man who had once served in Loyalist corps, but were now found in arms against the king. Many who had submitted to Clinton [page 313], and accepted protection, and had remained at home quietly during the recent revolt, were imprisoned, their property taken from them or destroyed, and their families treated with the utmost rigor. See note 3, page 337.

[4] Charles, Earl Cornwallis, was born, in Suffolk, England, in 1738. He was educated for military life, and commenced his career in 1759. After the Revolution in America, he was made governor-general of India [note 2, page 224], then lord-lieutenant of Ireland, and again governor of India. He died near Benares, East Indies, in 1805.

[5] His advanced corps were attacked by the Americans under Colonel Davie, on their arrival at Charlotte, but after a severe skirmish, the patriots were repulsed.

was operating on the east side of the Catawba, Major Patrick Ferguson was sent to embody the militia who favored the king, among the mountains west of the Broad River. Many profligate and worthless men joined his standard, and on the first of October, 1780, he crossed the Broad River at the Cherokee ford, in Yorkville district, and encamped among the hills of King's Mountain, with about fifteen hundred men. Several corps of Whig militia united to oppose him,[1] and on the 7th of October, they fell upon his camp on King's Mountain, there, a cluster of high, wooded, gravelly hills, about two miles below the southern line of North Carolina. A very severe engagement ensued, and the British were totally defeated. Ferguson was slain,[2] and three hundred of his men were killed and wounded. The spoils of victory, which cost the Americans only twenty men, were eight hundred prisoners, and fifteen hundred stand of arms. This defeat was to Cornwallis, what the affair at Bennington[3] was to Burgoyne, and it gave the Republicans hope.

Nearer the sea-board, in the mean while, the patriots were daily gaining strength. Marion and his men[4] were striking the banding Tories here and there, and annoying British outposts continually; while Colonel Pickens and Clarke were hourly augmenting their forces in Georgia and south-western Carolina. Sumter, too, undismayed by his recent defeat, again appeared in the field;[5] and other leaders were coming forth between the Yadkin and Broad Rivers. Alarmed by the defeat of Ferguson, and these demonstrations on flank and rear, Cornwallis withdrew [October 14] to South Carolina, and toward the close of October [27th], made his head quarters at Winnsborough, midway between the Broad and Catawba Rivers, in Fairfield district. Here he remained until called to the pursuit of Greene,[6] a few weeks later.

Victory after victory was achieved by Marion and his brigade, until late in October, when they pushed forward to assail the British post at Georgetown, for the purpose of obtaining necessary supplies. Hitherto Marion had confined his operations to forays upon British and Tories; now he undertook a more

[1] These were commanded by Colonels William Campbell, Isaac Shelby, Benjamin Cleveland, John Sevier, Joseph Winston, Charles McDowell, and James Williams. Their united forces amounted to nearly eighteen hundred men.

[2] On the spot where Ferguson was slain, a plain stone has been erected to the memory of that officer, and of Americans who were killed. The following inscriptions upon the stone, give the names: *North side.*—"Sacred to the memory of Major WILLIAM CHRONICLE, Captain JOHN MATTOCKS, WILLIAM ROBB, and JOHN BOYD, who were killed here fighting in defense of America, on the seventh of October, 1780." *South side.*—"Colonel FERGUSON, an officer belonging to his Britannic majesty, was here defeated and killed." Ferguson's rank is incorrectly given, on the monument. He was only a major; but his good conduct was placing him in the way of speedy promotion. He was a son of the eminent Scotch jurist, James Ferguson, and came to America in 1777. He was in the battle on the Brandywine, in the autumn of that year [page 273], and accompanied Sir Henry Clinton to South Carolina [page 306] at the close of 1779. [3] Page 277. [4] Page 317.

[5] Sumter collected a small force in the vicinity of Charlotte, and returned to South Carolina. For some weeks he annoyed the British and Tories very much, and Lord Cornwallis, who called him *The Carolina Game Cock*, used great endeavors to crush him. On the night of the 12th of November, Major Wemyss, at the head of a British detachment, fell upon him near the Broad River, but was repulsed. Eight days afterward he had a severe engagement with Tarleton, at Blackstock's plantation, on the Tyger River, in Union district. He had now been joined by some Georgians under Colonels Clarke and Twiggs. The British were repulsed, with a loss, in killed and wounded, of about three hundred. The Americans lost only three killed and five wounded. Sumter was among the latter, and he was detained from the field several months, by his wounds.

[6] Page 332.

serious business. The garrison was on the alert, and in a severe skirmish with a large party near the town, the Partisan was repulsed. He then retired to Snow's Island, at the confluence of Lynch's Creek and the Pedee, where he fixed his camp, and secured it by such works of art as the absence of natural defenses required. It was chiefly high river swamp, dry, and covered with a heavy forest, filled with game. From that island camp, Marion sent out and led detachments as occasion required; and for many weeks, expeditions which accomplished wonderful results, emanated from that point. Their leader seemed to be possessed of ubiquitous powers, for he struck blows at different points in rapid succession. The British became thoroughly alarmed, and the destruction of his camp became, with them, an object of vital importance.[1] That work was accomplished in the spring of 1781, when a party of Tories penetrated to Marion's camp, during his absence, dispersed the little garrison, destroyed the provisions and stores found there, and then fled. The Partisan was not disheartened by this misfortune, but pursued the marauder some distance, and then wheeling, he hastened through the then overflowed swamps to confront Colonel Watson, who was in motion with a body of fresh troops, in the vicinity of the Pedee.

While these events were progressing at the South, others of great importance were transpiring at the North. As we have observed,[2] military operations were almost suspended in this region during the year, and there were no offensive movements worthy of notice, except an invasion of New Jersey, in June. On the 6th of that month (before the arrival of Clinton from Charleston), Knyphausen[3] dispatched General Matthews from Staten Island, with about five thousand men, to penetrate New Jersey. They took possession of Elizabethtown [June 7], and burned Connecticut Farms (then a hamlet, and now the village of *Union*), on the road from Elizabethtown to Springfield. When the invaders arrived at the latter place, they met detachments which came down from Washington's camp at Morristown, and by them were driven back to the coast, where they remained a fortnight. In the mean while Clinton arrived, and joining Matthews with additional troops [June 22], endeavored to draw Washington into a general battle, or to capture his stores at Morristown. Feigning an expedition to the Highlands, Clinton deceived Washington, who, with a considerable force, marched in that direction, leaving General Greene in command at Springfield. Perceiving the success of his stratagem, he, with Knyphausen, marched upon Greene, witn about five thousand infantry, a considerable body of cavalry and almost twenty pieces of artillery. After a severe

---

[1] Here was the scene of the interview between Marion and a young British officer from Georgetown, so well remembered by tradition, and so well delineated by the pen of Simms and the pencil of White. The officer who came to treat respecting prisoners, was led blindfolded to the camp of Marion. There he first saw the diminutive form of the great partisan leader, and around him, in groups, were his followers, lounging beneath magnificent trees draped with moss. When their business was concluded, Marion invited the young Briton to dine with him. He remained, and to his utter astonishment he saw some roasted potatoes brought forward on a piece of bark, of which the general partook freely, and invited his guest to do the same. "Surely, general," said the officer, "this can not be your ordinary fare!" "Indeed it is," replied Marion, "and we are fortunate on this occasion, entertaining company, to have more than our usual allowance." It is related that the young officer gave up his commission on his return, declaring that such a people could not be, and ought not to be subdued.

[2] Page 309.

[3] Page 259.

Marion's Encampment on the Pedee.

skirmish at Springfield, the British were defeated [June 23, 1780], and setting fire to the village, they retreated, and passed over to Staten Island.

Good news for the Americans came from the East, a few days after this invasion. It was that of the arrival, at Newport, Rhode Island, on the 10th of July [1780], of a powerful French fleet, under Admiral Ternay, bearing six thousand land troops under the Count de Rochambeau. This expedition had been expected for some time, it having sailed from Brest early in April.

The whole matter had been arranged with the French government by La Fayette, who had returned from France in May, and brought the glad tidings to the Americans. With wise forethought, the relation between Washington and Rochambeau had been settled by the French government. In order to prevent any difficulties in relation to command, between the American and French officers, the king commissioned Washington a lieutenant-general of the empire. This allowed him to take precedence of Rochambeau, and made him commander-in-chief of the allied armies. Soon after his arrival, Rochambeau, by appointment, met Washington at Hartford, in Connecticut, to confer upon their future movements. The season being so far advanced, that it was thought imprudent for the French army to enter upon active duties during the current campaign, it was determined to have the main body of it remain in camp, on Rhode Island, while the cavalry should be cantoned at Lebanon, in Connecticut, the place of residence of Jonathan Trumbull, governor of that State. That eminent man was the only chief magistrate of a colony who retained his office after the change from royal to Republican rule; and throughout the war, he was one of the most efficient of the civil officers among the patriots.[1]

The arrival of the French caused Clinton to be more circumspect in his movements, and he made no further attempts to entice Washington to fight. Yet he was endeavoring to accomplish by his own strategy, and the treason of an American officer, what he could not achieve by force. At different times during the war, the British officials in America had tampered, directly or indirectly, with some Americans, supposed to be possessed of easy virtue, but it was late in the contest before one could be found who was wicked enough to be a traitor. Finally, a recreant to the claims of patriotism appeared, and while the French army were landing upon Rhode Island, and were preparing for winter quarters there, Clinton was bargaining with Benedict Arnold for the strong military post of West Point,[2] and its dependencies among the Hudson Highlands, and with it the liberties of America, if possible.

Arnold was a brave soldier, but a bad man.[3] He fought nobly for freedom, from the beginning of the war, until 1778, when his passions gained the mastery over his judgment and conscience. Impulsive, vindictive, and unscrupulous, he was personally unpopular, and was seldom without a quarrel with some of his companions-in-arms. Soon after his appointment to the command at Philadelphia,[4] he was married to the beautiful young daughter of Edward Shippen, one of the leading loyalists of that city. He lived in splendor, at an expense far beyond his income. To meet the demands of increasing creditors, he engaged in fraudulent acts which made him hated by the public, and caused charges of dishonesty and malpractices in office to be preferred against him, before the Continental Congress. A court-martial, appointed to try him, con-

---

[1] Jonathan Trumbull was born at Lebanon, Connecticut, in June, 1710, and was educated at Harvard College. He prepared for the ministry, but finally became a merchant. He was a member of the Connecticut Assembly at the age of twenty-three years. He was chosen governor of Connecticut in 1769, and for fourteen consecutive years he was elected to that office. He died at Lebanon, in August, 1785, at the age of seventy-five years. See page 323.

[2] During the spring and summer of 1778, the passes of the Hudson Highlands were much strengthened. A strong redoubt called Fort Clinton (in honor of George Clinton, then governor of New York), was erected on the extreme end of the promontory of West Point. Other redoubts were erected in the rear; and upon Mount Independence, five hundred feet above the Point, the strong fortress of Fort Putnam was built, whose gray ruins are yet visible. Besides these, an enormous iron chain, each link weighing more than one hundred pounds, was stretched across the Hudson at West Point, to keep British ships from ascending the river. It was floated upon timbers, linked together with iron, and made a very strong obstruction. Two of these floats, with the connecting links, are preserved at Washington's Head Quarters, at Newburgh; and several links of the great chain may be seen at the Laboratory, at West Point.

[3] While yet a mere youth, he attempted *murder*. A young Frenchman was an accepted suitor of Arnold's sister. The young tyrant (for Arnold was always a despot among his play-fellows) disliked him, and when he could not persuade his sister to discard him, he declared he would shoot the Frenchman if he ever entered the house again. The opportunity soon occurred, and Arnold discharged a loaded pistol at him, as he escaped through a window. The young man left the place forever, and Hannah Arnold lived the life of a maiden. Arnold and the Frenchman afterward met at Honduras, and fought a duel, in which the Frenchman was severely wounded.

[4] Note 3, page 287.

victed him, but sentenced him to a reprimand only. Although Washington performed that duty with the utmost delicacy, Arnold felt the disgrace. It awakened vengeful feelings which, operating with the pressure of debt, made him listen with complacency to the suggestions of a bad nature. He made treasonable overtures to Sir Henry Clinton, and by a correspondence of several months (under an assumed name, and with propositions couched in commercial phrases) with the accomplished Major Andrè,[1] Clinton's adjutant-general, he bargained with the British commander to betray West Point and its dependencies into his hands. For this service he was to receive a brigadier's commission, and fifty thousand dollars in cash.

The traitor managed the affair very adroitly. For a long time, Washington had been suspicious of Arnold's integrity, but was unwilling to believe him capable of treason. Under pretense of having private business in Connecticut, Arnold left Philadelphia, passed through Washington's camp on the Hudson, and on his return, he suggested to the chief that he would be glad to have command of West Point. He made many patriotic professions, and his desires were gratified. He was appointed to the command of that post, in August, 1780, and then all his thoughts were turned to the one great object of the betrayal of

[1] Arnold's hand-writing was disguised, and he signed his letters *Gustavus*. Andrè's letters were signed *John Anderson*. A correspondence was carried on between them for more than a year.

his trust. The time chosen for the consummation of his treasonable designs, was when Washington was absent, in September, in conference with the French officers at Hartford, Connecticut.[1] Up to the time of his taking command of West Point, Arnold and Andrè had negotiated in writing. They had never met, but now a personal conference was necessary. For that purpose, Andrè went up the Hudson in the sloop of war, *Vulture*, which anchored off Teller's Point, just above the mouth of the Croton River. Andrè was taken ashore, near Haverstraw, on the west side of the Hudson, where, by previous appointment, he met Arnold. Before they parted [Sept. 22, 1780], the whole matter was arranged. Clinton was to sail up the river with a strong force, and after a show of resistance, Arnold was to surrender West Point and its dependencies into his hands. But all did not work well. Some Americans dragged an old iron six-pound cannon (yet preserved at Sing Sing) to the end of Teller's Point, and with it so galled the *Vulture*, that she was driven from her anchorage, and, dropping down the river, disappeared from Andrè's view. He was consequently compelled to cross to the eastern side of the Hudson in disguise, and make his way toward New York, by land. At Tarrytown, twenty-seven miles from the city, he was stopped [Sept. 23] and searched by three young militia men,[2] who, finding papers concealed in his boots,[3] took him to the nearest American post. Colonel Jameson, the commander, could not seem to comprehend the matter, and unwisely allowed Andrè to send a letter to Arnold, then at his quarters opposite West Point. The alarmed and warned traitor immediately fled down the river in his barge, and escaped to the *Vulture* in safety, leaving behind him his young wife and infant son, who were kindly treated by Washington.[4]

The unfortunate Major Andrè was tried and found guilty as a spy, and was hanged on the 2d of October, 1780, at Tappan opposite Tarrytown, while the real miscreant escaped. Strenuous efforts were made to gain possession of Arnold, and save Andrè, but they failed,[5] and that accomplished officer, betrayed by circumstances, as he said in a letter to Washington, "into the vile condition of an enemy in disguise," suffered more because of the sins of others, than of his own. Washington would have spared Andrè, if the stern rules of war had permitted.

---

[1] Page 323.

[2] John Paulding, David Williams, and Isaac Van Wart, all residents of Westchester county. Andrè offered them large bribes if they would allow him to pass, but they refused, and thus saved their country from ruin.

[3] These papers are well preserved. After being in private hands more than seventy years, they were purchased, and deposited in the New York State Library, in 1853.

[4] Washington returned from Hartford on the very morning of Arnold's escape, and reached his quarters (yet standing opposite West Point) just after the traitor had left. The evidences of his treason were there, and officers were sent in pursuit, but in vain. Washington sent the wife and son of Arnold to New York, whither the traitor was conveyed by the *Vulture*. That infant, who was named James Robertson Arnold, was born at West Point. He became a distinguished officer in the British army, having passed through all the grades of office, from lieutenant. On the accession of Queen Victoria, in 1835, he was made one of her aids-de-camp, and rose to the rank of major-general, with the badge of a Knight of the Royal Hanoverian Guelphic Order.

[5] Serjeant Champe, of Lee's legion [page 333], went into New York City, in the disguise of a deserter, joined the corps which had been placed under Arnold's command, and had every thing arranged for carrying off the traitor, in a boat, to the New Jersey shore. On the very day when he was to execute his scheme, at night, Arnold's corps were ordered to Virginia, and Champe was compelled to accompany it. There he escaped, and joined Lee in the Carolinas.

The young soldier has always been more pitied than blamed; while the name of Arnold will ever be regarded with the bitterest scorn.[1] Although he did not accomplish his wicked schemes, he received the stipulated reward for his treasonable services. And history, too, has given him *its* reward of recorded shame, while those who were instrumental in securing André, and with him the evidences of the foul treason, are honored by the nation with its everlasting gratitude. Thankful for deliverance from the dangers of treason, Congress voted [Nov. 3, 1780] each of the three young militia men, a silver medal and a pension of two hundred dollars a year, for life. And marble monuments have been erected to their memories;[3] while the sentiment of sympathy for the unfortunate André, has also caused a memorial to him, to be erected at Tarrytown, upon the spot where he was executed.

CAPTOR'S MEDAL.[2]

And now another year drew to a close, and yet the patriots were not subdued. England had already expended vast treasures and much blood in endeavors to subjugate them; and, on account of the rebellion, had involved herself in open war with France and Spain. Notwithstanding all this, and unmindful of the fact that a large French land and naval armament was already on the American shores,[4] she seemed to acquire fresh vigor as every new obstacle presented itself. And when the British ministry learned that Holland, the maritime rival of England, was secretly negotiating a treaty with the United States for loans of money and other assistance, they caused a declaration of war against that government to be immediately proclaimed [Dec. 20, 1780], and procured from Parliament immense appropriations of men and money, ships and stores, to sustain the power of Great Britain on land and sea.

CHAPTER VIII.

SEVENTH YEAR OF THE WAR FOR INDEPENDENCE. [1781.]

ONE of the noblest displays of true patriotism, for which the war for Independence was so remarkable, signalized the opening of the year 1781. Year

[1] Benedict Arnold was born in Norwich, Connecticut, in January, 1730. He was bred to the business of an apothecary, and for some time carried on that, with bookselling, in New Haven. We have already met him in his career during the war, up to the time of his treason. We shall meet him again, in Virginia [page 330], with the enemy. At the close of the war, he went to England, then to Nova Scotia, but he was everywhere despised. He died in London, in June, 1801, where, just three years afterward, his wife also died.

[2] On one side is the word "FIDELITY," and on the other, "VINCIT AMOR PATRIÆ"—"The love of country conquers."

[3] To Paulding, in St. Peter's church-yard, about two miles from Peekskill, and to Van Wart in Greenburg church-yard, a little more than that distance from Tarrytown. Williams was buried in Schoharie county, where a monument is about to be erected to his memory.

[4] Page 323.

after year the soldiers had suffered every privation, from lack of money and clothing. Faction had now corrupted the Continental Congress, and the public welfare suffered on account of the tardiness of that body in the performance of its legitimate duties. Continental money had become almost worthless,[1] and the pay of officers and men was greatly in arrears. The frequent promises of Congress had been as frequently unfulfilled, and the common soldiers had cause to be dissatisfied with the illiberal interpretation which their officers gave to the terms of enlistment.[2] They had asked in vain for aid; and finally, on the first day of January, 1781, thirteen hundred of the Pennsylvania line, whose time, as they understood it, had expired, left the camp at Morristown,[3] with the avowed determination of marching to Philadelphia, and in person demanding justice from the national legislature. General Wayne[4] was in command of the Pennsylvania troops, and was much beloved by them. He exerted all his influence, by threats and persuasions, to bring them back to duty until their grievances should be redressed. They would not listen to his remonstrances; and, on cocking his pistol, they presented their bayonets to his breast, saying, "We respect and love you; often have you led us into the field of battle, but we are no longer under your command; we warn you to be on your guard; if you fire your pistol, or attempt to enforce your commands, we shall put you instantly to death." Wayne appealed to their patriotism; they pointed to the impositions of Congress. He reminded them of the strength their conduct would give to the enemy; they exhibited their tattered garments and emaciated forms. They avowed their willingness to support the cause of freedom, for it was dear to their hearts, if adequate provision could be made for their comfort, and then boldly reiterated their intention to march directly to Philadelphia, and demand from Congress a redress of their grievances.

Finding threats and persuasions useless, Wayne concluded to accompany the mutineers. When they reached Princeton, they presented the general with a written programme of their demands. It appeared reasonable; but not being authorized to promise them any thing, the matter was referred to Congress. That body immediately appointed a commission to confer with the insurgents. The result was a compliance with their just demands, and the disbanding of a large part of the Pennsylvania line, for the winter, which was filled by new recruits in the spring.[5]

---

[1] Page 245. Thirty dollars in paper were then worth only one in silver.

[2] The terms, as expressed, were, that they should "serve for three years, or during the war;" that is, for three years if the war continued, or be discharged sooner if the war should end sooner. The officers claimed that they were bound to serve as long as the war should continue.

[3] The head-quarters of Washington were now at New Windsor, just above the Hudson Highlands. The Pennsylvania troops were cantoned at Morristown, New Jersey; and the New Jersey troops were at Pompton, in the same State.

[4] Page 298.

[5] Intelligence of this revolt reached Washington and Sir Henry Clinton on the same day. Washington took measures immediately to suppress the mutiny, and prevent the bad influence of its example. Sir Henry Clinton, mistaking the spirit of the mutineers, thought to gain great advantage by the event. He dispatched two emissaries, a British sergeant, and a New Jersey Tory named Ogden, to the insurgents, with the written offer that, on laying down their arms and marching to New York, they should receive their arrearages, and the amount of the depreciation of the Continental currency, in hard cash; that they should be well clothed, have a free pardon for all past offenses, and be taken under the protection of the British government; and that no military service

On the 18th of January, a portion of the New Jersey line, at Pompton, followed the example of their comrades at Morristown. The mutiny was soon quelled [January 27], but by harsher means than Wayne had employed. General Robert Howe[1] was sent by Washington, with five hundred men, to restore order. Two of the ringleaders were hanged, and the remainder quietly submitted. These events had a salutary effect. They aroused Congress and the people to the necessity of more efficient measures for the support of the army. Taxes were imposed and cheerfully paid; a special agent, sent abroad to obtain loans, was quite successful,[2] and a national bank[3] was established at Philadelphia, and placed under the charge of Robert Morris,[4] to whose superintendence Congress had recently intrusted the public Treasury. To his efforts and financial credit, the country was indebted for the means to commence offensive operations in the spring of 1781. He collected the taxes, and by the free use of his ample private fortune, and his public credit, he supplied the army with flour and other necessaries, and doubtless prevented their disbanding by their own act.

Let us now turn our attention to events in the South. While half-starved, half-naked troops were making such noble displays of patriotism amid the snows

---

should be required of them, unless voluntarily offered. Sir Henry requested them to appoint agents to treat with his and adjust the terms of a treaty; and, not doubting the success of his plans, he went to Staten Island himself, with a large body of troops, to act as circumstances might require. Like his masters at home, he entirely misapprehended the spirit and the incentives to action of the American soldiers. They were not mercenary—not soldiers by profession, fighting merely for hire. The protection of their homes, their wives and little ones, and the defense of holy principles, which their general intelligence understood and appreciated, formed the motive-power and the bond of union of the American army; and the soldier's money stipend was the least attractive of all the inducements which urged him to take up arms. Yet as it was necessary to his comfort, and even his existence, the want of it afforded a just pretext for the assumption of powers delegated to a few. The mutiny was a democratic movement; and, while the patriot felt justified in using his weapons to redress grievances, he still looked with horror upon the armed oppressors of his country, and regarded the act and stain of treason, *under any circumstances*, as worse than the infliction of death. Clinton's proposals were, therefore, rejected with disdain. "See, comrades," said one of the leaders, "he takes us for traitors. Let us show him that the American army can furnish but one Arnold, and that America has no truer friends than we." They immediately seized the emissaries, who, being delivered, with Clinton's papers, into the hands of Wayne, were tried and executed as spies, and the reward which had been offered for their apprehension was tendered to the mutineers who seized them. They sealed the pledge of their patriotism by nobly refusing it, saying, "Necessity wrung from us the act of demanding justice from Congress, but we desire no reward for doing our duty to our bleeding country!" A committee of Congress, appointed to report on the condition of the army, said, a short time previous to this event, that it was "unpaid for five months; that it seldom had more than six days' provisions in advance, and was, on several occasions, for sundry successive days, without meat; that the medical department had neither sugar, coffee, tea, chocolate, wine, nor spirituous liquors of any kind, and that every department of the army was without money, and had not even the shadow of credit left."

[1] Page 292.

[2] Colonel John Laurens [See page 348], a son of Henry Laurens [page 348], had been sent to France to ask for aid. While earnestly pressing his suit, with Vèrgennes, the French minister, one day, that official said, that the king had every disposition to favor the United States. This patronizing expression kindled the indignation of the young diplomatist, and he replied with emphasis, "Favor, sir! The respect which I owe to my country will not admit the term. Say that the obligation is mutual, and I will acknowledge the obligation. But, as the last argument I shall offer to your Excellency, the sword which I now wear in defense of France, as well as my own country, unless the succor I solicit is immediately accorded, I may be compelled, within a short time, to draw against France, as a British subject." This had the effect intended. The French dreaded a reconciliation of the colonies with Great Britain, and soon a subsidy of one million two hundred thousand dollars, and a further sum, as a loan, was granted. The French minister also gave a guaranty for a Dutch loan of about two millions of dollars.

[3] This was called the *Bank of North America*, and was the first institution of the kind established in this country.

[4] Page 264.

of New Jersey, Arnold, the arch-traitor,[1] now engaged in the service of his royal master, was commencing a series of depredations upon lower Virginia, with about sixteen hundred British and Tory troops, and a few armed vessels. He arrived at Hampton Roads[2] on the 30th of December. Anxious to distinguish himself, he pushed up the James River, and after destroying [January 5, 1781] a large quantity of public and private stores at Richmond, and vicinity, he went to Portsmouth [Jan. 20], opposite Norfolk, and made that his head-quarters. Great efforts were made by the Americans to seize and punish the traitor. The Virginia militia men were collected in great numbers, for the purpose; and Jefferson, then governor of that State, offered a reward of five thousand guineas for his capture.[3] La Fayette was sent into Virginia, with twelve hundred men, to oppose him; and a portion of the French fleet went [March 8, 1781] from Rhode Island, to shut him up in the Elizabeth River, and assist in capturing him. But all these efforts failed. He was brave, vigilant, and exceedingly cautious. Admiral Arbuthnot[4] pursued and attacked the French fleet on the 16th of March, and compelled it to return to Newport; and General Phillips soon afterward joined Arnold [March 26], with more than two thousand men, and took the chief command. In April, the traitor accompanied Phillips on another expedition up the James River, and after doing as much mischief as possible between Petersburg and Richmond, he returned to New York.[5] We shall meet Arnold presently on the New England coast.[6]

During the year 1781, the southern States became the most important theater of military operations. General Greene[7] was appointed, on the 30th of October, 1780, to succeed General Gates in the direction of the southern army. He first proceeded to Hillsborough, to confer with Governor Nash, and other civil officers of North Carolina, and arrived at the head-quarters of the army, at Charlotte, on the second of December. On the following day he took formal command, and Gates immediately set out for the head-quarters of Washington, in East Jersey, to submit to an inquiry into his conduct at Camden,[8] which Congress had ordered. Greene, with his usual energy, at once prepared to confront or pursue the enemy, as occasion might require. He arranged his little army into two divisions. With the main body he took post at Cheraw, east of the Pedee, and General Morgan was sent with the remainder (about a thousand strong) to occupy the country near the junction of the Pacolet and Broad Rivers. Cornwallis, who was just preparing to march into North Car-

---

[1] Page 325. [2] Page 243. [3] Page 326. [4] Page 310.

[5] General Phillips sickened and died at Petersburg. Lord Cornwallis, who arrived from North Carolina soon afterward [page 338] took the chief command. In a skirmish, a short distance from Petersburg, on the 27th of April [1781], in which Arnold was engaged, he took some Americans prisoners. To one of them he put the question, "If the Americans should catch me, what would they do to me?" The soldier promptly replied, "They would bury with military honors the leg which was wounded at Saratoga, and hang the remainder of you upon a gibbet."

[6] Page 340.

[7] Nathanial Greene was born, of Quaker parents, in Rhode Island, in 1740. He was an anchor-smith, and was pursuing his trade when the Revolution broke out. He hastened to Boston after the skirmish at Lexington, and from that time until the close of the war, he was one of the most useful officers in the army. He died near Savannah, in June, 1786, and was buried in a vault in that city. His sepulchre can not now be identified. No living person knows in what vault his remains were deposited, and there is no record to cast light upon the question.

[8] Page 315.

olina again,[1] when Greene made this disposition of his army, found himself in a dangerous position, for he was placed between the two divisions. Unwilling to leave Morgan in his rear, he sent Tarleton to capture or disperse his com-

mand. The Americans retreated before this superior force, but were overtaken at the *Cowpens*, in Spartanburg district, and compelled to fight.[2] There, well posted upon an eminence, Morgan[3] and his brave followers turned upon their pursuers. Tarleton was disconcerted by this movement, for he expected to overtake the Americans while on the wing; yet, feeling confident of an easy victory, he quickly arranged his line in battle order. It was now nine o'clock in the morning [January 17, 1781]. At a signal from Tarleton, his advance gave a shout, and rushed furiously to the contest, under cover of artillery, and an incessant discharge of musketry.

GENERAL MORGAN.

[1] Page 318.

[2] The scene of the battle is among the Thicketty Mountains, west of the Broad River. It was called *Cowpens* from the fact, that some time before the Revolution, some traders at Camden kept herds of cows in that fertile region.

[3] Daniel Morgan, commander of the famous rifle corps of the Revolution, was born in New Jersey, in 1738, and was in the humble sphere of a wagoner, when called to the field. He had been a soldier under Braddock, and joined Washington at Cambridge, in 1775. He served with distinction in the army of the Revolution, and was a farmer in Virginia after the war, where he died in 1802.

The Americans were prepared to receive them, and combatted with them for more than two hours, with skill and bravery. The British were defeated, with a loss of almost three hundred men in killed and wounded, five hundred made prisoners, and a large quantity of arms, ammunition, and stores. It was a brilliant victory; and Congress gave Morgan a gold medal, as a token of its approbation. Colonels Howard[1] and Washington,[2] whose soldierly conduct won the battle, received each a silver medal.

COLONEL WASHINGTON.

When the battle was ended, Morgan pushed forward with his prisoners, intending to cross the Catawba, and make his way toward Virginia. Cornwallis started in pursuit of him, as soon as he heard of the defeat of Tarleton. He destroyed his heavy baggage, and hastened with his whole army toward the Catawba to intercept Morgan and his prisoners, before they should cross that stream. But he was too late. He did not reach that river until in the evening, two hours after Morgan had crossed. Then feeling confident of his prey, he deferred his passage of the stream until morning. A heavy rain during the night filled the river to its brim; and while the British were detained by the flood, Morgan had reached the banks of the Yadkin, where he was joined by General Greene and his escort.

One of the most remarkable military movements on record, now occurred. It was the retreat of the American army, under Greene, from the Catawba, through North Carolina, into Virginia. When the waters of the Catawba had subsided, the next day, Cornwallis crossed, and resumed his pursuit. He reached the western bank of the Yadkin on the 3d of February [1781], just as the Americans were safely landed on the eastern shore. There he was again arrested in his progress by a sudden swelling of the floods. Onward the patriots pressed, and soon again Cornwallis was in full chase. At Guilford Court-house, the capital of Guilford county, Greene was joined [February 7], by his main body from Cheraw,[3] and all continued the flight, for they were not strong enough to turn and fight. After many hardships and narrow escapes during the retreat, the Americans reached the Dan on the 13th of February, and

---

[1] John Eager Howard, of the Maryland line. He was born in Baltimore county in 1752. He went into military service at the commencement of the war. He was in all the principal battles of the Revolution, was chosen governor of Maryland in 1778, was afterwad United States Senator, and died in October, 1827.

[2] William Washington, a relative of the general. He was born in Stafford county, Virginia. He entered the army under Mercer, who was killed at Princeton [page 269], and greatly distinguished himself at the South, as a commander of a corps of cavalry. Taken prisoner at Eutaw Springs [page 338], he remained a captive till the close of the war, and died in Charleston, in March, 1810. In a personal combat with Tarleton in the battle at the Cowpens, Washington wounded his antagonist in his hand. Some months afterward, Tarleton said, sneeringly, to Mrs. Willie Jones, a witty American lady, of Halifax, North Carolina, "Colonel Washington, I am told, is illiterate, and can not write his own name." "Ah! colonel," said Mrs. Jones, "you ought to know better, for you bear evidence that he can *make his mark.*" At another time he expressed a desire to see Colonel Washington. Mrs. Ashe, Mrs. Jones's sister, instantly replied, "Had you looked behind you at the Cowpens you might have had that pleasure." Stung by this keen wit, Tarleton placed his hand upon his sword. General Leslie [page 347], who was present, remarked, "Say what you please, Mrs. Ashe; Colonel Tarleton knows better than to insult a lady in my presence."

[3] Page 330.

crossed its rising waters safely into the friendly bosom of Halifax county, in Virginia. When Cornwallis arrived, a few hours later [February 14], the stream was too much swollen to allow him to cross. For the third time the waters, as if governed by a special Providence, interposed a barrier between the pursuers and the pursued. Mortified and dispirited, the earl here abandoned the chase, and moving sullenly southward through North Carolina, he established his camp at Hillsborough.

General Greene remained in Virginia only long enough to refresh his troops, and receive recruits,[1] and then he re-crossed the Dan [February 23], to oppose Cornwallis in his efforts to embody the loyalists of North Carolina under the royal banner. Colonel Lee,[2] with his cavalry, scoured the country around the head waters of the Haw and Deep Rivers, and by force and stratagem foiled the efforts of Tarleton, who was recruiting in that region. On one occasion he defeated and dispersed [March 2] a body of three hundred loyalists under Colonel Pyle,[3] near the Alamance Creek, after which the Tories kept quiet, and very few dared to take up arms. Greene, in the mean while, had moved cautiously forward, and on the first of March [1781], he found himself at the head of almost five thousand troops. Feeling strong enough now to cope with Cornwallis, he sought an engagement with him, and on the 15th they met, and fiercely contended, near Guilford Court-house, about five miles from the present village of Greensborough, in Guilford county, North Carolina. That battle, which continued for almost two hours, was one of the severest of the war. Although the Americans were repulsed and the British became masters of the field, the victory was almost as destructive for Cornwallis as a defeat. "Another such victory," said Charles Fox in the British House of Commons, "will ruin the British army."[4] Both parties suffered severely; and, in some degree, the line of the Scotch ballad might be applied to them:

COLONEL HENRY LEE.

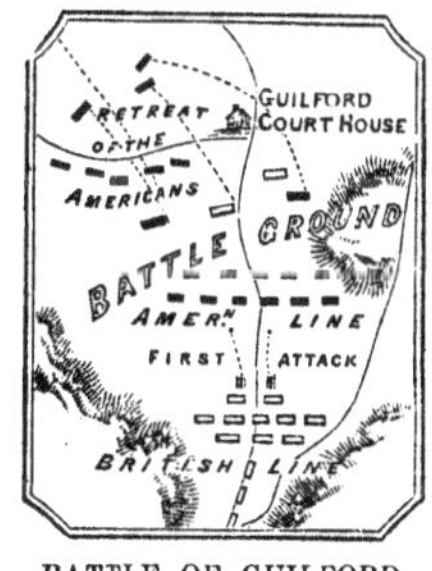

BATTLE OF GUILFORD.

"They baith did fight, they baith did beat, they baith did rin awa."

[1] On his way south, to take command of the southern army, he left the Baron Steuben [page 291] in Virginia, to gather recruits, provisions, &c., and forward them to him. This service the Baron performed with efficiency.

[2] Henry Lee was born in Virginia, in 1756. He entered the military service as captain of a Virginia company in 1776, and in 1777 joined the continental army. At the head of a legion, he performed extraordinary services during the war, especially at the South. He was afterward governor of Virginia, and a member of Congress. He died in 1818.

[3] Lee sent two young countrymen, whom he had captured, to the camp of Pyle, to inform that leader that Tarleton was approaching, and wished to meet him. Pyle had never seen Tarleton, and when he came up he supposed Lee and his party to be that of the renowned British officer. Friendly salutations were expressed, and at a word, the Americans fell upon the loyalists, killed almost a hundred of them, and dispersed the remainder. This event took place two or three miles from the scene of the Regulator battle mentioned on page 223.

[4] That statesman moved in committee, "That his majesty's ministers ought immediately to take every possible means for concluding peace with our American colonies." Young William Pitt, the

The battalions of Cornwallis were so shattered,[1] that he could not maintain the advantage he had gained; while the Americans retreated in good order to the Reedy Fork. Thoroughly dispirited, he abandoned Western Carolina, and moved [March 19] with his whole army, to Wilmington, near the sea-board. Greene rallied his forces and pursued the British as far as Deep River, in Chatham county. There he relinquished the pursuit, and prepared to re-enter South Carolina.

Lord Rawdon,[2] one of the most efficient of Cornwallis's chief officers, was now in command of a British force at Camden. On the 6th of April, Greene marched directly for that place, and on the 19th, he encamped on Hobkirk's Hill, about a mile from Rawdon's intrenchments. Six days afterward [April 25, 1781], he was surprised[3] and defeated by Rawdon, after a sharp battle for several hours, in which the Americans lost, in killed, wounded, and missing, two hundred and sixty-six men. The British lost two hundred and fifty-eight.[4] The British retired to their works at Camden, and Greene, with his little army, encamped for the night on the north side of Sanders's Creek.[5] Greene conducted his retreat so well, that he carried away all his artillery and baggage, with fifty British prisoners, who were captured by Colonel Washington.[6]

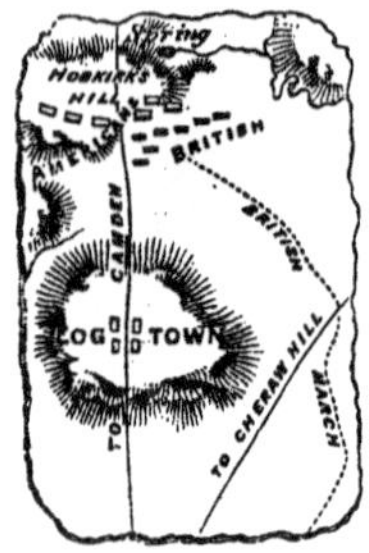

HOBKIRK'S HILL.

This defeat was unexpected to Greene,[7] yet he was not the man to be

successor of his father, the Earl of Chatham, inveighed eloquently against a further prosecution of the war. He averred that it was "wicked, barbarous, unjust, and diabolical—conceived in injustice, nurtured in folly—a monstrous thing that contained every characteristic of moral depravity and human turpitude—as mischievous to the unhappy people of England as to the Americans." Yet, as in former years, the British government was blind and stubborn still.

[1] The Americans lost in killed and wounded, about four hundred men, besides almost a thousand who deserted to their homes. The loss of the British was over six hundred. Among the officers who were killed was Lieutenant-Colonel Webster, who was one of the most efficient men in the British army. On this occasion, Greene's force was much superior in number to that of Cornwallis, and he had every advantage of position. Events such as are generally overlooked by the historian, but which exhibit a prominent trait in the character of the people of North Carolina, occurred during this battle, and deserve great prominence in a description of the gloomy picture, for they form a few touches of radiant light in the midst of the sombre coloring. While the roar of cannon boomed over the country, groups of women, in the Buffalo and Alamance congregations, who were under the pastoral charge of the Reverend Dr. Caldwell, might have been seen engaged in common prayer to the God of Hosts for his protection and aid; and in many places, the solitary voice of a pious woman went up to the Divine Ear, with the earnest pleadings of faith, for the success of the Americans. The battling hosts were surrounded by a cordon of *praying women* during those dreadful hours of contest.

[2] Page 315.

[3] Greene was breakfasting at a spring on the eastern slope of Hobkirk's Hill, when Rawdon's army, by a circuitous rout through a forest, fell upon him. Some of his men were cleaning their guns, others were washing their clothes, and all were unsuspicious of danger.

[4] The number killed was remarkably small. Only eighteen of the Americans, and thirty-eight of the British, were slain on the battle-field.

[5] Page 315.

[6] He had captured two hundred, but hastily paroling the officers and some of the men, he took only fifty with him.

[7] Greene had some desponding views of the future at this time. To Luzerne, the French minister at Philadelphia, he earnestly wrote: "This distressed country cannot struggle much longer without more effectual support. * * * We fight, get beaten, rise, and fight again. The whole country is one continued scene of blood and slaughter." To La Fayette, he wrote: "You may depend upon it, that nothing can equal the sufferings of our little army, but their merit." To Governor Reed, of Pennsylvania, he wrote: "If our good friends, the French, cannot lend a helping hand to save these sinking States, they must and will fall." At that time, the French army had remained for several months inactive, in New England.

crushed by adversity. On the morning succeeding the battle, he retired as far as Rugeley's Mills, and then crossing the Wateree, he took a strong position for offensive and defensive operations. The two armies were now about equal in numbers, and Greene's began to increase. Alarmed by this, and for the

Rebecca Motte

safety of his posts in the lower country, Rawdon set fire to Camden and retreated [May 10, 1781] to Nelson's Ferry, on the Santee. He had ordered Lieutenant-Colonel Cruger[1] to abandon Ninety-six[2] and join Brown at Augusta,[3] and had also directed Maxwell, the commander of Fort Granby,[4] to leave that post, and retire to Orangeburg,[5] on the North Edisto. But his orders and his movements were made too late. Within the space of a week, four important posts fell into the hands of the Americans,[6] and Greene was making rapid marches toward Ninety-six. Lee had pressed forward and co-operated with Pinckney in

---

[1] Page 313.

[2] So called because it was ninety-six miles from the frontier fort, Prince George, on the Keowee River. Its site is occupied by the pleasant village of Cambridge, in Abbeville District, one hundred and forty-seven miles north-west from Charleston.

[3] Page 313.

[4] On the western side of the Congaree, two miles from the present city of Columbia, South Carolina.

[5] On the east bank of the North Edisto, about sixty-five miles south of Columbia.

[6] Lee and Marion were the principal leaders against these posts. Orangeburg was taken on the 11th of May; Fort Motte on the 12th; the post at Nelson's Ferry on the 14th, and Fort Granby on the 16th. Fort Watson, situated on the Santee, a few miles above Nelson's Ferry, was taken on the 16th of April. Nelson's Ferry is at the mouth of Eutaw Creek, on the Santee, about fifty miles from Charleston. Fort Motte was near the junction of the Wateree and Congaree Rivers, and was, because of its geographical position, the most important of all these posts. It was composed of the fine residence of Rebecca Motte (a widowed mother, with six children), and temporary fortifications constructed around it. Mrs. Motte, who was an ardent Whig, had been driven to her farm-house upon an eminence near by. Marion and Lee appeared before Fort Motte with a considerable force, but having only one piece of artillery, could make but slight impression. The expected approach

holding the country-between Ninety-six and Augusta, to prevent a junction of the garrisons at either of those places; and thus, by skillful operations, the Americans completely paralyzed the lately potent strength of the enemy. At the beginning of June [1781], the British possessed only three posts in South Carolina, namely, Charleston, Nelson's Ferry, and Ninety-six.

On the 22d of May [1781], Greene commenced the siege of Ninety-six,[1] with less than a thousand regulars and a few raw militia. Kosciuszko,[2] the brave Pole, was his chief engineer, and the post being too strong to be captured by assault, the Americans commenced making regular approaches, by parallels.[3] Day after day the work went slowly on, varied by an occasional sortie. For almost a month, the efforts of the Americans were unavailing. Then hearing of the approach of Rawdon, with a strong force, to the relief of Cruger, they made an unsuccessful effort, on the 18th of June, to take the place by storm. They raised the siege the following evening [June 19], and retreated beyond the Saluda. Rawdon pursued them a short distance, when he wheeled and marched to Orangeburg.

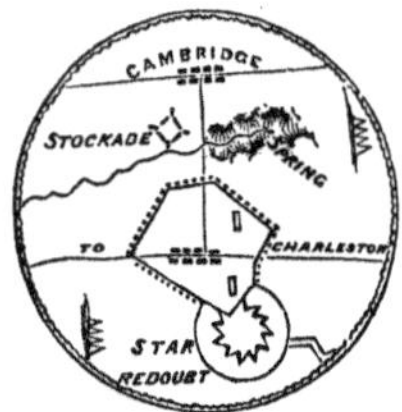

FORT NINETY-SIX.

Although unsuccessful at Ninety-six, detachments of the Republican army were victorious elsewhere. While this siege was progressing, Lee and Pickens, with Clarke and others of Georgia, were making successful efforts on the Savannah River. Lee captured Fort Galphin, twelve miles below Augusta, on the 21st of May, and then he sent an officer to that post, to demand of Brown an instant surrender of his garrison. Brown refused, and the siege of Augusta was commenced on the 23d. It continued until the 4th of June, when a general as-

GENERAL PICKENS.

of Rawdon, would not allow them to make the slow process of a regular siege. Lee proposed to hurl some burning missile upon the building, and consume it. To this destruction of her property, Mrs. Motte at once consented, and bringing out a bow and some arrows, which had been brought from the East Indies, these were used successfully for the purpose of conveying fire to the dry roof. The house was partially destroyed, when the British surrendered. The patriotic lady then regaled both the American and British officers with a good dinner at her own table. Colonel Horry (one of Marion's officers), in his narrative, mentions some pleasing incidents which occurred at the table of Mrs. Motte, on this occasion. Among the prisoners was Captain Ferguson, an officer of considerable reputation. Finding himself near Horry, Ferguson said, "You are Colonel Horry, I presume, sir." Horry replied in the affirmative, when Ferguson continued, "Well, I was with Colonel Watson when he fought your General Marion on Sampit. I think I saw you there with a party of horse, and also at Nelson's Ferry, when Marion surprised our party at the house. But," he continued, "I was hid in high grass, and escaped. You were fortunate in your escape at Sampit, for Watson and Small had twelve hundred men." "If so," replid Horry, "I certainly was fortunate, for I did not suppose they had more than half that number." "I consider myself," added the captain, "equally fortunate in escaping at Nelson's Old Field." "Truly you were," answered Horry dryly, "for Marion had but thirty militia on that occasion." The officers present could not suppress laughter. When Greene inquired of Horry how he came to affront Captain Ferguson, he replied, "He affronted himself by telling his own story."

[1] The principal work was a star redoubt [note 3, page 192]. There was a picketed inclosure [note 1, page 127] around the little village; and on the west side of a stream running from a spring (*a*) was a stockade [note 2, page 183] fort. The besiegers encamped at four different points around the works.

[2] Page 277.

[3] These are trenches, dug in a zig-zag line in the direction of the fortress to be assailed. The

sault was agreed upon. Brown now proposed a surrender; and the following day [June 5, 1781] the Americans took possession of that important post. They lost fifty-one men, killed and wounded; the British lost fifty-two killed, and three hundred and thirty-four (including the wounded) were made prisoners. At the close of the siege, Lee and Pickens[1] hastened to join Greene before Ninety-six, and all, on the approaoh of Rawdon, retreated beyond the Saluda, as we have observed.

The two chief commanders of the belligerent forces now changed relative positions. When Rawdon retired toward Orangeburg, Greene became his pursuer, and sent a message to Marion and Sumter, then on the Santee, to take a position in front of the enemy, so as to retard his progress.[2] Finding Rawdon strongly intrenched at Orangeburg, Greene deemed it prudent not to attack him. The Americans crossed the Congaree, and the main body encamped on the *High Hills of Santee*, in Santee district, there to pass the hot and sickly season. Leaving his troops at Orangeburg, in the command of Colonel Stewart (who had come up from Charleston with a reinforcement), Rawdon went to the sea-board and embarked for England.[3]

Early in August, Greene was reinforced by North Carolina troops, under General Sumner; and at the close of that month he crossed the Wateree and Congaree, and marched upon Orangeburg. Stewart (who had been joined by

earth is cast up in such a way that the workmen are shielded from shots from the assailed works, and in this way they get near enough to undermine a fort, or erect a battery, so as to have a powerful effect.

[1] Andrew Pickens was born in Pennsylvania, in 1739. In childhood he went to South Carolina, and was one of the first in the field for liberty, in the upper country of that State. He was a very useful officer, and good citizen. He died in 1817, at the age of seventy-eight years.

[2] It is related that the message to Sumter from Greene was conveyed by Emily Geiger, the daughter of a German planter in Fairfield district. He prepared a letter to that officer, but none of his men appeared willing to attempt the hazardous service, for the Tories were on the alert, as Rawdon was approaching the Congaree. Greene was delighted by the boldness of a young girl, not more than eighteen years of age, who came forward and volunteered to carry the letter to Sumter. With his usual caution, he communicated the contents of the letter to Emily, fearing she might lose it on the way. The maiden mounted a fleet horse, and crossing the Wateree at the Camden Ferry, pressed on toward Sumter's camp. Passing through a dry swamp on the second day of her journey, she was intercepted by some Tory scouts. Coming from the direction of Greene's army, she was an object of suspicion, and was taken to a house on the edge of the swamp, and confined in a room. With proper delicacy, they sent for a woman to search her person. No sooner was she left alone, than she ate up Greene's letter piece by piece. After a while, the matron arrived, made a careful search, but discovered nothing. With many apologies, Emily was allowed to pursue her journey. She reached Sumter's camp, communicated Greene's message, and soon Rawdon was flying before the Americans toward Orangeburg. Emily Geiger afterward married Mr. Thurwits, a rich planter on the Congaree.

[3] A short time before he sailed, Rawdon was a party to a cruel transaction which created a great deal of excitement throughout the South. Among those who took British protection after the fall of Charleston in 1780 [page 311], was Colonel Isaac Hayne, a highly respectable Carolinian. When General Greene, the following year, confined the British to Charleston alone, and their protection had no force, Hayne considered himself released from the obligations of his parole, took up arms for his country, and was made a prisoner. Colonel Balfour was then in chief command at Charleston, and from the beginning seemed determined on the death of Hayne. Without even the form of a trial, that patriot was condemned to be hanged. Not one, not even the prisoner, supposed that such a cruelty was contemplated, until the sentence was made public, and he was informed that he had but two days to live. The men of the city pleaded for him; the women signed petitions, and went in troops, and upon their knees, implored a remission of his sentence. All was in vain. Rawdon had exerted his influence to save the prisoner, but finally he consented to his execution, as a traitor, and he became as inexorable as Balfour. Greene was inclined to retaliate, but, fortunately, hostilities soon afterward ceased, and the flow of blood was stopped.

Cruger from Ninety-six), immediately retreated to Eutaw Springs, near the south-west bank of the Santee, and there encamped. Greene pursued; and on the morning of the 8th of September [1781], a severe battle commenced. The British were driven from their camp; and Greene's troops, like those of Sumter at Hanging Rock,[1] scattered among the tents of the enemy, drinking and plundering. The British unexpectedly renewed the battle, and after a bloody conflict of about four hours, the Americans were obliged to give way. Stewart felt insecure, for the partisan legions were not far off, and that night the British retreated toward Charleston. The next day [Sept. 9, 1781], Greene advanced and took possession of the battle-field, and then sent detachments in pursuit of the enemy. Both parties claimed the honor of a victory. It belonged to neither, but the advantage was with the Americans. Congress and the whole country gave warm expressions of their appreciation of the valor of the patriots. The skill, bravery, caution, and acuteness of Greene, were highly applauded; and Congress ordered a gold medal, ornamented with emblems of the battle, to be struck in honor of the event, and presented to him, together with a British standard, captured on that occasion. The Americans lost, in killed, wounded, and missing, five hundred and fifty-five. The British lost six hundred and ninety-three.

While these events were transpiring upon the upper waters of the Santee,[2] Marion, Sumter, Lee, and other partisans, were driving British detachments from post to post, in the lower country, and smiting parties of loyalists in every direction. The British finally evacuated all their interior stations, and retired to Charleston, pursued almost to the verge of the city by the bold American scouts and partisan troops. At the close of the year [1781] the British at the South were confined to Charleston and Savannah; and besides these places, they did not hold a single post south of New York. Late in the season [November] Greene moved his army to the vicinity of Charleston,[3] placing it between that city and the South Carolina Legislature, then in session at Jacksonborough; while Wayne, at the opening of 1782, was closely watching the British at Savannah.

We left Cornwallis, after the battle at Guilford Court-house, making his way toward Wilmington,[4] then in possession of a small British garrison, under Major Craig. Cornwallis arrived there on the seventh of April, 1781, and remained long enough to recruit and rest his shattered army. Apprised of Greene's march toward Camden, and hoping to draw him away from Lord Rawdon, then encamped there,[5] he marched into Virginia, joined the forces of Phillips and Arnold, at Petersburgh,[6] and then attempted the subjugation of that State. He left Wilmington on the 25th of April, crossed the Roanoke at

[1] Page 315.

[2] At Columbia, the Saluda and Wateree join, and form the Congaree. This, with other and smaller tributaries, form the Santee. The Wateree, above Camden, is called the Catawba.

[3] After the battle at Eutaw Springs, Greene again encamped on the High Hills of Santee, from whence he sent out expeditions toward Charleston. These were successful, and the enemy was kept close upon the sea-board during the remainder of the war.

[4] Page 334.

[5] Page 315.

[6] Page 330.

Halifax, and on the 20th of May, reached Petersburg. La Fayette was then in Virginia,[1] but his force was too small effectually to oppose the invaders, and the State seemed doomed to British rule.

For the purpose of bringing La Fayette into action, Cornwallis penetrated the country beyond Richmond, and destroyed an immense amount of property.[2] He also sent out marauding parties in various directions,[3] and for several weeks the whole State was kept in great alarm. He finally proceeded [June, 1781] slowly toward the coast, closely pursued by La Fayette, Wayne, and Steuben. While lying at Williamsburg, he received [June 29] orders from General Clinton, to take post near the sea, in order to reinforce the garrison at New York, if necessary, which was now menaced by the combined American and French armies. He crossed the James River [July 9] at Old Jamestown, where he was attacked by Wayne before he could embark his troops. Wayne struck a severe blow, and then skillfully and hastily retreated back to the main army under La Fayette, then only two miles distant. His loss was inconsiderable, but the attack damaged the British seriously. After crossing the river, Cornwallis proceeded by land to Portsmouth, opposite Norfolk; but disliking that situation, he went to Yorktown, on the York River, and commenced fortifying that place and Gloucester Point, opposite.

The French army under Rochambeau,[4] in the mean while, had left New England, and made its way to the Hudson River, where it joined [July 6, 1781] that of the Americans, in the vicinity of Dobbs' Ferry.[5] At that time, Washington, who had the immediate command of the American forces, contemplated an attack upon the British in New York city. For six weeks the two armies remained in Westchester waiting for the arrival of the Count De Grasse, an eminent French naval commander, to co-operate in the attack. While preparing to strike the blow, Clinton was reinforced [August 11] by nearly three thousand troops from Europe; and intelligence came from De Grasse that he could not then leave the West Indies. Thus foiled, Washington turned his thoughts to Virginia; and when, a few days afterward, he learned from De Barras, the successor of Ternay,[6] in command of the French

COUNT DE ROCHAMBEAU.

[1] Page 330.

[2] The principal object of Cornwallis in marching beyond Richmond, was to prevent a junction with La Fayette of troops under Wayne, then approaching through Maryland. But the marquis was too expert, outmarched the earl, and met Wayne on the 10th of June.

[3] Colonel Simcoe, commander of an active corps called the *Queen's Rangers*, was sent to capture or destroy stores at the junction of the Fluvanna and Rivanna Rivers. Cornwallis also dispatched Tarleton to attempt the capture of Governor Jefferson and the Legislature, who had fled from Richmond to Charlottesville, near the residence of Mr. Jefferson. Seven members of the Legislature fell into his hands [June 4], and Mr. Jefferson narrowly escaped capture by fleeing from his house to the mountains.

[4] The Count Rochambeau was born at Vendome, in France, in 1725. He was a distinguished officer in the French army, and after his return from America, was made a Field Marshal by his king. He was pensioned by Bonaparte, and died in 1807.

[5] Page 257.

[6] Admiral Ternay died at Newport, soon after the arrival of the fleet there, in the summer of 1780. His remains were deposited in Trinity Church-yard there, and a marble slab was placed over his grave.

COUNT DE GRASSE.

fleet at Newport, that De Grasse was about to sail for the Chesapeake, he resolved to march southward, and assist La Fayette against Cornwallis. He wrote deceptive letters to General Greene in New Jersey, and sent them so as to be intercepted by Sir Henry Clinton.[1] He thus blinded the British commander to his real intentions; and it was not until the allied armies had crossed the Hudson, passed through New Jersey, and were marching from the Delaware toward the head of Chesapeake Bay,[2] that Clinton was convinced that an attack upon the city of New York was not the object of Washington's movements. It was then too late for successful pursuit, and he endeavored to recall the Americans by sending Arnold to desolate the New England coast. Although there was a terrible massacre perpetrated by the invaders at Fort Griswold[3] [September 6, 1781], and New London, opposite (almost in sight of the traitor's birthplace),[4] was burned, it did not check the progress of Washington toward that goal where he was to win the greatest prize of his military career. Nor did reinforcements sent by water to aid Cornwallis, effect their object, for when Admiral Graves arrived off the Capes [September 5], De Grasse was there to guard the entrance to the Chesapeake.[5] He went out to fight Graves, but after a partial action, both withdrew, and the French fleet was anchored [September 10] within the Capes.[6]

While Cornwallis was fortifying Yorktown and Gloucester, and the hostile fleets were in the neighboring waters, the allied armies, twelve thousand strong,[7] were making their way southward. They arrived before Yorktown on the 28th of September, 1781; and after compelling the British to abandon their outworks, commenced a regular siege. The place was completely invested on the 30th, the line of the allied armies extending in a semi-circle, at a distance of almost two miles from the British works, each wing resting upon the York River. Having completed some batteries, the Republicans opened a heavy cannonade upon the town and the British works on the evening of the 9th of Oc-

---

[1] These letters directed Greene to prepare for an attack on New York.

[2] This is generally called in the letters and histories of the time, "Head of Elk," the narrow, upper part of the Chesapeake being called Elk River. There stands the village of Elkton.

[3] Arnold landed at the mouth of the Thames, and proceeded to attack Fort Trumbull, near New London. The garrison evacuated it, and the village was burned. Another division of the expedition went up on the east side of the Thames, attacked Fort Griswold at Groton, and after Colonel Ledyard had surrendered it, he and almost every man in the fort were cruelly murdered, or badly wounded. There is a monument to their memory at Groton.

[4] He was born at Norwich, at the head of the Thames, a few miles north of New London. See note 1, page 327.

[5] Graves intended to intercept a French squadron, which was on its way with heavy cannons and military stores for the armies at Yorktown. He was not aware that De Grasse had left the West Indies.

[6] The place of anchorage was in Lynn Haven Bay. The hostile fleets were in sight of each other for five successive days, but neither party was anxious to renew the combat.

[7] Including the Virginia militia, the whole of the American and French forces employed in the siege, amounted to a little over sixteen thousand men. Of the Americans, about seven thousand were regular troops, and four thousand militia. The French troops numbered about five thousand, including those brought by De Grasse from the West Indies.

tober. On the following evening they hurled red-hot balls among the British shipping in front of the town, and burned several vessels. Hour after hour, disasters were gathering a fearful web of difficulty around Cornwallis. Despairing of aid from Clinton, and perceiving his strong fortifications crumbling, one by one, under the terrible storm of iron from a hundred heavy cannons, he attempted to escape on the night of the 16th, by crossing to Gloucester, breaking through the French troops stationed there, and making forced marches toward New York. When the van of his troops embarked, the waters of the York River were perfectly calm, although dark clouds were gathering in the horizon. Then a storm arose as sudden and as fearful as a summer tornado, dispersed the boats, compelled many to put back, and the attempt was abandoned.[1] Hope now faded; and on the 19th, Cornwallis surrendered the posts at Yorktown and Gloucester, with almost seven thousand British soldiers, and his shipping and seamen, into the hands of Washington and De Grasse.[2]

SIEGE OF YORKTOWN.

The ceremony, on the occasion of the surrender, was exceedingly imposing. The American army was drawn up on the right side of the road leading from Yorktown to Hampton (see map), and the French army on the left. Their lines extended more than a mile in length. Washington, upon his white charger, was at the head of the American column; and Rochambeau, upon a powerful bay horse, was at the head of the French column. A vast concourse of people, equal in number, according to eye-witnesses, to the military, was also assembled from the surrounding country to participate in the joy of the event. Universal silence prevailed as the vanquished troops slowly marched out of their intrenchments, with their colors cased, and their drums beating a British tune, and passed between the columns of the combined armies. All were eager to look upon Lord Cornwallis, the terror of the South,[3] in the hour of his adversity. They were dis-

[1] Note 4, page 247.

[2] The British lost one hundred and fifty-six killed, three hundred and twenty-six wounded, and seventy missing. The combined armies lost, in killed and wounded, about three hundred. Among the spoils were seventy-five brass, and one hundred and sixty iron cannons; seven thousand seven hundred and ninety-four muskets; twenty-eight regimental standards; a large quantity of musket and cannon-balls; and nearly eleven thousand dollars in specie in the military chest. The army was surrendered to Washington, and the shipping and seamen to De Grasse. The latter soon afterward left the Chesapeake, and went to the West Indies. Rochambeau remained with his troops in Virginia during the winter, and the main body of the American army marched north, and went into winter quarters on the Hudson. A strong detachment, under General St. Clair [page 276], was sent south to drive the British from Wilmington, and reinforce the army of General Greene, then lying near Charleston.

[3] The conduct of Lord Cornwallis, during his march of over fifteen hundred miles through the Southern States, was often disgraceful to the British name. He suffered dwelling-houses to be plundered of every thing that could be carried off; and it was well known that his lordship's table

appointed; he had given himself up to vexation and despair, and, feigning illness, he sent General O'Hara with his sword, to lead the vanquished army to the field of humiliation. Having arrived at the head of the line, General O'Hara advanced toward Washington, and, taking off his hat, apologized for the absence of Earl Cornwallis. The commander-in-chief pointed him to General Lincoln for directions. It must have been a proud moment for Lincoln, for only the year before he was obliged to make a humiliating surrender of his army to British conquerors at Charleston.[1] Lincoln conducted the royal troops to the field selected for laying down their arms, and there General O'Hara delivered to him the sword of Cornwallis. Lincoln received it, and then politely handed it back to O'Hara, to be returned to the earl.

The delivery of the colors of the several regiments, twenty-eight in number, was next performed. For this purpose, twenty-eight British captains, each bearing a flag in a case, were drawn up in line. Opposite to them, at a distance of six paces, twenty-eight American sergeants were placed in line to receive the colors. An ensign was appointed by Colonel Hamilton, the officer of the day, to conduct this interesting ceremony.[2] When the ensign gave the order for the British captains to advance two paces, to deliver up their colors, and the American sergeants to advance two paces to receive them, the former hesitated, and gave as a reason, that they were unwilling to surrender their flags to non-commissioned officers. Hamilton, who was at a distance, observed this hesitation, and rode up to inquire the cause. On being informed, he willingly spared the feelings of the British captains, and ordered the ensign to receive them himself, and hand them to the American sergeants. The scene is depicted in the engraving.

Clinton appeared at the entrance to Chesapeake Bay a few days afterward, with seven thousand troops, but it was too late. The final blow which struck down British power in America had been given. The victory was complete; and Clinton returned to New York, amazed and disheartened.

Great was the joy throughout the colonies when intelligence of the capture of the British army reached the people. From every family altar where a love of freedom dwelt—from pulpits, legislative halls, the army, and from Congress,[3]

---

was furnished with plate thus obtained from private families. His march was more frequently that of a marauder than an honorable general. It is estimated that Virginia alone lost, during Cornwallis's attempt to reduce it, thirty thousand slaves. It was also estimated, at the time, from the best information that could be obtained, that, during the six months previous to the surrender at Yorktown, the whole devastations of his army amounted in value to about fifteen millions of dollars.

[1] Page 311.

[2] Ensign Robert Wilson, of General James Clinton's New York Brigade. He was the youngest commissioned officer in the army, being then only eighteen years of age. He was afterward a magistrate in central New York for a number of years, and was for some time postmaster at Manlius, in Onondago county. He died in 1811.

[3] A messenger, with a dispatch from Washington, reached Philadelphia at midnight. Soon the watchmen in the streets cried, "Past twelve o'clock, and Cornwallis is taken." Before dawn the exulting people filled the streets; and at an early hour, Secretary Thomson [page 227] read that cheering letter to the assembled Congress. Then that august body went in procession to a temple of the living God [Oct. 24th, 1781], and there joined in public thanksgivings to the King of kings, for the great victory. They also resolved that a marble column should be erected at Yorktown, to commemorate the event; and that two stands of colors should be presented to Washington, and two pieces of cannon to each of the French commanders, Rochambeau and De Grasse.

SURRENDER OF FLAGS AT YORKTOWN.

there went up a shout of thanksgiving and praise to the Lord God Omnipotent, for the success of the allied troops, and these were mingled with universal eulogies of the great leader and his companions in arms. The clouds which had lowered for seven long years, appeared to be breaking, and the splendors of the dawn of peace burst forth, like the light of a clear morning after a dismal night of tempest and woe. And the desire for peace, which had long burned in the bosom of the British people, now found such potential expression, as to be heeded by the British ministry. The intelligence of the fate of Cornwallis and his party, fell with all the destructive energy of a bomb-shell in the midst of the war-party in Parliament;[1] and the stoutest declaimers in favor of bayonets and gunpowder, Indians and German mercenaries,[2] as fit instruments for enslaving a free people, began to talk of the *expediency* of peace. Public opinion soon found expression in both Houses of Parliament; and Lord North[3] and his compeers, who had misled the nation for twelve years, gave way under the pressure of the peace sentiment, and retired from office on the 20th of March, 1782. The advocates of peace then came into power; and early in the following May, Sir Guy Carleton[4] arrived in New York, with propositions for a reconciliation.

CHAPTER IX.

CLOSING EVENTS OF THE WAR FOR INDEPENDENCE. [1782—1789.]

General Greene, with the main body of the Southern army, was yet on the High Hills of Santee, when, on the 30th of October [1781], intelligence of the capture of Cornwallis reached him. The day of its arrival was made jubilant with rejoicings by the army. The event seemed to be a guaranty for the future security of the Republicans in the South, and Governor Rutledge[5] soon called a Legislative Assembly, to meet at Jacksonborough, to re-establish civil authority. An offer of pardon for penitents, brought hundreds of Tories from the British lines at Charleston, to accept the clemency. The North Carolina Tories were dismayed, for immediately after the surrender of Cornwallis, St. Clair[6] had marched upon Wilmington, when the frightened enemy immediately abandoned that post, and Major Craig, the commander, and a few followers, took post upon St. John's Island, near Charleston. Yet the vigilance of the Americans was not allowed to slumber, for a wary foe yet occupied the capitals of South Carolina and Georgia. Marion and his men kept "watch and ward" over the region between the Cooper and the Santee,[7] while Greene's main

---

[1] Lord George Germaine said that Lord North received the intelligence "as he would have done a cannon-ball in his breast." He paced the room, and throwing his arms wildly about, kept exclaiming, "O, God! it is all over, it is all over!"

[2] Page 246. [3] Page 224. [4] Page 240. [5] Page 310. [6] Page 276.

[7] On one occasion, Marion's brigade suffered a severe defeat, while the commander was attend-

army lay near the Edisto; and Wayne, always vigilant, kept the enemy as close within his intrenchments at Savannah. Washington, who returned to the North immediately after the surrender, was, at the same time, keeping Clinton and his army close prisoners in New York.

Benj[a]. Thompson

While the theater of war was thus narrowing, British statesmen of all parties, considering the capture of Cornwallis and his army as the death-blow to all hope for future conquests, turned their attention to measures for an honorable termination of the unnatural war. General Conway, the firm and long-tried friend of the Americans, offered a resolution in Parliament in February [1782], which was preliminary to the enactment of a decree for commanding the cessation of hostilities. It was lost by only *one vote*. Thus encouraged,

---

ing his duties as a member of the South Carolina Legislature. He left his men in command of Colonel Horry, and near the Santee, Colonel Thompson (afterward the eminent Count Rumford) attacked the corps, with a superior force, and dispersed it. Marion arrived during the engagement, rallied his brigade, and then retired beyond the Santee, to reorganize and recruit. Benjamin Thompson was a native of Massachusetts, and was born in March, 1753. He became a schoolmaster, and while acting in that capacity, he married a rich widow. Already his mind was filled with scientific knowledge, and now he pursued his studies and investigations with energy. When the Revolution broke out, he refused to take part in political matters. The Whigs drove him to Boston for British protection, and he was sent to England by Lord Howe, with dispatches. Toward the close of the war, he commanded a corps of Tories at New York and Charleston. He returned to Europe, became acquainted with the sovereign of Bavaria, made himself exceedingly useful, was raised to the highest dignity, and was created a count. After suffering many vicissitudes, he died, near Paris, in August, 1814. His daughter, the Countess of Rumford, who was born in America, died at Concord, New Hampshire, in 1852. See Lossing's *Eminent Americans*.

the opposition pressed the subject warmly upon the attention of the House of Commons and the nation, and on the 4th of March, Conway moved "That the House would consider as enemies to his majesty and the country all those who should advise, or by any means attempt, the further prosecution of offensive

war on the Continent of North America." The resolution was carried without a division, and the next day the attorney-general introduced a plan for a truce with the Americans. Orders for a cessation of hostilities speedily went forth to the British commanders in America, and preparations were soon made for evacuating the cities of Savannah and Charleston.

When General Leslie, the British commander at Charleston, was apprised of these proceedings in Parliament, he proposed to General Greene a cessation of hostilities. Like a true soldier, Greene referred the matter to Congress, and did not for a moment relax his vigilance. Leslie also requested Greene to allow him to purchase supplies for his army, at the same time declaring his intention to evacuate Charleston. Greene was unwilling thus to nourish a viper, until his power to injure was destroyed, and he refused. Leslie then resorted to force to obtain provisions. Already he had made several efforts to penetrate the country for the purpose, and now, late in August, he attempted to ascend the Combahee,[1] when he was opposed by the Americans under General Gist, of

---

[1] Page 42.

the Maryland line. Colonel John Laurens[1] volunteered in the service; and in a skirmish at day-break, on the 25th of August, he was killed. He was greatly beloved by all, and his death was mourned with real sorrow. His was almost the last life sacrificed in that glorious old war. The blood of one other was shed at Stono Ferro,[2] a few weeks afterward, when Captain Wilmot was killed in a skirmish with a British foraging party.

Several weeks previous to this, the British had evacuated Savannah. That event occurred on the 11th of July, when General Wayne, in consideration of the eminent services of Colonel James Jackson,[3] appointed him to "receive the keys of the city of Savannah" from a committee of British officers. He performed the duty with great dignity, and on the same day the American army entered the city. Royal power then ceased in Georgia, forever. On the 14th of December following, the British evacuated Charleston, and the next day, the Americans, under General Greene, took possession of it, greeted from windows, balconies, and even house-tops, with cheers, waving of handkercniefs, and cries of "God bless you, gentlemen! Welcome! Welcome!" The British remained in New York almost a year longer (until the 25th of November, 1783), under the command of Sir Guy Carleton, who had succeeded Sir Henry Clinton, because the final negotiations for peace were not completed, by ratification, until near that time.

Measures were now taken by Congress and the British government to arrange a treaty of peace. The United States appointed five commissioners for the purpose, in order that different sections of the Union might be represented. These consisted of John Adams, John Jay, Benjamin Franklin, Thomas Jefferson, and Henry Laurens. These met Richard Oswald, the English commissioner, at Paris, and there, on the 30th of November, 1782, they signed a preliminary treaty.[4] French and English commissioners also signed a treaty of peace on the 20th of January following. Congress ratified the action of its commissioners in April, 1783, yet negotiations were in progress until September following, when a definitive treaty was signed [September 3, 1783] at Paris.[5] In that treaty, England acknowledged the Independence of the United States; allowed ample boundaries, extending northward to the Great Lakes,

---

[1] Note 2, page 329. [2] Page 296.

[3] James Jackson was one of the most eminent men in Georgia. He was born in England, in September, 1757, and came to America in 1772. He studied law at Savannah, and was an active soldier during the whole war for Independence. When a little past thirty years of age, he was elected governor of Georgia, but declined the honor on account of his youth. He was a member of the United States Senate for some time, and was governor of his State for two years. He died, while at Washington, as United States senator, in 1808, and his remains are in the Congressional burial-ground. See his portrait on page 347.

[4] Vèrgennes, the French minister, was dissatisfied with the manner in which the matter had been conducted. It was understood, by the terms of the alliance between the United States and France (and expressly stated in the instructions of the commissioners), that no treaty should be signed by the latter without the knowledge of the other. Yet it was done on this occasion. A portion of the American commissioners doubted the good faith of Vèrgennes, because he favored Spanish claims. Dr. Franklin, however, trusted Vèrgennes implicitly, and the latter appears to have acted honorably, throughout. The cloud of dissatisfaction soon passed away, when Franklin, with soft words, explained the whole matter.

[5] It was signed, on the part of England, by David Hartley, and on that of the United States, by Dr. Franklin, John Adams, and John Jay.

and westward to the Mississippi, and an unlimited right of fishing on the banks of Newfoundland. The two Floridas were restored to Spain. At the same time, definitive treaties between England, France, Spain, and Holland, were signed by their respective commissioners,[1] and the United States became an active power among the nations of the earth.[2]

A great work had now been accomplished, yet the joy of the American people, in view of returning peace and prosperity, was mingled with many gloomy apprehensions of evil. The army, which, through the most terrible sufferings, had remained faithful, and become conqueror, was soon to be disbanded; and thousands, many of them made invalids by the hard service in which they had been engaged, would be compelled to seek a livelihood in the midst of the desolation which war had produced.[3] For a long time the public treasury had been empty, and neither officers nor soldiers had received any pay for their services. A resolution of Congress, passed in 1780 [October 21], to allow the officers half pay for life, was ineffective, because funds were wanting. Already the gloomy prospect had created wide-spread murmurings in the army, and there were many men who sighed for a stronger government. They ascribed the weakness of the Confederation to its republican form, and a change, to be wrought by the army, was actually proposed to Washington. Nicola, a foreign officer in a Pennsylvania regiment, made the proposition, in a well-written letter, and not only urged the necessity of a monarchy, but endeavored to persuade Washington to become king, by the voice of the army. The sharp rebuke of the commander-in-chief [May, 1782], checked all further movements in that direction.

The general discontent soon assumed another shape, and on the 11th of March, 1783, a well-written address was circulated through the American camp (then near Newburg), which advised the army to take matters into its own hands, make a demonstration that should arouse the fears of the people and of Congress, and thus obtain justice for themselves.[4] For this purpose a meeting of officers was called, but the great influence of Washington prevented a response. The commander-in-chief then summoned all the officers together, laid the matter before them [March 15], and obtained from them a patriotic expression of their faith in the "justice of Congress and the country." In a few days the threatening cloud passed away, and soon after this event Congress made arrangements for granting to the officers full pay for five years, instead of half pay for life; and to the soldiers full pay for four months, in partial liquidation of their claims. This arrangement was not satisfactory, and discon-

[1] That between Great Britain and Holland was signed on the second.

[2] John Adams was the first minister of the United States to Great Britain. He was politely received by King George the Third; and that monarch was faithful to his promises to preserve inviolate the covenant he had made by acknowledging the independence of the new Republic.

[3] The army, consisting of about ten thousand men, was then encamped on the Hudson, near Newburg.

[4] This address was anonymous, but it was afterward acknowledged to be the production of John Armstrong, then a major, and one of General Gates's aids. It is believed that Gates and other officers were the instigators of the scheme, and that Armstrong acted under their direction. He was an accomplished writer, and was much in public life after the war. He was United States minister to France for six years, from 1804. He was Secretary of War in 1814; and died in Dutchess county, New York, in 1843, in the eighty-fifth year of his age.

tent still prevailed.[1] In the mean while [March 2] the preliminary treaty had arrived. On the eighth anniversary of the skirmish at Lexington [April 19, 1783], a cessation of hostilites was proclaimed in the army, and on the 3d of November following, the army was disbanded by a general order of Congress. A small force was retained under a definite enlistment, until a peace establishment should be organized.[2] These were now at West Point, under the command of General Knox. The remainder of that glorious band of patriots then quietly returned to their homes, to enjoy, for the remnant of their lives, the blessings of the liberty they had won, and the grateful benedictions of their countrymen. Of the two hundred and thirty thousand Continental soldiers, and the fifty-six thousand militia who bore arms during the war, not more than six hundred now [1856] remain among us ![3] And the average of these must be full ninety years.

The British army evacuated the city of New York on the 25th of November, 1783. With their departure, went, forever, the last instrument of royal power in these United States. On the morning of that day—a cold, frosty, but clear and brilliant morning—the American troops, under General Knox,[4] who had come down from West Point and encamped at Harlem, marched to the Bowery Lane, and halted at the present junction of Third Avenue and the Bowery. Knox was accompanied by George Clinton,[5] the governor of the State of New York, with all the principal civil officers. There they remained until about one o'clock in the afternoon, when the British left their posts in that vicinity and marched to Whitehall.[6] The American troops followed, and

GOVERNOR CLINTON.

[1] In May, 1783, a portion of the Pennsylvania troops, lately arrived from the South, marched to Philadelphia, where they were joined by others, and for three hours they stood at the door of the State House, and demanded immediate pay from Congress. St. Clair, then in command there, pacified them for the moment, and Washington soon quelled the mutiny. See page 328.

[2] A great portion of the officers and soldiers had been permitted, during the summer, to visit their homes on furlough. The proclamation of discharge, by Congress, was followed by Washington's farewell address to his companions in arms, written at Rocky Hill, New Jersey, on the 3d of November. He had already issued a circular letter (Newburg, June 8th, 1783) to the governors of all the States on the subject of disbanding the army. It was designed to be laid before the several State Legislatures. It is a document of great value, because of the soundness of its doctrines, and the weight and wisdom of its counsels. Four great points of policy constitute the chief theme of his communication, namely, *an indissoluble union of the States; a sacred regard for public justice; the organization of a proper peace establishment; and a friendly intercourse among the people of the several States, by which local prejudice might be effaced.* "These," he remarks, "are the pillars on which the glorious fabric of our independency and national character must be supported." No doubt this address had great influence upon the minds of the whole people, and made them yearn for that more efficient union which the Federal Constitution soon afterward secured.

[3] Great Britain sent to America, during the war, one hundred and twelve thousand five hundred and eighty-four troops for the land service, and more than twenty-two thousand seamen. Of all this host, not one is known to be living. One of them (John Battin) died in the city of New York, in June, 1852, at the age of one hundred years and four months.

[4] Henry Knox, the able commander of the artillery during the Revolution, was born in Boston, in 1740. He entered the army at the commencement of the war. He was President Washington's Secretary of War, and held that office eleven years. He died at Thomaston, in Maine, in 1806.

[5] Like Governors Trumbull [page 323] and Rutledge [page 310], Clinton, in a civil capacity, was of immense service to the American cause. He was born in Ulster county, New York, in 1739. He was governor about eighteen years, and died in 1812, while Vice-President of the United States. See page 404.

[6] Now the South Ferry to Brooklyn.

before three o'clock General Knox took formal possession of Fort George amid the acclamations of thousands of emancipated freemen, and the roar of artillery upon the Battery.

On Thursday, the 4th of December, Washington met his officers, yet re-

maining in service, at his quarters, corner of Broad and Pearl-streets, New York, for the last time. The scene, as described by Marshall,[1] the best of the early biographers of Washington, was one of great tenderness. The commander-in-chief entered the room where they were all waiting, and taking a glass of wine in his hand, he said, "With a heart full of love and gratitude, I now take

---

[1] John Marshall, the eminent Chief Justice of the United States, was born in Fauquier county, Virginia, in 1755, and was the eldest of fifteen children by the same mother. He entered the military service, in the Virginia militia, against Dunmore [page 244], in 1775, and was in the battle at the Great Bridge [see page 243]. He remained in service, as an excellent officer, until early in 1780, when he studied law, and became very eminent in his profession. He was again in the field in 1781. In 1782 he was a member of the Virginia Legislature. He was chosen Secretary of War in 1800, and the next year was elevated to the Chief Justiceship of the United States. His *Life of Washington* was published in 1805. Judge Marshall died at Philadelphia in 1835, in the eightieth year of his age. He was an exceedingly plain man, in person and habits, and always carried his own marketing home in his hands. On one occasion, a young housekeeper was swearing lustily because he could not hire a person to carry his turkey home for him. A plain man, standing by, offered to perform the service, and when they arrived at the door, the young man asked, "What shall I pay you?" "Oh, nothing," replied the old man; "you are welcome; it was on my way, and no trouble." "Who is that polite old gentleman who brought home my turkey for me?" inquired the young man of a bystander. "That," he replied, "is John Marshall, Chief Justice of the United States." The astonished young man exclaimed, "Why did he bring home my turkey?" "To give you a severe reprimand," replied the other, "and to learn you to attend to your own business." The lesson was never forgotten.

leave of you. I most devoutly wish that your latter days may be as prosperous and happy as your former ones have been glorious and honorable." Having drank, he continued, "I can not come to each of you to take my leave, but shall be obliged to you if each will come and take me by the hand." Knox, who stood nearest to him, turned and grasped his hand, and, while the tears flowed down the cheeks of each, the commander-in-chief kissed him. This he did to each of his officers, while tears and sobs stifled utterance. Washington soon left the room, and passing through corps of light infantry, he walked in silence to Whitehall, where he embarked in a barge for Elizabethtown, on his way to Annapolis, in Maryland, where Congress was in session. There, on the 23d of December, he resigned into its custody the commission which he received [June 16, 1775] from that body more than eight years before.[1] His address on that occasion was simple and touching, and the response of General Mifflin,[2] the president, was equally affecting. The spectacle was one of great moral sublimity. Like Cincinnatus, Washington, having been instrumental, under Providence, in preserving the liberties of his country and achieving its independence, laid down the cares of State and returned to his plow.

GENERAL MIFFLIN.

A few months before the final disbanding of the army, many of the officers, then at Newburg, on the Hudson, met [June 19, 1783] at the head-quarters of the Baron Steuben, situated about two miles from the Fishkill Ferry, and there formed an association, which they named the SOCIETY OF THE CINCINNATI. The chief objects of the Society were to promote cordial friendship and indissoluble union among themselves; to commemorate, by frequent re-unions, the great struggle they had just passed through; to use their best endeavors for the promotion of human liberty; to cherish good feeling between the respective States; and to extend benevolent aid to those of the Society whose circumstances might require it. They formed a General Society, and elected Washington its first president. They also made provision for the formation of auxiliary State societies. To perpetuate the Association, it was provided, in the constitution, that the eldest male descendant of an original member should be entitled to bear the ORDER, and enjoy the privileges of the Society. The *Order*[3] consists of a gold eagle, suspended upon a ribbon, on the breast of which is a medallion

ORDER.

[1] Page 238. At the same time Washington rendered the account current of his expenditures, for reconnoitering, traveling, secret service, and miscellaneous expenses, amounting to about $74,480. He would receive nothing in compensation for his own services as commander-in-chief.

[2] Thomas Mifflin was born in Philadelphia in 1744. He was a Quaker [note 7, page 94], but joined the patriot army in 1775, and rapidly rose to the rank of major-general. He was a member of Congress after the war, and also governor of Pennsylvania. He died in January, 1800.

[3] An *order* is a badge, or visible token of regard or distinction, conferred upon persons for meritorious services. On the breast of Baron Steuben on page 291, is the order of *Fidelity*, presented to him by Frederic the Great of Prussia, for his services in the army of that monarch. Some of the

with a device, representing Cincinnatus receiving the Roman senators.[1] Several State societies are yet [1856] in existence.

The war was ended, and peace was guarantied, but the people had much to do in the adjustment of public affairs, so as to lay the foundations of permanent prosperity, and thus secure the liberty and independence proclaimed and acknowledged. The country was burdened with a heavy debt, foreign and domestic,[2] and the *Articles of Confederation*[3] gave Congress no power to discharge them, if it had possessed the ability. On its recommendation, however, the individual States attempted to raise their respective quotas, by direct taxation. But all were impoverished by the war, and it was found to be impossible to provide means even to meet the arrears of pay due the soldiers of the Revolution. Each State had its local obligations to meet, and Congress could not coerce compliance with its recommendations.

This effort produced great excitement in many of the States, and finally, in 1787, a portion of the people of Massachusetts openly rebelled. Daniel Shays, who had been a captain in the continental army, marched at the head of a thousand men, took possession of Worcester, and prevented a session of the Supreme Court. He repeated the same at Springfield. The insurrection soon became so formidable, that Governor Bowdoin was compelled to call out several thousand militia, under General Lincoln, to suppress it. Lincoln captured one hundred and fifty of the insurgents, and their power was broken. A free pardon was, finally, offered to all privates who had engaged in the rebellion. Several leaders were tried, and sentenced to death, but none were executed, for it was perceived that the great mass of the people sympathized with them. This episode is known as *Shays's Rebellion.*

We have already noticed the fact that the Pope was unfriendly to England,[4] and looked with favor upon the rebellious movements of her colonies. Soon after the treaty of peace was concluded [Sept. 3, 1783], the Pope's Nuncio at Paris made overtures to Franklin, on the subject of appointing an apostolic vicar for the United States. The matter was referred to Congress, and that body properly replied, that the subject being purely spiritual, it was beyond their control. The idea of entire separation between the State and spiritual governments—the full exercise of freedom of conscience—was thus early enun-

---

orders conferred by kings are very costly, being made of gold and silver, and precious stones. The picture of the *order* of the Cincinnati, given on the preceding page, is half the size of the original.

[1] Cincinnatus was a noble Roman citizen. When the Romans were menaced with destruction by an enemy, the Senate appointed delegates to invite Cincinnatus to assume the chief magistracy of the nation. They found him at his plow. He immediately complied, raised an army, subdued the enemy, and, after bearing the almost imperial dignity for fourteen days, he resigned his office, and returned to his plow. How like Cincinnatus were Washington and his compatriots of the War for Independence!

[2] According to an estimate made by the Register of the Treasury in 1790, the entire cost of the War for Independence, was at least *one hundred and thirty millions* of dollars, exclusive of vast sums lost by individuals and the several States, to the amount, probably, of *forty millions* more. The treasury payments amounted to almost *ninety-three millions*, chiefly in continental bills. The foreign debt amounted to *eight millions* of dollars; and the domestic debt, due chiefly to the officers and soldiers of the Revolution, was more than *thirty millions* of dollars.

[3] Note 1, page 267, and Supplement.

[4] Page 266.

ciated. The Pope accordingly appointed John Carroll,[1] of Maryland, a cousin of Charles Carroll, one of the signers of the Declaration of Independence, to the high office of Apostolic-Vicar. He was consecrated Bishop of Baltimore, and was ultimately made Archbishop of the United States. At about the same

time, the Church of England in America sought a reorganization, and Samuel Seabury, an Episcopal minister of New London, Connecticut, at the request of the Churchmen of that State, proceeded to England to obtain ordination as bishop. The English bishops were not allowed to confer the dignity unless the recipient would take the oath of allegiance to the king of England, as head of the Church. This, Seabury (although a loyalist during the war) could not do, and he sought and obtained ordination from Scotch bishops. Such was the commencement of the two most prominent prelatical Churches in the United States. The Methodist Church, which has since flourished so wonderfully, was then just taking firm root.

---

[1] John Carroll was born in Maryland in 1735, and at the age of thirteen years, was sent to Europe to be educated. He was ordained a priest in 1769, and became a teacher at St. Omer and at Liege. When the Jesuits were expelled from France, he went to England, and returned to his native country in 1775. He accompanied a Congressional committee to Canada, in 1776, to endeavor to persuade that Roman Catholic colony to join the others in the revolt. Throughout the war he was attached to the Repulican cause. He was appointed Vicar-General in 1786, and was consecrated a bishop in 1790. He was made archbishop in 1808. He died in Baltimore in 1815, at the age of eighty years. His usual signature was † J. Bis[h]. of Baltimore.

For a long time it had been clearly perceived that, while the *Articles of Confederation* formed a sufficient constitution of government during the progress of the war, they were not adapted to the public wants in the new condition of an independent sovereignty in which the people found themselves. There appeared a necessity for a greater centralization of power by which the general government could act more efficiently for the public good. To a great extent, the people lost all regard for the authority of Congress, and the commercial affairs of the country became wretchedly deranged. In truth, every thing seemed to be tending toward utter chaos, soon after the peace in 1783,[1] and the leading minds engaged in the struggle for Independence, in view of the increasing and magnified evils, and the glaring defects of the *Articles of Confederation*, were turned to the consideration of a plan for a closer union of the States, and for a general government founded on the principles of the Declaration of Independence, from which the confederation in question widely departed.

The sagacious mind of Washington early perceived, with intense anxiety, the tendency toward ruin of that fair fabric which his wisdom and prowess had helped to rear, and he took the initial step toward the adoption of measures which finally resulted in the formation of the present Constitution of the United States.[2] At his suggestion, a convention, for the purpose of consulting on the best means of remedying the defects of the Federal Government, was held at Annapolis, in Maryland, in September, 1786. Only five States (Virginia, Delaware, Pennsylvania, New Jersey and New York) were represented. They met on the 11th of that month, and John Dickenson[3] was chosen chairman. They finally appointed a committee to prepare a draft of a report to be made to the Legislatures of the several States, then represented. The committee reported on the 14th, but there not being a representation from a majority of the States, it was thought advisable to postpone further action. They adjourned, after recommending the appointment of deputies to meet in convention at Philadelphia, in May following. The report was adopted and transmitted to Congress. On the 21st of February, 1787, a committee of that body,[4] to whom the report of the commissioners was referred, reported thereon, and strongly recommended to the different Legislatures to send forward delegates to meet in the proposed convention at Philadelphia. Propositions were made by delegates from New York and Massachusetts, and finally the following resolution, submitted by the latter, after being amended, was agreed to:

"*Resolved*, That in the opinion of Congress, it is expedient that on the second Monday in May next, a convention of delegates, who shall have been appointed by the several States, be held at Philadelphia, for the sole and express purpose of revising the *Articles of Confederation*, and reporting to Congress and the several Legislatures such alterations and provisions therein as shall, when agreed to in Congress, and confirmed by the States, render the

---

[1] Page 348. [2] Page 359. [3] Page 219.

[4] The committee consisted of Messrs. Dana, Varnum, S. M. Mitchell, Smith, Cadwalader, Irvine, N. Mitchell, Forest, Grayson, Blount, Bull, and Few.

Federal Constitution adequate to the exigences of the government and the preservation of the Union."

This resolution, with a preamble, was immediately transmitted to the several Speakers of State Legislatives Assemblies, and they were laid before the representatives of the people in all the States of the Confederacy. While a feeling generally prevailed, that *something* must be done to avert the threatened anarchy, toward which governmental operations were rapidly tending, great caution was observed in the delegation of powers to those who should be appointed members of the proposed convention.[1] In May, 1787,[2] delegates from all the States, except New Hampshire and Rhode Island,[3] assembled at Philadelphia, in the room where Congress was in session when the Declaration of Independence was adopted.[4] Washington, who was a delegate from Virginia, was, on motion of Robert Morris, chosen President. Able statesmen were his associates,[5] and they entered earnestly upon their duties. They had not proceeded far, however, before they perceived that the *Articles of Confederation* were so radically defective, and their powers so inadequate to meet the wants of the country, that, instead of trying to amend that old code, they went diligently to work to form a new Constitution. For some time they made but little progress. There were

---

[1] The great question that came up before the members, at the very commencement of the session of the Convention, was, "What powers do we possess? Can the amendments to the *Articles of Confederation* be carried so far as to establish an entirely new system?"

[2] The day fixed for the assembling of the Convention, was the 14th of May. On that day, delegates from only half the States were present. The remainder of the delegates did not all arrive before the 25th.

[3] Ignorant and unprincipled men, who were willing to liquidate public and private debts by the agency of unstable paper money, controlled the Assembly of Rhode Island, and that body refused to elect delegates to the Convention. But some of the best and most influential men in the State joined in sending a letter to the Convention, in which they expressed their cordial sympathy with the object of that national assembly, and promised their adhesion to whatever the majority might propose. The following are the names of the delegates:

New Hampshire.—John Langdon, John Pickering, Nicholas Gilman, and Benjamin West.

Massachusetts.—Francis Dana, Elbridge Gerry, Nathaniel Gorham, Rufus King, and Caleb Strong.

Connecticut.—William Samuel Johnson, Roger Sherman, and Oliver Ellsworth.

New York.—Robert Yates, John Lansing, Jr., and Alexander Hamilton.

New Jersey.—David Brearley, William Churchill Houston, William Paterson, John Neilson, William Livingston, Abraham Clark, and Jonathan Dayton.

Pennsylvania.—Thomas Mifflin, Robert Morris, George Clymer, Jared Ingersoll, Thomas Fitzsimmons, James Wilson, Gouverneur Morris, and Benjamin Franklin.

Delaware.—George Reed, Gunning Bedford, Jr., John Dickenson, Richard Bassett, and Jacob Brown.

Maryland.—James M'Henry, Daniel of St. Thomas Jenifer, Daniel Carroll, John Francis Mercer, and Luther Martin.

Virginia.—George Washington, Patrick Henry, Edmund Randolph, John Blair, James Madison, Jr., George Mason, and George Wythe. Patrick Henry having declined his appointment, James M'Clure was nominated to supply his place.

North Carolina.—Richard Caswell, Alexander Martin, William Richardson Davie, Richard Dobbs Spaight, and Willie Jones. Richard Caswell having resigned, William Blount was appointed a deputy in his place. Willie Jones having also declined his appointment, his place was supplied by Hugh Williamson.

South Carolina.—John Rutledge, Charles Pinckey, Charles C. Pinckney, and Pierce Butler.

Georgia.—William Few, Abraham Baldwin, William Pierce, George Walton, William Houston, and Nathaniel Pendleton.

[4] Page 250.

[5] The members who were most conspicuous as debaters in the Convention, were Randolph, Madison, and Mason, of Virginia; King, Gerry, and Gorham, of Massachusetts; Gouverneur Morris, Wilson, and Dr. Franklin, of Pennsylvania; Johnson, Sherman, and Ellsworth, of Connecticut; Lansing and Hamilton, of New York; the two Pinckneys, of South Carolina; Paterson, of New Jersey; Martin, of Maryland; Dickenson, of Delaware; and Dr. Williamson, of North Carolina.

Franklin in the Federal Convention.

great diversities of opinion,[1] and it seemed, after several days, that the convention must, of necessity, dissolve without accomplishing any thing. Some proposed a final adjournment. At this momentous crisis, Dr. Franklin arose, and said to the President, "How has it happened, sir, that while groping so long in the dark, divided in our opinions, and now ready to separate without accomplishing the great objects of our meeting, that we have hitherto not once thought of humbly applying to the Father of Lights to illuminate our understandings? In the beginning of the contest with Britain, when we were sensible of danger, we had daily prayers in this room for divine protection. Our prayers, sir, were heard, and graciously answered." After a few more remarks, he moved that "henceforth, prayers, imploring the assistance of Heaven, and its blessings on our deliberations, be held in this Assembly every morning before we proceed to business." The resolution was not adopted, as the convention, except three or four members, thought prayers unnecessary, because in this case they would be merely formal. Objections were also made, because there were no funds to defray the expenses of such clerical services.

After long and animated debates, the Convention referred all propositions, reports, etc., which had been agreed to from time to time, to a Committee of Detail, consisting of Rutledge, Randolph, Gorham, Ellsworth,[2] and Wilson. The Convention then adjourned, and ten days afterward [August 6, 1787] it met, and that committee reported a rough sketch of the Constitution, as it now stands. Now, again, long and sometimes angry debates were had. Amendments were made, and all were referred to a committee for final revision. That committee submitted the following resolution on the 12th of September, which was adopted:

---

[1] Edmund Randolph submitted a plan on the 29th of May, in a series of Resolutions, which was known as the "Virginia Plan." It proposed to form a general government, composed of a legislature, and an executive and judiciary department; a revenue, and an army and navy, independent of the control of the several States; to have power to conduct war, establish peace, and make treaties; to have the exclusive privilege of coining money, and the general supervision of all national transactions. Upon general principles, this plan was highly approved; but in that Convention there were many ardent and pure patriots, who looked upon the preservation of the State sovereignties as essential, and regarded this proposition as an infringement upon State Rights. Mr. Paterson also submitted a plan for amending the *Articles of Confederation*. It proposed to enlarge the powers of Congress, but left its resources and supplies to be found through the medium of the State governments. This was one of the most serious defects of the old League—a dependence of the general government upon the State governments for its vitality. Other propositions were submitted from time to time, and the most intense solicitude was felt by every member. Subjects of the most vital interest were ably discussed, from day to day; but none created more earnest debate than a proposition for the general government to assume the debts of the States contracted in providing means for carrying on the war. The debts of the several States were unequal. Those of Massachusetts and South Carolina amounted to more than ten millions and a half of dollars, while the debts of all the other States did not extend, in the aggregate, to fifteen millions. This assumption was finally made, to the amount of twenty-one millions five hundred thousand dollars. See page 370.

[2] Oliver Ellsworth was one of the soundest men in the Convention, and was ever one of the most beloved of the New England patriots. He was born in Windsor, Connecticut, in April, 1745. He was educated at Yale College, and at Princeton, and at the age of twenty-five, he commenced the practice of law at Hartford. He was an eloquent speaker, and became very eminent in his profession. He was a member of the Continental Congress in 1777, and in 1784 he was appointed Judge of the Superior Court of Connecticut. He was the first United States senator from Connecticut, under the new Constitution, and in 1796 he was appointed Chief Justice of the United States. He was an embassador to the French court from 1799 to 1801. He died in November, 1807, at the age of sixty-two years. See next page.

"*Resolved unanimously*, That the said report, with the resolutions and letters accompanying the same, be transmitted to the several Legislatures, in order to be submitted to a convention of delegates chosen in each State by the people thereof, in conformity to the resolves of the Convention, made and provided, in that case."

The new Constitution, when submitted to the people,[1] found many and able opposers. State rights, sectional interests, radical democracy, all had numerous friends, and these formed the phalanx of opposition. All the persuasive eloquence of its advocates, with pen and speech, was needed to convince the people of its superiority to the *Articles of Confederation*, and the necessity for its ratification. Among its ablest supporters was Alexander Hamilton,[2] whose

---

[1] The Convention agreed to the revised Constitution on the 15th of September, and on the 17th it was signed by the representatives of all the States then present, except Randolph, Gerry, and Mason. The Constitution was submitted to Congress on the 28th, and that body sent copies of it to all the State Legislatures. State Conventions were then called to consider it; and more than a year elapsed before the requisite number of States had ratified it. These performed that act in the following order: Delaware, Dec. 7, 1787; Pennsylvania, Dec. 12, 1787; New Jersey, Dec. 18, 1787; Georgia, Jan. 2, 1788; Connecticut, Jan. 9, 1788; Massachusetts, Feb. 6, 1788; Maryland, April 28, 1788; South Carolina, May 23, 1788; New Hampshire, June 21, 1788; Virginia, June 26, 1788; New York, July 26, 1788; North Carolina, Nov. 21, 1788; Rhode Island, May 29, 1790.

[2] Alexander Hamilton was born on the Island of Nevis, British West Indies, in January, 1757. He was of Scotch and French parentage. He became a clerk to a New York merchant at St. Croix, and he was finally brought to New York to be educated. He was at King's (now Columbia) College, and was distinguished as a good speaker and writer, while yet a mere lad. When the Revolution broke out, he espoused the Republican cause, entered the army, became Washington's favorite aid and secretary, and was an efficient officer until its close. He made the law his profession, and, as an able financier, he was made the first Secretary of the Treasury, under the new Constitu-

pen and sword had been identified with the career of Washington during almost the whole War for Independence. He gave to its advocacy the whole weight of his character and power of his genius; and, aided by Jay and Madison, he scattered broadcast among the people, those able papers called ***The Federalist.*** These, like Paine's *Crisis*, stirred the masses; and soon eleven States, in Con-

vention assembled, gave the Federal Constitution their support, and ratified it. Congress then fixed the time for choosing electors for President and Vice-President,[1] and provided for the organization of the new government. On Wednesday, the 4th day of March, 1789, the old Continental Congress[2] expired, and the FEDERAL CONSTITUTION became the organic law of the Republic. This was the crowning act of the War for Independence,[3] and then the UNITED STATES OF AMERICA commenced their glorious career as a powerful empire among the nations of the earth.

---

tion. He was shot in a duel, by Aaron Burr, in July, 1804, at the early age of forty-seven years. His widow, daughter of General Schuyler, died in November, 1854, in the ninety-seventh year of her age.

[1] These are men elected by the people in the various States, to meet and choose a President and Vice-President of the United States. Their number is equal to the whole number of Senators and Representatives to which the several States are entitled. So the people do not vote directly for the Chief Magistrate. Formerly, the man who received the highest number of votes was declared to be President, and he who received the next highest number was proclaimed Vice-President. Now these are voted for as distinct candidates for separate offices. See Article II. of the Federal Constitution, Supplement. The first electors were chosen on the first Wednesday in February, 1789. The inauguration of the first President did not take place [page 366] until the 30th of April following.

[2] Page 226.

[3] For details of the history, biography, scenery, relics, and traditions of the War for Independence, see Lossing's *Pictorial Field Book of the Revolution.*

Congress was in session at New York while the Convention at Philadelphia was busy in preparing the Federal Constitution. During that time it disposed of the subject of organizing a Territorial Government for the vast region northward of the Ohio River, within the domain of the United States.[1] On the 11th of July, 1787, a committee of Congress reported "An Ordinance for the Government of the Territory of the United States North-west of the Ohio." This

report embodied a bill, whose provisions in regard to personal liberty and distribution of property, were very important. It contained a special proviso that the estates of all persons dying intestate, in the territory, should be equally divided among all the children, or next of kin in equal degree, thus striking down the unjust law of primogeniture, and asserting a more republican principle. The bill, also, provided and declared, that "there shall be neither slavery nor involuntary servitude in the said territory, otherwise than in the punishment of crimes whereof the party shall have been duly convicted." This ordinance was adopted on the 13th, after adding a clause relative to the reclamation of fugitives from labor, similar to that incorporated in the Federal Constitution a few weeks later.[2]

This ordinance, together with the fact that Indian titles to seventeen millions of acres of land in that region, had been lately extinguished by treaty

[1] Page 390. [2] See the Federal Constitution, Article IV., Section 2, Clause 3.

with several of the dusky tribes,[1] caused a sudden and great influx of immigrants into the country along the northern banks of the Ohio. Manasseh Cutler, Rufus Putnam, Winthrop Sargent, and other New Englanders, organized the "Ohio Company," and entered into a contract for the sale of a tract of five millions of acres, extending along the Ohio from the Muskingum to the Sciota.[2] A similar contract was entered into with John Cleves Symmes, of New Jersey, for the sale of two millions of acres, between the Great and Little Miamis. These were the first steps taken toward the settlement of the vast *North-west Territory*, which embraced the present States of Ohio, Indiana, Illinois, Michigan, and Wisconsin. It was estimated that, during the year following the organization of that Territory [1788], full twenty thousand men, women, and children had passed down the Ohio River, to become settlers upon its banks. Since, then, how wonderful has been the progress of settlement beyond the Alleghanies! How wide and deep has been the ever-flowing tide of emigration thither! The original THIRTEEN STATES have now [1856] expanded into THIRTY-ONE, and vast territories, destined to become numerous other States, are rapidly filling with people.

---

[1] The Six Nations [page 25], the Wyandots [page 23], the Delawares [page 20], and the Shawnees [page 19].

[2] Rufus Putnam, who had been an active officer during the War for Independence, was one of the most efficient of the Ohio settlers. He was born in Worcester county, Massachusetts, in 1738. He entered the provincial army in 1757, and continued in service during the remainder of the French and Indian War. He entered the army of the Revolution in 1775, and at near the close of the war, he was promoted to brigadier-general. He went to the Ohio country, with abcut forty settlers, in 1788. They pitched their tents at the mouth of the Muskingum River, formed a settlement, and called it Marietta. Suspicious of the Indians, they built a stockade, and called it *Campus Martius*. In 1780, President Washington commissioned General Putnam Supreme Judge of the North-west Territory; and in 1792, he was appointed a brigadier, under Wayne. He was appointed surveyor-general of the United States in 1796; helped to frame the Constitution of Ohio in 1802; and then retired to private life. He died at Marietta in 1824. at the age of eighty-six years. He is called the FATHER OF OHIO.

INAUGURATION OF WASHINGTON.

SIXTH PERIOD.

THE CONFEDERATION.

CHAPTER I.

WASHINGTON'S ADMINISTRATION.
1789—1797.

GOUVERNEUR MORRIS.

WHEN the *Federal Constitution*[1] had received the approval of the people, and was made the supreme law of the Republic, all minds and hearts seemed spontaneously turned toward Washington as the best man to perform the responsible duties of chief magistrate of the nation. On the 6th of April, 1789, he was chosen President of the United States by the unanimous vote of the electors,[2] and John Adams was made Vice-President. The journey of Washington from Mount Vernon to New York, was like a triumphal march. He had scarcely left his porter's lodge, when he was met by a company of gentlemen from Alexandria, who escorted him to that town. Everywhere the people gathered to see him as he passed along the road. Towns sent out committees to receive him, and public addresses and entertainments

---

[1] We have observed that Gouverneur Morris was one of the committee to make the final revision of the Constitution. The committee placed it in his hands, and that instrument, in language and general management, is the work of that eminent man. Gouverneur Morris was born near New York, in 1752. He was a lawyer, and was always active in public life. In 1792 he was appointed minister to France, and after his return he was a legislator for many years. He died in 1816.

[2] Note 1, page 361.

were given in his honor, in many places. Militia companies escorted him from place to place, and firing of cannons and ringing of bells, announced his approach to the large towns. At Trenton, his reception was peculiar and gratifying. It was arranged by the ladies. Over Trenton bridge an arch was thrown, which was adorned with laurel leaves and flowers from the conservatories. Upon the

crown, and formed of leaves and flowers, were the words, "DECEMBER 26, 1776;"[1] and on the sweep beneath was the sentence, also formed of flowers: "THE DEFENDER OF THE MOTHERS WILL BE THE PROTECTOR OF THE DAUGHTERS." Beneath that arch the President was met by a troupe of females. As he approached, a group of little girls, bearing each a basket, commenced strewing flowers in the road, and the whole company, young and old, joined in singing the following ode, written for the occasion by Governor Howell:

"Welcome, mighty chief, once more
Welcome to this grateful shore.
Now no mercenary foe
Aims again the fatal blow—
    Aims at THEE the fatal blow.
Virgins fair and matrons grave,
Those thy conquering arm did save,
Build for THEE triumphal bowers—
Strew your HERO'S way with flowers!"

---

[1]. Page 262.

Washington reached New York on the 23d of April, 1789. On the 30th he appeared upon the street-gallery of the old City Hall[1] in New York, and there, in the presence of an immense concourse of people assembled in front, the oath of office was administered to him by Chancellor Livingston.[2]

After delivering an impressive address to the members of both Houses of Congress, the President and the representatives of the people went in solemn procession to St. Paul's Church, and there invoked the blessings of the Supreme Ruler upon the new government just inaugurated.

Men were never called upon to perform duties of greater responsibility, than those which demanded the consideration of Washington and his compeers. The first session of Congress[3] was chiefly occupied in the organization of the new government, and in the elaborating of schemes for the future prosperity of the Republic. The earliest efforts of that body were directed to the arrangement of a system of revenues, in order to adjust and regulate the wretched financial

[1] It stood on the site of the present Custom House, corner of Wall and Broad-streets. In the picture on page 364, a correct representation of its street-gallery is given.

[2] One of the committee [note 2, page 251] to draft the Declaration of Independence. He was born in New York in 1747, became a lawyer, and was always an active public man. He was minister to France in 1801, when he purchased Louisiana for the United States. See page 390. He joined Robert Fulton in steamboat experiments [page 398], and died in 1813.

[3] Members of the House of Representatives are elected to seats for two years, and they hold two sessions or sittings during that time. Each full term is called a *Congress*. Now [1856–57] our representatives are in the third session of the thirty-fourth Congress. The second was an extra session of a few days. Senators are elected by the State Legislatures to serve six years.

affairs of the country.[1] This subject was brought forward by Madison,[2] the tacitly acknowledged leader in the House of Representatives, two days after the votes for President and Vice-President had been counted. Pursuant to his suggestion, tonnage duties were levied, and also a tariff, or duties upon foreign goods imported into the United States. These duties were made favorable to American shipping. This was the commencement of our present, though considerably modified, revenue system.

Having made provision for the collection of revenue, Congress next turned its attention to the reorganization of the executive departments. Three—Treasury, War, and Foreign Affairs—were created, the heads of which were to be styled secretaries, instead of ministers, as in Europe. These the President might appoint or dismiss with the concurrence of the Senate. They were to constitute a cabinet council, always ready for consultation with the President, on public affairs, and bound to give him their opinions in writing, when required.

It may be instructive to take a brief retrospective view of the progress of legislative action concerning the commerce of the United States from the close of the Revolution until the time in question. In March, 1783, the younger Pitt[3] proposed in the British Parliament, a scheme for the temporary regulation of commercial intercourse between Great Britain and the United States. Its chief feature was the free admission into the British West India ports of American vessels laden with the products of American industry—the West India people, in turn, to be allowed like free trade with the United States. The proposition was rejected, and soon an order went forth from the Privy Council,[4] for the entire exclusion of American vessels from West India ports, and prohibiting the importation there of several products of the United States, even in British bottoms. Notwithstanding this unwise and narrow policy was put in force, Mr. Adams, the American minister at the court of St. James, proposed, in 1785, to place the navigation and trade between all the dominions of the British crown and all the territories of the United States, upon a basis of perfect reciprocity. This generous offer was not only declined, but the minister was haughtily assured that no other would be entertained. Whereupon Mr. Adams immediately recommended the United States to pass navigation acts for the benefit of their commerce.

Some individual States attempted to legislate upon commercial matters and the subject of duties for revenue, but their efforts were comparatively fruitless. The importance of having the united action of all the States, in framing general navigation laws, was clearly perceived, and this perception was one of the chief causes which led to the Convention that formed the Federal Constitution.[5] The new government was inaugurated in due time, and, as we have mentioned, the earliest efforts of Congress, under the new order of things, were the consideration of schemes for imposing discriminating duties.[6] These

---

[1] Page 353. [2] Note 5, page 356. [3] Page 217.
[4] Note 1, page 400. [5] Page 355. [6] Page 366.

measures immediately opened the blind eyes of British legislators to the necessity of a reciprocity in trade between the two countries. They saw that American commerce was no longer at the mercy of thirteen distinct legislative bodies, as under the old Confederation, nor subject to the control of the king and his council. They perceived that its interests were guarded and its strength nurtured, by a central power, of wonderful energy, and soon haughty Britain became the suppliant. Soon after the passage of the revenue laws by Congress, a committee of Parliament proposed to ask the United States to consent to an arrangement precisely the same as that suggested by Mr. Adams, six years before, which was so scornfully rejected. The proposition was met by generous courtesy on the part of the United States; yet it was not until 1816, when the second war for Independence[1] had been some time closed, that reciprocity treaties fairly regulated the commerce between the two countries.

During the period here referred to, another great commercial interest, then in embryo, was under contemplation and discussion, by a few men of forecast. It was that of the production of COTTON. Primarily it is an agricultural interest, but now, when nearly all the cotton used on the continent of Europe is grown in the United States, it has become a great commercial interest. Among the first and most powerful advocates of the cultivation of this plant, was Tench Coxe,[2] of Philadelphia, who, as early as 1785, when he was only thirty years of age, published the fact that he "felt pleasing convictions that the United States, in its extensive regions south of Anne Arundel and Talbot counties, Maryland, would certainly become a great cotton-producing country." And while the Federal Convention was in session in Philadelphia, in 1787,[3] Mr. Coxe delivered a powerful public address on that and kindred subjects, having for his object the establishment of a society for the encouragement of manufactures and the useful arts. Before that time, not a bale of cotton had ever been exported from the United States to any other country, and no planter had adopted its cultivation, as a "crop."[4]

The Senate was engaged upon the important matter of a Federal judiciary, while the House was employed on the Revenue bills. A plan, embodied in a bill drafted by Ellsworth of Connecticut,[5] was, after several amendments, concurred in by both Houses. By its provisions, a national judiciary was established, consisting of a supreme court, having one chief justice, and five associate

[1] Page 409.

[2] Tench Coxe was born in Philadelphia, in May, 1755, and, as we have mentioned in the text, was one of the earliest advocates of the cotton culture. From 1787 until his death, there was never an important industrial movement in which he was not greatly interested, or in which his name did not appear prominent. In 1794, while he was the Commissioner of Revenue, at Philadelphia, he published a large octavo volume, containing his views, as expressed in speech and writing, on the subject of the cotton culture. In 1806, he published an essay on naval power and the encouragement of manufactures. The following year he published an essay on the cultivation of cotton, and from time to time thereafter, he wrote and published his views on these subjects. He died in July, 1824, at the age of more than sixty-eight years. See next page.

[3] Page 356.

[4] It has been estimated that the entire produce of cotton, in all countries, in 1791, was four hundred and ninety millions of pounds, and that the United States produced only one twenty-fifth of the entire quantity. In the year 1855–56, the twelve cotton-growing States of the Union produced three millions, five hundred and twenty-six thousand, three hundred and sixty-two bales, of four hundred pounds each, making an aggregate of *one billion, four hundred and ten millions, five hundred and forty-four thousand, eight hundred* pounds. The whole world did not produce as much cotton as this, annually, previous to the year 1834.

[5] Page 360.

justices, who were to hold two sessions annually, at the seat of the Federal Government.[1] Circuit and district courts were also established, which had jurisdiction over certain specified cases. Each State was made a district, as were also the Territories of Kentucky[2] and Maine.[3] The districts, except Kentucky

and Maine, were grouped together into three circuits. An appeal from these lower courts to the Supreme Court of the United States, was allowed, as to points of law, in all civil cases when the matter in dispute amounted to two thousand dollars. A marshal was to be appointed by the President, for each district, having the general powers of a sheriff, who was to attend all courts, and was authorized to serve all processes. A district attorney, to act for the United States in all cases in which the Federal Government might be interested, was also to be appointed for each district. Such, in brief outline, and in general terms, was the Federal judiciary, organized at the commencement of the Government, and still in force, with slight modifications.

The next business of importance that engaged the attention of Congress,

[1] John Jay [page 379] of New York, one of the most active and acute lawyers in the country, was apppointed the first Chief Justice of the United States; and Edmund Randolph, of Virginia, was made Attorney-General. Randolph succeeded Patrick Henry as governor of Virginia, in 1786, and was very active in the Convention of 1787. See note 1, page 359. He succeeded Jefferson as Secretary of State, and died in 1813. John Rutledge [page 210], of South Carolina; James Wilson, of Pennsylvania; William Cushing, of Massachusetts; Robert H. Harrison, of Maryland; and John Blair, of Virginia, were appointed associate judges. [2] Page 377. [3] Page 452.

was the proposed amendments to the Federal Constitution, made by the minorities of the several conventions which ratified that instrument. This subject was brought forward by Madison, in justice to these minorities, and pursuant to pledges which he had found it necessary to give, in order to secure its ratification in Virginia. These amounted, in the aggregate, to one hundred and forty-seven,[1] besides separate bills of rights proposed by Virginia and New York. Many of these amendments were identical in spirit, as, for example, the nine propositions by Massachusetts were repeated by New Hampshire. And it is a singular fact, that of all the proposed amendments, not one, judged by subsequent experience, was of a vital character. How well this illustrates the profound wisdom embodied in our Constitution! Sixteen amendments were finally agreed to by Congress, ten of which were subsequently ratified by the States, and became a part of the Federal compact.[2] After a session of almost six months, Congress adjourned,[3] on the 29th of September [1789], and Washington, having appointed his cabinet council,[4] made a brief tour through the northern and eastern States, to make himself better acquainted with the people and their resources.[5]

On the 8th of January, 1790, the second session of the first Congress commenced, during which Alexander Hamilton,[6] the first Secretary of the Treasury, made some of those able financial reports which established the general line of national policy for more than twenty years. On his recommendation, the general government assumed the public foreign and domestic debt incurred by the late war,[7] and also the State debts contracted during that period. The foreign debt, including interest, due to France and to private lenders in Holland, with a small sum to Spain, amounted to $11,710,378. The domestic debt, registered and unregistered, including interest, and some claims, principally the outstanding continental money,[8] amounted to $42,414,085. Nearly one third of this was the arrears of interest. As the government certificates, continental

[1] The minority of the Pennsylvania Convention proposed 14; of Massachusetts, 9; of Maryland, 28; of South Carolina, 4; of New Hampshire, 12; of Virginia, 20; of New York, 32.

[2] See Supplement.

[3] A few days before the adjournment, a resolution was adopted, requesting the President of the United States to recommend a day of public thanksgiving and prayer, to be observed by the people of the nation, in acknowledgment of the many signal favors of the Almighty, in permitting them to establish, in peace, a free government.

GENERAL KNOX.

[4] Alexander Hamilton was appointed Secretary of the Treasury; Henry Knox, Secretary of War; and Thomas Jefferson, Secretary of Foreign Affairs. Jefferson was then United States minister at the court of France, and did not enter upon his duties until March, 1790. The office of Secretary of the Navy was not created until the presidency of Mr. Adams. Naval affairs were under the control of the Secretary of War. General Knox was one of the most efficient officers of the Revolution, having, from the beginning, the chief command of the artillery. He entered the army as captain of artillery, and rose to the rank of major-general. Note 4, page 350.

[5] Washington was everywhere received with great honors; and Trumbull, author of *M'Fingal*, wrote to his friend, Oliver Wolcott: "We have gone through all the popish grades of worship; and the President returns all fragrant with the odor of incense."

[6] Note 2, page 360

[7] Note 2, page 253. In that note the amount given is the *principal*, without the interest.

[8] Page 245.

bills, and other evidences of debt, were now held chiefly by speculators, who had purchased them at reduced rates, the idea had been put forth by prominent men, that it would be proper and expedient to apply a scale of depreciation, as in the case of the paper money toward the close of the war,[1] in liquidating these claims. But Hamilton opposed it as dishonest and impolitic, arguing, in support of the latter objection, that public credit was essential to the new Federal Government. He therefore urged that all the debts of the government should be met according to the terms of the contract. He proposed the funding of the public debt, in a fair and economical way, by which the public creditors should receive their promised six per cent. interest, until the Government should be able to pay the principal, the Secretary assuming that, in five years, the United States might effect loans at five, and even at four per cent., with which these claims might be liquidated. He proposed to have the proceeds of the post-office[2] as a sinking fund, for the gradual extinction of the debt. After much debate, the propositions of Hamilton, in general, were agreed to by Congress, on the 9th of March, 1790.[3] A system of revenue from imposts and internal excise, proposed by Hamilton, was also adopted. A petition from the Society of Friends, or Quakers, presented on the 11th of February, on the subject of slavery, caused long, and, sometimes, acrimonious debates. An act was also passed, during this session, making the District of Columbia the permanent seat of the Federal Government, after the lapse of ten years from that date.

The First Congress commenced its third session[4] in December, 1790, and before its close, measures were adopted which laid the foundations of public credit and national prosperity, deep and abiding. During the two years in which the new government had been engaged in the business of organization, a competent revenue had been provided for; the public debt, national and State, had been funded, and the interest thereon had been provided for; a national judiciary, wise in all its features, had been established; and the nation, in its own estimation and that of other States of the world, had taken a proud position in the great political family. North Carolina [Nov. 21, 1789] and Rhode Island [May 29, 1790], had already become members of the Confederacy, by ratifying the Constitution;[5] and during this session, Vermont[6] had been admitted [Feb. 18, 1791] as a sovereign State. Settlements were now rapidly spreading beyond the Alleghanies,[7] and the subject of territorial organizations

[1] Note 3, page 245. [2] Page 373.

[3] The President was authorized to borrow $12,000,000, if necessary, to pay off the foreign debt; and a new loan was to be opened, payable in certificates, of the domestic debt, at their par value, and in continental bills of credit, at the rate of one hundred for one. Congress also authorized an additional loan, payable in certificates of the State debts, to the amount of $21,500,000. These certificates were those which had been issued for services or supplies, during the war. A new board of commissioners was appointed, with full power to settle all claims on general principles of equity. [4] Note 3, page 366. [5] Page 360.

[6] Vermont was originally called the *New Hampshire Grants*, and was claimed by both New York and New Hampshire. In 1777, the people met in convention, and proclaimed the territory an independent State. After purchasing the claims of New York for $30,000, it was admitted into the Union.

[7] The first census, or enumeration of the inhabitants of the United States, was completed in 1791. The number of all sexes and colors, was 3,929,000. The number of slaves was 695,000.

was pressed upon the consideration of Congress. Already the *North-western Territory*, as we have seen,[1] had been established [July, 1787], and Tennessee had been constituted [March 26, 1790] the *Territory South-west of the Ohio.*[2]

The subject of a national currency early engaged the attention of Congress, and at the commencement of the last session of the First Congress, a bill for the establishment of a national bank was introduced into the Senate, in accordance with the suggestion and plan of Hamilton. At that time the whole banking capital in the United States was only $2,000,000, invested in the *Bank of North America*, at Philadelphia, established by Robert Morris ;[3] the *Bank of New York*, in New York city, and the *Bank of Massachusetts*, in Boston. The charter was limited to twenty years ; its location was to be in the city of Philadelphia, and its management to be intrusted to twenty-five directors. Although chartered in January, 1791, the National Bank did not commence its operations, in corporate form, until in February, 1794, when it began with a capital of $10,000,000.

Early in the first session of the second Congress, the important subject of a national mint received the attention of the representatives of the people. That subject had been frequently discussed. As early as 1782, the topic of coins and currency had been presented to the Continental Congress, by Gouverneur Morris, in an able report, written at the request of Robert Morris. In 1784, Mr. Jefferson, as chairman of a committee appointed for the purpose, submitted a report, agreeing with Morris in regard to a decimal system, but entirely disagreeing with him in the details.[4] He proposed to strike four coins, namely, a golden piece of the value of ten dollars ; a dollar, in silver ; a tenth of a dollar, in silver ; and a hundredth of a dollar, in copper. In 1785, Congress adopted Mr. Jefferson's report, and made legal provision, the following year, for a coinage upon that basis. This was the origin of our *cent*, *dime*, *dollar*, and *eagle*. Already several of the States had issued copper coins ;[5] but the Federal Constitution vested the right of coinage solely in the Federal Government. The establishment of a Mint was delayed, however, and no special action in that direction was taken until 1790, when Mr. Jefferson, then Secretary of

---

[1] Page 362.

[2] The subject of the public lands of the United States has always been one of interest. The first act of Congress, on the subject of limited sales, was in accordance with a scheme proposed by Hamilton, in 1790, which provided in some degree for the protection of small purchasers. Previous to that, not less than a tract of four thousand acres could be purchased. This was calculated to make labor subservient to wealth, in new settlements. Hamilton's scheme was highly approved. The minimum price of public land, previous to 1800, was two dollars per acre ; since then, one dollar and twenty-five cents. The extent of the public domain has greatly increased, by accessions, within a few years. At the close of 1855, there remained unsold about 96,000,000 of acres of surveyed public domain, and of the unsurveyed, about 136,000,000 of acres, worth, in the aggregate, about $276,000,000. The average cost to the government, per acre, of acquiring title, surveying, selling, and managing, is about 22 cents per acre, while it sells at $1.25 per acre, or a net profit of $1.03.

[3] Note 3, page 263.

[4] Morris attempted to harmonize the moneys of all the States. Starting with an ascertained fraction as an unit, for a divisor, he proposed the following table of moneys:

Ten units to be equal to one penny.
Ten pence to one bill.
Ten bills one dollar (or about seventy-five cents of our currency).
Ten dollars one crown.

[5] Note 4, page 122.

State, urged the matter upon the attention of Congress. Still there was delay, until on the 2d of April, 1792, laws were enacted for the establishment of a Mint. During three years from that time, its operations were chiefly experimental, and long debates were had concerning the devices for the new coins.[1] The Mint was finally put into full operation, in 1795,[2] and has continued to increase in its issues of coin, ever since.[3]

A bill for the organization of a post-office system, was passed during the same session that measures were adopted for the establishment of a Mint. Very soon after the commencement of the first session of the first Congress, a letter was received from Ebenezer Hazzard [July 17, 1789], then postmaster-general under the old Confederation, suggesting the importance of some new regulations for that department. A bill for the temporary establishment of the post office was passed soon afterward. The subject was brought up, from time to time, until the present system was organized in 1792. The postmaster-general was not made a cabinet officer until the first year [1829] of President Jackson's administration.[4]

British agents on the north-western frontier continued to tamper with the Indians, and excite them to hostilities against the United States, for several years after the peace of 1783.[5] And, contrary to the terms of that treaty, the British held possession of western posts belonging to the United States. These facts caused a prevalent belief that the British government yet hoped for an opportunity to bring the new Republic back to colonial dependence. The public mind in America became excited, and the fact, that Sir John Johnston[6] was the British Indian agent on that frontier, and Sir Guy Carleton (then Lord Dorchester) was again governor of Canada,[7] strengthened that opinion and apprehension. Finally, in the spring of 1790, the fostered discontents of the Indians were developed into open hostilities. Attempts at pacific arrangements were fruitless, and General Harmer was sent into the Indian country north of the present Cincinnati, with quite a strong force, to desolate their villages and

---

[1] The Senate proposed the head of the *President* of the United States who should occupy the chair at the time of the coinage. In the House, the head of *Liberty* was suggested, as being less aristocratic than that of the President—having less the stamp of royalty. The head of Liberty was finally adopted.

[2] The first mint was located in Philadelphia, and remained the sole issuer of coin, in the United States, until 1835, when a branch was established in each of the States of Georgia, North Carolina, and Louisiana—in Charlotte, Dahlonega, and New Orleans. These three branches went into operation in the years 1837–'38.

[3] From 1793 to 1795, the value of the whole issue was a little more than a million and a half of dollars. For the last three or four years, the amount has exceeded sixty millions annually. Previous to the year 1830, almost the entire supply of gold for our coinage was furnished by foreign countries. North Carolina was the first State of the Union that sent gold to the mint from its mines. Since then, almost every State has made contributions, some very small. But the youngest State of all, California [See page 497], has outstripped them all, having sent to the mint, at the close of 1854, gold to the amount of $264,250,000 of the $273,609,000 worth, the amount of the entire deposit of domestic gold. Altogether, the yield of the California mines now [1856] may be fairly estimated, in round numbers, at, at least, $500,000,000.

[4] Page 459. The operations of the post-office department increased very rapidly year after year. In 1795, the number of post-office routes was 453 over 13,207 miles of travel. The revenue of the department was $160,620. Now [1856] the number of routes is over 25,000; the number of miles traveled, full 220,000; and the revenue nearly $7,000,000.

[5] Page 348. [6] Note 2, page 278. [7] Page 240.

crops, as Sullivan did those of the Senecas in 1779.[1] In this he succeeded, but in two battles [Oct. 17 and 22, 1790], near the present village of Fort Wayne, in Indiana, he was defeated, with considerable loss. The following year, an expedition of Kentucky volunteers, under General Scott, marched against the Indians on the Wabash. General Wilkinson led a second expedition against them, in July following, and in September, General St. Clair,[2] then governor of the North-west Territory, marched into the Indian country, with two thousand men. While in camp near the northern line of Darke county, Ohio, on the borders of Indiana, he was surprised and defeated [Nov. 4, 1791] by the Indians, with a loss of about six hundred men.

The defeat of St. Clair produced great alarm on the whole north-western frontier. Even the people of Pittsburg[3] did not feel secure, and the border settlers called loudly for help. Fortunately the Indians did not follow up the advantage they had gained, and for a while hostilities ceased. Commissioners were appointed to treat with them, but through the interference of British officials, their negotiations were fruitless. General Wayne[4] had been appointed, in the mean while, to succeed St. Clair in military command, and apprehending that the failure of the negotiations would be followed by an immediate attack upon the frontier settlements, he marched into the Indian country in the autumn of 1793. He spent the winter at Greenville,[5] near the place of St. Clair's defeat, where he built Fort Recovery. The following summer [1794] he pushed forward to the Maumee River, and built Fort Defiance;[6] and on the St. Mary's he erected Fort Adams as an intermediate post. On the 16th of August he went down the Maumee, with three thousand men, and not far from the present Maumee City,[7] he fought and defeated the Indians, on the 20th of the same month. He then laid waste their country, and after a successful campaign of about ninety days, he went into winter quarters at Greenville. There, the following year, the chiefs and warriors of the western tribes, in all about eleven hundred, met [August 3, 1795] commissioners of the United States, made a treaty of peace, and ceded to the latter a large tract of land in the present States of Michigan[8] and Indiana. After that, the United States had very little trouble with the western Indians until just before the breaking out of the war of 1812–15.[9]

Party spirit, which had been engendered during the discussions of the Federal Constitution,[10] gradually assumed distinct forms, and during the second session of the second Congress, it became rampant among the people, as well as in the national legislature. Hamilton and Jefferson, the heads of distinct departments[11] in Washington's cabinet, differed materially concerning important public measures, and then, under the respective leadership of those statesmen,

---

[1] Page 304. [2] Page 276. [3] Page 205. [4] Page 298. [5] In Darke county, Ohio.

[6] At the junction of the Au Glaize with the Maumee River, in the south-east part of Williams county, Ohio.

[7] In the town of Waynesfield. The British then occupied a fort at the Maumee Rapids, near by.

[8] The British held possession of Detroit, and nearly all Michigan, until 1796. See page 380.

[9] Page 409. [10] Page 360. [11] Page 367.

WAYNE'S DEFEAT OF THE INDIANS.

were drawn those lines of party distinction known as *Federalist* and *Republican*, which continued for a quarter of a century. The *Federalist* party was composed of those who favored great concentration of power in the general government. The *Republicans*, on the contrary, were for diffusing power among the people. Here were antagonistic points of great difference, and the warfare between the parties was acrimonious in the extreme.

During the summer of 1792, very little of public interest occurred, except the admission [June 1] of Kentucky[1] into the Union, but the marshalling of forces for the presidential election, which was to take place in the autumn. Washington yearned for the quiet of private life, and had expressed his determination to withdraw from public station on the expiration of his presidential term; but it was made evident to his mind, that the great majority of the people desired his continuance in office, and that the public safety demanded it. Under these circumstances, he consented to be a candidate, and he and Adams were re-elected by large majorities.

Yet the Republican party was daily gaining strength, partly from developments within the body politic of the United States, and partly from events then transpiring in Europe. A bloody revolution was in progress in France. The people there had abolished monarchy, and murdered their king, and the new Republic in name (a political chaos in reality), having the avowed sympathies of the Republican party in America,[2] sent M. Genet[3] as its minister to the United States, to obtain the co-operation of the American people. The French Republic had declared war against England, Spain, and Holland, and needed transatlantic assistance. Remembering the recent alliance,[4] and sympathizing with all efforts for popular freedom, the Republican party here, and also many of the Federalists, received Genet (who arrived at Charleston, South Carolina, in April, 1793) with open arms, and espoused his cause.

But Genet's zeal outstripped his prudence, and defeated his plans. Without waiting for an expression of opinions or intentions from the government of the United States, he began to fit out privateers[5] in our ports, to depredate upon English, Dutch, and Spanish property;[6] and when Washington prudently issued [May 9, 1793] a proclamation, declaring it to be the duty and the inter-

---

[1] Kentucky, which had been settled chiefly by Virginians, and was claimed as a part of the territory of that State, was now erected into a sovereign member of the confederation. Its first settlement, as we have seen [note 2, page 300], was at Boonesboro', by Daniel Boone, in 1775.

[2] There was a general burst of enthusiasm in the United States, on receipt of the intelligence of the advent of Liberty in France, and public demonstrations of it were made in several places. In Boston, an ox, roasted whole, was placed upon a car drawn by sixteen horses, and with the American and French flags displayed from its horns, was paraded through the streets, followed by carts, bearing bread and two hogsheads of punch, which were distributed among the people. A civic feast was held at Faneuil Hall, over which Samuel Adams [note 1, page 221] presided. In Philadelphia the anniversary of the French alliance [page 283] was celebrated by a public dinner, at which General Mifflin [page 352] presided; and in other places festivals were held.

[3] Edmund Charles Genet was the son of a distinguished public man in France. He married, in this country, a daughter of Governor George Clinton [note 5, page 350], and remained in the United States. He died at Greenbush, opposite Albany, in 1834, aged about seventy-two years.

[4] Page 283.

[5] Note 1, page 246.

[6] These cruisers brought captured vessels into our ports, and French consuls actually held courts of admiralty, and authorized the sale of the prizes. All this was done before Genet was recognized as a minister by the American government.

est of the people of the United States to preserve a strict neutrality toward the contending powers of Europe, Genet persisted, and tried to excite hostility between our people and their government. Washington finally requested and obtained his recal, and Fauchet, who succeeded him in 1794, was instructed to assure the President that the French government disapproved of Genet's conduct. No doubt the prudence and firmness of Washington, at this time, saved our Republic from utter ruin.

A popular outbreak in western Pennsylvania, known in history as *The Whiskey Insurrection*, gave the new government much trouble in 1794. An excise law, passed in 1791, which imposed duties on domestic distilled liquors, was very unpopular. A new act, passed in the spring of 1794, was equally unpopular; and when, soon after the adjournment of Congress, officers were sent to enforce it in the western districts of Pennsylvania, they were resisted by the people, in arms. The insurrection became general throughout all that region, and in the vicinity of Pittsburg many outrages were committed. Buildings were burned, mails were robbed, and government officers were insulted and abused. At one time there were between six and seven thousand insurgents under arms. The local militia would have been utterly impotent to restore order, if their aid had been given. Indeed, most of the militia assembled in response to a call made by the leaders of the insurgents, and these composed a large portion of the "rebels." The insurgent spirit extended into the border counties of Virginia; and the President and his cabinet, perceiving, with alarm, this imitation of the lawlessness of French politics, took immediate steps to crush the growing hydra. The President first issued two proclamations [August 7, and September 25], but without effect. After due consideration, and the exhaustion of all peaceable means, he ordered out a large body of the militia of Virginia, Maryland, Pennsylvania, and New Jersey, who marched to the insurgent district, in October [1794], under the command of General Henry Lee, then governor of Virginia.[1] This last argument was effectual; and soon this insurrection, like that of Shays's, of Massachusetts, some years earlier,[2] which threatened the stability of the Federal Government, was allayed.

Another cloud was now rising in the political horizon. While these internal commotions were disturbing the public tranquillity, a bitter feeling was growing up between the American and British governments. Each accused the other of infractions of the treaty of 1783,[3] and the disputes, daily assuming a more bitter tone, threatened to involve the two nations in another war. The Americans complained that no indemnification had been made for negroes carried away at the close of the Revolution;[4] that the British held military posts on their frontiers, contrary to the treaty;[5] that British emissaries had excited the hostility of the Indians;[6] and that, to retaliate on France, the English had

---

[1] Page 333. [2] Page 353. [3] Page 348.

[4] During the last two years of the war in the Carolinas and Georgia, and at the final evacuation, the British plundered many plantations, and sold the negroes in the West Indies.

[5] Note 8, page 374. [6] Page 373.

captured our neutral vessels, and impressed our seamen into the British service.[1] The British complained that stipulations concerning the property of loyalists,[2] and also in relation to debts contracted in England before the Revolution, had not been complied with. In order to avert an event so very undesirable as a war with Great Britain, the President proposed to send a special envoy to the British court, in hopes of bringing to an amicable settlement, all matters in dispute between the two governments. The Federal Legislature approved of it,

and on the 19th of April, 1794, John Jay[3] was appointed an envoy extraordinary for the purpose.

The special minister of the United States was received with great courtesy in England, where he arrived in June; and he negotiated a treaty which, at the time, was not very satisfactory to a large portion of his countrymen. It honestly provided for the collection of debts here, by British creditors, which had

[1] This practice was one of the causes which finally produced a war between the two nations, in 1812. See page 409.

[2] The loyalists, or Tories [note 4, page 226], who had fled from the country during the progress, or at the close of the War for Independence, and whose property had been confiscated, endeavoured to regain their estates, and also indemnity for their other losses. The British government finally paid to these sufferers more than $15,000,000.

[3] John Jay was a descendant of a Huguenot family [page 49], and was born in the city of New York in 1745. He was early in the ranks of active patriots, and rendered very important services during the Revolution. After the war he was one of the most efficient of our countrymen in laying the foundations of our Federal Government, and of establishing the civil government of his native State, of which he was chief magistrate at one time. He retired from public life in 1801, and died in 1829, at the age of eighty-four years. His residence was at Bedford, Westchester county, New York.

been contracted before the Revolution, but it procured no redress for those who had lost negroes. It secured indemnity for unlawful captures on the seas, and the evacuation of the forts on the frontiers (yet held by the British), by the 1st of June, 1796. In order to secure certain points of great importance, Jay was

compelled to yield others; and he finally signed a treaty, defective, in some things, and objectionable in others, but the best that could then be obtained. The treaty gave rise to violent debates in Congress,[1] and in State Legislatures, but was ratified by the Senate on the 24th of June, 1795.[2] The wisdom,

[1] The debates, on that occasion, developed talent of the highest order, and present a memorable epoch in the history of American politics and statesmanship. Albert Gallatin then established his title to the leadership of the opposition in the House of Representatives, while Fisher Ames, in a speech of wonderful power, in favor of the treaty and the Administration, won for himself the laurels of an unrivaled orator. He was then in feeble health; and when he arose to speak, thin and pale, he could hardly support himself on his feet, and his voice was feeble. Strength seemed to come as he warmed with the subject, and his eloquence and wisdom poured forth as from a mighty and inexhaustible fountain. So powerful was his speech, that a member opposed to him moved that the question on which he had spoken should be postponed until the next day, "that they should not act under the influence of an excitement of which their calm judgment might not approve." In allusion to this speech, John Adams bluntly said: "There was n't a dry eye in the House, except some of the jackasses that occasioned the necessity of the oratory." Fisher Ames was born in Dedham, Massachusetts, in April, 1756. His health was delicate from infancy. He was so precocious that he commenced the study of Latin when six years of age, and was admitted to Harvard College at the age of twelve. He chose the law for a profession, and soon stood at the head of the bar in his native district. He was a warm advocate of the Federal Constitution. He was the first representative of his district in the Federal Congress. He died on the 4th of July, 1808, at the age of forty-eight years.

[2] Great excitement succeeded. In several cities mobs threatened personal violence to the sup-

and policy, and true patriotism of Mr. Jay were soon made manifest. In October following, a treaty was concluded with Spain, by which the boundaries between the Spanish territories of Louisiana and Florida, and the United States, were defined. That treaty also secured to the United States the free navigation of the Mississippi, and the use of New Orleans, as a port, for ten years.

As soon as one excitement was fairly allayed, causes for others appeared; and during the whole time of Washington's administration of eight years, when the policy of the new government had to be established, and its machinery put in operation, the greatest wisdom, circumspection, and conservative action, on the part of officials, were continually demanded. Difficulties appeared like little clouds on the distant horizon, sometimes as mere specks, at others, in alarming shapes. These were chiefly in connection with trade, especially in foreign lands. American commerce was rapidly expanding, and now began to find its way into the Mediterranean Sea. There it was met by Algerine pirates, who seized the merchandise, and held the seamen in captivity, in order to procure ransom-money. These depredations, which finally gave rise to efforts to organize a navy, had continued many years before the government took active measures to suppress them. President Washington called the attention of Congress to the subject, toward the close of 1790; and at the same time, Jefferson, then Secretary of State, gave many interesting details, in his annual report, on the subject of these piracies. A commissioner was sent to treat with the Dey, or Governor, of Algiers on the subject, but that semi-barbarian robber argued in reply: "If I were to make peace with everybody, what should I do with my corsairs? what should I do with my soldiers? They would take off my head for the want of other prizes, not being able to live on their miserable allowance."

In the spring of 1794, Congress, on account of these depredations, passed an Act to provide for a naval armament, and appropriated almost seven hundred thousand dollars for the purpose. But the United States, in the absence of the proposed navy, was compelled to make a treaty of peace in the autumn of 1795 [November 28], with the Dey of Algiers, by which an annual tribute was to be given for the redemption of captives, in accordance with the long-established usages of European nations.[1] This was humiliating, but could not then be avoided. Congress had given the President power to provide by purchase or otherwise, and equip, several vessels. To this end he put forth his energies immediately, and in July [1794], he commissioned captains and superintendents, naval constructors and navy agents, six each, and ordered the construction of six ships. The treaty with the Dey of Algiers caused work on

porters of the treaty. Mr Jay was burned in effigy [note 6, page 215], Mr. Hamilton was stoned at a public meeting, and the British minister at Philadelphia was insulted.

[1] Between the years 1785 and 1793, the Algerine pirates captured and carried into Algiers, fifteen American vessels, used the property, and made one hundred and eighty officers and seamen slaves of the most revolting kind. In 1795, the United States agreed, by treaty, to pay eight hundred thousand dollars for captives, then alive, and in addition, to make the dey, or governor, a present of a frigate worth a hundred thousand dollars. An annual tribute of twenty-three thousand dollars was also to be paid. This was complied with until the breaking out of the war of 1812. See pages 390 and 445.

these vessels to be suspended in 1795. Soon the folly of not completing the little navy, so well begun, was made manifest, when British cruisers commenced the practice of taking seamen from American vessels, and impressing them into the English service.[1] The ships of the French Republic soon afterward commenced depredations upon American commerce; and in 1797, when war with that government seemed inevitable,[2] Congress, on the urgent recommendation of President Adams, caused the frigates *United States*, *Constellation*, and *Constitution* to be completed, equipped, and sent to sea. This was the commencement of the American navy,[3] which, in after years, though weak in numbers, performed many brilliant exploits. From this time the navy became the cherished arm of the national defense; and chiefly through its instrumentality, the name and power of the United States began to be properly appreciated in Europe, at the beginning of the present century.

Now [1796], the administration of Washington was drawing to a close. It had been one of vast importance and incessant action. All disputes with foreign nations, except France,[4] had been adjusted; government credit was established, and the nation was highly prosperous.[5] The embryos of new empires beyond the Alleghanies, had been planted; and the last year of his administration was signalized by the admission [June, 1796] of Tennessee into the Union of States, making the number of confederated republics, sixteen.

During the closing months of Washington's administration, the first great struggle among the people of the United States, for ascendancy between the *Federalists* and *Republicans*,[6] took place. The only man on whom the nation now could possibly unite, was about to retire to private life. He issued his admirable *Farewell Address* to his countrymen—that address so full of wisdom, patriotism, and instruction—early in the autumn of 1796 [September 19], and then the people were fully assured that some other man must be chosen to fill his place. There was very little time for preparation or electioneering, for the choice must be made in November following. Activity the most extraordinary appeared among politicians, in every part of the Union. The Federalists nominated John Adams for the high office of Chief Magistrate, and the Republicans nominated Thomas Jefferson for the same. The contest was fierce, and party spirit, then in its youthful vigor, was implacable. The result was a vic-

---

[1] Page 401. [2] Page 385.

[3] Congress had created the office of Secretary of the Navy, as an executive department, and on the 30th of April, 1798, Benjamin Stoddart, of Georgetown, in the District of Columbia, was appointed to that chair. Hitherto the business of the war and navy departments had been performed by the Secretary of War.

[4] The French government was highly displeased because of the treaty made with England, by Mr. Jay, and even adopted hostile measures toward the United States. It wanted the Americans to show an active participation with the French in hatred of the English, and therefore the strict neutrality observed by Washington, was exceedingly displeasing to the French Committee of Public Safety. The conclusion of the treaty with Algiers, independently of French intervention, and the success of the negotiation with Spain, excited the jealousy of the French rulers. In a word, because the United States, having the strength, assumed the right to stand alone, the French were offended, and threatened the grown-up child with personal chastisement.

[5] Commerce had wonderfully expanded. The exports had, in five years, increased from nineteen millions of dollars to more than fifty-six millions of dollars, and the imports in about the same ratio.

[6] Page 377.

tory for both parties—Adams being elected President, and Jefferson, having the next highest number of votes, was chosen Vice-President.[1] On the 4th of March, 1797, Washington retired from office, and Adams was inaugurated the second President of the United States. The great leader of the armies in the War for Independence was never again enticed from the quiet pursuits of agriculture at Mount Vernon, to the performance of public duties.

CHAPTER II.

ADAMS'S ADMINISTRATION. [1797—1801.]

JOHN ADAMS[2] was in the sixty-second year of his age when, dressed in a full suit of pearl-colored broadcloth, and with powdered hair, he stood in Independence Hall [March 4, 1797], in Philadelphia, and took the oath of office,

John Adams

[1] The whole number of electoral votes [see note 1, page 361] was one hundred and thirty-eight, making seventy necessary to a choice. John Adams received seventy-one, and Jefferson sixty seven.

[2] John Adams was born at Braintree, Massachusetts, in October, 1735. He chose the law as a profession, but being a good writer and fair speaker, he entered the political field quite early, and with Hancock, Otis, and others, he took an active part in the earlier Revolutionary movements, in Boston and vicinity. He was a member of the Continental Congress, from which he was transferred to the important post of a minister to the French and other courts in Europe. He was one of the most industrious men in Congress. In the course of the eighteen months preceding his de-

as President of the United States, administered by Chief Justice Ellsworth.[1] He was pledged, by his acts and declarations, to the general policy of Washington's administration, and he adopted, as his own, the cabinet council left by his predecessor.[2] He came into office at a period of great trial for the Republic. Party spirit and sectional differences were rife in its bosom, and the relations of the United States with France were becoming more and more unfriendly.

C C Pinckney

Already Charles Cotesworth Pinckney, the American minister at the French court, had been ordered to leave their territory by the Directory, then the supreme executive power in France.[3] Depredations upon American commerce had also been authorized by them; and the French minister in the United

parture for Europe, Mr. Adams had been on ninety different committees, and was chairman of *thirty-five* of them. He was, at one time, intrusted with no less than six missions abroad, namely, to treat for peace with Great Britain; to make a commercial treaty with Great Britain; to negotiate the same with the States General of Holland; the same with the Prince of Orange; to pledge the faith of the United States to the Armed Neutrality; and to negotiate a loan of ten millions of dollars. He was a signer of the Declaration of Independence; and died on the fiftieth anniversary of that great act [1826], with the words "Independence forever!" upon his lips. He was in the ninety-second year of his age. See page 459.

[1] Page 360.

[2] Timothy Pickering, Secretary of State; Oliver Wolcott, Secretary of the Treasury; James M'Henry, Secretary of War; and Charles Lee, Attorney-General. Washington's first cabinet had all resigned during the early part of his second term of office (the President is elected for four years), and the above-named gentlemen were appointed during 1795 and 1796.

[3] The Republican government of France was administered by a council called the *Directory*. It was composed of five members, who ruled in connection with two representative bodies, called, respectively, the *Council of Ancients*, and the *Council of Five Hundred*. The *Directory* was the head, or executive power of the government.

States had grossly insulted the government. President Adams perceived the necessity of prompt and energetic action, and he convened an extraordinary session of Congress, on the 15th of May. With the concurrence of the Senate, the President appointed [July] three envoys,[1] with Pinckney at their head, to proceed to France, and endeavor to adjust all difficulties. They met at Paris, in October, but were refused an audience with the Directory, unless they should first pay a large sum of money into the French treasury. Overtures for this purpose were made by unofficial agents. The demand was indignantly refused; and then it was that Pinckney uttered that noble sentiment, "Millions for defense, but not one cent for tribute!" The two Federalist envoys (Marshall and Pinckney) were ordered out of the country, while Mr. Gerry, who was a Republican, and whose party sympathized with the measures of France, was allowed to remain. The indignant people of the United States censured Mr. Gerry severely for remaining. He, too, soon found that nothing could be accomplished with the French rulers, and he returned home.

The fifth Congress assembled at Philadelphia, on the 13th of November, 1797. Perceiving the vanity of further attempts at negotiation with France, Congress, and the country generally, began to prepare for war. Quite a large standing army was authorized [May, 1798]; and as Washington approved of the measure, he was appointed [July] its commander-in-chief, with General Alexander Hamilton as his first lieutenant. Washington consented to accept the office only on condition that General Hamilton should be the acting commander-in-chief, for the retired President was unwilling to enter into active military service again. A naval armament, and the capture of French vessels of war, was authorized; and a naval department, as we have observed,[2] with Benjamin Stoddart at its head, was created. Although there was no actual declaration of war made by either party, yet hostilities were commenced on the ocean, and a vessel of each nation suffered capture;[3] but the army was not summoned to the field.

The proud tone of the French Directory was humbled by the dignified and decided measures adopted by the United States, and that body made overtures for a peaceful adjustment of difficulties. President Adams immediately appointed [Feb. 26, 1799] three envoys[4] to proceed to France, and negotiate for

---

[1] Charles Cotesworth Pinckney, Elbridge Gerry, and John Marshall. Pinckney was an active patriot in South Carolina during the Revolution. He was born in Charleston, in February, 1746, and was eduated in England. He studied law there, and on his return to his native country, in 1769, he commenced a successful professional career in Charleston. He took part early in Republican movements, held military offices during the War for Independence, and when war with France seemed certain, in 1797, Washington appointed him next to Hamilton in command. He died, in August, 1825, in the eightieth year of his age. Gerry was one of the signers of the Declaration of Independence, and Marshall had been an active patriot and soldier. See page 351. The latter, as Chief Justice of the United States, administered the oath of office to several Presidents.

[2] Page 382.

[3] The United States frigate *Constellation*, captured the French frigate *L'Insurgente*, in February, 1799. That frigate had already taken the American schooner *Retaliation*. On the 1st of February, 1800, the *Constellation* had an action with the French frigate *La Vengeance*, but escaped capture after a loss of one hundred and sixty men, in killed and wounded.

[4] W. V. Murray, Oliver Ellsworth, and Patrick Henry. Mr. Henry declined, and William R. Davie [note 5, page 318], of North Carolina, took his place.

peace, but when they arrived, the weak Directory was no more. The government was in the hands of Napoleon Bonaparte [Nov. 1799] as First Consul,[1] whose audacity and energy now saved France from anarchy and utter ruin. He promptly received the United States embassadors, concluded a treaty [Sept. 30, 1800], and gave such assurances of friendly feelings that, on the return of the ministers, the provisional army of the United States, whose illustrious commander-in-chief had, in the mean while, been removed by death, was disbanded.

Two unpopular domestic measures were adopted in the summer of 1798, known as the *Alien* and *Sedition* laws. The first authorized the President to expel from the country any alien (not a citizen) who should be suspected of conspiring against the Republic. An apology for the law was, that it was computed that there were more than thirty thousand Frenchmen in the United States, all of whom were devoted to their native country, and were mostly associated, by clubs or otherwise. Besides these, there were computed to be in the country at least fifty thousand persons who had been subjects of Great Britain, some of whom had found it unsafe to remain at home. The Sedition law authorized the suppression of publications calculated to weaken the authority of the government. At that period there were two hundred newspapers published in the United States, of which about one hundred and seventy-five were in favor of the federal administration; the remainder were chiefly under the control of aliens. These measures were unpopular, because they might lead to great abuses. In Virginia and Kentucky, the legislatures declared them to be decidedly unconstitutional, and they were finally repealed.

The nation suffered a sad bereavement near the close of the last year of the century. Washington, the greatest and best-beloved of its military and civil leaders, died at Mount Vernon on the 14th of December, 1799, when almost sixty-eight years of age. No event since the foundation of the government, had made such an impression on the public mind. The national grief was sincere, and party spirit was hushed into silence at his grave. All hearts united in homage to the memory of him who was properly regarded as the FATHER OF HIS COUNTRY. Congress was then in session at Philadelphia, and when Judge Marshall[2] announced the sad event, both Houses[3] immediately adjourned for the day. On re-assembling the next day, appropriate resolutions were passed, and the President was directed to write a letter of condolence to Mrs. Washington,[4] in the name of Congress. Impressive funeral ceremonies were

---

[1] Bonaparte, Cambaceres, and the Abbe Sieyes became the ruling power in France, with the title of Consuls, after the first had overthrown the Directory. Bonaparte was the First Consul, and was, in fact, an autocrat, or one who rules by his own will. [2] Page 351. [3] Note 3, page 366.

[4] Martha Dandridge, who first married Daniel Parke Custis, and afterward, while yet a young widow, was wedded to Colonel Washington, was born in Kent county, Virginia, in 1732, about three months later than her illustrious husband. Her first husband died when she was about twenty-five years of age, leaving her with two children, and a large fortune in lands and money. She was married to Colonel Washington, in January, 1759. She was ever worthy of such a husband; and while he was President of the United States, she presided with dignity over the executive mansion, both in New York and Philadelphia. When her husband died, she said: "'Tis well; all is now over; I shall soon follow him; I have no more trials to pass through." In little less than thirty months afterward, she was laid in the family vault at Mount Vernon. Her grandson, and adopted son of Washington (also the last surviving executor of his will) is yet [December, 1856] living on the banks of the Potomac, opposite Washington City.

observed by that body, and throughout the country.[1] General Henry Lee,[2] of Virginia, on the invitation of Congress, delivered [December 26, 1799] an eloquent funeral oration before the national legislature; and the recommendation of Congress, for the people of the United States to wear crape on their left arms for thirty days, was generally complied with. The whole nation put on tokens of mourning.

M Washington

The death of Washington also made a profound impression in Europe. To the people there, who were aspiring for freedom, it seemed as if a bright star had disappeared from the firmament of their hopes. Rulers, also, joined in demonstrations of respect. Soon after the event of his death was known in France, Bonaparte, then First Consul,[3] rendered unusual honors to his name. On the 9th of February [1800], he issued the following order of the day to the army: "Washington is dead! This great man fought against tyranny; he established the liberties of his country. His memory will always be dear to the French people, as it will be to all free men of the two worlds; and especially to French soldiers, who, like him and the American soldiers, have combatted for liberty and equality." Bonaparte also ordered, that during ten days black crape should be suspended from all the standards and flags throughout the French Republic. Splendid ceremonies in the *Champs de Mars*, and a funeral oration in the *Hôtel des Invalides*, were also given, at both of which

[1] Congress resolved to erect a mausoleum, or monument, at Washington City, to his memory, but the resolution has never been carried into effect. A magnificent one, composed of white marble, is now in course of erection there, to be paid for by individual subscriptions.

[2] Note 2, page 333. [3] Note 1, page 395.

the First Consul, and all the civil and military authorities of the capital were present. Lord Bridport, commander of a British fleet of almost sixty vessels, lying at Torbay, on the coast of France, when he heard of the death of Washington, lowered his flag half-mast, and this example was followed by the whole fleet. And from that time until the present, the name of Washington has inspired increasing reverence at home and abroad, until now it may be said that the praise of him fills the whole earth.

After the close of the difficulties with France, very little of general interest occurred during the remainder of Mr. Adams's administration, except the removal of the seat of the Federal government to the District of Columbia,[1] in the summer of 1800; the admission into the Union [May, 1800] of the country between the western frontier of Georgia and the Mississippi River, as the *Mississippi Territory;* and the election of a new President of the United States. Now, again, came a severe struggle between the Federalists and Republicans, for political power.[2] The former nominated Mr. Adams and Charles Cotesworth Pinckney,[3] for President; the latter nominated Thomas Jefferson and Aaron Burr,[4] for the same office. In consequence of dissensions among the Federalist leaders, and the rapid development of ultra-democratic ideas among the people, the Republican party was successful. Jefferson and Burr had an equal number of electoral votes. The task of choosing, therefore, was transferred to the House of Representatives, according to the provisions of the Federal Constitution. The choice finally fell upon Mr. Jefferson, after thirty-five ballotings; and Mr. Burr was proclaimed Vice-President.

During the year 1800, the last of Adams's administration, the second enumeration of the inhabitants of the United States took place. The population was then five millions, three hundred and nineteen thousand, seven hundred and sixty-two—an increase of one million, four hundred thousand in ten years. The Federal revenue, which amounted to four millions, seven hundred and seventy-one thousand dollars in 1790, was increased to almost thirteen millions in 1800.

CHAPTER III.

JEFFERSON'S ADMINISTRATION. [1801—1809].

Thomas Jefferson,[5] the third President of the United States, was in the fifty-eighth year of his age when, on the 4th of March, 1801, he was duly

---

[1] Page 371. The District is a tract ten miles square on each side of the Potomac, ceded to the United States by Maryland and Virginia in 1790. The city of Washington was laid out there in 1791, and the erection of the Capitol was commenced in 1793, when [April 18] President Washington laid the corner stone of the north wing, with Masonic honors. The two wings were completed in 1808, and these were burned by the British in 1814. See page 436. The central portion of the Capitol was completed in 1827, the wings having been repaired soon after the conflagration. Altogether it covered an area of a little more than an acre and a half of ground. In course of time it became too small, and now [1856] an extension of it is in progress. The addition is in the form of wings, north and south, projecting both east and west beyond the main building.

[2] Page 377. [3] Note 1, page 385. [4] Note 4, page 241, and page 397.

[5] Thomas Jefferson was born in Albemarle county, Virginia, in April, 1743. He was educated

inaugurated the Chief Magistrate of the Republic, in the new Capitol, at Washington City. His inaugural speech, which was looked for with great anxiety, as a foreshadowing of the policy of the new President, was manly and conservative, and it allayed many apprehensions of his opponents. From its tone, they

Th: Jefferson

imagined that few of the Federal office-holders would be disturbed; but in this they soon found themselves mistaken. The Federal party, while in power, having generally excluded Republicans from office, Jefferson felt himself justified in giving places to his own political friends. He therefore made many removals from official station throughout the country; and then was commenced the second act in the system of political proscription,[1] which has not always proved wise or salutary. He retained, for a short time, Mr. Adams's Secretaries of the Treasury and Navy (Samuel Dexter and Benjamin Stoddart), but called

---

at William and Mary College, studied law with the eminent George Wythe, and had his patriotism first inflamed by listening to Patrick Henry's famous speech [note 1, page 214] against the Stamp Act. He first appeared in public life in the Virginia Assembly, in 1769, and was one of the most active workers in that body, until sent to perform more important duties in the Continental Congress. The inscription upon his monument, written by himself, tells of the most important of his public labors: "Here lies buried THOMAS JEFFERSON, Author of the Declaration of Independence; of the Statute of Virginia for religious freedom; and Father of the University of Virginia." He was governor of his own State, and a foreign minister. He lived until the fiftieth anniversary of the Declaration of Independence [July 4, 1826], and at almost the same hour when the spirit of Adams took its flight [page 457], his also departed from the body, when he was at the age of eighty-three years.

[1] Page 461.

Republicans to fill the other seats in his cabinet.[1] He set vigorously at work to reform public abuses, as far as was in his power; and so conciliatory were his expressed views in reference to the great body of his opponents, that many Federalists joined the Republican ranks, and became bitter denouncers of their former associates and their principles.

President Jefferson's administration was signalized at the beginning by the repeal of the Excise Act,[2] and other obnoxious and unpopular laws. His suggestions concerning the reduction of the diplomatic corps, hauling up of the navy in ordinary, the abolition of certain offices, and the revision of the judiciary, were all taken into consideration by Congress, and many advances in jurisprudence were made. Vigor and enlightened views marked his course; and even his political opponents confessed his forecast and wisdom, in many things. During his first term, one State and two Territories were added to the confederacy. A part of the North-western Territory[3] became a State, under the name of Ohio,[4] in the autumn of 1802; and in the spring of 1803, Louisiana was purchased [April] of France for fifteen millions of dollars. This result was brought about without much difficulty, for the French ruler was desirous of injuring England, and saw in this an excellent way to do it. In violation of a treaty made in the year 1795, the Spanish governor of Louisiana closed the port of New Orleans in 1802. Great excitement prevailed throughout the western settlements; and a proposition was made in Congress to take forcible possession of the Territory. It was ascertained that, by a secret treaty, the country had been ceded to France, by Spain. Negotiations for its purchase were immediately opened with Napoleon, and the bargain was consummated in April, 1803. The United States took peaceable possession in the autumn of that year. It contained about eighty-five thousand mixed inhabitants, and about forty thousand negro slaves. When this bargain was consummated, Napoleon said, prophetically, "This accession of territory strengthens forever the power of the United States; and I have just given to England a maritime rival that will sooner or later humble her pride." Out of it two Territories were formed, called respectively the *Territory of New Orleans* and the *District of Louisiana.*

We have already adverted to the depredations of Algerine corsairs upon American commerce. The insolence of the piratical powers on the southern shores of the Mediterranean,[5] at length became unendurable; and the United States government resolved to cease paying tribute to them. The Bashaw of Tripoli thereupon declared war [June 10, 1801] against the United States; and Captain Bainbridge was ordered to cruise in the Mediterranean to protect

---

[1] James Madison, Secretary of State; Henry Dearborn, Secretary of War; Levi Lincoln, Attorney General. Before the meeting of Congress in December, he appointed Albert Gallatin [note 1, page 380, and note 6, page 443], Secretary of the Treasury, and Robert Smith, Secretary of the Navy. They were both Republicans. [2] Page 378. [3] Page 362.

[4] No section of the Union had increased, in population and resources, so rapidly as Ohio. When, in 1800, it was formed into a distinct Territory, the residue of the *North-western Territory* remained as one until 1809. Then the Territories of *Indiana* and *Illinois* were formed. When Ohio was admitted as a State, it contained a population of about seventy-two thousand souls.

[5] Morocco, Algiers, Tunis, and Tripoli, in Africa. They are known as the *Barbary Powers.*

American commerce.[1] In 1803, Commodore Preble was sent thither to humble the pirates. After bringing the Emperor of Morocco to terms, he appeared before Tripoli with his squadron. One of his vessels (the Philadelphia), commanded by Bainbridge,[2] struck on a rock in the harbor, while reconnoitering;

and before she could be extricated, she was captured [October 31, 1803] by the Tripolitans. The officers were treated as prisoners of war, but the crew were made slaves.

---

[1] Captain Bainbridge had been on that coast the previous year. He arrived at Algiers in September, 1800, in the frigate *George Washington*, with the annual tribute money [page 381]. The dey, or governor, demanded the use of his vessel to carry an ambassador to Constantinople. Bainbridge remonstrated, when the dey haughtily observed: "You pay me tribute, by which you become my slaves, and therefore I have a right to order you as I think proper." Bainbridge was obliged to comply, for the castle guns would not allow him to pass out of the harbor. He sailed for the East, and had the honor of first displaying the American flag before the ancient city of Constantinople. The Sultan regarded it as a favorable omen of future friendship, because *his* flag bore a *crescent* or half-moon, and the American a group of *stars*.

UNITED STATES FRIGATE.

[2] William Bainbridge was born in New Jersey, in 1774. He was captain of a merchant vessel at the age of nineteen years, and entered the naval service in 1798. He was distinguished during the second War for Independence [page 409], and died in 1833.

The credit of the American navy was somewhat repaired, early in the following year, when Lieutenant Decatur,[1] with only seventy-six volunteers, sailed into the harbor of Tripoli, in the evening of February 3, 1804, and runing alongside the *Philadelphia* (which lay moored near the castle, and guarded by a large number of Tripolitans), boarded her, killed or drove into the sea all of her turbaned defenders, set her on fire, and under cover of a heavy cannonade from the American squadron, escaped, without losing a man.[2] As they left the burning vessel, the Americans raised a shout, which was answered by the guns of the batteries on the shore, and by the armed vessels at anchor near. They went out into the Mediterranean unharmed, sailed for Syracuse, and were received there with great joy by the American squadron, under Commodore Preble. This bold act humbled and alarmed the bashaw;[3] yet his capital withstood a heavy bombardment, and his gun-boats gallantly sustained a severe action [August 3] with the American vessels.

LIEUTENANT DECATUR.

In the following year, through the aid of Hamet Caramelli, brother of Jessuff, the reigning bashaw (or governor) of Tripoli, favorable terms of peace were secured. The bashaw was a usurper, and Hamet, the rightful heir to the throne,[4] was an exile in Egypt. He readily concerted, with Captain William Eaton, American consul at Tunis, a plan for humbling the bashaw, and obtaining his own restoration to rightful authority. Captain Eaton acted under the sanction of his government; and early in March [March 6, 1805], he left Alexandria, with seventy United States seamen, accompanied by Hamet and his followers, and a few Egyptian troops. They made a journey of a thousand miles across the Libyan desert, and on the 27th of April, captured Derne, a Tripolitan city on the Mediterranean. Three weeks later [May 18], they had a successful battle with Tripolitan troops; and on the 18th of June they again defeated the forces of the bashaw, and

MOHAMMEDAN SOLDIER.

---

[1] Stephen Decatur was born in Maryland in 1779. He entered the navy at the age of nineteen years. After his last cruise in the Mediterranean, he superintended the building of the gun-boats. He rose to the rank of commodore; and during the second War for Independence [page 409], he was distinguished for his skill and bravery. He afterward humbled the Barbary Powers [note 5, page 390]; and was esteemed as one among the choicest flowers of the navy. He was killed, at Bladensburg, in a duel with Commodore Barron, in March, 1820, when forty-one years of age.

[2] While the American squadron was on its way to Syracuse, it captured a small Tripolitan vessel, bound to Constantinople, with a present of female slaves for the Sultan. This was taken into service, and named the *Intrepid*, and was the vessel with which Decatur performed his bold exploit at Tripoli. This act greatly enraged the Tripolitans, and the American prisoners were treated with the utmost severity. The annals of that day give some terrible pictures of white slavery on the southern shores of the Mediterranean Sea.

[3] Bashaw, or Pacha [Pag-shaw], is the title of the governor of a province, or town, in the dominions of the Sultan (or emperor) of Turkey. The Barbary States [note 5, page 390] are all under the Sultan's rule.

[4] The bashaw, who was a third son, had murdered his father and elder brother, and compelled Hamet to fly for his life. With quite a large number of followers, he fled into Egypt.

DECATUR BURNING THE PHILADELPHIA.

pressed forward toward Tripoli. The terrified ruler had made terms of peace [June 4, 1805] with Colonel Tobias Lear, American consul-general[1] in the Mediterranean, and thus disappointed the laudable ambition of Eaton, and the hopes of Hamet.[2]

While these hostile movements were occurring in the East, the President

had, in a confidential message to Congress, in January, 1803, proposed the first of those peaceable conquests which have opened, and are still opening, to civilization and human industry, the vast inland regions of our continent. He recommended an appropriation for defraying the expenses of an exploring expedition across the continent from the Mississippi to the Pacific Ocean. The appropriation was made, and presently an expedition, consisting of thirty individuals, under Captains Lewis and Clarke, was organized. They left the banks of the Mississippi on the 14th of May, 1804, and were absent about twenty-seven months. It was very successful, particularly in geographical discoveries, and

---

[1] A consul is an officer appointed by a government to reside in a foreign port, to have a general supervision of the commercial interests of his country there. In some cases they have powers almost equal to a minister. Such is the case with consuls within the ports of Mohammedan countries. The word *consul* was applied to Napoleon [page 387] in the ancient Roman sense. It was the title of the chief magistrate of Rome during the Republic. The treaty made by Lear provided for an exchange of prisoners, man for man, as far as they would go. Jessuff had about two hundred more prisoners than the Americans held, and for these, a ransom of $60,000 was to be paid. It was also stipulated that the wife and children of Hamet should be given up to him.

[2] Hamet afterward came to the United States, and applied to Congress for a remuneration for his services in favor of the Americans. He was unsuccessful; but Congress voted $2,400 for his temporary relief.

furnished the first reliable information respecting the extensive country between the Mississippi and the Pacific Ocean. During the same year, the election for President of the United States recurred. Aaron Burr, having lost the confidence of the Democratic party,[1] was not re-nominated for Vice-President. George Clinton[2] was put in his place; and Jefferson and Clinton were elected by a great majority[3] over their Federal opponents, Charles Cotesworth Pinckney,[4] of South Carolina, who was nominated for President, and Rufus King,[5] of New York, for Vice-President.

A serious difficulty commenced in the West during the second year [1805] of Mr. Jefferson's second administration. The fertile valleys of the Ohio and Mississippi were then very rapidly filling with adventurers, and the materials for new States, strong and ample, were gathering. Michigan was erected into a Territory in 1805; and all along the Mississippi, extensive settlements were taking root and flourishing. The tide of population was full and unceasing, and was composed, chiefly, of adventurous characters, ready for any enterprise that should offer the result of great gain. Taking advantage of the restless spirit of these adventurers, and the general impression that the Spanish population of Louisiana would not quietly submit to the jurisdiction of the United States,[6] Aaron Burr[7] thought to make them subservient to his own ambitious purposes. His murder of Hamilton in a duel,[8] on the 12th of July, 1804, made him everywhere detested; and, perceiving his unpopularity in the fact of his having been superseded in the office of Vice-President of the United States, by George Clinton,[9] he sought a new field for achieving personal aggrandisement. In April, 1805, he departed for the West, with several nominal objects in view, but chiefly in relation to pecuniary speculations. These seemed to conceal his real design of effecting a strong military organization, for the purpose of invading the Spanish possessions in Mexico. General Wilkinson,[10] then in the West, and the commander-in-chief of the Federal army, became his associate. Wil-

[1] Page 377. [2] Page 350.

[3] The great popularity of Jefferson's administration was shown by the result of this election. He received in the electoral college [note 1, page 361] one hundred and sixty-two votes, and Mr. Pinckney only fourteen. [4] Page 384.

[5] Rufus King was born in 1755, and was in Harvard College in 1775, when hostilities with Great Britain commenced, and the students were dispersed. He chose the law for a profession, and became very eminent as a practitioner. He was in Sullivan's army, on Rhode Island [page 289], in 1778; and in 1784, the people, appreciating his talents and his oratorical powers, elected him to a seat in the Legislature of Massachusetts. He was an efficient member of the Federal Convention, in 1787, and nobly advocated the Constitution afterward. He removed to New York, was a member of the State Legislature, was also one of the first United States Senators from New York, and in 1796 was appointed minister to Great Britain. From 1813 to 1826 he was a member of the United States Senate, and in 1825 was again sent to England as minister plenipotentiary. He died, near Jamaica, Long Island, in April, 1827, at the age of seventy-two years. [6] Page 390.

[7] Aaron Burr was born in New Jersey, in 1756. In his twentieth year he joined the continental army, and accompanied Arnold [note 4, page 241] in his expedition against Quebec, in 1775. His health compelled him to leave the army in 1779, and he became a distinguished lawyer and active public man. He died on Staten Island, near New York, in 1836, at the age of eighty years.

[8] Note 2, page 360. A political quarrel led to fatal results. Burr had been informed of some remarks made by Hamilton, in public, derogatory to his character, and he demanded a retraction. Hamilton considered his demand unreasonable, and refused compliance. Burr challenged him to fight, and Hamilton reluctantly met him on the west side of the Hudson, near Hoboken, where they fought with pistols. Hamilton discharged his weapon in the air, but Burr took fatal aim, and his antagonist fell. Hamilton died the next day. [9] Page 350. [10] Page 410.

kinson had just been appointed governor of Louisiana, and his official position secured precisely the advantage which Burr sought.

Burr went down the Ohio; and one beautiful morning at the close of April [1805], he appeared at the house of Blennarhasset, an Irishman possessed of

fine education, a large fortune, and an accomplished and enthusiastic wife.[1] To him he unfolded his grand military scheme; and the imaginations of Blennarhasset and his wife were fired. Dreams of immense wealth and power filled their minds; and when Burr had departed from the quiet home of this gentleman, the sunshine of his house faded. Blennarhasset was a changed man. He placed his wealth and reputation in the keeping of an unprincipled demagogue, and lost both. At that time, the brave and noble Andrew Jackson[2] was in command of the militia of Tennessee. In May, Burr appeared at the door of that stern patriot, and before he left it, he had won Jackson's confidence, and his promise of co-operation. He also met Wilkinson at St. Louis, and there gave him some hints of a greater scheme than he had hitherto unfolded, which, that officer alleged, made him suspicious that Burr's ultimate aim was damage

[1] His residence was upon an island a little below the mouth of the Muskingum River. There he had a fine library, beautiful conservatories, and a variety of luxuries hitherto unseen in that wilderness region. His home was an earthly paradise, into which the vile political serpent crawled, and despoiled it with his slime. Blennarhasset became poor, and died in 1831. His beautiful and accomplished wife was buried by the Sisters of Charity, in the city of New York, in the year 1842.

[2] Page 460.

to the Union. However, the schemer managed the whole matter with great skill. He made friends with many of the dissatisfied military and naval officers, and won their sympathies;[1] and in the summer of 1806, he was very active in the organization of a military expedition in the West. The secresy with

which it was carried on, excited the suspicions of many good men beyond the mountains, among whom was Jackson. Burr was suspected of a design to dismember the Union, and to establish an independent empire west of the Alleghanies, with himself at the head. Those suspicions were communicated to the Federal Government, which, having reason to suspect Burr of premeditated treason, put forth the strong arm of its power, and crushed the viper in its egg. Burr was arrested [February, 1807], near Fort Stoddart, on the Tombigbee River, in the present State of Alabama, by Lieutenant (afterward Major-General) Gaines,[2] taken to Richmond, in Virginia, and there tried on a charge of treason. He was acquitted. The testimony showed that his probable design was an invasion of Mexican provinces, for the purpose of establishing there an independent government.

While Burr's scheme was ripening, difficulties with Spain were increasing, and the United States were brought to the verge of a war with that country.

[1] Many in the West supposed the government was secretly favoring Burr's plans against Mexico, and, having no suspicions of any other designs, some of the truest men of that region became, some more and some less, involved in the meshes of his scheme.

[2] Page 467.

At the same time, the continued impressment of American seamen into the English navy, and the interruptions to American commerce by the British government, irritated the people of the United States, and caused the President to recommend partial non-intercourse with Great Britain. This policy was adopted by Congress [April 15, 1806], the prohibition to take effect in November following. This was one of the first of the retaliatory measures of the American government toward that of Great Britain.

The following year [1807] is remarkable in American history as the era of the commencement of successful steamboat navigation. Experiments in that direction had been made in this country many years before, but it was reserved for Robert Fulton[1] to bear the honor of success. He spent a long time in France, partly in the pursuit of his profession as a portrait-painter, and in the study of the subject of steam navigation. Through the kindness of Joel Barlow, then [1797] in Paris (in whose family he remained seven years), he was enabled to study the natural sciences, modern languages, and to make experiments. There he became acquainted with Robert R. Livingston,[2] and through his influence and pecuniary aid, on his return to America, he was enabled to construct a steamboat, and to make a voyage on the Hudson from New York to Albany, "against wind and tide," in thirty-six hours.[3] He took out his first patent in 1809. Within fifty years, the vast operations connected with steamboat navigation, have been brought into existence. Now the puff of the steam-engine is heard upon the waters of every civilized nation on the face of the globe.

FULTON'S STEAMBOAT.

And now the progress of events in Europe began to disturb the amicable relations which had subsisted between the governments of the United States and Great Britain since the ratification of Jay's treaty.[4] Napoleon Bonaparte was upon the *throne* of France as emperor; and in 1806 he was King of Italy, and his three brothers were made ruling monarchs. He was upon the full tide of his success and conquests, and a large part of continental Europe was now

---

[1] Robert Fulton was born in Pennsylvania, in 1765, and was a student of West, the great painter, for several years. He had more genius for mechanics than the fine arts, and when he turned his efforts in that direction, he became very successful. He died in 1815, soon after launching a steamship of war, at the age of fifty years. At that time there were six steamboats afloat on the Hudson, and he was building a steamship, designed for a voyage to St. Petersburg, in Russia.

[2] Page 366.

[3] This was the *Clermont*, Fulton's experimental boat. It was one hundred feet in length, twelve feet in width, and seven in depth. The engine was constructed by Watt and Bolton, in England, and the hull was made by David Brown, of New York. The following advertisement appeared in the Albany *Gazette*, September 1st, 1807: "The *North River Steamboat* will leave Paulus's Hook [Jersey City] on Friday, the 4th of September, at 9 in the morning, and arrive at Albany on Saturday, at 9 in the afternoon. Provisions, good berths, and accommodations are provided. The charge to each passenger is as follows:

"To	Newburg,	dollars,	3,	time,	14	hours.
"	Poughkeepsie,	"	4,	"	17	"
"	Esopus,	"	5,	"	20	"
"	Hudson,	"	5½,	"	30	"
"	Albany,	"	7,	"	36	"

[4] Page 380.

prostrate at his feet. Although England had joined the continental powers against him [1803], in order to crush the Democratic revolution commenced in France, and the English navy had almost destroyed the French power at sea, all Europe was yet trembling in his presence. But the United States, by

maintaining a strict neutrality, neither coveted his favors nor feared his power: at the same time American shipping being allowed free intercourse between English and French ports, enjoyed the vast advantages of a profitable carrying trade between them.

The belligerents, in their anxiety to damage each other, ceased, in time, to respect the laws of nations toward neutrals, and adopted measures at once destructive to American commerce, and in violation of the most sacred rights of the United States. In this matter, Great Britain took the lead. By an order in council,[1] that government declared [May 16, 1806] the whole coast of Europe, from the Elbe, in Germany, to Brest, in France, to be in a state of blockade. Napoleon retaliated by issuing [November 21] a decree at Berlin, which declared all the ports of the British islands to be in a state of blockade. This was intended as a blow against England's maritime superiority, and it was

[1] The British privy council consists of an indefinite number of gentlemen, chosen by the sovereign, and having no direct connection with the cabinet ministers. The sovereign may, under the advice of this council, issue orders or proclamations which, if not contrary to existing laws, are binding upon the subjects. These are for temporary purposes, and are called *Orders in Council.*

the beginning of what he termed the *continental system*, the chief object of which was the ruin of Great Britain. The latter, by another order [January 7, 1807], prohibited all coast trade with France; and thus the gamesters played with the world's peace and prosperity. In spite of pacific attempts to put an end to these ungenerous measures, American vessels were seized by both English and French cruisers, and American commerce dwindled to a domestic coast trade.[1] The United States lacked a navy to protect her commerce on the ocean, and the swarms of gun-boats[2] which Congress, from time to time, had authorized as a substitute, were quite inefficient, even as a coast-guard.

A FELUCCA GUN-BOAT.

The American merchants and all in their interest, so deeply injured by the "orders" and "decrees" of the warring monarchs, demanded redress of grievances. Great excitement prevailed throughout the country, and the most bitter feeling was beginning to be felt against Great Britain. This was increased by her haughty assertion and offensive practice of the doctrine that she had the right to search American vessels for suspected deserters from the British navy, and to carry away the suspected without hinderance.[3] This right was strenuously denied, and its policy vehemently condemned, because American seamen might be thus forced into the British service, under the pretense that they were deserters. Indeed this had already happened.[4]

Clouds of difficulty now gathered thick and black. A crisis approached. Four seamen on board the United States frigate *Chesapeake*, were claimed as deserters from the British armed ship *Melampus*.[5] They were demanded, but Commodore Barron, of the *Chesapeake*, refused to give them up. The

---

[1] In May, 1806, James Monroe [page 447] and William Pinkney, were appointed to assist in the negotiation of a treaty with Great Britain, concerning the rights of neutrals, the imprisonment of seamen, right of search, &c. A treaty was finally signed, but as it did not offer security to American vessels against the aggressions of British ships in searching them and carrying off seamen, Mr. Jefferson refused to submit it to the Senate, and rejected it. The Federalists condemned the course of the President, but subsequent events proved his wisdom. Mr. Pinkney, one of the special envoys, was a remarkable man. He was born at Annapolis, Maryland, in March, 1764. He was admitted to the bar, at the age of twenty-two years, and became one of the most profound statesmen and brilliant orators of the age. He was a member of the Maryland Senate, in 1811, when President Madison appointed him Attorney-General for the United States. He was elected a member of Congress, and in 1816 was appointed United States minister to St. Petersburg. After a short service in the Senate, his health gave way, and he died in February, 1822, in the fifty-ninth year of his age.

[2] These were small sailing vessels, having a cannon at the bow and stern, and manned by fully armed men, for the purpose of boarding other vessels.

[3] England maintains the doctrine that a British subject can never become an alien. At the time in question, she held that she had the right to take her native-born subjects wherever found, and place them in the army or navy, even though, by legal process, they had become citizens of another nation. Our laws give equal protection to the native and adopted citizen, and would not allow Great Britain to exercise her asserted privilege toward a Briton who had become a citizen of the United States.

[4] During nine months, in the years 1796 and 1797, Mr. King [page 395], the American minister in London, had made application for the release of two hundred and seventy-one seamen (a greater portion of whom were Americans), who had been seized on the false charge of being deserters, and pressed into the British service.

[5] A small British squadron, of which the *Melampus* was one, was lying in Lynn Haven Bay, at the mouth of the Chesapeake Bay, at this time. It was commanded by Admiral Berkeley.

Chesapeake left the capes of Virginia on a cruise, on the 22d of June, 1807, and on the same day she was chased and attacked by the British frigate *Leopard.* Unsuspicious of danger and unprepared for an attack, Barron surrendered his vessel, after losing three men killed and eighteen wounded. The four men were then taken on board the *Leopard*, and the *Chesapeake* returned to Hampton Roads.[1] Investigation proved that three of the seamen, who were colored men, were native Americans, and that the fourth had been impressed into the British service, and had deserted.

Forbearance was no longer a virtue. The outrage upon the *Chesapeake* aroused the nation, and provoked retaliatory measures. All parties joined in one loud voice of indignation, and many were very anxious for a declaration of war with England. The President, however, proposed a pacific course, as long as any hope for justice or reconciliation remained. He issued a proclamation, in July [1807], ordering all British armed vessels to leave the waters of the United States immediately, and forbidding any one to enter until full satisfaction for the present insult, and security against future aggressions, should be made. Although the British government understood the attack on the *Chesapeake* as an outrage, yet diplomacy, which is seldom honest, was immediately employed to mistify the plain question of law and right.[2] In the mean while, France and England continued to play their desperate game, to the detriment of commerce, unmindful of the interests of other nations, or the obligations of international law. A British order in council[3] was issued on the 11th of November, 1807, forbidding neutral nations to trade with France or her allies, except upon payment of tribute to Great Britain. Napoleon retaliated, by issuing, on the 17th of December, a decree at Milan, forbidding all trade with England or her colonies; and authorizing the confiscation of any vessel found in his ports, which had submitted to English search, or paid the exacted tribute. In other words, any vessel having goods upon which any impost whatever should have been paid to Great Britain, should be *denationalized*, and subject to seizure and condemnation. These edicts were, of course, destructive to the principal part of the foreign commerce of the United States. In this critical state of affairs, the President convened Congress several weeks [Oct. 25, 1807] earlier than usual; and in a confidential message [December 18], he recommended to that body the passage of an act, levying a commercial embargo. Such an act was passed [December 22], which provided for the detention of all vessels, American and foreign, at our ports; and ordered American vessels abroad to return home immediately, that the seamen might be

---

[1] Page 297.

[2] The President forwarded instructions to Mr. Monroe, our minister to England, to demand immediate satisfaction for the outrage, and security against similar events in future. Great Britain thereupon dispatched an envoy extraordinary (Mr. Rose) to the United States, to settle the difficulty in question. The envoy would not enter into negotiations until the President should withdraw his proclamation, and so the matter stood until November, 1811 (more than four years), when the British government declared the attack on the *Chesapeake* to have been unauthorized, and promised pecuniary aid to the families of those who were killed at that time. But Britain would not relinquish the right of search, and so a cause for quarrel remained.

[3] Note 1, page 400.

trained for the inevitable war. Thus the chief commerce of the world was brought to a full stop.

The operation of the embargo law was the occasion of great distress, especially in commercial communities, yet it was sustained by the great body of the

American people. It put patriotism and firmness to a severe test. It bore extremely hard upon seamen and their employers, for it spread ruin throughout the shipping interest. It was denounced by the Federal party, chiefly for political effect;[1] and as it failed to obtain from England and France any acknowledgment of American rights, it was repealed on the 1st of March, 1809, three days before Mr. Jefferson retired from office. Congress, at the same time, passed [March 1, 1809] a law which forbade all commercial intercourse with France and England, until the "orders in council" and the "decrees" should be repealed.

[1] Mr. Jefferson truly wrote to a friend: "The Federalists are now playing a game of the most mischievous tendency, without, perhaps, being themselves aware of it. They are endeavoring to convince England that we suffer more from the embargo than they do, and that, if they will hold out awhile, we must abandon it. It is true, the time will come when we must abandon it; but if this is before the repeal of the orders in council, we must abandon it only for a state of war." John Quincy Adams, who had resigned his seat in the Senate of the United States, because he differed from the majority of his constituents in supporting the measures of the administration, wrote to the President to the effect, that from information received by him, it was the determination of the ruling party (Federalists) in Massachusetts, and even throughout New England, if the embargo was persisted in, no longer to submit to it, but to separate themselves from the Union; and that such was the pressure of the embargo upon the community, that they would be supported by the people. This was explicitly denied, in after years, by the Federalist leaders.

In the midst of the excitement on account of the foreign relations of the United States, another Presidential election was held. Who should be the Democratic candidate? was a question of some difficulty, the choice lying between Messrs. Madison and Monroe, of Virginia. For some time, a portion of the Democratic party in that State, under the leadership of the eminent John Randolph,[1] of Roanoke, had differed from the Administration on some points of its foreign policy; yet, while they acted with the Federalists on many occasions, they studiously avoided identification with that party. Mr. Madison was the firm adherent of Jefferson, and an advocate and apologist of his measures, while Mr. Monroe[2] rather favored the views of Mr. Randolph and his friends. The strength of the two candidates was tried in a caucus of the Democratic members of the Virginia Legislature, and also in a caucus of the Democratic members of Congress. Mr. Madison, having a large majority on both occasions, was nominated for the office of President, and George Clinton for that of Vice-President. Charles Cotesworth Pinckney and Rufus King were the Federalist candidates. Madison and Clinton were elected. At the close of eight years' service, as Chief Magistrate of the United States, Mr. Jefferson left office [March 4, 1809], and retired to his beautiful *Monticello*, in the bosom of his native Virginia.

CHAPTER IV.

MADISON'S ADMINISTRATION. [1809—1817.]

WHEN James Madison, the fourth President of the Republic, took the chair of state, the country was overspread with gloom and despondency. Although somewhat highly colored, the report of a committee of the Massachusetts Legislature, in January, 1809, gives, doubtless, a fair picture of the condition of affairs. It said: "Our agriculture is discouraged; the fisheries abandoned; navigation forbidden; our commerce at home restrained, if not

[1] John Randolph was seventh in descent from Pocahontas [page 66], the beloved daughter of the emperor of the Powhatans. He was born at Petersburg, in Virginia, in June, 1773. He was in delicate health from infancy. He studied in Columbia College, New York, and William and Mary College, in Virginia. Law was his chosen profession; yet he was too fond of literature and politics to be confined to its practice. He entered public life in 1799, when he was elected to a seat in Congress, where he was a representative of his native State, in the lower House, for thirty years, with the exception of three intervals of two years each. During that time he was a member of the Senate for two years. He opposed the war in 1812. His political course was erratic. Jackson appointed him minister to St. Petersburg in 1830. His health would not permit him to remain there. On his return he was elected to Congress, but consumption soon laid him in the grave. He died at Philadelphia, in May, 1833. Mr. Randolph was a strange compound of moral and intellectual qualities. He was at times almost an atheist; at others, he was imbued with the deepest emotions of piety and reverence for Deity. It is said that, on one occasion, he ascended a lofty spur of the Blue Ridge, at dawn, and from that magnificent observatory saw the sun rise. As its light burst in beauty and glory over the vast panorama before him, he turned to his servant and said, with deep emotion, "Tom, if any body says there is no God, tell them they lie!" Thus he expressed the deep sense which his soul felt of the presence of a Great Creator.

[2] Page. 447.

annihilated; our commerce abroad cut off; our navy sold, dismantled, or degraded to the service of cutters, or gun-boats;[1] the revenue extinguished; the course of justice interrupted; and the nation weakened by internal animosities and divisions, at the moment when it is unnecessarily and improvidently exposed to war with Great Britain, France, and Spain." This was the language of the opponents of the administration, and must be taken with some allowance. That party was strongly opposed to Mr. Madison, because they

believed that he would perpetuate the policy of Mr. Jefferson. But when, dressed in a suit of plain black, he modestly pronounced his inaugural address [March 4, 1809], the tone and sentiment of which fell like oil upon the troubled waters, those of his most implacable political enemies who heard him, could not refrain from uttering words of approbation; and hopes were entertained by the whole nation, that his measures might change the gloomy aspect of affairs.

To all unbiassed minds, no man appeared better fitted for the office of Chief Magistrate of the Republic, at that time of general commotion, than Mr. Madison.[2] He had been Secretary of State during the whole administration of Mr.

---

[1] Page 401.

[2] James Madison was born in Virginia, in March, 1751. He was educated at Princeton, New Jersey, and was diverted from the intended practice of the law by the charms and excitements of political life. He assisted in framing the first Constitution of Virginia, in 1776. He was a member of his State Legislature and of the Executive Council, and in 1780 was a delegate in the Continental Congress. In public life, there, and in his State councils, he was ever the champion of popular liberty. As a member of the Federal Convention, and supporter of the Constitution, he

Jefferson, and was familiar with every event which had contributed to produce the existing hostile relations between the United States and Great Britain. His cabinet was composed of able men,[1] and in the eleventh Congress, which convened on the 22d of May, 1809, in consequence of the critical state of affairs,[2] there was a majority of his political friends. Yet there was a powerful party in the country (the Federalists) hostile to his political creed, and opposed to a war with England, which now seemed probable.

At the very beginning of Madison's administration, light beamed upon the future. Mr. Erskine, the British minister, assured the President, that such portions of the orders in council[3] as affected the United States, should be repealed by the 10th of June. He also assured him that a special envoy would soon arrive, to settle all matters in dispute between the two governments. Supposing the minister to be authorized by his government to make these assurances, the President, as empowered by Congress, issued a proclamation [April 19, 1809], permitting a renewal of commercial intercourse with Great Britain, on that day. But the government disavowed Erskine's act, and the President again [August 10] proclaimed non-intercourse. The light had proved deceitful. This event caused great excitement in the public mind; and had the President then declared war against Great Britain, it would doubtless have been very popular.

Causes for irritation between the two governments continually increased, and, for a time, political intercourse was suspended. France, too, continued its aggressions. On the 23d of March, 1810, Bonaparte issued a decree at Rambouillet, more destructive in its operations to American commerce, than any measures hitherto employed. It declared forfeit every American vessel which had entered French ports since March, 1810, or that might thereafter enter; and authorized the sale of the same, together with the cargoes—the money to be placed in the French treasury. Under this decree, many American vessels were lost, for which only partial remuneration has since been obtained.[4] Bonaparte justified this decree by the plea, that it was made in retaliation for the American decree of non-intercourse.[5] Three months later [May, 1810], Congress offered to resume commercial intercourse with either France or England, or both, on condition that they should repeal their obnoxious orders and decrees, before the 3d of March, 1811.[6] The French emperor, who was always governed by expediency, in defiance of right and justice, feigned compliance, and by giving assurance [August] that such repeal should take effect in Novem-

---

was one of the wisest and ablest; and his voluminous writings, purchased by Congress, display the most sagacious statesmanship. As a Republican, he was conservative. For eight years he was President of the United States, when he retired to private life. He died in June, 1836, at the age of eighty-five years.

[1] Robert Smith, Secretary of State; Albert Gallatin, Secretary of the Treasury; William Eustis, Secretary of War; Paul Hamilton, Secretary of the Navy; Cæsar Rodney, Attorney-General.

[2] Its session lasted only about five weeks, because peace seemed probable.

[3] Note 1, page 400. [4] Page 468. [5] Page 402.

[6] The act provided, that if either government should repeal its obnoxious acts, and if the other government should not do the same within three months thereafter, then the first should enjoy commercial intercourse with the United States, but the other should not.

ber, caused the President to proclaim such resumption of intercourse. It was a promise intended to be broken at any moment when policy should dictate. American vessels continued to be seized by French cruisers, as usual, and confiscated; and in March, 1811, Napoleon declared the decrees of Berlin[1] and Milan[2] to be the fundamental laws of the empire. A new envoy from France, who arrived in the United States at about this time, gave official notice to the government, that no remuneration would be made for property seized and confiscated.

The government of Great Britain acted more honorably, though wickedly. She continued her hostile orders, and sent ships of war to cruise near the principal ports of the United States, to intercept American merchant vessels and send them to England as lawful prizes. While engaged in this nefarious business, the British sloop of war[3] *Little Belt*, Captain Bingham, was met [April 16, 1811], off the coast of Virginia, by the American frigate *President*, Commodore Rogers.[4] That officer hailed the commander of the sloop, and received a cannon shot in reply. A brief action ensued, when Captain Bingham, after having eleven men killed and twenty-one wounded, gave a satisfactory answer to Rogers. The conduct of both officers was approved by their respective governments. That of the United States condemned the act of Bingham as an outrage without palliation; and the government and people felt willing to take up arms in defense of right, justice, and honor. Powerful as was the navy of Great Britain, and weak as was that of the United States, the people of the latter were willing to accept of war as an alternative for submission, and to measure strength on the ocean. The British navy consisted of almost *nine hundred* vessels, with an aggregate of one hundred and forty-four thousand men. The American vessels of war, of large size, numbered only *twelve*, with an aggregate of about three hundred guns. Besides these, there were a great number of gun-boats, but these were hardly sufficient for a coast-guard. Here was a great disparity; and for a navy so weak to defy a navy so strong, seemed madness. It must be remembered, however, that the British navy was necessarily very much scattered, for that government had interests to protect in various parts of the globe.

The protracted interruption of commercial operations was attended with very serious effect upon the trade and revenue of the United States, and all parties longed for a change, even if it must be brought about by war with European governments. The Congressional elections in 1810 and 1811, proved that the policy of Mr. Madison's administration was sustained by a large majority of the American people, the preponderance of the Democratic party being kept up in both branches of the Federal Legislature. The opposition, who, as a party, were unfavorable to hostilities, were in a decided minority, and the government had more strength in its councils than at any time during Jefferson's administration.

For several years war with England had seemed inevitable, and now [1811]

[1] Page 400. [2] Page 402. [3] Page 415.
[4] He died in the Naval Asylum, Philadelphia, in August, 1838.

many causes were accelerating the progress of events toward such a result. Among these, the hostile position of the Indian tribes on the north-western frontier of the United States, was one of the most powerful. They, too, had felt the pressure of Bonaparte's commercial system. In consequence of the exclusion of their furs from the continental markets, the Indian hunters found their traffic reduced to the lowest point. The rapid extension of settlements north of the Ohio was narrowing their hunting-grounds, and producing a rapid diminution of game; and the introduction of whiskey, by the white people, was spreading demoralization, disease, and death among the Indians. These evils, combined with the known influence of British emissaries, finally led to open hostilities.

In the spring of 1811, it became certain that Tecumseh, a Shawnee[1] chief, who was crafty, intrepid, unscrupulous, and cruel, and who possessed the qualities of a great leader, almost equal to those of Pontiac,[2] was endeavoring to emulate that great Ottawa by confederating the tribes of the north-west in a war against the people of the United States. Those over whom himself and twin-brother, the Prophet,[3] exercised the greatest control, were the Delawares, Shawnees, Wyandots, Miamies, Kickapoos, Winnebagoes, and Chippewas.[4] During the summer, the frontier settlers became so alarmed by the continual military and religious exercises of the savages, that General Harrison,[5] then governor of the Indiana Territory,[6] marched, with a considerable force, toward the town of the Prophet, situated at the junction of the Tippecanoe and Wabash Rivers, in the upper part of Tippecanoe county, Indiana. The Prophet appeared and proposed a conference, but Harrison, suspecting treachery, caused his soldiers to sleep on their arms [Nov. 6, 1811] that night. At four o'clock the next morning [Nov. 7] the savages fell upon the American camp, but after a bloody battle until dawn, the Indians were repulsed. The battle of Tippecanoe was one of the most desperate ever fought with the Indians, and the loss was heavy on both sides.[7] Tecumseh was not present on this occasion, and it is said the Prophet took no part in the engagement.

These events, so evidently the work of British interference, aroused the spirit of the nation, and throughout the entire West, and in the Middle and Southern States, there was a desire for war. Yet the administration fully appreciated the deep responsibility involved in such a step; and having almost the entire body of the New England people in opposition, the President and his friends hesitated. The British orders in council[8] continued to be rigorously enforced; insult after insult was offered to the American flag; and the British press insolently boasted that the United States "could not be kicked into a

---

[1] Page 19. [2] Page 204.

[3] In 1809, Governor Harrison had negotiated a treaty with the Miamies [page 19] and other tribes, by which they sold to the United States a large tract of land on both sides of the Wabash. The Prophet was present and made no objection; but Tecumseh, who was absent, was greatly dissatisfied. The British emissaries took advantage of this dissatisfaction, to inflame him and his people against the Americans.

[4] Page 17. [5] Page 474. [6] Note 4, page 390.

[7] Harrison had upward of sixty killed, and more than a hundred wounded.

[8] Note 1, page 400.

war." Forbearance became no longer a virtue; and on the 4th of April, 1812, Congress laid another embargo[1] upon vessels in American waters, for ninety days. On the 1st of June, the President transmitted a special message to Congress, in which he reviewed the difficulties with Great Britain, strongly portrayed the aggressions inflicted upon us by that nation, and intimated the necessity of war. The message was referred to the Committee on Foreign Relations, in the House of Representatives, a majority of whom[2] agreed upon, and reported a manifesto [June 3], as the basis of a declaration of war. On the following day [June 4, 1812], a bill, drawn up by Mr. Pinckney, the Attorney-General of the United States,[3] declaring war to exist between the United States and Great Britain, was presented by Mr. Calhoun. During the proceedings on this subject, Congress sat with closed doors. The measure was finally agreed to, by both Houses, by fair majorities. It passed the House of Representatives by a vote of 79 to 49. On the 17th it passed the Senate by a vote of 19 to 13, and on that day it received the signature of the President.[4] Two days afterward [June 19], the President issued a proclamation which formally declared war against Great Britain.[5] This is known in history as THE WAR OF 1812; or

THE SECOND WAR FOR INDEPENDENCE.[6]

Congress, having authorized the President to declare war, took immediate measures to sustain that declaration. It passed an act which gave him authority to enlist twenty-five thousand men, to accept fifty thousand volunteers, and to call out one hundred thousand militia for the defense of the sea-coast and frontiers. Fifteen millions of dollars were appropriated for the army, and almost three millions for the navy. But at the very threshhold of the new order

[1] Page 402. Four days after this [April 8] Louisiana was admitted into the Union as a State.

[2] John C. Calhoun, of South Carolina; Felix Grundy, of Tennessee; John Smilie, of Pennsylvania; John A. Harper, of New Hampshire; Joseph Desha, of Kentucky; and Ebenezer Seaver, of Massachusetts.

[3] Page 400.

[4] The following are the words of that important bill: "*Be it enacted, etc.*, That war be, and the same is hereby declared to exist between the United Kingdom of Great Britain and Ireland, and the dependencies thereof, and the United States of America and their Territories; and that the President of the United States is hereby authorized to use the whole land and naval force of the United States to carry the same into effect, and to issue to private armed vessels of the United States, commissions, or letters of marque, and general reprisal, in such form as he shall think proper, and under the seal of the United States, against the vessels, goods, and effects of the government of the said United Kingdom of Great Britain and Ireland, and the subjects thereof."

[5] The chief causes for this act were the impressment of American seamen by the British; the blockade of French ports without an adequate force to sustain the act; and the British *Orders in Council*. The Federalists in Congress presented an ably-written protest, which denied the necessity or the expediency of war.

[6] This is an appropriate title, for, until the termination of that war, the United States were only nominally free. Blessed with prosperity, the people dreaded war, and submitted to many acts of tyranny and insult from Great Britain and France, rather than become involved in another conflict. Socially and commercially, the United States were dependent upon Europe, and especially upon England; and the latter was rapidly acquiring a dangerous political interest here, when the war broke out. The war begun in 1775 was really only the first great step toward independence; the war begun in 1812, first thoroughly accomplished it. Franklin once heard a person speaking of the Revolution as the *War of Independence*, and reproved him, saying, "Sir, you mean the Revolution; the war of *Independence* is yet to come. It was a war *for* Independence, but not *of* Independence."

of things, the administration was met by determined opposition. The Federal members of the House of Representatives published an address to their constituents, in which they set forth the state of the country at that time, the course of the administration and its supporters in Congress, and the reasons of the minority for opposing the war. This was fair and honorable. But outside of Congress, a party, composed chiefly of Federalists, with some disaffected Democrats, was organized under the name of the *Peace party*. Its object was to cast such obstructions in the way of the prosecution of the war, as to compel the government to make peace. This movement, so unpatriotic, the offspring of the lowest elements of faction, was frowned upon by the most respectable members of the Federal party, and some of them gave the government their hearty support, when it was necessary, in order to carry on the war with vigor and effect.

The first care of the government, in organizing the army, was to select efficient officers. Nearly all of the general officers of the Revolution were in their graves, or were too old for service, and even those of subordinate rank in that war, who yet remained, were far advanced in life. Yet upon them the chief duties of leadership were devolved. Henry Dearborn[1] was appointed major-general and commander-in-chief; and his principal brigadiers were James Wilkinson,[2] Wade Hampton,[3] William Hull,[4] and Joseph Bloomfield—all of them esteemed soldiers of the Revolution.

GENERAL DEARBORN.

Hull was governor of the Territory of Michigan, and held the commission of a brigadier-general. When war was declared, he was marching, with a little more than two thousand troops, from Ohio, to attempt the subjugation of the hostile Indians.[5] Congress gave him discretionary powers for invading Canada; but caution and preparation were necessary, because the British authorities, a long time in expectation of war, had taken measures accordingly.[6] Feeling strong enough for the enemy, Hull, on the 12th of July, 1812, crossed the Detroit River with his whole force, to attack Fort Malden, a British post near the present village of Amherstburg. At Sandwich, he encamped, and by a fatal delay, lost every advantage which an immediate attack might have secured. In the mean while, Fort

[1] Henry Dearborn was a native of New Hampshire, and a meritorious officer in the continental army. He accompanied Arnold to Quebec, and was distinguished in the battles which ruined Burgoyne [page 281]. He held civil offices of trust after the Revolution. He returned to private life in 1815, and died at Roxbury, near Boston, in 1829, at the age of seventy-eight years.

[2] Pages 396 and 426. [3] Note 3, page 427. [4] Note 4, page 411. [5] Page 408.

[6] Canada then consisted of two provinces. The old French settlements on the St. Lawrence, with a population of about three hundred thousand, constituted Lower Canada; while the more recent settlements above Montreal, and chiefly upon the northern shore of Lake Ontario, including about one hundred thousand inhabitants, composed Upper Canada. These were principally the families of American loyalists, who were compelled to leave the States at the close of the Revolution. Then each province had its own governor and Legislature. The regular military force, which was scattered over a space of more than a thousand miles, did not exceed two thousand men; hence the British commanders were compelled to call for volunteers, and they used the Indians to good effect, in their favor.

Mackinaw, one of the strongest posts of the United States in the north-west,[1] was surprised and captured [July 17, 1812] by an allied force of British and Indians; and on the 5th of August, a detachment under Major Van Horne, sent by Hull to escort an approaching supply-party to camp, were defeated by some British and Indians near Brownstown, on the Huron River.[2] These events, and the reinforcement of the garrison at Malden, by General Brock, the British commander-in-chief, caused Hull to recross the river on the 7th of August, abandon the expedition against Canada, and take post at Detroit, much to the disappointment of his troops, who were anxious to measure strength with the enemy.

On the 9th of August, General Brock crossed the river with seven hundred British troops and six hundred Indians, and demanded an instant surrender of Detroit, threatening at the same time to give free rein to Indian cruelty in the event of refusal. Hull's excessive prudence determined him to surrender, rather than expose his troops to the hatchet. When the assailants approached, and at the moment when the Americans were hoping for and expecting a command to fire, he ordered his troops to retire within the fort, and hung a white flag upon the wall, in token of submission. The army, fort, stores, garrison, and Territory, were all surrendered [August 16, 1812], to the astonishment of the victor himself, and the deep mortification of the American troops. Hull was afterward tried by a court-martial[3] [1814], on charges of treason and cowardice. He was found guilty of the latter, and sentenced to be shot, but was pardoned by the President on account of his revolutionary services. The whole country severely censured him; and the rage of the war party, increased by the taunts of the Federalists, because of the disastrous termination of one of the first expeditions of the campaign, was unbounded. The difficulties with which Hull was surrounded—his small force (only about eight hundred effective men); the inexperience of his officers, and the rawness of his troops; his lack of information, because of the interception of his communications; and the number and character of the enemy—were all kept out of sight, while bitter denunciations were poured upon his head. In after years, he was permitted fully to vindicate his character, and the sober judgment of this generation, guided by historic truth, must acquit him of all crime, and even serious error, and pity him as a victim of untoward circumstances.[4]

[1] Formerly spelled Michilimackinac. It was situated upon an island of that name, near the Straits of Mackinaw or Michilimakinac.

[2] On the 8th, Colonel Miller and several hundred men, sent by Hull to accomplish the object of Van Horne, met and defeated Tecumseh [page 408] and his Indians, with a party of British, near the scene of Van Horne's failure.

[3] He was taken to Montreal a prisoner, and was afterward exchanged for thirty British captives. He was tried at Albany, New York.

[4] Hull published his *Vindication* in 1824; and in 1848, his grandson published a large octavo volume, giving a full and thorough vindication of the character of the general, the material for which was drawn from official records. Hull's thorough knowledge of the character of the foe who menaced him, and a humane desire to spare his troops, was doubtless his sole reason for surrendering the post. A good and brave man has too long suffered the reproaches of history. William Hull was born in Connecticut in 1753. He rose to the rank of major in the continental army, and was distinguished for his bravery. He was appointed governor of the Michigan Territory in 1805. After the close of his unfortunate campaign, he never appeared in public life. He died near Boston in 1825.

At about this time, a tragedy occurred near the head of Lake Michigan, which sent a thrill of horror through the land. Captain Heald, with a company of fifty regulars, occupied Fort Dearborn, on the site of the present large city of Chicago.[1] Hull ordered him to evacuate that post in the deep wilderness, and hasten to Detroit. He left the public property in charge of friendly Indians, but had proceeded only a short distance from the fort, along the beach, when he was attacked by a body of Indians. Twenty-six of the regular troops, and all of the militia, were slaughtered. A number of women and children were murdered and scalped; and Captain Heald, with his wife, though severely wounded, escaped to Michilimackinac.[2] His wife also received six wounds, but none proved mortal. This event occurred on the day before Hull's surrender [Aug. 15, 1812] at Detroit, and added to the gloom that overspread, and the indignation that flashed through, the length and breadth of the land.

While these misfortunes were befalling the Army of the North-west,[3] the opponents of the war were casting obstacles in the way of the other divisions of the American troops operating in the State of New York, and preparing for another invasion of Canada.[4] The governors of Massachusetts, New Hampshire, and Connecticut, refused to allow the militia of those States to march to the northern frontier on the requisition of the President of the United States. They defended their unpatriotic position by the plea that such a requisition was unconstitutional, and that the war was unnecessary. The British government, in the mean while, had declared the whole American coast in a state of blockade, except that of the New England States, whose apparent sympathy with the enemies of their country, caused them to be regarded as ready to leave the Union, and become subject to the British crown. But there was sterling patriotism sufficient there to prevent such a catastrophe, even if a movement, so fraught with evil, had been contemplated. Yet the effect was chilling to the best friends of the country, and the President felt the necessity of extreme circumspection.

Unmindful of the intrigues of its foes, however, the administration persevered; and during the summer of 1812, a plan was matured for invading Canada on the Niagara frontier. The militia of the State of New York were placed, by Governor Tompkins, under the command of Stephen Van Rensselaer,[5]

---

[1] Chicago is built upon the verge of Lake Michigan and the borders of a great prairie, and is one of the wonders of the material and social progress of the United States. The Pottawatomie Indians [page 18], by treaty, left that spot to the white people in 1833. The city was laid out in 1830, and lots were first sold in 1831. In 1840, the population was 4,470. Now [1856] it can not be less than 80,000!

[2] Page 411.

[3] The forces under General Harrison were called the *Army of the North-west;* those under General Stephen Van Rensselaer, at Lewiston, on the Niagara River, the *Army of the Center;* and those under General Dearborn, at Plattsburg and at Greenbush, near Albany, the *Army of the North.*

[4] Page 410.

[5] Stephen Van Rensselaer, a lineal descendant of one of the earliest and best known of the Patroons [note 10, page 139] of the State of New York, was born at the manor-house, near Albany, in November, 1764. The War for Independence had just closed when he came into possession of his immense estate, at the age of twenty-one years. He engaged in politics, was a warm supporter of the Federal Constitution, and was elected Lieutenant-Governor of New York in 1795. He was very little engaged in politics after the defeat of the Federal party in 1800 [page 388]. After the Second War for Independence, he was elected to a seat in Congress; and, by his casting vote in the New York delegation, he gave the Presidency of the United States to John Quincy Adams.

who was commissioned a Major-General. Intelligence of the surrender of Hull[1] had inspired the Americans with a strong desire to wipe out the disgrace; and the regiments were filled without much difficulty. These forces were concentrated chiefly at Lewiston, on the Niagara frontier, under Van Rensselaer, and at Plattsburg, on Lake Champlain, and Greenbush, near Albany, under General Dearborn.

The first demonstration against the neighboring province was made on the Niagara, in mid-autumn. In anticipation of such movement, British troops were strongly posted on the heights of Queenstown, opposite Lewiston; and on the morning of the 13th of October [1812], two hundred and twenty-five men, under Colonel Solomon Van Rensselaer,[2] crossed over to attack them. The commander was severely wounded, at the landing; but his troops pressed forward, under Captains Wool[3] and Ogilvie, successfully assaulted a battery near

---

Here closed his political life, and he passed the remainder of his days in the performance of social and Christian duties. He was for several years president of the Board of Canal Commissioners, and, while in that office, he died in January, 1840, in the seventy-fifth year of his age.

[1] Page 411.

[2] Solomon Van Rensselaer was one of the bravest and best men of his time; and to his efforts, more than to those of any other man, the salvation of the American army on the northern frontier, at this time, was due. He died at Albany on the 3d of April, 1852.

[3] John E. Wool, now [1856] Major-General in the army of the United States.

the summit of the hill, and gained possession of Queenstown Heights. But the victory was not yet complete. General Sir Isaac Brock approached from Fort George, with six hundred men, and attempted to regain the battery. The British were repulsed, and Brock was killed.[1] In the mean while, General Stephen Van Rensselaer, who had crossed over, returned to Lewiston, and was using his most earnest efforts to send reinforcements; but only about one thousand troops, many of them quite undisciplined, could be induced to cross the river. These were attacked in the afternoon [Oct. 13, 1812] by fresh troops from Fort George, and a body of Chippewa Indians, and were nearly all killed or made prisoners, while at least fifteen hundred of their companions-in-arms cowardly refused to cross to their aid. The latter excused their conduct by the plea, put into their mouths by the opponents of the war, that they considered it wrong to invade the enemy's country, the war being avowedly a defensive one. The enemies of the administration applauded them for their conscientiousness, while a victory that might have led to reconciliation and peace, was lost at the winning moment. General Van Rensselaer, disgusted with the inefficiency everywhere displayed, left the service, and was succeeded by General Alexander Smyth, of Virginia This officer accomplished nothing of importance during the remainder of the season; and when the troops went into winter quarters [Dec.], there appeared to have been very few achievements made by the American army worthy of honorable mention in history.

While the army was suffering defeats, and became, in the mouths of the opponents of the administration, a staple rebuke, the little navy had acquitted itself nobly, and the national honor and prowess had been fully vindicated upon the ocean. At this time the British navy numbered one thousand and sixty vessels, while that of the United States, exclusive of gun-boats,[2] numbered only twenty. Two of these were unseaworthy, and one was on Lake Ontario. Nine of the American vessels were of a class less than frigates, and all of them could not well compare in appointments with those of the enemy. Yet the Americans were not dismayed by this disparity, but went out boldly in their ships to meet the war vessels of the proudest maritime nation upon the earth.[3] Victory after victory told of their skill and prowess. On the 19th of August, 1812, the United States frigate *Constitution*, Commodore Isaac Hull,[4] fought the British frigate *Guerriere*,[5] Captain Dacres, off the American coast, in the present track of ships to Great Britain. The contest continued about forty minutes, when

---

[1] Sir Isaac Brock was a brave and generous officer. There is a fine monument erected to his memory on Queenstown Heights, a short distance from the Niagara River. [2] Page 401.

[3] At the time of the declaration of war, Commodore Rogers [page 407] was at Sandy Hook, New York, with a small squadron, consisting of the frigates *President*, *Congress*, *United States*, and the sloop-of-war *Hornet*. He put to sea on the 21st of June, in pursuit of a British squadron which had sailed as a convoy of the West India fleet. After a slight engagement, and a chase of several hours, the pursuit was abandoned at near midnight. The frigate *Essex* [page 430] went to sea on the 3d of July; the *Constitution*, on the 12th. The brigs *Nautilus*, *Viper*, and *Vixen* were then cruising off the coast, and the sloop *Wasp* was at sea on her return from France.

[4] Isaac Hull was made a lieutenant in the navy in 1798, and was soon distinguished for skill and bravery. He rendered important service to his country, and died in Philadelphia in February, 1843.

[5] This vessel had been one of a British squadron which gave the *Constitution* a long and close chase about a month before, during which the nautical skill of Hull was most signally displayed.

Dacres surrendered;[1] and his vessel was such a complete wreck, that the victor burned her. The *Constitution*, it is said, was so little damaged, that she was ready for action the following day. This victory had a powerful effect on the public mind in both countries.

On the 18th of October, 1812, the United States sloop-of-war, *Wasp*, Captain Jones, captured the British brig *Frolic*, off the coast of North Carolina, after a very severe conflict for three-quarters of an hour. The slaughter on board the *Frolic* was dreadful. Only three officers and one seaman, of eighty-four, remained unhurt. The others were killed or badly wounded. The *Wasp* lost only ten men. Her term of victory was short, for the same afternoon, the British seventy-four gun ship *Poictiers* captured both vessels. A week afterward [October 25], the frigate *United States*, Commodore Decatur,[2] fought the British frigate *Macedonian*, west of the Canary Islands, for almost two hours. After being greatly damaged, and losing more than one hundred men, in killed and wounded, the *Macedonian* surrendered. Decatur lost only five killed and seven wounded; and his vessel was very little injured. A few weeks afterward [December 29, 1812], the *Constitution*, then commanded by Commodore Bainbridge,[3] became a victor, after combatting the British frigate *Java* for almost three hours, off San Salvador, on the coast of Brazil. The *Java* had four hundred men on board, of whom almost two hundred were killed or wounded. The *Constitution* was again very little injured; but she made such havoc with the *Java*, that Bainbridge, finding her incapable of floating long, burned her [January 1, 1813], three days after the action.

SLOOP-OF-WAR.

The Americans were greatly elated by these victories. Nor were they confined to the national vessels. Numerous privateers, which now swarmed upon the ocean, were making prizes in every direction, and accounts of their exploits filled the newspapers. It is estimated that during the year 1812, upward of fifty British armed vessels, and two hundred and fifty merchantmen, with an aggregate of more than three thousand prisoners, and a vast amount of booty, were captured by the Americans. These achievements wounded British pride in a tender part, for England claimed the appellation of "mistress of the seas." They also strengthened the administration; and at the close of the year, naval armaments were in preparation on the lakes, to assist the army in a projected invasion of Canada the following spring.

At the close of these defeats upon land, and these victories upon the ocean, the election of President and Vice-President of the United States, and also of members of Congress, occurred. The administration was strongly sustained by the popular vote. Mr. Madison was re-elected, with Elbridge Gerry[4] as Vice-President—George Clinton having died at Washington in April of that year.[5]

[1] On the *Guerriere* were seventy-nine killed and wounded. The *Constitution* lost seven killed and seven wounded.
[2] Page 392.
[3] Page 391.
[4] Note 1, page 385.
[5] Note 5, page 350.

A fraction of the Democratic party, and most of the Federalists, voted for De Witt Clinton[1] for President, and Jared Ingersoll, for Vice-President. Notwithstanding the members of Congress then elected, were chiefly Democrats, it was evident that the opposition was powerful and increasing, particularly in the eastern States, yet the President felt certain that the great body of the people were favorable to his war policy.

CHAPTER V.

THE SECOND WAR FOR INDEPENDENCE. [1813.]

During the autumn of 1812, the whole western country, incensed by Hull's surrender, seemed filled with the zeal of the old Crusaders.[2] Michigan had to be recovered,[3] and the greatest warlike enthusiasm prevailed. Volunteers had gathered under local leaders, in every settlement. Companies were formed and equipped in a single day, and were ready to march the next. For several weeks the volunteers found employment in driving the hostile Indians from post to post, in the vicinity of the extreme western settlements. They desolated their villages and plantations, after the manner of Sullivan, in 1779,[4] and the fiercest indignation against the white people was thus excited among the tribes, which, under the stimulus of their British allies, led to terrible retaliations.[5] So eager were the people for battle, that the snows of winter in the great wilderness, did not keep them from the field. The campaign of 1813 opened with the year. Almost the entire northern frontier of the United States was the chief theatre of operations. The army of the *West*,[6] under General Harrison,[7] was concentrating at the head of Lake Erie; that of the *Centre*,[8] now under Dearborn, was on the banks of the Niagara River; and that of the *North*,[9] under Hampton, was on the borders of Lake Champlain. Sir George Prevost was the successor of Brock[10] in command of the British army in Canada, assisted by General Proctor in the direction of Detroit,[11] and by General Sheaffe in the vicinity of Montreal and the lower portions of Lake Champlain.

Brave and experienced leaders had rallied to the standard of Harrison in the north-west. Kentucky sent swarms of her young men, from every social

---

[1] Page 456. [2] Note 5, page 38. [3] Page 411. [4] Page 304.

[5] Harrison early took steps to relieve the frontier posts. These were Fort Harrison, on the Wabash; Fort Wayne, on the Miami of the lakes; Fort Defiance [Note 6, page 374]; and Fort Deposit, to which the Indians laid siege on the 12th of September. Generals Winchester, Tupper, and Payne, and Colonels Wells, Scott, Lewis, Jennings, and Allen, were the chief leaders against the savages. Operations were carried on vigorously, further west. Early in October, almost four thousand volunteers, chiefly mounted riflemen, under General Hopkins, had collected at Vincennes [page 303] for an expedition against the towns of the Peoria and other Indians, in the Wabash country. It was this formidable expedition, sanctioned by Governor Shelby, which produced the greatest devastation in the Indian country. [6] Note 3, page 412. [7] Page 474.

[8] Note 3, page 412. [9] Note 3, page 412. [10] Page 411. [11] Page 412.

rank, led by the veteran Shelby,[1] and the yeomanry of Ohio and its neighborhood hastened to the field. So numerous were the volunteers, that Harrison was compelled to issue an order against further enlistments, and many a warm heart, beating with desire for military glory, was chilled by disappointment. General Harrison chose the west end of Lake Erie as his chief place of muster,

with the design of making a descent upon the British at Malden and Detroit,[2] and by securing possession of those posts, recover Michigan and the forts west of it. Early in January [10th, 1813], General Winchester, on his way from the southward, with eight hundred young men, chiefly Kentuckians, reached the Maumee Rapids.[3] There he was informed [January 13, 1813] that a party of British and Indians had concentrated at Frenchtown, on the river Raisin,[4] twenty-five miles south of Detroit. He immediately sent a detachment,

---

[1] Isaac Shelby was born in Maryland, in 1750. He entered military life in 1774, and went to Kentucky as a land-surveyor, in 1775. He engaged in the War of the Revolution, and was distinguished in the battle on King's Mountain [page 319] in 1780. He was made governor of Kentucky in 1792, and soon afterward retired to private life, from which he was drawn, first in 1812, to the duties of Chief Magistrate of his State, and again, in 1813, to lead an army to the field against his old enemy. He died in 1826, when almost seventy-six years of age.

[2] Page 412.

[3] Note 7, page 374.

[4] Opposite the flourishing village of Monroe, Michigan, two or three miles from Lake Erie. The Raisin derived its name from the fact, that in former years great quantities of grapes clustered upon its banks.

under Colonels Allen and Lewis, to protect the inhabitants in that direction. Finding Frenchtown in the possession of the enemy, they successfully attacked [January 18] and routed them, and held possession until the arrival of Winchester [January 20], with almost three hundred men, two days afterward.

General Proctor, who was at Malden, eighteen miles distant, heard of the advance of Winchester, and proceeded immediately and secretly, with a combined force of fifteen hundred British and Indians, to attack him. They fell upon the American camp at dawn, on the morning of the 22d of January. After a severe battle and heavy loss on both sides, Winchester,[1] who had been made a prisoner by the Indians, surrendered his troops on the condition, agreed to by Proctor, that ample protection to all should be given. Proctor, fearing the approach of Harrison, who was then on the Lower Sandusky, immediately marched for Malden, leaving the sick and wounded Americans behind, without a guard. After following him some distance, the Indians turned back [January 23], murdered and scalped[2] the Americans who were unable to travel, set fire to dwellings, took many prisoners to Detroit, in order to procure exorbitant ransom prices, and reserved some of them for inhuman torture. The indifference of Proctor and his troops, on this occasion, was criminal in the highest degree, and gave just ground for the dreadful suspicion, that they encouraged the savages in their deeds of blood. Oftentimes after that, the war-cry of the Kentuckians was, "Remember the River Raisin!" The tragedy was keenly felt in all the western region, and especially in Kentucky, for the slain, by bullet, arrow, tomahawk, and brand, were generally of the most respectable families in the State; many of them young men of fortune and distinction, with numerous friends and relations.

Harrison had advanced to the Maumee Rapids, when the intelligence of the affair at Frenchtown reached him. Supposing Proctor would press forward to attack him, he fell back [January 23, 1813]; but on hearing of the march of the British toward Malden, he advanced [February 1] to the rapids, with twelve hundred men, established a fortified camp there, and called it Fort Meigs,[3] in honor of the governor of Ohio. There he was besieged by Proctor several weeks afterward [May 1], who was at the head of more than two thousand British and Indians. On the fifth day of the siege, General Clay[4] arrived [May 5] with twelve hundred men, and dispersed the enemy. A large portion of his troops, while unwisely pursuing the fugitives, were surrounded and captured; and Proctor returned to the siege. The impatient Indians, refusing to listen to Tecumseh,[5] their leader, deserted

FORT MEIGS.

[1] James Winchester was born in Maryland in 1756. He was made brigadier-general in 1812; resigned his commission in 1815; and died in Tennessee in 1826. [2] Note 4, page 14.

[3] Fort Meigs was erected on the south side of the Maumee, nearly opposite the former British post [note 8, page 374], and a short distance from the present village of Perrysburg.

[4] Green Clay was born in Virginia in 1757, was made a brigadier of Kentucky volunteers early in 1813, and died in October, 1826.

[5] Page 408. Tecumseh came with the largest body of Indians ever collected on the northern frontier.

the British on the eighth day [May 8]; and twenty-four hours afterward, Proctor abandoned the siege and returned to Malden [May 9], to prepare for a more formidable invasion. Thus terminated a siege of thirteen days, during which time the fortitude and courage of the Americans were wonderfully displayed in the presence of the enemy. The Americans lost in the fort, eighty-one killed, and one hundred and eighty-nine wounded.

For several weeks after the siege of Fort Meigs, military operations were suspended by both parties. Here, then, let us take a brief retrospective glance. Congress assembled on the 2d of November, 1812, and its councils were divided by fierce party spirit, which came down from the people. The Democrats had a decided majority, and therefore the measures of the administration were sustained. The British government now began to show some desire for reconciliation. Already the orders in council had been repealed, and the Prince Regent[1] demanded that hostilities should cease. To this the President replied, that being now at war, the United States would not put an end to it, unless full provisions were made for a general settlement of differences, and a cessation of the practice of impressment, pending the negotiation. At about the same time a law was passed, prohibiting the employment of British seamen in American vessels. The British also proposed an armistice, but upon terms which the Americans could not accept. Indeed, all propositions from that quarter were inconsistent with honor and justice, and they were rejected. When these attempts at reconciliation had failed, the Emperor Alexander of Russia offered his mediation. The government of the United States instantly accepted it,[2] but the British government refused it; and so the war went on. Congress made provision for prosecuting it with vigor; and the hope lighted by Alexander's offer, soon faded.

The American troops in the West had remained at Fort Meigs and vicinity. Toward the close of July [July 21, 1813], about four thousand British and Indians, under Proctor and Tecumseh,[3] again appeared before that fortress, then commanded by General Clay. Meeting with a vigorous resistance, Proctor left Tecumseh to watch the fort, while he marched [July 28], with five hundred regulars and eight hundred Indians, to attack Fort Stephenson, at Lower Sandusky,[4] which was garrisoned by about one hundred and fifty young men,[5] commanded by Major Croghan, a brave soldier,

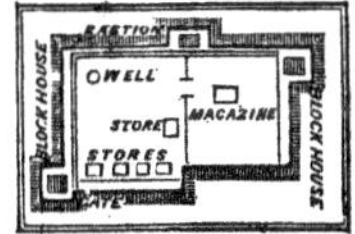

FORT SANDUSKY.

[1] When, in consequence of mental infirmity, George the Third became incompetent to reign, in February, 1811, his son, George, Prince of Wales, and afterward George the Fourth, was made regent, or temporary ruler of the realm. He retained the office of king, *pro tempore*, until the death of his father, in 1820.

[2] The President appointed, as commissioners, or envoys extraordinary, to negotiate a treaty of peace with Great Britain, under the Russian mediation, Albert Gallatin, John Quincy Adams, and James A. Bayard. Mr. Adams was then American minister at the Russian court, and was joined by Messrs. Gallatin and Bayard in June following.

[3] Page 408.

[4] On the west bank of the Sandusky River, about fifteen miles south from Sandusky Bay. The area within the pickets [note 1, page 127] was about an acre. The fort was made of regular embankments of earth and a ditch, with bastions and block-houses [note 3, page 192] and some rude log buildings within.

[5] The greater portion of the garrison were very young men, and some of them were mere youths.

then only twenty-one years of age.[1] Proctor's demand for surrender was accompanied by the usual menace of Indian massacre; but it did not intimidate Croghan.[2] After a severe cannonade[3] had made a breach, about five hundred of the besiegers attempted to rush in and take the place by assault [Aug. 2, 1813]; but so terribly were they met by grape-shot[4] from the only cannon in the fort, that they recoiled, panic-stricken, and the whole body fled in confusion, leaving one hundred and fifty of their number killed or wounded. The Americans lost only one man killed, and seven wounded. This gallant defense was universally applauded,[5] and it had a powerful effect upon the Indians.

MAJOR CROGHAN.

Proctor and Tecumseh left for Detroit, after this noble defense of Fort Stephenson, and the British abandoned all hope of capturing these western American posts, until they should become masters of Lake Erie. But while the events just narrated were in progress, a new power appeared in the conflict in the West and North, and complicated the difficulties of the enemy. In the autumn of 1812, Commodore Chauncey had fitted out a small naval armament at Sackett's Harbor, to dispute the mastery, on Lake Ontario, with several British armed vessels then afloat.[6] And during the summer of 1813, Commodore Oliver Hazzard Perry had prepared, on Lake Erie, an American squadron of nine vessels,[7] mounting fifty-four guns, to co-operate with the Army of the West. The British had also fitted out a small squadron of six vessels, carrying sixty-three guns, commanded by Commodore Barclay. Perry's fleet was ready by the 2d of August, but some time was occupied in getting several of his vessels over the bar in the harbor of Erie. The hostile fleets met near the western extremity of Lake Erie on the morning of the 10th of September, 1813, and a very severe battle ensued. The brave Perry managed with the skill of an old admiral, and the courage of the proudest soldier. His flag-ship, the *Lawrence*, had to bear the brunt of the battle, and very soon she became an unmanageable wreck, having all her crew, except four or five, killed or wounded. Perry then left her, in an open boat, and hoisted his flag on the *Niagara* at the moment when that of the *Lawrence* fell. With this vessel he

[1] George Croghan was a nephew of George Rogers Clarke [page 300]. He afterward rose to the rank of colonel, and held the office of inspector-general. He died at New Orleans in 1849.

[2] In reply to Proctor's demand and threat, he said, in substance, that when the fort should be taken there would be none left to massacre, as it would not be given up while there was a man left to fight.

[3] The British employed six six-pounders and a howitzer, in the siege. A howitzer is a piece of ordnance similar to a mortar, for hurling bomb-shells.

[4] Note 4, page 242.

[5] Major Croghan was immediately promoted to the rank of lieutenant-colonel; and the ladies of Chillicothe gave him an elegant sword.

[6] Chauncey's squadron consisted of six vessels, mounting thirty-two guns, in all. The British squadron consisted of the same number of vessels, but mounting more than a hundred guns. Notwithstanding this disparity, Chauncey attacked them near Kingston [note 5, page 180] early in November, damaged them a good deal, and captured and carried into Sackett's Harbor, a schooner belonging to the enemy. He then captured another schooner, which had $12,000 in specie on board, and the baggage of the deceased General Brock. See page 414.

[7] *Lawrence* (flag-ship), 20 guns; *Niagara*, 20; *Caledonian*, 3; shooner *Ariel*, 4; *Scorpion*, 2; *Somers*, 2 guns and 2 swivels; sloop *Trippe*, and schooners *Tigress* and *Porcupine*, of 1 gun each.

PERRY ON LAKE ERIE.

passed through the enemy's line, pouring broadsides, right and left, at half pistol-shot distance. The remainder of the squadron followed, with a fair wind, and the victory was soon decided. At four o'clock in the afternoon, every British vessel had surrendered to him;[1] and before sunset, he had sent a messenger to General Harrison with the famous dispatch, "*We have met the enemy, and they are ours.*" This victory was hailed with unbounded demon-

strations of joy. For a moment, party rancor was almost forgotten; and bonfires and illuminations lighted up the whole country.

Perry's victory was followed by immediate and energetic action on the part of Harrison. The command of Lake Erie now being secured, and a reinforcement of four thousand Kentucky volunteers, under Governor Shelby, the old hero of King's Mountain,[2] having arrived [Sept. 17, 1813], the general proceeded to attack Malden and attempt the recovery of Detroit. The fleet conveyed a portion of the troops across the lake [Sept 27], but on their arrival at Malden, it had been deserted by Proctor, who was fleeing, with Tecumseh and his Indians, toward the Moravian village, on the Thames, eighty miles from

---

[1] The carnage was very great, in proportion to the numbers engaged. The Americans lost twenty-seven killed, and ninety-six wounded. The British lost about two hundred in killed and wounded, and six hundred prisoners. Perry's treatment of his prisoners received the highest applause. Commodore Barclay declared that his humane conduct was sufficient to immortalize him. That brave commander was born at Newport, Rhode Island, in 1785. He entered the service as midshipman, in 1798. He continued in active service after the close of the Second War for Independence, and died of yellow fever, in the West India seas, in 1819. It was his brother, Commodore M. C. Perry, who effected a treaty with Japan in 1854. See page 512.

[2] Page 417.

Detroit.[1] A body of Americans took possession of Detroit on the 29th of September; and on the 2d of October, Harrison and Shelby, with Colonel Richard M. Johnson and his cavalry (thirty-five hundred strong), started in pursuit of the enemy.[2] They overtook them [Oct. 5] at the Moravian town, when a desperate battle ensued. Tecumseh was slain;[3] and then his dismayed followers, who had fought furiously, broke and fled. Almost the whole of Proctor's command were killed or made prisoners, and the general himself narrowly escaped, with a few of his cavalry. Here the Americans recaptured six brass field-pieces which had been surrendered by Hull, on two of which were engraved the words, "Surrendered by Burgoyne at Saratoga."[4] These pieces are now at the United States military post of West Point, on the Hudson.[5]

The battle on the Thames was a very important one. By that victory, all that Hull[6] had lost was recovered; the Indian confederacy[7] was completely broken up, and the war on the north-western borders of the Union was terminated. The name of Harrison was upon every lip; and throughout the entire Republic, there was a general outburst of gratitude. He was complimented by Congress, and by various public bodies; and a member of the House of Representatives asserted, in his place, that his victory was "such as would have secured to a Roman general, in the best days of the republic, the honors of a triumph." Security now being given to the frontier, General Harrison dismissed a greater portion of the volunteers; and leaving General Cass, with about a thousand regulars, to garrison Detroit, proceeded [Oct. 23, 1813] to Niagara, with the remainder of his troops, to join the Army of the Center,[8] which had been making some endeavors to invade Canada. In the mean while, an Indian war had been kindled in the South;[9] and on the ocean, the laurel wreaths of triumph won by the Americans during 1812,[10] had been interwoven with garlands of cypress on account of reverses. Let us turn a moment to the operations of the Army of the North.[11]

Hostilities were kept up on portions of the northern frontier, during the winter, as well as in the West. In February [1813], a detachment of British soldiers crossed the St. Lawrence on the ice, from Prescott to Ogdensburg, and under pretense of seeking for deserters, committed robberies. Major Forsyth, then in command of riflemen there, retaliated. This was resented, in turn, by

---

[1] In the present town of Orford, West Canada.

[2] Commodore Perry, and General Cass, (now [1856] United States Senator from Michigan,) accompanied General Harrison as volunteer aids. The Americans moved with such rapidity, that they traveled twenty-six miles the first day.

[3] Tecumseh was then only about forty years of age. He was a man of great ability, and had he been born and educated in civilized society, his powerful intellect would have made him one of the most distinguished characters of the age. He possessed great dignity, and always maintained it in his deportment. On one occasion he was to attend a conference held with Harrison. A circle of the company had been formed; and when he came and entered it, there was no seat for him, Harrison's aid having taken the one by the side of the general, intended for him. Harrison perceived that Tecumseh was offended, and told his aid to invite the chief to the seat near him. The aid politely said to Tecumseh, "Your father requests you to take a seat by his side." The offended chief drew his blanket around him, and, with an air of great dignity, said, "The Great Spirit is my father, and I will repose on the bosom of my mother;" and then sat down upon the ground.

[4] Page 281. [5] Note 2, page 324. [6] Page 411. [7] Page 408.

[8] Page 412. [9] Page 428. [10] Page 415. [11] Page 412.

a British force of twelve hundred men, who crossed on the 21st of February, and after a conflict of an hour, drove out the few military defenders of Ogdensburg, plundered and destroyed a large amount of property, and then returned to Canada.[1] These events accelerated the gathering of the militia in that quarter. Bodies of new levies arrived, almost daily, at Sackett's Harbor, but these, needing discipline, were of little service, as a defense of the country between that point and Ogdensburg.

Being unable to afford assistance to the exposed points in that region, General Dearborn, the commander-in-chief,[2] resolved to attempt the capture of York (now Toronto), the capital of Upper Canada, and the principal depository of British military stores for the supply of western garrisons. He embarked seventeen hundred troops on board the fleet of Commodore Chauncey,[3] at Sackett's Harbor, on the 25th of April; and two days afterward [April 27], they landed on the beach at York, about two miles west from the British works, in the face of a galling fire from regulars and Indians, under General Sheaffe. These were soon driven back to their fortifications, and the Americans, under General Pike,[4] pressed forward, captured two redoubts, and were advancing upon the main work, when the magazine of the fort blew up,[5] hurling stones and timbers in every direction, and producing great destruction of life among the assailants. General Pike was mortally wounded, but he lived long enough to know that the enemy had fled, and that the American flag waved in triumph over the fort at York.[6] The command then devolved on Colonel Pearce; and at four o'clock in the afternoon, the town was in possession of the Americans. General Dearborn, who had remained with the fleet, landed soon after the fall of Pike, but did not assume the immediate command until after the surrender of the town.

GENERAL PIKE.

When the victory was completed, the fleet and troops returned [May 1] to Sackett's Harbor, but soon afterward proceeded to attack Fort George, on the western shore of Niagara River, near its mouth. After a brief defense [May 27, 1813], the garrison fled to Burlington Heights, at the western extremity of Lake Ontario,[7] thirty-five miles distant, closely pursued by a much larger force,

---

[1] The Americans lost, in killed and wounded, twenty men. The British loss was about double that number.
[2] Page 410.
[3] Page 420.

[4] General Dearborn had given the command of this expedition to Brigadier-General Zebulon M. Pike, a brave and useful officer, who had been at the head of an expedition, a few years earlier, to explore the country around the head waters of the Mississippi. He was born in New Jersey, in 1779. He died on board the flag-ship of Commodore Chauncey, with the captured British flag under his head, at the age of thirty-four years. In the burial-ground attached to Madison barracks, at Sackett's Harbor, is a dilapidated wooden monument erected over the remains of General Pike and some of his companions in arms. When the writer visited the spot, in 1855, it was wasting with decay, and falling to the earth. Such a neglect of the burial-place of the illustrious dead, is a disgrace to our government.

[5] The British had laid a train of wet powder communicating with the magazine, for the purpose, and when they retreated, they fired it.

[6] General Sheaffe escaped, with the principal part of the troops, but lost all his baggage, books, papers, and a large amount of public property.

[7] At the head of Burlington Bay, in Canada.

under Generals Chandler[1] and Winder.[2] In this affair, Colonel (now Lieutenant-General) Scott was distinguished for his skill and bravery. On the night of the 6th of June, the British fell upon the American camp, at Stony Creek,[3] but were repulsed. It was very dark, and in the confusion both of the American generals were made prisoners.

A British squadron appeared before Sackett's Harbor on the same day [May 27] that the Americans attacked Fort George: and two days afterward [May 29] Sir George Prevost and a thousand soldiers landed in the face of a severe fire from some regulars[4] stationed there. The regular force of the Americans consisted of only a few seamen, a company of artillery, and about two hundred invalids—not more than five hundred men in all. General Jacob Brown, the commander at that station, rallied the militia, and their rapid gathering, at and near the landing-place, back of Horse Island, so alarmed Prevost, lest they should cut off his retreat, that he hastily re-embarked, leaving almost the whole of his wounded behind. Had he been aware of the condition of his opposers, he could have made an easy conquest of Sackett's Harbor. The raw militia had become panic-stricken at the first, and when Prevost retreated, they, too, were endeavoring to make their way to places of safety in the country.

A change in the administration of military affairs occurred soon after the event at Sackett's Harbor. For some time, the infirmities of General Dearborn, the commander-in-chief,[5] had disqualified him for active participation in the operations of the army, and in June [1813] he withdrew from the service. He was succeeded in command by General James Wilkinson,[6] who, like Dearborn, had been an active young officer in the War for Independence. General John Armstrong,[7] then Secretary of War, had conceived another invasion of Canada, by the united forces of the armies of the Center and North.[8] For this purpose a little more than seven thousand men were concentrated at French Creek on the 5th of November, 1813, and on that morning went down the St. Lawrence in boats, with the intention of co-operating with about four thousand troops under Hampton,[9] in an attack upon Montreal. They landed the same evening, a few miles abave the British fort at Prescott, opposite Ogdensburg. It being foggy, Wilkinson attempted to pass down the river upon the flotilla commanded by General Brown. The fog cleared away, and the moon revealed the Amer-

[1] John Chandler was a native of Massachusetts. Some years after the war he was United States Senator from Maine. He died at Augusta, in that State, in 1841. [2] Page 436.

[3] In the present township of Saltfleet, Canada West. In this affair the Americans lost, in killed, wounded, and missing, one hundred and fifty-four.

[4] Note 6, page 185. [5] Page 410.

[6] James Wilkinson was born in Maryland, in 1757, and studied medicine. He joined the continental army at Cambridge, in 1775, and continued in service during the war. He commanded the western division of the United States army at the beginning of the century, and became somewhat involved, as we have seen [page 396], in Burr's scheme, in 1806. He died near the city of Mexico, in 1825, at the age of sixty-eight years.

[7] Note 4, page 349. John Armstrong was a son of Colonel John Armstrong, of Pennsylvania [page 191], and was born at Carlisle, in that State, in 1758. He served in the War of the Revolution; was Secretary of the State of Pennsylvania; minister to France in 1804; Secretary of War in 1813; and died in Dutchess county, New York, in 1843. [8] Note 3, page 412.

[9] Page 410.

icans to the garrison of the fort. The latter immediately opened a heavy fire, and being thus annoyed by the enemy on shore, and by gun-boats[1] in his rear, Wilkinson landed Brown and a strong detachment to go forward and disperse quite a large force near Williamsburg, and to cover the descent of the boats. A severe battle ensued [November 11] in which the Americans lost more than three hundred men in killed and wounded, and the British about two hundred. This is known as the battle of Chrysler's Field. The locality is on the northern shore of the St. Lawrence, a little more than thirty miles below Ogdensburg, and about ninety above Montreal.

General Wilkinson arrived at St. Regis[2] the next day, with the main body, when he was informed that no troops from the army of the North would join him.[3] He therefore abandoned the expedition against Montreal, and went into winter quarters at French Mills (now Fort Covington, in St. Lawrence county), about nine miles east of St. Regis. A little later, some stirring events occurred on the Niagara frontier. General M'Clure, commander at Fort George,[4] burnt the Canadian village of Newark on the 10th of December. Two days later [December 12, 1813] he was compelled by the British to abandon Fort George. A strong force of British and Indians then surprised and captured [December 19] Fort Niagara, on the east side of the Niagara River, near its mouth;[5] and in retaliation for the burning of Newark, they laid Youngstown, Lewiston, Manchester (now Niagara Falls), and the Tuscarora Indian village, in Niagara county, in ashes. On the 30th, the little villages of Black Rock and Buffalo[6] were also consumed, and a large amount of public and private property was destroyed. With these events ended the campaign of 1813, in the North.

FORT NIAGARA, 1813.

Affairs in the extreme South assumed a serious aspect during the summer of 1813. In the spring of that year, Tecumseh (who was slain on the Thames a few months later)[7] went among the Southern tribes, to arouse them to wage war upon the white people. The powerful Creeks[8] yielded to his persuasions; and late in August [30th], a large party of them surprised and captured Fort Mimms, on the Alabama River,[9] and massacred almost three hundred men,

[1] Page 401.
[2] This is an old French and Indian settlement on the St. Lawrence, at the mouth of the St. Regis River, about fifty miles below Ogdensburg. The dividing line (45th degree) between the United States and Canada, passes through the center of the village.
[3] There was an enmity between Wilkinson and Hampton, and Armstrong resolved to command the expedition himself, to prevent trouble on account of precedence. He joined the army at Sackett's Harbor, but soon returned to Washington, for he and Wilkinson could not agree. To the jealousies and bickerings of these old officers, must the disasters of the land troops be, in a great degree, attributed. General Hampton did move forward toward Canada, but finally fell back to Plattsburg, and leaving the command with General Izard, returned to South Carolina. He died at Columbia, South Carolina, in 1835, aged eighty-one years.
[4] Page 414.
[5] Page 200.
[6] Buffalo was then a small village, containing about fifteen hundred inhabitants, and was utterly destroyed. It is now [1856] one of the stateliest commercial cities on the continent, with a population of not much less than one hundred thousand.
[7] Page 424.
[8] Page 30.
[9] On the east side of the Alabama, about ten miles above its junction with the Tombigbee.

women, and children. This event aroused the whole South. General Andrew Jackson,[1] accompanied by General Coffee, marched into the Creek country, with twenty-five hundred Tennessee militia, and prosecuted a subjugating war against them, with great vigor.

On the 3d of November, General Coffee,[2] with nine hundred men, surrounded an Indian force at Tallushatchee,[3] and killed two hundred of them. Not a warrior escaped. Within ten weeks afterward, bloody battles had been fought at Talladega[4] [November 8], Autossee[5] [November 29], and Emucfau[6] [January 22d, 1814], and several skirmishes had also taken place. The Americans were always victorious, yet they lost many brave soldiers. At length the Creeks established a fortified camp at the Great Horseshoe Bend of the Tallapoosa River,[7] and there a thousand warriors, with their women and children, determined to make a last defensive stand. The Americans surrounded them, and Jackson, with the main body of his army, attacked them on the 27th of March, 1814. The Indians fought desperately, for they saw no future for themselves, in the event of defeat. Almost six hundred warriors were slain, for they disdained to surrender. Only two or three were made prisoners, with about three hundred women and children. This battle crushed the power and spirit of the Creek nation, and soon afterward the chiefs of the remnant signified their submission.[8] It was a sad scene to the eyes of the benevolent and good, to see these ancient tribes of our land, who were then making rapid strides in the progress of civilization, so utterly ruined by the destroying hand of war. They found that *might* made *right*, in the view of their subjugators, and they were compelled to make a treaty of peace upon the terms dictated by their conquerors. Thus, time after time since the advent of the white people here, have the hands of the stronger been laid upon the weaker, until now nothing but *remnants* of once powerful nations remain.

The naval operations upon the ocean, during the year 1813, were very important. Many and severe conflicts between public and private armed vessels of the United States and Great Britain, occurred; and at the close of the year, the balance-sheet of victories showed a preponderance in favor of the former.[9] Toward the end of February, the United States sloop of war *Hornet*, Cap-

---

[1] Page 460.

[2] John Coffee was a native of Virginia. He did good service during the second War for Independence, and in subsequent campaigns. He died in 1834.

[3] South side of Tallushatchee Creek, near the village of Jacksonville, in Benton county, Alabama.

[4] A little east of the Coosa River, in the present Talladega county.

[5] On the bank of the Tallapoosa, twenty miles from its junction with the Coosa, in Macon county.

[6] On the west bank of the Tallapoosa, at the mouth of Emucfau Creek, in Tallapoosa county.

[7] Called Tohopeka by the Indians. Near the north-east corner of Tallapoosa county.

[8] Among those who bowed in submission was Weathersford, their greatest leader. He appeared suddenly before Jackson, in his tent, and standing erect, he said: "I am in your power; do with me what you please. I have done the white people all the harm I could. I have fought them, and fought them bravely. My warriors are all gone now, and I can do no more. When there was a chance for success, I never asked for peace. There is none now, and I ask it for the remnant of my nation."

[9] More than seven hundred British vessels were taken by the American navy and privateers, during the years 1812 and 1813.

tain Lawrence, fought [Feb. 24, 1813] the British brig *Peacock*, off the mouth of Demarara River, South America. The *Peacock* surrendered, after a fierce conflict of fifteen minutes, and a few moments afterward she sank, carrying down with her nine British seamen and three Americans. The loss of the *Peacock*, in killed and wounded, was thirty-seven; of the *Hornet* only five. The generous conduct of Captain Lawrence, toward his enemy on this occasion, drew from the officers of the *Peacock*, on their arrival in New York, a public letter of thanks.[1] This, of itself, was a wreath of honor for the victor, more glorious than his triumph in the sanguinary conflict.

On his return to the United States, Captain Lawrence was promoted to the command of the frigate *Chesapeake;* and on the 1st of June, 1813, he sailed from Boston harbor, in search of the British frigate, *Shannon*, which had recently appeared off the New England coast, and challenged any vessel, of equal size, to meet her. Lawrence found the boaster the same day, about thirty miles from Boston light; and at five in the afternoon, a furious action began. The two vessels soon became entangled. Then the Britons boarded the *Chesapeake*, and after a desperate hand-to-hand struggle, hoisted the British flag. Lawrence was mortally wounded at the beginning of the action; and when he was carried below, he uttered those brave words of command, which Perry afterward displayed on his flag-ship on Lake Erie, "*Don't give up the ship!*" The combat lasted only fifteen minutes; but in that time, the *Chesapeake* had forty-eight killed and ninety-eight wounded; the *Shannon* twenty-three killed, and fifty-six wounded. The body of Lawrence,[2] with that of Ludlow, the second in command, was carried to Halifax, in the victorious *Shannon*, and there buried with the honors of war. This event caused great sadness in America, and unbounded joy in England.[3]

CAPTAIN LAWRENCE.

Another disaster followed the loss of the *Chesapeake*. It was the capture of the American brig *Argus*, Captain Allen, in August. The *Argus*, in the spring [1813], had conveyed Mr. Crawford, United States minister, to France, and for two months had greatly annoyed British shipping in the English Chan-

---

[1] They said, "So much was done to alleviate the uncomfortable and distressing situation in which we were placed, when received on board the ship you command, that we can not better express our feelings than by saying, we ceased to consider ourselves prisoners; and every thing that friendship could dictate, was adopted by you and the officers of the *Hornet*, to remedy the inconvenience we otherwise should have experienced, from the unavoidable loss of the whole of our property and clothes, by the sudden sinking of the *Peacock*." The crew of the *Hornet* divided their clothing with the prisoners.

[2] Captain James Lawrence was a native of New Jersey, and received a midshipman's warrant at the age of sixteen years. He was with Decatur at Tripoli [page 392]. He died four days after receiving the wound, at the age of thirty-one years. A beautiful monument, in the form of a truncated column and pedestal, was erected to his memory in Trinity church-yard, New York. This, in time, became dilapidated, and a few years since, a new one, of another form, was erected near the south entrance to the church, a few feet from Broadway.

[3] A writer of the time observed: "Never did any victory—not those of Wellington in Spain, nor even those of Nelson—call forth such expressions of joy on the part of the British; a proof that our naval character had risen somewhat in their estimation."

nel. Several vessels were sent out to capture her; and on the 14th of August, the sloop of war[1] *Pelican*, after a brief, but severe action, defeated the *Argus*. In less than a month afterward [Sept. 10], Perry gained his great victory on Lake Erie;[2] and the British brig *Boxer*, Captain Blythe, had surrendered [Sept. 5, 1813], to the United States brig *Enterprise*, Lieutenant Burrows, after an engagement of forty minutes, off the coast of Maine. Blythe and Burrows, young men of great promise, were both slain during the action, and their bodies were buried in one grave at Portland, with military honors.

A distressing warfare upon the coast between Delaware Bay and Charleston, was carried on during the spring and summer of 1813, by a small British squadron under the general command of Admiral Cockburn. His chief object was to draw the American troops from the northern frontier to the defense of the seaboard, and thus lessen the danger that hung over Canada. It was a sort of amphibious warfare—on land and water—and was marked by many acts of unnecessary cruelty. The British had talked of "chastising the Americans into submission," and the method now employed was the instrument. On the 4th of February, 1813, two ships of the line, three frigates, and other British vessels, made their appearance at the capes of Virginia.[3] At about the same time, another British squadron entered the Delaware River, destroyed the American shipping there in March, and in April cannonaded the town of Lewiston. In May, Frenchtown, Havre de Grace, Georgetown, and Fredericktown, on the Chesapeake, were plundered and burned; and then the combined British fleet entered Hampton Roads,[4] and menaced Norfolk. While attempting to go up to that city, the enemy were nobly repulsed [Jan. 22, 1813] by the Americans upon Craney Island,[5] under the command of Major Faulkner, assisted by naval officers. The British then fell upon Hampton [Jan. 25]; and having surfeited themselves with plunder, withdrew. Cockburn[6] sailed down the North Carolina coast, marauding whenever opportunity offered, and carried away a large number of negroes and sold them in the West Indies. In pleasant contrast to this, was the deportment of Commodore Hardy, whose squadron was employed during the same season, in blockading the New England coast. Although he landed upon our shores frequently, yet his conduct was always that of a high-minded gentleman and generous enemy.[7]

During the year 1813, the United States frigate *Essex*, Captain Porter, made a long and successful cruise in the Atlantic and Pacific Oceans. It occupied the time from April until October. The *Essex* carried at her masthead the popular motto, "*Free Trade and Sailor's Rights;*" and, while in

---

[1] Page 415. [2] Page 423. [3] Page 64. [4] Note 3, page 297.

[5] Craney Island is low and bare, and lies at the mouth of the Elizabeth River, about five miles below Norfolk. At the time in question, there were some unfinished fortifications upon it, remains of which may yet [1856] be seen.

[6] Cockburn died in England in 1853, at an advanced age.

[7] Congress had passed an act, offering a reward of half their value for the destruction of British ships, by other means than those of the armed vessels of the United States. This was to encourage the use of torpedoes. The cruel forays upon the southern coasts seemed to warrant this species of dishonorable warfare. It was employed against Hardy's squadron. He was justly indignant, and protested against it as unmanly.

the Pacific, she captured twelve British whale-ships, with an aggregate of three hundred and two men, and one hundred and seven guns. The *Essex* was finally captured in the harbor of Valparaiso [March, 28, 1814], on the western coast of South America, by the British frigate *Phœbe*, and sloop of war *Cherub*, after one of the most desperately fought battles of the war. It is said that thousands of the inhabitants of Valparaiso covered the neighboring heights as spectators of the conflict. Perceiving the overpowering advantage of the British, their sympathies were strongly elicited in favor of the *Essex*. When any thing in her favor appeared, loud shouts went up from the multitude; and when she was finally disabled and lost, they expressed their feelings in groans and tears. The *Essex* lost one hundred and fifty-four, in killed and wounded. Captain Porter[1] wrote to the Secretary of the Navy, "We have been unfortunate, but not disgraced."

COMMODORE PORTER.

CHAPTER VI.

SECOND WAR FOR INDEPENDENCE, CONTINUED. [1814, 1815.]

DURING the year 1814, the war was prosecuted by both parties with more zeal and vigor than hitherto. The means for supporting it were much augmented by the government of the United States, notwithstanding the public credit was much depreciated, and treasury notes fell as low as seventeen per cent. below par. At the same time, Great Britain seemed to put forth increased energy, and her vessels of war hovered along our entire coast, and kept the sea-port towns in a state of continual alarm. Early in that year, the victorious career of Napoleon, in Europe, was checked by the allied powers. Almost all of the governments of continental Europe, with that of England, had combined to crush him, and sustain the sinking Bourbon dynasty. Their armies were allied in a common cause. These, approaching from different directions, reached Paris, at the close of March, 1814, when the Russian and Prussian emperors entered the city.[2] Hoping to secure the crown to his son, Napoleon abdicated in his favor on the 4th of April, and retired to Elba. Peace for Europe

[1] Commodore David Porter was among the most distinguished of the American naval commanders. He was a resident minister of the United States in Turkey, and died, near Constantinople, in March, 1843.

[2] Russians, one hundred and fifty thousand strong, advanced from Switzerland; Blucher led one hundred and thirty thousand Prussians from Germany; Bernadotte, the old companion-in-arms of Napoleon, was at the head of one hundred thousand Swedes, and marched through Holland; and the English, in great power, advanced from Spain, under Wellington. A battle at Montmartre left Paris exposed to the enemy, and Alexander and Frederic took possession of the capital on the 31st of March.

seemed certain. British troops were withdrawn from the continent, and early in the summer of 1814, fourteen thousand of Wellington's veterans were sent to Canada[1] to operate against the United States. Considering the moral and material weakness of the American army, hitherto, the circumstance of the continual employment of the British troops on the continent, was highly favorable to the United States. Had Europe been at peace, the result of this second War for Independence might have been quite different.

The favorite project of the public authorities continued to be the invasion of Canada;[2] and to oppose it, was the chief solicitude of the British officers on our northern frontiers. The principal force of the enemy in Upper Canada, was placed under the chief command of Lieutenant-General Drummond, late in the season; while the American army on the Niagara frontier was commanded by General Brown, at the same time. General Wilkinson was still in the vicinity of the St. Lawrence, and toward the close of February, he broke up his camp at French Mills,[3] and retired to Plattsburg; while General Brown, with two thousand men, marched to Sackett's Harbor, preparatory to his departure for the Niagara. Late in March, Wilkinson proceeded to erect a battery at Rouse's Point, at the foot of Lake Champlain; and at La Colle, three miles below, he had an unsuccessful engagement [March 30] with the British. The disastrous result of this affair brought Wilkinson into disrepute, and he was tried by a court-martial, but acquitted of all charges alleged against him. He had been suspended from all command, in the mean while, and the charge of the troops was given to General Izard.

GENERAL BROWN.

Preparations had been making on Lake Ontario, during the winter and spring, by both parties, to secure the control of that inland sea. Sir James Yeo was in command of a small British squadron, and on the 5th of May [1814], he appeared before Oswego, accompanied by about three thousand land troops and marines.[4] Oswego was then defended by only about three hundred troops under Colonel Mitchell, and a small flotilla under Captain Woolsey. The chief object of the expedition was to capture or destroy a large quantity of naval and military stores, deposited at Oswego Falls,[5] but the gallant band of Americans at the harbor defeated the project. They withstood an attack, by land and water, for almost two days, before they yielded to a superior force. Afraid to penetrate the country toward the Falls, in the face of such determined opponents, the British withdrew on the morning of the 7th [May, 1814],

---

[1] These were embarked at Bourdeaux, in France, and sailed directly for the St. Lawrence, without even touching the shores of England.

[2] Page 410.

[3] Page 427.

[4] The fort on the east side of the river was then in quite a dilapidated state, and formed but a feeble defense for the troops. It was strengthened after this attack.

[5] At the present village of Fulton, on the east side of Oswego River, and about twelve miles from the harbor.

after losing two hundred and thirty-five men, in killed and wounded. The Americans lost sixty-nine.

Toward the close of June, General Brown marched from Sackett's Harbor[1] to the Niagara frontier; and on the morning of the 3d of July, Generals Scott and Ripley[2] crossed the river, with a considerable force, and captured Fort Erie, which was situated on the Canada side of the Niagara River, nearly opposite Black Rock. The garrison withdrew to the intrenched camp of the British General Riall, then at Chippewa,[3] a few miles below. On the morning of the 4th [July, 1814], Brown advanced, and on the 5th the two armies had a sanguinary battle in the open fields at Chippewa. The British were repulsed, with a loss of about five hundred men, and retreated to Burlington Heights,[4] where they were reinforced by troops under General Drummond, who assumed the chief command in person. The Americans lost a little more than three hundred.

General Drummond was mortified by this discomfiture of his veteran troops by what he considered raw Americans, and he resolved to wipe out the stain. Collecting every regiment from Burlington and York, with some from Kingston and Prescott, he prepared for a renewal of combat. With a force about one third greater than that of Brown,[5] he immediately advanced to meet the Americans. The latter had encamped at Bridgewater, near Niagara Falls; and there, at the close of a sultry day, and within the sound of the great cataract's thunder, one of the most destructive battles of the war began.[6] It commenced at sunset and ended at midnight [July 25, 1814], when the Americans had lost eight hundred and fifty-eight men in killed and wounded, and the British twenty more than that. The Americans were left in quiet possession of the field, but were unable to carry away the heavy artillery which they had captured.[7] Brown and Scott being wounded,[8] the command devolved on Ripley, and the following day [July 26] he withdrew to Fort Erie, where General Gaines,[9] a senior officer, who arrived soon afterward, assumed the chief command.

Having recovered from his wound, Drummond again advanced, with five

---

[1] Page 432.

[2] Winfield Scott, now [1856] Lieutenant-General, and commander-in-chief of the army of the United States. See page 485. General James Ripley remained in the army after the war, and died on the 2d of March, 1839.

[3] On the Canada shore, about two miles above Niagara Falls.

[4] Page 425.

[5] Jacob Brown was born in Pennsylvania, in 1775. He engaged in his country's service in 1813, and soon became distinguished. He was made Major-General in 1814. He was commander-in-chief of the United States army in 1821, and held that rank and office when he died, in 1828.

[6] The hottest of the fight was in and near an obscure road known as Lundy's Lane. This battle is known by the respective names of *Bridgewater*, *Lundy's Lane*, and *Niagara Falls*.

[7] After the Americans had withdrawn, a party of the British returned and carried off their artillery. This event was so magnified, in the English accounts of the battle, as to make the victory to appear on the side of the British.

[8] The British Generals Drummond and Riall were also wounded. General Scott led the advance in the engagement, and for an hour maintained a most desperate conflict, when he was reinforced. It was quite dark, and General Riall and his suite were made prisoners by the gallant Major Jesup. A British battery upon an eminence did terrible execution, for it swept the whole field. This was assailed and captured by a party under Colonel Miller, who replied, when asked by General Brown if he could accomplish it, "I'll try, sir." Three times the British attempted to recapture this battery. In the last attempt, Drummond was wounded.

[9] Page 398.

thousand men, and on the 4th of August appeared before Fort Erie, and commenced preparations for a siege. From the 7th until the 14th, there was an almost incessant cannonade between the besiegers and the besieged. On the 15th, Drummond made a furious assault, but was repulsed, with a loss of almost a thousand men. Very little was done by either party for nearly a month after this affair, when General Brown, who had assumed command again, ordered a sortie [Sept. 17] from the fort. It was successful; and the Americans pressed forward, destroyed the advanced works of the besiegers, and drove them toward Chippewa. Informed, soon afterward, that General Izard was approaching,[1] with reinforcements for Brown, Drummond retired to Fort George.[2] The Americans abandoned and destroyed Fort Erie in November [November 5], and, crossing the river, went into winter-quarters at Buffalo, Black Rock, and Batavia.

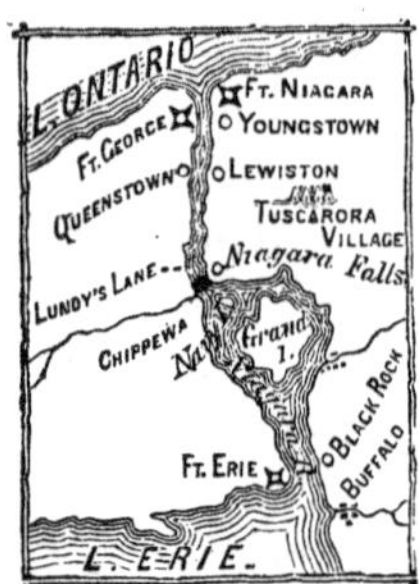

NIAGARA FRONTIER.

Let us consider the military operations in northern New York, for a moment. Very little of interest transpired in the vicinity of Lake Champlain until toward the close of summer, when General Izard[3] marched [August, 1814] from Plattsburg, with five thousand men, to reinforce General Brown on the Niagara frontier, leaving General Macomb[4] in command, with only fifteen hundred men. Taking advantage of this circumstance, General Prevost, who led an army of fourteen thousand men, chiefly Wellington's veterans, to the invasion of the United States, marched for Plattsburg. During the spring and summer, the British and Americans had each constructed a small fleet on Lake Champlain, and those were now ready for operations; the former under Commodore Downie, and the latter under Commodore Macdonough.[5]

General Prevost arrived near Plattsburg on the 6th of September, when

---

[1] Note 3, page 427.

[2] Page 425.

[3] George Izard was born in South Carolina, in 1777, and made military life his profession. After the war he left the army. He was governor of Arkansas Territory in 1825, and died at Little Rock, Arkansas, in 1828.

[4] Alexander Macomb was born in the fort in Detroit, in 1782, and entered the army at the age of seventeen years. He was made a brigadier in 1814. In 1835, he was commander-in-chief of the armies of the United States, and died in 1841.

[5] Thomas Macdonough was a native of Delaware. He was twenty-eight years of age at the time of the engagement at Plattsburg. The State of New York gave him one thousand acres of land on Plattsburg Bay, for his services. He died in 1825, at the age of thirty-nine years. Macdonough was always remarkable for cool courage. On one occasion, while first lieutenant of a vessel lying in the harbor of Gibraltar, an armed boat from a British man-of-war boarded an American brig anchored near, in the absence of the commander, and carried off a seaman. See page 401. Macdonough manned a gig, and with an inferior force, made chase and recaptured the seaman. The captain of the man-of-war came aboard Macdonough's vessel, and, in a great rage, asked him how he dared to take the man from his majesty's boat. "He was an American seaman, and I did my duty," was the reply. "I'll bring my ship alongside, and sink you," angrily cried the Briton. "That you can do," coolly responded Macdonough; "but while she swims, that man you will not have." The captain, roaring with rage, said, "Supposing *I* had been in the boat, would you have dared to commit such an act?" "I should have made the attempt, sir," was the calm reply. "What!" shouted the captain, "if I were to impress men from that brig, would you interfere?" "You have only to try it, sir," was Macdonough's tantalizing reply. The haughty Briton was over-matched, and he did not attempt to try the metal of such a brave young man. There were cannon-balls in his coolness, full of danger.

Macomb's little army, and quite a large body of militia under General Mooers, retired to the south side of the Saranac, and prepared to dispute its passage by the invaders. On the morning of the 11th, the British fleet came around Cumberland Head, with a fair wind, and attacked Macdonough's squadron in Plattsburg Bay.[1] At the same time, the British land troops opened a heavy cannonade upon the Americans. After a severe engagement of two hours and

twenty minutes, Macdonough became victor, and the whole British fleet was surrendered to him.[2] The land forces fought until dark, and every attempt of the British to cross the Saranac was bravely resisted. During the evening, Prevost hastily retreated, leaving his sick and wounded, and a large quantity of military stores, behind him. The British loss, in killed, wounded, and deserted, from the 6th to the 11th, was about twenty-five hundred; that of the Americans, only one hundred and twenty-one. The victory was applauded with the greatest enthusiasm throughout the land, and gave emphasis to the effect of another at Baltimore, which had been recently achieved.

[1] When the British squadron appeared off Cumberland Head, Macdonough knelt on the deck of the *Saratoga* (his flag-ship), in the midst of his men, and prayed to the God of Battles for aid. A curious incident occurred during the engagement that soon followed. A British ball demolished a hen-coop on board the *Saratoga*. A cock, released from his prison, flew into the rigging, and crowed lustily, at the same time flapping his wings with triumphant vehemence. The seamen regarded the event as a good omen, and they fought like tigers, while the cock cheered them on with his crowings, until the British flag was struck and the firing ceased.

[2] The Americans lost, in killed and wounded, one hundred and sixteen; the British one hundred and ninety-four. Among them was Commodore Downie, whose remains lie under a monument at Plattsburg.

So wide was the theater of war, that in our rapid view of it, the shifting scenes carry us alternately from the northern frontier to the western and southern borders, and then upon the Atlantic and its coasts. The latter were experiencing much trouble, while the whole frontier from the Niagara to the St. Lawrence was in commotion. The principal ports from New York to Maine were blockaded by British war-vessels; and early in the spring, a depredating warfare again[1] commenced on the shores of the Chesapeake. These were but feebly defended by a small flotilla,[2] under the veteran, Commodore Barney;[3] and when, about the middle of August, a British squadron, of almost sixty sail, arrived in the bay, with six thousand troops, under General Ross, destined for the capture of Washington city, it proved of little value. Ross landed [Aug. 19, 1814] at Benedict, on the Patuxent (about twenty-five miles from its mouth), with five thousand men, and marched toward Washington city.[4] Barney's flotilla, lying higher up the stream, was abandoned and burned, and his marines joined the gathering land forces, under General Winder. Ross was one of Wellington's most active commanders, and Winder had only three thousand troops to oppose him, one-half of whom were undisciplined militia. A sharp engagement took place [Aug. 24] at Bladensburg,[5] a few miles from Washington city, when the militia fled, and Barney, fighting gallantly at the head of his seamen and marines, was made prisoner.[6] Ross pushed forward to Washington city the same day, burned the capitol, President's house, and other public and private buildings [August 24], and then hastily retreated [August 25] to his shipping.[7]

The British ministry were greatly elated by the destruction of the public buildings and property at Washington, but their jubilant feelings were not shared by the best of the English people at large. The act was denounced, in severe terms, on the floor of the British House of Commons; and throughout civilized Europe, it was considered a disgrace to the perpetrators and abettors. General Ross, however, seemed to glory in it as heartily as did the marauder, Cockburn; and, flushed with success, he proceeded to attack Baltimore, where the veteran, General Smith,[8] was in command. That officer, in connection with

---

[1] Page 430.

[2] It consisted of a cutter (a vessel with one mast), two gun-boats [page 401], and nine barges, or boats propelled by oars.

[3] He was born in Baltimore in 1759. He entered the naval service of the Revolution in 1775, and was active during the whole war. He bore the American flag to the French National Convention in 1796, and entered the French service. He returned to America in 1800, took part in the War of 1812, and died at Pittsburg in 1818.

[4] Another small squadren was sent up the Potomac, but effected little else than plunder.

[5] Note 1, page 392.

[6] Until the latest moment, it was not known whether Washington or Baltimore was to be attacked. Winder's troops, employed for the defense of both cities, were divided. The loss of the British, in killed, wounded, and by desertion, was almost a thousand men; that of the Americans was about a hundred killed and wounded, and a hundred and twenty taken prisoners. The President and his Cabinet were at Bladensburg when the British approached, but returned to the city when the conflict began, and narrowly escaped capture.

[7] Washington then contained about nine hundred houses, scattered, in groups, over a surface of three miles. The Great Bridge across the Potomac was also burnt. The light of the conflagration was distinctly seen at Baltimore, forty miles distant.

[8] Samuel Smith, the brave commander of Fort Mifflin [page 275] in 1777. He was born in

General Stricker, rallied the militia of the city and vicinity, and soon almost fifteen thousand men were under arms, to defend the town. Ross landed [Sept. 12, 1814], with almost eight thousand troops, at North Point, fourteen miles from the city, while a portion of the fleet went up the Patapsco to bombard Fort M'Henry. He immediately pressed forward, but was soon met by the advanced corps of General Stricker, and a slight skirmish ensued. Ross was killed, and the command devolved on Colonel Brooke, who continued to advance. A severe battle now commenced, which continued an hour and a quarter, when the Americans fell back, in good order, toward the city. In this engagement the British lost about three hundred men; the Americans, one hundred and sixty-three. Both parties slept on their arms that night; and the following morning [Sept. 13], the British advanced, as if to attack the city. The fleet, in the mean while, had opened its bombs and cannons upon the fort, whose garrison, under Major Armistead, made a most gallant defense. The bombardment continued most of the day and night, and no less than fifteen hundred bombshells were thrown. The people in the city felt in immediate danger of an attack from the land troops; but toward the morning of the 14th, these silently embarked, and the disheartened and discomfited enemy withdrew.[1] This defense was hailed as an important victory.[2]

The whole Atlantic coast, eastward from Sandy Hook,[3] was greatly annoyed by small British squadrons, during the summer of 1814. These captured many American coasting vessels, and sometimes menaced towns with bombardment. Finally, in August, Commodore Hardy[4] appeared before Stonington, and opened a terrible storm of bombshells and rockets[5] upon the town. The attack continued four successive days [August 9–12], and several times land forces attempted to debark, but were always driven back by the militia. The object of this unprovoked attack seems to have been, to entice the American forces from New London, so that British shipping might go up the Thames, and destroy some American frigates, then near Norwich. The expedient signally failed, and no further attempt of a similar kind was made on the Connecticut coast.

Further eastward, that part of Maine which lies between the Penobscot River and Passamaquoddy Bay, became a scene of stirring events. On the first

---

Pennsylvania in 1752; entered the revolutionary army in 1776; afterward represented Baltimore in Congress many years; and died in April 1839.

[1] General Smith estimated the entire loss of the British, in their attack upon Baltimore, at "between six and seven hundred."

[2] An event, connected with this attack on Baltimore, was the origin of the stirring song, *The Star-Spangled Banner*, which was written by Francis S. Key, of that city, to the air of "Anacreon in Heaven." A gentleman left Baltimore with a flag of truce, to attempt the release of a friend on board the British fleet. He was not allowed to return, lest he should disclose the intended attack on the city. From a British vessel he was compelled to see the bombardment of Fort M'Henry. He watched the American flag over the fort, all day, with great anxiety. The darkness of the night hid it from view. With eager eyes, he looked in that direction at dawn, and, to his great joy, he saw the *star-spangled banner* yet waving over the ramparts.

[3] Page 289. [4] Page 430.

[5] Rockets used for setting fire to towns and shipping, are made similar to the common "sky-rockets," but filled with inflammable substances, which are scattered over buildings and the rigging of ships.

of September [1814], the governor of Nova Scotia and Admiral Griffith entered the Penobscot River, seized the town of Castine, and, by proclamation, took possession of the country, then inhabited by about thirty thousand people. A few days afterward, the United States frigate *John Adams* entered the Penobscot after a successful cruise, and ran upon the rocks. While having her injuries repaired, she was attacked by several of the British sailing vessels and barges, manned by about a thousand men. Finding resistance to be vain, Captain Morris, her commander, fired her magazine, and blew her up.

Difficulties again appeared in the south-west. We have already considered Jackson's successful warfare upon the Creek Indians.[1] In the course of the summer of 1814, he wrung from them a treaty, which completed their downfall, as a nation, and the war at the South was considered ended. They agreed to surrender a large portion of their beautiful and fertile country, as indemnity for the expenses of the war; to allow the United States to make roads through the remainder; and also not to hold intercourse with any British or Spanish posts. But the common enemy, favored by the Spaniards at Pensacola, soon appeared, and the Creeks again lifted their heads in hope, for a moment. A British squadron, cruising in the Gulf of Mexico, took possession of the forts at Pensacola, by permission of the Spanish authorities, and there fitted out an expedition against Fort Bower (now Fort Morgan), at the entrance to Mobile Bay,[2] then commanded by Major Lawrence. General Jackson then had his head-quarters at Mobile. The enemy appeared off Mobile Point on the 15th of September, and commenced the attack, by land and water, at about four o'clock in the afternoon. Fort Bower was garrisoned by resolute men, and was armed with twenty pieces of cannon. Lawrence and his little band made a gallant defense; and soon the British were repulsed, with the loss of a ship of war and many men. Among the British land troops on the occasion, were two hundred Creek warriors.

Jackson, now a Major-General in the army, and commander of the south-western military district, assuming all the authority he was entitled to, held the Spanish governor of Florida responsible for the act of giving shelter to the enemies of the United States. Failing to obtain any satisfactory guaranty for the future, he marched from Mobile with about two thousand Tennessee militia and some Choctaw warriors, against Pensacola. On the 7th of November [1814] he stormed the town, drove the British to their shipping, and finally from the harbor, and made the governor beg for mercy, and surrender Pensacola and all its military works, unconditionally. The British fleet disappeared the next day [November 8], and the victor retraced his steps [November 9]. His return was timely, for he was needed where extreme danger was menacing the whole southern country. On his arrival at Mobile, he found messages from New Orleans, begging his immediate march thither, for the British in the Gulf of Mexico, reinforced by thousands of troops from England, were about to invade Louisiana. Jackson instantly obeyed the summons, and arrived there

[1] Page 427.

[2] On the east side, about thirty miles south from Mobile.

on the 2d of December. He found the people of New Orleans in the greatest alarm, but his presence soon restored quiet and confidence. By vigorous, and even rigorous measures (for he declared martial law),[1] he soon placed the city in a state of comparative security,[2] and when the British squadron, bearing General Packenham and about twelve thousand troops, many of them Wellington's veterans, entered Lake Borgne, he felt confident of success, even against such fearful odds.

On the 14th of December, a British fleet of barges, about forty in number, and conveying twelve hundred men, captured a flotilla of five American gun-boats, in Lake Borgne, which were under the command of Lieutenant (late Commodore) Thomas Ap Catesby Jones. In the engagement the Americans lost, in killed and wounded, about forty; the British loss was about three hundred. The destruction of these gun-boats gave the enemy power to choose his point of attack; and eight days afterward [Dec. 22], about twenty-four hundred of the British, under General Keane, reached the Mississippi, nine miles below New Orleans. An American detachment, led by Jackson in person, fell upon their camp the following night [Dec. 23, 1814], but withdrew to a stronger position, after killing or wounding four hundred of the British. The Americans lost about one hundred.

And now preparations were instantly made for the great battle which soon afterward ensued. Jackson concentrated his troops (about three thousand in number, and mostly militia) within a line of intrenchments[3] cast up four miles below the city of New Orleans, where they were twice cannonaded by the British, but without much effect. Finally, on the morning of the 8th of January, 1815, General Packenham, the British commander-in-chief, advanced with his whole force, numbering more than twelve thousand men, to make a general assault. Having been reinforced by about three thousand militia (chiefly Kentuckians), Jackson now had six thousand expert marksmen concealed behind his intrenchments, or stationed at the batteries on his extended line. A deep and ominous silence prevailed behind these defenses, until the British had approached within reach of the batteries, when the Americans opened a terrible cannonade. Yet the enemy continued to advance until within range of the American muskets and rifles. Volley after volley then poured a deadly storm of lead upon the

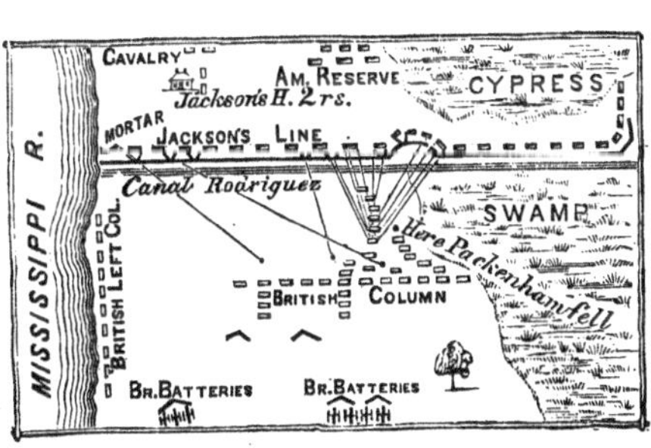

BATTLE OF NEW ORLEANS.

[1] Note 8, page 170.

[2] All the inlets, or bayous, were obstructed, and the banks of the Mississippi were so fortified as to prevent the ascent of vessels. A battery was erected on Chef Menteur, at the entrance to Lake Pontchartrain.

[3] These intrenchments were a mile in length, extending from the river so far into the swamp, as to be impassable at the extremity. Along this line were eight distinct batteries, with heavy cannons; and on the opposite side of the river was a battery with fifteen cannons.

invaders. The British column soon wavered; General Packenham fell in front of his troops, with not less than a thousand dead and wounded lying around him; and, utterly amazed by the terrible fire of the Americans, the entire army fled in confusion, leaving seven hundred dead, and more than a thousand wounded, on the field. The fugitives hastened to their encampment [Jan. 9],

William C. C. Claiborne

and finally to their ships [Jan. 18], and escaped.[1] The Americans were so safely intrenched, that they lost only *seven killed and six wounded*, in this victorious battle. It was the crowning victory,[2] and last land battle of moment, of the SECOND WAR FOR INDEPENDENCE.[3]

While the victory of the Americans at New Orleans saved that city from plunder and destruction,[4] and the whole Southern country from invasion, the

---

[1] While these operations were in progress on the Mississippi, the British fleet had not been inactive. Some vessels bombarded Fort St. Philip, below New Orleans, on the 11th of January, and continued the attack for eight days without success. In the mean while, Admiral Cockburn [page 430] was pursuing his detestable warfare along the Carolina and Georgia coasts, menacing Charleston and Savannah with destruction, and landing at obscure points to plunder the inhabitants.

[2] During 1814, the war continued on the ocean, yet there were no battles of great importance. The *Peacock* captured the British brig *Epervier*, on the 29th of April, off the coast of Florida. The *Wasp*, Captain Blakely, also made a successful cruise, but after capturing her thirteenth prize, disappeared, and was never heard of again. Probably lost in a storm. The *President*, Commodore Decatur, was captured off Long Island, on the 16th of January, 1815; and on the 20th of February following, the *Constitution*, Commodore Stewart, had a severe action with the British frigate *Cyane*, and sloop-of-war *Levant*, and captured both. Soon after this, the British brig *Penguin* was captured, but the proclamation of peace had then ended the war.

[3] Page 409.

[4] It is asserted, upon good authority, that Packenham's watchword, as he led his troops toward the city, was "Booty and Beauty," thereby indicating that plunder and ravishment should be the soldiers' reward! We can hardly believe Sir Edward really contemplated such barbarity.

JACKSON AT NEW ORLEANS.

brave Jackson, whose skill and prowess had been chiefly instrumental in producing that result, was mercilessly assailed by some persons in official station, who could not appreciate his pure motives and sturdy patriotism. Perceiving the necessity of prompt and vigorous action, Jackson had taken all power into his hands, on his arrival at New Orleans, and declared martial law.[1] Governor Claiborne[2] wisely and generously seconded the measure, and surrendering all authority into the hands of General Jackson, led a large body of the militia of his State to the field. Three days after the battle, the news of peace arrived; and Judge Hall immediately ordered the arrest of Jackson, on a charge of contempt of court.[3] He was tried; and the judge fined him a thousand dollars. The people hissed the official; bore the brave general upon their shoulders from the court-room to the street, and then the immense crowd sent up a shout, such as went over the land with emphasis thirteen years later, when he was a candidate for the Chief Magistracy of the nation[4]—"Hurrah for Jackson!" The blow aimed at him recoiled with fearful force upon his persecutors.

The country was made vocal with rejoicings on account of the victory at New Orleans; and Congress honored General Jackson with thanks and a gold medal. A little more than a month after the battle, a proclamation by the President [Feb. 18, 1815], that peace had been secured by treaty, spread a smile of tranquillity and happiness over the whole Union.[5] For more than a year, efforts toward that end had been put forth. As early as December, 1813, the British government had sent overtures of peace to that of the United States. They were forwarded by the British schooner *Bramble*, which arrived at Annapolis, in Maryland, on the 1st of January, 1814, bearing a flag of truce. The President at once informed Congress of the fact, and immediate action was had. The overtures were promptly met, in a conciliatory spirit, by the government of the United States, and commissioners were appointed by the two powers to negotiate a treaty.[6] For a long time the American commissioners were treated with neglect by the British government. They

---

[1] Note 8, page 170.

[2] William C. C. Claiborne was born in Virginia in 1775, and was educated at William and Mary College. He became an assistant clerk of the Federal House of Representatives at the age of sixteen years; and at the age of twenty-nine, President Jefferson appointed him governor of the Louisiana Territory. He had already become conspicuous as a lawyer in the West; and at the age of twenty-two he was a judge of the Supreme Court of Tennessee. He was elected to Congress the following year, and was a distinguished man in that body. He was elected governor of Louisiana when it became a State in 1812, and was acting in that capacity when the British menaced New Orleans. He left that office in 1817, when he was elected to the United States Senate. But his death was near, and he never entered that assembly. He died in November, 1817, in the forty-second year of his age.

[3] A member of the Louisiana Legislature assailed Jackson by a newspaper publication. Jackson ordered his arrest. Judge Hall granted a writ of *habeas corpus*. Jackson, in the proper exercise of his power under martial law, not only refused obedience to the mandates of the writ, but arrested the judge, and sent him out of the city. For this "contempt of court" Jackson himself was arrested. His noble defence was written by Edward Livingston.

[4] Page 459.

[5] As we have observed, intelligence of the signing of the treaty reached New Orleans three days after the battle. It was not formally proclaimed until more than a month afterward.

[6] The United States commissioners were John Quincy Adams, James A. Bayard, Henry Clay, John Russel, and Albert Gallatin. Those of Great Britain were Admiral Lord Gambier, Henry Goulbourn, and William Adams. These commissioners are all dead. Mr. Clay, who died in 1852, was the last survivor.

were suffered to remain in England unnoticed, for months, and then the ministry, proposing first one place, and then another, for the negotiations, exhibited a trifling spirit, derogatory to true dignity. For half a year the treaty was prolonged in this way, until, finally, the commissioners of the two governments met in the city of Ghent, in Belgium, in the month of August, 1814. On the 24th of December following, a treaty was signed, which both governments speedily ratified. It stipulated a mutual restoration of all places and possessions taken during the war, or which might be taken after signing the treaty; declared that all captures at sea should be relinquished, if made within specified times thereafter, in different parts of the world; and that each party should mutually put a stop to Indian hostilities, and endeavor to extinguish the traffic in slaves. The boundaries, imperfectly adjusted by the treaty of 1783,[1] were all settled; but the subject of impressment of seamen, which was the chief cause of the war,[2] of paper blockades,[3] and orders in council,[4] were all passed by without specific notice, in the treaty. With this treaty ended the war, which had been in progress for two years and eight months; and the proclamation of the fact was an occasion of the most sincere rejoicing throughout the United States and Great Britain, for it was an unnatural contest—a conflict between brethren of the same blood, the same religion, the same laws, and the same literature.

During these negotiations, the war, as we have seen, was vigorously prosecuted, and the opposition of the *Federalists* grew more intense.[5] It reached its culmination in December, when delegates, appointed by several New England Legislatures,[6] met [Dec. 15, 1814] in convention at Hartford, for the purposes of considering the grievances of the people, caused by a state of war, and to devise speedy measures for its termination.[7] This convention, whose sessions were secret, was denounced as treasonable by the administration party; but patriotism appears to have prevailed in its councils, whatever may have been the designs of some. Its plans for disunion or secession, if any were formed, were rendered abortive soon after its adjournment, by the proclamation of peace, followed by the appointment of a day for national thanksgiving to the Almighty for the blessed event. That day was observed throughout the Union.

The short time which remained of the session of Congress, after the proclamation of peace, was occupied by that body in adapting the affairs of the government to the new condition of things. The army was reduced to a peace establment of ten thousand men, and various acts, necessary for the public good during a state of war, were repealed. The naval establishment, however, was kept up; and the depredations of Algerine cruisers caused Congress to author-

---

[1] Page 348. [2] Note 5, page 409.
[3] A port being blockaded by proclamation, without ships of war being there to maintain it. This practice is no longer in vogue. [4] Note 1, page 400. [5] Page 410.
[6] New Hampshire and Vermont were unrepresented, except by three county delegates. The Federalists in Vermont, especially, were now in a weak majority; and Governor Gilman, of New Hampshire, the members of whose council were Democratic, could not call a meeting of the Legislature to appoint delegates.
[7] George Cabot was appointed President of the Convention, and Theodore Dwight, a former member of Congress from Connecticut, and then editor of the *Hartford Union*, was its secretary. The Convention was composed of twenty-six members.

ize the President to send a squadron to the Mediterranean Sea. The results of the war, though apparently disastrous to all concerned at the time, were seen, subsequently, to have been highly beneficial to the United States, not so much in a material as in a moral aspect. The total cost of the war to the United States was about one hundred millions of dollars, and the loss of lives, by battles and other casualties incident to the war, has been estimated at thirty thousand persons. The cost of blood and treasure to the British nation was much greater. During the war, the Americans captured, on the ocean and on the lakes, fifty-six British vessels of war, mounting 886 cannons; and 2,360 merchant vessels, mounting 8,000 guns. There were also lost on the American coast, during the war, by wreck or otherwise, twenty-nine British ships of war, mounting about 800 guns. The Americans lost only twenty-five vessels of war and a much less number of merchant-ships than the British.

The clouds of an almost three years' war had scarcely disappeared from the firmament, when others suddenly arose. The contest with England had but just ended, when the United States were compelled to engage in a brief

WAR WITH ALGIERS.

As we have observed,[1] the United States had paid tribute to Algiers since 1795. Every year, as his strength increased, the ruler of that Barbary State became more insolent,[2] and, finally, believing that the United States navy had been almost annihilated by the British in the late contest, he made a pretense for renewing depredations upon American commerce, in violation of the treaty. The American government determined to pay tribute no longer, accepted the challenge, and in May, 1815, Commodore Decatur[3] proceeded with a squadron to the Mediterranean, to humble the pirate. Fortunately, the Algerine fleet was cruising in the Mediterranean, in search of American vessels. On the 17th of June [1815], Decatur met and captured the flag-ship (a frigate) of the Algerine admiral, and another vessel with almost six hundred men, and then sailed for the Bay of Algiers. He immediately demanded [June 28] the instant surrender of all American prisoners, full indemnification for all property destroyed, and absolute relinquishment of all claims to tribute from the United States, in future. Informed of the fate of a part of his fleet, the Dey[4] yielded to the humiliating terms, and signed a treaty [June 30] to that effect. Decatur then sailed for Tunis, and demanded and received [July, 1815] from the bashaw, forty-six thousand dollars, in payment for American vessels which he had allowed the English to capture in his harbor. The same demand, on the same account, was made upon the bashaw of Tripoli,[5] and Decatur received [August] twenty-five thousand dollars from him and the restoration of prisoners. This cruise in the Mediterranean gave full security to American commerce in those

---

[1] Page 381.

[2] Page 381. In 1812, the Dey compelled Mr. Lear, the American consul [page 395], to pay him $27,000 for the safety of himself, family, and a few Americans, under the penalty of all being made slaves.

[3] Page 392. [4] Note 3, page 392. [5] Page 392.

seas, and greatly elevated the character of the government of the United States in the opinion of Europe. Now was accomplished, during a single cruise, what the combined powers of Europe dared not to attempt.

Now the eventful administration of Mr. Madison drew to a close, and very little of general interest occurred, except the chartering of a new United States Bank,[1] with a capital of $35,000,000, to continue twenty years; and the admission of Indiana [December, 1816] into the union of States. On the 16th of March, 1816, a caucus of Democratic members of Congress, nominated James Monroe of Virginia (who had been Madison's Secretary of War for a few months), for President of the United States, and Daniel D. Tompkins[2] of New-York, for Vice-President. The *Federalists*, whose power, as a party, was now rapidly passing away, nominated Rufus King[3] for President, and votes were given to several persons for Vice-President. Monroe and Tompkins were elected by large majorities. Mr. Monroe's election was by an almost unanimous vote of the electoral college.[4] Only one (in New Hampshire) was cast against him.

CHAPTER VII.

MONROE'S ADMINISTRATION. [1817—1825].

On the 4th of March, 1817, James Monroe,[5] the fifth President of the United States, was inaugurated at Washington City. The oath of office was administered by Chief Justice Marshall,[6] in the presence of Mr. Madison, the judges of the Supreme Court, and a large congregation of citizens. His address on that occasion was liberal and temperate in its tone, and gave general satisfaction to the people. The commencement of his administration was hailed as the dawn of an era of good feeling and national prosperity.[7] He selected his cabinet from the Republican party, and never since the formation of the gov-

---

[1] Page 372.

[2] Daniel D. Tompkins was born in 1774. He was a prominent Democrat when Jefferson was elected [page 389] President of the United States. He was chief justice of New York and also Governor of the State. He died on Staten Island, in 1825.

[3] Page 395.

[4] Note 1, page 361.

[5] James Monroe was born in Westmoreland county, Virginia, in April, 1759. He was educated at William and Mary College, and his youth was spent amid the political excitements, when the War for Independence was kindling. He joined the Continental army, under Washington, in 1776, and during the campaigns of 1777 and 1778, he was aid to Lord Stirling. After the battle of Monmouth, he left the army and commenced the study of law under Jefferson. He was again in the field when Arnold and Phillips invaded his State, in 1781 [page 330]. The next year, he was a member of the Virginia Legislature, and at the age of twenty-five, was elected a delegate to the Continental Congress. He was in active life as a legislator, foreign minister, Governor of Virginia, and President of the United States, until his retirement from the latter office in 1825. He died in the city of New York, on the 4th of July, 1831, when in the seventy-second year of his age. His remains lie unmarked by any monument, except a simple slab, in a cemetery on the north side of Second-street, in the city of New York.

[6] Page 351.

[7] President Monroe, soon after his inauguration, made a long tour of observation, extending to Portland, in Maine, on the east, and to Detroit, on the west, in which he was occupied more than three months. He was everywhere received with the kindest attentions and highest honors, and his journey was conducive to the national good.

ernment, had a President been surrounded with abler counselors.[1] Monroe was a judicious and reliable man; and when we reflect upon the condition of the country at that time—in a transition state from war and confusion to peace and order—his elevation to the presidency seems to have been a national blessing.

The administration of Mr. Monroe was marked by immense expansion in the material growth of the United States. During the war, a large number of manufacturing establishments had been nurtured into vigorous life by great demands and high prices; but when peace returned, and European manufactures flooded the country at very low prices, wide-spread ruin ensued, and thousands of men were compelled to seek other employments. The apparent misfortune was a mercy in disguise, for the nation. Beyond the Alleghanies, millions of fertile acres, possessing *real* wealth, were awaiting the tiller's industry and skill.[2] Agriculture beckoned the bankrupts to her fields. Homes in

---

[1] His cabinet consisted of John Quincy Adams, Secretary of State; William H. Crawford, Secretary of the Treasury; John C. Calhoun, Secretary of War; Benjamin Crowninshield, Secretary of the Navy; and William Wirt, Attorney-General. He offered the War Department to the venerable Governor Shelby, of Kentucky [page 417], who declined it. Calhoun was appointed in December, 1817. Crowninshield, who was in Madison's cabinet, continued in office until the close of November, 1818, when Smith Thompson, of New York, was appointed in his place.

[2] The progress of the States and Territories west of the Alleghanies [note 3, page 19], in wealth and population, is truly wonderful. A little more than fifty years ago, those immense lakes, Ontario, Erie, Michigan, Huron, and Superior, were entirely without commerce, and an Indian's canoe was almost the only craft seen upon them. In 1853, the value of traffic upon these waters and the navigable rivers, was estimated at five hundred and sixty-two millions of dollars. See note 4, page 537. Twenty-five years ago [1831] there were less than five thousand white people in the vast

the East were deserted; emigration flowed over the mountains in a broad and vigorous stream; and before the close of Monroe's administration, four new sovereign States had started into being[1] from the wilderness of the great West, and one in the East.[2]

The first year of Monroe's administration was chiefly distinguished by the admission [December 10, 1817] of a portion of the Mississippi Territory into the Union, as a State,[3] and the suppression of two piratical and slave-dealing establishments near the southern and south-western borders of the Republic. One of them was at the mouth of the St. Mary's, Florida, and the other at Galveston, Texas. In addition to a clandestine trade in slaves, these buccaneers,[4] under pretense of authority from some of the Spanish republics of South America,[5] were endeavoring to liberate the Floridas from the dominion of Spain. In November, 1817, United States troops proceeded to take possession of Amelia Island, the rendezvous of the pirates on the Florida coast, and the Galveston establishment soon disappeared for want of support.

Other serious difficulties arose at about the same time. A motley host, composed chiefly of Seminole Indians,[6] Creeks dissatisfied with the treaty of 1814,[7] and runaway negroes, commenced murderous depredations upon the frontier settlements of Georgia and the Alabama Territory, toward the close of 1817. General Gaines[8] was sent to suppress these outrages, and to remove every Indian from the territory which the Creeks had ceded to the United States, in 1814. His presence aroused the fiercest ire of the Indians, who, it was ascertained, were incited to hostilities by British subjects, protected by the Spanish authorities in Florida. Gaines was placed in a perilous position, when General Jackson, with a thousand mounted Tennessee volunteers, hastened [December, 1817] to his aid. In March, 1818, he invaded Florida, took possession [April] of the weak Spanish post of St. Mark, at the head of Apalachee Bay,[9] and sent the civil authorities and troops to Pensacola.[10] At St. Mark he secured the persons of Alexander Arbuthnot and Robert C. Ambrister, who, on being tried [April 26] by a court martial, were found guilty of being the principal emissaries among the southern Indians, inciting them to hostilities.

---

region between Lake Michigan and the Pacific Ocean; now [1856] the number is probably two and a half millions. Chicago was then a mere hamlet; now [1856] it is a fine city, with not less than eighty thousand inhabitants. And never was the growth of the Great West more rapid than at the present.

[1] Mississippi, December 10, 1817; Illinois, December 3, 1818; Alabama, December 14, 1819; and Missouri, March 2, 1821.

[2] Maine, March 3, 1820.

[3] The Territory was divided. The western portion was made a State, and the eastern was erected into a Territory, named Alabama, after its principal river. It included a portion of Georgia, given for a consideration. See page 455.

[4] Note 6, page 149.

[5] During the first quarter of the present century, nearly all of the countries in Central and South America, which, since the conquests of Cortez [page 43] and Pizarro [note 4, page 44], had been under the Spanish yoke, rebelled, and forming republics, became independent of Spain. It was the policy of our government to encourage these republics, by preventing the establishment of monarchical power on the American continent. This is known as the "Monroe doctrine," a term frequently used in political circles.

[6] Page 30.

[7] Note 8, page 428.

[8] Page 308. Edmund P. Gaines was born in Virginia, in 1777. He entered the army in 1799, and rose gradually until he was made Major-General for his gallantry at Fort Erie [page 433] in 1814. He remained in the army until his death, in 1849.

[9] Page 44.

[10] Page 438.

JACKSON AT PENSACOLA.

They were both executed on the 30th of the same month.[1] Jackson soon afterward marched for Pensacola, it being known that the Spanish authorities there had encouraged the Indians in making depredations in Alabama. The Spanish governor protested against this invasion of his territory; but Jackson, satisfied of his complicity with the Indians, pushed forward and seized Pensacola on the 24th of May. The governor and a few followers fled on horseback to Fort Barrancas, at the entrance to Pensacola Bay. This fortress was captured by Jackson three days afterward [May 27], and the Spanish authorities and troops were sent to Havana.

For this invasion of the territory of a friendly power, and his summary proceedings there, General Jackson was much censured. His plea, in justification, was the known interference of the Spanish authorities in Florida, in our domestic affairs, by sheltering those who were exciting the Indians to bloody deeds; and the absolute necessity of prompt and efficient measures at the time. He was sustained by the government and the voice of the people. These measures developed the necessity for a general and thorough settlement of affairs on the southern boundary of the Republic, and led to the important treaty[2] concluded at Washington City, in February, 1819, by which Spain ceded to the United States the whole of the Floridas, and the adjacent islands. That country was erected into a Territory in February, 1821; and in March ensuing, General Jackson was appointed the first governor of the newly-acquired domain.

We have observed that the vast region of Louisiana, purchased from France in 1803, was divided into two Territories.[3] The *Louisiana Territory* was admitted into the Union as a State, in 1812;[4] and while the treaty concerning Florida was pending, the southern portion of the remainder of the Territory extending westward of that State to the Pacific Ocean, which was erected into the "Missouri Territory" in 1812, was formed into a separate government in 1819, and called Arkansas. In December, the same year, Alabama was

---

[1] Arbuthnot was a Scotch trader from New Providence, one of the Bermuda Islands. He had a store on the Suwaney River, where many of the hostile Indians and negroes congregated. Ambrister was a young Englishman, about twenty-one years of age, who had borne a lieutenant's commission in the British service. He was also at the Suwaney settlements, and put himself at the head of the Indians and negroes.

[2] Made by John Quincy Adams for the United States, and Don Onis, the Spanish embassador at Washington. Hitherto, the United States had claimed a large portion of Texas, as a part of Louisiana. By this treaty, Texas was retained by the Spaniards. The cession was made as an equivalent for all claims against Spain for injury done the American commerce, to an amount not exceeding five millions of dollars. The treaty was not finally ratified until February, 1821.

[3] Page 390.

[4] The admirable penal code of Louisiana, which has ever stood the test of severe criticism, is the work of Edward Livingston, who was appointed the principal of a commission appointed to codify the laws of that State. The code, of which he was the sole author, was adopted in 1824. Mr. Livingston was born upon the "Manor," in Columbia county, New York, in 1764. He was educated at Princeton, studied law under Chancellor Lansing, and became eminent in his profession. He became a member of Congress in 1794, then attorney for the district of New York, and finally, he went to New Orleans to retrieve a broken fortune. He was an aid to General Jackson, in the battle at New Orleans, in January, 1815, and his pen wrote the noble defense of that soldier, when he was persecuted by civil officers in that city. See page 443. When the last page of his manuscript code of laws for Louisiana was ready for the press, a fire consumed the whole, and he was two years reproducing it. That work is his monument. Mr. Livingston was Secretary of State under President Jackson; and in 1833, he was sent to France, as the resident minister of the United States. He died in Dutchess county, New York, in May, 1837.

admitted into the Union; and at the same time, Missouri and Maine were making overtures for a similar position. Maine was admitted in March, 1820,[1] but the entrance of Missouri was delayed until August, 1821, by a violent and protracted debate which sprung up between the Northern and the Southern members of Congress on the subject of slavery, elicited by the proposition for its admission.

It was during the session of 1818–19, that a bill was introduced into Congress, which contained a provision forbidding the existence of slavery or involuntary servitude in the new State of Missouri, when admitted. Heated debates immediately occurred, and the subject was postponed until another session. The whole country, in the mean while, was agitated by disputes on the subject; and demagogues, as usual at the North and at the South, raised the cry of *Disunion of the Confederation!* Both parties prepared for the great struggle; and when the subject was again brought before Congress [November 23, 1820], angry disputes and long discussions ensued. A compromise was finally agreed to [February 28, 1821], by which slavery should be allowed in Missouri and in all territory south of thirty-six degrees and thirty minutes north latitude (southern boundary of Missouri), and prohibited in all the territory northerly and westerly of these limits. This is known as *The Missouri Compromise.*[2] Under this compromise, Missouri was admitted on the 21st of August, 1821, and

[1] Page 129.

[2] Page 501.

the excitement on the subject ceased. The Confederation was now composed of twenty-four sovereign States.

While the Missouri question was pending, a new election for President and Vice-President of the United States, took place. Never, since the foundation of the government, had there been an election so quiet, and so void of party virulence. Mr. Monroe was re-elected President, and Mr. Tompkins[1] Vice-President [November, 1820], by an almost unanimous vote—the old Federal party,[2] as an organization, being nearly extinct. The administration had been very popular, and the country was blessed with general prosperity. Two other measures, besides those already noticed, received the warmest approbation of the people. The first was an act of Congress, passed in March, 1818, in pursuance of Monroe's recommendation, making provision, in some degree, for the surviving officers and soldiers of the Revolution. It was subsequently extended, so as to include the widows and children of those who were deceased. The other was an arrangement made with Great Britain, in October, 1818, by which American citizens were allowed to share with those of that realm, in the valuable Newfoundland fisheries. At the same time, the northern boundary of the United States, from the Lake of the Woods to the Rocky Mountains, was defined.[3]

Few events of general importance, aside from the rapid progress of the country in all its industrial and governmental operations, occurred during the remainder of Monroe's administration, except the suppression of piracy among the West India Islands, and the visit of General La Fayette[4] to the United States, as the nation's guest. The commerce of the United States had been greatly annoyed and injured by swarms of pirates who infested the West India seas. A small American squadron, under Commodore Perry,[5] had been sent thither in 1819, to chastise the buccaneers. Perry died of the yellow fever in the performance of his duty, and very little was done at that time. About four years later [1822], a small American squadron destroyed more than twenty piratical vessels on the coast of Cuba; and the following year the work was completed by a larger force, under Commodore Porter.[6] The second-named event was of a more pleasing character. La Fayette, the companion-in-arms of Washington[7] during the Revolutionary struggle, arrived at New York, from France, in August, 1824, and during about eleven succeeding months, he made a tour of over five thousand miles, throughout the United States. He was everywhere greeted with the warmest enthusiasm, and was often met by men who had served under him in the first War for Independence. When he was prepared to return, an American frigate, named *Brandywine*, in compliment to him,[8] was sent by the United States government to convey him back to France.

Mr. Monroe's administration now drew toward a close, and in the autumn

---

[1] Page 446. [2] Page 374. [3] Page 479.
[4] Page 273. [5] Page 423. [6] Page 431. [7] Page 273.
[8] La Fayette's first battle for freedom in America, was that on the Brandywine Creek, in September, 1777, where he was wounded in the leg. See note 5, page 273.

of 1824, the people were called upon to select his successor. It soon became evident that a large proportion of the old politicians of the Democratic party had decided to support William H. Crawford, the Secretary of the Treasury, for the succession. Four candidates, representing the different sections of the Union,[1] were finally put in nomination. The result was, that the choice devolved upon the House of Representatives, for the second time.[2] That body, by an election held in February, 1825, chose John Quincy Adams for President. John C. Calhoun had been chosen Vice-President by the people. The election and final choice produced great excitement throughout the country, and engendered political rancor equal to that which prevailed during the administration of the elder Adams. Mr. Monroe's administration closed on the 4th of March ensuing, and he resigned to his successor the Chief Magistracy of a highly-prosperous nation.

CHAPTER VIII.

JOHN QUINCY ADAMS'S ADMINISTRATION. [1825—1829.]

At about half-past twelve o'clock, on the 4th day of March, 1825, John Quincy Adams,[3] son of the second President of the United States, entered the hall of the House of Representatives, and took his seat in the chair of the Speaker. He was dressed in a suit of black cloth, and, being small in stature, did not present a more dignified appearance than hundreds of his fellow-citizens around him. He appeared, as he really was, a plain Republican—one of the people. When silence was obtained, he arose and delivered his inaugural address; then descending, he placed himself on the right hand of a table, and took the oath of office, administered by Chief-Justice Marshall. The Senate being in session, Mr. Adams immediately nominated his cabinet officers,[4] and

[1] John Quincy Adams in the *East*, William H. Crawford in the *South*, Andrew Jackson and Henry Clay in the *West*.

[2] Page 388.

[3] John Quincy Adams, the sixth President of the United States, was born at Quincy, Massachusetts, on the 11th of July, 1767. He went to Europe, with his father, at the age of eleven years; and, in Paris, he was much in the society of Franklin and other distinguished men. At the age of fourteen years he accompanied Mr. Dana to St. Petersburg, as private secretary to that embassador. He traveled much alone, and finally returned, and finished his education at Harvard College. He became a lawyer, but public service kept him from that pursuit. He was made United States minister to the Netherlands in 1794, and afterward held the same office at Lisbon and Berlin. He was a member of the United States Senate in 1803; and in 1809 he was sent as minister to the Russian court. After negotiating a treaty of peace at Ghent [page 443], he was appointed minister to the English court. In 1817 he was made Secretary of State, by Mr. Monroe. Having served one term as President of the United States, he retired; and from 1831, he was a member of Congress until his death, which occurred in the Speaker's room, at the Federal Capitol, on the 22d of February, 1848, when in the eighty-first year of his age.

[4] Henry Clay, Secretary of State; Richard Rush, Secretary of the Treasury; James Barbour, Secretary of War; Samuel L. Southard (continued in office), Secretary of the Navy; and William Wirt (continued), Attorney-General. There was considerable opposition in the Senate to the confirmation of Henry Clay's nomination. He had been charged with defeating the election of General Jackson, by giving his influence to Mr. Adams, on condition that he should be appointed his Secre-

all but one were confirmed by a unanimous vote of that body. His political views were consonant with those of Mr. Monroe, and the foreign and domestic policy of his administration were generally conformable to those views. The amity which existed between the United States and foreign governments, and the absence of serious domestic troubles, made the administration of Mr. Adams

J. Q. Adams

a remarkably quiet one, and gave the executive opportunities for adjusting the operations of treaties with the Indian tribes, and the arrangement of measures for the promotion of those great staple interests of the country—agriculture, commerce, and manufactures. Discords, which the election had produced, excited the whole country during Mr. Adams's administration, with the agitations incident to excessive party zeal, and bitter party rancor; yet the President, thoroughly acquainted with all the public interests, and as thoroughly skilled in every art of diplomacy and jurisprudence, managed the affairs of State with a fidelity and sagacity which command our warmest approbation.

One of the most exciting topics, for thought and discussion, at the beginning of Adams's administration [1825], was a controversy between the Federal Government and the chief magistrate of Georgia, concerning the lands of the Creek Indians, and the removal of those aboriginals from the territory of that State. When Georgia relinquished her claims to considerable portions of the Mississippi Territory,[1] the Federal Government agreed to purchase, for that State,

---

tary of State. This, however, was only a bubble on the surface of political strife, and had no truthful substance. In the Senate, there were twenty-seven votes in favor, and fourteen against confirming the nomination of Mr. Clay.

[1] Note 2, page 447.

the Indian lands within its borders, "whenever it could be peaceably done upon reasonable terms." The Creeks, who, with their neighbors, the Cherokees, were beginning to practice the arts of civilized life, refused to sell their lands. Troup, the governor of Georgia, demanded the immediate fulfillment of the contract. He caused a survey of the lands to be made, and prepared to distribute

them by lottery, to the citizens of that State. Impatient at the tardiness of the United States in extinguishing the Indian titles and removing the remnants of the tribes, according to stipulation, the governor assumed the right to do it himself. The United States took the attitude of defenders of the Indians, and, for a time, the matter bore a serious aspect. The difficulties were finally settled, and the Creeks[1] and Cherokees[2] gradually removed to the rich wilderness beyond the Mississippi.

At about this time a great work of internal improvement was completed. The Erie Canal, in the State of New York, was finished in 1825. It was the most important and stupendous public improvement ever undertaken in the United States; and, though it was the enterprise of the people of a single State, that originated and accomplished the labor of forming the channel of a river through a large extent of country, it has a character of nationality. Its earliest advocate was Jesse Hawley, who, in a series of articles published in 1807 and 1808, signed *Hercules*, set forth the feasibility and great importance of such a connection of the waters of Lake Erie and the Hudson River.[3] His

---

[1] Page 30. [2] Page 27.

[3] In a manuscript letter now before the writer, dated "Albany, 4th March, 1822," Dewitt Clinton says to Jesse Hawley, to whom the letter is addressed: "In answer to your letter, I have no

views were warmly seconded by Gouverneur Morris,[1] Dewitt Clinton, and a few others, and its final accomplishment was the result, chiefly, of the untiring efforts, privately and officially, of the latter gentleman, while a member of the Legislature and governor of the State of New York. It is three hundred and sixty-three miles in length, and the first estimate of its cost was $5,000,000. Portions of it have since been enlarged, to meet the increasing demands of its commerce; and in 1853, the people of the State decided, by a general vote, to have it enlarged its entire length. That work is now [1856] in progress.

A most remarkable coincidence occurred on the 4th of July, 1826, the fiftieth anniversary of American Independence. On that day, and almost at the same hour, John Adams and Thomas Jefferson expired. They were both members of the committee who had framed the Declaration of Independence,[2] both signed it,[3] both had been foreign ministers,[4] both had been Vice-Presidents, and then Presidents of the United States, and both had lived to a great age.[5] These coincidences, and the manner and time of their death, produced a profound impression upon the public mind. In many places throughout the Union, eulogies or funeral orations were pronounced, and these, collected, form one of the most remarkable contributions to our historical and biographical literature.

After the difficulties with Georgia were settled, the remaining years of Mr. Adams's administration were so peaceful and prosperous, that public affairs present very few topics for the pen of the general historian.[6] The most important movement in foreign policy, was the appointment, early in 1826, of commissioners[7] to attend a congress of representatives of the South American Republics,[8] held at Panama [July, 1826], on the Pacific coast. This appointment

---

hesitation in stating that the first suggestion of a canal from Lake Erie to the Hudson River, which came to my knowledge, was communicated in essays under the signature of *Hercules*, on Internal Navigation, published in the *Ontario Messenger*, at Canandaigua. The first number appeared on the 27th of October, 1807, and the series of numbers amounted, I believe, to fourteen. The board of Canal Commissioners, which made the first tour of observation and survey, in 1810, were possessed of the writings of *Hercules*, which were duly appreciated, as the work of a sagacious inventor and elevated mind. And you were at that time, and since, considered the author." Dewitt Clinton was a son of General James Clinton, of Orange county, New York. He was born in March, 1769. He was mayor of New York ten years, and was elected governor of the State in 1817, and again in 1820 and 1826. He died suddenly while in that office, in February, 1828.

[1] Page 364.

[2] Note 2, page 251.

[3] Jefferson was its author, and Adams its principal supporter, in the Continental Congress.

[4] Note 2, page 383, and note 5, page 388.

[5] Mr. Adams died at Quincy, Massachusetts, at the age of almost ninety-one years. Mr. Jefferson died at Monticello, Virginia, at the age of almost eighty-three years.

[6] An event occurred in 1826 which produced great excitement throughout the country, and led to the formation of a new, and for a time, quite a powerful political party. William Morgan, of Western New York, announced his intention to publish a book, in which the secrets of Free Masonry were to be disclosed. He was suddenly seized at Canandaigua one evening, placed in a carriage, and was never heard of afterward. Some Free Masons were charged with his murder, and the report of an investigating committee, appointed by the New York State Legislature, confirmed the suspicion. The public mind was greatly agitated, and there was a disposition to exclude Free Masons from office. An Anti-Masonic party was formed, and its organization spread over several States. In 1831, a national anti-Masonic convention was held at Philadelphia, and William Wirt, of Virginia, was nominated for the office of President of the United States. Although the party polled a considerable vote, it soon afterward disappeared.

[7] R. C. Addison, and John Sargeant, commissioners; and William B. Rochester, of New York, their secretary.

[8] Note 5, page 448. As early as 1823, General Bolivar, while acting as President of Colombia,

produced much discussion in Congress, chiefly on party grounds. The result of the congress at Panama was comparatively unimportant, so far as the United States was concerned, and appears to have had very little influence on the affairs of South America.

During the administration of Mr. Adams, the policy of protecting home

manufactures, by imposing a heavy duty upon foreign articles of the same kind, assumed the shape of a settled national policy, and the foundations of the *American System*, as that policy is called, was then laid. The illiberal commercial policy of Great Britain, caused tariff laws to be enacted by Congress as early as 1816, as retaliatory measures.[1] In 1824, imposts were laid on foreign fabrics, with a view to encourage American manufactures. In July, 1827, a national convention was held at Harrisburg, in Pennsylvania, to discuss the subject of protective tariffs. Only four of the slave States sent delegates. The result of the convention was a memorial to Congress, asking an augmentation of duties on several articles then manufactured in the United States. The Secretary of the Treasury called attention to the subject in his report in Decem-

invited the governments of Mexico, Peru, Chili, and Buenos Ayres, to unite with him in forming a general congress at Panama, and the same year arrangements between Colombia, Mexico, and Peru were made, to effect that object. In the spring of 1825, the United States government was invited to send a delegation to the proposed congress. The objects of the congress were, to settle upon some line of policy having the force of international law, respecting the rights of those republics; and to consult upon measures to be taken to prevent further colonization on the American continent by European powers, and their interference in then existing contests.

[1] Page 367.

ber following. Congress, at an early period of the session of 1827–'28, took up the matter, and a Tariff Bill became a law in May following. The *American System* was very popular with the manufacturers of the North, but the cotton-growing States, which found a ready market for the raw material in England, opposed it. The tariff law, passed on the 15th of May, 1828, was very obnoxious to the Southern people.[1] They denounced it as oppressive and unconstitutional, and it led to menaces of serious evils in 1831 and 1832.[2]

The Presidential election took place in the autumn of 1828, when the public mind was highly excited. For a long time the opposing parties had been marshaling their forces for the contest. The candidates were John Quincy Adams and General Andrew Jackson. The result was the defeat of Mr. Adams, and the election of General Jackson. John C. Calhoun,[3] of South Carolina, was elected Vice-President, and both had very large majorities. During the contest, the people appeared to be on the verge of civil war, so violent was the party strife, and so malignant were the denunciations of the candidates. When it was over, perfect tranquillity prevailed, the people cheerfully acquiesced in the result, and our sytem of government was nobly vindicated before the world.

President Adams retired from office on the 4th of March, 1829. He left to his successor a legacy of unexampled national prosperity, peaceful relations with all the world, a greatly diminished national debt, and a surplus of more than five millions of dollars in the public treasury. He also bequeathed to the Republic the tearful gratitude of the surviving soldiers of the Revolution, among whom had been distributed in pensions,[4] during his administration, more than five millions of dollars.

CHAPTER IX.

JACKSON'S ADMINISTRATION. [1829—1837]

THERE were incidents of peculiar interest connected with the inauguration of Andrew Jackson,[5] the seventh President of the United States. President

[1] The chief articles on which heavy protective duties were laid, were woolen and cotton fabrics. At that time, the value of annual imports of cotton goods from Great Britain was about $8,000,000; that of woolen goods about the same. The exports to Great Britain, of cotton, rice, and tobacco, alone (the chief products of the Southern States), was about $24,000,000 annually. These producers feared a great diminution of their exports, by a tariff that should almost wholly prohibit the importation of three millions of dollars' worth of British cotton and woolen fabrics, annually.

[2] Page 463.

[3] John C. Calhoun was born in South Carolina in 1782. He first appeared in Congress in 1811, and was always distinguished for his consistency, especially in his support of the institution of slavery, and the doctrine of State rights. He was a sound and incorruptible statesman, and commanded the thorough respect of the whole country. He died at Washington city, while a member of the United States Senate, in March, 1850.

[4] Page 453.

[5] Andrew Jackson was born in Mecklenberg county, North Carolina, in March, 1767. His parents were from the north of Ireland, and belonged to that Protestant community known as Scotch-Irish. In earliest infancy, he was left to the care of an excellent mother, by the death of his father. He first saw the horrors of war, and felt the wrongs of oppression, when Colonel

Adams had convened the Senate on the morning of the 4th of March, 1829, and at twelve o'clock that body adjourned for an hour. During that time, the President elect entered the Senate chamber, having been escorted from Gadsby's Hotel, by a few surviving officers and soldiers of the old War for Independence. These had addressed him at the hotel, and now, in presence of the chief officers of government, foreign ministers, and a large number of ladies, he thus replied to them:

"RESPECTED FRIENDS—Your affectionate address awakens sentiments and recollections which I feel with sincerity and cherish with pride. To have around my person, at the moment of undertaking the most solemn of all duties to my country, the companions of the immortal Washington, will afford me satisfaction and grateful encouragement. That by my best exertions, I shall be able to exhibit more than an imitation of his labors, a sense of my own imper-

Buford's troops were massacred [page 313, and note 1, page 314] in his neighborhood, in 1780. He entered the army, and suffered in the cause of freedom, by imprisonment, and the death of his mother while she was on an errand of mercy. He studied law, and became one of the most eminent men in the Western District of Tennessee, as an advocate and a judge. He was ever a controlling spirit in that region. He assisted in framing a State constitution for Tennessee, and was the first representative of that State in the Federal Congress. He became United States senator in 1797, and was soon afterward appointed Judge of the Supreme Court of his State. He settled near Nashville, and for a long time was chief military commander in that region. When the War of 1812 broke out, he took the field, and in the capacity of Major-General, he did good service in the southern country, till its close. He was appointed the first Governor of Florida, in 1821, and in 1823, was again in the United States Senate. He retired to private life at the close of his presidential term, and died at his beautiful residence, *The Hermitage*, near Nashville, in June, 1845, at the age of seventy-eight years.

fections, and the reverence I entertain for his virtues, forbid me to hope. To you, respected friends, the survivors of that heroic band who followed him, so long and so valiantly, in the path of glory, I offer my sincere thanks, and to Heaven my prayers, that your remaining years may be as happy as your toils and your lives have been illustrious." The whole company then proceeded to the eastern portico of the capitol, where, in the presence of a vast assembly of citizens, the President elect delivered his inaugural address, and took the oath of office, administered by Chief Justice Marshall.[1] That jurist again administered the same oath to President Jackson on the 4th of March, 1835, and a few months afterward went down into the grave.

President Jackson was possessed of strong passions, an uncorrupt heart, and an iron will. Honest and inflexible, he seized the helm of the ship of state with a patriot's hand, resolved to steer it according to his own conceptions of the meaning of his guiding chart, *The Constitution*, unmindful of the interference of friends or foes. His instructions to the first minister sent to England, on his nomination—"Ask nothing but what is right; submit to nothing wrong"—indicate the character of those moral and political maxims by which he was governed. His audacity amazed his friends and alarmed his opponents; and no middle men existed. He was either thoroughly loved or thoroughly hated; and for eight years he braved the fierce tempests of party strife,[2] domestic perplexities,[3] and foreign arrogance,[4] with a skill and courage which demands the admiration of his countrymen, however much they may differ with him in matters of national policy. The gulf between him and his political opponents was so wide, that it was difficult for the broadest charity to bridge it. To those who had been his true friends during the election struggle, he extended the grateful hand of recognition, and after having his inquiries satisfied, "Is he capable? is he honest?" he conferred official station upon the man who pleased him, with a stoical indifference to the clamor of the opposition. The whole of President Adams's cabinet officers having resigned, Jackson immediately nominated his political friends for his counselors, and the Senate confirmed his choice.[5]

Among the first subjects of general and commanding interest which occupied the attention of President Jackson, at the commencement of his administration, were the claims of Georgia to lands held by the powerful Cherokee tribe of Indians, and lying within the limits of that State. Jackson favored the views of the Georgia authorities, and the white people proceeded to take possession of the Indians' land. Trouble ensued, and the southern portion of the Republic was

---

[1] Page 351.

[2] Following the precedent of Jefferson [page 389], he filled a large number of the public offices with his political friends, after removing the incumbents. These removals were for all causes; and during his administration, they amounted to six hundred and ninety out of several thousands, who were removable. The entire number of removals made by all the preceding Presidents, from 1790 to 1829, was seventy-four.

[3] Page 464.

[4] Page 468.

[5] Martin Van Buren, Secretary of State; Samuel D. Ingham, Secretary of the Treasury; John H. Eaton, Secretary of War; John Branch, Secretary of the Navy; and John McPherson Berrian, Attorney-General. It having been determined to make the Postmaster-General a cabinet officer, William T. Barry was appointed to that station.

again menaced with civil war. The matter was adjudicated by the Supreme Court of the United States, and on the 30th of March, 1832, that tribunal decided against the claims of Georgia. But that State, favored by the President, resisted the decision. The difficulty was finally adjusted; and in 1838, General Winfield Scott[1] was sent thither, with several thousand troops, to remove the Cherokees, peaceably if possible, but forcibly if necessary, beyond the Mississippi. Through the kindness and conciliation of Scott, they were induced to migrate. They had become involved in the difficulties of their Creek neighbors,[2] but were defended against the encroachments of the Georgians during Adams's administration. But in December, 1829, they were crushed, as a nation, by an act of Congress, and another of the ancient communities of the New World was wiped from the living record of empire. The Cherokees[3] were more advanced in the arts of civilized life than the Creeks.[4] They had churches, schools, and a printing-press, and were becoming successful agriculturists. It appeared cruel in the extreme to remove them from their fertile lands and the graves of their fathers, to the wilderness; yet it was, doubtless, a proper measure for insuring the prosperity of both races. But now [1856], again, the tide of civilization is beating against their borders. Will they not be borne upon its powerful wave, further into the wilderness?

Another cause for public agitation appeared in 1832. In his first annual message [December, 1829] Jackson took strong ground against the renewal of the charter of the United States Bank,[5] on the ground that it had failed in the great end of establishing a uniform and sound currency, and that such an institution was not authorized by the Federal Constitution. He again attacked the bank in his annual message in 1830, and his objections were renewed in that of 1831. At the close of 1831, the proper officers of the bank, for the first time, petitioned for a renewal of its charter. That petition was presented in the Senate on the 9th of January, 1832, and on the 13th of March, a select committee to whom it was referred, reported in favor of renewing the charter for fifteen years. Long debates ensued; and, finally, a bill for re-chartering the bank passed both Houses of Congress: the Senate on the 11th of June, by twenty-eight against twenty votes; and by the House of Representatives on the 3d of July, by one hundred and seven against eighty-five. Jackson vetoed[6] it on the 10th of July, and as it failed to receive the support of two thirds of the members of both Houses, the bank charter expired, by limitation, in 1836. The commercial community, regarding a national bank as essential to their prosperity, were alarmed; and prophecies of panics and business revulsions, everywhere uttered, helped to accomplish their own speedy fulfillment.

An Indian war broke out upon the north-western frontier, in the spring of 1832. Portions of some of the western tribes,[7] residing within the domain

---

[1] Page 485. [2] Page 427. [3] Page 27. [4] Page 30. [5] Page 446.

[6] That is, refused to sign it, and returned it to Congress, with his reasons, for reconsideration by that body. The Constitution gives the President this power, and when exercised, a bill can not become law without his signature, unless it shall, on reconsideration, receive the votes of two thirds of the members of both Houses of Congress. See Article I, Section 7, of the *Constitution*, in the Supplement.

[7] Sacs, Foxes, and Winnebagoes. See page 18.

of the present State of Wisconsin,[1] led by Black Hawk,[2] a fiery Sac chief, commenced warfare upon the frontier settlers of Illinois, in April of that year. After several skirmishes with United States troops and Illinois militia, under General Atkinson,[3] the Indians were driven beyond the Mississippi. Black Hawk was captured in August, 1832, and taken to Washington City; and then, to impress his mind with the strength of the nation he had foolishly made war with, he was conducted through several of the eastern cities. This brief strife, which appeared quite alarming at one time, is known in history as the "Black Hawk War."[4]

This cloud in the West had scarcely disappeared, when one loomed up in the South far more formidable in appearance, and charged with menacing thun-

der that, for a while, shook the entire fabric of the Confederation. The discontents of the cotton-growing States, produced by the tariff act of 1828,[5] assumed the form of rebellion in South Carolina, toward the close of 1832. An act of Congress, imposing additional duties upon foreign goods, passed in

---

[1] That domain was not erected into a Territory until four years after that event; now it is a rich, populous, and flourishing State. [2] Page 18.

[3] Henry Atkinson was a native of North Carolina, and entered the army as captain, in 1808. He was retained in the army after the second War for Independence, was made Adjutant-General, and was finally appointed to the command of the Western Army. He died at Jefferson Barracks, in June, 1842.

[4] Black Hawk returned to his people, but was, with difficulty, restored to his former dignity of chief. He died in October, 1840, and was buried on the banks of the Mississippi. [5] Page 459.

the spring of 1832, led to a State convention in South Carolina, in November following. It assembled on the 19th of that month, and the Governor of South Carolina was appointed its president. That assembly declared the tariff acts unconstitutional, and therefore null and void. It resolved that duties should not be paid; and proclaimed that any attempt to enforce the collection of duties in the port of Charleston, by the general government, would be resisted by arms, and would produce the withdrawal of South Carolina from the Union. The State Legislature, which met directly after the adjournment of the convention, passed laws in support of this determination. Military preparations were immediately made, and civil war appeared inevitable. Then it was that the executive ability of the President, so much needed, was fully displayed. Jackson promptly met the crisis by a proclamation, on the 10th of December, which denied the right of a State to nullify *any* act of the Federal Government; and warned those who were engaged in fomenting a rebellion, that the laws of the United States would be strictly enforced by military power, if necessary. This proclamation met the hearty response of every friend of the Union, of whatever party, and greatly increased that majority of the President's supporters, who had just re-elected him to the Chief Magistracy of the Republic.[1] The nullifiers[2] of South Carolina, though led by such able men as Calhoun[3] and Hayne,[4] were obliged to yield for the moment; yet their zeal and determination in the cause of State Rights, were not abated. Every day the tempest-cloud of civil commotion grew darker and darker; until, at length, Henry Clay,[5] a warm friend of the American system,[6] came forward, in Congress [February 12, 1833], with a bill, which provided for a gradual reduction of the obnoxious duties, during the succeeding ten years. This compromise measure was accepted by both parties. It became a law on the 3d of March, and discord between the North and the South soon ceased, but only for a season.[7]

---

[1] Jackson was re-elected by a large majority, in November, 1832, over Henry Clay, the opposing candidate. Martin Van Buren, of New York, was elected Vice-President.

[2] Those who favored the doctrine that a State might nullify the acts of the Federal government, were called *nullifiers*, and the dangerous doctrine itself was called *nullification*.

[3] Page 458. Mr. Calhoun, who had quarreled, politically, with Jackson, had recently resigned the office of Vice-President of the United States, and was one of the ablest men in Congress. He asserted the State Rights doctrine boldly on the floor of Congress, and held the same opinion until his death.

[4] Robert Y. Hayne was one of the ablest of southern statesmen. The debate between Hayne and Webster, in the Senate of the United States, during the debates on this momentous subject, is regarded as one of the most eminent, for sagacity and eloquence, that ever marked the proceedings of that body. Mr. Hayne was born near Charleston, South Carolina, in November, 1791. He was admitted to the bar in 1812, and the same year volunteered his services for the defense of the sea-board, and entered the army as lieutenant. He arose rapidly to the rank of Major-General of the militia of his State, and was considered one of the best disciplinarians of the South. He had extensive practice at the bar, before he was twenty-two years of age, and it was always lucrative. He was a member of the South Carolina Assembly in 1814, where he was distinguished for eloquence. He was chosen Speaker in 1818. For ten years he represented South Carolina in the Senate of the United States; and he was chairman of the Committee of the Convention of South Carolina, which reported the "ordinance of nullification." He was soon afterward chosen Governor of his State. He died in September, 1841, in the fiftieth year of his age. [5] Page 500. [6] Page 459.

[7] It is said that Mr. Clay introduced the Compromise Bill with the concurrence of Mr. Calhoun. The latter had proceeded to the verge of treason, in his opposition to the general government, and President Jackson had threatened him with arrest, if he moved another step forward. Knowing

President Jackson's hostility to the United States Bank was again manifested in his annual message to Congress, in December, 1832, when he recommended the removal of the public funds from its custody, and a sale of the stock of the bank, belonging to the United States.[1] Congress, by a decided vote, refused to authorize the measure; but after its adjournment, the President assumed the responsibility of the act, and directed William J. Duane, the Secretary of the Treasury, to withdraw the government funds (then almost $10,000,000), and deposit them in certain State banks. During a northern tour which the President had made in the summer of 1833, he had urged Mr. Duane (then in Philadelphia) to make the removal, but he would only consent to the appointment of an agent to inquire upon what terms the local banks would receive the funds on deposit. The President then ordered him, peremtorily, to remove them from the bank. The Secretary refused compliance, and was dismissed from office. His successor, Roger B. Taney (the present [1856] Chief-Justice of the United States) obeyed the President; and in October, 1833, the act was accomplished. The effect produced was sudden and widespread commercial distress. The business of the country was plunged from the height of prosperity to the depths of adversity, because its intimate connection with the National Bank rendered any paralysis of the operations of that institution fatal to commercial activity. The amount of loans of the bank, on the 1st of October, was over sixty millions of dollars, and the amount of the funds of the United States, then on deposit in the bank, was almost ten millions of dollars. The fact, that the connection of the bank with the business of the country was so vital, confirmed the President in his opinion of the danger of such an enormous moneyed institution.

A large portion of the government funds were removed in the course of four months, and the whole amount in about nine months. Intense excitement prevailed throughout the country; yet the President, supported by the House of Representatives, persevered and triumphed. Numerous committees, appointed by merchants, mechanics, manufacturers, and others, waited upon him, to ask him to take some measures for relief. He was firm; and to all of them he replied, in substance, that "the government could give no relief, and provide no remedy; that the banks were the occasion of all the evils which existed, and that

---

the firmness and decision of the President, Mr. Calhoun dared not take the fatal step. He could not recede, nor even stand still, without compromising his character with his southern friends. In this extremity, he arranged with Mr. Clay to propose a measure which would satisfy both sides, and save both his neck and his reputation. In justice to Mr. Calhoun, it is proper to say, that in the discussion of the matter in the Senate, he most earnestly disclaimed any hostile feelings toward the Union, on the part of South Carolina. The State authorities, he asserted, had looked only to a judicial decision upon the question, until the concentration of the United States troops at Charleston and Augusta, by order of the President, compelled them to make provision to defend themselves. Several of the State Legislatures hastened to condemn the nullification doctrine as destructive to the Federal Constitution. Massachusetts, Connecticut, New York, Delaware, Indiana, Missouri, and Georgia, all thus spoke out plainly in favor of the Union. Georgia, however, at the same time, expressed its reprobation of the tariff system, which had brought about the movement in South Carolina, and proposed a convention of the States of Virginia, North and South Carolina, Georgia, Alabama, Tennessee, and Mississippi, to devise measures to obtain relief from it.

[1] By the law of 1816, for chartering the bank, the funds of the United States were to be deposited with that institution, and to be withdrawn only by the Secretary of the Treasury.

those who suffered by their great enterprise had none to blame but themselves; that those who traded on borrowed capital ought to break." The State banks received the government funds on deposit, and loaned freely. Confidence was gradually restored, and apparent general prosperity[1] returned. Now [1856], after the lapse of more than twenty years, the wisdom and forecaste of General Jackson, evinced by his distrust of the United States Bank, appears to be universally acknowledged. The necessity for such an institution is no longer admitted, and its dangerous power, if wickedly exercised, may be plainly seen.[2]

Trouble again appeared on the southern borders of the Union. Toward the close of 1835, the Seminole Indians, in Florida, guided by their head sachem, Micanopy, and led by their principal chief, Osceola,[3] commenced a distressing warfare upon the frontier settlements of Florida. The cause of the outbreak was an attempt to remove them to the wilderness bepond the Mississippi. In his annual message in December, 1830, President Jackson recommended the devotion of a large tract of land west of the Mississippi, to the use of the Indian tribes yet remaining east of that stream, forever. Congress passed laws in accordance with the proposition, and the work of removal commenced, first by the Chickasaws and Choctaws.[4] We have seen that trouble ensued with the Creeks and Cherokees,[5] and the Seminoles in East Florida were not disposed to leave their ancient domain. Some of the chiefs in council made a treaty in May, 1832, and agreed to remove; but other chiefs, and the great body of the nation, did not acknowledge the treaty as binding. In 1834, the President sent General Wiley Thompson to Florida, to prepare for a forcible removal of the Seminoles, if necessary. The tone and manner assumed by Osceola, at that time, displeased Thompson, and he put the chief in irons and in prison for a day. The proud leader feigned penitence, and was released. Then his wounded pride called for revenge, and fearfully he pursued it, as we shall observe presently. The war that ensued was a sanguinary one, and almost four years elapsed before it was wholly terminated. Osceola, with all the cunning of a Tecumseh,[6] and the heroism of a Philip,[7] was so successful in stratagem, and brave in conflict, that he baffled the skill and courage of the United States troops for a long time. He had agreed to fulfill treaty stipulations,[8] in December [1835], but instead

OSCEOLA.

---

[1] Page 470.

[2] The course of President Jackson, toward the bank, was popular in many sections, but in the commercial States it caused a palpable diminution of the strength of the administration. This was shown by the elections in 1834. Many of his supporters joined the Opposition, and this combined force assumed the name of "Whigs"—the old party name of the Revolution—while the administration party adhered to the name of "Democrats."

[3] Page 468. [4] Page 30. [5] Page 27. [6] Page 424. [7] Page 124.

[8] Osceola had promised General Thompson that the delivery of certain cattle and horses belonging to the Indians should be made during the first fortnight of December, 1835, and so certain was Thompson of the fulfillment of this stipulation, that he advertised the animals for sale.

of compliance, he was then at the head of a war party, murdering the unsuspecting inhabitants on the borders of the everglade haunts of the savages.

At that time General Clinch was stationed at Fort Drane,[1] in the interior of Florida, and Major Dade was dispatched from Fort Brooke, at the head of Tampa Bay, with more than a hundred men, for his relief. That young commander,[2] and all but four of his detachment, were massacred [Dec. 28, 1835] near Wahoo Swamp.[3] On the same day, and only a few hours before, Osceola, and a small war party, killed and scalped General Thompson, and five of his friends, who were dining at a store a few yards from Fort King.[4] The assailants disappeared in the forest before the deed was known at the fort. Two days afterward [Dec. 31], General Clinch and his troops had a battle with the Seminoles on the Withlacoochee; and in February [Feb. 29, 1836], General Gaines[5] was assailed near the same place,[6] and several of his men were killed. The battle-ground is about fifty miles from the mouth of the river.

SEAT OF SEMINOLE WAR.

The Creeks aided their brethren in Florida, by attacking white settlers within their domain,[7] in May, 1836. Success made them bold, and they attacked mail-carriers, stages, steamboats, and finally villages, in Georgia and Alabama, until thousands of white people were fleeing for their lives from place to place, before the savages. General Winfield Scott[8] was now in chief command in the South, and he prosecuted the war with vigor. The Creeks were finally subdued; and during the summer, several thousands of them were removed to their designated homes beyond the Mississippi. In October, Governor Call, of Georgia, marched against the Seminoles with almost two thousand men. A detachment of upward of five hundred of these, had a severe contest [Nov. 21] with the Indians at Wahoo Swamp, near the scene of Dade's massacre; yet, like all other engagements with the savages in their swampy fastnesses, neither party could claim a positive victory.[9] The year [1836] closed with no prospect

---

[1] About forty miles north-east from the mouth of the Withlacoochee River, and eight south-west from Orange Lake.

[2] Francis L. Dade was a native of Virginia. After the War of 1812–15, he was retained in the army, having risen from third lieutenant to major. A neat monument has been erected to the memory of himself and companions in death, at West Point, on the Hudson.

[3] Near the upper waters of the Withlacoochee, about fifty miles north from Fort Brooke. Three of the four survivors soon died of their wounds, and he who lived to tell the fearful narrative (Ransom Clarke), afterward died from the effects of his injuries on that day.

[4] On the southern borders of Alachua county, about sixty miles south-west from St. Augustine. Osceola scalped [note 4, page 14] General Thompson with his own hands, and thus enjoyed his revenge for the indignity he had suffered.

[5] Page 433. Edmund P. Gaines was born in Virginia in 1777, and entered the army in 1799. He was breveted a major-general in 1814, and presented by Congress with a gold medal for his gallantry at Fort Erie. He died in 1849.

[6] South side of the river, in Dade county. The place where Gaines was assaulted is on the north side, in Alachua county. [7] Page 30. [8] Page 433.

[9] In this warfare the American troops suffered dreadfully from the poisonous vapors of the swamps, the bites of venomous serpents, and the stings of insects. The Indians were inaccessible in their homes amid the morasses, for the white people could not follow them.

of peace, either by treaty or by the subjugation of the Indians. The war continued through the winter. Finally, after some severe encounters with the United States troops, several chiefs appeared in the camp of General Jessup[1] (who was then in supreme command) at Fort Dade,[2] and on the 6th of March, 1837, they signed a treaty which guarantied immediate peace, and the instant departure of the Indians to their new home beyond the Mississippi. But the lull was temporary. The restless Osceola caused the treaty to be broken; and during the summer of 1837, many more soldiers perished in the swamps while pursuing the Indians. At length, Osceola, with several chiefs and seventy warriors, appeared [Oct. 21] in Jessup's camp under the protection of a flag. They were seized and confined;[3] and soon afterward, the brave chief was sent to Charleston, where he died of a fever, while immured in Fort Moultrie.[4] This was the hardest blow yet dealt upon the Seminoles; but they continued to resist, notwithstanding almost nine thousand United States troops were in their territory at the close of 1837.

On the 25th of December, a large body of Indians suffered a severe repulse on the northern border of Macaco Lake,[5] from six hundred troops under Colonel Zachary Taylor.[6] That officer had succeeded General Jessup, and for more than two years afterward, he endured every privation in efforts to bring the war to a close. In May, 1839, a treaty was made which appeared to terminate the war; but murder and robberies continued, and it was not until 1842 that peace was finally secured. This war, which lasted seven years, cost the United States many valuable lives, and millions of treasure.

In the autumn of 1836, the election of a successor to President Jackson took place, and resulted in the choice of Martin Van Buren, of New York. Energy had marked every step of the career of Jackson as Chief Magistrate, and at the close of his administration, the nation stood higher in the esteem of the world than it had ever done before. At the close of his first term, our foreign relations were very satisfactory, except with France. That government had agreed to pay about $5,000,000, by instalments, as indemnification for French spoliations on American commerce, under the operation of the several decrees of Napoleon, from 1806 to 1811.[7] The French government did not promptly comply with the agreement, and the President assumed a hostile tone, which caused France to perform her duty. Similar claims against Portugal

---

[1] Thomas S. Jessup was born in Virginia in 1788. He was a brave and useful officer during the war of 1812–15, and was retained in the army. He was breveted major-general in 1828, and was succeeded in command in Florida by Colonel Zachary Taylor, in 1838. He is now [1856] a resident of Washington city.

[2] On the head waters of the Withlachoochee, about forty miles north-east from Fort Brooke, at the head of Tampa Bay. See map on page 467.

[3] General Jessup was much censured for this breach of faith and the rules of honorable warfare. His excuse was the known treachery of Osceola, and a desire to put an end to bloodshed by whatever means he might be able to employ.

[4] On Sullivan's Island, upon the site of Fort Sullivan of the Revolution [page 249]. Near the entrance gate to the fort is a small monument erected to the memory of Osceola.

[5] Sometimes called Big Water Lake. The Indian name is O-ke-cho-bee, and by that title the battle is known.

[6] The brave leader in the Mexican War [page 481], and afterward President of the United States. See page 498.

[7] See pages 400 to 407, inclusive.

were made, and payment obtained. A treaty of reciprocity had been concluded with Russia and Belgium, and everywhere the American flag commanded the highest respect. Two new States (Arkansas and Michigan) had been added to the Union. The original thirteen had doubled, and great activity prevailed in every part of the Republic. Satisfaction with the administration generally prevailed, and it was understood that Van Buren would continue the policy of his predecessor, if elected. He received a large majority; but the people, having failed to elect a Vice-President, the Senate chose Richard M. Johnson, of Kentucky, who had been a candidate with Van Buren, to fill that station.

Much excitement was produced, and bitter feelings were engendered, toward President Jackson, by his last official act. A circular was issued from the Treasury department on the 11th of July, 1836, requiring all collectors of the public revenue to receive nothing but gold and silver in payment. This was intended to check speculations in the public lands, but it also bore heavily upon every kind of business. The "specie circular" was denounced; and so loud was the clamor, that toward the close of the session in 1837, both Houses of Congress adopted a partial repeal of it. Jackson refused to sign the bill, and by keeping it in his possession until after the adjournment of Congress, prevented it becoming a law. On the 4th of March, 1837, he retired from public life, to enjoy that repose which an exceedingly active career entitled him to. He was then seventy years of age.

CHAPTER X.

VAN BUREN'S ADMINISTRATION. [1837—1841.]

Martin Van Buren,[1] the eighth President of the United States, seemed to stand, at the time of his inauguration—on the 4th of March, 1837—at the opening of a new era. All of his predecessors in the high office of Chief Magistrate of the Republic, had been descended of Britons, and were engaged in the old struggle for Independence Van Buren was of Dutch descent, and was born after the great conflict had ended, and the birth of the nation had occurred. The day of his inauguration was a remarkably pleasant one. Seated by the side of the venerable Jackson, in a phæton made from the wood of the frigate *Constitution*, which had been presented to the President by his political

[1] Martin Van Buren was born at Kinderhook, Columbia county, New York, in December, 1782. He chose the profession of law. In 1815, he became Attorney-General of his native State, and in 1828 was elected Governor of the same. Having served his country in the Senate of the United States, he was appointed minister to England in 1831, and was elected Vice-President of the United States in the autumn of 1832. Since his retirement from the presidency in 1841, Mr. Van Buren has spent a greater portion of his time on his estate in his native town. He visited Europe at the close of 1853, and was the first of the chief magistrates of the Republic who crossed the Atlantic after their term of office had expired. Ex-President Fillmore followed his example in 1855, and spent several months abroad. Mr. Van Buren is still [December, 1856] living, at the ripe age of seventy-four years. His residence is Kinderhook, New York.

friends in New York, he was escorted from the presidential mansion to the capitol by a body of infantry and cavalry, and an immense assemblage of citizens. Upon a rostrum, erected on the ascent to the eastern portico of the capitol, he delivered his inaugural address, and took the prescribed oath of office, administered by Chief Justice Taney.[1]

M. Van Buren

At the moment when Mr. Van Buren entered the presidential mansion as its occupant, the business of the country was on the verge of a terrible convulsion and utter prostration. The distressing effects of the removal of the public funds from the United States Bank,[2] in 1833 and 1834, and the operations of the "specie circular,"[3] had disappeared, in a measure, but as the remedies for the evil were superficial, the cure was only apparent. The chief remedy had been the free loaning of the public money to individuals by the State deposit banks;[4] but a commercial disease was thus produced, more disastrous than the panic of 1833–34. A sudden expansion of the paper currency was the result. The State banks which accepted these deposits, supposed they would remain undisturbed until the government should need them for its use. Considering them as so much capital, they loaned their own funds freely. But in January, 1836, Congress authorized the Secretary of the Treasury to distribute all the public funds, except five millions of dollars, among the several States, according to their representation. The funds were

[1] He appointed John Forsyth Secretary of State; Levi Woodbury, Secretary of the Treasury; Joel R. Poinsett, Secretary of War; Mahlon Dickinson, Secretary of the Navy; Amos Kendall, Postmaster-General; and Benjamin F. Butler, Attorney-General. All of them, except Mr. Poinsett, held their respective offices under President Jackson.

[2] Page 465. [3] Page 469. [4] Page 466.

accordingly taken from the deposit banks, after the 1st of January, 1837, and these banks being obliged to curtail their loans, a serious pecuniary embarrassment was produced. The immediate consequences of such multiplied facilities for obtaining bank loans, were an immensely increased importation of foreign goods, inordinate stimulation of all industrial pursuits and internal improvements, and the operation of a spirit of speculation, especially in real estate, which assumed the features of a mania, in 1836. A hundred cities were founded, and a thousand villages were "laid out" on broad sheets of paper, and made the basis of vast money transactions. Borrowed capital was thus diverted from its sober, legitimate uses, to the fostering of schemes as unstable as water, and as unreal in their fancied results as dreams of fairy-land. Overtrading and speculation, which had relied for support upon continued bank loans, was suddenly checked by the necessary bank contractions, on account of the removal of the government funds from their custody; and during March and April, 1837, there were mercantile failures in the city of New York alone, to the amount of more than a hundred millions of dollars.[1] Fifteen months before [December, 1835], property to the amount of more than twenty millions of dollars had been destroyed by fire in the city of New York, when five hundred and twenty-nine buildings were consumed. The effects of these failures and losses were felt to the remotest borders of the Union, and credit and confidence were destroyed.

Early in May, 1837, a deputation from the merchants and bankers of New York, waited upon the President, and solicited him to defer the collection of duties on imported goods, rescind the "specie circular," and to call an extraordinary session of Congress to adopt relief measures. The President declined to act on their petitions. When his determination was known, all the banks in New York suspended specie payments [May 10, 1837], and their example was speedily followed in Boston, Providence, Hartford, Albany, Philadelphia, Baltimore, and in smaller towns throughout the country. On the 16th of May the Legislature of New York passed an act, authorizing the suspension of specie payments for one year. The measure embarrassed the general government, and it was unable to obtain gold and silver to discharge its own obligations. The public good now demanded legislative relief, and an extraordinary session of Congress was convened by the President on the 4th of September. During a session of forty-three days, it did little for the general relief, except the passage of a bill authorizing the issue of treasury notes, not to exceed in amount ten millions of dollars.[2]

During the year 1837, the peaceful relations which had long existed between the United States and Great Britain, were somewhat disturbed by a revolution-

---

[1] In two days, houses in New Orleans stopped payment, owing an aggregate of twenty-seven millions of dollars; and in Boston one hundred and sixty-eight failures took place in six months.

[2] In his message to Congress at this session, the President proposed the establishment of an independent treasury, for the safe keeping of the public funds, and their entire and total separation from banking institutions. This scheme met with vehement opposition. The bill passed the Senate, but was lost in the House. It was debated at subsequent sessions, and finally became a law on the 4th of July, 1840. This is known as the *Sub-Treasury Scheme.*

ary movement in Canada which, at one time, seemed to promise a separation of that province from the British crown. The agitation and the outbreak appeared simultaneously in Upper and Lower Canada. In the former province, the most conspicuous leader was William Lyon M'Kenzie, a Scotchman, of rare abilities as a political writer and an agitator, and a republican in sentiment; and in the latter province, Louis Joseph Papineau, a large land-owner, and a very influential man among the French population. The movements of the Revolutionary party were well planned, but local jealousies prevented unity of action, and the scheme failed. It was esteemed a highly patriotic effort to secure independence and nationality for the people of the Canadas, and, as in the case of Cuba, at a later period,[1] the warmest sympathies of the Americans were enlisted, especially at the North. Banded companies and individuals joined the rebels;[2] and so general became this active sympathy on the northern frontier, that peace between the two governments was jeoparded. President Van Buren issued a proclamation, calling upon all persons engaged in the schemes of invasion of Canada, to abandon the design, and warning them to beware of the penalties that must assuredly follow such infractions of international laws. In 1838, General Scott was sent to the frontier to preserve order, and was assisted by proclamations of the Governor of New York. Yet secret revolutionary associations, called "Hunter's Lodges," continued for a long time. For about four years, that cloud hung upon our northern horizon, when, in September, 1841, President Tyler issued an admonitory proclamation, specially directed to the members of the Hunter's Lodges, which prevented further aggressive movements. The leaders of the revolt were either dead or in exile, and quiet was restored.

While this excitement was at its height, long disputes concerning the boundary between the State of Maine and the British province of New Brunswick, ripened into armed preparations for settling the matter by combat. This, too, threatened danger to the peaceful relations between the two governments. The President sent General Scott to the theater of the dispute, in the winter of 1839, and by his wise and conciliatory measures, he prevented bloodshed, and produced quiet. The whole matter was finally settled by a treaty [August 20, 1842], negotiated at Washington City, by Daniel Webster for the United States, and Lord Ashburton for Great Britain. The latter had been sent as special minister for the purpose. Besides settling the boundary question, this agreement, known as the Ashburton Treaty, provided for the final suppression of the slave-trade, and for the giving up of criminal fugitives from justice, in certain cases.

A new presidential election now approached. On the 5th of May, 1840, a

[1] Page 502.

[2] A party of Americans took possession of Navy Island, situated in the Niagara River about two miles above the Falls, and belonging to Canada. They numbered seven hundred strong, well provisioned, and provided with twenty pieces of cannon. They had a small steamboat named *Caroline*, to ply between Schlosser, on the American side, and Navy Island. On a dark night in December, 1837, a party of royalists from the Canada shore crossed over, cut the *Caroline* loose, set her on fire, and she went over the great cataract while in full blaze. It was believed that some persons were on board the vessel at the time.

national Democratic convention assembled at Baltimore, and unanimously nominated Mr. Van Buren for President. No nomination was made for Vice-President, but soon afterward, Richard M. Johnson[1] and James K. Polk were selected as candidates for that office, in different States. A national Whig[2] convention had been held at Harrisburg, in Pennsylvania, on the 4th of December previous [1839], when General William H. Harrison, of Ohio, the popular leader in the North-West, in the War of 1812,[3] was nominated for President, and John Tyler, of Virginia, for Vice-President. Never, before, was the country so excited by an election, and never before was a presidential contest characterized by such demoralizing proceedings.[4] The government, under Mr. Van Buren, being held responsible by the opposition for the business depression which yet brooded over the country, public speakers arrayed vast masses of the people against the President, and Harrison and Tyler were elected by overwhelming majorities. And now, at the close of the first fifty years of the Republic, the population had increased from three and a half millions, of all colors, to seventeen millions. A magazine writer of the day,[5] in comparing several administrations, remarked that "The great events of Mr. Van Buren's administration, by which it will hereafter be known and designated, is the *divorce of bank and State*[6] in the fiscal affairs of the Federal government, and the return, after half a century of deviation, to the original design of the Constitution."

CHAPTER XI.

HARRISON'S AND TYLER'S ADMINISTRATION. [1841—1845.]

THE city of Washington was thronged with people from every State in the Union, on the 4th of March, 1841, to witness the ceremonies of the inauguration of General William Henry Harrison,[7] the ninth President of the United States. He

---

[1] Page 424 [2] Note 2, page 466. [3] Pages 416 to 424, inclusive.

[4] Because General Harrison lived in the West, and his residence was associated with pioneer life, a log-cabin became the symbol of his party. These cabins were erected all over the country, in which meetings were held; and, as the hospitality of the old hero was symbolized by a barrel of cider, made free to all visiters or strangers, who "never found the latch-string of his log-cabin drawn in," that beverage was dealt out unsparingly to all who attended the meetings in the cabins. These meetings were scenes of carousal, deeply injurious to all who participated in them, and especially to the young. Thousands of drunkards, in after years, dated their departure from sobriety to the "Hard Cider" campaign of 1840.

[5] *Democratic Review*, April, 1840.

[6] This is in allusion to the sub-treasury scheme. Mr. Van Buren remarked to a friend, just previous to sending his message to Congress, in which he proposed that plan for collecting and keeping the public moneys: "We can not know how the immediate convulsion may result; but the people will, at all events, eventually come right, and posterity at least will do me justice. Be the present issue for good or for evil, it is for posterity that I will write this message."

[7] William Henry Harrison, son of one of the signers of the Declaration of Independence, was born near the banks of the James River, in Charles City county, Virginia, in February, 1773. He was educated at Hampden Sydney College, and was prepared, by studies, for a physician, but entered the army as ensign in the United States artillery, in 1791. He was Secretary of the North-

was then an old man, having passed almost a month beyond the age of sixty-eight years. Yet there was a vigor in his movements quite remarkable for one of that age, and who had passed through so many hardships and physical labors. From a platform over the ascent to the eastern portico of the Capitol, where Mr. Van Buren delivered his inaugural address, General Harrison, in a clear

voice, read his. He was frequently interrupted by cheers during the reading. When it was concluded, Chief Justice Taney administered the oath of office, and three successive cannon peals announced the fact that the Republic had a new President. Harrison immediately nominated his cabinet officers,[1] and these were all confirmed by the Senate, then in session.

President Harrison's inaugural speech was well received by all parties, and the dawn of his administration gave omens of a brighter day for the country. When his Address went over the land, and the wisdom of his choice of cabinet

---

western Territory in 1797; and at the age of twenty-six years, was elected the first delegate to Congress from that domain. He was afterward appointed governor of Indiana Territory, and was very active during the War of 1812. See pages 416 to 424 inclusive. At its close he retired to his farm at North Bend, on the banks of the Ohio. He served in the national council for four years [1824 to 1828] as United States senator, when he was appointed minister to Colombia, one of the South American republics. He was finally raised to the highest post of honor in the nation. His last disease was pneumonia, or bilious pleurisy, which terminated his life in a few days. His last words were (thinking he was addressing his successor in office): "Sir, I wish you to understand the principles of the government. I wish them carried out. I ask nothing more."

[1] Daniel Webster, Secretary of State; Thomas Ewing, Secretary of the Treasury; John Bell, Secretary of War; George E. Badger, Secretary of the Navy; Francis Granger, Postmaster-General; and J. J. Crittenden, Attorney-General.

counselors was known, prosperity was half restored, for confidence was re-enthroned in the commercial world. But all the hopes which centered in the new President were soon extinguished, and the anthems of the inaugural day were speedily changed to solemn requiems. Precisely one month after he uttered his oath of office, the new President died. That sad event occurred on the 4th day of April, 1841. Before he had fairly placed his hand upon the machinery of the government, it was paralyzed, and the only official act of general importance performed by President Harrison during his brief administration, was the issuing of a proclamation, on the 17th of March, calling an extraordinary session of Congress, to commence at the close of the following May, to legislate upon the subjects of finance and revenue.[1]

In accordance with the provisions of the Constitution, the Vice-President became the official successor of the deceased President; and on the 6th of April the oath of office was administered to

JOHN TYLER.[2]

He retained the cabinet appointed by President Harrison until September following, when all but the Secretary of State resigned.[3]

The extraordinary session of Congress called by President Harrison, commenced its session on the appointed day [May 31, 1841], and continued until the 13th of September following. The Sub-Treasury act[4] was repealed, and a general Bankrupt law was enacted. This humane law accomplished a material benefit. Thousands of honest and enterprising men had been crushed by the

---

[1] The predecessors of Harrison had called extraordinary sessions of Congress, as follows: John Adams, on the 16th of May, 1797; Thomas Jefferson, on the 17th of October, 1808, to provide for carrying the treaty of Louisiana into effect; James Madison, on the 23d of May, 1809, and also on the 25th of May, 1813; and Martin Van Buren, on the 4th of September, 1837.

[2] On the 4th of April, the members of Harrison's cabinet dispatched Fletcher Webster, chief clerk in the State Department, with a letter to Mr. Tyler, announcing the death of the President. Mr. Tyler was then at Williamsburg. So great was the dispatch, both by the messenger and the Vice-President, that the latter arrived in Washington on Tuesday morning, the 6th of April, at four o'clock. As doubts might arise concerning the validity of his oath of office as Vice-President, while acting as President, Mr. Tyler took the oath anew, as Chief Magistrate, before Judge Cranch, of Washington city. On the following day he attended the funeral of President Harrison. John Tyler was born in Charles City county, Virginia, in March, 1790. He was so precocious that he entered William and Mary College at the age of twelve years. He graduated at the age of seventeen, studied law, and at nineteen he was a practicing lawyer. At the age of twenty he was elected a member of the Virginia Legislature, where he served for several years. He was elected to Congress to fill a vacancy caused by death, in 1816, when only twenty-six years of age. He was there again in 1819. In 1825 he was elected governor of Virginia. He was afterward sent to the Senate of the United States; and he was much in public life until the close of his Presidential career. Since then he has lived in retirement at Sherwood Forest, his pleasant estate, a few miles from Charles City court-house.

[3] He then appointed Walter Forward, Secretary of the Treasury; John C. Spencer, Secretary of War; Abel P. Upshur, Secretary of the Navy; Charles A. Wickliffe, Postmaster-General; and Hugh S. Legarè, Attorney-General. Mr. Tyler had the misfortune to lose three of his cabinet officers, by death, in the course of a few months. Mr. Legarè accompanied the President to Boston, on the occasion of celebrating the completion of the Bunker Hill monument [page 235], in June, 1843, and died there. On the 28th of February following, the bursting of a gun on board the steamship *Princeton*, while on an excursion upon the Potomac, killed Mr. Upshur, then Secretary of State; Mr. Gilmer, Secretary of the Navy; and several other distinguished gentlemen. The President and many ladies were on board. Among the killed was Mr. Gardiner, of the State of New York, whose daughter the President soon afterward married.

[4] Note 2, page 471.

recent business revulsion, and were so laden with debt as to be hopelessly chained to a narrow sphere of action. The law relieved them; and while it bore heavily upon the creditor class, for a while, its operations were beneficent and useful. When dishonest men began to make it a pretense for cheating, it was repealed. But the chief object sought to be obtained during this session,

namely, the chartering of a Bank of the United States, was not achieved. Two separate bills[1] for that purpose were vetoed[2] by the President, who, like Jackson, thought be perceived great evils to be apprehended from the workings of such an institution. The course of the President was vehemently censured by the party in power, and the last veto led to the dissolution of his cabinet. Mr. Webster patriotically remained at his post, for great public interests would have suffered by his withdrawal, at that time.

The year 1842 (second of Mr. Tyler's administration) was distinguished by the return of the United States Exploring Expedition; the settlement of the North-eastern boundary question; essential modifications of the tariff; and domestic difficulties in Rhode Island. The exploring expedition, commanded by Lieutenant Wilkes, of the United States navy, had been sent, several years before, to traverse and explore the great southern ocean. It coasted along what

[1] One was passed on the 16th of August, 1841; the other, modified so as to meet the President's objections, as it was believed, passed September 9th.

[2] Note 6, page 462.

is supposed to be an Antarctic continent, for seventeen hundred miles in the vicinity of latitude 66 degrees south, and between longitude 96 and 154 degrees east. The expedition brought home a great many curiosities of island human life, and a large number of fine specimens of natural history, all of which are now [1856] in the custody of the National Institute, Patent Office building, in Washington city. The expedition made a voyage of about ninety thousand miles, equal to almost four times the circumference of the globe. The modifications of the tariff were important. By the compromise act of 1832,[1] duties on foreign goods were to reach the minimum of reduction at the close of 1842, when the tariff would only provide *revenue*, not *protection to manufactures*, like that of 1828.[2] The latter object appeared desirable; and by an act passed on the 29th of June, 1842, high tariffs were imposed on many foreign articles. The President vetoed it; but another tariff bill, less objectionable, received his assent on the 9th of August.

The difficulties in Rhode Island originated in a movement to adopt a State Constitution of government, and to abandon the old charter given by Charles the Second,[3] in 1663, under which the people had been ruled for one hundred and eighty years. Disputes arose concerning the proper method to be pursued in making the change, and these assumed a serious aspect. Two parties were formed, known, respectively, as the "suffrage," or radical party; the other as the "law and order," or conservative party. Each formed a Constitution, elected a governor and legislature,[4] and finally armed [May and June, 1843] in defense of their respective claims. The State was on the verge of civil war, and the aid of Federal troops had to be invoked, to restore quiet and order. A free Constitution, adopted by the "law and order" party in November, 1842, to go into operation on the first Tuesday in May, 1843, was sustained, and became the law of the land.

During the last year of President Tyler's administration, the country was much agitated by discussions concerning the proposed admission of the independent republic of Texas, on our south-west frontier, as a State of the Union. The proposition was warmly opposed at the North, because the annexation would increase the area and political strength of slavery, and lead to a war with Mexico.[5] A treaty for admission, signed at Washington on the 12th of April,

---

[1] Page 464. [2] Page 459. [3] Page 158.

[4] The "suffrage" party elected Thomas W. Dorr, governor, and the "law and order" party chose Samuel W. King for chief magistrate. Dorr was finally arrested, tried for and convicted of treason, and sentenced to imprisonment for life. The excitement having passed away, in a measure, he was released in June, 1845, but was deprived of all the civil rights of a citizen. These disabilities were removed in the autumn of 1853.

[5] Texas was a part of the domain of that ancient Mexico conquered by Cortez [page 43]. In 1824, Mexico became a republic under Generals Victoria and Santa Anna, and was divided into States united by a Federal Constitution. One of these was Texas, a territory which was originally claimed by the United States as a part of Louisiana, purchased [page 390] from France in 1803, but ceded to Spain in 1820. In 1821–22, a colony from the United States, under Stephen F. Austin, made a settlement on both sides of the Colorado River; and the Spanish government favoring immigration thither, caused a rapid increase in the population. There were ten thousand Americans in that province in 1833. Santa Anna became military dictator; and the people of Texas, unwilling to submit to his arbitrary rule, rebelled. A war ensued; and on the 2d of March, 1836, a convention declared Texas *independent*. Much bloodshed occurred afterward; but a final

1844, was rejected by the Senate on the 8th of June following. To the next Congress the proposition was presented in the form of a joint resolution, and received the concurrence of both Houses on the 1st of March, 1845, and the assent of the President on the same day. This measure had an important bearing upon the Presidential election in 1844. It became more and more popular with the people throughout the Union, and James K. Polk, of Tennessee, who was pledged in favor of the measure, was nominated for the office of President of the United States, by the National Democratic Convention, assembled at Baltimore on the 27th of May, 1844. George M. Dallas was nominated for Vice-President at the same time; and in November following, they were both elected. The opposing candidates were Henry Clay and Theodore Frelinghuysen. The last important official act of President Tyler was the signing, on the 3d of March, 1845, of the bill for the admission of Florida and Iowa into the Union of States.

CHAPTER XII.

POLK'S ADMINISTRATION. [1845—1849.]

NEVER before had so large a concourse of people assembled at the Federal city, to witness the inauguration of a new Chief Magistrate of the nation, as on the 4th of March, 1845, when James Knox Polk,[1] of Tennessee, the tenth President of the United States, took the oath of office, administered by Chief Justice Taney. The day was unpleasant. A lowering morning preceded a rainy day, and the pleasures of the occasion were marred thereby. The address of the President, on that occasion, clearly indicated that energetic policy which distinguished his administration. On the day of his inauguration he nominated his cabinet officers,[2] and the Senate being in session, immediately confirmed them.

Among the most important topics which claimed the attention of the administration, were the annexation of Texas, and the claims of Great Britain to a large portion of the vast territory of Oregon, on the Pacific coast. The former

---

battle at San Jacinto, in which the Texans were led by General Houston, one of the present [1856] United States senators from Texas, vindicated the position the people had taken, and terminated the strife. Texas remained an independent republic until its admission into our Federal Union in 1845.

[1] James K. Polk was born in Mecklenburg county, North Carolina, in November, 1795. While he was a child, his father settled in Tennessee; and the first appearance of young Polk in public life, was as a member of the Tennessee Legislature, in 1823. He had been admitted to the bar three years before, but public life kept him from the practice of his profession, except at intervals. He was elected to Congress in 1825, and was in that body almost continually until elevated to the Presidential chair. He was elected Speaker of the House of Representatives in 1835, and continued in the performance of the duties of that office during five consecutive sessions. He was elected governor of Tennessee in 1839, and President of the United States in 1844. He retired to his residence, near Knoxville, Tennessee, at the close of his term, in 1849, and died there in June of the same year.

[2] James Buchanan, Secretary of State; Robert J. Walker, Secretary of the Treasury; William L. Marcy, Secretary of War; George Bancroft, Secretary of the Navy; Cave Johnson, Postmaster-General; and John Y. Mason, Attorney-General.

demanded and received the earliest consideration. On the last day of his official term, President Tyler had sent a messenger to the Texan Government, with a copy of the joint resolutions of the American Congress,[1] in favor of annexation. These were considered by a convention of delegates, called for the purpose of forming a State Constitution for Texas. That body approved of the measure, by resolution, on the 4th of July, 1845. On that day Texas became

one of the States of our Confederation. The other momentous subject (the claims of Great Britain to certain portions of Oregon), also received prompt attention. That vast territory, between the Rocky Mountains and the Pacific, had been, for some time, a subject of dispute between the two countries.[2] In 1818, it was mutually agreed that each nation should equally enjoy the privileges of all the bays and harbors on the coast, for ten years. This agreement was renewed in 1827, for an indefinite time, with the stipulation, that either party might rescind it by giving the other party twelve months' notice. Such notice

[1] The communication was made through A. J. Donelson, the "American" candidate for Vice-President of the United States, in 1856, who was our Chargé d'Affaires to the Texan Government.

[2] Captain Grey, of Boston, entered the mouth of the Columbia River in 1792, and Captains Lewis and Clarke explored that region, from the Rocky Mountains westward, in 1804–'5. In 1811, the late J. J. Astor established a trading station at the mouth of the Columbia River. The British doctrine, always practiced by them, that the entrance of a vessel of a civilized nation into the mouth of a river, gives title, by the right of discovery, to the territory watered by that river and its tributaries, clearly gave Oregon to 54 degrees 40 minutes, to the United States, for the discovery of Captain Grey, in 1792, was not disputed.

was given by the United States in 1846, and the boundary was then fixed by treaty, made at Washington city, in June of that year. Great Britain claimed the whole territory to 54° 40′ north latitude, the right to which was disputed by the United States. The boundary line was finally fixed at latitude 49°; and in 1848, a territorial government was established. In March, 1853, Oregon was divided, and the northern portion was made a separate domain, by the title of Washington Territory.

The annexation of Texas, as had been predicted, caused an immediate rupture between the United States and Mexico; for the latter claimed Texas as a part of its territory, notwithstanding its independence had been acknowledged by the United States, England, France, and other governments. Soon after [March 6, 1845] Congress had adopted the joint resolution for the admission of that State into the Union,[1] General Almonte, the Mexican minister at Washington, formally protested against that measure, and demanded his passports. On the 4th of June following, General Herrera, President of Mexico, issued a proclamation, declaring the rights of Mexico, and his determination to defend them—by arms, if necessary. But, independent of the act complained of, there already existed a cause for serious disputes between the United States and Mexico.[2] Ever since the establishment of republican government by the latter, in 1824, it had been an unjust and injurious neighbor. Impoverished by civil wars, its authorities did not hesitate to replenish its Treasury by plundering American vessels in the Gulf of Mexico, or by confiscating the property of American merchants within its borders. The United States government remonstrated in vain, until, in 1831, a treaty was formed, and promises of redress were made. But aggressions continued; and in 1840, the aggregate amount of American property which had been appropriated by Mexicans, was more than six millions of dollars. The claim for this amount remained unsettled[3] when the annexation of Texas occurred [July 4, 1845], and peaceful relations between the two governments were suspended.

The President being fully aware of the hostile feelings of the Mexicans, ordered [July] General Zachary Taylor,[4] then in command of troops in the South-West, to proceed to Texas, and take a position as near the Rio Grande,[5] as prudence would allow. This force, about fifteen hundred strong, was called the "Army of Occupation," for the defense of Texas. At the same time, a strong squadron, under Commodore Conner, sailed for the Gulf of Mexico, to protect American interests there. General Taylor first landed on the 25th of July on St. Joseph's Island,[6] and then embarked for Corpus Christi, a Mexican

---

[1] Page 478.

[2] Pronounced May-hee-co by the Spaniards.

[3] Commissioners appointed by the two governments to adjust these claims, met in 1840. The Mexican commissioners acknowledged two millions of dollars, and no more. In 1843 the whole amount was acknowledged by Mexico, and the payment was to be made in instalments of three hundred thousand dollars each. Only three of these instalments had been paid in 1845, and the Mexican government refused to decide whether the remainder should be settled or not.

[4] Taylor's actual rank in the army list was only that of Colonel. He had been made a Brigadier-General by *brevet*, for his good conduct in the Florida War [page 468]. A title by *brevet* is only honorary. Taylor held the *title* of Brigadier-General, but received only the *pay* of a Colonel.

[5] Great or Grand river. Also called *Rio Bravo del Norte*—Brave North river.

[6] There the flag of the United States was first displayed in power over Texas soil.

village beyond the Nueces, and near its mouth. There he formed a camp [September, 1845], and remained during the succeeding autumn and winter. It was during the gathering of this storm of war on our south-western frontier, that the difficulties with Great Britain, concerning Oregon, occurred, which we have already considered.

By a dispatch dated January 13, 1846, the Secretary of War ordered General Taylor to advance from Corpus Christi to near the mouth of the Rio Grande, opposite the Spanish city of Matamoras, because Mexican troops were then gathering in that direction, with the evident intention of invading Texas. This was disputed territory between Texas and the Mexican province of Tamaulipas; and when, on the 25th of March, he encamped at Point Isabel, on the coast, about twenty-eight miles from Matamoras, General Taylor was warned by the Mexicans that he was upon foreign soil. Regardless of menaces, he left his stores at Point Isabel, under Major Monroe and four hundred and fifty men, and with the remainder of his army advanced [March 28, 1846] to the bank of the Rio Grande, where he established a fortified camp, and commenced the erection of a fort.[1]

President Herrera's desire for peace with the United States made him unpopular, and the Mexican people elected General Paredes[2] to succeed him. That officer immediately dispatched General Ampudia[3] with a large force, to Matamoras, to drive the Americans beyond the Nueces. Ampudia arrived on the 11th of April, 1846, and the next day he sent a letter to General Taylor, demanding his withdrawal within twenty-four hours. Taylor refused compliance, and continued to strengthen his camp. Ampudia hesitated; and on the 24th of that month he was succeeded in command by the more energetic Arista,[4] the commander-in-chief of the northern division of the army of Mexico, whose reported reinforcements made it probable that some decisive action would soon take place. This change of affairs was unfavorable to the Americans, and the situation of the "Army of Occupation" was now becoming very critical. Parties of armed Mexicans had got between Taylor and his stores at Point Isabel, and had cut off all inter-communication. Arista's army was hourly gathering strength; and already an American reconnoitering party, under Captain Thornton,[5] had been killed or captured [April 24] on the Texas side of the Rio Grande. This was the first blood shed in

THE WAR WITH MEXICO.

When he had nearly completed the fort opposite Matamoras, General Taylor hastened [May 1], with his army, to the relief of Point Isabel, which was menaced by a large Mexican force[6] collected in his rear. He left a regiment

[1] It was named Fort Brown, in honor of Major Brown, the officer in command there. It was erected under the superintendence of Captain Mansfield, and was large enough to accommodate about two thousand men.

[2] Pronounced Pa-ray-dhes.

[3] Pronounced Am-poo-dhee-ah.

[4] Pronounced Ah-rees-tah.

[5] General Taylor had been informed that a body of Mexican troops were crossing the Rio Grande, above his encampment, and he sent Captain Thornton, with sixty dragoons, to reconnoitre. They were surprised and captured. Sixteen Americans were killed, and Captain Thornton escaped by an extraordinary leap of his horse.

[6] General Taylor was apprised of this force of fifteen hundred Mexicans, by Captain Walker,

of infantry and two companies of artillery, under Major Brown (in whose honor, as we have just observed, the fortification was named), to defend the fort, and reached Point Isabel the same day, without molestation. This departure produced great joy in Matamoras, for the Mexicans regarded it as a cowardly retreat. Preparations were immediately made to attack Fort Brown; and on the morning of the 3d of May [1846], a battery at Matamoras opened a heavy cannonade and bombardment upon it, while quite a large body of troops crossed the river, to attack it in the rear. General Taylor had left orders that, in the event of an attack, and aid being required, heavy signal-guns should be fired at the fort. For a long time the little garrison made a noble defense, and silenced the Mexican battery; but when, finally, the enemy gathered in strength in the rear, and commenced planting cannons, and the heroic Major Brown was mortally wounded,[1] the signals were given [May 6], and Taylor prepared to march for the Rio Grande. He left Point Isabel on the evening of the 7th, with a little more than two thousand men, having been reinforced by Texas volunteers, and marines from the American fleet then blockading the mouth of the Rio Grande. At noon, the next day [May 8], they discovered a Mexican army, under Arista, full six thousand strong, drawn up in battle array upon a portion of a prairie flanked by ponds of water, and beautified by trees, which gave it the name of Palo Alto. As soon as his men could take refreshments, Taylor formed his army, and pressed forward to the attack. For five hours a hot contest was maintained, when, at twilight, the Mexicans gave way and fled, and victory, thorough and complete, was with the Americans. It had been an afternoon of terrible excitement and fatigue, and when the firing ceased, the victors sank exhausted upon the ground. They had lost, in killed and wounded, fifty-three;[2] the Mexicans lost about six hundred.

At two o'clock in the morning of the 9th of May, the deep slumbers of the little army were broken by a summons to renew the march for Fort Brown. They saw no traces of the enemy until toward evening, when they discovered them strongly posted in a ravine, called Resaca de la Palma,[3] drawn up in battle order. A shorter, but bloodier conflict than that at Palo Alto, the previous day, ensued, and again the Americans were victorious. They lost, in killed and wounded, one hundred and ten; the Mexican loss was at least one thousand. General La Vega[4] and a hundred men were made prisoners, and

---

the celebrated Texas Ranger, who had been employed by Major Monroe to keep open a communication between Point Isabel and Taylor's camp. Walker had fought them with his single company, armed with revolving pistols, and after killing thirty, escaped, and, with six of his men, reached Taylor's camp.

[1] He lost a leg by the bursting of a bomb-shell [note 2, page 296], and died on the 9th of May. He was born in Massachusetts in 1788; was in the war of 1812; was promoted to Major in 1843; and was fifty-eight years of age when he died.

[2] Among the fatally wounded was Captain Page, a native of Maine, who died on the 12th of July following, at the age of forty-nine years. Also, Major Ringgold, commander of the Flying Artillery, who died at Point Isabel, four days afterward, at the age of forty-six years.

[3] Pronounced Ray-sah-kah day la Pal-mah, or Dry River of Palms. The ravine is supposed to be the bed of a dried-up stream. The spot is on the northerly side of the Rio Grande, about three miles from Matamoras. In this engagement, Taylor's force was about one thousand seven hundred; Arista had been reinforced, and had about seven thousand men.

[4] Lay Vay-goh. He was a brave officer, and was captured by Captain May, who, rising in his

eight pieces of cannon, three standards, and a quantity of military stores, were captured. The Mexican army was completely broken up. Arista saved himself by solitary flight, and made his way alone across the Rio Grande. After suffering a bombardment for one hundred and sixty hours, the garrison at Fort Brown were relieved, and the terrified Mexicans were trembling for the safety of Matamoras.

When intelligence of the first bloodshed, in the attack upon Captain Thornton and his party, on the 24th of April, and a knowledge of the critical situation of the little Army of Occupation, reached New Orleans, and spread over the land, the whole country was aroused; and before the battles of Palo Alto and Resaca de la Palma [May 8, 9] were known in the States, Congress had declared [May 11, 1846] that, "by the act of the Republic of Mexico, a state of war exists between that government and the United States;" authorized the President to raise fifty thousand volunteers, and appropriated ten millions of dollars [May 13] toward carrying on the contest. Within two days, the Secretary of War and General Scott[1] planned [May 15] a campaign, greater in the territorial extent of its proposed operations, than any recorded in history. A fleet was to sweep around Cape Horn, and attack the Pacific coast of Mexico; an "Army of the West" was to gather at Fort Leavenworth,[2] invade New Mexico, and co-operate with the Pacific fleet; and an "Army of the Center" was to rendezvous in the heart of Texas,[3] to invade Old Mexico from the north. On the 23d of the same month [May], the Mexican government made a formal declaration of war against the United States.

When news of the two brilliant victories reached the States, a thrill of joy went throughout the land, and bonfires, illuminations, orations, and the thunder of cannons, were seen and heard in all the great cities. In the mean while, General Taylor was in Mexico, preparing for other brilliant victories.[4] He crossed the Rio Grande, drove the Mexican troops from Matamoras, and took possession of that town on the 18th of May. There he remained until the close of August, receiving orders from government, and reinforcements, and preparing to march into the interior. The first division of his army, under General Worth,[5] moved toward Monterey[6] on the 20th. Taylor, with the remainder (in all, more than six thousand men), followed on the 3d of September; and on the 19th, the whole army[7] encamped within three miles of the doomed city, then

stirrups, shouted, "Remember your regiment! Men, follow!" and, with his dragoons, rushed forward in the face of a heavy fire from a battery, captured La Vega, killed or dispersed the gunners, and took possession of the cannons.

[1] Page 485.

[2] A strong United States post on the southern bank of the Missouri River, on the borders of the Great Plains. These plains extend to the eastern slopes of the Rocky Mountains.

[3] At San Antonia de Bexar, the center of Austin's settlement [note 5, page 477], south of the Colorado river.

[4] On the 30th of May he was rewarded for his skill and bravery by a commission as Major-General, by *brevet*. See note 4, page 480.

[5] William J. Worth was born in Columbia county, New York, in 1704. He was a gallant soldier during the War of 1812–15; was retained in the army, and for his gallantry at Monterey, was made a Major-General by *brevet*, and received the gift of a sword from Congress. He was of great service during the whole war with Mexico. He died in Texas in May, 1849.

[6] Pronounced Mon-tar-ray. It is the capital of New Leon.

[7] The principal officers with General Taylor, at this time, were Generals Worth, Quitman, Twiggs, Butler, Henderson, and Hamer.

defended by General Ampudia,[1] with more than nine thousand troops. It was a strongly built town, at the foot of the great Sierra Madre, well fortified by both nature and art, and presented a formidable obstacle in the march of the victor toward the interior. But having secured the Saltillo road,[2] by which supplies for the Mexicans in Monterey were to be obtained, General Taylor commenced a siege on the 21st of September. The conflict continued almost four days, a part of the time within the streets of the city, where the carnage was dreadful. Ampudia surrendered the town and garrison on the fourth day[3] [September 24], and leaving General Worth in command there, General Taylor encamped at Walnut Springs, three miles distant, and awaited further orders from his government.[4]

When Congress made the declaration of war, and authorized the raising of an army from the great body of the people, General Wool[5] was commissioned to muster and prepare for serviee, the gathering volunteers. He performed this duty so promptly, that by the middle of July, twelve thousand of them had been inspected, and mustered into service. Nine thousand of them were sent to the Rio Grande, to reinforce General Taylor, and the remainder repaired to Bexar,[6] in Texas, where they were disciplined by General Wool, in person, preparatory to marching into the province of Chihuahua,[7] in the heart of Mexico. Wool went up the Rio Grande with about three thousand men, crossed the river at Presidio, and on the last day of October, reached Monclova, seventy miles north-west from Monterey. His kindness to the people won their confidence and esteem, and he was regarded as a friend. There he was informed of the capture of Monterey, and guided by the advice of General Taylor, he abandoned the project of penetrating Chihuahua, and marched to the fertile district of Parras, in Coahuila, where he obtained ample supplies for his own and Taylor's forces.

The armistice[8] at Monterey ceased on the 13th of November, by order of the United States government. General Worth, with nine hundred men, took possession of Saltillo [November 15, 1846], the capital of Coahuila,[9] and General Taylor, leaving General Butler in command at Monterey, marched for Victoria, the capital of Tamaulipas, with the intention of attacking Tampico,

---

[1] Page 481.

[2] This road passed through the mountains along the San Juan river, and is the only communication between Monterey and the fertile provinces of Coahuila and Durango. The command of this road was obtained after a severe contest with Mexican cavalry, on the 20th of May, by a party under General Worth.

[3] The Mexican soldiers were permitted to march out with the honors of war; and, being short of provisions, and assured that Santa Anna, now at the head of the Mexicans, desired peace, General Taylor agreed to a cessation of hostilities for eight weeks, if permitted by his government.

[4] The Americans lost in killed, wounded, and missing, five hundred and sixty-one. The number lost by the Mexicans was never ascertained, but it was supposed to be more than one thousand.

[5] John Ellis Wool is a native of New York. He entered the army in 1812, and soon rose to the rank of Lieutenant-Colonel, for gallant conduct on Queenstown Heights [page 413]. He has belonged to the army ever since. He was breveted brigadier in 1826, and for gallant conduct at Buena Vista, in 1847, was breveted Major-General.

[6] Austin's settlement. See note 5, page 477.

[7] Pronounced Chee-wah-wah.

[8] The agreement for a cessation of hostilities is so called.

[9] Pronounced Co-ah-weel-ah.

on the coast. That place had already surrendered[1] [November 14], and being informed that Santa Anna was collecting a large force at San Luis Potosi,[2] he returned to Monterey, to reinforce General Worth, if necessary. Worth was joined by Wool's division, near Saltillo, on the 20th of December, and Taylor again advanced and took possession of Victoria, on the 29th.

And now the conquering Taylor was compelled to endure a severe trial of his temper and patriotism. General Scott[3] had arrived before Vera Cruz [January, 1847], for the purpose of invading Mexico from that point, and being the senior officer, took the supreme command. Just as Taylor was preparing for a vigorous winter campaign, he received an order from General Scott, to send him a large portion of his best officers and troops to assist against Vera Cruz, and to act thereafter only on the defensive.[4] Taylor was deeply mortified, but, like a true soldier, instantly obeyed, and he and General Wool were left with an aggregate force of only about five thousand men (only five hundred regulars) to oppose an army of twenty thousand, now gathering at San Luis Potosi, under Santa Anna. They united their forces at Agua Nueva,[5] twenty miles south from Saltillo, on the San Luis road, early in February [Feb. 4, 1847], and weak as he was, Taylor determined to fight the Mexicans, who were now advancing upon him. The opportunity was not long delayed. The Americans fell back [Feb. 21] to Buena Vista,[6] within eleven miles of Saltillo, and there, in a narrow defile in the mountains, encamped in battle order. At about noon the next day [Feb. 22]—the anniversary of the birth of Washington—the Mexican army approached within two miles of them; and Santa Anna, assuring Taylor that he was surrounded by twenty thousand troops, and could not escape, ordered him to surrender within an hour. Taylor politely refused the request, and both armies prepared for battle.[7] There was some skirmising dur-

GENERAL SCOTT.

[1] Commodore Connor, who commanded the "Home Squadron" in the Gulf, captured Tampico. Tobasco and Tuspan were captured by Commodore Perry [page 512], in October following.

[2] Santa Anna was elected provisional President of Mexico, in December, and in violation of his peace promises to Commodore Connor, he immediately placed himself at the head of the army.

[3] Winfield Scott was born in Virginia in 1786. He was admitted to law practice at the age of twenty years. He joined the army in 1808, was made Lieutenant-Colonel in 1812, and passed through the war that ensued, with great honor to himself and his country. He was breveted major-general in 1814, and was made general-in-chief of the army in 1841. His successes in Mexico greatly added to his laurels; and Congress, after a delay of several years, honored him with the commission of Lieutenant-General, on the 15th of February, 1855. He is now [1856] considered one of the greatest captains of the age.

[4] The necessity for this order was as painful to General Scott as it was mortifying to General Taylor. Before leaving Washington, Scott wrote a long private letter to Taylor, apprising him of this necessity, expressing his sincere regrets, and speaking in highest praise of the victories already achieved in Mexico.

[5] Pronounced Ag-wah New-vah, or New Water.

[6] Pronounced Bwe-naw Ves-tah—Pleasant View. This was the name of a hacienda (plantation) at Angostura.

[7] Santa Anna wrote as follows:

"CAMP AT ENCATADA, February 22d, 1847.

"GOD AND LIBERTY!—You are surrounded by twenty thousand men, and can not, in any human probability, avoid suffering a rout, and being cut to pieces with your troops; but as you de-ing the afternoon, when the battle-cry of the Americans was, "*The Memory of Washington!*" Early the following morning [Feb. 23] a terrible conflict commenced. It was desperate and bloody, and continued until sunset. Several times the overwhelming numbers of the Mexicans appeared about to crush the little band of Americans; and finally Santa Anna made a desperate assault[1] upon the American center, commanded by Taylor in person. It stood like a rock before a billow; and by the assistance of the artillery of Bragg, Washington, and Sherman, the martial wave was rolled back, the Mexicans fled in confusion, and the Americans were masters of the bloody field. During the night succeeding the conflict, the Mexicans all withdrew, leaving their dead and wounded behind them.[2] The invaders were now in possession of all the northern Mexican provinces, and Scott was preparing to storm Vera Cruz[3] and march to the capital.[4] In the course of a few months General Taylor left Wool in command [Sept., 1847], and returned home, everywhere receiving tokens of the highest regard from his countrymen. Let us now consider other operations of the war during this period.

REGION OF TAYLOR'S OPERATIONS.

The command of the "Army of the West"[5] was given to General Kearney,[6] with instructions to conquer New Mexico and California. He left Fort Leavenworth in June, and after a journey of nine hundred miles over the Great Plains and among the mountain ranges, he arrived at Santa Fé, the capital of New

serve consideration and particular esteem, I wish to save you from such a catastrophe, and for that purpose give you this notice, in order that you may surrender at discretion, under the assurance that you will be treated with the consideration belonging to the Mexican character; to which end you will be granted an hour's time to make up your mind, to commence from the moment that my flag of truce arrives in your camp. With this view, I assure you of my particular consideration.

"ANTONIO LOPEZ DE SANTA ANNA.

"To General Z. Taylor, Commanding the Forces of the U. S."

General Taylor did not take the allotted time to make up his mind, but instantly sat down and wrote the following reply:

"HEAD-QUARTERS, ARMY OF OCCUPATION, Near Buena Vista, Feb. 22d, 1847.

"SIR: In reply to your note of this date, summoning me to surrender my forces at discretion, I beg leave to say that I decline acceding to your request. With high respect, I am, sir, your obedient servant, Z. TAYLOR, Major-General U. S. Army."

[1] To deceive the Americans, Santa Anna resorted to the contemptible trick of sending out a flag in token of surrender, at the moment of making the assault, hoping thereby to cause his enemy to be less vigilant. Taylor was too well acquainted with Mexican treachery to be deceived.

[2] The Americans lost two hundred and sixty-seven killed, four hundred and fifty-six wounded, and twenty-three missing. The Mexicans lost almost two thousand. They left five hundred of their comrades dead on the field. Among the Americans slain was Lieutenant-Colonel Clay, son of the distinguished Henry Clay, of Kentucky. Page 500.

[3] Page 489.

[4] On the day of the battle at Buena Vista, General Minon, with eight hundred cavalry, was driven from Saltillo by Captain Webster and a small party of Americans. On the 26th of February, Colonels Morgan and Irvin defeated a party at Agua Frio; and on the 7th of March, Major Giddings was victorious at Ceralvo.

[5] Page 483.

[6] Stephen W. Kearney was a native of New Jersey. He was a gallant soldier in the War of 1812–15. He was breveted a Brigadier in 1846, and Major-General in December the same year, for gallant conduct in the Mexican War. He died at Vera Cruz, in October, 1848, at the age of fifty-four years.

Mexico, on the 18th of August. He met with no resistance;[1] and having taken peaceable possession of the country, and constituted Charles Bent its governor, he marched toward California. He soon met an express from Commodore Stockton[2] and Lieutenant-Colonel Fremont, informing him that the conquest of California had already been achieved.

Fremont had been sent with a party of about sixty men to explore portions of New Mexico and California. When he arrived in the vicinity of Monterey, on the Pacific coast, he was opposed by a Mexican force under General Castro. Fremont aroused all the American settlers in the vicinity of San Francisco Bay, captured a Mexican post and garrison, and nine cannons, and two hundred and fifty muskets, at Sonoma Pass [June 15, 1846], and then advanced to Sonoma, and defeated Castro and his troops. The Mexican authorities were effectually driven out of that region of the country; and on the 5th of July, the American Californians declared themselves independent, and placed Fremont at the head of the government. Two days afterward, Commodore Sloat, then in command of the squadron in the Pacific, bombarded and captured Monterey; and on the 9th, Commodore Montgomery took possession of San Francisco. Commodore Stockton arrived on the 15th, and with Colonel Fremont, took possession of the city of Los Angelos on the 17th of August. On receiving this information, Kearney sent the main body of his troops to Santa Fé, and with one hundred men he pushed forward to Los Angelos, near the Pacific coast, where he met [Dec. 27, 1847] Stockton and Fremont. In company with these officers, he shared in the honors of the final important events [Jan. 8, 1847], which completed the conquest and pacification of California. Fremont, the real liberator of that country, claimed the right to be governor, and was supported by Stockton and the people; but Kearney, his superior officer, would not acquiesce. Fremont refused to obey him; and Kearney departed, sailed to Monterey, and there, in conjunction with Commodore Shubrick, he assumed the office of governor, and proclaimed [Feb. 8, 1847] the annexation of California to the United States. Fremont was ordered home to be tried for disobedience of orders. He was deprived of his commission; but the President, valuing him as one of the ablest officers in the army, offered it to him again. Fremont refused it, and went again to the wilderness and engaged in exploration.[3]

---

[1] The governor and four thousand Mexicans troops fled at his approach, and the people, numbering about six thousand, quietly submitted.

[2] Robert F. Stockton is a son of one of the New Jersey signers of the Declaration of Independence. He entered the navy in 1811, and was appointed commodore in 1838. He left the navy in May, 1850, and has since been a member of the United States Senate from New Jersey.

[3] John Charles Fremont was born at Savannah, Georgia, in January, 1813. His father was a Frenchman; his mother a native of Virginia. He was born while his parents were on a journey, and his infancy was spent among the wilds of the south-west. At the age of thirteen he commenced the study of law, but was soon afterward placed in a good school for the enlargement of his education. He was very successful; and after leaving school became a teacher in Charleston, and then instructor in mathematics on board a sloop-of-war. As a civil engineer, he had few equals, and in this capacity he made many explorations, in the service of private individuals and the government, as lieutenant. His several explorations are among the wonders of the age. In 1846, the citizens of Charleston, South Carolina, presented him with an elegant sword, in a gold scabbard, as a testimonial of their appreciation of his great services to the country; and in 1850, the King of Prussia,

Other stirring events were occurring in the same direction at this time. While Kearney was on his way to California, Colonel Doniphan, by his command, was engaged, with a thousand Missouri volunteers, in forcing the Navajo Indians to make a treaty of peace. This was accomplished on the 22d of November, 1846, and then Doniphan marched toward Chihuahua, to join General Wool. At Braceti, in the valley of the Rio del Norte, they met a large

Mexican force on the 22d of December, under General Ponce de Leon. He sent a black flag to Doniphan, with the message, "We will neither ask nor give quarter." The Mexicans then advanced and fired three rounds. The Missourians fell upon their faces, and the enemy, supposing them to be all slain, rushed forward for plunder. The Americans suddenly arose, and delivering a deadly fire from their rifles, killed two hundred Mexicans, and dispersed the remainder in great confusion. Doniphan then pressed forward, and when within eighteen miles of the capital of Chihuahua, he was confronted [Feb. 28, 1847] by four thousand Mexicans. These he completely routed,[1] and then pressing forward to the city of Chihuahua, he entered it in triumph, raised the

through the venerable Baron Von Humboldt, sent him the grand golden medal struck for those who have made essential progress in science. When California became a State, he was elected its first United States senator [1851]; and at the "Republican" National Convention, held at Philadelphia, in June, 1856, he was nominated for the high office of President of the United States.

[1] The Americans lost, in killed and wounded, only eighteen men; the Mexicans lost about six hundred.

flag of the United States upon its citadel, in the midst of a population of forty thousand [March 2], and took possession of the province in the name of his government. After resting six weeks he marched to Saltillo [May 22], where General Wool was encamped. From thence he returned to New Orleans, having made a perilous march from the Mississippi, of about five thousand miles. The conquest of all Northern Mexico,[1] with California, was now complete, and General Scott was on his march for the great capital. Let us now consider

GENERAL SCOTT'S INVASION OF MEXICO.

The Mexican authorities having scorned overtures for peace made by the government of the United States in the autumn of 1846, it was determined to conquer the whole country. For that purpose General Scott was directed to collect an army, capture Vera Cruz,[2] and march to the Mexican capital. His rendezvous was at Lobos Island, about one hundred and twenty-five miles north from Vera Cruz; and on the 9th of March, 1847, he landed near the latter with an army of about thirteen thousand men, borne thither by a powerful squadron commanded by Commodore Connor.[3] He invested the city on the 13th; and five days afterward [March 18], having every thing ready for an attack,[4] he summoned the town and fortress, for the last time, to surrender A refusal was the signal for opening a general cannonade, and bombardment from his batteries and the fleet. The siege continued until the 27th, when the city, the strong castle of San Juan d'Ulloa, with five thousand prisoners, and five hundred pieces of artillery, were surrendered to the Americans. The latter had only forty men killed, and about the same number wounded. At least a thousand Mexicans were killed, and a great number were maimed. It is estimated that during this siege, not less than six thousand seven hundred shots and shells were thrown by the American batteries, weighing, in the aggregate, more than forty thousand pounds.

INTRENCHMENTS AT VERA CRUZ.

Two days after the siege [March 29, 1847], General Scott took possession of Vera Cruz, and on the 8th of April, the advanced force of his army, under General Twiggs, commenced their march for the interior by way of Jalapa.[5] Santa Anna had advanced, with twelve thousand men, to Cerro Gordo, a diffi-

---

[1] Some conspiracies in New Mexico against the new government, ripened into revolt, in January, 1847. Governor Bent and others were murdered at Fernando de Taos on the 19th, and massacres occurred in other quarters. On the 23d, Colonel Price, with three hundred and fifty men, marched against and defeated the insurgents at Canada, and finally dispersed them at the mountain gorge called the Pass of Embudo.

[2] This city was considered the key to the country. On an island opposite was a very strong fortress called the castle of San Juan d'Ulloa [pronounced San-whan-dah-oo-loo-ah], always celebrated for its great strength, and considered impregnable by the Mexicans.

[3] Page 480.

[4] The engineering operations were performed very skillfully under the direction of Colonel Totten, an officer of the War of 1812. For his bravery at Vera Cruz, he was made Brigadier-General, by brevet. He is now [1856] about seventy years of age.

[5] Pronounced Hah-lah-pah.

cult mountain pass at the foot of the eastern chain of the Cordilleras. He was strongly fortified, and had many pieces of cannon well placed for defense. Scott had followed Twiggs with the main body. He had left a strong garrison at Vera Cruz, and his whole army now numbered about eight thousand five hundred men. Having skillfully arranged his plans, he attacked the enemy on the 18th of April. The assault was successful. More than a thousand Mexicans were killed or wounded, and three thousand were made prisoners. Having neither men to guard, nor food to sustain the prisoners, General Scott dismissed them on parole.[1] The boastful Santa Anna narrowly escaped capture by fleeing upon a mule taken from his carriage.[2] The Americans lost, in killed and wounded, four hundred and thirty-one.

The victors entered Jalapa on the 19th of April; and on the 22d, General Worth unfurled the stars and stripes upon the castle of Perote, on the summit of the eastern Cordilleras, fifty miles from Jalapa. This was considered the strongest fortress in Mexico next to Vera Cruz, yet it was surrendered without resistance. Among the spoils were fifty-four pieces of cannon, and mortars, and a large quantity of munitions of war. Onward the victorious army marched; and on the 15th of May [1847] it entered the ancient walled and fortified city of Puebla,[3] without opposition from the eighty thousand inhabitants within. Here the Americans rested, after a series of victories almost unparalleled. Within two months, an army averaging only about ten thousand men, had taken some of the strongest fortresses on this continent, made ten thousand prisoners, and captured seven hundred pieces of artillery, ten thousand stand of arms, and thirty thousand shells and cannon-balls. Yet greater conquests awaited them.

General Scott remained at Puebla until August,[4] when, being reinforced by fresh troops, sent by way of Vera Cruz, he resumed his march toward the capital, with more than ten thousand men, leaving a large number sick in the hospital.[5] Their route was through a beautiful region, well watered, and clothed with the richest verdure, and then up the slopes of the great Cordilleras. From their lofty summits, and almost from the same spot where Cortez and his followers stood amazed more

ROUTE OF THE U. S. ARMY FROM VERA CRUZ TO MEXICO.

---

[1] Note 6, page 311.

[2] Before the battle, Santa Anna said, "I will die fighting rather than the Americans shall proudly tread the imperial city of Azteca." So precipitate was his flight that he left all his papers behind him, and his wooden leg. He had been so severely wounded in his leg, while defending Vera Cruz against the French, in 1838, that amputation became necessary, and a wooden one was substituted.

[3] Pronounced Pweb-lah.

[4] During this long halt of the American army, the government of the United States made unavailing efforts to negotiate for peace. The Mexican authorities refused the olive branch, and boasted of their patriotism, valor, and strength, while losing post after post, in their retreat toward the capital.

[5] At one time there were eighteen hundred men sick at Puebla; and at Perote seven hundred died during the summer, notwithstanding the situations of these places, on lofty table-lands, were considered exceedingly healthful.

Bombardment of Vera Cruz.

than three centuries before,[1] Scott and his army looked down [August 10, 1847] upon that glorious panorama of intervales, lakes, cities, and villages, in the great valley of Mexico—the capital of the Aztec Empire[2]—the seat of "the Halls of the Montezumas."[3]

General Twiggs[4] cautiously led the advance of the American army toward the city of Mexico, on the 11th of August, and encamped at St. Augustine, on the Acapulco road, eight miles south of the capital. Before him lay the strong fortress of San (or St.) Antonio, and close on his right were the heights of Churubusco, crowned with embattled walls covered with cannons, and to be reached in front only by a dangerous causeway. Close by was the fortified camp of Contreras, containing six thousand Mexicans, under General Valencia; and between it and the city was Santa Anna, and twelve thousand men, held in reserve. Such was the general position of the belligerents when, a little after midnight on the 20th of August [1847], General Smith[5] marched to the attack of the camp at Contreras. The battle opened at sunrise. It was sanguinary, but brief, and the Americans were victorious. Eighty officers and three thousand private soldiers were made prisoners; and the chief trophies were thirty-three pieces of artillery. In the mean while, Generals Pierce[6] and Shields,[7] with a small force, kept Santa Anna's powerful reserve at bay.

General Scott now directed a similar movement against Cherubusco. Santa Anna advanced; and the whole region became a battle-field, under the eye and control of the American commander-in-chief. The invaders dealt blow after blow successfully. Antonio yielded, Churubusco was taken, and Santa Anna abandoned the field and fled to the capital. It was a memorable day in Mexico. An army, thirty thousand strong, had been broken up by another less than one third its strength in numbers; and at almost every step the Americans were successful. Full four thousand of the Mexicans were killed or wounded, three thousand were made prisoners, and thirty seven pieces of cannon were taken, all in one day. The Americans lost, in killed and wounded, almost eleven

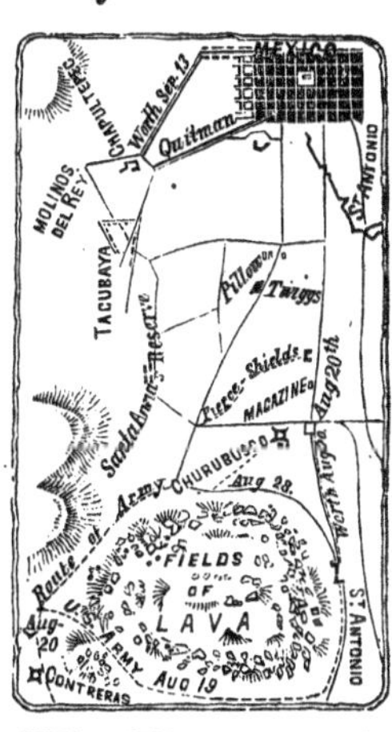

OPERATIONS NEAR MEXICO.

[1] Page 43.

[2] According to the faint glimmerings of ancient Mexican history which have come down to us, the Aztecs, who occupied that country when it first became known to Europeans [page 43], came from the North, and were more refined than any other tribes, which, from time to time, had held possession of the country. They built a city within the borders of Lake Tezcuco, and named it Mexico, in honor of *Mexitli*, their god of war. Where the present great cathedral stands, they had erected an immense temple, dedicated to the sun, and there offered human sacrifices. It is related, that at its consecration, almost sixty thousand human beings were sacrificed. The temple was built about the year 1480, by the predecessor of Montezuma, the emperor found by Cortez.

[3] This expression, referring to the remains of the palace of Montezuma in Mexico, was often used during the war.

[4] David E. Twiggs was born in Georgia in 1790. He was a major at the close of the War of 1812–15, and was retained in the army. He was breveted a Major-General after the battle at Monterey, and for his gallantry there received the gift of a sword from Congress.

[5] General Persifer F. Smith, of Louisiana.

[6] Page 514.

[7] General James Shields, of Illinois, afterward a representative of that State in the Senate of the United States.

hundred. They might now have entered the city of Mexico in triumph, but General Scott preferred to bear the olive branch, rather than the palm. As he advanced to Tacubaya, [August 21], within three miles of the city, a flag came from Santa Anna to ask for an armistice, preparatory to negotiations for peace.[1] It was granted, and Nicholas P. Trist, who had been appointed, by the United States government, a commissioner to treat for peace, went into the capital [August 24] for the purpose. Scott made the palace of the archbishop, at Tacubaya, his head-quarters, and there anxiously awaited the result of the conference, until the 5th of September, when Mr. Trist returned, with the intelligence that his propositions were not only spurned with scorn, but that Santa Anna had violated the armistice by strengthening the defenses of the city. Disgusted with the continual treachery of his foe, Scott declared the armistice at an end, on the 7th of September, and prepared to storm the capital.

The first demonstration against the city was on the morning of the 8th of September, when less than four thousand Americans attacked fourteen thousand Mexicans, under Santa Anna, at *El Molinos del Rey* (the King's Mills) near Chepultepec. They were at first repulsed, with great slaughter; but returning to the attack, they fought desperately for an hour, and drove the Mexicans from their position. Both parties suffered dreadfully. The Mexicans left almost a thousand dead on the field, and the Americans lost about eight hundred. And now the proud Chepultepec was doomed. It was a lofty hill, strongly fortified, and the seat of the military school of Mexico. It was the last place to be defended outside the suburbs of the city. Scott erected four heavy batteries to bear upon it, on the night of the 11th of September; and the next day [September 12, 1847], a heavy cannonade and bombardment commenced. On the 13th, the assailants commenced a furious charge, routed the enemy, with great slaughter, and unfurled the American flag over the shattered castle of Chepultepec. The Mexicans fled to the city along an aqueduct, pursued by General Quitman[2] to its very gates. That night, Santa Anna and his army, with the officers of government, fled from the doomed capital; and at four o'clock the following morning [September 14], a deputation from the city authorities waited upon General Scott, and begged him to spare the town and treat for peace. He would make no terms, but ordered Generals Worth and Quitman[3] to move forward, and plant the stripes and stars upon the National Palace. The victorious generals entered at ten o'clock, and on the Grand *Plaza*,[4] took formal possession of the Mexican Empire. Order soon reigned in the capital. Santa Anna made some feeble efforts to regain lost power, and failed. He appeared before Puebla on the 22d of September, where Colonel Childs had been besieged since the 13th. The approach of General Lane frightened him away; and in a battle with the troops of that leader at Huamantla, Santa

---

[1] Note 1, page 242.

[2] John A. Quitman is a native of New York, and is now [1856] about fifty-seven years of age. He led volunteers to the Mexican war, and was breveted and presented with a sword by Congress, for his gallantry. He was Governor of Mississippi in 1851.

[3] The approach of each was along separate aqueducts. See map, page 493.

[4] Place. This is the large public square in the city of Mexico.

General Scott Entering the City of Mexico

Anna was defeated. On the 18th of October he was again defeated at Atlixco, and there his troops deserted him. Before the close of October, he was a fugitive, stripped of every commission, and seeking safety, by flight, to the shores of the Gulf.[1] The president of the Mexican Congress assumed provisional authority; and on the 2d of February, 1848, that body concluded a treaty of peace, with commissioners of the United States at Gaudaloupe Hidalgo. This treaty was finally agreed to by both governments, and on the 4th of July following, President Polk proclaimed it. It stipulated the evacuation of Mexico by the American army, within three months; the payment of three millions of dollars in hand, and twelve millions of dollars, in four annual instalments, by the United States to Mexico, for the territory acquired by conquest; and in addition, to assume debts due certain citizens of the United States to the amount of three millions five hundred thousand dollars. It also fixed boundaries, and otherwise adjusted matters in dispute. New Mexico and California now became Territories of the United States.

During the same month that a treaty of peace was signed at Gaudaloupe Hidalgo, a man employed by Captain Sutter, who owned a mill twenty-five miles up the American fork of the Sacramento River, discovered gold. It was very soon found in other localities, and during the summer, rumors of the fact reached the United States. These rumors assumed tangible form in President Polk's message in December, 1848; and at the beginning of 1849, thousands were on their way to the land of gold. Around Cape Horn, across the Isthmus of Panama, and over the great central plains of the continent, men went by hundreds; and far and wide in California, the precious metal was found. From Europe and South America, hundreds flocked thither; and the Chinese came also from Asia, to dig gold. The dreams of the early Spanish voyagers,[2] and those of the English who sought gold on the coasts of Labrador,[3] and up the rivers in the middle of the continent,[4] have been more than realized. Hundreds yet [1856] continue to go thither, and the gold seems inexhaustible.[5]

The war with Mexico, and the settlement of the Oregon boundary question[6] with Great Britain, were the most prominent events, having a relation to foreign powers, which distinguished Mr. Polk's administration. Two measures of a domestic character, appear prominently among many others which mark his administration as full of activity. These were the establishment of an independent treasury system,[7] by which the national revenues are collected in gold and silver, or treasury notes, without the aid of banks; and a revision of the tariff laws in 1846, by which protection to American manufacturers was lessened. It was during the last year of his administration that Wisconsin was admitted [May 29, 1848] into the Union of States, making the whole number thirty. At about this time, the people of the Union were preparing for another presidential election. The popularity which General Taylor had gained by his brilliant victories in Mexico, caused him to be nominated for that exalted station, in many parts of the Union, even before he returned home;[8] and he was

[1] Note 6, page 515. [2] Page 43. [3] Page 52. [4] Page 56. [5] Note 3, page 373. [6] Page 479. [7] Note 2, page 471. [8] Page 486.

chosen to be a candidate for that office, by a national convention held at Philadelphia in June, 1848. His opponent was General Lewis Cass, of Michigan, now [1856] United States senator from that State.[1] General Taylor was elected by a large majority, with Millard Fillmore, of New York, as Vice-President.

CHAPTER XIII.

TAYLOR'S ADMINISTRATION. [1849—1850.]

THE 4th of March, 1849, was Sunday, and the inauguration of Zachary Taylor,[2] the twelfth President of the United States, did not take place until the

next day. Again people had gathered at the Federal city from all parts of the Union, and the day being pleasant, though cloudy, a vast concourse were

[1] Note 2, page 424.

[2] Zachary Taylor was born in Virginia, in November, 1784. He went with his father to Kentucky the following year, and his childhood was passed near the present city of Louisville. He entered the United States army in 1807. He was a distinguished subaltern during the war of 1812–15, and attained the rank of major. He was of great service in the Florida War [page 468]; and when hostilities with Mexico appeared probable, he was sent in that direction, and, as we have seen, displayed great skill and bravery. He died in July, 1850, having performed the duties of President for only sixteen months.

assembled in front of the eastern portico of the capitol, long before the appointed hour for the interesting ceremonies. In a clear and distinct voice, he pronounced his inaugural address, and then took the oath of office administered by Chief Justice Taney. On the following day he nominated his cabinet officers,[1] and the appointments were immediately confirmed by the Senate. With the heart of a true patriot and honest man, Taylor entered upon his responsible duties with a sincere desire to serve his country as faithfully in the cabinet, as he had done in the field.[2] He had the sympathies of a large majority of the people with him, and his inauguration was the promise of great happiness and prosperity for the country.

When President Taylor entered upon the duties of his office, thousands of adventurers were flocking to California from all parts of the Union, and elements of a new and powerful State were rapidly gathering there. Statesmen and politicians perceived the importance of the new Territory, and soon the question whether slavery should have a legal existence there, became an absorbing topic in Congress and among the people. The inhabitants of California decided the question for themselves. In August, 1849, General Riley, the military Governor of the Territory, established a sort of judiciary by proclamation, with Peter H. Burnet as Chief Justice. Before that time there was no statute law in California. By proclamation, also, Governor Riley summoned a convention of delegates to meet at Monterey, to form a State Constitution. Before it convened, the inhabitants in convention at San Francisco, voted against slavery; and the Constitution, prepared and adopted at Monterey, on the first of September, 1849, excluded slavery from the Territory, forever. Thus came into political form the crude elements of a State, the birth and maturity of which seems like a dream. All had been accomplished within twenty months from the time when gold was discovered near Sutter's Mill.

Under the Constitution, Edward Gilbert and G. H. Wright, were elected delegates for California in the Federal House of Representatives; and the State Legislature, at its first session, elected John Charles Fremont[3] and William M. Gwinn, United States senators. When the latter went to Washington, they carried their Constitution with them, and presented a petition [February, 1850] asking for the admission of that Territory into the Union as a free and independent State.[4] The article of the Constitution which excluded slavery, became a cause for violent debates in Congress, and of bitter sectional feeling between the people of the North and the South. The Union, so strong in the hearts of the people, was shaken to its center, and prophets of evil foolishly

---

[1] He appointed John M. Clayton, Secretary of State; William M. Meredith, Secretary of the Treasury; George W. Crawford, Secretary of War; William B. Preston, Secretary of the Navy; Thomas Ewing, Secretary of the Interior (a new office recently established, in which some of the duties before performed by the State and Treasury departments are attended to); Jacob Collamer, Postmaster-General; and Reverdy Johnson, Attorney-General.

[2] Page 481 to page 486, inclusive.

[3] Page 488.

[4] At this time our government was perplexed by the claims of Texas to portions of the Territory of New Mexico, recently acquired [page 497], and serious difficulty was apprehended. Early in 1850, the inhabitants of New Mexico petitioned Congress for a civil government, and the Mormons of the Utah region also petitioned for the organization of the country they had recently settled, into a Territory of the United States.

predicted its speedy dissolution. As in 1832,[1] there were menaces of secession from the Union, by Southern representatives, and never before did civil war appear so inevitable. Happily for the country, some of the ablest statesmen and patriots the Republic had ever gloried in, were members of the national Legislature, at that time, and with consummate skill they directed and controlled the storm. In the midst of the tumult and alarm in Congress, and throughout the land, Henry Clay again[2] appeared as the potent peace-maker

H. Clay

between the Hotspurs of the North and South; and on the 25th of January, 1850, he offered, in the Senate a plan of compromise which met the difficulty. Eleven days afterward [February 5, 1850] he spoke nobly in defense of his plan, denounced secession as treason, and implored his countrymen to make

[1] Page 381.

[2] Page 464. Henry Clay was born in Hanover county, Virginia, in April, 1777. His early education was defective, and he arose to greatness by the force of his own genius. His extraordinary intellectual powers began to develop at an early age, and at nineteen he commenced the study of the law. When admitted to practice, at the age of twenty, he went over the mountains to the fertile valleys of Kentucky, and there laid the foundations of his greatness as a lawyer and orator. The latter quality was first fully developed when a convention was called to revise the Constitution of Kentucky. Then he worked manfully and unceasingly to procure the election of delegates who would favor the emancipation of the slaves. He became a member of the Kentucky Legislature in 1803, and there he took a front rank. He was chosen to fill a vacant seat in the United States Senate in 1806, and in 1811 he was elected a member of the House of Representatives, and became its Speaker. From that time until his death, he was continually in public life. He long held a front rank among American statesmen, and died, while a member of the United States Senate, in the city of Washington, at the close of June, 1852.

every sacrifice but honor, in support of the Union. Mr. Clay's plan was warmly seconded by Daniel Webster;[1] and other senators approving of compromise, submitted propositions. Finally, on motion of Senator Foote of Mississippi, a committee of thirteen was appointed to consider the various plans and report a bill. The committee consisted of six northern and six southern senators, and these chose the thirteenth. The Senate appointed Mr. Clay chairman of the committee, and on the 8th of May following, he reported a bill. It was discussed for four months, and on the 9th of September, each measure included in the bill having been thoroughly considered separately, the famous *Compromise Act* of 1850, having passed both Houses of Congress, became a law. Because several measures, distinct in their objects, were embodied in the act, it is sometimes known as the "Omnibus Bill." The most important stipulations of the act were, 1st. That California should be admitted into the Union as a State, with its anti-slavery Constitution, and its territorial extent from Oregon to the Mexican possessions; 2d. That the vast country east of California, containing the Mormon settlements near the Great Salt Lake,[2] should be erected into a Territory called Utah, without mention of slavery; 3d. That New Mexico should be erected into a Territory, within satisfactory boundaries, and without any stipulations respecting slavery, and that ten millions of dollars should be paid to Texas from the Federal treasury, in purchase of her claims; 4th. That the slave-trade in the District of Columbia should be abolished; 5th. A law providing for the arrest in the northern or free States, and return to their masters, of all slaves who should escape from bondage. The last measure of the Compromise Act produced, and continues to produce, much dissatisfaction at the North; and the execution, evasion, and violation of the law, in several instances, have led to serious disturbances and much bitter sectional feeling.[3]

While the great Compromise question was under discussion, the nation was called to lament the loss of its Chief Magistrate. President Taylor was seized with a malady, similar in its effects to cholera, which terminated his earthly career on the 9th of July, 1850. In accordance with the provisions of the Constitution,[4] he was immediately succeeded in office by

MILLARD FILLMORE,[5]

who, on the 10th of July, took the oath to "preserve, protect, and defend the Constitution of the United States." President Taylor's cabinet resigned; but the new President, with great delicacy, declined to consider their resignations

---

[1] Page 503. [2] Page 503. [3] Page 529. [4] Article II., section 1, of the Federal Constitution.

[5] Millard Fillmore was born in January, 1800, in Cayuga county, New York. His early education was limited, and at a suitable age he was apprenticed to a wool-carder. At the age of nineteen, his talent attracted the attention of Judge Wood, of Cayuga county, and he took the humble apprentice under his charge, to study the science of law. He became eminent in his profession. He was elected to the Assembly of his native State in 1829, and in 1832, was chosen to represent his district in Congress. He was re-elected in 1837, and was continued in office several years. In 1844, he was an unsuccessful candidate for the office of Governor of his native State, and in 1848 he was elected Vice-President of the United States. The death of Taylor gave him the presidency, and he conducted public affairs with dignity and skill. In the summer of 1856, he was nominated for the office of President of the United States, by the "American" party, with A. J. Donelson for Vice-President. See Note 1, page 479.

until after the obsequies of the deceased President had been performed. At his request, they remained in office until the 15th of the month, when President Fillmore appointed new heads of the departments.[1]

The administration of President Taylor had been brief, but it was distin-

guished by events which will have an important bearing upon the future destiny of our Republic. One of these was an invasion of Cuba by a force under General Lopez, a native of that island, which was organized and officered in the United States, in violation of existing neutrality laws. For a long time the native Cubans had been restive under the rigorous rule of Spanish Governor-Generals,[2] and a desire for independence burned in the hearts of many of the best men there. Among these was Lopez, who, in forming this invading expedition, counted largely upon this feeling for co-operation. He landed at Car-

[1] Daniel Webster, Secretary of State; Thomas Corwin, Secretary of the Treasury; Charles M. Conrad, Secretary of War; Alexander H. H. Stuart, Secretary of the Interior; William A. Graham, Secretary of the Navy; John J. Crittenden, Attorney-General; Nathan K. Hall, Postmaster-General. Daniel Webster was born in Salisbury, New Hampshire, in January, 1782, and was educated chiefly at the Phillips Academy at Andover, and Dartmouth College at Hanover. He studied law in Boston, and was admitted to the bar in 1805. He commenced practice in his native State, and soon became eminent. He first appeared in public life in 1813, when he took his seat as a member of the Federal House of Representatives. At that session his speeches were remarkable, and a southern member remarked, "The North has not his equal, nor the South his superior." Although in public life a greater portion of the time from that period until his death, yet he always had an extensive and lucrative law practice. He stood foremost as a constitutional lawyer; and for many years he was peerless as a statesman. He died at Marshfield, Massachusetts, in October, 1852, at the age of almost seventy-one years.

[2] Page 40.

denas on the 19th of April, 1850, expecting to be joined by some of the Spanish troops and native Cubans, and by concerted action to rid the island of cruel bondage. But the people and troops did not co-operate with him, and disappointed, he returned to the United States to prepare for a more formidable expedition. We shall meet him again presently.

Dan'l Webster

During Taylor's administration, one sovereign State and three Territories were added to the Confederacy, and preparations were made for organizing other local governments within the domain of the United States. That State was California, and the Territories were of those of New Mexico, Utah, and Minnesota.[1] The greater portion of the inhabitants of Utah are of the religious sect called Mormons, who, after suffering much in Missouri and Illinois, from their opposers, left those States in 1848, and penetrated the deep wilderness in the interior of our continent; and near the Great Salt Lake, in the midst of the savage Utah tribes, they have built a large city, made extensive plantations, and founded an empire almost as large, in territorial extent, as that of

---

[1] *Minnesota* (sky-colored water) is the Indian name of the river St. Peter, the largest tributary of the Mississippi, in that region. It was a part of the vast Territory of Louisiana, and was organized in March, 1849. An embryo village at the Falls of St. Anthony, named St. Paul, was made the capital, and it now contains more than ten thousand souls. Its growth is unprecedented, even in the wonderful progress of other cities of the West, and it promises to speedily equal Chicago in its population. The whole region of Minnesota is very attractive; and it has been called the New England of the West.

Alexander the Great.[1] The sect was founded in 1827, by a shrewd young man named Joseph Smith, a native of central New York, who professed to have received a special revelation from Heaven, giving him knowledge of a book which had been buried many centuries before, in a hill near the village of Palmyra, whose leaves were of gold, upon which were engraved the records of the ancient people of America, and a new gospel for man. He found dupes, believers, and followers; and now [1856] there are Mormon missionaries in every quarter of the globe, and the communion numbers, probably, not less than two hundred thousand souls. There is about a sufficient number in Utah (60,000) to entitle them to a State constitution, and admission into the Union. Their permission of polygamy, or men having more than one wife, will be a serious bar to their admission, for Christianity and sound morality forbid the custom. The Mormons have poetically called their country Deseret—the land of the Honey Bee—but Congress has entitled it Utah, and by that name it must be known in history.

JOSEPH SMITH.

The country inhabited by the Mormons is one of the most remarkable on the face of the globe. It consists of a series of extensive valleys and rocky margins, spread out into an immense basin, surrounded by rugged mountains, out of which no waters flow. It is midway between the States on the Mississippi and the Pacific Ocean, perfectly isolated from habitable regions, and embracing a domain covering sixteen degrees of longitude in the Utah latitude. On the east are the sterile spurs of the Rocky Mountains, stretching down to the vast plains traversed by the Platte river; on the west, extending nearly a thousand miles toward the Pacific, are arid salt deserts, broken by barren mountains; and north and south are immense mountain districts. The valleys afford pe-

[1] The Mormon exodus was one of the most wonderful events on record, when considered in all its phases. In September, 1846, the last lingering Mormons at Nauvoo, Illinois, where they had built a splendid temple, were driven away at the point of the bayonet, by 1,600 troops. In February preceding, some sixteen hundred men, women, and children, fearful of the wrath of the people around them, had crossed the Mississippi on the ice, and traveling with ox-teams and on foot, they penetrated the wilderness to the Indian country, near Council Bluffs, on the Missouri. The remnant who started in autumn, many of whom were sick men, feeble women, and delicate girls, were compelled to traverse the same dreary region. The united host, under the guidance of Brigham Young, who is yet their temporal and spiritual leader, halted on the broad prairies of Missouri the following summer, turned up the virgin soil, and planted. Here leaving a few to cultivate and gather for wanderers who might come after them, the host moved on, making the wilderness vocal with preaching and singing. Order marked every step of their progress, for the voice of Young, whom they regarded as a seer, was to them as the voice of God. On they went, forming *Tabernacle Camps*, or temporary resting-places in the wilderness. No obstacles impeded their progress. They forded swift-running streams, and bridged the deeper floods; crept up the great eastern slopes of the Rocky Mountains, and from the lofty summits of the Wasatch range, they beheld, on the 20th of July, 1847, the valley where they were to rest and build a city, and the placid waters of the Great Salt Lake, glittering in the beams of the setting sun. To those weary wanderers, this moutain top was a Pisgah. From it they saw the Promised Land—to them a scene of wondrous interest. Westward, lofty peaks, bathed in purple air, pierced the sky; and as far as the eye could reach, north and south, stretched the fertile Valley of Promise, and here and there the vapors of hot springs, gushing from rocky coverts, curled above the hills, like smoke from the hearth-fires of home. The Pilgrims entered the valley on the 21st of July, and on the 24th the President and High Council arrived. There they planted a city, the Jerusalem—the Holy City—of the Mormon people.

MORMON EMIGRATION.

rennial pasturage, and the soil is exceedingly fertile. Wild game abounds in the mountains; the streams are filled with excellent fish; the climate is delightful at all seasons of the year; and "breathing is a real luxury." Southward, over the rim of the great basin, is a fine cotton-growing region, into which the Mormons are penetrating. The vast hills and mountain slopes present the finest pasturage in the world for sheep, alpacas, and goats. The water-power of the whole region is immense. Iron mines everywhere abound, and in the Green river basin, there are inexhaustible beds of coal. In these great natural resources and defenses, possessed by a people of such indomitable energy and perseverance as the Mormons, we see the vital elements of a powerful mountain nation in the heart of our continent, and in the direct pathway from the Atlantic to the Pacific States, that may yet play a most important part, for good or evil, in the destinies of our country and of the world.

The most important measures adopted during the early part of Fillmore's administration, was the Compromise act, already considered.[1] During his official career, the President firmly supported all the requirements of the act, and his judicious and conservative course kept the waters of public opinion comparatively calm, notwithstanding the workings of the Fugitive Slave Law frequently produced much local excitement, where it happened to be executed, or, as was frequently the case, resisted. At the close of his administration, in the spring of 1853, there was very little disquietude in the public mind on the subject of slavery.

In the spring of 1851, Congress made important changes in the general post-office laws, chiefly in the reduction of letter postage, fixing the rate upon a letter weighing not more than half an ounce, and pre-paid, at three cents, to any part of the United States, excepting California and the Pacific Territories. This measure was a salutary one, and has been productive of much social and commercial advantage, for interchanges of thought are proportionately more frequent than before, and friendly intercourse and business transactions by letters are far more extensive. At the same time, electro-magnetic telegraphing had become quite perfect; and by means of the subtle agency of electricity, communications were speeding over thousands of miles of iron wire, with the rapidity of lightning. The establishment of this instantaneous communication between distant points is one of the most important achievements of this age of invention and discovery; and the names of Fulton and Morse[2] will be

PROFESSOR MORSE.

[1] Page 399.

[2] In 1832, Professor Samuel F. B. Morse had his attention directed to the experiments of Franklin upon a wire of a few miles in length, on the banks of the Schuylkill, in which the velocity of electricity was found to be so inappreciable that it was supposed to be instantaneous. Professor Morse, pondering upon this subject, suggested that electricity might be made the means of recording characters as signs of intelligence at a distance; and in the autumn of 1832 he constructed a portion of the instrumentalities for that purpose. In 1835 he showed the first complete instrument for *telegraphic recording*, at the New York city University. In 1837 he com-

forever indissolubly connected in the commercial and social history of our Republic.

During the summer of 1851, there was again considerable excitement produced throughout the country because other concerted movements were made at different points, in the organization of a military force for the purpose of invading Cuba.[1] The vigilance of the government of the United States was awakened, and orders were given to Federal marshals to seize suspected men, vessels, and munitions of war. The steamboat *Cleopatra* was seized at New York; and several gentlemen, of the highest respectability, were arrested on a charge of a violation of existing neutrality laws. In the mean while, the greatest excitement prevailed in Cuba, and forty thousand Spanish troops were concentrated there, while a considerable naval force watched and guarded the coasts. These hinderances caused the dispersion of the armed bands who were preparing to invade Cuba, and quiet was restored for awhile. But in July, the excitement was renewed. General Lopez[2] made a speech to a large crowd in New Orleans, in favor of an invading expedition. Soon afterward [August, 1851], he sailed from that port with about four hundred and eighty followers, and landed [August 11] on the northern coast of Cuba. There he left Colonel Crittenden,[3] of Kentucky, with one hundred men, and proceeded toward the interior. Crittenden and his party were captured, carried to Havana, and on the 16th were shot. Lopez was attacked on the 13th, and his little army dispersed. He had been greatly deceived. There yet appeared no signs of revolution in Cuba, and he became a fugitive. He was arrested on the 28th, with six of his followers, taken to Havana, and on the 1st of September was executed. Since that event no successful effort to organize an invading expedition has been made, notwithstanding there is still [1856] a strong feeling in some sections favorable to it.

---

pleted a more perfect machinery. In 1838 he submitted the matter and the telegraphic instruments to Congress, asking their aid to construct a line of sufficient length "to test its practicability and utility." The committee to whom the subject was referred, reported favorably, and proposed an appropriation of $30,000 to construct the first line. The appropriation, however, was not made until the 3d of March, 1843. The posts for supporting the wires were erected between Washington and Baltimore, a distance of forty miles. In the spring of 1844 the line was completed, and the proceedings of the Democratic convention, then sitting in Baltimore, which nominated James K. Polk for the Presidency of the United States, was the first use, for public purposes, ever made by the telegraph, whose wires now [1856] extend a distance of almost fifty thousand miles in the United States and Canadas. Professor Morse's system of Recording Telegraphs is adopted generally on the continent of Europe, and has been selected by the government of Australia for the telegraphic systems of that country. A very ingenious machine for recording telegraphic communications with printing types, so as to avoid the necessity of copying, was constructed, a few years ago, by House, and is now extensively used. Professor Morse is the eldest son of Rev. Jedediah Morse, the first American geographer. He was born in Charlestown, Massachusetts, in 1791, and was graduated at Yale College in 1810. He studied painting, in England, and was very successful. He was one of the founders of the National Academy of Design in New York, and he was the first to deliver a course of lectures upon art, in America. He became a professor in the University of the city of New York, and there perfected his magnetic telegraph. Mr. Morse now [1856] resides on his beautiful estate of Locust Grove, near Po'keepsie, New York. He has received many testimonials of appreciation from eminent individuals and societies abroad; and in the summer of 1856 he departed for Russia, having received an invitation from the Emperor Alexander to be present at his coronation. He returned at the close of October.

[1] Page 502. [2] Page 502.

[3] William L. Crittenden. He had been a second lieutenant in the United States infantry, by brevet, but resigned in 1849.

In the autumn of 1851, more accessions were made to the vastly-extended possessions of the United States, by the purchase of twenty-one millions of acres of land in Minnesota, from the Upper Sioux tribes.[1] The amount paid for this tract was about three hundred and five thousand dollars, to be given when the Indians should reach their reservation in Upper Minnesota, and sixty-eight thousand dollars a year, for fifty years. At about the same time, another broad region was purchased of the Lower Sioux;[2] and now [1856] a white population is flowing thither, to take the place of the Indians, and make "the wilderness blossom as the rose." On account of the rapid progress of immigration from abroad and inter-emigration at home, and the wonderful prosperity of business of all kinds, the greatest activity everywhere prevailed, and forecast perceived a vast and speedy increase of population and national wealth. Already new States and Territories were sending additional representatives to the seat of the Federal Government, and the capitol was becoming too narrow.[3] In view of future wants, its extension was decided upon; and on the 4th of July, 1851, the President laid the corner-stone of the addition.[4]

In the month of May, 1845, Sir John Franklin, a veteran English explorer, with two vessels and one hundred and thirty-eight men, left Great Britain in search of the long-sought-for north-west passage to the East Indies.[5] Since the spring of 1846, no certain tidings of him have been received, and several expeditions have been sent in search of him.[6] Among others, Henry Grinnell, a wealthy merchant of New York, sent two vessels, at his own expense, in quest of the missing mariner. The expedition left New York in May, 1850, under the command of Lieutenant De Haven, of the United States navy. It penetrated the polar waters to the southern entrance of Wellington Channel, where the graves of three of Franklin's men, made in April, 1846, were discovered. After ineffectual attempts to pass up that channel to the supposed open circumpolar sea beyond, the expedition returned in October, 1851, without accomplishing its benevolent object. Yet the search for the brave Sir John and his com-

---

[1] Page 31.

[2] About $225,000 were paid for this tract, and a promised annual payment of $30,000 for fifty years. Altogther, the United States government paid about $3,000,000 for Indian lands in the autumn of 1851.

[3] Each State is entitled to two senators. The number of States now [1856] being thirty-one, the Senate is composed of sixty-two members. The number of Representatives to which each State is entitled, is determined by the number of inhabitants. The present number of the members in the House of Representatives is two hundred and thirty-four.

[4] Note 1, page 388. On the occasion of laying the corner-stone, an oration was pronounced by Daniel Webster, in the course of which he said: "If, therefore, it shall hereafter be the will of God that this structure shall fall from its base, that its foundations be upturned, and the deposit beneath this stone brought to the eyes of men, be it then known, that on this day the Union of the United States of America stands firm—that their Constitution still exists unimpaired, and with all its usefulness and glory, growing every day stronger in the affections of the great body of the American people, and attracting, more and more, the admiration of the world."

[5] Note 2, page 47, also page 52, and note 8, page 59.

[6] In 1855, an overland exploring party, was dispatched by the Hudson's Bay Fur Company to examine the localities on the northern coast of America, where it was supposed Franklin and his associates perished. At the mouth of the Great Fish, or Black River, Esquimaux informed them that about four years before, a party of white men had perished from famine and exhaustion in the vicinity of Montreal Island. Some articles known to have belonged to Sir John Franklin's party, were found among the Esquimaux, and seem to confirm the belief that these brave adventurers actually perished about the year 1851, on the northern borders of North America.

panions was not abandoned. From England another expedition was sent; and Mr. Grinnell, in connection with the government of the United States, sent another on the same errand, under the command of Dr. Elisha K. Kane, the surgeon and naturalist of the former enterprise. It sailed from New York on the 31st of May, 1853, and on the 10th of September following they were frozen in on the coast of Greenland, at the most northerly point ever reached. There they passed the winter, and the following summer was spent in exploring the shores, their vessel all the while remaining fast in the ice. The winter of 1854 and 1855 was one of unexampled severity, and they suffered inconceivable hardships. Their stock of fuel was exhausted, and even rats became choice morsels of food. Disease fell upon them; and at one time it appeared as if all must inevitably perish. But the indomitable perseverance of Dr. Kane[1] and his party overcame all; and they were rewarded by the discovery of the long-suspected open polar sea, beyond the great ice-belt that girdles the North Pole. The long absence of the expedition excited fears for their safety, and another was sent to their relief. Dr. Kane and his party, compelled to abandon their vessels, had voyaged in open boats thirteen hundred miles to a Danish settlement on Greenland, and were about to take passage for England when the Relief Expedition found them. On the 18th of September, 1855, they all sailed for New York, where they arrived on the 11th of October. In the mean while, the great problem which, for three hundred years, has perplexed the maritime world, had been worked out by an English navigator. The fact of a north-west passage around the Arctic coast of North America, from Baffin's Bay to Behring's Straits, has been unquestionably demonstrated by Captain M'Clure, of the ship *Investigator*, who was sent in search of Sir John Franklin in October, 1853. Having passed through

DR. KANE.

[1] Elisha Kent Kane was born in Philadelphia in February, 1822, and he took his degree in the Medical University of Pennsylvania in 1843. He entered the American navy as assistant-surgeon, and was attached as a physician to the first American embassy to China. While in the East, he visited many of the Islands, and met with wild adventures. After that he ascended the Nile to the confines of Nubia, and passed a season in Egypt. After traveling through Greece and a part of Europe, on foot, he returned to the United States in 1846. He was immediately sent to the coast of Africa, where he narrowly escaped death from fever. Soon after his recovery he went to Mexico as a volunteer in the war then progressing, where his bravery and endurance commanded universal admiration. His horse was killed under him, and himself was badly wounded. He was appointed senior surgeon and naturalist to the "Grinnell Expedition," sent in search of Sir John Franklin; and after his return he prepared an interesting account of the exploration. He was appointed to the command of a second expedition, which sailed in May, 1853. Governed by the suggestions of a theory which had long occupied his mind, he prepared more for land than water explorations. Supposing Greenland to be the southern cape of a polar continent, it was the intention of Dr. Kane to sail as far north along that coast as the ice would allow, and then leave his vessels and make an overland journey northward, in quest of supposed green fields under a mild atmosphere, and an open sea within the polar circle; and, perhaps, there find the temporary home of Franklin and his men. The rigors of those northern winters prevented a full carrying out of his plan, but he accomplished wonders in behalf of geographical science. The record of this wonderful expedition, prepared by himself, has been published in two superb volumes, illustrated by engravings from drawings by Dr. Kane. The hardships which he had endured made great inroads on the health of Dr. Kane (who was a very light man, weighing only 106 pounds); and in October, 1856, he sailed for England, and from thence to Havana, where he died on the 16th of February, 1857.

Behring's Straits, and sailed eastward, he reached a point with sleds upon the ice, which had been penetrated by navigators from the East (Captain Parry and others), thus establishing the fact that there is a water connection between Baffin's Bay and those Straits. Already the mute whale had demonstrated this fact to the satisfaction of naturalists. The same species are found in Behring's Straits and Baffin's Bay; and as the waters of the tropical regions would be like a sea of fire to them, they must have had communication through the polar channels.

Toward the close of 1851 [December], Louis Kossuth, the exiled governor of Hungary, arrived in New York, from England, on a mission to the United States in quest of aid for his oppressed country. His wonderful efforts in behalf of liberty in Hungary during and after the European revolutions in 1848,[1] and his extraordinary talent as an orator, secured for him a reception in Great Britain and in the United States, such as the most powerful emperor might be proud of. His journey throughout a greater portion of the States was like a continued ovation. He was welcomed by a deputation from all classes and pursuits; and many thousands of dollars were raised in aid of Hungary, by voluntary contributions. His noble advocacy of correct international law[2] and universal brotherhood, his unwearied labors in behalf of his smitten country, and his devotion to the cause of human freedom in general, endeared him to the great majority of the people of the United States. The policy of our government forbade its lending material aid; but Kossuth received an expression of its warmest sympathies.[3] His advent among us, and his bold enunciation of hitherto unrecognized national duties, are important and interesting events in the history of our republic.

Some ill-feeling between Great Britain and the United States was engendered during the summer of 1852, when the subject of difficulties concerning the fisheries[4] on the coast of British America was brought to the notice of Congress, and for several months there were indications of a serious disturbance of the amicable relations between the governments of the United States and Great Britain. American fishers were charged with a violation of the treaty of 1818, which stipulated that they should not cast their lines or nets in the bays of the British possessions, except at a distance of three miles or more from the shore. Now, the British government claimed the right to draw a line from head-land

---

[1] In February, 1848, the French people drove Louis Phillippe from his throne, and formed a temporary republic. The revolutionary spirit spread; and within a few months, almost every country on the continent of Europe was in a state of agitation, and the monarchs made many concessions to the people. Hungary made an effort to become free from the rule of Austria, but was crushed by the power of a Russian army.

[2] He asserted that grand principle, that one nation has no right to interfere with the domestic concerns of another, and that all nations are bound to use their efforts to prevent such interference.

[3] Matters connected with his reception, visit, and desires, occupied much of the attention of Congress, and elicited warm debates during the session of 1852. The Chevalier Hulseman, the Austrian minister at Washington, formally protested against the reception of Kossuth, by Congress; and because his protest was not heeded, he retired from his post, and left the duties of his office with Mr. Auguste Belmonte, of New York. Previous to this, Hulseman issued a written protest against the policy of our government in relation to Austria and Hungary, and that protest was answered, in a masterly manner, in January, 1851, by Mr. Webster, the Secretary of State.

[4] Pages 47 and 453.

to head-land of these bays, and to exclude the Americans from the waters within that line.[1] An armed naval force was sent to sustain this claim, and American vessels were threatened with seizure if they did not comply. The government of the United States regarded the assumption as illegal, and two steam vessels of war (*Princeton* and *Fulton*) were sent to the coast of Nova Scotia to protect the rights of American fishermen. The dispute was amicably settled by mutual concessions, in October, 1852, and the cloud passed by.

During the summer of 1853, another important measure of national concern was matured and put in operation. The great importance of commercial intercourse with Japan, because of the intimate relations which must soon exist between our Pacific coast and the East Indies, had been felt ever since the foundation of Oregon[2] and California.[3] An expedition, to consist of seven ships of war, under the command of Commodore Perry, a brother of the "Hero of Lake Erie,"[4] was fitted out for the purpose of carrying a letter from the President of the United States to the emperor of Japan, soliciting the negotiation of a treaty of friendship and commerce between the two nations, by which the ports of the latter should be thrown open to American vessels, for purposes of trade. The mission of Commodore Perry was highly successful. He negotiated a treaty, by which ports on different Islands should be open to American commerce;[5] that steamers from California to China should be furnished with supplies of coals; and that American sailors shipwrecked on the Japanese coasts should receive hospitable treatment. Subsequently a peculiar construction of the treaty on the part of the Japanese authorities, in relation to the permanent residence of Americans there, threatened a disturbance of the amicable relations which had been established.

The relations between the United States and old Spain, on account of Cuba, became interesting in the autumn of 1852. The Spanish authorities of Cuba, being thoroughly alarmed by the attempts at invasion,[6] and the evident sympathy in the movement of a large portion of the people of the United States, became excessively suspicious, and many little outrages were committed at Havana, which kept alive an irritation of feeling inconsistent with social and commercial friendship.[7] The idea became prevalent in Cuba and in Europe, that it was the policy of the government of the United States to ultimately acquire absolute possession

---

[1] This stipulation was so construed as to allow American fishermen to catch cod within the large bays where they could easily carry on their avocation at a greater distance than three miles from any land. Such had been the common practice, without interference, until the assumption of exclusive right to their bays was promulgated by the British.

[2] Page 479. [3] Page 487. [4] Page 423.

[5] Previous to this, the Dutch had monopolized the trade of Japan. See note 5, page 59.

[6] Pages 502 and 508.

[7] In the autumn of 1852 an officer of the steamship *Crescent City*, which conveyed the United States mails, passengers, and freight between New Orleans and New York, was charged by the Spanish authorities with having written articles published in the New York papers, on Cuban affairs, which were very offensive. He was forbidden to land in Havana; and in November, when the *Crescent City*, on her way to New York, entered that harbor, no communication between her and the shore was allowed, and she was obliged to proceed to sea, with passengers and mails that should have been left at Havana. A more flagrant outrage of a similar character was committed in the spring of 1854. See page 521.

of that island, and thus have the control over the commerce of the Gulf of Mexico (the door to California), and the trade of the West India group of islands, which are owned, chiefly, by France and England. To prevent such a result, the cabinets of France and England asked that of the United States to enter with them into a treaty which should secure Cuba to Spain, by agreeing to disclaim "now and forever hereafter, all intention to obtain possession of the Island of Cuba," and "to discountenance all such attempts, to that effect, on the part of any power or individual whatever." On the 1st of December, 1852, Edward Everett, then Secretary of State, issued a response to this extraordinary proposition, which the American people universally applauded for its keen logic and patriotic and enlightened views. He told France and England plainly, that the question was an American, and not an European one, and not properly within the scope of their interference; that while the United States Government disclaimed all intention to violate existing neutrality laws, it would not relinquish the right to act in relation to Cuba independent of any other power; and that it could not see with indifference "the Island of Cuba fall into the hands of any other power than Spain."[1] Lord John Russell, the English prime-minister, answered this letter, in February, 1853, and thus ended the diplomatic correspondence on the subject of the proposed "Tripartite Treaty," as it was called.

At a national Democratic convention, held at Baltimore early in June, 1852, Franklin Pierce, of New Hampshire, was nominated for President of the United States, and William R. King, of Alabama, for Vice-President. At a Whig convention, held at the same place on the 16th of June, General Winfield Scott was nominated for the Chief Magistracy, and William A. Graham, of North Carolina, for Vice-President. The Democratic nominees were elected in November following. Mr. King never entered upon the duties of his office. Failing health compelled him to leave the country before the oath of office could be administered to him. He went to Cuba, remained a few months, and died on the 18th of April, 1853, soon after his return to his estate in Alabama, at the age of sixty-eight years.

The most important of the closing events of Mr. Fillmore's administration was the creation by Congress of a new Territory called Washington, out of the northern part of Oregon.[2] The bill for this purpose became a law on the 2d of March, 1853.

---

[1] As early as 1823, when the Spanish provinces in South America were in rebellion or forming into independent republics, President Monroe, in a special message upon the subject, promulgated the doctrine, since acted upon, that the United States ought to resist the extension of foreign domain or influence upon the American continent, and not allow any European government, by colonizing or otherwise, to gain a foothold in the New World not already acquired. [See note 5, page 448.] This was directed specially against the efforts expected to be made by the allied sovereigns who had crushed Napoleon, to assist Spain against her revolted colonies in America, and to suppress the growth of Democracy there. It became a settled policy of our government, and Mr. Everett reasserted it in its fullest extent. Such expression seemed to be important and seasonable, because it was well known that Great Britain was then making strenuous efforts to obtain potent influence in Central America, so as to prevent the United States from acquiring exclusive property in the routes across the isthmus from the Gulf of Mexico to the Pacific Ocean.

[2] Page 479.

CHAPTER XIV.

PIERCE'S ADMINISTRATION. [1853—1857.]

A DRIVING sleet filled the air on the 4th of March, 1853, when Franklin Pierce,[1] the fourteenth President of the United States, stood upon the rude platform of New Hampshire pine, erected for the purpose over the steps of the eastern portico of the Federal capitol, and took the oath of office administered

by Chief Justice Taney. The military display on that occasion, was larger than had ever been seen in the streets of the Federal city, and it was estimated that at least twenty thousand strangers were in Washington on the morning of the inauguration. Among that great assembly there was one who bore a near

[1] Franklin Pierce was born at Hillsborough, New Hampshire, in November, 1804. He is the son of General Benjamin Pierce, an active officer in the old War for Independence, and one of the most useful men in New Hampshire. In 1820, when sixteen years of age, young Pierce became a student in Bowdoin College, at Brunswick, Maine. He was graduated in 1824, chose law as a profession, and was admitted to practice at the bar in 1827. He became a warm politician, and partisan of General Jackson in 1828; and the next year, when he was twenty-five years of age, he was elected a member of the Legislature of his native State. There he served four years. He was elected to Congress in 1833, and served his constituents in the House of Representatives for four years. In 1837, the Legislature of New Hampshire elected him to a seat in the Federal Senate. He resigned his seat in June, 1842, and remained in private life until 1845, when he was appointed United States District Attorney for New Hampshire. He was commissioned a Brigadier-General in March, 1847, and joined the army in Mexico, under General Scott. After the war, he retired from public life, where he remained until called to the highest office in the gift of the people.

relationship to the great Washington,[1] and had been present at the inauguration of every President of the United States since the formation of our Federal government in 1789.[2] Untrammeled by special party pledges, the new Chief Magistrate entered upon the duties of his office under pleasant auspices; and his inaugural address, full of promise and patriotism, received the general approval of his countrymen. Three days afterward [March 7] the Senate, in special session, confirmed his cabinet appointments,[3] and the administration now [1856] drawing to a close began its work.

The most serious difficulty which President Pierce was called upon to encounter, at the commencement of his administration, was a dispute concerning the boundary line between the Mexican province of Chihuahua[4] and New Mexico.[5] The Mesilla valley, a fertile and extensive region, was claimed by both Territories; and under the direction of Santa Anna,[6] who was again President of the Mexican Republic in 1854, Chihuahua took armed possession of the disputed territory. For a time war seemed inevitable between the United States and Mexico. The dispute was finally settled by negotiations; but events are continually transpiring on the borders of the two countries, calculated to produce much irritation of feeling. The people of Mexico are becoming every year more impatient of the arbitrary rule of military leaders, and insurrection after insurrection continually disturb the Republic. The youth of the present generation will probably observe the rule of the United States eventually extended over the whole of that unhappy country.

A few days after the expedition under the command of Dr. Kane left New York, in May, 1853, another, consisting of four armed vessels and a supply-ship, sailed from Norfolk, under the command of Captain Ringgold, of the United States Navy. Its destination was the eastern coast of Asia, and its object a thorough exploration of those regions of the Pacific Ocean yet to be traversed by vessels passing between the ports of our western frontier and China, and of the whaling grounds of the Sea of Okotsk and Behring's Straits. This expedition returned in the summer of 1856, having accomplished many of the objects for which it was sent out. In the mean while, plans had been sug-

---

[1] George Washington Parke Custis, of Arlington House, Virginia, a grandson of Mrs. Washington, and adopted son of the *Father of his Country*. He is now [Dec., 1856] the only surviving executor of the last Will of Washington.

[2] Page 361.

[3] William L. Marcy, Secretary of State; James Guthrie, Secretary of the Treasury; Robert McClelland, Secretary of the Interior; Jefferson Davis, Secretary of War; James C. Dobbin, Secretary of the Navy; James Campbell, Postmaster-General; Caleb Cushing, Attorney-General.

[4] Note 7, page 484.

[5] Page 497.

[6] Antonio Lopez de Santa Anna is a native of Mexico, and first came into public life in 1821, during the excitements of revolution. He has been one of the chief revolutionists in that unhappy country. He was chosen President of the Republic in 1833. After an exciting career as a commanding General, he was again elected President in 1841, but was hurled from power in 1845. After the capture of the city of Mexico by the Americans under General Scott [page 491], he retired to the West Indies, and finally to Carthagena, where he resided until 1853, when he returned to Mexico, and was elected President again. In the summer of 1854, he was accused of a design to assume imperial power, and violent insurrections were the consequence. These resulted in his being again deprived of power; and now [1856] he is in exile. Few men have experienced greater vicissitudes than Santa Anna.

SANTA ANNA.

gested, and some matured, for the construction of one or more railways from the Mississippi valley across the continent to the Pacific coast. This subject yet [1856] occupies a prominent place in the public mind, and is next in importance, as a national question, to that of human slavery, now the great and absorbing topic of the time. The thirty-second Congress, at its last session,[1] authorized surveys for the selection of the best path for such railroad; and by mid-summer [1853] four expeditions were fitted out to explore as many different routes. One, under Major Stevens, was instructed to survey a northern route from the upper waters of the Mississippi to Puget's Sound. The course to be taken was from St. Paul's, in Minnesota, to the Great Bend of the Missouri river; thence on the table land between the Missouri and Saskatchawan rivers, to the most available pass in the Rocky Mountains. A second expedition, under Lieutenant Whipple, was directed to cross the continent from the Mississippi, along a line adjacent to the 36th parallel of latitude. It was to proceed from the Mississippi, along the head waters of the Canadian river, across the Rio Peco, and enter the valley of the Rio del Norte near Albuquerque, thence through Walker's Pass in the Rocky Mountains to the Pacific, on the coast of Southern California, near San Pedro, Los Angelos, or San Diego. A third, under Captain Gunnison, was to proceed through the Rocky Mountains, near the head waters of the Del Norte, by way of the Heurfano river, into the valley of the Greene and Grand rivers, thence westwardly along the Nicollet river of the Great Basin, and north, by way of the Great Salt Lake in Utah.[2] A fourth was to leave the more southern portions of the Mississippi, and reach the Pacific somewhere in Lower California—perhaps at San Diego. These expeditions[3] were intended, by their combined operations, to sweep the whole area of our territory between the Mississippi and the Pacific. Their work is not yet [1856] accomplished. They have been compelled to encounter the most discouraging obstacles,[4] but the results will be of infinite importance, not only to our country, but to the world. These, taken in connection with the operations of portions of the navy of the United States, in explorations, certainly rank among the most important movements of the age. Who can estimate the effect of a consummation of these gigantic plans, upon the growth and prosperity of the United States, when the Pacific's shores shall be reached by railways, and steamships shall ply regularly between their termini and that "farther India,"

AN OCEAN STEAMSHIP.

[1] Note 3, page 366. [2] Page 504.

[3] Late in the autumn of 1853, Colonel Fremont started with a number of men, to explore the Cochatope Pass, in mid-winter, and ascertain, by his own observation, whether the snows were so deep at that season of the year, as to render railroad travel through there impracticable. He and his party suffered terribly. Forty-five days they fed on mules, which, from want of food, could go no further, and were killed and eaten—every particle, even to the entrails! They were met and relieved by another party on the 19th of February, 1854. This was Fremont's fifth and last exploring expedition.

[4] In February, 1854, the Indians of the Wasatch Mountains attacked Captain Gunnison's party, and slew the leader and several of his men. Their remains were afterward found by another party, when the spring sun had melted the snow.

whose wealth the commercial world has so long coveted?[1] The beaten tracks of commerce will be changed, and teeming marts will burst into existence where now the dwindling tribes of the forest build their wigwams,[2] and gaze musingly upon the sunset, the emblem of their own destiny.[3]

In the year 1851 an immense building, made of iron and glass, was erected in Hyde Park, London, under royal patronage;[4] and within it an exhibition of the industry of all nations was opened on the 1st of May of that year. It was a WORLD'S FAIR; and representatives from every civilized nation of the globe were there, mingling together as brothers of one family, and all equally interested in the perfection of each other's productions. The idea was one of great moral grandeur, for it set an insignia of dignity upon labor, hitherto withheld by those who bore scepters and orders. There men of all nations and creeds received a lesson upon the importance of brotherhood among the children of men, such as the pen and tongue could not teach; and they are now diffusing the blessings of that lesson among their several peoples, the fruits of which will be seen by future generations. Pleased with the idea of a "World's Fair," Americans repeated its development upon their own free soil. In the heart of the commercial metropolis of the New World—the city of New York—a "Crystal Palace" was erected; and on the 14th of July, 1853, an exhibition of the industry of all nations was opened there with imposing ceremonies led by the presiding Chief Magistrate of the United States.[5] For several months the Palace was thronged with delighted visitors; and on the 4th of May, 1854, it was re-opened with impressive ceremonies as a *perpetual* exhibition. There, in that beautiful Palace, Labor was crowned as the supreme dignity of a nation and of the world.[6] Although the

CRYSTAL PALACE IN NEW YORK.

[1] Note 4, page 38. [2] Page 13. [3] Page 33.

[4] The chief patron was Prince Albert, husband of Victoria, queen of Great Britain.

[5] On that occasion, prayer was read by Dr. Wainwright, provisional bishop of the Protestant Episcopal Church in the diocese of New York (since deceased); an address was pronounced by Theodore Sedgwick, president of the Association by which the building was erected; and on the 16th of the month, a grand entertainment was given by the directors to distinguished guests, among whom were the President of the United States, and members of his cabinet; Sir Charles Lyell, the eminent English geologist, and others.

[6] One of the speakers on that occasion [Elihu Burritt] said: "Worthy of the grandest circumstances which could be thrown around a human assembly, worthy of this occasion and a hundred like this, is that beautiful idea, the coronation of Labor. * * * Not American labor, not British labor, not French labor, not the labor of the New World or the Old, but the labor of mankind as one undivided brotherhood—labor as the oldest, the noblest, prerogative of duty and humanity." And Rev. E. H. Chapin closed with the beautiful invocation: "O! genius of Art, fill us with the inspiration of still higher and more spiritual beauty. O! instruments of invention, enlarge our dominion over reality. Let iron and fire become as blood and muscle, and in this electric net-work let heart and brain inclose the world with truth and sympathy. And thou, O! beautiful dome of light, suggestive of the brooding future, the future of human love and divine communion, expand and spread above the tribes of men, a canopy broad as the earth, and glorious as the upper heaven."

whole proceedings were but an ephemeral show, and the scheme of a *perpetual exhibition* has utterly failed, the event will ever remain a prominent initial letter, beautifully illuminated, on the pages of our history.

In the same month [July, 1853] an event occurred which greatly increased the respect of foreign nations for the flag of the United States. A Hungarian refugee,[1] named Martin Koszta, had taken the legal measures to become a naturalized citizen of our republic. While engaged in business at Smyrna, on the Mediterranean, he was seized, by order of the Austrian consul-general,[2] and taken on board an Austrian brig to be conveyed to Trieste as a rebel refugee, notwithstanding he carried an American protection. Captain Ingraham, of the United States sloop-of-war[3] *St. Louis*, then lying in the harbor of Smyrna, immediately claimed Koszta as an American citizen. On the refusal of the Austrian authorities to release the prisoner, Ingraham cleared his vessel for action [July 2], and threatened to fire upon the brig if Koszta was not delivered up within a given time. The Austrians yielded to the powerful arguments of forty well-shotted cannons, and Koszta was placed in the custody of the French consul, to await the action of the respective governments. Ingraham's course was everywhere applauded; and Congress signified its approbation by voting him an elegant sword. The pride of the Austrian government was severely wounded, and it issued a protest against the proceedings of Captain Ingraham, and sent it to all the European courts. Mr. Hulseman, the Austrian minister at Washington,[4] demanded an apology, or other redress, from our government, and menaced the United States with the displeasure of his royal master. But no serious difficulty occurred. It was plainly perceived that the Austrians were in the wrong; and Koszta, under the protection of the United States flag, returned to this land of free opinions.

CAPTAIN INGRAHAM.

On the first Monday in December, 1853, the thirty-third Congress (first session)[5] assembled in the Federal capitol. A greater degree of good feeling was exhibited among members of both Houses, from all parts of the Union, than had been witnessed since the excitement incident to the slavery agitation in 1850.[6] The people regarded the session as one of great moment, for subjects of vast national importance would necessarily occupy the attention of their representatives. The construction of a railway to the Pacific Ocean[7] was a topic of paramount importance to be discussed. There were treaties in progress respecting boundaries and claims between the United States and their southern neighbors, Mexico and Central America, chiefly concerning grants of territory for inter-oceanic communications across the Isthmus; and boundary lines between

[1] When Austria, by the aid of Russia [note 1, page 511], crushed the rebellion in Hungary, in 1848, many of the active patriots became exiles in foreign lands. A large number came to the United States, and many of them became naturalized citizens—that is, after due legal preparation, took an oath to support the Constitution and laws of the United States, and to perform faithfully all the duties of a citizen. [2] Note 1, page 395. [3] Page 415.
[4] Note 3, page 511. [5] Note 3, page 366. [6] Page 500. [7] Page 516.

New Mexico, California, and Old Mexico. The government of the Sandwich Islands was then making earnest overtures for annexing that ocean empire to our republic. This was a matter of great interest; for these Islands are destined to be of vast importance in the operations of the future commerce of the Pacific Ocean. A great majority of the white people there are Americans by birth; and the government, in all its essential operations, is controlled by Americans, notwithstanding the ostensible ruler is a native king. The consuls of France and England, when they perceived a disposition on the part of the king to have his domain annexed to the United States, charged the scheme upon certain American missionaries, and officially protested against their alleged conduct. They declared that France and England would not remain indifferent spectators of such a movement. The missionaries, as well as the United States commissioner, disclaimed any tampering with the native authorities on the subject; at the same time, the latter, in a published reply to the protest, denied the right of foreign governments to interfere to prevent such a result, if it should be deemed mutually desirable. Preliminary negotiations were commenced, and a treaty was actually formed, when, on the 15th of December, 1854, King Kamehameha died, at the age of forty-nine years, and was succeeded by his son, Prince Alexander Liholiho. The new king immediately ordered the discontinuance of negotiations with the United States, and the subject of annexation has not since been revived. That such annexation will finally occur, is surely prophesied by the history of the past and the teachings of the present.

Just as the preliminaries were arranged in Congress for entering vigorously upon the business of the session, the chairman of the Senate Committee on Territories (Mr. Douglas, of Illinois) presented a bill [Jan., 1854] which became the chief topic for discussion in and out of Congress. In the center of our continent is a vast region, almost twice as large, in territorial extent, as the original thirteen States,[1] stretching between Missouri, Iowa, and Minnesota, and the Pacific Territories, from the thirty-seventh parallel of north latitude to the British possessions,[2] and embracing one fourth of all the public lands of the United States. The bill alluded to proposed to erect this vast region into two Territories, the southern portion below the fortieth parallel to be named *Kansas*, and the northern and larger portion, *Nebraska*. It defined the boundaries of *Nebraska*, as follows: "Beginning at a point in the Missouri River where the fortieth parallel north latitude crosses the same; thence west on said parallel to the summits of the highlands separating the waters flowing into the waters of the Green River, or Colorado of the West, from the waters flowing into the great lakes; thence northward on the said highlands to the summit of the Rocky Mountains; thence on said summit northward to the forty-ninth parallel of north latitude; thence east on said parallel to the western boundary of the Territory of Minnesota; thence southward on said boundary to the Missouri River; thence down the main channel of said river to the place of beginning." It also thus defines the boundaries of *Kansas:* "Beginning at a point

[1] Page 174.

[2] Page 480.

on the western boundary of the State of Missouri where the thirty-seventh parallel of north latitude crosses the same; thence west on said parallel to the eastern boundary of New Mexico; thence north on said boundary to latitude thirty-eight; thence following said boundary westward to the summit of the highlands dividing the waters flowing into the Colorado of the West, or Green River, from the waters flowing into the great basin; thence northward on said summit to the fortieth parallel of latitude; thence east on said parallel to the western boundary of the State of Missouri; thence south with the western boundary of said State, to the place of beginning."

The Kansas-Nebraska Bill, as it was called, contained a provision which would nullify the Compromise of 1820,[1] and allow the inhabitants of those Territories to decide for themselves whether they would have the institution of slavery or not. This proposition surprised Congress and the whole country, and it became a subject of discussion throughout the Union. The slavery agitation was aroused in all its strength and rancor, and the whole North became violently excited. Public meetings were held by men of all parties, and petitions and remonstrances against the measure, especially in its relation to *Nebraska*, were poured into the Senate,[3] while the debate on the subject was progressing, from the 30th of January [1854] until the 3d of March. On the latter day the bill passed that body by the decisive vote of thirty-seven to fourteen. The measure encountered great opposition in the House of Representatives; and by means of several amendments, its final defeat seemed almost certain, and the excitement subsided. At about the same time a bill was reported in the Senate [March 10], providing for the construction of a railway to the Pacific Ocean; and on the same day when the Nebraska Bill passed that body [March 7], the House of Representatives adopted one called the Homestead Bill, which provided that any free white male citizen, or any one who may have declared his intentions to become one previous to the passage of this act, might select a quarter section [one hundred and sixty acres] of land, on the public domain, and on proof being given that he had occupied and cultivated it for five years,, he might receive a title to it, in fee, without being required to pay any thing for it. This bill was discussed in both Houses for several weeks; and finally an amendment, graduating the prices of all the public lands, was adopted in its stead. It provided that all lands which have been in market ten years shall be subject to entry at one dollar per acre; fifteen years, at seventy-five cents; and so on, in the same ratio—those which have been in the market for thirty years being offered at twelve and a half cents. It also provided that every person availing himself of the act should make affidavit that he enters the land for his own use; and no one can acquire more than three hundred and twenty acres, or two quarter sections.

The public mind had become comparatively tranquil when, on the 9th of

---

[1] Page 452. [2] Page 501.

[3] A petition against the measure was presented to the Senate immediately after the passage of the bill by that body, signed by three thousand clergymen of New England.

May, the Nebraska bill was again called up in the House of Representatives. It became the absorbing subject for discussion. During a fortnight, violent debates, with great acrimony of feeling, occurred, and on one occasion there was a session of thirty-six consecutive hours' duration, when an adjournment took place in the midst of great confusion. The country, meanwhile, was much excited, for the decision of the question was one of great moment in its relation to the future. While it was pending, the suspense became painful. It did not last long. The final question was taken on the 22d, and the bill was passed by a vote of one hundred and thirteen to one hundred. Three days afterward [May 25], the Senate agreed to it as it came from the House by a vote of thirty-five to thirteen, and it received the signature of the President on the last day of May.[1]

New difficulties with the Spanish authorities of Cuba[2] appeared, while the Nebraska subject was under discussion. Under cover of a shallow pretense, the American steamship, *Black Warrior*, was seized in the harbor of Havana [February 28, 1854], and the vessel and cargo declared confiscated. The outrage was so flagrant, that a proposition was immediately submitted to the lower House of Congress, to suspend the neutrality laws, and compel the Havana officials to behave properly. These are agreements made between the governments of the United States and Old Spain, to remain neutral or inactive when either party should engage in war with another. Under the provisions of such laws, any number of citizens of the United States, who may be engaged in hostilities against Spain, would forfeit the protection of their government, and become liable to punishment, for a violation of law. It was on this account that Crittenden and his party were shot at Havana,[3] without the right of claiming the interference of the government of the United States in their behalf. The President sent a special messenger to the government at Madrid, with instructions to the American minister to demand immediate redress, in the form of indemnity to the owners of the *Black Warrior*. But the Spanish government justified the act of the Cuban authorities, when such formal demand was made. In the mean while the perpetrators of the outrage became alarmed, and the Captain General (or Governor) of Cuba, with pretended generosity, offered to give up the vessel and cargo, on the payment by the owners, of a fine of six thousand dollars. They complied, but under protest.[4] The matter was finally settled amicably between the governments of the United States and Spain,[5] and

[1] A few days after the final passage of the Nebraska bill, the city of Boston was made a theater of great excitement, by the arrest of a fugitive slave there, and a deputy-marshal was shot dead, during a riot. United States troops from Rhode Island were employed, to sustain the officers of the law, and a local military force was detailed, to assist in the protection of the court and the parties concerned, until the trial of the alleged fugitive was completed. The United States Commissioner decided in favor of the claimant of the slave, and he was conveyed to Virginia by a government vessel. This commotion in Boston is known as the *Burns Riot*—the name of the fugitive slave being Burns. [2] Page 502. [3] Page 508.

[4] Protesting against an act which a party is *compelled* to perform, leaves the matter open for a future discussion and final settlement.

[5] The President of the United States having been informed that expeditions were preparing in different parts of the Union, for the purpose of invading Cuba, issued a proclamation against such movements, on the 1st of June, 1854, and called upon all good citizens to respect the obligations of existing treaties, between the governments of our Republic and Spain.

since then nothing has materially disturbed the friendly relations between the two countries. The conduct of the government officials of Cuba may at any time terminate that friendship, so long as they are allowed to take shelter behind the imperial throne at Madrid. The commercial transactions, and the continual passenger intercourse between the United States and that island, have now become so important and extensive, that it is felt to be a necessity for the Spanish authorities there to be made immediately responsible for any outrage they may commit. The people of the United States do not feel disposed to tolerate irresponsible despotisms so near the line of their commercial operations. And so strong is the indignation of the people of some portions of our Union, against the Cuban officials—so attractive is that "Queen of the Antilles" to the acquisitiveness of another portion, and so powerful is the tendency of a spirit of adventure toward an invasion of the island, to assist the native population in casting off the Spanish yoke[1]—that a rupture may at any time occur.

The impending difficulties with Spain, in the summer of 1854, led to an important conference of some of the American ministers plenipotentiary in Europe. In August, 1854, the President directed Mr. Buchanan,[2] then American embassador at London, Mr. Mason, embassador at Paris, and Mr. Soulé, embassador at Madrid, to meet at some convenient place, to confer upon the best means of settling the difficulties about Cuba, and gaining possession of the island, by purchase or otherwise. They accordingly met at Ostend, a seaport town in Belgium, on the 9th of October, 1854. After remaining there three days, they adjourned to Aix-la-Chapelle, in Rhenish Prussia, and from thence, on the 18th of the same month, they addressed a letter to the United States government, which embodied their views. In that letter, they recommended the purchase of Cuba; or, if negotiation toward that end should fail—"if Spain," they said, "actuated by stubborn pride and a false sense of honor, should refuse to sell Cuba to the United States," then, "by every law, human and divine, we [the United States] shall be justified in wresting it from Spain, if we possess the power." This doctrine, that "might makes right," has been strongly condemned, when promulgated by other nations, and a large proportion of the people of the Union do not coincide with the views of their embassadors on that occasion. The President did not deem it advisable to follow the course indicated by the embassadors, and since then nothing has been done in relation to the political position of Cuba toward the United States.

Early in the summer of 1854, a treaty was negotiated and ratified by the United States and Mexico, by which the boundaries between the two governments were defined and settled. By it, the dividing line begins in the Gulf of Mexico, three leagues from land, opposite the mouth of the Rio Grande, thence up the middle of that river, to the point where the parallel of 31° 47′ north latitude, crosses the same; thence due west one hundred miles; thence south to the parallel of 31° 20′ north latitude; thence along the said parallel to the 111th meridian of longitude west of Greenwich; thence in a straight line to a

---

[1] Page 41.

[2] Page 532.

point in the Colorado river, twenty English miles below the junction of the Gila and Colorado rivers; thence up the middle of the Colorado until it intersects the present line between the United States and Mexico. The decision of the commissioners appointed to run the boundary, under the treaty, was to be final; the United States were to be released from all obligations imposed by the treaty of Guadaloupe Hidalgo,[1] to defend the Mexican frontier against the Indians, and in consideration for this release, and for the territory ceded by Mexico, the United States agreed to pay ten millions of dollars—seven millions on the ratification of the treaty, and the remainder as soon as the boundary line should be established. These conditions have been complied with, and nothing except private invasions of the Mexican territory, by armed citizens of the United States, now [1856] seems likely to disturb the present friendly relations between the two governments.

At about the same time, a reciprocity treaty was negotiated between the United States and Great Britain, which lowered, and in some instances effaced, the barriers to free commerce between the British provinces in America and our Confederation. It provided that the fisheries of the provinces, except those of Newfoundland,[2] should be open to American citizens; that disputes respecting fisheries should be settled by arbitration; that the British should have a right to participate in the American fisheries as far as the 36th degree of north latitude; that there should be free commerce between the provinces and the United States, in flour, breadstuffs, fruits, fish, animals, lumber, and a variety of natural productions in their unmanufactured state. It stipulated that the St. Lawrence River and the Canadian canals should be thrown open to American vessels; and the United States government agreed to urge the respective States to admit British vessels into their canals, upon similar terms. This treaty was submitted to the provincial Legislatures, and to the governments of the contracting powers, and was ratified by all.

Ever since the war with Mexico, and the extension of the territory of the United States in the direction of Central America, and down the Pacific coast, the relations of the Federal government toward the provinces of that region have been most of the time in a state of feverish discontent. The temptations presented by those countries, so rich in mineral and agricultural wealth, to the cupidity of the floating elements of society in the United States, have been too great for the easy virtue of adventurers, and from time to time, intelligence of some foray or some actual invasion of territory comes from thence, to alarm our government, call out proclamations and warnings against the infraction of international laws or treaty stipulations, and to excite the ire, the jealousy, or the pugnacity of England, France, and Spain.

Upon the Caribbean Sea, in the State of Nicaragua, is a region known as the Musquito coast, inhabited, chiefly, by a degraded race of natives, but occupying an important commercial position, in prospective. It has been the desire of the people of the United States interested in commercial

---

[1] Page 497

[2] Page 47.

operations, to have the control of that region, for purposes of transportation from ocean to ocean, and for free communication, by a short land route, with our State and Territories on the Pacific coast. It is equally the interest of Great Britain, as a commercial nation, to have control of that future great highway of commerce, by canal or otherwise;[1] and these conflicting interests have at times menaced the friendly relations between England and the United States. In June, 1854, the little village of Greytown, on the Musquito coast, was bombarded by a United States vessel, in punishment for alleged outrages upon American citizens by the local authorities, who claimed to derive their power exclusively from the Musquito king. The English claimed, that by some arrangement with that monarch, that region was under the protection of her majesty's government, and the bombardment was denounced as an insult to Great Britain. For awhile the cloud of difficulty appeared ominous of evil, but it passed away in course of time, it being clearly perceived that the question at issue was not of sufficient importance for two nations, so allied by multifarious ties, to engage in a war with each other.

Another speck of difficulty occurred in the far south-west. An alleged grant of territory, by the king of the Musquito Indians, to two British subjects, led to serious misunderstandings. Colonel H. L. Kinney fitted out an expedition, composed of alleged emigrants, to settle upon that claim by permission of the grantees, when the government of Nicaragua, which claimed jurisdiction over the Musquito Territory, protested against the movement as an invasion of its domain, and in violation of the neutrality laws of the United States. This movement occurred in the autumn and early winter of 1854; and on the 16th of January following, the Nicaraguan minister at Washington made a representation to our government, setting forth the facts that the English had attempted to establish a protectorate over the Musquito country; that the United States had long ago taken the ground (and since maintained it) that no European government should interfere with the domestic concerns of the republics of Central America,[2] and that the latter had thus virtually denied the right of the Musquito king, acting under British influenee, to make any grants of lands

---

[1] A railway across the Isthmus of Panama has been constructed, and the first trains passed over it, from Aspinwall to Panama, on the 28th of January, 1855. The project of a ship-canal across the Isthmus of Darien, or Panama, has occupied the attention of statesmen and commercial men for many years. The first actual exploration of the Isthmus, with a view to cutting a ship-canal across it, was made in 1853, by a party of twenty-three, under the direction of William Kennish, of New York. They were sent out by J. C. Prevost, commander of the British steamship *Virago*, in pursuance of orders from the commander of the British squadron then in the Pacific. They commenced on the Pacific coast, and traveled northward to the Atlantic shore. For ten days they traversed a dense forest which covered a fine, fertile, and well-watered plain, which, at no time, rose more than fifty feet above the level of the sea. The party became short of provisions; and having separated, for some prudent purpose, a portion of them were murdered and plundered by the Indians. The survivors returned to the *Virago*, without accomplishing much. In January, 1854, Lieutenant Strain, of the United States Navy, with a party of twenty, started from the Atlantic side to explore the Isthmus. They suffered dreadfully; and as nothing was heard from them for several weeks, it was supposed that all had perished. Their provisions became exhausted, and some died from famine. The Indians, however, did not molest them, but fled to the mountains. When Lieutenant Strain and the survivors reached the Pacific coast, they were destitute of both clothing and food. Since then no attempt has been made to explore that dreary region.

[2] The "Monroe Doctrine." See note 5, page 448.

whatever.[1] In reply to this, Colonel Kinney assured our government [January 28, 1855] that the object of his expedition was the peaceable one of settling upon and improving the lands of the granted tract. To this the government answered [Feb. 4], that if the emigrants chose to go in a peaceable manner, abandon all claims to the protection of the United States, and submit themselves to the jurisdiction of another power, the Federal government would not interfere. But the President and his cabinet had reasons for changing their views and actions a few months later, when it appeared probable that the expedition was not as peacefully inclined as at first supposed. In June [1855], Colonel Kinney was arrested in New York and Philadelphia, on a charge of attempting to violate the neutrality laws, and was admitted to bail in both cases. Notwithstanding these legal interpositions, Kinney secretly departed for Nicaragua, with half-a-dozen followers; and a few weeks afterward he published a card, calling upon those who had enlisted, to join him at once, by whatever conveyance they might obtain. In the mean while, the government of Nicaragua had issued a decree [Jan. 1, 1855], at Grenada, calling upon all citizens to aid the authorities in repelling the invasion, prohibiting Kinney and his companions from entering the territory, and directing them to be immediately seized and conducted to the seat of government.

And now another phase of this emigration scheme was developed. Colonel William Walker, who, the year before, had invaded Sonora from California with a few followers, and had been repulsed, was again prepared for adventures. Colonel Kinney invited Walker to join him in improving his grant on Lake Nicaragua, and in developing its mineral resources. Walker soon left San Francisco, ostensibly for that purpose, with three hundred armed men. He arrived on the coast of Nicaragua on the 27th of June, and the next day his hostile intentions were developed in an attempt to take possession of the town of Rivas. He had been led to believe that large numbers of the inhabitants, tired of despotic rule, would join him, but in this he was mistaken. Even one hundred and fifty Central American troops, under General Castillon, who had joined him, deserted when they saw the forces of Nicaragua approaching; and Walker and his men, with the courage of desperation, cut their way through their opposers, reached the coast, and escaped in a schooner.

In August, Colonel Walker again landed not far from Rivas, and unsuccessfully attempted to recruit from California passengers. In the mean while, Colonel Kinney was pursuing his peaceful course, having concluded a contract for a very large portion of the Musquito Territory. The white people in that region, assuming independence of Nicaragua, organized a government, and on the 6th of September [1855], elected Kinney Chief Magistrate, with a Council of Five, as assistants. On the 3d of the same month, Walker, taking advantage of revolutionary movements in Nicaragua, had a battle with about four hundred government troops, at Virgin Bay. The government party were

---

[1] For some time the British had been endeavoring to obtain a controlling influence in this region, and they had induced the chief of the Musquito nation to assume authority independent of the State of Nicaragua.

defeated, and on the 12th of October, Walker marched upon Grenada, the capital of Nicaragua, and captured it. When order was restored, the citizens, in public meeting, offered the presidency to the conqueror, but he declined the honor. General Rivas, a Nicaraguan, was placed in the presidential chair, while Walker, intent upon strengthening his army in order to maintain his conquest, was receiving large reinforcements from the Atlantic States, and from California. The British consul at Realejo recognized the new government, and it also received the favorable regard of Colonel Wheeler,[1] the American minister at Grenada. The new government now asserted its claim to the Musquito Territory,[2] and when Colonel Kinney visited Grenada, to negotiate with the government on the subject of his grant, he was arrested on a charge of treasonable practices, and ordered to leave the country.

The establishment of political power in Central America, by armed adventurers from the United States, produced a great deal of uneasiness among the governments of the Isthmus, and in the winter of 1856, an alliance of all the other States in that region, against Nicaragua, was attempted. The latter, in the mean while, had made some arrangements with the British government, independent of the United States, for the settlement of the Musquito question, and the king of that country was placed on an equal footing with other native chiefs. Thus ended the Kinney government.

Early in March, 1856, Costa Rica made a formal declaration of war against Nicaragua; and on the 10th of the same month, Walker made a corresponding declaration. The former government called upon all the Central American States to "unite and destroy the invaders from the North," while Walker declared that he was there by invitation of the Liberal party in Nicaragua.

On the 20th of March hostilities commenced, and on the 11th of April a sanguinary conflict occurred, in which the Nicaraguans were the victors, and forced the Costa Ricans to retreat from the country. Walker's rule became unpopular, because of his forced loan from the citizens of Grenada, but he found strength by the refusal, at that time, of other States to join the Costa Ricans. But soon President Rivas himself, jealous of the Americans, became alienated from Walker, abandoned the government, and proclaimed against it. On the 24th of June [1856] a new election for President was held, when Walker received two thirds of the popular vote, and was inaugurated Chief Magistrate on the 12th of July. And now a general league of all the Central American States against him, was consummated, with Rivas in active command. In the mean while Walker's government had been acknowledged as legitimate

---

[1] Colonel John H. Wheeler was a resident of western North Carolina, and while on his way to New York, to embark for Nicaragua, two of his slaves, who attended him, were detained in Philadelphia [July 18, 1855], through the instrumentality of persons there who sought to make them free. One of these (Passmore Williamson) was ordered by Judge Kane (father of Dr. Kane, the Arctic explorer), of the United States District Court, to bring the slaves before him. Williamson declared that the slaves had never been in his custody, and of course he could not produce them. On motion of Colonel Wheeler, Judge Kane committed Williamson to prison, for contempt of court, where he remained for several months. This case, in connection with other questions in regard to slavery, produced great excitement throughout the country. Williamson, after his release, commenced a suit for false imprisonment against Judge Kane.

[2] Page 523.

by the United States, and his minister cordially received [July] at Washington.[1] Thus strengthened, he declared all the ports of the Central American States in a condition of blockade, and adopted severe measures toward all disaffected Nicaraguans. He managed affairs with vigor and skill; and finally, on the 13th of October, he had a severe battle with his enemies at Grenada, and utterly vanquished them.[2] The league against Nicaragua appeared to be weak indeed; and it seemed as if the hardy element of the North would control the political affairs of that little republic, until in the course of time it should become a permanent State, under North American rule.

Such, in brief, is the history of the attempts to establish a large State—the planting of a new and free empire—in the most important portion of Central America, by the prowess of men from the bosom of our Republic. Placing out of sight the means employed to attain this end, the effort challenges our natural sympathies, because it may be firmly rooting, in a virgin soil, the principles of free government. We can not but regard this movement as one that will be followed by the establishment of a permanent State, destined, in the progress of events, to become a member of our broad and expanding confederation.

During the spring of 1855, Cuba was in a state of continual alarm, from apprehensions of another invasion from the United States,[3] supported by an insurrection in the island. An extensive conspiracy had been detected, many suspected persons were arrested, and some were tried and executed. Among these was Estrampes, an alleged citizen of the United States, who was executed on the 30th of March, notwithstanding the strong protest of the United States consul. At about the same time, the United States steamers had been brought to, on their passage, by Spanish armed vessels, and our government dispatched a strong squadron to the Gulf to prevent and punish any indignity offered to our flag. This movement made the Cuban authorities more circumspect.

Civilization has been compelled to encounter hostilities from the natives of our continent at almost every step of its progress; and even now, when they have been driven back toward the shores of the Pacific, and they have dwindled in numbers to a handfull, in comparison with their former strength, they continue, occasionally, to lift a feeble hand of resistance to the on-flowing tide of emigration, which presages their final and complete extinction.[4] Toward the close of 1855, the Indians of Oregon and Washington Territories,[5] commenced hostilities upon the settlers; and ever since, the people there have suffered all the horrors of savage warfare upon them. In July, the Indians had murdered several miners in Rogue River Valley; and later in the season, a battle, which lasted fifty hours, was fought in Yakimaw county, between United States troops

---

[1] Several months before, Rivas had sent as minister, Colonel Parker H. French, but the United States government refused to receive him. The accepted minister was Father Vijil, a Roman Catholic priest. His stay in Washington was brief.

[2] The army of the League against Nicaragua, about four thousand strong, took possession of Massaya on the 11th of October. On the same day, Walker, with a little more than eight hundred men, marched against them. He drove the enemy out, early on the morning of the 12th. At about 10 o'clock, he received intelligence that quite a force had attacked Grenada. He immediately marched thither, and soon dispersed them, with very little loss on his part.

[3] Page 521. [4] Note 4, page 32. [5] Page 479.

and a large body of Indians. Nearly one fifth of the former were killed or wounded, and the remainder saved themselves by a desperate retreat, leaving baggage and stores behind them. The Indians were well armed, and there appeared to be a general combination among those extreme western tribes to exterminate the settlers. Still later in the season, whole families were massacred; and General Wool,[1] then stationed at San Francisco, proceeded to Portland, in Oregon, to organize a campaign against them.

On the 7th and 8th of December, 1855, a desperate battle was fought near the Walla-Walla River, between some volunteers and a large body of Indians, who lost their chief in the engagement, and were defeated. At about the same time, seven hundred Indians attacked the town of Seattle, in Washington Territory, north of Oregon, when the place was saved by the aid of some gallant marines from the sloop-of-war *Decatur*, lying there, the guns of which were turned upon the savages. During the winter and spring of 1856, these hostilities became quite general in both Territories, and General Wool seemed to be almost powerless in quelling them. On the 25th of March, eight hundred Indians attacked a place in Oregon, called the Cascades, burned every building in the town, and a steamboat, and murdered several citizens. Further north the savages laid waste the whole country; and it appeared, at one time, as if the settlements must be abandoned. Suspicions have been awakened that the depredations in Washington Territory have been instigated by persons connected with the English Hudson's Bay Company, who have married Indian women. Finally, late in summer, the troubles in Oregon were brought to an end, but further north, the knife, and hatchet, and musket were fearfully menacing the white settlements during the autumn. In the mean while there has been troubles with the Indians in California, on the borders of New Mexico and Texas, and in Florida, where a portion of those Seminoles, who have refused to go west of the Mississippi,[2] seem disposed to defy the strong arm of the white people.

Again, at the close of 1854 and during the winter and spring of 1855, circumstances occurred which disturbed the existing harmony of feeling between the governments of the United States and Great Britain. It had been apparent that enlistments of recruits for the English army in the Crimea were going on in American cities, under the sanction of British officials. This fact was certified by the trial of two men at Philadelphia early in the autumn of 1855, on a charge of violating the neutrality laws of the United States. It was then clearly proved that enlistments had been made under the direct sanction of Mr. Crampton, the British minister at Washington. The United States government immediately remonstrated with that of Great Britain, and demanded the recall of Minister Crampton. The latter refused to comply; and timid persons on both sides of the Atlantic prophesied inevitable war between the two countries. After waiting several months, and participating in a friendly diplomatic correspondence with the British Government, the President dismissed Mr. Cramp-

---

[1] Note 3, page 413.

[2] Page 468.

ton, and also the British consuls at New York, Philadelphia, and Cincinnati, because of their complicity in violating neutrality laws. This action did not disturb the friendly relations between the two governments, as had been anticipated. The American minister (Mr. Dallas) remained in London, but the British government had not, in December, 1856, filled the place made vacant by the departure of its representative from Washington.

Indian wars,[1] foreign relations, and almost every other public topic, were, for many months previous to the presidential election in November, 1856, completely overshadowed by the great question of the extension of human slavery into Territories of the United States, then free; and upon that issue was the struggle for ascendancy in the choice of a Chief Magistrate for the Republic, which occurred on the 4th of that month. It has been observed that the passage of the Kansas-Nebraska Act[2] [May 27, 1854], and the repeal of the Missouri Compromise Act,[3] were regarded as ominous of much future trouble. That trouble came with swift feet. The repeal of the Missouri Compromise left *all* territory belonging to the United States open to the social institutions of every section of the Union. Then commenced one of the most desperate struggles between the pro-slavery and anti-slavery people of our country, which had yet been seen. It was a struggle for immediate supremacy in Kansas, and future dominion in all the States yet to be admitted into the Confederation. Emigration to Kansas from the free States was at once urged by the opposers of slavery; and on the 24th of July, 1854 (two months after the repeal of the Missouri Compromise Act), an Emigrant Aid Society, which had been incorporated by the Legislature of Massachusetts in April previous, was formed in Boston. This movement excited the friends of slavery to action; and in Missouri, combinations were at once formed to counteract it, under the various names of "Social Band," "Friends' Society," "Blue Lodge," "The Sons of the South," etc. Emigration soon commenced flowing into Kansas from the free States; and during the period from August to October, 1854, several towns were formed by these people.[4] The Missourians also went into the Territory, and founded several towns;[5] and in October, the appointed governor of Kansas, A. H. Reeder, arrived. With the election in March following [1855], when a Territorial Legislature was chosen, commenced a reign of terror in Kansas, and for more than a year civil war raged in that beautiful land. All classes of men carried deadly weapons about their persons, and a slight or accidental quarrel frequently produced unusual violence. Finally, Governor Reeder departed for Washington [April 19, 1855] to consult with the Federal Government on the affairs of the Territory.

Early in the autumn of 1855, and while the exasperation of both parties in Kansas was at its height, the free State men of the Territory held a convention [Sept. 5], and nominated Governor Reeder as a delegate in Congress, in place

---

[1] Page 527. [2] Page 521. [3] Pages 452 and 501.

[4] The free State settlers founded the towns of Lawrence, Topeka, Boston (now called Manhattan), Grasshopper Falls, Pawnee, and other settlements.

[5] They founded Kickapoo, Doniphan, Atchison, and other places on the Missouri River.

of General Whitfield, who had been chosen at a previous election, not, as was alleged, by the votes of actual settlers, but by those of people from Missouri. Reeder was elected in October; and when, on the 4th of February, 1856, General Whitfield was admitted, provisionally, to a seat in Congress, he contested it with him. On the 11th of November [1855], the free State convention completed a State Constitution, and submitted it to the people; and on the 17th of January following, elections under it were held. On the 24th of that month, the President of the United States sent a special message to Congress, in which he represented the formation of the free State government in Kansas as an act of rebellion.

Troubles still continued. Violence and bloodshed prevailed in that unhappy Territory. The accounts from Kansas being very contradictory and alarming, the House of Representatives, on the 19th of March, appointed a committee of three to proceed thither, investigate the whole matter, and report. They returned to Washington in June; and on the 1st of July the majority of the committee presented their report, which concluded with the following summing up:

"*First.* That each election in the Territory, held under the organic or alleged Territorial law, has been carried by organized invasions from the State of Missouri, by which the people of the Territory have been prevented from exercising the rights secured to them by the organic law.

"*Second.* That the alleged Territorial Legislature was an illegally-constituted body, and had no power to pass valid laws, and their enactments are, therefore, null and void.

"*Third.* That these alleged laws have not, as a general thing, been used to protect persons and property and to punish wrong, but for unlawful purposes.

"*Fourth.* That the election under which the sitting delegate, John W. Whitfield, holds his seat, was not held in pursuance of any valid law, and that it should be regarded only as the expression of the choice of those resident citizens who voted for him.

"*Fifth.* That the election under which the contesting delegate, Andrew H. Reeder, claims his seat, was not held in pursuance of law, and that it should be regarded only as the expression of the choice of the resident citizens who voted for him.

"*Sixth.* That Andrew H. Reeder received a greater number of votes of resident citizens than John W. Whitfield, for delegate.

"*Seventh.* That in the present condition of the Territory, a fair election can not be held without a new census, a stringent and well-guarded election law, the selection of impartial judges, and the presence of United States troops at every place of election.

"*Eighth.* That the various elections held by the people of the Territory, preliminary to the formation of the State government, have been as regular as the disturbed condition of the Territory would allow; and that the Constitution passed by the convention, held in pursuance of said elections, embodies the will of a majority of the people.

"As it is not the province of your committee to suggest remedies for the existing troubles in the Territory of Kansas, they content themselves with the foregoing statement of facts."

The minority report declared the statements of the majority to be *ex parte*, and in many cases untrue; and thus, after a long investigation, and the excitation of high hopes that the committee would unanimously agree, and suggest some plan for the pacification of the Territory, both parties were dissatisfied with the result. As the autumn advanced, and the presidential election approached, disturbances were less frequent and general. Isolated cases of violence, committed by persons of both parties, frequently occurred, and order was not fully restored when the year drew toward a close. The time when peace and prosperity shall prevail in that unhappy country, was yet an unsolved question. The events which have transpired there, appear as a foul blot upon our national escutcheon; and the year 1856 will be looked back upon by American citizens with the deepest mortification, as an era of national disgrace. But the time has not yet arrived to write a truthful history of events there. There is now too much of the smoke of error to perceive the truth in its clearness. The pabulum of all the difficulty is the question of the extension of slavery over territory yet free, compounded with the selfish ambition of demagogues who are governed by those seven controlling principles—five loaves and two fishes.

The question of the extension of slavery has now assumed a form and dimension, which loom above all other national topics. Under its influence new political organizations have grown up; and in the presidential campaign of 1856, three contestants for the office of Chief Magistrate of the Republic, appeared, each the representative of a distinct party. For more than a year previously, a new organization, composed of men of all political creeds, united in opposition to the extension of slavery, had been gathering force and bulk, until, when the presidential contest came on [November 4, 1856], it had assumed giant proportions in the Free States, and was looked upon kindly by many in the slave States. This is known as the *Republican* party. Long before its advent, another organization, at first secret in its operations, and known as the *American* or *Know-Nothing* party, had become a great political power in the country, its chief bond of union being opposition to foreign influence, and the domination of Roman Catholicism in our political affairs. The old *Democratic* party, dating its modern organization at the election of President Jackson in 1828,[1] had become divided and weakened; while the old *Whig* party[2] was virtually annihilated as a distinct organization, having real vitality. Thus appeared the several partisan forces early in 1856, when the leaders of each prepared to choose their respective standard-bearers for the presidential campaign.

The *American* party held a national convention in Philadelphia, in February, 1856; and on the 22d of that month, nominated ex-President Fillmore,[3] for re-election to the high office he had once held. Andrew J. Donelson, of Tennessee,[4] was nominated for Vice-President. Subsequently, some of the Americans, disagreeing with their brethren on the subject of slavery, repudiated that nomination, but Mr. Fillmore continued his position as a nominee, and went into the election, having the support of a large number of the old Whig party. The two wings of the Democratic party became partially reconciled later in the season; and on the 2d of June, delegates from each met in national convention at Cincinnati. After several ballotings, on the 5th, James Buchanan[5] of Pennsylvania was unanimously nominated for President, and John C. Breckinridge, of Kentucky, for Vice-President. A national convention of Republican delegates assembled at Philadelphia on the 17th of June,

[1] Page 459. [2] Note 2, page 466. [3] Note 5, page 501.
[4] Note 1, page 479. [5] Page 522.

and nominated John C. Fremont,[1] of California, for President, and William L. Dayton, of New Jersey, for Vice-President. The Democratic and Republican conventions promulgated, by resolutions, their respective principles and policy, to which the candidate of each subscribed, while the nominee of the American party referred his countrymen to his past acts as the exponents of his principles.

James Buchanan

Never, since the election of General Harrison, in 1840,[2] had there been so much excitement in the country, as during the presidential campaign of 1856. The great question of the extension of slavery was the leading topic with the Republicans; while all parties used extraordinary efforts in support of their respective candidates. The contest finally ended on the 4th of November, and resulted in the election of James Buchanan,[3] as President of the United

[1] Page 488. [2] Page 473.

[3] James Buchanan was born in Franklin county, Pennsylvania, on the 23d of April, 1791. He was educated at Dickenson College, where he was graduated at the age of eighteen years. In 1809 he was admitted to the bar, and was soon in successful practice in his native State. In 1814, when only twenty-three years of age, he was elected to a seat in the Legislature of Pennsylvania. This was his first prominent appearance in public life. In 1815 he distinguished himself in his State Legislature as an opponent of the United States Bank, and became one of the foremost men in the Republican party. He was elected to Congress in 1820, and there he soon became distinguished as a speaker and debater. After ten years' service, he retired from Congress in 1831, when President Jackson appointed him minister to Russia. In 1833 he was elected to the United States Senate, where he also served ten years. President Polk called him to his cabinet, as Secretary of State; and in 1849 he again retired to private life. In 1853 he was appointed minister to England; and in June, 1856, he was nominated for President of the United States. In November following he was elected to that high office. Mr. Buchanan was then in the sixty-sixth year of his age.

States, and of John C. Breckinridge, as Vice-President. The people of our beloved Union—the great conservative masses who cling to it as the ark of freedom for the world—acquiesced gracefully in the choice of the majority, and, with true faith, will ever hope for good things, while, with true love for our free institutions, they will work nobly for their perpetuation. Mr. Buchanan was inaugurated the fifteenth President of the United States, on the 4th of March, 1857.

The question of slavery still looms up, dark and ominous, asking for a solution. In it are involved the principles of moral right, political and social expediency, and a great pecuniary interest. It has ever been a vexing and perplexing question, and has produced more heart-burnings—more "envy, hatred, and malice, and all uncharitableness," among our people, than all other national questions which have arisen since the birth of the Republic. The prolific seed of the institution was brought here and planted, early; and its mighty fruition is now our GREAT AND ABIDING TROUBLE. In the same year when the Pilgrim Fathers,[1] fleeing from spiritual slavery, landed on the bleak shores of Massachusetts Bay, a Dutch vessel carried Africans to Virginia, and sold them to the English settlers there.[2] To the humane impulses of Las Casas, a sagacious Romish priest, Western Africa is indebted for all its troubles connected with the foreign slave-trade. He had long witnessed the sufferings of the weak and gentle natives of the West India Islands, under the cruel rigors of Spanish bondage.[3] He saw them perish by thousands; and, moved by pity, he suggested that the more hardy Africans, who were continually at war with each other, and sold their captives into slavery, should be substituted. The sanction of the Pope to this traffic was speedily obtained; and before the close of the 16th century, the whole Atlantic coast of Africa between the tropics, became one great slave mart. That traffic had no justification in English laws, nor early colonial statutes; yet it was permitted as a matter of policy; and custom, in process of time, assumed the dignity of common law.

When the Declaration of Independence was promulgated, its precepts struck at the root of human bondage in every form; and efforts were made, in several States, to eradicate the institution, sometimes in the form of propositions for immediate, and at others for gradual, emancipation. It had been expelled from England by the decision of Lord Mansfield, just before the kindling of the American Revolution;[4] and the most enlightened men in the colonies, regarding it with great disfavor, attempts were made, from time to time, to limit it.

---

[1] Page 77. [2] Note 6, page 105. [3] Page 41.

[4] This decision was in the case of James Somerset, a native of Africa, who was carried to Virginia, and sold as a slave, taken to England by his master, and there induced to assert his freedom. The first case of a similar nature on record in England, was in 1697, when it was held that negroes "being usually bought and sold among merchants, as merchandise, and also being infidels, there might be a property in them sufficient to maintain trover." This position was overruled by Chief Justice Holt, who decided that "so soon as a negro lands in England, he is free." To this decision Cowper alludes, when he says, "Slaves can not breathe in England." In 1702, Justice Holt also decided that "there is no such thing as a slave by the law of England." In 1729, an opinion was obtained, that "negroes legally enslaved elsewhere might be held as slaves in England, and that baptism was no bar to the master's claim." This was held as good law until Mansfield's decision above mentioned.

Among others, the famous ordinance of 1787, for the government of the territory of the United States, north-west of the Ohio,[1] known as the *North-western Territory*, stands forth prominent.[2]

Although the words "slave" and "slavery" do not appear in the Federal Constitution, yet the institution is recognized there by fair implication, and the force of its provisions may not be evaded.[3] This was one of the important compromises which the framers found necessary in order to have the sanction of a requisite number of States for that instrument.[4] There stand the clauses, impregnable against sophistry, and their force can only be shaken or destroyed by actual amendment of the Constitution, in prescribed form. But to the several States, power to abolish the institution from within their respective limits, was conceded; and in the course of years, several of the northern members of the Confederacy cast off the system by legislative enactments.[5] In Delaware, Maryland, Virginia, and Kentucky, there has been wide-spread discontent with slavery, as a social and economical institution. The ethical features of the question seem to admit of little controversy. It is its material features—its relation to the material and social interests of our common country, in which are involved vast private pecuniary interests—that claim attention. In this view of the case, all of the perplexing lineaments of the question are to be seen. These should be discussed with candor and forbearance. Harshness of speech is not argument, and never produces conviction. Harshness of action is not manly, and irritates rather than convinces; and mutual recriminations, ungenerous expressions, and flippant censures, only tend to alienate the affections of those who ought to live as brothers, conceding to each other sincerity of feeling and honesty of motives. To us and our institutions the nations of the Old World, aspiring to be free, are looking with anxious hearts and straining eyes, as the main hope of freedom for the race. Let us be true to our mission as the ark-bearers of Human Liberty; and let each, in the spirit of true brotherly kindness, say to his neighbor, on all occasions—If thou hast a truth to utter, speak, and leave the result to God.

We dare not attempt to lift the vail of the future, or predict the events of

---

[1] Page 362.

[2] In 1784, efforts were made in the Continental Congress to restrict slavery. A select committee was appointed, consisting of Thomas Jefferson (the author of the Declaration of Independence), as chairman, and Messrs. Chase of Maryland (one of the signers of the Declaration), and Howell of Rhode Island. They reported a plan for the government of the *Western Territory*, then including the whole region west of the old thirteen States, as far south as the thirty-first degree of north latitude, and embracing several of our present slave States. The plan contemplated the ultimate division of this territory into seventeen States, eight of them below the latitude of the present city of Louisville, in Kentucky. Among the rules for the government of that region, reported by Mr. Jefferson, was the following: "That after the year 1800 of the Christian era, there shall be neither slavery nor involuntary servitude in any of the said States, otherwise than in punishment of crimes, whereof the party shall have been convicted to be personally guilty." This clause was stricken out [April 19, 1784], on motion of Mr. Spaight, of North Carolina, seconded by Mr. Read, of South Carolina. A majority of the States were against striking it out, but the Articles of Confederation required a vote of nine States to carry a proposition. See *Journals of Congress*. In the ordinance of 1787 [see page 362], this rule, omitting the words "after the year 1800 of the Christian era," was incorporated.

[3] See Federal Constitution, Supplement, No. VII.

[4] Vermont was the only State in which slavery never existed.

[5] Note 4, page 177.

to-morrow. Never was the human mind so active as now. There is a comparative quiet in the political and social atmosphere of the nations, but it is only the calm before the storm. There are cruel wrongs to be redressed—fearful reckonings to be made; and in those days, the people of the United States will bear a conspicuous part as umpires.

Here, on the verge of great events yet to be developed in the Old and New World, we pause in our wonderful story of the discovery,[1] settlement,[2] and colonization[3] of this beautiful land, and the establishment of one of the noblest Republics the world ever saw, covering with the broad ægis of its power, a territory as extensive as that of old Rome in her palmiest days, when she was mistress of the world.[4] At the present we are engaged in the marvelous labor of founding new States, with a facility and power hitherto unknown. In our history, the nineteenth century will be distinguished as the era of the birth of mighty empires—empires brought forth in the wildernesses of a vast continent—at whose baptism, statesmen and gospel-bearers, brave soldiers and gentle women, stand as sponsors, while the children of the forest look on in sorrow, for the ring of the hammer upon every corner-stone of the structures of civilization, is the knell of their extinction. Over them the free eagle may perch, as the emblem of their former sovereignty; but the setting sun just above the peaks of the western hills, or over the billows of the Pacific, more truly symbolizes their present and their future. Let us not take special pride in the extent and physical grandeur of our beloved country, but endeavor to have our hearts and minds thoroughly penetrated with the glorious thoughts of Alcæus of Mytelene, who asked and answered—

"What constitutes a State?
Not high-raised battlement, or labored mound,
Thick wall or moated gate;
Not cities proud, with spires and turrets crowned;
Not bays, and broad-armed ports,
Where, laughing at the storms, rich navies ride;
Not starred and spangled courts,
Where low-browed baseness wafts perfume to pride.
No: men, high-minded men,
With powers as far above dull brutes endued,

---

[1] Page 40. [2] Page 61. [3] Page 104.

[4] The territorial extent of our Republic is ten times as large as that of Great Britain and France combined; three times as large as the whole of France, Britain, Austria, Prussia, Spain, Portugal, Belgium, Holland, and Denmark together; one and a half times as large as the Russian empire in Europe, and only one sixth less than the area covered by the sixty States and Empires of Europe. The entire area in 1853, was 2,983,153 square miles. The internal trade of the United States is of vast extent. Its value amounted in 1853 (Lake and Western River trade), to more than $560,000,000, in which about 11,000,000 of our people are directly or indirectly interested. According to the seventh enumeration of inhabitants of the United States, made in 1850, the total number was 23,191,876, of whom 19,553,068, are white people; 434,495, free colored; and 3,204,313 slaves. Taking the increase of population from 1840 to 1850, as a basis for calculation, we may safely conclude the population of the United States to be, at this time [December, 1856], about 28,000,000. The most accessible works, in which are given, in detail, the progress of political events in the United States, from the formation of the Constitution until the present time, are Hildreth's *History of the United States*, second series; and Williams's *Statesman's Manual*. The former closes with the year 1821; the latter is continued to the present year.

In forest, brake, or den,
As brutes excel cold rocks and brambles rude—
Men, who their duties know,
But know their rights, and knowing, dare maintain;
Prevent the long-aimed blow,
And crush the tyrant while they rend the chain—
These constitute a *State*."

Or with the more subtle thoughts of our own Simms, of South Carolina, who wrote—

"The moral of the race is in the State,
The secret germ for great development,
Through countless generations:—all the hopes,
The aims, the great ambition, the proud works,
Virtues, performances, high desires, and deeds,
With countless pure and precious sentiments,
Nursed in some few brave souls, that, still apart
From the rude hunger of the multitude,
Light fires, build altars, image out the God
That makes the grand ideal.
* * * . A State 's the growth
Of the great family of a thousand years,
With all its grand community of thought,
Affections, faith, sentiments, as well
As its material treasures. These are naught
If that the faith, the virtues, and the will
Be lacking to the race. The guardian State
Keeps these immaculate. They are not yours,
Or mine; nor do they rest within the charge
Of the mere feeders at the common crib,
Of all the myriads keeping pace with us,
Some seventy years of march."

Founding New States.

SUPPLEMENT.

STATE PAPERS.

SUPPLEMENT.

I.

THE STAMP ACT.

THE idea of producing a revenue by the sale of stamps and stamped paper in America was promulgated almost forty years before its final development in legislative enactment in 1765.[1] Sir William Keith advised the policy as early as 1728. In 1739 the London merchants advised the ministry to adopt the measure, and public writers from time to time suggested various ideas predicated upon the same idea. In 1750, Douglas, in his work on British America, recommended the levying of a stamp duty upon all legal writings and instruments. Dr. Franklin regarded the plan favorably; and Governor Sharpe of Maryland, was confident, in 1754, that Parliament would speedily make a statute for raising money by means of stamp duties. Lieutenant-Governor Delancey spoke in favor of it in the New York Assembly in 1755, and the following year, Governor Shirley, of Massachusetts, urged Parliament to adopt a stamp tax. The British press urged the measure in 1757, and it was confidently stated, that at least three hundred thousand dollars annually might thus be drawn from the colonies, without the tax being sensibly felt. But William Pitt would not listen to the recommendation, for, like Walpole, twenty-five years before, he preferred to draw money into the treasury by the exercise of a liberal commercial policy toward the Americans. Notwithstanding public opinion in England appeared to be decidedly favorable to the measure, it was not proposed by the ministry until 1764. It became a law in 1765, and was repealed in 1766. Had not ministers been deceived by the representations of the stupid and selfish royal governors in America, it probably would never have been enacted. Those men were frequently too indolent or indifferent to make themselves acquainted with the real temper of the people. Regarding the mass as equally servile as their flatterers, they readily commended that fatal measure which proved the spark that lighted the flames of Revolution, and severed forever the political connection between Great Britain and thirteen of her American colonies.

The following is a copy of the famous Stamp Act of 1765:

WHEREAS, by an act made in the last session of Parliament, several duties were granted, continued, and appropriated toward defraying the expenses of

[1] Page 213.

defending, protecting, and securing the British colonies and plantations in America; and whereas it is just and necessary that provision be made for raising a further revenue within your majesty's dominions in America, toward defraying the said expenses; we, your majesty's most dutiful and loyal subjects, the Commons of Great Britain, in Parliament assembled, have therefore resolved to give and grant unto your majesty the several rates and duties hereinafter mentioned; and do humbly beseech your majesty that it may be enacted, and be it enacted by the king's most excellent majesty, by and with the advice and consent of the lords spiritual and temporal, and commons, in this present Parliament assembled, and by the authority of the same, that from and after the first day of November, one thousand seven hundred and sixty-five, there shall be raised, levied, collected, and paid unto his majesty, his heirs, and successors, throughout the colonies and plantations in America, which now are, or hereafter may be, under the dominion of his majesty, his heirs and successors:

For every skin or piece of vellum or parchment, or sheet or piece of paper, on which shall be engrossed, written, or printed, any declaration, plea, replication, rejoinder, demurrer, or other pleading, or any copy thereof, in any court of law within the British colonies and plantations in America, a stamp duty of three pence.

For every skin or piece of vellum or parchment, or sheet or piece of paper, on which shall be engrossed, written, or printed, any special bail, and appearance upon such bail in any such court, a stamp duty of two shillings.

For every skin or piece of vellum or parchment, or sheet or piece of paper, on which may be engrossed, written, or printed, any petition, bill, answer, claim, plea, replication, rejoinder, demurrer, or other pleading, in any court of chancery or equity within the said colonies and plantations, a stamp duty of one shilling and sixpence.

For every skin or piece of vellum or parchment, or sheet or piece of paper, on which shall be engrossed, written, or printed, *any copy* of any petition, bill, answer, claim, plea, replication, rejoinder, demurrer, or other pleading in any such court, a stamp duty of three pence.

For every skin or piece of vellum or parchment, or sheet or piece of paper, on which shall be engrossed, written, or printed, any motion, libel, answer, allegation, inventory, or renunciation in ecclesiastical matters, in any court of probate, court of the ordinary, or other court exercising ecclesiastical jurisdiction within the said colonies and plantations, a stamp duty of *one shilling*.

For every skin or piece of vellum or parchment, or sheet or piece of paper, on which shall be engrossed, written, or printed, any copy of any will (other than the probate thereof), monition, libel, answer, allegation, inventory, or renunciation in ecclesiastical matters, in any such court, a stamp duty of *six pence*.

For every skin or piece of vellum or parchment, or sheet or piece of paper, on which shall be engrossed, written, or printed, any donation, presentation, collation, or institution, of or to any benefice, or any writ or instrument for the like purpose, or any register, entry, testimonial, or certificate of any degree taken in any university, academy, college, or seminary of learning within the said colonies and plantations, a stamp duty of *two pounds.*

For every skin or piece of vellum or parchment, or sheet or piece of paper, on which shall be engrossed, written, or printed, any monition, libel, claim, answer, allegation, information, letter of request, execution, renunciation, inventory, or other pleading, in any admiralty court within the said colonies and plantations, a stamp duty of *one shilling.*

For every skin or piece of vellum or parchment, or sheet or piece of paper, on which any copy of any such monition, libel, claim, answer, allegation, information, letter of request, execution, renunciation, inventory, or other pleading, shall be engrossed, written, or printed, a stamp duty of *six pence.*

For every skin or piece of vellum or parchment, or sheet or piece of paper, on which shall be engrossed, written, or printed, any appeal, writ of error, writ of dower, *ad quod damnum*, certiorari, statute merchant, statute staple, attestation, or certificate, by any officer, or exemplification of any record or proceeding, in any court whatsoever, within the said colonies and plantations (except appeals, writs of error, certiorari, attestations, certificates, and exemplifications, for, or relating to the removal of any proceedings from before a single justice of the peace), a stamp duty of *ten shillings.*

For every skin or piece of vellum or parchment, or sheet or piece of paper, on which shall be engrossed, written, or printed, any writ of covenant for levying fines, writ of entry for suffering a common recovery, or attachment issuing out of, or returnable into, any court within the said colonies and plantations, a stamp duty of *five shillings.*

For every skin or piece of vellum or parchment, or sheet or piece of paper, on which shall be engrossed, written, or printed, any judgment, decree, sentence, or dismission, or any record of *nisi prius* or *postea*, in any court within the said colonies and plantations, a stamp duty of *four shillings.*

For every skin or piece of vellum or parchment, or sheet or piece of paper, on which shall be engrossed, written, or printed, any affidavit, common bail, or appearance, interrogatory, deposition, rule, order or warrant of any court, or any *dedimus potestatem*, *capias subpœna*, summons, compulsory citation, commission, recognizance, or any other writ, process, or mandate, issuing out of, or returnable into, any court, or any office belonging thereto, or any other proceeding therein, whatsoever, or any copy thereof, or of any record not herein before charged, within the said colonies and plantations (except warrants relating to criminal matters, and proceedings thereon, or relating thereto,) a stamp duty of *one shilling.*

For every skin or piece of vellum or parchment, or sheet or piece of paper, on which shall be engrossed, written, or printed, any note or bill of lading, which shall be signed for any kind of goods, wares, or merchandise, to be exported from, or any cocket or clearance granted within the said colonies and plantations, a stamp duty of four pence.

For every skin or piece of vellum or parchment, or sheet or pieee of paper, on which shall be engrossed, written, or printed, letters of mart or commission for private ships of war, within the said colonies and plantations, a stamp duty of *twenty shillings.*

For every skin or piece of vellum or parchment, or sheet or piece of paper, on which shall be engrossed, written, or printed, any grant, appointment, or admission of, or to, any public beneficial office or employment, for the space of one year, or any lesser time, of or above *twenty pounds per annum*, sterling money, in salary, fees, and perquisites, within the said colonies and plantations (except commissions and appointments of officers of the army, navy, ordnance, or militia, of judges, and of justices of the peace), a stamp duty of *ten shillings.*

For every skin or piece of vellum or parchment, or sheet or piece of paper, on which any grant of any liberty, privilege, or franchise, under the seal or sign-manual of any governor, proprietor, or public officer, alone, or in conjunction with any other person or persons, or with any council, or any council and assembly, or any exemplification of the same, shall be engrossed, written, or printed, within the said colonies and plantations, a stamp duty of *six pounds.*

For every skin or piece of vellum or parchment, or sheet or piece of paper, on which shall be engrossed, written, or printed, any license for retailing of spirituous liquors, to be granted to any person who shall take out the same, within the said colonies and plantations, a stamp duty of *twenty shillings.*

For every skin or piece of vellum or parchment, or sheet or piece of paper, on which shall be engrossed, written, or printed, any license for retailing of wine, to be granted to any person who shall not take out a license for retailing of spirituous liquors, within the said colonies and plantations, a stamp duty of *four pounds.*

For every skin or piece of vellum or parchment, or sheet or piece of paper, on which shall be engrossed, written, or printed, any license for retailing of wine, to be granted to any person who shall take out a license for retailing of spirituous liquors, within the said colonies and plantations, a stamp duty of *three pounds.*

For every skin or piece of vellum or parchment, or sheet or piece of paper, on which shall be engrossed, written, or printed, any probate of will, letters of administration, or of guardianship for any estate above the value of twenty pounds, sterling money, within the British colonies and plantations upon the continent of America, the islands belonging thereto, and the Bermuda and Bahama Islands, a stamp duty of *five shillings.*

For every skin or piece of vellum or parchment, or sheet or piece of paper, on which shall be engrossed, written, or printed, any such probate, letters of administration or of guardianship, within all other parts of the British dominions in America, a stamp duty of *ten shillings.*

For every skin or piece of vellum or parchment, or sheet or piece of paper, on which shall be engrossed, written, or printed, any bond for securing the payment of any sum of money, not exceeding the sum of ten pounds sterling money, within the British colonies and plantations upon the continent of America, the islands belonging thereto, and the Bermuda and Bahama Islands, a stamp duty of *six pence.*

For every skin or piece of vellum or parchment, or sheet or piece of paper, on which shall be engrossed, written, or printed, any bond for securing the payment of any sum of money above ten pounds, and not exceeding twenty pounds sterling money, within such colonies, plantations and islands, a stamp duty of *one shilling.*

For every skin or piece of vellum or parchment, or sheet or piece of paper, on which shall be engrossed, written, or printed, any bond for securing the payment of any sum of money above twenty pounds, and not exceeding forty pounds sterling money, within such colonies, plantations, and islands, a stamp duty of *one shilling and six pence.*

For every skin or piece of vellum or parchment, or sheet or piece of paper, on which shall be engrossed, written, or printed, any order or warrant for surveying or setting out any quantity of land, not exceeding one hundred acres, issued by any governor, proprietor, or any public officer, alone, or in conjunction with any other person or persons, or with any council, or any council and assembly, within the British colonies and plantations in America, a stamp duty of *six pence.*

For every skin or piece of vellum or parchment, or sheet or piece of paper, on which shall be engrossed, written, or printed, any such order or warrant for surveying or setting out any quantity of land above one hundred, and not exceeding two hundred acres, within the said colonies and plantations, a stamp duty of *one shilling.*

For every skin or piece of vellum or parchment, or sheet or piece of paper, on which shall be engrossed, written, or printed, any such order or warrant for surveying or setting out any quantity of land above two hundred, and not exceeding three hundred and twenty acres, and in proportion for every such order or warrant for surveying or setting out every other three hundred and twenty acres within the said colonies and plantations, a stamp duty of *one shilling and six pence.*

For every skin or piece of vellum or parchment, or sheet or piece of paper, on which shall be engrossed, written, or printed, any original grant, or any deed, mesne conveyance, or other instrument whatsoever, by which any quantity of land, not exceeding one hundred acres, shall be granted, conveyed, or assigned, within the British colonies or plantations upon the continent of America, the islands belonging thereto, and the Bermuda and Bahama Islands (except leases for any term not exceeding the term of twenty-one years), a stamp duty of *one shilling and six pence.*

For every skin or piece of vellum or parchment, or sheet or piece of paper, on which shall be engrossed, written, or printed, any such original grant, or any such deed, mesne conveyance, or other instrument whatsoever, by which any quantity of land above one hundred, and not exceeding two hundred acres, shall be granted, conveyed, or assigned, within such colonies, plantations, and islands, a stamp duty of *two shillings.*

For every skin or piece of vellum or parchment, or sheet or piece of paper, on which shall be engrossed, written, or printed, any such original grant, or any such deed, mesne conveyance, or other instrument whatsoever, by which any quantity of land above two hundred, and not exceeding three hundred and twenty acres, shall be granted, conveyed, or assigned, and in proportion for every such grant, deed, mesne conveyance, or other instrument, granting, conveying, or assigning, overy other three hundred and twenty acres, within such colonies, plantations, and islands, a stamp duty of *two shillings and six pence.*

For every skin or piece of vellum or parchment, or sheet or piece of paper, on which shall be engrossed, written, or printed, any such original grant, or any such deed, mesne conveyance, or other instrument whatsoever, by which any quantity of land, not exceeding one hundred acres, shall be granted, conveyed, or assigned, within all other parts of the British dominions in America, a stamp duty of *three shillings.*

For every skin or piece of vellum or parchment, or sheet or piece of paper, on which shall be engrossed, written, or printed, any such original grant, or any such deed, mesne conveyance, or other instrument whatsoever, by which any quadtity of land above one hundred, and not exceeding two hundred acres, shall be granted, conveyed, or assigned, within the same parts of the said dominions, a stamp duty of *four shillings.*

For every skin or piece of vellum or parchment, or sheet or piece of paper, on which shall be engrossed, written, or printed, any such original grant, or any such deed, mesne conveyance, or other instrument whatsoever, by which any quantity of land above two hundred, and not exceeding three hundred and twenty acres, shall be granted, conveyed, or assigned, and in proportion for every such grant, deed, mesne conveyance, or other instrument, granting, conveying, or assigning, every other three hundred and twenty acres, within the same parts of the said dominions, a stamp duty of *five shillings.*

For every skin or piece of vellum or parchment, or sheet or piece of paper, on which shall be engrossed, written, or printed, any grant, appointment, or admission, of or to any beneficial office or employment, not herein before charged, above the value of twenty pounds per annum sterling money, in salary, fees, and perquisites, or any exemplification of the same, within the British colonies and plantations upon the continent of America, the islands belonging thereto, and the Bermuda and Bahama Islands (except commissions of officers of the army, navy, ordnance, or militia, and of justices of the peace), a stamp duty of *four pounds.*

For every skin or piece of vellum or parchment, or sheet or piece of paper, on which shall be engrossed, written, or printed, any such grant, appointment, or admission, of or to any such public beneficial office or employment, or any exemplificatton of the same, within all other parts of the British dominions in America, a stamp duty of *six pounds.*

For every skin or piece of vellum or parchment, or sheet or piece of paper, on which shall be engrossed, written, or printed, any indenture, lease, conveyance, contract, stipulation, bill of sale, charter party, protest, articles of apprenticeship or covenant (except the hire of servants not apprentices, and also except such other matters as herein before charged), within the British colonies and plantations in America, a stamp duty of *two shillings and six pence.*

For every skin or piece of vellum or parchment, or sheet or piece of paper, on which any warrant or order for auditing any public accounts, beneficial warrant, order, grant, or certificate, under any public seal, or under the seal or sign-manual of any governor, proprietor, or public officer, alone, or in conjunction with any person or persons, or with any council, or any council and assembly, hot herein before charged, or any passport or let-pass, surrender of office, or policy of assurance, shall be engrossed, written, or printed, within the said colonies and plantations (except warrants or orders for the service of the army, navy, ordnance, or militia, and grants of offices under twenty pounds per annum, in salary, fees, and perquisites), a stamp duty of *five shillings.*

For every skin or piece of vellum or parchment, or sheet or piece of paper, on which shall be engrossed, written, or printed, any notarial act, bond, deed, letter of attorney, procuration, mortgage, release, or other obligatory instrument, not herein before charged, within the said colonies and plantations, a stamp duty of *two shillings and three pence.*

For every skin or piece of vellum or parchment, or sheet or piece of paper, on which shall be engrossed, written, or printed, any register, entry, or enrollment of any grant, deed, or other instrument whatsover, herein before charged, within the said colonies and plantations, a stamp duty of *three pence.*

For every skin or piece of vellum or parchment, or sheet or piece of paper, on which shall be engrossed, written, or printed, any register, entry, or enrollment of any grant, deed, or other instrument whatsoever, not herein before charged, within the said colonies and plantations, a stamp duty of *two shillings.*

And for and upon every pack of playing-cards, and all dice, which shall be sold or used within the said colonies and plantations, the several stamp duties following (that is to say):

For every pack of such cards, one shilling.

For every pair of such dice, ten shillings.

And for and upon every paper called a *pamphlet*, and upon every newspaper, containing public news or occurrences, which shall be printed, dispersed, and made public, within any of the said colonies and plantations, and for and upon such advertisements as are hereinafter mentioned, the respective duties following (that is to say):

For every such pamphlet and paper contained in a half sheet, or any lesser piece of paper which shall be so printed, a stamp duty of one half penny for every printed copy thereof.

For every such pamphlet and paper (being larger than a half sheet, and not exceeding one whole sheet), which shall be printed, a stamp duty of one penny for every printed copy thereof.

For every pamphlet and paper, being larger than one whole sheet, and not exceeding six sheets in octavo, or in a lesser page, or not exceeding twelve sheets in quarto, or twenty sheets in folio, which shall be so printed, a duty after the rate of one shilling for every sheet of any kind of paper which shall be contained in one printed copy thereof.

For every advertisement to be contained in any gazette, newspaper, or other paper, or any pamphlet which shall be so printed, a duty of two shillings.

For every *almanac*, or calendar, for any one particular year, or for any time less than a year, which shall be written or printed on one side only of any one sheet, skin, or piece of paper, parchment, or vellum, within the said colonies and plantations, a stamp duty of *two pence.*

For every other almanac or calendar, for any one particular year, which shall be written or printed within the said colonies and plantations, a stamp duty of *four pence.*

And for every almanac or calendar, written or printed in the said colonies and plantations, to serve for several years, duties to the same amount respectively shall be paid for every such year.

For every skin or piece of vellum or parchment, or sheet or piece of paper, on which any instrument, proceeding, or other matter or thing aforesaid, shall be engrossed, written, or printed, within the said colonies or plantations, in any other than the English language, a stamp duty of double the amount of the respective duties before charged thereon.

And there shall be also paid, in the said colonies and plantations, a duty of six pence for every twenty shillings, in any sum not exceeding fifty pounds sterling money, which shall be given, paid, contracted, or agreed for, with, or in relation to, any clerk or apprentice, which shall be put or placed to or with any master or mistress, to learn any profession, trade, or employment. II. And also a duty of one shilling for every twenty shillings, in any sum exceeding fifty pounds, which shall be given, paid, contracted, or agreed for, with, or in relation to, any such clerk or apprentice.

Finally, the produce of all the aforementioned duties shall be paid into his majesty's treasury, and there held in reserve, to be used from time to time by the Parliament, for the purpose of defraying the expenses necessary for the defense, protection, and security of the said colonies and plantations.

II.

STATE PAPERS PUT FORTH BY THE STAMP ACT CONGRESS, IN 1765.

DECLARATION OF RIGHTS.[1]

THE members of this Congress, sincerely devoted, with the warmest sentiments of affection and duty, to his Majesty's person and government, inviolably attached to the present happy establishment of the Protestant succession, and with minds deeply impressed by a sense of the present and impending misfortunes of the British colonies on this continent; having considered, as maturely as time will permit, the circumstances of the said colonies, esteem it our indispensable duty to make the following declarations of our humble opinion, respecting the most essential rights and liberties of the colonists, and of the grievances under which they labor, by reason of several late acts of Parliament.

I. That his majesty's subjects in these colonies owe the same allegiance to the crown of Great Britain that is owing from his subjects born within the realm, and all due subordination to that august body the Parliament of Great Britain.

II. That his majesty's liege subjects in these colonies are entitled to all the inherent rights and liberties of his natural-born subjects within the kingdom of Great Britain.

III. That it is inseparably essential to the freedom of a people, and the undoubted right of Englishmen, that no taxes be imposed on them but with their own consent, given personally, or by their representatives.

IV. That the people of these colonies are not, and, from local circumstances, can not be, represented in the House of Commons in Great Britain.

V. That the only representatives of the people of these colonies are persons chosen therein by themselves, and that no taxes ever have been, or can be constitutionally imposed on them, but by their respective Legislatures.

VI. That all supplies to the crown being free gifts of the people, it is unreasonable and inconsistent with the spirit of the British constitution for the people of Great Britain to grant to his majesty the property of the colonists.

VII. That trial by jury is the inherent and invaluable right of every British subject in these colonies.

VIII. That the late act of Parliament, entitled, *An act for granting and applying certain stamp duties, and other duties, in the British colonies and*

---

[1] Adopted October 19, 1765. Written by John Cruger, of New York.

plantations in America, &c., by imposing taxes on the inhabitants of these colonies, and the said act, and several other acts, by extending the jurisdiction of the courts of admiralty beyond its ancient limits, have a manifest tendency to subvert the rights and liberties of the colonists.

IX. That the duties imposed by several late acts of Parliament, from the peculiar circumstances of these colonies, will be extremely burdensome and grievous; and, from the scarcity of specie, the payment of them absolutely impracticable.

X. That as the profits of the trade of these colonies ultimately center in Great Britain, to pay for the manufactures which they are obliged to take from thence, they eventually contribute very largely to all supplies granted there to the crown.

XI. That the restrictions imposed by several late acts of Parliament on the trade of these colonies, will render them unable to purchase the manufactures of Great Britain.

XII. That the increase, prosperity, and happiness of these colonies depend on the full and free enjoyment of their rights and liberties, and an intercourse with Great Britain mutually affectionate and advantageous.

XIII. That it is the right of the British subjects in these colonies to petition the king, or either House of Parliament.

Lastly, That it is the indispensable duty of these colonies, to the best of sovereigns, to the mother country, and to themselves, to endeavor, by a loyal and dutiful address to his majesty, and humble applications to both Houses of Parliament, to procure the repeal of the act for granting and applying certain stamp duties, of all clauses of any other acts of Parliament, whereby the jurisdiction of the admiralty is extended as aforesaid, and of the other late acts for the restriction of American commerce.

PETITION TO THE KING.[1]

The petition of the Freeholders and other Inhabitants of the colonies of Massachusetts Bay, Rhode Island and Providence Plantations, New York, New Jersey, Pennsylvania, the government of the counties of New Castle, Kent, and Sussex, upon Delaware, and province of Maryland,

Most humbly showeth,

That the inhabitants of these colonies, unanimously devoted with the warmest sentiments of duty and affection to your sacred person and government, and inviolably attached to the present happy establishment of the Protestant succession in your illustrious house, and deeply sensible of your royal attention to

[1] Adopted October 22, 1765. Written by Robert R. Livingston, of New York.

their prosperity and happiness, humbly beg leave to approach the throne, by representing to your majesty, that these colonies were originally planted by subjects of the British crown, who, animated with the spirit of liberty, encouraged by your majesty's royal predecessors, and confiding in the public faith for the enjoyment of all the rights and liberties essential to freedom, emigrated from their native country to this continent, and, by their successful perseverance, in the midst of innumerable dangers and difficulties, together with a profusion of their blood and treasure, have happily added these vast and extensive dominions to the Empire of Great Britain.

That, for the enjoyment of these rights and liberties, several governments were early formed in the said colonies, with full power of legislation, agreeably to the principles of the English constitution; that, under these governments, these liberties, thus vested in their ancestors, and transmitted to their posterity, have been exercised and enjoyed, and by the inestimable blessings thereof, under the favor of Almighty God, the inhospitable deserts of America have been converted into flourishing countries; science, humanity, and the knowledge of divine truths diffused through remote regions of ignorance, infidelity, and barbarism; the number of British subjects wonderfully increased, and the wealth and power of Great Britain proportionably augmented.

That, by means of these settlements and the unparalleled success of your majesty's arms, a foundation is now laid for rendering the British empire the most extensive and powerful of any recorded in history; our connexion with this empire we esteem our greatest happiness and security, and humbly conceive it may now be so established by your royal wisdom, as to endure to the latest period of time; this, with the most humble submission to your majesty, we apprehend will be most effectually accomplished by fixing the pillars thereof on liberty and justice, and securing the inherent rights and liberties of your subjects here, upon the principles of the English constitution. To this constitution, these two principles are essential; the rights of your faithful subjects freely to grant to your majesty such aids as are required for the support of your government over them, and other public exigencies; and trials by their peers. By the one they are secured from unreasonable impositions, and by the other from the arbitrary decisions of the executive power. The continuation of these liberties to the inhabitants of America, we ardently implore, as absolutely necessary to unite the several parts of your wide-extended dominions, in that harmony so essential to the preservation and happiness of the whole. Protected in these liberties, the emoluments Great Britain receives from us, however great at present, are inconsiderable, compared with those she has the fairest prospect of acquiring. By this protection, she will forever secure to herself the advantages of conveying to all Europe the merchandize which America furnishes, and for supplying, through the same channel, whatsoever is wanted from thence. Here opens a boundless source of wealth and naval strength. Yet these immense advantages, by the abridgment of those invaluable rights and liberties, by which our growth has been nourished, are in danger of being forever lost, and our subordinate legislatures in effect rendered useless by the late acts of

Parliament imposing duties and taxes on these colonies, and extending the jurisdiction of the courts of admiralty here, beyond its ancient limits; statutes by which your majesty's commons in Britain undertake absolutely to dispose of the property of their fellow-subjects in America without their consent, and for the enforcing whereof, they are subjected to the determination of a single judge, in a court unrestrained by the wise rules of the common law, the birthright of Englishmen, and the safeguard of their persons and properties.

The invaluable rights of taxing ourselves and trial by our peers, of which we implore your majesty's protection, are not, we most humbly conceive, unconstitutional, but confirmed by the Great Charter of English liberties. On the first of these rights the honorable House of Commons found their practice of originating money, a right enjoyed by the kingdom of Ireland, by the clergy of England, until relinquished by themselves; a right, in fine, which all other your majesty's English subjects, both within and without the realm, have hitherto enjoyed.

With hearts, therefore, impressed with the most indelible characters of gratitude to your majesty, and to the memory of the kings of your illustrious house, whose reigns have been signally distinguished by their auspicious influence on the prosperity of the British dominions; and convinced by the most affecting proofs of your majesty's paternal love to all your people, however distant, and your unceasing and benevolent desires to promote their happiness; we most humbly beseech your majesty that you will be graciously pleased to take into your royal consideration the distresses of your faithful subjects on this continent, and to lay the same before your majesty's Parliament, and to afford them such relief as, in your royal wisdom, their unhappy circumstances shall be judged to require.

And your petitioners will pray, &c.

MEMORIALS TO PARLIAMENT.[1]

To the right honorable the Lords, spiritual and temporal, of Great Britain, in Parliament assembled:

The memorial of the Freeholders and other Inhabitants of the colonies of Massachusetts Bay, Rhode Island and Providence Plantations, New York, New Jersey, Pennsylvania, the government of the counties of New Castle, Kent, and Sussex, upon Delaware, and province of Maryland, in America,

Most humbly showeth,

That his majesty's liege subjects in his American colonies, though they acknowledge a due subordination to that august body the British Parliament, are entitled, in the opinion of your memorialists, to all the inherent rights and

[1] Adopted October 23, 1765. Written by James Otis, of Massachusetts.

liberties of the natives of Great Britain, and have, ever since the settlement of the said colonies, exercised those rights and liberties, as far as their local circumstances would permit.

That your memorialists humbly conceive one of the most essential rights of these colonists, which they have ever till lately uninterruptedly enjoyed, to be trial by jury.

That your memorialists also humbly conceive another of these essential rights, to be the exemption from all taxes, but such as are imposed on the people by the several legislatures in these colonies, which rights they have also till of late enjoyed. But your memorialists humbly beg leave to represent to your lordships, that the act granting certain stamp duties in the British colonies in America, &c., fills his majesty's American subjects with the deepest concern, as it tends to deprive them of the two fundamental and invaluable rights and liberties above mentioned; and that several other late acts of Parliament, which extend the jurisdiction and power of courts of admiralty in the plantations beyond their limits in Great Britain, thereby make an unnecessary, unhappy distinction, as to the modes of trial between us and our fellow-subjects there, by whom we never have been excelled in duty and loyalty to our sovereign.

That from the natural connexion between Great Britain and America, the perpetual continuance of which your memorialists most ardently desire, they conceive that nothing can conduce more to the interest of both, than the colonists' free enjoyment of their rights and liberties, and an affectionate intercourse between Great Britain and them. But your memorialists (not waiving their claim to these rights, of which, with the most becoming veneration and deference to the wisdom and justice of your lordships, they apprehend, they cannot reasonably be deprived), humbly represent, that, from the peculiar circumstances of these colonies, the duties imposed by the aforesaid act, and several other late acts of Parliament, are extremely grievous and burdensome; and the payment of the several duties will very soon, for want of specie, become absolutely impracticable; and that the restrictions on trade by the said acts, will not only distress the colonies, but must be extremely detrimental to the trade and true interest of Great Britain.

Your memorialists, therefore, impressed with a just sense of the unfortunate circumstances of the colonies, the impending destructive consequences which must necessarily ensue from the execution of these acts, and animated with the warmest sentiments of filial affection for their mother country, most earnestly and humbly entreat your lordships will be pleased to hear their counsel in support of this memorial, and take the premises into your most serious consideration, and that your lordships will also be thereupon pleased to pursue such measures for restoring the just rights and liberties of the colonies, and preserving them forever inviolate; for redressing their present, and preventing future grievances, thereby promoting the united interests of Great Britain and America, as to your lordships, in your great wisdom, shall seem most conducive and effectual to that important end.

And your memorialists will pray, &c.

To the honorable the Knights, Citizens, and Burgesses, of Great Britain, in Parliament assembled:

The petition of his Majesty's dutiful, loyal subjects, the Freeholders and other Inhabitants of the colonies of Massachusetts Bay, Rhode Island and Providence Plantations, New York, New Jersey, Pennsylvania, the government of the counties of Newcastle, Kent, and Sussex, upon Delaware, and province of Maryland, in America,

Most humbly showeth,

That the several late acts of Parliament, imposing divers duties and taxes on the colonies, and laying the trade and commerce under very burdensome restrictions; but, above all, the act for granting and applying certain stamp duties in America, have filled them with the deepest concern and surprise, and they humbly conceive the execution of them will be attended with consequences very injurious to the commercial interests of Great Britain and her colonies, and must terminate in the eventual ruin of the latter. Your petitioners, therefore, most ardently implore the attention of the honorable House to the united and dutiful representation of their circumstances, and to their earnest supplications for relief from their regulations, that have already involved this continent in anxiety, confusion, and distress. We most sincerely recognize our allegiance to the crown, and acknowledge all due subordination to the Parliament of Great Britain, and shall always retain the most grateful sense of their assistance and approbation; it is from and under the English constitution we derive all our civil and religious rights and liberties; we glory in being subjects of the best of kings, having been born under the most perfect form of government. But it is with the most ineffable and humiliating sorrow that we find ourselves of late deprived of the right of granting our own property for his majesty's service, to which our lives and fortunes are entirely devoted, and to which, on his royal requisitions, we have been ready to contribute to the utmost of our abilities.

We have also the misfortune to find that all the penalties and forfeitures mentioned in the Stamp Act, and divers late acts of trade extending to the plantations, are, at the election of the informers, recoverable in any court of admiralty in America. This, as the newly-elected court of admiralty has a general jurisdiction over all British America, renders his majesty's subjects in these colonies liable to be carried, at an immense expense, from one end of the continent to the other. It always gives us great pain to see a manifest distinction made therein between the subjects of our mother country and the colonies, in that the like penalties and forfeitures recoverable there only in his majesty's courts of record, are made cognizable here by a court of admiralty. By this means we seem to be, in effect, unhappily deprived of two privileges essential to freedom, and which all Englishmen have ever considered as their best birthrights—that of being free from all taxes but such as they have consented to in person, or by their representatives, and of trial by their peers.

Your petitioners further show, that the remote situation, and other circumstances of the colonies, render it impracticable that they should be represented but in their respective subordinate legislatures; and they humbly conceive that the Parliament, adhering strictly to the spirit of the constitution, have never hitherto taxed any but those who were therein actually represented; for this reason, we humbly apprehend, they never have taxed Ireland, nor any other of the subjects without the realm. But were it ever so clear, that the colonies might in law be reasonably represented in the honorable House of Commons, yet we conceive that very good reasons, from inconvenience, from the principles of true policy, and from the spirit of the British constitution, may be adduced to show, that it would be for the real interest of Great Britain, as well as her colonies, that the late regulations should be rescinded, and the several acts of Parliament imposing duties and taxes on the colonies, and extending the jurisdiction of the courts of admiralty here, beyond their ancient limits, should be repealed.

We shall not attempt a minute detail of all the reasons which the wisdom of the honorable House may suggest, on this occasion, but would humbly submit the following particulars to their consideration:

That money is already very scarce in these colonies, and is still decreasing by the necessary exportation of specie from the continent for the discharging of our debts to British merchants; that an immensely heavy debt is yet due from the colonists for British manufactures; and that they are still heavily burdened with taxes to discharge the arrearages due for aids granted by them in the late war; that the balance of trade will ever be much against the colonies, and in favor of Great Britain, whilst we consume her manufactures; the demand of which must ever increase in proportion to the number of inhabitants settled here, with the means of purchasing them. We, therefore, humbly conceive it to be the interest of Great Britain to increase rather than diminish those means, as the profit of all the trade of the colonies ultimately centers there to pay for her manufactures, as we are not allowed to purchase elsewhere, and by the consumption of which, at the advanced prices the British taxes oblige the makers and venders to set on them, we eventually contribute very largely to the revenues of the crown.

That, from the nature of American business, the multiplicity of suits and papers used in matters of small value, in a country where freeholds are so minutely divided, and property so frequently transferred, a stamp duty must be ever very burdensome and unequal.

That it is extremely improbable that the honorable House of Commons should at all times be thoroughly acquainted with our condition, and all facts requisite to a just and equal taxation of the colonies.

It is also humbly submitted whether there be not a material distinction, in reason and sound policy, at least, between the necessary exercise of parliamentary jurisdiction in general acts, and the common law, and the regulations of trade and commerce, through the whole empire, and the exercise of that jurisdiction by imposing taxes on the colonies.

That the several subordinate provincial legislatures have been molded into forms as nearly resembling that of the mother country, as by his majesty's royal predecessors was thought convenient; and these legislatures seem to have been wisely and graciously established, that the subjects in the colonies might, under the due administration thereof, enjoy the happy fruits of the British government, which in their present circumstances they can not be so fully and clearly availed of any other way.

Under these forms of government we and our ancestors have been born or settled, and have had our lives, liberties, and properties, protected; the people here, as everywhere else, retain a great fondness of their old customs and usages; and we trust that his majesty's service, and the interest of the nation, so far from being obstructed, have been vastly promoted by the provincial legislatures.

That we esteem our connection with and dependence on Great Britain, as one of our greatest blessings, and apprehend the latter will be sufficiently secure, when it is considered that the inhabitants in the colonies have the most unbounded affection for his majesty's person, family, and government, as well as for the mother country, and that their subordination to the Parliament is universally acknowledged.

We, therefore, most humbly entreat that the honorable House would be pleased to hear our counsel in support of this petition, and to take our distressed and deplorable case into their serious consideration, and that the acts and clauses of acts so grievously restraining our trade and commerce, imposing duties and taxes on our property, and extending the jurisdiction of the court of admiralty beyond its ancient limits, may be repealed; or that the honorable House would otherwise relieve your petitioners, as in your great wisdom and goodness shall seem meet.

And your petitioners shall ever pray, &c.

MEMBERS OF THE STAMP ACT CONGRESS.

The following delegates were present at the organization of the Convention:

Massachusetts.—James Otis, Oliver Partridge, Timothy Ruggles.

New York.—Robert R. Livingston, John Cruger, Philip Livingston, William Bayard, Leonard Lispenard.

New Jersey.—Robert Ogden, Hendrick Fisher, Joseph Borden.

Rhode Island.—Metcalf Bowler, Henry Ward.

Pennsylvania.—John Dickenson, John Morton, George Bryan.

Delaware.—Thomas M'Kean, Cæsar Rodney.

Connecticut.—Eliphalet Dyer, David Rowland, William Samuel Johnson.

Maryland.—William Murdock, Edward Tilghman, Thomas Ringgold.

South Carolina.—Thomas Lynch, Christopher Gadsden, John Rutledge.

Timothy Ruggles, of Massachusetts, was elected chairman of the Congress, and John Cotten, its clerk.

III.

STATE PAPERS PUT FORTH BY THE FIRST CONTINENTAL CONGRESS, IN 1774.[1]

TO THE PEOPLE OF GREAT BRITAIN.[2]

WHEN a nation, led to greatness by the hand of liberty, and possessed of all the glory that heroism, munificence, and humanity can bestow, descends to the ungrateful task of forging chains for her friends and children, and, instead of giving support to freedom, turns advocate for slavery and oppression, there is reason to suspect she has ceased to be virtuous, or been extremely negligent in the appointment of her rulers.

In almost every age, in repeated conflicts, in long and bloody wars, as well civil as foreign, against many and powerful nations, against the open assaults of enemies, and the more dangerous treachery of friends, have the inhabitants of your island, your great and glorious ancestors, maintained their independence, and transmitted the rights of men and the blessings of liberty to you, their posterity.

Be not surprised, therefore, that we, who are descended from the same common ancestors; that we, whose forefathers participated in all the rights, the liberties, and the Constitutions you so justly boast of, and who have carefully conveyed the same fair inheritance to us, guarantied by the plighted faith of government and the most solemn compacts with British sovereigns, should refuse to surrender them to men who found their claims on no principles of reason, and who prosecute them with a design, that, by having our lives and property in their power, they may, with the greatest facility, enslave you. The cause of America is now the object of universal attention: it has at length become very serious. This unhappy country has not only been oppressed, but abused and misrepresented; and the duty we owe ourselves and posterity, to your interest, and the general welfare of the British empire, leads us to address you on this very important subject. *Know, then*, that we consider ourselves, and do insist, that we are and ought to be, as free as our fellow-subjects in Britain, and that no power on earth has a right to take our property from us without our consent. That we claim all the benefits secured to the subject by the English Constitution, and particularly that inestimable one of trial by jury. That we hold it essential to English liberty, that no man be condemned un-

[1] Page 228.

[2] Adopted October 21, 1774.—*Journals of Congress*, vol. i., p. 36. This was written by John Jay, of New York. See page 379.

heard, or punished for supposed offenses, without having an opportunity of making his defense. That we think the Legislature of Great Britain is not authorized, by the Constitution, to establish a religion fraught with sanguinary and impious tenets, or to erect an arbitrary form of government, in any quarter of the globe. These rights we, as well as you, deem sacred; and yet, sacred as they are, they have, with many others, been repeatedly and flagrantly violated.

Are not the proprietors of the soil of Great Britain lords of their own property? can it be taken from them without their consent? will they yield it to the arbitrary disposal of any man, or number of men whatever? You know they will not. Why, then, are the proprietors of the soil in America less lords of their property than you are of yours? or why should they submit it to the disposal of your Parliament, or of any other parliament or council in the world not of their election? Can the intervention of the sea that divides us cause disparity in rights? or can any reason be given why English subjects who live three thousand miles from the royal palace, should enjoy less liberty than those who are three hundred miles distant from it?

Reason looks with indignation on such distinctions, and freemen can never perceive their propriety. And yet, however chimerical and unjust such discriminations are, the Parliament assert they have a right to bind us in all cases, without exception, whether we consent or not; that they may take and use our property when and in what manner they please; that we are pensioners on their bounty for all that we possess, and can hold it no longer than they vouchsafe to permit. Such declarations we consider as heresies in English politics; and which can no more operate to deprive us of our property, than the interdicts of the Pope can divest kings of scepters which the laws of the land and the voice of the people have placed in their hands.

At the conclusion of the late war[1]—a war rendered glorious by the abilities and integrity of a minister to whose efforts the British empire owes its safety and its fame; at the conclusion of this war, which was succeeded by an inglorious peace, formed under the auspices of a minister of principles and of a family unfriendly to the Protestant cause, and inimical to liberty: we say, at this period, and under the influence of that man, a plan for inslaving your fellow-subjects in America was concerted, and has ever since been pertinaciously carrying into execution.

Prior to this era you were content with drawing from us the wealth produced by our commerce. You restrained our trade in every way that would conduce to your emoluments. You exercised unbounded sovereignty over the sea. You named the ports and nations to which alone our merchandise should be carried, and with whom alone we should trade; and though some of these restrictions were grievous, we nevertheless did not complain; we looked up to you as to our parent State, to which we were bound by the strongest ties, and were happy in being instrumental to your prosperity and your grandeur.

We call upon you yourselves to witness our loyalty and attachment to the

---

[1] The French and Indian War. See page 179.

common interest of the whole empire: did we not, in the last war, add all the strength of this vast continent to the force which repelled our common enemy? did we not leave our native shores, and meet disease and death to promote the success of the British arms in foreign climates? did you not thank us for our zeal, and even reimburse us large sums of money, which you professed we had advanced beyond our proportion, and far beyond our abilities? You did.

To what causes, then, are we to attribute the sudden change of treatment, and that system of slavery which was prepared for us at the restoration of peace?

Before we had recovered from the distresses which ever attend war, an attempt was made to drain this country of all its money by the oppressive Stamp Act. Paint, glass, and other commodities, which you would not permit us to purchase of other nations, were taxed; nay, although no wine is made in any country subject to the British state, you prohibited our procuring it of foreigners without paying a tax, imposed by your Parliament, on all we imported. These and many other impositions were laid upon us most unjustly and unconstitutionally, for the express purpose of raising a revenue. In order to silence complaint, it was, indeed, provided that this revenue should be expended in America, for its protection and defense. These exactions, however, can receive no justification from a pretended necessity of protecting and defending us: they are lavishly squandered on court favorites and ministerial dependants, generally avowed enemies to America, and employing themselves by partial representations to traduce and embroil the colonies. For the necessary support of government here we ever were and ever shall be ready to provide; and whenever the exigences of the State may require it, we shall, as we have heretofore done, cheerfully contribute our full proportion of men and money. To enforce this unconstitutional and unjust scheme of taxation, every fence that the wisdom of our British ancestors had carefully erected against arbitrary power has been violently thrown down in America, and the inestimable right of trial by jury taken away in cases that touch both life and property. It was ordained that, whenever offenses should be committed in the colonies against particular acts, imposing various duties and restrictions upon trade, the prosecutor might bring his action for penalties in the courts of admiralty; by which means the subject lost the advantage of being tried by an honest uninfluenced jury of the vicinage, and was subjected to the sad necessity of being judged by a single man, a creature of the crown, and according to the course of a law which exempts the prosecutor from the trouble of proving his accusation, and obliges the defendant either to evince his innocence or suffer. To give this new judiciary the greater importance, and as if with design to protect false accusers, it is further provided, that the judge's certificate of there having been probable causes of seizure and prosecution shall protect the prosecutors from actions at common law for recovery of damages.

By the course of our laws, offenses committed in such of the British dominions in which courts are established and justice duly and regularly administered, shall be there tried by a jury of the vicinage. There the offenders and the witnesses are known, and the degree of credibility to be given to their testimony can be ascertained.

In all these colonies, justice is regularly and impartially administered, and yet, by the construction of some, and the direction of other acts of Parliament, offenders are to be taken by force, together with all such persons as may be pointed out as witnesses, and carried to England, there to be tried in a distant land by a jury of strangers, and subject to all the disadvantages that result from want of friends, want of witnesses, and want of money.

When the design of raising a revenue, from the duties imposed on the importation of tea in America, had in a great measure been rendered abortive, by our ceasing to import that commodity, a scheme was concerted by the ministry with the East India Company, and an act passed enabling and encouraging them to transport and vend it in the colonies. Aware of the danger of giving success to this insidious maneuver, and of permitting a precedent of taxation thus to be established among us, various methods were adopted to elude the stroke. The people of Boston, then ruled by a governor whom, as well as his predecessor, Sir Francis Bernard, all America considers as her enemy, were exceedingly embarrassed. The ships which had arrived with the tea were, by his management, prevented from returning. The duties would have been paid, the cargoes landed and exposed to sale; a governor's influence would have procured and protected many purchasers. While the town was suspended by deliberations on this important subject, the tea was destroyed. Even supposing a trespass was thereby committed, and the proprietors of the tea entitled to damages, the courts of law were open, and judges, appointed by the crown, presided in them. The East India Company, however, did not think proper to commence any suits, nor did they even demand satisfaction, either from individuals, or from the community in general. The ministry, it seems, officially made the case their own, and the great council of the nation descended to intermeddle with a dispute about private property. Divers papers, letters, and other unauthenticated *ex parte* evidence, were laid before them; neither the persons who destroyed the tea, nor the people of Boston, were called upon to answer the complaint. The ministry, incensed by being disappointed in a favorite scheme, were determined to recur from the little arts of finesse to open force and unmanly violence. The port of Boston was blocked up by a fleet, and an army placed in the town. Their trade was to be suspended, and thousands reduced to the necessity of gaining subsistence from charity, till they should submit to pass under the yoke, and consent to become slaves, by confessing the omnipotence of Parliament, and acquiescing in whatever disposition they might think proper to make of their lives and property.

Let justice and humanity cease to be the boast of your nation! Consult your history, examine your records of former transactions; nay, turn to the annals of the many arbitrary states and kingdoms that surround you, and show us a single instance of men being condemned to suffer for imputed crimes, unheard, unquestioned, and without even the specious formality of a trial; and that, too, by laws made expressly for the purpose, and which had no existence at the time of the fact committed. If it be difficult to reconcile these proceedings to the genius and temper of your laws and Constitution, the task will become more arduous when we call upon our ministerial enemies to justify, not only condemning men untried and by hearsay, but involving the innocent in one common punishment with the guilty, and for the acts of thirty or forty, to bring poverty, distress, and calamity on thirty thousand souls, and those not your enemies, but your friends, brethren, and fellow-subjects.

It would be some consolation to us if the catalogue of American oppressions ended here. It gives us pain to be reduced to the necessity of reminding you that, under the confidence reposed in the faith of government, pledged in a royal charter from the British sovereign, the forefathers of the present inhabitants of Massachusetts Bay left their former habitations, and established that great, flourishing, and loyal colony. Without incurring or being charged with a forfeiture of their right, without being heard, without being tried, and without justice, by an act of Parliament their charter is destroyed, their liberties violated, their Constitution and form of government changed; and all this upon no better pretense than because in one of their towns a trespass was committed upon some merchandise said to belong to one of the companies, and because the ministry were of opinion that such high political regulations were necessary to due subordination and obedience to their mandates.

Nor are these the only capital grievances under which we labor; we might tell of dissolute, weak, and wicked governors having been set over us; of Legislatures being suspended for asserting the rights of British subjects; of needy and ignorant dependants on great men advanced to the seats of justice, and to other places of trust and importance; of hard restrictions on commerce, and a great variety of lesser evils, the recollection of which is almost lost under the pressure and weight of greater and more poignant calamities.

But mark the progression of the ministerial plan for inslaving us.

Well aware that such hardy attempts to take our property from us, to deprive us of that valuable right of trial by jury, to seize our persons and carry us for trial to Great Britain, to blockade our ports, to destroy our charters, and change our form of government, would occasion, and had already occasioned, great discontent in the colonies, which might produce opposition to these measures, an act was passed to protect, indemnify, and screen from punishment, such as might be guilty even of murder, in endeavoring to carry their oppressive edicts into execution; and by another act the dominion of Canada is to be so extended, modeled, and governed, as that, by being disunited from us, detached from our interests, by civil as well as religious prejudices, that by their numbers daily swelling with Catholic emigrants from Europe, and by their devotion to administration, so friendly to their religion, they might become formidable to us, and, on occasion, be fit instruments in the hands of power to reduce the ancient, free Protestant colonies to the same state of slavery with themselves.

This was evidently the object of the act; and in this view, being extremely dangerous to our liberty and quiet, we can not forbear complaining of it as hostile to British America. Superadded to these considerations, we can not help deploring the unhappy condition to which it has reduced the many English settlers who, encouraged by the royal proclamation, promising the enjoyment of all their rights, have purchased estates in that country. They are now the subjects of an arbitrary government, deprived of trial by jury, and, when imprisoned, can not claim the benefit of the *habeas corpus* act, that great bulwark and palladium of English liberty; nor can we suppress our astonishment that a British Parliament should ever consent to establish in that country a religion that has deluged your island in blood, and dispersed impiety, bigotry, persecution, murder, and rebellion, through every part of the world.

This being a true state of facts, let us beseech you to consider to what end they lead.

Admit the ministry, by the powers of Britain and the aid of our Roman Catholic neighbors, should be able to carry the point of taxation, and reduce us to a state of perfect humiliation and slavery. Such an enterprise would doubtless make some addition to your national debt, which already presses down your liberty, and fills you with pensioners and placemen. We presume also that your commerce will be somewhat diminished. However, suppose you should prove victorious, in what condition will you then be? What advantages, or what laurels will you reap from such a conquest?

May not a ministry with the same armies inslave you? It may be said, you will cease to pay them; but remember the taxes from America, the wealth, and, we may add, the men, and particularly the Roman Catholics of this vast continent, will then be in the power of your enemies; nor will you have any reason to expect that, after making slaves of us, many among us should refuse to assist in reducing you to the same abject state.

Do not treat this as chimerical. Know that in less than half a century the quit-rents reserved to the crown, from the numberless grants of this vast continent, will pour large streams of wealth into the royal coffers; and if to this be added the power of taxing America at pleasnre, the crown will be rendered independent of you for supplies, and will possess more treasures than may be necessary to purchase the remains of liberty in your island. In a word, take care that you do not fall into the pit that is preparing for us.

We believe there is yet much virtue, much justice, and much public spirit in the English nation. To that justice, we now appeal. You have been told that we are seditious, impatient of government, and desirous of independency. Be assured that these are not facts, but calumnies. Permit us to be as free as yourselves, and we shall ever esteem a union with you to be our greatest glory and our greatest happiness; we shall ever be ready to contribute all in our power to the welfare of the empire; we shall consider your enemies as our enemies, and your interest as our own. But if you are determined that your ministers shall wantonly sport with the rights of mankind—if neither the voice of justice, the dictates of the law, the principles of the Constitution, nor the suggestions of humanity, can restrain your hands from shedding human blood in such an impious cause, we must tell you that we will never submit to be hewers of wood or drawers of water for any ministry or nation n the world.

Place us in the same situation that we were at the close of the last war, and our former harmony will be restored.

But, lest the same supineness, and the same inattention to our common interest, which you have for several years shown, should continue, we think it prudent to anticipate the consequences.

By the destruction of the trade of Boston, the ministry have endeavored to induce submission to their measures. The like fate may befall us all. We will endeavor, therefore, to live without trade, and recur, for subsistence, to the fertility and bounty of our native soil, which will afford us all the necessaries, and some of the conveniences, of life. We have suspended our importation from Great Britain and Ireland; and in less than a year's time, unless our grievances should be redressed, we shall discontinue our exports to those kingdoms and to the West Indies.

It is with the utmost regret, however, that we find ourselves compelled, by the overruling principles of self-preservation, to adopt measures detrimental in their consequences to numbers of our fellow-subjects in Great Britain and Ireland. But we hope that the magnanimity and justice of the British nation will furnish a Parliament of such wisdom, independence, and public spirit, as may save the violated rights of the whole empire from the devices of wicked ministers and evil counselors, whether in or out of office; and thereby restore that harmony, friendship and fraternal affection, between all the inhabitants of his majesty's kingdoms and territories, so ardently wished for by every true and honest American.

The Congress then resumed the consideration of the memorial to the inhabitants of the British colonies, and the same, being debated by paragraphs, and amended, was approved, and is as follows:

TO THE INHABITANTS OF THE SEVERAL ANGLO-AMERICAN COLONIES.[1]

We, the delegates appointed by the good people of these colonies to meet at Philadelphia in September last, for the purposes mentioned by our respective constituents, have, in pursuance of the trust reposed in us, assembled, and taken into our most serious consideration, the important matters recommended to the Congress. Our resolutions thereupon will be herewith communicated to you. But as the situation of public affairs grows daily more and more alarming; and as it may be more satisfactory to you to be informed by us in a collective body, than in any other manner, of those sentiments that have been approved, upon a full and free discussion, by the representatives of so great a part of America, we esteem ourselves obliged to add this address to these resolutions.

In every case of opposition by a people to their rulers, or of one State to another, duty to Almighty God, the Creator of all, requires that a true and

[1] Adopted October 21, 1774.—*Journals of Congress*, vol. i., p. 43. This was written by William Livingston, afterward Governor of New Jersey.

impartial judgment be formed of the measures leading to such opposition, and of the causes by which it has been provoked or can in any degree be justified, that, neither affection on one hand, nor resentment on the other, being permitted to give a wrong bias to reason, it may be enabled to take a dispassionate view of all circumstances, and to settle the public conduct on the solid foundations of wisdom and justice.

From counsels thus tempered arise the surest hopes of the divine favor, the firmest encouragement of the parties engaged, and the strongest recommendation of their cause to the rest of mankind.

With minds deeply impressed by a sense of these truths, we have diligently, deliberately, and calmly inquired into and considered those exertions, both of the legislative and executive power of Great Britain, which have excited so much uneasiness in America, and have with equal fidelity and attention considered the conduct of the colonies. Upon the whole, we find ourselves reduced to the disagreeable alternative of being silent and betraying the innocent, or of speaking out and censuring those we wish to revere. In making our choice of these distressing difficulties, we prefer the course dictated by honesty and a regard for the welfare of our country.

Soon after the conclusion of the late war, there commenced a memorable change in the treatment of these colonies. By a statute made in the fourth year of the present reign, a time of profound peace, alleging "the expediency of new provisions and regulations for extending the commerce between Great Britain and his majesty's dominions in America, and the necessity of raising a revenue in the said dominions, for defraying the expenses of defending, protecting, and securing the same," the Commons of Great Britain undertook to give and grant to his majesty many rates and duties to be paid in these colonies. To enforce the observance of this act, it prescribes a great number of severe penalties and forfeitures; and in two sections makes a remarkable distinction between the subjects in Great Britain and those in America. By the one, the penalties and forfeitures incurred there are to be recovered in any of the king's courts of record at Westminster, or in the court of exchequer in Scotland; and by the other, the penalties and forfeitures incurred here are to be recovered in any court of record, or in any court of admiralty or vice-admiralty, at the election of the informer or prosecutor.

The inhabitants of these colonies, confiding in the justice of Great Britain, were scarcely allowed sufficient time to receive and consider this act, before another, well known by the name of the Stamp Act, and passed in the fifth year of this reign, engrossed their whole attention. By this statute, the British Parliament exercised, in the most explicit manner, a power of taxing us, and extending the jurisdiction of courts of admiralty and vice-admiralty in the colonies to matters arising within the body of a county, and directed the numerous penalties and forfeitures thereby inflicted to be recovered in the said courts.

In the same year a tax was imposed upon us by an act establishing several new fees in the customs. In the next year the Stamp Act was repealed, not because it was founded in an erroneous principle, but, as the repealing act recites, because "the continuance thereof would be attended with many inconveniences, and might be productive of consequences greatly detrimental to the commercial interest of Great Britain."

In the same year, and by a subsequent act, it was declared, "that his majesty in Parliament, of right, had power to bind the people of these colonies by statutes in all cases whatsoever." In the same year another act was passed for imposing rates and duties payable in these colonies. In this statute, the Commons, avoiding the terms of giving and granting, "humbly besought his majesty that it might be enacted," etc. But from a declaration in the preamble, that the rates and duties "were in lieu of" several others granted by the statute first before mentioned for raising a revenue, and from some other expressions, it appears that these duties were intended for that purpose.

In the next year (1767) an act was made "to enable his majesty to put the customs and other duties in America under the management of commissioners," etc.; and the king thereupon erected the present expensive board of commissioners, for the express purpose of carrying into execution the several acts relating to the revenue and trade in America.

After the repeal of the Stamp Act, having again resigned ourselves to our ancient unsuspicious affections for the parent State, and anxious to avoid any controversy with her, in hopes of a favorable alteration in sentiments and measures toward us, we did not press our objections against the above-mentioned statutes made subsequent to that repeal.

Administration, attributing to trifling causes a conduct that really proceeded from generous motives, were encouraged in the same year (1767) to make a bolder experiment on the patience of America.

By a statute commonly called the Glass, Paper, and Tea Act, made fifteen months after the repeal of the Stamp Act, the Commons of Great Britain resumed their former language, and again undertook to "give and grant rates and duties to be paid in these colonies," for the express purpose of "raising a revenue to defray the charges of the administration of justice, the support of civil government, and defending the king's dominions," on this continent. The penalties and forfeitures incurred unter this statute are to be recovered in the same manner with those mentioned in the foregoing acts.

To this statute, so naturally tending to disturb the tranquillity then universal throughout the colonies, Parliament, in the same session, added another no less extraordinary.

Ever since the making the present peace a standing army has been kept in these colonies. From respect for the mother country, the innovation was not only tolerated, but the provincial Legislatures generally made provision for supplying the troops.

The Assembly of the province of New York having passed an act of this kind, but differing in some articles from the directions of the act of Parliament made in the fifth year of this reign, the House of Representatives in that colony was prohibited, by a statute made in the last session mentioned, from making any bill, order, resolution, or vote, except for adjourning or choosing a speaker, until provision shall be made by the said Assembly for furnishing the troops within that province not only with all such necessaries as were required by the statute which they were charged with disobeying, but also with those required by two other subsequent statutes, which were declared to be in force until the twenty-fourth day of March, 1769.

These statutes of the year 1767 revived the apprehensions and discontents that had entirely subsided on the repeal of the Stamp Act; and, amid the just fears and jealousies thereby occasioned, a statute was made in the next year (1768) to establish courts of admiralty and vice-admiralty on a new model, expressly for the end of more effectually recovering of the penalties and forfeitures inflicted by acts of Parliament framed for the purpose of raising a revenue in America, etc. The immediate tendency of these statutes is to subvert the right of having a share in legislation, by rendering assemblies useless; the right of property, by taking the money of the colonists without their consent; the right of trial by jury, by substituting in their places trials in admiralty and vice-admiralty courts, where single judges preside, holding their commissions during pleasure, and unduly to influence the courts of common law by rendering the judges thereof totally dependent on the crown for their salaries.

These statutes, not to mention many others exceedingly exceptionable, compared one with another, will be found not only to form a regular system in which every part has great force, but also a pertinacious adherence to that system for subjugating these colonies, that are not, and from local circumstances can not be, represented in the House of Commons, to the uncontrollable and unlimited power of Parliament, in violation of their undoubted rights and liberties, in contempt of their humble and repeated supplications.

This conduct must appear equally astonishing and unjustifiable, when it is considered how unprovoked it has been by any behavior of these colonies. From their first settlement, their bitterest enemies never fixed on any of them any charge of disloyalty to their sovereign or disaffection to their mother country. In the wars she has carried on they have exerted themselves, whenever required, in giving her assistance, and have rendered her services which she has publicly acknowledged to be extremely important. Their fidelity, duty, and usefulness during the last war were frequently and affectionately confessed by his late majesty and the present king.

The reproaches of those who are most unfriendly to the freedom of America are principally leveled against the province of Massachusetts Bay, but with what little reason will appear by the following declarations of a person, the truth of whose evidence in their favor will not be questioned. Governor Bernard thus addresses the two Houses of Assembly in his speech on the 24th of April, 1762: "The unanimity and dispatch with which you have complied with the repuisitions of his majesty require my particular acknowledgment, and it gives me additional pleasure to observe that you have therein acted under no other influence than a due sense of your duty, both as members of a general empire and as the body of a particular province."

In another speech, on the 27th of May in the same year, he says, "Whatever shall be the event of the war, it must be no small satisfaction to us that this province has contributed its full share to the support of it. Every thing that hath been required of it hath been complied with; and the execution of the powers committed to me for raising the provincial troops hath been as full and complete as the grant of them. Never before were regiments so easily levied, so well composed, and so early in the field, as they have been this year: the common people seem to be animated with the spirit of the General Court, and to vie with them in their readiness to serve the king."

Such was the conduct of the people of Massachusetts Bay during the last war. As to their behavior before that period, it ought not to have been forgot in Great Britain that not only on every occasion they had constantly and cheerfully complied with the frequent royal requisitions, but that chiefly by their vigorous efforts Nova Scotia was subdued in 1710, and Louisbourg in 1745.

Foreign quarrels being ended, and the domestic disturbances that quickly succeeded on account of the Stamp Act being quieted by its repeal, the Assembly of Massachusetts Bay transmitted an humble address of thanks to the king and divers noblemen, and soon after passed a bill for granting compensation to the sufferers in the disorders occasioned by that act.

These circumstances, and the following extracts from Governer Bernard's letters, in 1768, to the Earl of Shelburne, Secretary of State, clearly show with what grateful tenderness they strove to bury in oblivion the unhappy occasion of the late discords, and with what respectful deference they endeavored to escape other subjects of future controversy. "The House," says the governor, "from the time of opening the session to this day, has shown a disposition to avoid all dispute with me, every thing having passed with as much good humor as I could desire, except only their continuing to act in addressing the king, remonstrating to the Secretary of State, and employing a separate agent. It is the importance of this innovation, without any willfulness of my own, which induces me to make this remonstrance at a time when I have a fair prospect of having in all other business nothing but good to say of the proceedings of the House.

"They have acted in all things, even in their remonstrance, with temper and moderation; they have avoided some subjects of dispute, and have laid a foundation for removing some causes of former altercation.

"I shall make such a prudent and proper use of this letter as I hope will perfectly restore the peace and tranquillity of this province, for which purpose considerable steps have been made by the House of Representatives."

The vindication of the province of Massachuetts Bay contained in these letters will have greater force if it be considered that they were written several months after the fresh alarm given to the colonies by the statutes passed in the preceding year.

In this place it seems proper to take notice of the insinuation of one of those statutes, that the interference of Parliament was necessary to provide for "defraying the charges of the administration of justice, the support of civil government, and defending the king's dominions in America."

As to the first two articles of expense, every colony had made such provision as by their respective Assemblies, the best judges on such occasions, was thought expedient and suitable to their several circumstances; respecting the last, it is well known to all men the least acquainted with American affairs, that the colonies were established, and generally defended themselves, without the least assistance from Great Britain; and that, at the time of her taxing them by the statutes before-mentioned, most of them were laboring under very heavy debts contracted in the last war. So far were they from sparing their money when their sovereign constitutionally asked their aids, that, during the course of that war, Parliament repeatedly made them compensations for the expenses of those strenuous efforts which, consulting their zeal rather than their strength, they had cheerfully incurred.

Severe as the acts of Parliament before-mentioned are, yet the conduct of administration hath been equally injurious and irritating to this devoted country.

Under pretense of governing them, so many new institutions, uniformly rigid and dangerous, have been introduced, as could only be expected from incensed masters for collecting the tribute, or, rather the plunder of conquered provinces.

By an order of the king, the authority of the commander-in-chief, and under him of the brigadier-generals, in time of peace, is rendered supreme in all civil governments in America, and thus an uncontrollable military power is vested in officers not known to the Constitutions of these colonies.

A large body of troops, and a considerable armament of ships of war, have been sent to assist in taking their money without their consent.

Expensive and oppressive officers have been multiplied, and the acts of corruption industriously practiced to divide and destroy.

The judges of the admiralty and vice-admiralty courts are empowered to receive their salaries and fees from the effects to be condemned by themselves.

The commissioners of the customs are empowered to break open and enter houses without the authority of any civil magistrate, founded on legal information.

Judges of courts of common law have been made entirely dependent on the crown for their commissions and salaries. A court has been established at Rhode Island for the purpose of taking colonists to England to be tried. Humble and reasonable petitions from the representatives of the people have been frequently treated with contempt, and assemblies have been repeatedly and arbitrarily dissolved.

From some few instances it will sufficiently appear on what pretenses of justice those dissolutions have been founded.

The tranquillity of the colonies having been again disturbed, as has been mentioned, by the statutes of the year 1767, the Earl of Hillsborough, Secretary of State, in a letter to Governor Bernard, dated April 22d, 1768, censures the "presumption" of the House of Representatives for "resolving upon a measure of so inflammatory a nature as that of writing to the other colonies on the subject of their intended representations against some late acts of Parliament," then declares that "his majesty considers this step as evidently tending to create unwarrantable combinations, to excite an unjustifiable opposition to the constitutional authority of Parliament," and afterward adds, "it is the king's pleasure that, as soon as the General Court is again assembled at the time prescribed by the charter, you should require of the House of Representatives, in his majesty's name, to rescind the resolutions which gave birth to the circular letter of the speaker, and to declare their disapprobation of and dissent to that rash and hasty proceeding."

"If the new Assembly should refuse to comply with his majesty's reasonable expectation, it is the king's pleasure that you should immediately dissolve them."

This letter being laid before the House, and the resolution not being rescinded, according to order the Assembly was dissolved. A letter of a similar nature was sent to other governors, to procure resolutions approving the conduct of the representatives of Massachusetts Bay to be rescinded also; and the Houses of Representatives in other colonies refusing to comply, assemblies were dissolved.

These mandates spoke a language to which the ears of English subjects had for several generations been strangers. The nature of assemblies implies a power and right of deliberation; but these commands, proscribing the exercise of judgment on the propriety of the requisitions made, left to the assemblies only the election between dictated submission and threatened punishment: a punishment, too, founded on no other act than such as is deemed innocent even in slaves, of agreeing in petitions for redress of grievances that equally affect all.

The hostile and unjustifiable invasion of the town of Boston soon followed these events in the same year, though that town, the province in which it is situated, and all the colonies, from abhorrence of a contest with their parent State, permitted the execution even of those statutes against which they were so unanimously complaining, remonstrating, and supplicating.

Administration, determined to subdue a spirit of freedom which English ministers should have rejoiced to cherish, entered into a monopolizing combination with the East India Company to send to this continent vast quantities of tea, an article on which a duty was laid by a statute that in a particular manner attacked the liberties of America, and which, therefore, the inhabitants of these colonies had resolved not to import. The cargo sent to South Carolina was stored and not allowed to be sold. Those sent to Philadelphia and New York were not permitted to be landed. That sent to Boston was destroyed, because Governor Hutchinson would not suffer it to be returned.

On the intelligence of these transactions arriving in Great Britain, the public-spirited town last mentioned was singled out for destruction, and it was determined the province it belongs to should partake of its fate. In the last session of Parliament, therefore, were passed the acts for shutting up the port of Boston, indemnifying the murderers of the inhabitants of Massachusetts Bay, and changing their chartered constitution of government. To enforce these acts, that province is again invaded by a fleet and army.

To mention these outrageous proceedings is sufficient to explain them. For though it is pretended the province of Massachusetts Bay has been particularly disrespectful to Great Britain, yet, in truth, the behavior of the people in other colonies has been an equal "opposition to the power assumed by Parliament." No step, however, has been taken against any of the rest. This artful conduct conceals several designs. It is expected that the province of Massachusetts Bay will be irritated into some violent action that may displease the rest of the continent, or that may induce the people of Great Britain to approve the meditated vengeance of an imprudent and exasperated ministry. If the unexampled pacific temper of that province shall disappoint this part of the plan, it is hoped the other colonies will be so far intimidated as to desert their brethren suffering in a common cause, and that, thus disunited, all may be subdued.

To promote these designs another measure has been pursued. In the session of Parliament last mentioned, an act was passed for changing the government of Quebec, by which act the Roman Catholic religion, instead of being tolerated, as stipulated by the treaty of peace, is established, and the people there are deprived of a right to an assembly, trials by jury, and the English laws in civil cases are abolished, and instead thereof the French laws are established, in direct violation of his majesty's promise by his royal proclamation, under the faith of which many English subjects settled in that province; and the limits of that province are extended so as to comprehend those vast regions that lie adjoining to the northerly and westerly boundaries of these colonies.

The authors of this arbitrary enactment flatter themselves that the inhabitants, deprived of liberty, and artfully provoked against those of another religion, will be proper instruments for assisting in the oppression of such as differ from them in modes of government and in faith.

From the detail of facts herein-before recited, as well as from authentic intelligence received, it is clear, beyond a doubt, that a resolution is formed and now carrying into execution to extinguish the freedom of these colonies, by subjecting them to a despotic government.

At this unhappy period we have been authorized and directed to meet and consult together for the welfare of our common country. We accepted the important trust with diffidence, but have endeavored to discharge it with integrity. Though the state of these colonies would certainly justify other measures than we have advised, yet weighty reasons determined us to prefer those which we have adopted. In the first place, it appeared to us a conduct becoming the character these colonies have ever sustained, to perform, even in the midst of the unnatural distresses and immediate dangers which surround them, every act of loyalty, and therefore we were induced once more to offer to his majesty the petitions of his faithful and oppressed subjects in America. Secondly, regarding with the tender affection which we knew to be so universal among our countrymen, the people of the kingdom from which we derive our origin, we could not forbear to regulate our steps by an expectation of receiving full conviction that the colonists are equally dear to them. Between these provinces and that body subsists the social band, which we ardently wish may never be dissolved, and which can not be dissolved, until their minds shall become indisputably hostile, or their inattention shall permit those who are thus hostile to persist in prosecuting, with the powers of the realm, the destructive measures already operating against the colonists, and in either case shall reduce the latter to such a situation that they shall be compelled to renounce every regard but that of self-preservation. Notwithstanding the violence with which affairs have been impelled, they have not yet reached that fatal point. We do not incline to accelerate their motion, already alarmingly rapid; we have chosen a method of opposition that does not preclude a hearty reconciliation with our fellow-citizens on the other side of the Atlantic. We deeply deplore the urgent necessity that presses us to an immediate interruption of commerce that may prove injurious to them. We trust they will acquit us of any unkind intentions toward them, by reflecting that we are driven by the hands of violence into unexperienced and unexpected public convulsions, and that we are contending for freedom, so often contended for by our ancestors.

The people of England will soon have an opportunity of declaring their sentiments concerning our cause. In their piety, generosity, and good sense, we repose high confidence, and can not, upon a review of past events, be persuaded that they, the defenders of true religion, and the asserters of the rights of mankind, will take part against their affectionate Protestant brethren in the colonies, in favor of our open and their own secret enemies, whose intrigues, for several years past, have been wholly exercised in sapping the foundations of civil and religious liberty.

Another reason that engaged us to prefer the commercial mode of operation arose from an assurance that the mode will prove efficacious if it be persisted in with fidelity and virtue, and that your conduct will be influenced by these laudable principles, can not be doubted. Your own salvation and that of your posterity, now depends upon yourselves. You have already shown that you entertain a proper sense of the blessings you are striving to retain. Against the temporary inconveniences you may suffer from a stoppage of trade, you will weigh in the opposite balance the endless miseries you and your descendants must endure from an established arbitrary power. You will not forget the honor of your country, that you must, from your behavior, take its title, in the estimation of the world, to glory or to shame; and you will, with the deepest attention, reflect that if the peaceable mode of opposition recommended by us be broken and rendered ineffectual, as your cruel and haughty ministerial enemies, from a contemptuous opinion of your firmness, insolently predict will be the case, you must inevitably be reduced to choose either a more dangerous contest, or a final, ruinous, and infamous submission.

Motives thus cogent, arising from the emergency of your unhappy condition, must excite your utmost diligence and zeal to give all possible strength and energy to the pacific measures calculated for your relief; but we think ourselves bound in duty to observe to you, that the schemes agitated against these colonies have been so conducted as to render it prudent that you should extend your views to mournful events, and be, in all respects, prepared for every contingency. Above all things, we earnestly entreat you, with devotion of spirit, penitence of heart, and amendment of life, to humble yourselves, and implore the favor of Almighty God; and we fervently beseech his divine goodness to take you into his gracious protection.

ADDRESS TO THE INHABITANTS OF THE PROVINCE OF QUEBEC.[1]

Friends and Fellow-subjects:

WE, the delegates of the colonies of New Hampshire, Massachusetts Bay, Rhode Island and Providence Plantations, Connecticut, New York, New Jersey, Pennsylvania, the counties of Newcastle, Kent, and Sussex, on Delaware, Maryland, Virginia, North Carolina, deputed by the inhabitants of the said colonies to represent them in a general Congress at Philadelphia, in the province of Pennsylvania, to consult together concerning the best methods to obtain redress of our afflicting grievances, having accordingly assembled, and taken into our most serious consideration the state of public affairs on this continent, have thought proper to address your province, as a member therein deeply interested.

When the fortune of war, after a gallant and glorious resistance, had incorporated you with the body of English subjects, we rejoiced in the truly valuable addition, both on our own and your account, expecting, as courage and generosity are naturally united, our brave enemies would become our hearty friends, and that the Divine Being would bless to you the dispensations of his overruling providence, by securing to you and your latest posterity the inestimable advantages of a free English constitution of government, which it is the privilege of all English subjects to enjoy.

These hopes were confirmed by the king's proclamation, issued in the year 1763, plighting the public faith for the full enjoyment of those advantages.

Little did we imagine that any succeeding ministers would so audaciously and cruelly abuse the royal authority as to withhold from you the fruition of the irrevocable rights to which you were thus justly entitled.

But since we have lived to see the unexpected time when ministers of this flagitious temper have dared to violate the most sacred compacts and obligations, and as you, educated under another form of government, have artfully been kept from discovering the unspeakable worth of that form you are now undoubtedly entitled to, we esteem it our duty, for the weighty reasons hereinafter mentioned, to explain to you some of its most important branches.

"In every human society," says the celebrated Marquis Beccaria, "there

[1] Adopted October 26th, 1774.—*Journals of Congress*, vol. i., page 55. This was written by John Dickenson. See page 219. Peter Force, Esq., of Washington City, has a printed copy of the Journals of that Congress, on the margin of which, in the handwriting of Cæsar Rodney, one of the members, the authorship of these several state papers is thus given.

is an effort continually tending to confer on one part the height of power and happiness, and to reduce the other to the extreme of weakness and misery. The intent of good laws is to oppose this effort, and to diffuse their influence universally and equally."

Rulers stimulated by this pernicious "effort," and subjects animated by the just "intent of opposing good laws against it," have occasioned that vast variety of events that fill the histories of so many nations. All these histories demonstrate the truth of this simple position, that to live by the will of one man, or set of men, is the production of misery to all men.

On the solid foundation of this principle, Englishmen reared up the fabric of their Constitution with such a strength, as for ages to defy time, tyranny, treachery, internal and foreign wars; and, as an illustrious author[1] of your nation, hereafter mentioned, observes, "They gave the people of their colonies the form of their own government, and this government carrying prosperity along with it, they have grown great nations in the forests they were sent to inhabit."

In this form, the first grand right is that of the people having a share in their own government, by their representatives chosen by themselves, and, in consequence, of being ruled by laws which they themselves approve, not by the edicts of men over whom they have no control. This is a bulwark surrounding and defending their property, so that no portions of it can legally be taken from them but with their own full and free consent, when they in their judgment deem it just and necessary to give them for public services, and precisely direct the easiest, cheapest, and most equal methods in which they shall be collected.

The influence of this right extends still further. If money is wanted by rulers who have in any manner oppressed the people, they may retain it until their grievances are redressed, and thus peaceably procure relief without trusting to despised petitions or disturbing the public tranquillity.

The next great right is that of trial by jury. This provides that neither life, liberty, nor property can be taken from the possessor until twelve of his unexceptionable countrymen and peers of his vicinage, who, from that neighborhood, may reasonably be supposed to be acquainted with his character and the characters of his witnesses, upon a fair trial and full inquiry, face to face, in open court, before as many of the people as choose to attend, shall pass their sentence upon oath against him—a sentence that can not injure him without injuring their own reputation, and probably their interest also, as the question may turn on points that in some degree concern the general welfare; and if it does not, their verdict may form a precedent that, on a similar trial of their own, may militate against themselves.

Another right relates merely to the liberty of the person. If a subject be seized and imprisoned, though by order of government, he may, by virtue of this right, immediately obtain a writ termed a *habeas corpus* from a judge, whose sworn duty it is to grant it, and thereupon procure any illegal restraint to be quickly inquired into and redressed.

---

[1] Montesquieu.

A fourth right is that of holding lands by the tenure of easy rents, and not by rigorous and oppressive services, frequently forcing the possessors from their families and their business, to perform what ought to be done in all well-regulated states by men hired for the purpose.

The last right we shall mention regards the freedom of the press. The importance of this consists, besides the advancement of truth, science, morality, and arts in general, in its diffusion of liberal sentiments on the administration of government, its ready communication of thoughts between subjects, and its consequential promotion of union among them, whereby oppressive officers are shamed or intimidated into more honorable and just modes of conducting affairs.

These are the invaluable rights that form a considerable part of our mild system of government; that, sending its equitable energy through all ranks and classes of men, defends the poor from the rich, the weak from the powerful, the industrious from the rapacious, the peaceable from the violent, the tenants from the lords, and all from their superiors.

These are the rights without which a people can not be free and happy, and under the protecting and encouraging influence of which these colonies have hitherto so amazingly flourished and increased. These are the rights a profligate ministry are now striving by force of arms to ravish from us, and which we are with one mind resolved never to resign but with our lives.

These are the rights you are entitled to, and ought at this moment in perfection to exercise. And what is offered to you by the late act of Parliament in their place? Liberty of conscience in your religion? No. God gave it to you, and the temporal powers with which you have been and are connected firmly stipulated for your enjoyment of it. If laws divine and human could secure it against the despotic caprices of wicked men, it was secured before. Are the French laws in civil cases restored? It seems so. But observe the cautious kindness of the ministers who pretend to be your benefactors. The words of the statute are, "that those laws shall be the rule until they shall be varied or altered by any ordinances of the governor and council." Is the "certainty and lenity of the criminal law of England, and its benefits and advantages," commended in the said statute, and said to have been "sensibly felt by you," secured to you and your descendants? No. They too are subjected to arbitrary "alterations" by the governor and council; and a power is expressly reserved of appointing "such courts of criminal, civil, and ecclesiastical jurisdiction as shall be thought proper." Such is the precarious tenure of mere will by which you hold your lives and religion. The crown and its ministers are empowered, as far as they could be by Parliament, to establish even the Inquisition itself among you. Have you an Assembly composed of worthy men, elected by yourselves, and in whom you can confide, to make laws for you, to watch over your welfare, and to direct in what quantity and in what manner your money shall be taken from you? No. The power of making laws for you is lodged in the governor and council, all of them dependent upon and removable at the pleasure of a minister. Besides, another late statute, made without your consent, has subjected you to the impositions of excise, the horror of all free states, thus wresting your property from you by the most odious of taxes, and laying open to insolent tax-gatherers houses, the scenes of domestic peace and comfort, and called the castles of English subjects in the books of their law. And in the very act for altering your government, and intended to flatter you, you are not authorized to "assess, levy, or apply any rates and taxes but for the inferior purposes of making roads, and erecting and repairing public buildings, or for other local conveniences within your respective towns and districts." Why this degrading distinction? Ought not the property honestly acquired by Canadians to be held as sacred as that of Englishmen? Have not Canadians sense enough to attend to any other public affairs than gathering stones from one place and piling them up in another? Unhappy people! who are not only injured, but insulted. Nay, more! With such a superlative contempt of your understanding and spirit has an insolent ministry presumed to think of you, our respectable fellow-subjects, according to the information we have received, as firmly to persuade themselves that your gratitude for the injuries and insults they have recently offered to you will engage you to take up arms, and render yourselves the ridicule and detestation of the world, by becoming tools in their hands in taking that freedom from us which they have treacherously denied to you; the unavoidable consequences of which attempt, if successful, would be the extinction of all hopes of you or your posterity being ever restored to freedom; for idiocy itself can not believe that, when their drudgery is performed, they will treat you with less cruelty than they have us, who are of the same blood with themselves.

What would your countryman, the immortal Montesquieu, have said to such a plan of domination as has been framed for you? Hear his words, with an intenseness of thought suited to the importance of the subject: "In a free state, every man who is supposed a free agent ought to be concerned in his own government; therefore the legislative should reside in the whole body of the people or their representatives." "The political liberty of the subject is a tranquillity of mind, arising from the opinion each person has of his safety. In order to have this liberty, it is requisite the government be so constituted as that one man need not be afraid of another. When the power of making laws and the power of executing them are united in the same person, or in the same body of magistrates, there can be no liberty, because apprehensions may arise lest the same monarch or senate should enact tyrannical laws to execute them in a tyrannical manner."

"The power of judging should be exercised by persons taken from the body of the people, at certain times of the year, and pursuant to a form and manner prescribed by law. There is no liberty if the power of judging be not separated from the legislative and executive powers."

"Military men belong to a profession which may be useful, but is often dangerous." "The enjoyment of liberty, and even its support and preservation, consists in every man's being allowed to speak his thoughts and lay open his sentiments."

Apply these decisive maxims, sanctified by the authority of a name which all Europe reveres, to your own State. You have a governor, it may be urged, vested with the executive powers, or the powers of administration: in him and in your Council is lodged the power of making laws. You have judges, who are to decide every cause affecting your lives, liberty, or property. Here is, indeed, an appearance of the several powers being separated and distributed into different hands, for checks upon one another—the only effectual mode ever invented by the wit of men to promote their freedom and prosperity. But, scorning to be illuded by a tinseled outside, and exerting the natural sagacity of Frenchmen, examine the specious device, and you will find it, to use an expression of holy writ, "a whited sepulchre" for burying your lives, liberty, and property.

Your judges and your Legislative Council, as it is called, are dependent on your governor, and he is dependent on the servant of the crown in Great Britain. The legislative, executive, and judging powers are all moved by the nods of a minister. Privileges and immunities last no longer than his smiles. When he frowns, their feeble forms dissolve. Such a treacherous ingenuity has been exerted in drawing up the code lately offered to you, that every sentence beginning with a benevolent pretension concludes with a destructive power; and the substance of the whole, divested of its smooth words, is, that the crown and its ministers shall be as absolute throughout your extended province as the despots of Asia or Africa. What can protect your property from taxing edicts, and the rapacity of necessitous and cruel masters? your persons from *lettres-de-cachet*, jails, dungeons, and oppressive services? your lives and general liberty from arbitrary and unfeeling rulers? We defy you, casting your view upon every side, to discover a single circumstance promising from any quarter the faintest hope of liberty to you or your posterity, but from an entire adoption into the union of these colonies.

What advice would the truly great man before mentioned, that advocate of freedom and humanity, give you, were he now living, and knew that we, your numerous and powerful neighbors, animated by a just love of our invaded rights, and united by the indissoluble bands of affection and interest, called upon you by every obligation of regard for yourselves and your children, as we now do, to join us in our righteous contest, to make common cause with us therein, and take a noble chance for emerging from a humiliating subjection under governors, intendants, and military tyrants, into the firm rank and condition of English freemen, whose custom it is, derived from their ancestors, to make those tremble who dare to think of making them miserable?

Would not this be the purport of his address? "Seize the opportunity presented to you by Providence itself. You have been conquered into liberty, if you act as you ought. This work is not of man. You are a small people compared with those who, with open arms, invite you into a fellowship. A moment's reflection should convince you which will be most for your interest and happiness, to have all the rest of North America your unalterable friends, or your inveterate enemies. The injuries of Boston have roused and associated every colony from Nova Scotia to Georgia. Your province is the only link wanting to complete the bright and strong chain of union. Nature has joined your country to theirs. Do you join your political interests. For their own sakes they will never desert or betray you. Be assured that the happiness of a people inevitably depends on their liberty and their spirit to assert it. The value and extent of the advantages tendered to you are immense. Heaven grant you may not discover them to be blessings after they have bid you an eternal adieu."

We are too well acquainted with the liberality of sentiment distinguishing your nation, to imagine that difference of religion will prejudice you against a hearty amity with us. You know that the transcendant nature of freedom elevates those who unite in her cause above all such low-minded infirmities. The Swiss Cantons furnish a memorable proof of this truth. Their union is composed of Roman Catholic and Protestant States, living in the utmost concord and peace with one another, and thereby enabled, ever since they bravely vindicated their freedom, to defy and defeat every tyrant that has invaded them.

Should there be any among you, as there generally are in all societies, who prefer the favor of ministers and their own private interests to the welfare of their country, the temper of such selfish persons will render them incredibly active in opposing all public-spirited measures, from an expectation of being well rewarded for their sordid industry by their superiors; but we doubt not you will be upon your guard against such men, and not sacrifice the liberty and happiness of the whole Canadian people and their posterity to gratify the avarice and ambition of individuals.

We do not ask you, by this address, to commence acts of hostility against our common sovereign. We only invite you to consult your own glory and welfare, and not to suffer yourselves to be inveigled or intimidated by infamous ministers, so far as to become the instruments of their cruelty and despotism, but to unite with us in one social compact, formed on the generous principles of equal liberty, and cemented by such an exchange of beneficial and endearing offices as to render it perpetual. In order to complete this highly-desirable union, we submit it to your consideration, whether it may not be expedient for you to meet together in your several towns and districts, and elect deputies who, afterward meeting in a Provincial Congress, may choose delegates to represent your province in the Continental Congress to be held at Philadelphia on the tenth day of May, 1775.

In this present Congress, beginning on the fifth of the last month, and continued to this day, it has been with universal pleasure, and a unanimous vote, resolved that we should consider the violation of your rights, by the act for altering the government of your province, as a violation of our own, and that you should be invited to accede to our confederation, which has no other objects than the perfect security of the natural and civil rights of all the constituent members, according to their respective circumstances, and the preservation of a lasting and happy connection with Great Britain on the salutary and constitutional principles hereinbefore mentioned. For effecting these purposes, we have addressed an humble and loyal petition to his majesty, praying relief of our and your grievances, and have associated to stop all importations from Great Britain and Ireland, after the first day of December, and all exportations to those kingdoms and the West Indies, after the tenth day of next September, unless the said grievances are redressed.

That Almighty God may incline your minds to approve our equitable and necessary measures, to add yourselves to us, to put your fate, whenever you suffer injuries which you are determined to oppose, not on the small influence of your single province, but on the consolidated powers of North America, and may grant to our joint exertions an event as happy as our cause is just, is the fervent prayer of us, your sincere and affectionate friends and fellow-subjects.

By order of the Congress,

HENRY MIDDLETON, President.

PETITION OF CONGRESS TO THE KING.[1]

To the King's most excellent Majesty:

MOST GRACIOUS SOVEREIGN—We your majesty's faithful subjects, of the colonies of New Hampshire, Massachusetts Bay, Rhode Island and Providence Plantations, Connecticut, New York, New Jersey, Pennsylvania, the counties of Newcastle, Kent, and Sussex, on Delaware, Maryland, Virginia, North Carolina, and South Carolina, in behalf of ourselves and the inhabitants of these colonies, who have deputed us to represent them in general Congress, by this our humble petition beg leave to lay our grievances before the throne.

A standing army has been kept in these colonies ever since the conclusion of the late war, without the consent of our Assemblies; and this army, with a considerable naval armament, has been employed to force the collection of taxes.

The authority of the commander-in-chief, and under him the brigadier-general, has, in time of peace, been rendered supreme in all the civil governments of America.

The commander-in-chief of all your majesty's forces in North America has, in time of peace, been appointed governor of a colony.

The charges of usual officers have been greatly increased, and new, expensive, and oppressive offices have been multiplied.

The judges of admiralty and vice-admiralty courts are empowered to receive their salaries and fees from the effects condemned by themselves.

The officers of the customs are empowered to break open and enter houses without the authority of any civil magistrate, founded on legal information.

The judges of courts of common law have been made entirely dependent on one part of the Legislature for their salaries, as well as for the duration of their commissions.

---

[1] Adopted October 26th, 1774.—*Journals of Congress*, vol. i., p. 63. This was drawn up by John Adams, and corrected by John Dickenson.

Counselors, holding their commissions during pleasure, exercise legislative authority.

Humble and reasonable petitions, from the representatives of the people, have been fruitless.

The agents of the people have been discountenanced, and governors have been instructed to prevent the payment of the salaries.

Assemblies have been repeatedly and injuriously dissolved.

Commerce has been burdened with many useless and oppressive restrictions.

By several acts of Parliament, made in the fourth, fifth, sixth, seventh, and eighth years of your majesty's reign, duties are imposed on us for the purpose of raising a revenue; and the powers of admiralty and vice-admiralty courts are extended beyond their ancient limits, whereby our property is taken from us without our consent, the trial by jury in many civil cases is abolished, enormous forfeitures are incurred for slight offenses, vexatious informers are exempted from paying damages to which they are justly liable, and oppressive security is required from owners before they are allowed to defend their right.

Both Houses of Parliament have resolved that colonists may be tried in England for offenses alleged to have been committed in America, by virtue of a statute passed in the thirty-fifth year of Henry the Eighth, and in consequence thereof, attempts have been made to enforce that statute.

A statute was passed in the twelfth year of your majesty's reign, directing that persons charged with committing any offense therein described, in any place out of the realm, may be indicted and tried for the same in any shire or county within the realm, whereby inhabitants of these colonies may, in sundry cases by that statute made capital, be deprived of a trial by their peers of the vicinage.

In the last session of Parliament, an act was passed for blocking up the harbor of Boston; another, empowering the governor of the Massachusetts Bay to send persons indicted for murder in that province to another colony, or even to Great Britain, for trial, whereby such offenders may escape legal punishment; a third for altering the chartered constitution of government in that province; and a fourth for altering the limits of Quebec, abolishing the English and restoring the French laws, whereby great numbers of British Frenchmen are subjected to the latter, and establishing an absolute government and the Roman Catholic religion throughout those vast regions that border on the westerly and northerly boundaries of the free, Protestant English settlements; and a fifth for the better providing suitable quarters for officers and soldiers in his majesty's service in North America.

To a sovereign who glories in the name of Britain, the bare recital of these acts must, we presume, justify the loyal subjects who fly to the foot of his throne and implore his clemency for protection against them.

From this destructive system of colony administration, adopted since the conclusion of the last war, have flowed those distresses, dangers, fears, and jealousies that overwhelm your majesty's dutiful colonists with affliction; and we defy our most subtile and inveterate enemies to trace the unhappy differences between Great Britain and these colonies from an earlier period, or from other causes than we have assigned.

Had they proceeded on our part from restless levity of temper, unjust impulses of ambition, or artful suggestions of seditious persons, we should merit the opprobrious terms frequently bestowed on us by those we revere. But, so far from promoting innovations, we have only opposed them, and can be charged with no offense unless it be one to recieve injuries, and be sensible of them.

Had our creator been pleased to give us existence in a land of slavery, the sense of our condition might have been mitigated by ignorance and habit. But, thanks be to his adorable goodness, we were born the heirs of freedom, and ever enjoyed our right, under the auspices of your royal ancestors, whose family was seated on the throne to rescue and secure a pious and gallant nation from the popery and despotism of a superstitious and inexorable tyrant. Your majesty, we are confident, justly rejoices that your title to the crown is thus founded on the title of your people to liberty; and, therefore, we doubt not but your royal wisdom must approve the sensibility that teaches your subjects anxiously to guard the blessing they received from divine Providence, and thereby to prove the performance of that compact which elevated the illustrious house of Brunswick to the imperial dignity it now possesses.

The apprehension of being degraded into a state of servitude from the preeminent rank of English freemen, while our minds retain the strongest love of liberty, and clearly foresee the miseries preparing for us and our posterity, excites emotions in our breasts which, though we can not describe, we should not wish to conceal. Feeling as men, and thinking as subjects, in the manner we do, silence would be disloyalty. By giving this faithful information, we do all in our power to promote the great objects of your royal cares, the tranquillity of your government and the welfare of your people.

Duty to your majesty, and regard for the preservation of ourselves and our posterity, the primary obligations of nature and society, command us to entreat your royal attention; and, as your majesty enjoys the signal distinction of reigning over freemen, we apprehend the language of freemen can not be displeasing. Your royal indignation, we hope, will rather fall on those designing and dangerous men, who, daringly interposing themselves between your royal person and your faithful subjects, and for several years past incessantly employed to dissolve the bonds of society, by abusing your majesty's authority, misrepresenting your American subjects, and prosecuting the most desperate and irritating projects of oppression, have at length compelled us, by the force of accumulated injuries, too severe to be any longer tolerable, to disturb your majesty's repose by our complaints.

These sentiments are extorted from hearts that much more willingly would bleed in your majesty's service. Yet so greatly have we been misrepresented, that a necessity has been alleged of taking away our property from us without our consent, "to defray the charge of the administration of justice, the support of civil government, and the defense, protection, and security of the colonies."

But we beg leave to assure your majesty that such provision has been and will be made for defraying the first two articles as has been and shall be judged, by the Legislatures of the several colonies, just and suitable to their respective circumstances; and, for the defense, protection, and security of the colonies, their militia, if properly regulated, as they earnestly desire may immediately be done, would be fully sufficient, at least in times of peace; and in case of war, your faithful colonists will be ready and willing, as they ever have been, when constitutionally required, to demonstrate their loyalty to your majesty, by exerting their most strenuous efforts in granting supplies and raising forces. Yielding to no British subjects in affectionate attachment to your majesty's person, family, and government, we too dearly prize the privilege of expressing that attachment by those proofs that are honorable to the prince who receives them, and to the people who give them, ever to resign it to any body of men upon earth.

Had we been permitted to enjoy in quiet the inheritance left us by our forefathers, we should at this time have been peaceably, cheerfully, and usefully employed in recommending ourselves by every testimony of devotion to your majesty, and of veneration to the State from which we derive our origin. But though now exposed to unexpected and unnatural scenes of distress by a contention with that nation in whose parental guidance, on all important affairs, we have hitherto, with filial reverence, constantly trusted, and therefore can derive no instruction in our present unhappy and perplexing circumstances from any former experience, yet we doubt not the purity of our intention and the integrity of our conduct will justify us at that grand tribunal before which all mankind must submit to judgment.

We ask but for peace, liberty, and safety. We wish not a diminution of the prerogative, nor do we solicit the grant of any new right in our favor. Your royal authority over us, and our connection with Great Britain, we shall always carefully and zealously endeavor to support and maintain.

Filled with sentiments of duty to your majesty, and of affection to our parent State, deeply impressed by our education, and strongly confirmed by our reason, and anxious to evince the sincerity of these dispositions, we present this petition only to obtain redress of grievances and relief from fears and jealousies occasioned by the system of statutes and regulations, adopted since the close of the late war, for raising a revenue in America; extending the powers of courts of admiralty and vice-admiralty; trying persons in Great Britain for offenses alleged to be committed in America, affecting the province of Massachusetts Bay; and altering the government and extending the limits of Quebec; by the abolition of which system the harmony between Great Britain and these colonies, so necessary to the happiness of both, and so ardently desired by the latter, and the usual intercourse will be immediately restored. In the magnanimity and justice of your majesty and Parliament, we confide for a redress of our other grievances, trusting that, when the causes of our apprehensions are removed, our future conduct will prove us not unworthy of the regard we have been accustomed, in our happier days, to enjoy; for, appealing to that Being who searches thoroughly the hearts of his creatures, we solemnly profess that our councils have been influenced by no other motives than a dread of impending destruction.

Permit us, then, most gracious sovereign, in the name of all your faithful people in America, with the utmost humility, to implore you, for the honor of Almighty God, whose pure religion our enemies are undermining; for your glory, which can be advanced only by rendering your subjects happy, and keeping them united; for the interests of your family, depending on an adherence to the principles that enthroned it; for the safety and welfare of your kingdoms and dominions, threatened with almost unavoidable dangers and distresses, that your majesty, as the loving father of your whole people, connected by the same bonds of law, loyalty, faith, and blood, though dwelling in various countries, will not suffer the transcendant relation formed by these ties to be further violated, in uncertain expectation of effects that, if attained, never can compensate for the calamities through which they must be gained.

We, therefore, most earnestly beseech your majesty that your royal authority and interposition may be used for our relief, and that a gracious answer may be given to this petition.

That your majesty may enjoy every felicity through a long and glorious reign, over loyal and happy subjects, and that your descendants may inherit your prosperity and dominions till time shall be no more, is, and always will be, our sincere and fervent prayer.

IV.

A DECLARATION, BY THE SECOND CONTINENTAL CONGRESS. SETTING FORTH THE CAUSES AND NECESSITY OF THE PEOPLE TAKING UP ARMS.[1]

If it was possible for men, who exercise their reason, to believe that the Divine Author of our existence intended a part of the human race to hold an absolute property in, and an unbounded power over, others, marked out by his infinite goodness and wisdom, as the objects of a legal domination never rightfully resistible, however severe and oppressive, the inhabitants of these colonies might at least require from the Parliament of Great Britain some evidence that this dreadful authority over them has been granted to that body. But a reverence for our great Creator, principles of humanity, and the dictates of common sense, must convince all those who reflect upon the subject, that government was instituted to promote the welfare of mankind, and ought to be administered for the attainment of that end. The Legislature of Great Britain, however, stimulated by an inordinate passion for a power not only unjustifiable, but which they know to be peculiarly reprobated by the very constitution of that kingdom, and desperate of success in any mode of contest where regard should be had to truth, law, or right, have, at length, deserting those, attempted to effect their cruel and impolitic purpose of enslaving these colonies by violence, and have thereby rendered it necessary for us to close with their last appeal from reason to arms. Yet, however blinded that assembly may be by their intemperate rage for unlimited domination, so to slight justice and the opinion of mankind, we esteem ourselves bound by obligations of respect to the rest of the world to make known the justice of our cause.

Our forefathers, inhabitants of the island of Great Britain, left their native land to seek on these shores a residence for civil and religious freedom. At the expense of their blood, at the hazard of their fortunes, without the least charge to their country from which they removed, by unceasing labor and an unconquerable spirit, they effected settlements in the distant and inhospitable wilds of America, then filled with numerous and warlike nations of barbarians. Societies or governments vested with perfect Legislatures were formed under charters from the crown, and an harmonious intercourse was established between the colonies and the kingdom from which they derived their origin. The mutual benefits of this union became, in a short time, so extraordinary as to excite astonishment. It is universally confessed that the amazing increase of the

---

[1] Adopted July 6, 1775.—See *Journals of Congress*, vol. 1, p. 134.

wealth, strength, and navigation of the realm arose from this source; and the minister who so wisely and successfully directed the measures of Great Britain in the late war publicly declared, that these colonies enabled her to triumph over her enemies. Toward the close of that war it pleased our sovereign to make a change in his councils. From that fatal moment the affairs of the British empire began to fall into confusion, and gradually sliding from the summit of glorious prosperity, to which they had been advanced by the virtues and abilities of one man, are at length distracted by the convulsions that now shake it to its deepest foundations. The new ministry, finding the brave foes of Britain, though frequently defeated, yet still contending, took up the unfortunate idea of granting them a hasty peace, and of then subduing her faithful friends.

These devoted colonies were judged to be in such a state, as to present victories without bloodshed, and all the easy emoluments of statuteable plunder. The uninterrupted tenor of their peaceable and respectful behavior from the beginning of colonization—their dutiful, zealous, and useful services during the war, though so recently and amply acknowledged in the most honorable manner by his majesty, by the late king, and by Parliament, could not save them from the meditated innovations. Parliament was influenced to adopt the pernicious project, and, assuming a new power over them, have, in the course of eleven years, given such decisive specimens of the spirit and consequences attending this power, as to leave no doubt concerning the effects of acquiescence under it. They have undertaken to give and grant our money without our consent, though we have ever exercised an exclusive right to dispose of our own property; statutes have been passed for extending the jurisdiction of admiralty and vice-admiralty courts beyond their ancient limits; for depriving us of the accustomed and inestimable privilege of trial by jury, in cases affecting both life and property; for suspending the Legislature of one of the colonies; for interdicting all commerce with the capital of another; and for altering fundamentally the form of government established by charter, and secured by acts of its own Legislature solemnly confirmed by the crown; for exempting the "murderers" of colonists from legal trial, and, in effect, from punishment; for erecting in a neighboring province, acquired by the joint arms of Great Britain and America, a despotism dangerous to our very existence; and for quartering soldiers upon the colonists in time of profound peace. It has also been resolved in Parliament, that colonists charged with committing certain offenses shall be transported to England to be tried.

But why should we enumerate our injuries in detail? By one statute it is declared, that Parliament can "of right make laws to bind us in all cases whatsoever." What is to defend us against so enormous, so unlimited, a power? Not a single man of those who assume it is chosen by us, or is subject to our control or influence; but, on the contrary, they are all of them exempt from the operation of such laws, and an American revenue, if not diverted from the ostensible purposes for which it is raised, would actually lighten their own burdens in proportion as they increase ours. We saw the misery to which such despotism would reduce us. We for ten years incessantly and ineffectually besieged the throne as supplicants: we reasoned, we remonstrated with Parliament in the most mild and decent language.

Administration, sensible that we should regard these oppressive measures as freemen ought to do, sent over fleets and armies to enforce them. The indignation of the Americans was roused, it is true, but it was the indignation of a virtuous, loyal, and affectionate people. A Congress of delegates from the united colonies was assembled at Philadelphia on the fifth day of last September. We resolved again to offer an humble and dutiful petition to the king, and also addressed our fellow-subjects of Great Britain. We have pursued every temperate, every respectful measure; we have even proceeded to break off our commercial intercourse with our fellow-subjects, as the last peaceable admonition, that our attachment to no nation on earth should supplant our attachment to liberty. This, we flattered ourselves, was the ultimate step of the controversy; but subsequent events have shown how vain was the hope of finding moderation in our enemies.

Several threatening expressions against the colonies were inserted in his majesty's speech; our petition, though we were told it was a decent one, and that his majesty had been pleased to receive it graciously, and to promise laying it before his Parliament, was huddled into both Houses among a bundle of American papers, and there neglected. The Lords and Commons, in their address in the month of February, said, that "a rebellion at that time actually existed within the province of Massachusetts Bay; and that those concerned in it had been countenanced and encouraged by unlawful combinations and engagements, entered into by his majesty's subjects in several of the other colonies; and therefore they besought his majesty that he would take the most effectual measures to enforce due obedience to the laws and authority of the supreme Legislature." Soon after, the commercial intercourse of the whole colonies, with foreign countries, and with each other, was cut off by an act of Parliament: by another, several of them were entirely prohibited from the fisheries in the seas near their coasts, on which they always depended for their sustenance; and large reinforcements of ships and troops were immediately sent over to General Gage.

Fruitless were all the entreaties, arguments, and eloquence of an illustrious band of the most distinguished peers and commoners, who nobly and strenuously asserted the justice of our cause, to stay, or even to mitigate the heedless fury with which these accumulated and unexampled outrages were hurried on. Equally fruitless was the interference of the city of London, of Bristol, and many other respectable towns in our favor. Parliament adopted an insidious movement calculated to divide us, to establish a perpetual auction of taxations where colony should bid against colony, all of them uninformed what ransom would redeem their lives, and thus to extort from us, at the point of the bayonet, the unknown sums that should be sufficient to gratify, if possible to gratify, ministerial rapacity, with the miserable indulgence left to us of raising, in our own mode, the prescribed tribute. What terms more rigid and humiliating could have been dictated by remorseless victors to conquered enemies? In our circumstances to accept them, would be to deserve them.

Soon after the intelligence of these proceedings arrived on this continent, General Gage, who in the course of the last year had taken possession of the town of Boston, in the province of Massachusetts Bay, and still occupied it as a garrison, on the nineteenth day of April, sent out from that place a large detachment of his army, who made an unprovoked assault on the inhabitants of the said province, at the town of Lexington, as appears by the affidavits of a great number of persons, some of whom were officers and soldiers of that detachment, murdered eight of the inhabitants, and wounded many others. From thence the troops proceeded, in warlike array, to the town of Concord, where they set upon another party of the inhabitants of the same province, killing several and wounding more, until compelled to retreat by the country people suddenly assembled to repel this cruel aggression. Hostilities, thus commenced by the British troops, have been since prosecuted by them without regard to faith or reputation. The inhabitants of Boston being confined within that town by the general, their governor, and having, in order to procure their dismission, entered into a treaty with him, it was stipulated that the said inhabitants, having deposited their arms with their own magistrates, should have liberty to depart, taking with them their other effects. They accordingly delivered up their arms, but in open violation of honor, in defiance of the obligation of treaties, which even savage nations esteem sacred, the governor ordered the arms deposited as aforesaid, that they might be preserved for their owners, to be seized by a body of soldiers; detained the greatest part of the inhabitants in the town, and compelled the few who were permitted to retire, to leave their most valuable effects behind.

By this perfidy wives are separated from their husbands, children from their parents, the aged and the sick from their relations and friends, who wish to attend and comfort them; and those who had been used to live in plenty and even elegance, are reduced to deplorable distress.

The general, further emulating his ministerial masters, by a proclamation bearing date on the twelfth day of June, after venting the grossest falsehoods and calumnies against the good people of these colonies, proceeds to "declare them all, either by name or description, to be rebels and traitors, to supersede the course of the common law, and instead thereof to publish and order the use and exercise of the law martial." His troops have butchered our countrymen, have wantonly burned Charlestown, besides a considerable number of houses in other places; our ships and vessels are seized; the necessary supplies of provisions are intercepted; and he is exerting his utmost power to spread destruction and devastation around him.

We have received certain intelligence that General Carleton, the governor of Canada, is instigating the people of that province and the Indians to fall upon us; and we have but too much reason to apprehend that schemes have been formed to excite domestic enemies against us. In brief, a part of these colonies now feel, and all of them are sure of feeling, as far as the vengeance of administration can inflict them, the complicated calamities of fire, sword, and famine. We are reduced to the alternative of choosing an unconditional submission to the tyranny of irritated ministers, or resistance by force. The latter is our choice. We have counted the cost of this contest, and find nothing so dreadful as voluntary slavery. Honor, justice, and humanity, forbid us tamely to surrender that freedom which we received from our gallant ancestors, and which our innocent posterity have a right to receive from us. We can not endure the infamy and guilt of resigning succeeding generations to that wretchedness which inevitably awaits them, if we basely entail hereditary bondage upon them.

Our cause is just: our union is perfect: our internal resources are great, and, if necessary, foreign assistance is undoubtedly attainable. We gratefully acknowledge, as signal instances of the Divine favor toward us, that His Providence would not permit us to be called into this severe controversy until we were grown up to our present strength, had been previously exercised in warlike operations, and possessed of the means of defending ourselves. With hearts fortified with these animating reflections, we most solemnly, before God and the world, *declare*, that, exerting the utmost energy of those powers which our beneficent Creator hath graciously bestowed upon us, the arms we have been compelled by our enemies to assume, we will, in defiance of every hazard, with unabating firmness and perseverance, employ for the preservation of our liberties; being with one mind resolved to die freemen rather than to live slaves.

Lest this declaration should disquiet the minds of our friends and fellow-subjects in any part of the empire, we assure them that we mean not to dissolve that union which has long and so happily subsisted between us, and which we sincerely wish to see restored. Necessity has not yet driven us into that desperate measure, or induced us to excite any other nation to war against them. We have not raised armies with ambitious designs of separating from Great Britain, and establishing independent States. We fight not for glory nor for conquest. We exhibit to mankind the remarkable spectacle of a people attacked by unprovoked enemies, without any imputation or even suspicion of offense. They boast of their privileges and civilization, and yet proffer no milder conditions than servitude or death.

In our native land, in defense of the freedom that is our birthright, and which we ever enjoyed till the late violation of it—for the protection of our property, acquired solely by the honest industry of our forefathers and ourselves, against violence actually offered, we have taken up arms. We shall lay them down when hostilities shall cease on the part of the aggressors, and all danger of their being renewed shall be removed, and not before.

With an humble confidence in the mercies of the supreme and impartial Judge and Ruler of the universe, we most devoutly implore His divine goodness to protect us happily through this great conflict, to dispose our adversaries to reconciliation on reasonable terms, and thereby to relieve the empire from the calamities of civil war.

MEMBERS OF THE FIRST CONTINENTAL CONGRESS.

The following are the names of the members of the first Continental Congress, who assembled at Carpenter's Hall, Philadelphia, on the 5th of September, 1774. Many of these were members of the second Congress, also, which assembled at the same place on the 10th of May, 1775.

New Hampshire.—John Sullivan, Nathanial Folsom.

Massachusetts.—Thomas Cushing, Samuel Adams, John Adams, Robert Treat Paine.

Rhode Island and Providence Plantations.—Stephen Hopkins, Samuel Ward.

Connecticut.—Eliphalet Dyer, Roger Sherman, Silas Deane.

New York.—James Duane, John Jay, Isaac Low, John Alsop, William Floyd, Philip Livingston, Henry Wisner.

New Jersey.—James Kinsey, Stephen Crane, William Livingston, Richard Smith, John De Hart.

Pennsylvania.—Joseph Galloway, John Morton, Charles Humphreys, Thomas Mifflin, Samuel Rhodes, Edward Biddle, George Ross, John Dickenson.

Delaware.—Cæsar Rodney, Thomas M'Kean, George Read.

Maryland.—Robert Goldsborough, Samuel Chase, Thomas Johnson, Matthew Tilghman, William Paca.

Virginia.—Peyton Randolph, Richard Henry Lee, George Washington, Patrick Henry, Richard Bland, Benjamin Harrison, Edmund Pendleton.

North Carolina.—William Hooper, Joseph Hughes, Richard Caswell.

South Carolina.—Henry Middleton, John Rutledge, Thomas Lynch, Christopher Gadsden, Edward Rutledge.

The several sessions of the Continental Congress were commenced as follows: September 5, 1774, also May 10, 1775, at Philadelphia; December 20, 1776, at Baltimore; March 4, 1777, at Philadelphia; September 27, 1777, at Lancaster, Pennsylvania; September 30, 1777, at York, Pennsylvania; July 2, 1778, at Philadelphia; June 30, 1783, at Princeton, New Jersey; November 26, 1783, at Annapolis, Maryland; November 1, 1784, at Trenton, New Jersey; June 11, 1785, at New York, which, from that time, continued to be the place of meeting until the adoption of the Federal Constitution.

V.

THE DECLARATION OF INDEPENDENCE.

THE bold Resolution offered in the Continental Congress, by Richard Henry Lee, of Virginia, on the 7th of June, 1776, which declared the American colonies FREE AND INDEPENDENT STATES, was, as we have observed,[1] debated for three days, when the further consideration of it was postponed until the first of July, and a committee was appointed to draw up an accompanying Declaration. On the day specified, the motion was brought up in the committee of the whole House, Benjamin Harrison, of Virginia (father of the late President Harrison), in the chair. The draft of a Declaration of Independence was reported at the same time, and for three consecutive days, it was debated by paragraphs, seriatim. Many alterations, omissions, and amendments were made. The following is a copy of the original draft, from the pen of Thomas Jefferson, before any amendments were made in committee of the whole. The passages omitted by Congress are printed in italics, and the substitutions are given in notes at the bottom of the page:[2]

---

[1] Page 251.

[2] John Adams, in his autobiography, gives the following reasons why Mr. Jefferson was chosen to write the Declaration: "Mr. Jefferson had been now about a year a member of Congress, but

A Declaration by the Representatives of the UNITED STATES OF AMERICA, *in general Congress assembled:*

When, in the course of human events, it becomes necessary for one people to dissolve the political bands which have connected them with another, and to assume, among the powers of the earth, the separate and equal station to which the laws of nature and of nature's God entitle them, a decent respect to the opinions of mankind requires that they should declare the causes which impel them to the separation.

We hold these truths to be self-evident: that all men are created equal; that they are endowed by their Creator with *inherent and inalienable*[1] rights; that among these are life, liberty, and the pursuit of happiness; that, to secure these rights, governments are instituted among men, deriving their just powers from the consent of the governed; that, whenever any form of government becomes destructive of these ends, it is the right of the people to alter or *to* abolish it, and to institute new government, laying its foundation on such principles, and organizing its powers in such form, as to them shall seem most likely to effect their safety and happiness. Prudence, indeed, will dictate, that governments long established, should not be changed for light and transient

---

had attended his duty in the House a very small part of the time, and when there had never spoken in public. During the whole time I sat with him in Congress, I never heard him utter three sentences together.

"It will naturally be inquired how it happened that he was appointed on a committee of such importance. There were more reasons than one. Mr. Jefferson had the reputation of a masterly pen; he had been chosen a delegate in Virginia in consequence of a very handsome public paper which he had written for the House of Burgesses, which had given him the character of a fine writer. Another reason was, that Mr. Richard Henry Lee was not beloved by the most of his colleagues from Virginia, and Mr. Jefferson was sent up to rival and supplant him. This could be done only by the pen, for Mr. Jefferson could stand no competition with him, or any one else, in elocution and public debate.

"The committee had several meetings, in which were proposed the articles of which the Declaration was to consist, and minutes made of them. The committee then appointed Mr. Jefferson and me to draw them up in form, and clothe them in a proper dress. The sub-committee met, and considered the minutes, making such observations on them as then occurred, when Mr. Jefferson desired me to take them to my lodgings and make the draft. This I declined, and gave several reasons for so doing:

"1. That he was a Virginian, and I a Massachusettensian. 2. That he was a Southern man, and I a Northern one. 3. That I had been so obnoxious for my early and constant zeal in promoting the measure, that every draft of mine would undergo a more severe scrutiny and criticism in Congress than one of his composition. 4. And lastly, and that would be reason enough, if there were no other, I had a great opinion of the elegance of his pen, and none at all of my own. I therefore insisted that no hesitation should be made on his part. He accordingly took the minutes, and in a day or two produced to me his draft."

On the 8th of July, four days after the amended Declaration was adopted, Mr. Jefferson wrote the following letter, and sent it, with the original draft to Mr. Lee, who was then at his home in Virginia, with his sick wife:

"PHILADELPHIA, July 8, 1776.

"DEAR SIR—For news, I refer you to your brother, who writes on that head. I inclose you a copy of the Declaration of Independence, as agreed to by the House, and also as originally framed; you will judge whether it is the better or the worse for the critics. I shall return to Virginia after the 11th of August. I wish my successor may be certain to come before that time; in that case, I hope I shall see you, and not Wythe, in convention, that the business of government, which is of everlasting concern, may receive your aid. Adieu, and believe me to be your friend and servant,

"THOMAS JEFFERSON."

"TO RICHARD HENRY LEE, ESQ."

[1] Certain unalienable

causes. And, accordingly, all experience hath shown that mankind are more disposed to suffer, while evils are sufferable, than to right themselves by abolishing the forms to which they are accustomed. But when a long train of abuses and usurpations, *begun at a distinguished period, and* pursuing invariably the same object, evinces a design to reduce them under absolute despotism, it is their right, it is their duty, to throw off such government, and to provide new guards for their future security. Such has been the patient sufferance of these colonies; and such is now the necessity which constrains them to *expunge*[1] their former systems of government. The history of the present King of Great Britain is a history of *unremitting*[2] injuries and usurpations; *among which appears no solitary fact to contradict the uniform tenor of the rest; but* all *have*,[3] in direct object, the establishment of an absolute tyranny over these States. To prove this, let facts be submitted to a candid world; *for the truth of which we pledge a faith yet unsullied by falsehood.*

He has refused his assent to laws the most wholesome and necessary for the public good.

He has forbidden his governors to pass laws of immediate and pressing importance, unless suspended in their operation till his assent should be obtained; and when so suspended, he has *neglected utterly*[4] to attend to them.

He has refused to pass other laws for the accommodation of large districts of people, unless those people would relinquish the right of representation in the Legislature; a right inestimable to them, and formidable to tyrants only.

He has called together legislative bodies at places unusual, uncomfortable, and distant from the repository of their public records, for the sole purpose of fatiguing them into compliance with his measures.

He has dissolved representative Houses repeatedly *and continually*, for opposing with manly firmness his invasions of the rights of the people.

He has refused, for a long time after such dissolutions, to cause others to be elected, whereby the legislative powers, incapable of annihilation, have returned to the people at large for their exercise, the State remaining, in the mean time, exposed to all the dangers of invasion from without and convulsions within.

He has endeavored to prevent the population of these States; for that purpose obstructing the laws for naturalization of foreigners; refusing to pass others to encourage their migrations hither; and raising the conditions of new appropriations of lands.

He has suffered the administration of justice totally to cease in some of these States,[5] refusing his assent to laws for establishing judiciary powers.

He has made *our* judges dependent on his will alone, for the tenure of their offices and the amount and payment of their salaries.

He has erected a multitude of new offices *by a self-assumed power*, and sent hither swarms of officers to harass our people and eat out their substance.

---

[1] Alter [2] Repeated [3] Having [4] Utterly neglected
[5] He has obstructed the administration of justice, by

He has kept among us, in times of peace, standing armies *and ships of war*, without the consent of our Legislatures.

He has affected to render the military independent of, and superior to, the civil power.

He has combined with others to subject us to a jurisdiction foreign to our constitutions, and unacknowledged by our laws; giving his assent to their acts of pretended legislation:

For quartering large bodies of armed troops among us;

For protecting them, by a mock trial, from punishment for any murders which they should commit on the inhabitants of these States;

For cutting off our trade with all parts of the world;

For imposing taxes on us without our consent;

For depriving us[1] of the benefits of trial by jury;

For transporting us beyond the seas to be tried for pretended offenses;

For abolishing the free system of English laws in a neighboring province, establishing therein an arbitrary government, and enlarging its boundaries, so as to render it at once an example and fit instrument for introducing the same absolute rule into these *States*;[2]

For taking away our charters, abolishing our most valuable laws, and altering fundamentally the forms of our governments;

For suspending our own Legislatures, and declaring themselves invested with power to legislate for us in all cases whatsoever.

He has abdicated government here, *withdrawing his governors, and*[3] declaring us out of his *allegiance and* protection, and waging war against us.

He has plundered our seas, ravaged our coasts, burned our towns, and destroyed the lives of our people.

He is at this time transporting large armies of foreign mercenaries to complete the works of death, desolation, and tyranny, already begun with circumstances of cruelty and perfidy[4] unworthy the head of a civilized nation.

He has endeavored to bring on the inhabitants of our frontiers the merciless Indian savages, whose known rule of warfare is an undistinguished destruction of all ages, sexes, and conditions *of existence; he has excited treasonable insurrections of our fellow-citizens with the allurements of forfeiture and confiscation of our property.*

He has constrained *others*,[5] taken captive on the high seas, to bear arms against their country, to become the executioners of their friends and brethren, or to fall themselves by their hands.

He has waged cruel war against human nature itself, violating its most sacred rights of life and liberty in the persons of a distant people, who never offended him, captivating and carrying them into slavery in another hemisphere, or to incur miserable death in their transportation thither. This piratical warfare, the opprobrium of infidel powers, is the warfare of the CHRISTIAN *King of Great Britain. Determined to keep open a market*

[1] In many cases [2] Colonies. [3] By
[4] Scarcely paralleled in the most barbarous ages, and totally [5] Our fellow-citizens

where MEN *should be bought and sold, he has prostituted his negative for suppressing every legislative attempt to prohibit or to restrain this execrable commerce. And that this assemblage of horrors might want no fact of distinguished dye, he is now exciting those very people to rise in arms among us, and to purchase that liberty of which* he *has deprived them, by murdering the people upon whom* he *obtruded them: thus paying off former crimes committed against the* LIBERTIES *of one people with crimes which he urges them to commit against the* LIVES *of another.**

In every stage of these oppressions, we have petitioned for redress in the most humble terms: our repeated petitions have been answered only by repeated injury. A prince whose character is thus marked by every act which may define a tyrant, is unfit to be the ruler of a people *who mean to be free.*[1] *Future ages will scarce believe that the hardiness of one man adventured, within the short compass of twelve years only, to build a foundation, so broad and undisguised, for tyranny over a people fostered and fixed in principles of freedom.*

Nor have we been wanting in attentions to our British brethren. We have warned them, from time to time, of attempts by their Legislature to extend *a*[2] jurisdiction over *these our States.*[3] We have reminded them of the circumstances of our emigration and settlement here, *no one of which could warrant so strange a pretension; that these were effected at the expense of our own blood and treasure, unassisted by the wealth or the strength of Great Britain; that, in constituting, indeed, our several forms of government, we had adopted one common king, thereby laying a foundation for perpetual league and amity with them; but that submission to their Parliament was no part of our Constitution, nor ever in idea, if history may be credited; and* we[4] appealed to their native justice and magnanimity, *as well as to*[5] the ties of our common kindred, to disavow these usurpations, which *were likely to*[6] interrupt our connection and correspondence. They, too, have been deaf to the voice of justice and consanguinity; *and when occasions have been given them, by the regular course of their laws, of removing from their councils the disturbers of our harmony, they have, by their free election, re-established them in power. At this very time, too, they are permitting their chief magistrate to send over, not only soldiers of our common blood, but [Scotch† and] foreign mercenaries to invade and destroy us. These facts have given*

* It has been asserted that this paragraph was expunged because it was not palatable to those delegates who were slaveholders, and that it was stricken out lest it should cause them to cast a negative vote on the question. There is no proof that such selfish motives actuated any member of that assembly. It was a sacred regard for truth which caused it to be stricken out. No such charge as the paragraph contained could justly be made against George III., then under arraignment. The slave-trade was begun and carried on long before the reign of any of his house, and it is not known that he ever gave his assent to any thing relating to slavery, except to abolish it, and to declare the trade a piracy. By a resolution offered by Charles F. Mercer, of Virginia, and adopted by Congress in 1817, the slave-trade was declared "a piracy." Mr. Jefferson was the first American statesman, and probably the first writer of modern times, who denounced that infamous traffic as "a piratical warfare."—See *Life of Richard Henry Lee*, i., 176.

1 Free people
2 An unwarrantable
3 Us
4 Have
5 And we have conjured them by
6 Would inevitably

† Dr. Witherspoon, who was a Scotchman by birth, moved the striking out of the word *Scotch.*

the last stab to agonizing affection, and manly spirit bids us to renounce forever these unfeeling brethren. We must endeavor to forget our former love for them; we must, therefore, acquiesce in the necessity which denounces our separation, and hold them as we hold the rest of mankind, enemies in war, in peace, friends.

We might have been a free and great people together; but a communication of grandeur and of freedom, it seems, is below their dignity. Be it so, since they will have it. The road to happiness and to glory is open to us, too; we will climb it apart from them, and acquiesce in the necessity which denounces our eternal separation.

We, therefore, the representatives of the United States of America, in general Congress assembled, appealing to the Supreme Judge of the world for the rectitude of our intentions, do, in the name, and by the authority of the good people of these States,[1] *reject and renounce all allegiance and subjection to the kings of Great Britain, and all others who may hereafter claim by, through, or under them; we utterly dissolve all political connection which may heretofore have subsisted between us and the Parliament or people of Great Britain; and, finally, we do assert the colonies to be free and independent States;* and that, as free and independent States, they have full power to levy war, conclude peace, contract alliances, establish commerce, and to do all other acts and things which independent States may of right do. And for the support of this Declaration, we mutually pledge to each other our lives, our fortunes, and our sacred honor.

Mr. Lee's resolution, declaring the colonies "free and independent States," was adopted on the 2d of July, and that day, rather than the 4th, should be celebrated as our national anniversary. It was only the *form of the Declaration,* which accompanied the resolution, that was adopted on the latter day.

The debates on the question of the adoption of the Declaration of Independence were long and animated, for there was very little unanimity in feeling when they began in June. Richard Henry Lee, the Adamses, of Massachusetts, Dr. Witherspoon, of New Jersey, and Edward Rutledge, of South Carolina, were the chief speakers in favor of the measure; and John Dickenson, of Pennsylvania, against it. Although it was evident, from the first introduction of the resolution, that a majority of the colonies would vote for it, its friends were fearful that a *unanimous* vote could not be obtained, inasmuch as two of the Assemblies of Maryland and Pennsylvania had refused to sanction the measure, and those of Georgia, South Carolina, and New York, were silent. Anxiously did the friends of the measure endeavor to win the wavering, and at length they were successful. On the 4th of July, 1776, a unanimous vote of the thirteen colonies was given in favor of the great Declaration.[2] The record

[1] Colonies. See concluding paragraph of the Declaration, page 601.

[2] On the 9th of September, 1776, Congress resolved, "That in all continental commissions, and other instruments, where, heretofore, the words "United Colonies" have been used, the style be altered, for the future, to the "United States." From that day, the word "Colony" is not known in our history.

of the event was made in the following plain manner, in the journal of Congress for that day:[1]

"Agreeably to the order of the day, the Congress resolved itself into a committee of the whole, to take into their further consideration the Declaration; and, after some time, the president resumed the chair, and Mr. Harrison reported that the committee have agreed to a Declaration, which they desired him to report. The Declaration being read, was agreed to as follows:"

A DECLARATION BY THE REPRESENTATIVES OF THE UNITED STATES OF AMERICA, IN CONGRESS ASSEMBLED.

When, in the course of human events, it becomes necessary for one people to dissolve the political bands which have connected them with another, and to assume, among the powers of the earth, the separate and equal station, to which the laws of nature, and of nature's God entitle them, a decent respect to the opinions of mankind requires that they should declare the causes which impel them to the separation.

We hold these truths to be self-evident—that all men are created equal; that they are endowed by their Creator with certain inalienable rights; that among these are life, liberty, and the pursuit of happiness. That, to secure these rights, governments are instituted among men, deriving their just powers from the consent of the governed; that, whenever any form of government becomes destructive of these ends, it is the right of the people to alter or abolish it, and to institute a new government, laying its foundations on such principles, and organizing its powers in such form, as to them shall seem most likely to effect their safety and happiness. Prudence, indeed, will dictate that governments long established should not be changed for light and transient causes; and, accordingly, all experience hath shown that mankind are more disposed to suffer, while evils are sufferable, than to right themselves by abolishing the forms to which they are accustomed. But when a long train of abuses and usurpations, pursuing invariably the same object, evinces a design to reduce them under absolute despotism, it is their right, it is their duty, to throw off such a government, and to provide new guards for their future security. Such has been the patient sufferance of these colonies, and such is now the necessity which constrains them to alter their former systems of government. The history of the present King of Great Britain, is a history of repeated injuries and usurpations, all having in direct object the establishment of an absolute tyranny over these States. To prove this, let facts be submitted to a candid world.

He has refused his assent to laws the most wholesome and necessary for the public good.[2]

---

[1] The great importance of the event does not seem to have been realized even by many men in public life. Anderson, in his *Constitutional Gazette*, announced the fact thus, as a mere *on dit*, without comment or further reference to the subject: "On Tuesday last, the Continental Congress declared the United Colonies free and independent States."

[2] The colonial assemblies from time to time made enactments touching their commercial operations, the emission of a colonial currency, and concerning representatives in the imperial parliament,

He has forbidden his governors to pass laws of immediate and pressing importance, unless suspended in their operations till his assent should be obtained; and, when so suspended, he has utterly neglected to attend to them.[1]

He has refused to pass other laws for the accommodation of large districts of people, unless those people would relinquish the right of representation in the Legislature—a right inestimable to them, and formidable to tyrants only.[2]

He has called together legislative bodies at places unusual, uncomfortable, and distant from the repository of their public records, for the sole purpose of fatiguing them into compliance with his measures.[3]

He has dissolved representative houses repeatedly, for opposing, with manly firmness, his invasions on the rights of the people.[4]

---

but the assent of the sovereign to these laws was withheld. After the Stamp Act excitements [page 214], Secretary Conway informed the Americans that the tumults should be overlooked, provided the Assemblies would make provision for full compensation for all public property which had been destroyed. In complying with this demand, the Assembly of Massachusetts thought it would be "wholesome and necessary for the public good," to grant free pardon to all who had been engaged in the disturbances, and passed an act accordingly. It would have produced quiet and good feeling, but the royal assent was refused.

[1] In 1764, the Assembly of New York took measures to conciliate the SIX NATIONS, and other Indian tribes. The motives of the Assembly were misconstrued, representations having been made to the king that the colonies wished to make allies of the Indians, so as to increase their physical power and proportionate independence of the British crown. The monarch sent instructions to all his governors to desist from such alliances, or to suspend their operations until his assent should be given. He then "utterly neglected to attend to them." The Massachusetts Assembly passed a law in 1770, for taxing officers of the British government in that colony. The governor was ordered to withhold his assent to such tax-bill. This was in violation of the colonial charter, and the people justly complained. The Assembly was prorogued from time to time, and laws of great importance were "utterly neglected."

[2] A law was passed by Parliament in the spring of 1774, by which the popular representative system in the province of Quebec (Canada) was annulled, and officers appointed by the crown, had all power as legislators, except that of levying taxes. The Canadians being Roman Catholics, were easily pacified under the new order of things, by having their religious system declared the established religion of the province. But "large districts of people" bordering on Nova Scotia, felt this deprivation to be a great grievance. Their humble petitions concerning commercial regulations were unheeded, because they remonstrated against the new order of things, and Governor Carleton [page 240] plainly told them that they must cease their clamor about representatives, before they should have any new commercial laws. A bill for "better regulating the government in the province of Massachusetts Bay," passed that year, provided for the abridgment of the privileges of popular elections, to take the government out of the hands of the people, and to vest the nomination of judges, magistrates, and even sheriffs, in the crown. When thus deprived of "free representation in the Legislature," and the governor refused to issue warrants for the election of members of the Assembly, they called a convention of the freemen, and asked for the passage of "laws for the accommodation of large districts of people." These requests were disregarded, and they were told that no laws should be passed until they should quietly "relinquish the right of representation in the Legislature—a right inestimable to them, and formidable to tyrants only."

[3] In consequence of the destruction of tea in Boston Harbor [page 225] in 1773, the inhabitants of that town became the special objects of royal displeasure. The Boston Port Bill [page 225] was passed as a punishment. The custom-house, courts, and other public operations were removed to Salem, while the public records were kept in Boston, and so well guarded by two regiments of soldiers, that the patriotic members of the colonial Assembly could not have referred to them. Although compelled to meet at a place [page 225] "distant from the repository of the public records," and in a place extremely "uncomfortable," they were *not* fatigued into compliance, but in spite of the efforts of the governor, they elected delegates to a general Congress [page 227], and adopted other measures for the public good.

[4] When the British government became informed of the fact that the Assembly of Massachusetts, in 1768, had issued a circular [page 219] to other Assemblies, inviting their co-operation in asserting the principle that Great Britain had no right to tax the colonists without their consent, Lord Hillsborough, the Secretary for Foreign Affairs, was directed to order the governor of Massachusetts to require the Assembly of that province to rescind its obnoxious resolutions expressed in the circular. In case of their refusal to do so, the governor was ordered to dissolve them immediately. Other Assemblies were warned not to imitate that of Massachusetts, and when they

He has refused, for a long time after such dissolutions, to cause others to be elected, whereby the legislative powers, incapable of annihilation, have returned to the people at large for their exercise; the State remaining, in the mean time, exposed to all the dangers of invasions from without, and convulsions from within.[1]

He has endeavored to prevent the population of these States; for that purpose obstructing the laws for the naturalization of foreigners; refusing to pass others to encourage their migration hither, and raising the conditions of new appropriations of lands.[2]

He has obstructed the administration of justice, by refusing his assent to laws for establishing judiciary powers.[3]

He has made judges dependent on his will alone for the tenure of their offices, and the amount and payment of their salaries.[4]

---

refused to accede to the wishes of the king, as expressed by the several royal governors, they were repeatedly dissolved. The Assemblies of Virginia and North Carolina were dissolved for denying the right of the king to tax the colonies, or to remove offenders out of the country, for trial. [See page 221.] In 1774, when the several Assemblies entertained the proposition to elect delegates to a general Congress [page 227], nearly all of them were dissolved.

[1] When the Assembly of New York, in 1766, refused to comply with the provisions of the Mutiny Act [page 218], its legislative functions were suspended by royal authority [page 218], and for several months the State remained "exposed to all the dangers of invasion from without, and convulsions within." The Assembly of Massachusetts, after its dissolution in July, 1768, was not permitted to meet again until the last Wednesday of May, 1769, and then they found the place of meeting surrounded by a military guard, with cannons pointed directly at their place of meeting. They refused to act under such tyrannical restraint, and their legislative powers "returned to the people."

[2] Secret agents were sent to America soon after the accession of George the Third to the throne of England [page 212], to spy out the condition of the colonists. A large influx of liberty-loving German emigrants was observed, and the king was advised to discourage these immigrations. Obstacles in the way of procuring lands, and otherwise, were put in the way of all emigrants, except from England, and the tendency of French Roman Catholics to settle in Maryland, was also discouraged. The British government was jealous of the increasing power of the colonies, and the danger of having that power controlled by democratic ideas, caused the employment of restrictive measures. The easy conditions upon which actual settlers might obtain lands on the western frontier, after the peace of 1763 [page 211], were so changed, that toward the dawning of the Revolution, the vast solitudes west of the Alleghanies were seldom penetrated by any but the hunter from the sea-board provinces. When the War for Independence broke out, immigration had almost ceased. The king conjectured wisely, for almost the entire German population in the colonies, were on the side of the patriots.

[3] By an Act of Parliament in 1774, the judiciary was taken from the people of Massachusetts. The judges were appointed by the king, were dependent on him for their salaries, and were subject to his will. Their salaries were paid from moneys drawn from the people by the commissioners of customs [page 220], in the form of duties. The same act deprived them, in most cases, of the benefit of trial by jury; and the "administration of justice" was effectually obstructed. The rights for which Englishmen so manfully contended in 1688 [note 7, page 113], were trampled under foot. Similar grievances concerning the courts of law, existed in other colonies, and throughout the Anglo-American [note 1, page 195] domain there was but a semblance of justice left. The people met in conventions, when Assemblies were dissolved, and endeavored to establish "judiciary powers," but in vain, and were finally driven to rebellion.

[4] As we have observed in note 2, page 596, judges were made independent of the people. Royal governors were placed in the same position. Instead of checking their tendency to petty tyranny, by having them depend upon the colonial Assemblies for their salaries, these were paid out of the national treasury. Independent of the people, they had no sympathies with the people, and thus became fit instruments of oppression, and ready at all times to do the bidding of the king and his ministers. The colonial Assemblies protested against the measure, and out of the excitement which it produced, grew that power of the Revolution, the committees of correspondence [note 2, page 224]. When, in 1774, Chief Justice Oliver, of Massachusetts, declared it to be his intention to receive his salary from the crown, the Assembly proceeded to impeach him, and petitioned the governor for his removal. The governor refused compliance, and great irritation ensued.

He has erected a multitude of new offices, and sent hither swarms of officers to harass our people and eat out their substance.[1]

He has kept among us in times of peace, standing armies, without the consent of our Legislatures.[2]

He has affected to render the military independent of, and superior to, the civil power.[3]

He has combined with others to subject us to a jurisdiction foreign to our constitutions, and unacknowledged by our laws; giving his assent to their acts of pretended legislation:[4]

For quartering large bodies of armed troops among us;[5]

For protecting them, by a mock trial, from punishment for any murders which they should commit on the inhabitants of these States;[6]

For cutting off our trade with all parts of the world;[7]

---

[1] After the passage of the Stamp Act, stamp distributors were appointed in every considerable town. In 1766 and 1767, acts for the collection of duties created "swarms of officers," all of whom received high salaries; and when, in 1768, admiralty and vice-admiralty courts were established on a new basis, an increase in the number of officers was made. The high salaries and extensive perquisites of all of these, were paid with the people's money, and thus "swarms of officers" "eat out their substance."

[2] After the treaty of peace with France, in 1763 [page 211], Great Britain left quite a large number of troops in America, and required the colonists to contribute to their support. There was no use for this standing army, except to repress the growing spirit of democracy among the colonists, and to enforce compliance with taxation laws. The presence of troops was always a cause of complaint, and when, finally, the colonists boldly opposed the unjust measures of the British government, armies were sent hither to awe the people into submission. It was one of those "standing armies," kept here "without the consent of the Legislature," against which the patriots at Lexington, and Concord [page 233], and Bunker Hill [page 235], so manfully battled in 1775.

[3] General Gage, commander-in-chief of the British forces in America, was appointed governor of Massachusetts, in 1774; and to put the measures of the Boston Port Bill [page 225], into execution, he encamped several regiments of soldiers upon Boston Common. The military there, and also in New York, was made independent of, and superior to, the civil power, and this, too, in a time of peace, before the minute men [page 229] were organized.

[4] The establishment of a Board of Trade, to act independent of colonial legislation through its creatures (resident commissioners of customs) in the enforcement of revenue laws, was altogether foreign to the constitution of any of the colonies, and produced great indignation. The establishment of this power, and the remodelling of the admiralty courts, so as to exclude trial by jury therein, in most cases, rendered the government fully obnoxious to the charge in the text. The people felt their degradation under such petty tyranny, and resolved to spurn it. It was effectually done in Boston, as we have seen [page 220], and the government, after all its bluster, was obliged to recede. In 1774, the members of the council of Massachusetts (answering to our Senate) were, by a parliamentary enactment, chosen by the king, to hold the office during his pleasure. Almost unlimited power was also given to the governor, and the people were indeed subjected to "a jurisdiction foreign to their constitution," by these creatures of royalty.

[5] In 1774 seven hundred troops were landed in Boston, under cover of the cannons of British armed ships in the harbor; and early the following year, Parliament voted ten thousand men for the American service, for it saw the wave of rebellion rising high under the gale of indignation which unrighteous acts had spread over the land. The tragedies at Lexington and Concord soon followed, and at Bunker Hill the War for Independence was opened in earnest.

[6] In 1768, two citizens of Annapolis, in Maryland, were murdered by some marines belonging to a British armed ship. The trial was a mockery of justice, and in the face of clear evidence against them, they were acquitted. In the difficulties with the Regulators [page 223] in North Carolina, in 1771, some of the soldiers who had shot down citizens, when standing up in defense of their rights, were tried for murder and acquitted, while Governor Tryon mercilessly hung six prisoners, who were certainly entitled to the benefits of the laws of war, if his own soldiers were.

[7] The navigation laws [note 3, page 177] were always oppressive in character; and in 1764, the British naval commanders having been clothed with the authority of custom-house officers, completely broke up a profitable trade which the colonists had long enjoyed with the Spanish and French West Indies, notwithstanding it was in violation of the old Navigation Act of 1660 [note 4, page 109], which had been almost ineffectual. Finally, Lord North concluded to punish the

For imposing taxes on us without our consent;[1]

For depriving us, in many cases, of the benefits of trial by jury;[2]

For transporting us beyond seas, to be tried for pretended offenses;[3]

For abolishing the free system of English laws in a neighboring province, establishing therein an arbitrary government, and enlarging its boundaries, so as to render it at once an example and fit instrument for introducing the same absolute rule into these colonies;[4]

For taking away our charters, abolishing our most valuable laws, and altering, fundamentally, the forms of our governments;[5]

For suspending our own Legislatures, and declaring themselves invested with power to legislate for us in all cases whatsoever.[6]

He has abdicated government here, by declaring us out of his protection, and waging war against us.[7]

---

refractory colonists of New England, by crippling their commerce [page 231] with Great Britain, Ireland, and the West Indies. Fishing on the banks of Newfoundland was also prohibited, and thus, as far as parliamentary enactments could accomplish it, their "trade with all parts of the world" was cut off.

[1] In addition to the revenue taxes imposed from time to time, and attempted to be collected by means of writs of assistance [page 212], the Stamp Act [page 213] was passed, and duties upon paper, painters' colors, glass, tea, etc., were levied. This was the great bone of contention between the colonists and the imperial government. It was contention, on the one hand, for the great political truth, that *taxation and representation are inseparable*, and a lust for power, and the means for replenishing an exhausted treasury, on the other. The climax of the contention was the Revolution.

[2] This was especially the case, when commissioners of customs were concerned in the suit. After these functionaries were driven from Boston in 1768 [page 220], an act was passed which placed violations of the revenue laws under the jurisdiction of the admiralty courts, where the offenders were tried by a creature of the crown, and were deprived "of the benefits of trial by jury."

[3] A law of 1774 provided that any person in the province of Massachusetts, who should be accused of riot, resistance of magistrates or the officers of customs, murder, "or any other capital offense," might, at the option of the governor, be taken for trial to another colony, or transported to Great Britain, for the purpose. The minister pretended that impartial justice could not be administered in Massachusetts, but the facts of Captain Preston's case [page 222] refuted his arguments, in that direction. The bill was violently opposed in Parliament, yet it became law. It was decreed that Americans might be "transported beyond the seas, to be tried for pretended offenses," or real crimes.

[4] This charge is embodied in an earlier one [page 596], considered in note 2, page 596. The British ministry thought it prudent to take early steps to secure a footing in America, so near the scene of inevitable rebellion, as to allow them to breast, successfully, the gathering storm. The investing of a legislative council in Canada, with all powers except levying of taxes, was a great stride toward that absolute military rule which bore sway there within eighteen months afterward. Giving up their political rights for doubtful religious privileges, made them willing slaves, and Canada remained a part of the British empire, when its sister colonies rejoiced in freedom.

[5] This is a reiteration of the charge considered in note 2, page 596, and refers to the alteration of the Massachusetts charter, so as to make judges and other officers independent of the people, and subservient to the crown. The governor was empowered to remove and appoint all inferior judges, the attorney-general, provosts, marshals, and justices of the peace, and to appoint sheriffs independent of the council. As the sheriffs chose jurors, trial by jury might easily be made a mere mockery. The people had hitherto been allowed, by their charter, to select jurors; now the whole matter was placed in the hands of creatures of government.

[6] This, too, is another phase of the charge just considered. We have noticed the suppression of the Legislature of New York [page 218], and, in several cases, the governors, after dissolving colonial Assemblies, assumed the right to make proclamations stand in the place of statute law. Lord Dunmore assumed this right in 1775, and so did Sir James Wright, of Georgia, and Lord William Campbell, of South Carolina. They were driven from the country, in consequence.

[7] In his message to Parliament early in 1775, the king declared the colonists to be in a state of open rebellion, and by sending armies hither to make war upon them, he really "abdicated government," by thus declaring them "out of his protection." He sanctioned the acts of governors in employing the Indians against his subjects [note 4, page 237], and himself bargained for the em-

He has plundered our seas, ravaged our coasts, burned our towns, and destroyed the lives of our people.[1]

He is at this time transporting large armies of foreign mercenaries to complete the works of death, desolation, and tyranny, already begun with circumstances of cruelty and perfidy scarcely paralleled in the most barbarous ages, and totally unworthy the head of a civilized nation.[2]

He has constrained our fellow-citizens, taken captive on the high seas, to bear arms against their country, to become the executioners of their friends and brethren, or to fall themselves by their hands.[3]

He has excited domestic insurrection among us, and has endeavored to bring on the inhabitants of our frontiers, the merciless Indian savages, whose known rule of warfare is an undistinguished destruction of all ages, sexes, and conditions.[4]

In every stage of these oppressions we have petitioned for redress in the most humble terms; our repeated petitions have been answered only by repeated injury. A prince whose character is thus marked by every act which may define a tyrant, is unfit to be the ruler of a free people.[5]

Nor have we been wanting in our attentions to our British brethren.[6] We have warned them, from time to time, of attempts by their legislature to extend an unwarrantable jurisdiction over us. We have reminded them of the circumstances of our emigration and settlement here. We have appealed to their

---

ployment of German hirelings. And when, yielding to the pressure of popular will, his representatives (the royal governors) fled before the indignant people, he certainly "abdicated government."

[1] When naval commanders were clothed with the powers of custom-house officers and excisemen, they seized many American vessels; and after the affair at Lexington and Bunker Hill, British ships of war "plundered our seas" whenever an American vessel could be found. They also "ravaged our coasts and burnt our towns." Charlestown [page 236], Falmouth (now Portland, in Maine), and Norfolk were burnt; and Dunmore and others [page 241] "ravaged our coasts" and "destroyed the lives of our people." And at the very time when this Declaration was being read to the assembled Congress [page 252], the shattered fleet of Sir Peter Parker was sailing northward [page 249], after an attack upon Charleston, South Carolina.

[2] This charge refers to the infamous employment of German troops, known here as Hessians. See page 246.

[3] An act of Parliament, passed toward the close of December, 1775, authorized the capture of all American vessels, and also directed the treatment of the crews of armed vessels to be as slaves, and not as prisoners of war. They were to be enrolled for the "service of his majesty," and were thus compelled to fight for the crown, even against their own friends and countrymen. This act was loudly condemned on the floor of Parliament, as unworthy of a Christian people, and "a refinement of cruelty unknown among savage nations."

[4] This was done in several instances. Dunmore was charged [note 4, page 237] with a design to employ the Indians against the Virginians, as early as 1774; and while ravaging the Virginia coast, in 1775 and 1776, he endeavored to excite the slaves against their masters. He was also concerned with Governor Gage and others, under instructions from the British ministry, in exciting the Shawnees, and other savages of the Ohio country, against the white people. Emissaries were also sent among the Cherokees and Creeks, for the same purpose, and all of the tribes of the Six Nations, except the Oneidas, were found in arms with the British when war began. Thus excited, dreadful massacres occurred on the borders of the several colonies.

[5] For ten long years the colonies petitioned for redress of grievances, "in the most humble terms," and loyal manner. It was done by the Colonial Congress of 1765 [page 215], and also by the Continental Congresses of 1774 [page 228] and 1775 [page 238]. But their petitions were almost always "answered only by repeated injuries."

[6] From the beginning, the colonists appealed, in the most affectionate terms, to "their British brethren." The first address put forth by the Congress of 1774 [note 6, page 228] was "To the People of Great Britain; and the Congress of 1775 sent an affectionate appeal to the people of Ireland.

native justice and magnanimity, and we have conjured them by the ties of our common kindred, to disavow these usurpations, which would inevitably interrupt our connections and correspondence. They, too, have been deaf to the voice of justice and of consanguinity. We must, therefore, acquiesce in the

necessity which denounces our separation, and hold them as we hold the rest of mankind—enemies in war—in peace, friends.

We, therefore, the representatives of the United States of America, in general Congress assembled, appealing to the Supreme Judge of the world for the rectitude of our intentions, do, in the name and by the authority of the good people of these colonies, solemnly publish and declare that these united colonies are, and of right ought to be, free and independent States; that they are absolved from all allegiance to the British crown, and that all political connection between them and the State of Great Britain is, and ought to be, totally dissolved, and that, as free and independent States, they have full power to levy war, conclude peace, contract alliances, establish commerce, and do all other acts and things which independent States may of right do. And for the support of this Declaration, with a firm reliance on the protection of Divine Providence, we mutually pledge to each other our lives, our fortunes, and our sacred honor.

SIGNERS OF THE DECLARATION OF INDEPENDENCE.

The following is a list of the members of the Continental Congress, who signed the Declaration of Independence, with the places and dates of their birth, and the time of their respective deaths:

NAMES OF THE SIGNERS.	BORN AT	DELEGATE FROM	DIED.
Adams, John	Braintree, Mass., 19th Oct., 1735	Massachusetts,	4th July, 1826
Adams, Samuel	Boston, " 22d Sept., 1722	Massachusetts,	2d Oct., 1803
Bartlett, Josiah	Amesbury, " in Nov., 1729	New Hampshire,	19th May, 1795
Braxton, Carter	Newington, Va., 10th Sept., 1736	Virginia,	10th Oct., 1797
Carroll, Charles, of Carrollton	Annapolis, Md., 20th Sept., 1737	Maryland,	14th Nov., 1832
Chase, Samuel	Somerset co., Md., 17th April, 1741	Maryland,	19th June, 1811
Clark, Abraham	Elizabetht'n, N. J., 15th Feb., 1726	New Jersey,	—— June, 1794
Clymer, George	Philadelphia, Penn., in 1739	Pennsylvania,	24th Jan., 1813
Ellery, William	Newport, R. I., 22d Dec., 1727	R. I. & Prov. Pl.,	15th Feb., 1820
Floyd, William	Suffolk co., N. Y., 17th Dec., 1734	New York,	4th Aug., 1821
Franklin, Benjamin	Boston, Mass., 17th Jan., 1706	Pennsylvania,	17th April, 1790
Gerry, Elbridge	Marblehead, Mass., 17th July, 1744	Massachusetts,	23d Nov., 1814
Gwinnet, Burton	England, in 1732	Georgia,	27th May, 1777
Hall, Lyman	Connecticut, in 1731	Georgia,	—— Feb., 1790
Hancock, John	Braintree, Mass., in 1737	Massachusetts,	8th Oct., 1793
Harrison, Benjamin	Berkely, Virginia, ——	Virginia,	—— April, 1791
Hart, John	Hopewell, N. J., about 1715	New Jersey,	—— ——, 1780
Heyward, Thomas, jr.	St. Luke's, S. C., in 1746	South Carolina,	—— Mar., 1809
Hewes, Joseph	Kingston, N. J., in 1730	North Carolina,	10th Nov., 1779
Hooper, William	Boston, Mass., 17th June, 1742	North Carolina,	—— Oct., 1790
Hopkins, Stephen	Scituate, " 7th March, 1707	R. I. & Prov. Pl.,	19th July, 1785
Hopkinson, Francis	Philadelphia, Penn., in 1737	New Jersey,	9th May, 1790
Huntingdon, Samuel	Windham, Conn., 3d July, 1732	Connecticut,	5th Jan., 1796
Jefferson, Thomas	Shadwell, Va., 13th April, 1743	Virginia,	4th July, 1826
Lee, Francis Lightfoot	Stratford, " 14th Oct., 1734	Virginia,	—— April, 1797
Lee, Richard Henry	Stratford, " 20th Jan., 1732	Virginia,	19th June, 1794
Lewis, Francis	Landaff, Wales, in March, 1713	New York,	30th Dec., 1803
Livingston, Philip	Albany, N. Y., 15th Jan., 1716	New York,	12th June, 1778
Lynch, Thomas, jr.	St. George's, S. C., 5th Aug., 1749	South Carolina,	lost at sea, 1779
M'Keon, Thomas	Chester co., Pa., 19th March, 1734	Delaware,	24th June, 1817
Middleton, Arthur	Middleton Place, S. C., in 1743	South Carolina,	1st Jan., 1787
Morris, Lewis	Morrisania, N. Y., in 1726	New York,	22d Jan., 1798
Morris, Robert	Lancashire, England, Jan., 1733	Pennsylvania,	8th May, 1806
Morton, John	Ridley, Penn., in 1724	Pennsylvania,	—— April, 1777
Nelson, Thomas, jr.	York, Virginia, 26th Dec., 1738	Virginia,	4th Jan., 1789
Paca, William	Wye-Hill, Md., 31st Oct., 1740	Maryland,	—— ——, 1799
Paine, Robert Treat	Boston, Mass., in 1731	Massachusetts,	11th May, 1814
Penn, John	Caroline co., Va., 17th May, 1741	North Carolina,	—— Sept., 1788
Read, George	Cecil co., Maryland, in 1734	Delaware,	—— ——, 1798
Rodney, Cæsar	Dover, Delaware, in 1730	Delaware,	—— ——, 1783
Ross, George	New Castle, Del., in 1730	Pennsylvania,	—— July, 1779
Rush, Benjamin, M.D.	Byperry, Penn., 24th Dec., 1745	Pennsylvania,	19th April, 1813
Rutledge, Edward	Charleston, S. C., in Nov., 1749	South Carolina,	23d Jan., 1800
Sherman, Roger	Newton, Mass., 19th April, 1721	Connecticut,	23d July, 1793
Smith, James	Ireland, ——	Pennsylvania,	11th July, 1806
Stockton, Richard	Princeton, N. J., 1st Oct., 1730	New Jersey,	28th Feb., 1781
Stone, Thomas	Charles co., Md., in 1742	Maryland,	5th Oct., 1787
Taylor, George	Ireland, in 1716	Pennsylvania,	23d Feb., 1781
Thornton, Matthew	Ireland, in 1714	New Hampshire,	24th June, 1803
Walton, George	Frederick co., Va., in 1740	Georgia,	2d Feb., 1804
Whipple, William	Kittery, Maine, in 1730	New Hampshire,	28th Nov., 1785
Williams, William	Lebanon, Conn., 8th April, 1731	Connecticut,	2d Aug., 1811
Wilson, James	Scotland, about 1742	Pennsylvania,	28th Aug., 1798
Witherspoon, John	Yester, Scotland, 5th Feb., 1722	New Jersey,	15th Nov., 1794
Wolcott, Oliver	Windsor, Conn., 26th Nov., 1726	Connecticut,	1st Dec., 1797
Wythe, George	Elizabeth city, Va., in 1726	Virginia,	8th June, 1806

Among the signers of the Declaration of Independence, were men engaged in almost every vocation. There were twenty-four *lawyers*; fourteen *farmers*, or men devoted chiefly to agriculture; nine *merchants*; four *physicians*; one gospel *minister*, and three who were educated for that profession, but chose other avocations; and one *manufacturer*. A large portion of them lived to the age of three score and ten years. Three of them were over 90 years of age when they died; ten over 80; eleven over 70; fourteen over 60; eleven over

50; and six over 44. Mr. Lynch (lost at sea) was only 30. The aggregate years of life of the fifty-six patriots, were 3,687 years. The last survivor of the signers of the Declaration of Independence, was Charles Carroll, of Carrollton, who died on the 14th of November, 1832, when in the ninety-sixth year of his age.[1]

In allusion to the signers of the Declaration of Independence, and their compeers, the Abbè Raynal wrote, in 1781, in his essay on *The Revolution in America:* "With what grandeur, with what enthusiasm, should I not speak of those generous men who erected this grand edifice by their patience, their wisdom, and their courage! Hancock, Franklin, the two Adamses, were the greatest actors in this affecting scene; but they were not the only ones. Posterity shall know them all. Their honored names shall be transmitted to it by a happier pen than mine. Brass and marble shall show them to remotest ages. In beholding them, shall the friend of freedom feel his heart palpitate with joy —feel his eyes float in delicious tears. Under the bust of one of them has been written, HE WRESTED THUNDER FROM HEAVEN AND THE SCEPTER FROM TYRANTS.[2] Of the last words of this eulogy shall the whole of them partake."

"I ask," exclaimed Mirabeau, on the tribune of the National Assembly of France, while descanting upon our Declaration—"I ask if the powers who have formed alliances with the States have dared to read that manifesto, or to interrogate their consciences after the perusal? I ask whether there be at this day one government in Europe—the Helvetic and Batavian confederations and the British isles excepted—which, judged after the principles of the Declaration of Congress, on the 4th of July, 1776, is not divested of its rights." And Napoleon afterward, alluding to the same scene, said, "The finger of God was there!"

---

[1] Charles Carroll was born at Annapolis, in Maryland, on the 20th of September, 1737. He was educated in France, and after an absence of twenty-two years, he returned, and found his countrymen in a state of high excitement on account of the Stamp Act. He espoused the cause of the people, and all through the ensuing struggles and the long war, he was a faithful and unwavering patriot. He held a fluent pen, and was powerful in speech. In his native State, and in the national council, he was always a leading advocate of popular rights. He was elected to the Continental Congress, too late to *vote* for independence, but in time to affix his signature to the Declaration. It has become a record of history, that Mr. Carroll, after signing his name, was told that the British Government would not be able to identify him as the arch-traitor, because there were other Charles Carrolls in Maryland, and that he affixed "of Carrollton" to his name, with the remark, "Now, they can't make a mistake." This is not true, for it was his common way of signing his name. In a letter before the writer, sent to General Schuyler from Canada, by a committee of which Mr. Carroll was one, and which was written some time before the resolution concerning independence was introduced into Congress, his name has the suffix "of Carrollton." He retired from public life at the age of sixty-four years; and when, in 1826, Adams and Jefferson died, he alone, of all the signers, remained upon the earth. For portrait see page .

[2] This was written in Latin, as follows, by the celebrated Thurgot, Controller-General of the Finances of France: "*Eripuit cœlo fulmen sceptrumque tyrannis.*" It was the exergue of a medal, struck in Paris, in honor of Dr. Franklin.

VI.

ARTICLES OF CONFEDERATION.

As early as July, 1775, Doctor Franklin submitted to the consideration of Congress a sketch of articles of confederation between the colonies,[1] limiting the duration of their vitality to the time when reconciliation with Great Britain should take place; or, in the event of the failure of that desirable result, to be perpetual. At that time, Congress seemed to have no fixed plans for the future—the teeming present, with all its vast and novel concerns, engrossed their whole attention—and Dr. Franklin's plan seems not to have been discussed at all in the National Council. But when a Declaration of Independence was proposed, that idea alone suggested the necessity of a confederation of the States to carry forward the work to a successful consummation. Congress, therefore, on the 11th of June, 1776, resolved that a committee should be appointed to prepare, and properly digest, a form of confederation to be entered into by the several States. The committee appointed under the resolution consisted of one delegate from each State.[2] John Dickenson, of Pennsylvania, was chosen chairman, and through him the committee reported a draft of articles of confederation on the 12th of July. Almost daily debates upon the subject ensued until the 20th of August, when the report was laid aside, and was not taken up again for consideration until the 8th of April, 1777. In the mean while, several of the States had adopted Constitutions for their respective government, and Congress was practically acknowledged the supreme head in all matters appertaining to the war, public finances, etc. It emitted bills of credit, or paper money, appointed foreign ministers, and opened negotiations with foreign governments.

From the 8th of April until the 15th of November following, the subject was debated two or three times a week, and several amendments were made. As the confederation might be a permanent bond of union, of course local interests were considered prospectively. If the union had been designed to be temporary, to meet the exigences arising from the state of war in which the colonies then were, local questions could hardly have had weight enough to have elicited debate; but such was not the case, and of course the sagacious men who were then in Congress looked beyond the present, and endeavored to legislate accordingly. From the 7th of October until the 15th of November, the debates upon it were almost daily, and the conflicting interests of the several States were strongly brought into view by the different speakers. On

---

[1] Page 267.

[2] The committee consisted of Messrs. Bartlett, Samuel Adams, Hopkins, Sherman, R. R. Livingston, Dickenson, M'Kean, Stone, Nelson, Hewes, Edward Rutledge, and Gwinnett.

that day the following draft, containing all of the amendments, was laid before Congress, and after a spirited debate was adopted:

ARTICLE 1. The style of this confederacy shall be, "The United States of America."

ARTICLE 2. Each State retains its sovereignty, freedom, and independence, and every power, jurisdiction, and right, which is not by this confederation expressly delegated to the United States in Congress assembled.

ARTICLE 3. The said States hereby severally enter into a firm league of friendship with each other for their common defense, the security of their liberties, and their mutual and general welfare; binding themselves to assist each other against all force offered to, or attacks made upon them, or any of them, on account of religion, sovereignty, trade, or any other pretense whatever.

ARTICLE 4. The better to secure and perpetuate mutual friendship and intercourse among the people of the different States in this Union, the free inhabitants of each of these States, paupers, vagabonds, and fugitives from justice excepted, shall be entitled to all privileges and immunities of free citizens in the several States; and the people of each State shall have free ingress and regress to and from any other State, and shall enjoy therein all the privileges of trade and commerce, subject to the same duties, impositions, and restrictions, as the inhabitants thereof respectively, provided that such restrictions shall not extend so far as to prevent the removal of property imported into any State to any other State, of which the owner is an inhabitant; provided, also, that no imposition, duties, or restriction shall be laid by any State on the property of the United States, or either of them.

If any person guilty of or charged with treason, felony, or other high misdemeanor, in any State, shall flee from justice, and be found in any of the United States, he shall upon demand of the Governor or executive power of the State from which he fled, be delivered up and removed to the State having jurisdiction of his offense.

Full faith and credit shall be given in each of these States to the records, acts, and judicial proceedings of the courts and magistrates of every other State.

ARTICLE 5. For the more convenient management of the general interests of the United States, delegates shall be annually appointed in such manner as the Legislature of each State shall direct, to meet in Congress on the first Monday in November in every year, with a power reserved to each State to recall its delegates, or any of them, at any time within the year, and to send others in their stead for the remainder of the year.

No State shall be represented in Congress by less than two, nor by more than seven members; and no persan shall be capable of being a delegate for more than three years in any term of six years; nor shall any person, being a delegate, be capable of holding any office under the United States, for which he, or another for his benefit, receives any salary, fees, or emoluments of any kind.

Each State shall maintain its own delegates in a meeting of the States, and while they act as members of the committee of the States.

In determining questions in the United States, in Congress assembled, each State shall have one vote.

Freedom of speech and debate in Congress shall not be impeached or questioned in any court or place out of Congress; and the members of Congress shall be protected in their persons from arrests and imprisonments, during the time of their going to and from and attendance on Congress, except for treason, felony, or breach of the peace.

ARTICLE 6. No State, without the consent of the United States, in Congress assembled, shall send any embassy to, or receive any embassy from, or enter into any conference, agreement, alliance, or treaty, with any king, prince, or State; nor shall any person holding any office of profit or trust under the United States, or any of them, accept of any present, emolument, office, or title of any kind whatever, from any king, prince, or foreign State; nor shall the United States in Congress assembled, or any of them, grant any title of nobility.

No two or more States shall enter into any treaty, confederation, or alliance whatever between them, without the consent of the United States, in Congress assembled, specifying accurately the purposes for which the same is to be entered into and how long it shall continue.

No State shall lay any imposts or duties which may interfere with any stipulations in treaties entered into by the United States, in Congress assembled, with any king, prince, or State, in pursuance of any treaties already proposed by Congress to the courts of France and Spain.

No vessel of war shall be kept up in time of peace by any State, except such number only as shall be deemed necessary by the United States, in Congress assembled, for the defense of such State or its trade; nor shall any body of forces be kept up by any State in time of peace, except such number only as in the judgment of the United States, in Congress assembled, shall be deemed requisite to garrison the forts necessary for the defense of such State; but every State shall always keep up a well-regulated and disciplined militia, sufficiently armed and accoutered, and shall provide and have constantly ready for use, in public stores, a due number of field-pieces and tents, and a proper quantity of arms, ammunition, and camp equipage.

No State shall engage in any war without the consent of the United States in Congress assembled, unless such State be actually invaded by enemies, or shall have received certain advice of a resolution being formed by some nation of Indians to invade such State, and the danger is so imminent as not to admit of a delay till the United States, in Congress assembled, can be consulted; nor shall any State grant commissions to any ships or vessels of war, nor letters of marque or reprisal, except it be after a declaration of war by the United States, in Congress assembled, and then only against the kingdom or State, and the subjects thereof, against which war has been so declared, and under such regulations as shall be established by the United States, in Congress assembled, unless such State be infested by pirates, in which case, vessels of war may be fitted out for that occasion, and kept so long as the danger shall continue, or until the United States, in Congress assembled, shall determine otherwise.

ARTICLE 7. When land forces are raised by any State for the common defense, all officers of or under the rank of Colonel shall be appointed by the Legislature of each State respectively by whom such forces shall be raised, or in such manner as such State shall direct, and all vacancies shall be filled up by the State which first made the appointment.

ARTICLE 8. All charges of war, and all other expenses that shall be incurred for the common defense or general welfare, and allowed by the United States in Congress assembled, shall be defrayed out of a common treasury, which shall be supplied by the several States in proportion to the value of all land within each State granted to or surveyed for any person, as such land and the buildings and improvements thereon shall be estimated, according to such mode as the United States, in Congress assembled, shall from time to time direct and appoint.

The taxes for paying that proportion shall be laid and levied by the authority and direction of the Legislatures of the several States, within the time agreed upon by the United States, in Congress assembled.

ARTICLE 9. The United States, in Congress assembled, shall have the sole and exclusive right and power of determining on peace and war, except in the cases mentioned in the sixth article; of sending and receiving embassadors; entering into treaties and alliances—provided that no treaty of commerce shall be made whereby the legislative power of the respective States shall be restrained from imposing such imposts and duties on foreigners as their own people are subjected to, or from prohibiting exportation or importation of any species of goods or commodities whatsoever; of establishing rules for deciding in all cases what captures on land or water shall be legal, and in what manner prizes taken by land or naval forces in the service of the United States, shall be divided or appropriated; of granting letters of marque and reprisal in times of peace; appointing courts for the trial of piracies and felonies committed on the high seas, and establishing courts for receiving and determining finally appeals in all cases of captures; provided that no member of Congress shall be appointed a judge of any of the said courts.

The United States, in Congress assembled, shall also be the last resort, on appeal, in all disputes and differences now subsisting, or that hereafter may arise between two or more States concerning boundary, jurisdiction, or any other cause whatever; which authority shall always be exercised in the manner following: whenever the legislative or executive authority or lawful agent of any State in controversy with another shall present a petition to Congress, stating the matter in question, and praying for a hearing, notice thereof shall be given by order of Congress to the legislative or executive authority of the other State in controversy, and a day assigned for the appearance of the parties, by their lawful agents, who shall then be directed to appoint, by joint consent, commissioners or judges to constitute a court for hearing and determining the matter in question; but if they can not agree, Congress shall name three persons out of each of the United States, and from the list of such persons each party shall alternately strike out one, the petitioners beginning, until the number shall be reduced to thirteen; and from that number not less than seven, nor more than nine names, as Congress shall direct, shall, in the presence of Congress, be drawn out by lot; and the persons whose names shall be so drawn, or any five of them, shall be commissioners or judges, to hear and finally determine the controversy, so always as a major part of the judges, who shall hear the cause, shall agree in the determination; and if either party shall neglect to attend at the day appointed, without showing reasons which Congress shall judge sufficient, or, being present, shall refuse to strike, the Congress shall proceed to nominate three persons out of each State, and the Secretary of Congress shall strike in behalf of such person absent or refusing; and the judgment and sentence of the court, to be appointed in the manner before prescribed, shall be final and conclusive; and if any of the parties shall refuse to submit to the authority of such court, or to appear, or defend their claim or cause, the court shall nevertheless proceed to pronounce sentence or judgment, which shall in like manner be final and decisive—the judgment or sentence and other proceedings being in either case transmitted to Congress, and lodged among the acts of Congress for the security of the parties concerned; provided that every commissioner, before he sits in judgment, shall take an oath, to be administered by one of the judges of the Supreme or Superior Court of the State, where the cause shall be tried, "well and truly to hear and determine the matter in question, according to the best of his judgment, without favor, affection, or hope of reward;" provided, also, that no State shall be deprived of territory for the benefit of the United States.

All controversies concerning the private right of soil, claimed under different grants of two or more States, whose jurisdiction as they may respect such lands, and the States which passed such grants are adjusted, the said grants or either of them being at the same time claimed to have originated antecedent to such settlement of jurisdiction, shall, on the petition of either party to the Congress of the United States, be finally determined, as near as may be, in the same manner as is before prescribed for deciding disputes respecting territorial jurisdiction between different States.

The United States, in Congress assembled, shall also have the sole and exclusive right and power of regulating the alloy and value of coin struck by their own authority or by that of the respective States; fixing the standard of weights and measures throughout the United States; regulating the trade and managing all affairs with the Indians not members of any of the States—provided that the legislative right of any State within its own limits be not infringed or violated; establishing and regulating post-offices from one State to another throughout all the United States, and exacting such postage on the papers passing through the same as may be requisite to defray the expenses of the said office; appointing all officers of the land forces in the service of the United States, excepting regimental officers; appointing all the officers of the naval forces, and commissioning all officers whatever in the service of the United States; making rules for the government and regulation of the said land and naval forces, and directing their operations.

The United States, in Congress assembled, shall have authority to appoint a committee to sit in the recess of Congress, to be denominated "a Committee of the States," and to consist of one delegate from each State; and to appoint such other committees and civil officers as may be necessary for managing the general affairs of the United States under their direction; to appoint one of their number to preside, provided that no person be allowed to serve in the office of president more than one year in any term of three years; to ascertain the necessary sums of money to be raised for the service of the United States, and to appropriate and apply the same for defraying the public expenses; to borrow money or emit bills on the credit of the United States—transmitting every half year to the respective States an account of the sums of money so borrowed or emitted; to build and equip a navy; to agree upon the number of land forces, and to make requisitions from each State for its quota, in proportion to the number of white inhabitants in such State, which requisition shall be binding, and thereupon the Legislature of each State shall appoint the regimental officers, raise the men, and clothe, arm, and equip them, in a soldier-like manner, at the expense of the United States; and the officers and men so clothed, armed, and equipped, shall march to the place appointed, and within the time agreed on by the United States, in Congress assembled; but if the United States, in Congress assembled, shall, on consideration of circumstances, judge proper that any State should not raise men, or should raise a smaller number than its quota, or that any other State should raise a greater number of men than the quota thereof, such extra number shall be raised, officered, clothed, armed, and equipped, in the same manner as the quota of such State, unless the Legislature of such State shall judge that such extra number can not be safely spared out of the same; in which case they shall raise, officer, clothe, arm, and equip, as many of such extra number as they judge can be safely spared. And the officers and men so clothed, armed, and equipped, shall march to the place appointed, and within the time agreed on by the United States, in Congress assembled.

The United States, in Congress assembled, shall never engage in a war, nor grant letters of marque and reprisal in time of peace, nor enter into any treaties or alliances, nor coin money, nor regulate the value thereof, nor ascertain the sums and expenses necessary for the defense and welfare of the United States, or any of them, nor emit bills, nor borrow money on the credit of the United States, nor appropriate money, nor agree upon the number of vessels of war to be built or purchased, or the number of land or sea forces to be raised, nor appoint a commander-in-chief of the army or navy, unless nine States assent to the same; nor shall a question on any other point, except for adjourning from day to day, be determined unless by the votes of a majority of the United States, in Congress assembled.

The Congress of the United States shall have power to adjourn to any time within the year, and to any place within the United States, so that no period of adjournment be for a longer duration than the space of six months; and shall publish the journal of their proceedings monthly, except such parts thereof relating to treaties, alliances, or military operations, as in their judgment require secresy; and the yeas and nays of the delegates of each State on any question, shall be entered on the journal when it is desired by any delegate; and the delegates of a State or any of them, at his or their request, shall be furnished with a transcript of the said journal, except such parts as are above excepted, to lay before the Legislatures of the several States.

ARTICLE 10. The committee of the States, or any nine of them, shall be authorized to execute, in the recess of Congress, such of the powers of Congress as the United States, in Congress assembled, by the consent of nine States, shall from time to time think expedient to vest them with; provided that no power be delegated to the said committee, for the exercise of which, by the articles of confederation, the voice of nine States, in the Congress of the United States assembled, is requisite.

ARTICLE 11. Canada, acceding to this confederation, and joining in the measures of the United States, shall be admitted into, and entitled to, all the advantages of this union; but no other colony shall be admitted into the same, unless such admission be agreed to by nine States.

ARTICLE 12. All bills of credit emitted, moneys borrowed, and debts contracted, by or under the authority of Congress, before the assembling of the United States, in pursuance of the present confederation, shall be deemed and considered as a charge against the United States, for payment and satisfaction whereof the said United States and the public faith are hereby solemnly pledged.

ARTICLE 13. Every State shall abide by the decision of the United States, in Congress assembled, on all questions which, by this confederation, are submitted to them. And the articles of this confederation shall be inviolably observed by every State, and the Union shall be perpetual; nor shall any alteration at any time hereafter be made in any of them, unless such alteration be agreed to in a Congress of the United States, and be afterward confirmed by the Legislature of every State.

Congress directed these Articles to be submitted to the Legislatures of the several States, and, if approved of by them, they were advised to authorize their delegates to ratify the same in Congress, by affixing their names thereto.

Notwithstanding there was a general feeling that *something* must be speedily done, the State Legislatures were slow to adopt the articles. In the first place, they did not seem to accord with the prevailing sentiments of the people, as set forth in the Declaration of Independence; and in many things that Declaration and the Articles of Confederation were manifestly at variance. The former was based upon declared *right;* the foundation of the latter was asserted *power*. The former was based upon a superintending Providence, and the inalienable rights of man; the latter resting upon the "sovereignty of declared power; one ascending from the foundation of human government, to the laws of nature and of nature's God, written upon the heart of man; the other resting upon the basis of human institutions, and prescriptive law, and colonial charters."[1] Again, the system of representation proposed was highly objectionable, because

[1] John Quincy Adams's Jubilee Discourse, 1839.

each State was entitled to the same voice in Congress, whatever might be the difference in population. But the most objectionable feature of all was, that the *limits* of the several States, and also in whom was vested the control or possession of the crown-lands, was not only unadjusted, but wholly unnoticed. These and other defects caused most of the States to hesitate, at first, to adopt the Articles, and several of them for a long time utterly refused to accept them.

On the 22d of June, 1778, Congress proceeded to consider the objections of the States to the Articles of Confederation, and on the 27th of the same month, a form of ratification was adopted and ordered to be engrossed upon parchment, with a view that the same should be signed by such delegates as were instructed so to do by their respective Legislatures.

On the 9th of July, the delegates of New Hampshire, Massachusetts, Rhode Island, Connecticut, New York, Pennsylvania, Virginia, and South Carolina signed the Articles. The delegates from New Jersey, Delaware, and Maryland were not yet empowered to ratify and sign. Georgia and North Carolina were not represented, and the ratification of New York was conditioned that all the other States should ratify. The delegates from North Carolina signed the articles on the 21st of July; those of Georgia on the 24th of the same month; those of New Jersey, on the 26th of November; and those of Delaware, on the 22d of February and fifth of May, 1779. Maryland still firmly refused to ratify, until the question of the conflicting claims of the Union and of the separate States to the crown-lands should be fully adjusted. This point was finally settled by cessions of claiming States to the United States, of all unsettled and unappropriated lands for the benefit of the whole Union. This cession of the crown-lands to the Union originated the Territorial System, and the erection of the North-western Territory into a distinct government, similar to the existing States, having a local Legislature of its own. The insuperable objection of Maryland having been removed by the settlement of this question, her delegates signed the Articles of Confederation on the 1st day of March, 1781, four years and four months after they were adopted by Congress.[1] By this act of Maryland, they became the organic law of the Union, and on the 2d of March Congress assembled under the new powers.

---

[1] The following are the names of the delegates from the several States appended to the Articles of Confederation:

New Hampshire, Josiah Bartlett, John Wentworth, Jr.

Massachusetts Bay, John Hancock, Samuel Adams, Elbridge Gerry, Francis Dana, James Lovell, Samuel Holten.

Rhode Island, William Ellery, Henry Marchant, John Collins.

Connecticut, Roger Sherman, Samuel Huntington, Oliver Wolcott, Titus Hosmer, Andrew Adams.

New York, James Duane, Francis Lewis, William Duer, Gouverneur Morris.

New Jersey, John Witherspoon, Nathaniel Scudder.

Pennsylvania, Robert Morris, Daniel Roberdeau, Jonathan Bayard Smith, William Clingan, Joseph Reed.

Delaware, Thomas M'Kean, John Dickenson, Nicholas Van Dyke.

Maryland, John Hanson, Daniel Carroll.

Virginia, Richard Henry Lee, John Banister, Thomas Adams, John Harvie, Francis Lightfoot Lee.

North Carolina, John Penn, Cornelius Harnett, John Williams.

South Carolina, Henry Laurens, William Henry Drayton, Jonathan Matthews, Richard Hutson, Thomas Heyward, Jr.

Georgia, John Walton, Edward Telfair, Edward Langworthy.

VII.

CONSTITUTION OF THE UNITED STATES.[1]

Objects. WE the People of the United States, in order to form a more perfect Union, establish Justice, insure domestic Tranquility, provide for the common defence, promote the general Welfare, and secure the Blessings of Liberty to ourselves and our Posterity, do ordain and establish this Constitution for the United States of America.

ARTICLE I.

Legislative Powers. SECTION 1. All legislative powers herein granted shall be vested in a Congress of the United States, which shall consist of a Senate and House of Representatives.

[1] In 1853, the writer made a very careful copy of the Constitution of the United States, from the original in the State Department at Washington city, together with the autographs of the members of the Convention who signed it. In orthography, capital letters, and punctuation, the copy here

SECTION 2. The House of Representatives shall be composed of Members chosen every second Year by the People of the several States, and the Electors in each State shall have the Qualifications requisite for Electors of the most numerous Branch of the State Legislature.

House of Representatives.

No Person shall be a Representative who shall not have attained to the age of twenty-five Years, and been seven Years a Citizen of the United States, and who shall not, when elected, be an Inhabitant of that State in which he shall be chosen.

Qualifications of Representatives.

Representatives and direct Taxes shall be apportioned among the several States which may be included within this Union, according to their respective Numbers,[1] which shall be determined by adding to the whole Number of free Persons, including those bound to Service for a Term of Years, and excluding Indians not taxed, three fifths of all other Persons.[2] The actual Enumeration shall be made within three Years after the first Meeting of the Congress of the United States, and within every subsequent Term of ten Years, in such Manner as they shall by Law direct. The Number of Representatives shall not exceed one for every thirty Thousand;[3] but each State shall have at Least one Representative; and until such enumeration shall be made, the State of New Hampshire shall be entitled to choose three, Massachusetts eight, Rhode Island and Providence Plantations one, Connecticut five, New York six, New Jersey four, Pennsylvania eight, Delaware one, Maryland six, Virginia ten, North Carolina five, South Carolina five, and Georgia three.

Apportionment of Representatives.

given may be relied upon as correct, it having been subsequently carefully compared with a copy published by Mr. Hickey, in his useful little volume, entitled *The Constitution of the United States of America*, etc., and attested, on the 20th of July, 1846, by Nicholas P. Trist, chief clerk of the State Department. Most of the notes are from the *National Calendar*, a work published in 1828, by Peter Force, of Washington city, and carefully prepared by him. The most prominent American writers upon constitutional law, are the late Justice Story and Chancellor Kent. Joseph Story was born at Marblehead, Massachusetts, in September, 1779, and was educated at Harvard University. He studied law; and soon, on entering upon his practice, took a prominent position. He was a member of his State Legislature, and of the Federal Congress, and was chiefly instrumental in effecting the repeal of the Embargo Act [page 403]. He was only thirty-two years of age when President Madison made him an associate of the Supreme Court of the United States. From that time he discarded politics. In commercial and constitutional law he was peerless. His *Commentaries on the Constitution of the United States*, published in three volumes, in 1833, will ever be a standard work. Judge Story died at Cambridge, Massachusetts, in September, 1845, at the age of sixty-six years. His own words, applied to another, may be appropriately said of him: "Whatever subject he touched was touched with a master's hand and spirit. He employed his eloquence to adorn his learning, and his learning to give solid weight to his eloquence. He was always instructive and interesting, and rarely without producing an instantaneous conviction. A lofty ambition of excellence, that stirring spirit which breathes the breath of Heaven, and pants for immortality, sustained his genius in its perilous course."

[1] The constitutional provision, that direct taxes shall be apportioned among the several States, according to their respective numbers, to be ascertained by a census, was not intended to restrict the power of imposing direct taxes to States only.—*Loughborough* vs. *Blake*, 5 *Wheaton*, 319.

[2] Slaves. Every five slaves are accounted three persons, in making the apportionment.

[3] See laws United States, vol. ii., chap. 124; iii., 261; iv., 332. Acts of 17th Congress, 1st session, chap. x.; and of the 22d and 27th Congress.

Vacancies how filled.

When vacancies happen in the Representation from any State, the Executive Authority thereof shall issue Writs of Election to fill such Vacancies.

Speaker, how appointed.

The House of Representatives shall choose their Speaker and other Officers; and shall have the sole Power of Impeachment.

Number of Senators from each State.

SECTION 3. The Senate of the United States shall be composed of two Senators from each State, chosen by the Legislature thereof, for six Years; and each Senator shall have one Vote.[1]

Classification of Senators.

Immediately after they shall be assembled in Consequence of the first Election, they shall be divided as equally as may be into three Classes. The Seats of the Senators of the first Class shall be vacated at the Expiration of the second Year, of the second Class at the Expiration of the fourth Year, and of the third Class at the Expiration of the sixth Year, so that one third may be chosen every second year; and if Vacancies happen by Resignation, or otherwise, during the Recess of the Legislature of any State, the Executive thereof may make temporary Appointments until the next Meeting of the Legislature, which shall then fill such Vacancies.

Qualification of Senators.

No Person shall be a Senator who shall not have attained to the age of thirty Years, and been nine Years a Citizen of the United States, and who shall not, when elected, be an Inhabitant of that State for which he shall be chosen.

Presiding officer of the Senate.

The Vice-President of the United States shall be President of the Senate, but shall have no Vote, unless they be equally divided.

The Senate shall choose their other Officers, and also a President pro tempore, in the absence of the Vice-President, or when he shall exercise the Office of President of the United States.

Senate a court for trial of impeachments.

The Senate shall have full power to try all impeachments: When sitting for that Purpose, they shall be on Oath, or Affirmation. When the President of the United States is tried, the Chief Justice shall preside: and no Person shall be convicted without the Concurrence of two thirds of the Members present.

Judgment in case of conviction.

Judgment in Cases of Impeachment shall not extend further than to removal from Office, and Disqualification to hold and enjoy any Office of Honor, Trust, or Profit under the United States: but the party convicted shall nevertheless be liable and subject to Indictment, Trial, Judgment, and Punishment, according to Law.

---

[1] See art. v., clause 1.

Elections of Senators and Representatives.

SECTION 4. The Times, Places, and Manner of holding Elections for Senators and Representatives, shall be prescribed in each State by the Legislature thereof; but the Congress may at any time by Law make or alter such Regulations, except as to the places of chusing Senators.

Meeting of Congress.

The Congress shall assemble at least once in every Year, and such meeting shall be on the first Monday in December, unless they shall by Law appoint a different day.

Organization of Congress.

SECTION 5. Each House shall be the Judge of the Elections, Returns, and Qualifications of its own Members, and a Majority of each shall constitute a Quorum to do Business; but a smaller Number may adjourn from day to day, and may be authorized to compel the Attendance of absent Members, in such Manner, and under such Penalties as each House may provide.

Rules of proceeding.

Each House may determine the Rules of its Proceedings,[1] punish its Members for disorderly Behaviour, and, with the Concurrence of two thirds, expel a Member.

Journal of Congress.

Each House shall keep a Journal of its Proceedings, and from time to time publish the same, excepting such Parts as may in their Judgment require Secresy; and the Yeas and Nays of the Members of either House on any question shall, at the Desire of one fifth of those Present, be entered on the Journal.

Adjournment of Congress.

Neither House, during the Session of Congress, shall, without the Consent of the other, adjourn for more than three days, nor to any other Place than that in which the two Houses shall be sitting.

Compensation and privileges of members.

SECTION 6. The Senators and Representatives shall receive a Compensation for their Services, to be ascertained by Law, and paid out of the Treasury of the United States. They shall in all Cases, except Treason, Felony, and Breach of the Peace, be privileged from Arrest during their Attendance at

---

[1] To an action of trespass against the sergeant-at-arms of the House of Representatives of the United States, for assault and battery and false imprisonment, it is a legal justification and bar to plead that a Congress was held and sitting during the period of the trespasses complained, and that the House of Representatives had resolved that the plaintiff had been guilty of a breach of the privileges of the House, and of a high contempt of the dignity and authority of the same; and had ordered that the Speaker should issue his warrant to the sergeant-at-arms, commanding him to take the plaintiff into custody wherever to be found, and to have him before the said House to answer to the said charge; and that the Speaker did accordingly issue such a warrant, reciting the said resolution and order, and commanding the sergeant-at-arms to take the plaintiff into custody, etc., and deliver the said warrant to the defendant: by virtue of which warrant the defendant arrested the plaintiff, and conveyed him to the bar of the House, where he was heard in his defense touching the matter of said charge, and the examination being adjourned from day to day, and the House having ordered the plaintiff to be detained in custody, he was accordingly detained by the defendant until he was finally adjudged to be guilty and convicted of the charge aforesaid, and ordered to be forthwith brought to the bar and reprimanded by the Speaker, and then discharged from custody, and after being thus reprimanded, was actually discharged from the arrest and custody aforesaid.—*Anderson* vs. *Dunn*, 6 *Wheaton*, 204.

the Session of their respective Houses, and in going to and returning from the same; and for any Speech or Debate in either House, they shall not be questioned in any other Place.

Plurality of offices prohibited.

No Senator or Representative shall, during the Time for which he was elected, be appointed to any civil Office under the Authority of the United States, which shall have been created, or the Emoluments whereof shall have been increased during such time; and no Person holding any office under the United States, shall be a Member of either House during his Continuance in office.

Bills, how originated.

SECTION 7. All Bills for raising Revenue shall originate in the House of Representatives; but the Senate may propose or concur with Amendments as on other Bills.

How bills become laws.

Every Bill which shall have passed the house of Representatives and the Senate, shall, before it become a Law, be presented to the President of the United States: if he approve he shall sign it, but if not he shall return it, with his Objections, to that House in which it shall have originated, who shall enter the Objections at large on their Journal, and proceed to reconsider it. If, after such Reconsideration, two thirds of that House shall agree to pass the Bill, it shall be sent, together with the Objections, to the other House, by which it shall likewise be reconsidered, and if approved by two thirds of that House, it shall become a Law. But in all such Cases the Votes of both Houses shall be determined by Yeas and Nays, and the Names of the Persons voting for and against the Bill shall be entered on the Journal of each House respectively. If any Bill shall not be returned by the President within ten Days (Sunday excepted) after it shall have been presented to him, the Same shall be a Law, in like Manner as if he had signed it, unless the Congress by their Adjournment prevent its Return, in which Case it shall not be a Law.

Approval and veto powers of President.

Every Order, Resolution, or Vote to which the Concurrence of the Senate and House of Representatives may be necessary (except on a question of adjournment), shall be presented to the President of the United States; and before the Same shall take Effect, shall be approved by him, or being disapproved by him, shall be repassed by two thirds of the Senate and House of Representatives, according to the Rules and Limitations prescribed in the Case of a Bill.

Powers vested in Congress.

SECTION 8. The Congress shall have Power

To lay and collect Taxes,[1] Duties, Imposts, and Excises;

[1] The power of Congress to *lay and collect taxes, duties,* &c., extends to the District of Columbia, and to the Territories of the United States, as well as to the States.—*Loughborough* vs. *Blake,* 5

to pay the Debts and provide for the common Defense and general Welfare of the United States; but all Duties, Imposts, and Excises shall be uniform throughout the United States;

Powers vested in Congress.

To borrow Money on the credit of the United States;

To regulate Commerce with foreign Nations, and among the several States, and with the Indian tribes;

To establish an uniform Rule of Naturalization,[2] and uniform Laws on the subject of Bankruptcies[3] throughout the United States;

To coin Money, regulate the Value thereof, and of foreign Coin, and fix the Standard of Weights and Measures;

To provide for the Punishment of counterfeiting the Securities and current Coin of the United States;

To establish Post Offices and Post Roads;

To promote the progress of Science and useful Arts, by securing for limited Times to Authors and Inventors the exclusive Right to their respective Writings and Discoveries;[4]

To constitute Tribunals inferior to the Supreme Court;

To define and punish Piracies and Felonies committed on the high Seas, and Offenses against the Law of Nations;[5]

To declare War, grant Letters of Marque and Reprisal, and make Rules concerning Captures on Land and Water;

To raise and support Armies; but no Appropriation of Money to that Use shall be for a longer Term than two Years;

To provide and maintain a Navy;

To make Rules for the Government and Regulation of the Land and Naval Forces;

Wheaton, 318. But Congress are not bound to extend a direct tax to the District and Territories. —*Id.*, 318.

[2] Under the Constitution of the United States, the power of naturalization is exclusively in Congress.—*Chivac* vs. *Chivac*, 2 *Wheaton*, 259.

See Laws United States, vol. ii., chap. 30; ii., 261; iii., 71; iii., 288; iii., 400; iv., 564; vi., 32.

[3] Since the adoption of the Constitution of the United States, a State has authority to pass a bankrupt law, provided such law does not impair the obligation of contracts within the meaning of the Constitution (art. i., sect. 10), and provided there be no act of Congress in force to establish a uniform system of bankruptcy conflicting with such law.—*Sturgess* vs. *Crowninshield*, 4 *Wheaton*, 122, 192.

See Laws United States, vol. ii., chap. 368, sect. 2; iii., 66; iii., 158.

[4] The first copyright law was enacted in 1790, on the petition of Dr. David Ramsay, the historian, and others. See note 1, page 312.

[5] The act of the 3d March, 1819, chap. 76, sect. 5, referring to the law of nations for a definition of the crime of piracy, is a constitutional exercise of the power of Congress to define and punish that crime.—*United States* vs. *Smith*, 5 *Wheaton*, 153, 157.

Congress have power to provide for the punishment of offenses committed by persons on board a ship-of-war of the United States, wherever that ship may lie. But Congress have not exercised that power in the case of a ship lying in the waters of the United States—the words, within fort, arsenal, dockyard, magazine, or in *any other place or district of country under the sole and exclusive jurisdiction of the United States*, in the third section of the act of 1790, chap. 9, not extending to a ship-of-war, but only to objects in their nature, fixed and territorial.—*United States* vs. *Bevans*, 3 *Wheaton*, 890.

Powers vested in Congress.

To provide for calling forth the Militia to execute the Laws of the Union, suppress Insurrections, and repel Invasions;

To provide for organizing, arming, and disciplining the Militia, and for governing such Part of them as may be employed in the Service of the United States—reserving to the States respectively, the Appointment of the Officers, and the Authority of training the Militia according to the Discipline prescribed by Congress;[1]

To exercise exclusive Legislation in all Cases whatsoever, over such District (not exceeding ten Miles square) as may, by Cession of particular States, and the Acceptance of Congress, become the Seat of the Government of the United States,[2] and to exercise like Authority over all Places purchased by the Consent of the Legislature of the State in which the Same shall be, for the Erection of Forts, Magazines, Arsenals, Dockyards, and other needful Buildings;—And

To make all Laws which shall be necessary and proper for carrying into Execution the foregoing Powers, and all other Powers vested by this Constitution in the Government of the United States, or in any Department or Officer thereof.[3]

---

[1] Vide amendments, art. ii.

[2] Congress has authority to impose a direct tax on the District of Columbia, in proportion to the census directed to be taken by the Constitution.—*Loughborough* vs. *Blake*, 5 *Wheaton*, 317.

But Congress are not bound to extend a direct tax to the District and Territories.—*Id.*, 322.

The power of Congress to exercise exclusive jurisdiction in all cases whatsoever, within the District of Columbia, includes the power of taxing it.—*Id.*, 324.

[3] Whenever the terms in which a power is granted by the Constitution to Congress, or whenever the nature of the power itself requires that it should be exercised exclusively by Congress, the subject is as completely taken away from the State Legislatures as if they had been expressly forbidden to act on it.—*Sturgess* vs. *Crowninshield*, 4 *Wheaton*, 193.

Congress has power to incorporate a bank.—*M'Culloch* vs. *State of Maryland*, 4 *Wheaton*, 316.

The power of establishing a corporation is not a distinct sovereign power or end of government, but only the means of carrying into effect other powers which are sovereign. Whenever it becomes an appropriate means of exercising any of the powers expressly given by the Constitution to the government of the Union, it may be exercised by that government.—*Id.*, 411, 421.

If a certain means to carry into effect any of the powers expressly given by the Constitution to the government of the Union, be an appropriate measure, not prohibited by the Constitution, the degree of its necessity is a question of legislative discretion, not of judicial cognizance.—*Id.*, 421.

The act of the 19th April, 1816, chap. 44, to incorporate the subscribers to the bank of the United States, is a law made in pursuance of the Constitution.—*Id.*, 424.

The bank of the United States has constitutionally a right to establish its branches or offices of discount and deposit within any State.—*Id.*, 424.

There is nothing in the Constitution of the United States similar to the Articles of Confederation, which excludes incidental or implied powers.—*Id.*, 403.

If the *end* be legitimate, and within the scope of the Constitution, all the *means* which are appropriate, which are plainly adapted to that end, and which are not prohibited, may constitutionally be employed to carry it into effect.—*Id.*, 421.

The powers granted to Congress are not exclusive of similar powers existing in the States, unless where the Constitution has expressly, in terms, given an exclusive power to Congress, or the exercise of a like power is prohibited to the States, or there is a direct repugnancy or incompatibility in the exercise of it by the States.—*Houston* vs. *Moore*, 5 *Wheaton*, 49.

The example of the first class is to be found in the exclusive legislation delegated to Congress over places purchased by the consent of the Legislature of the State in which the same shall be, for forts, arsenals, dockyards, &c. Of the second class, the prohibition of a State to coin money or

SECTION 9. The Migration or Importation of such Persons as any of the States now existing shall think proper to admit, shall not be prohibited by the Congress prior to the Year one thousand eight hundred and eight, but a Tax or Duty may be imposed on such Importation, not exceeding ten dollars for each Person.[1] Immigrants, how admitted.

The Privilege of the Writ of Habeas Corpus[2] shall not be suspended, unless when in Cases of Rebellion or Invasion the public Safety may require it. Habeas Corpus.

No Bill of Attainder or ex post Facto law shall be passed.[3] Attainder.

No Capitation, or other direct, Tax shall be laid, unless in Proportion to the Census or Enumeration herein before directed to be taken. Taxes.

No Tax or Duty shall be laid on Articles exported from any State.

No Preference shall be given by any Regulation of Commerce or Revenue to the Ports of one State over those of another; nor shall Vessels bound to, or from, one State, be obliged to enter, clear, or pay Duties in another. Regulations regarding duties.

No Money shall be drawn from the Treasury, but in Consequence of Appropriations made by law; and a regular Statement and Account of the Receipts and Expenditures of all public Money shall be published from time to time. Money, how drawn.

No Title of Nobility shall be granted by the United States: And no Person holding any Office of Profit or Trust under them, shall, without the Consent of the Congress, accept of any Present, Emolument, Office, or Title, of any kind whatever, from any King, Prince, or Foreign State.[4] Titles of nobility prohibited.

---

emit bills of credit. Of the third class, the power to establish a uniform rule of naturalization, and the delegation of admiralty and maritime jurisdiction.—*Id.*, 49.

In all other classes of cases, the States retain concurrent authority with Congress.—*Id.*, 48.

But in cases of concurrent authority, where the laws of the States and of the Union are in direct and manifest collision on the same subject, those of the Union being the supreme law of the land, are of paramount authority, and the State so far, and so far only as such incompatibility exists, must necessarily yield.—*Id.*, 49.

The State within which a branch of the United States bank may be established, can not, without violating the Constitution, tax that branch.—*M'Culloch* vs. *State of Maryland*, 4 *Wheaton*, 425.

The State governments have no right to tax any constitutional means employed by the government of the Union to execute its constitutional powers.—*Id.*, 427.

The States have no power by taxation, or otherwise, to retard, impede, burden, or in any manner control, the operation of the constitutional laws enacted by Congress, to carry into effect the powers vested in the national government.—*Id.*, 436.

This principle does not extend to a tax paid by the real property of the bank of the United States, in common with the other real property in a particular State, nor to a tax imposed on the proprietary which the citizens of that State may hold in common with the other property of the same description throughout the State.—*Id.*, 436.

[1] This was a provision for the gradual extinction of the slave-trade, carried on between Africa and the United States.

[2] A writ for delivering a person from false imprisonment, or for removing a person from one court to another.

[3] Declaring an act penal or criminal which was innocent when committed. Attainder is a deprivation of power to inherit or transmit property, a loss of civil rights, &c.

[4] Note 1, page 267.

Powers of State defined.

SECTION 10. No State shall enter into any Treaty, Alliance, or Confederation; grant Letters of Marque and Reprisal; coin Money; emit Bills of Credit; make any Thing but gold and silver Coin a Tender in Payment of Debts; pass any Bill of Attainder, ex post facto Law, or Law impairing the Obligation of Contracts,[1] or grant any Title of Nobility.

No State shall, without the Consent of the Congress, lay any Imposts or Duties on Imports or Exports, except what may be absolutely necessary for executing its inspection Laws: and the net Produce of all Duties and Imposts, laid by any State on Imports or Exports, shall be for the Use of the Treasury of the United States; and all such Laws shall be subject to the Revision and Controul of the Congress.

---

[1] Where a law is in its nature a *contract*, where absolute rights have vested under that contract, a repeal of the law can not divest those rights.—*Fletcher* vs. *Peck*, 6 *Cranch*, 88.

A party to a contract can not pronounce its own deed invalid, although that party be a *sovereign State*.—*Id.*, 88.

A *grant* is a *contract executed*.—*Id.*, 89.

A law annulling conveyance is unconstitutional, because it is a law impairing the obligation of contracts within the meaning of the Constitution of the United States.—*Id.*

The court will not declare a law to be unconstitutional, unless the opposition between the Constitution and the law be clear and plain.—*Id.*, 87.

An act of the Legislature of a State, declaring that certain lands which should be purchased for the Indians should not thereafter be subject to any tax, constituted a contract which could not, after the adoption of the Constitution of the United States, be rescinded by a subsequent legislative act—such rescinding act being void under the Constitution of the United States.—*State of New Jersey* vs. *Wilson*, 7 *Cranch*, 164.

The present Constitution of the United States did not commence its operation until the first Wednesday in March, 1789, and the provision in the Constitution, that "no State shall make any law impairing the obligation of contracts," does not extend to a State law enacted before that day, and operating upon rights of property vesting before that time.—*Owings* vs. *Speed*, 5 *Wheaton*, 420, 421.

An act of a State Legislature, which discharges a debtor from all liability for debts contracted previous to his discharge, on his surrendering his property for the benefit of his creditors, is a law impairing "the obligation of contracts," within the meaning of the Constitution of the United States, so far as it attempts to discharge the contract; and it makes no difference in such a case, that the suit was brought in a State court of the State of which both the parties were citizens where the contract was made, and the discharge obtained, and where they continued to reside until the suit was brought.—*Farmers' and Mechanics' Bank* vs. *Smith*, 6 *Wheaton*, 131.

The act of New York, passed on the 3d of April, 1811 (which not only liberates the person of the debtor, but discharges him from all liability for any debt contracted previous to his discharge, on his surrendering his property in the manner it prescribes), so far as it attempts to discharge the contract, is a law impairing the obligation of contracts, within the meaning of the Constitution of the United States, and is not a good plea in bar of an action brought upon such contract.—*Sturgess* vs. *Crowninshield*, 4 *Wheaton*, 122, 197.

Statutes of limitation and usury laws, unless retro-active in their effect, do not impair the obligation of contracts, and are constitutional.—*Id.*, 206.

A State bankrupt or insolvent law (which not only liberates the person of the debtor, but discharges him from all liability for the debt), so far as it attempts to discharge the contract, is repugnant to the Constitution of the United States, and it makes no difference in the application of this principle, whether the law was passed *before* or *after* the debt was contracted.—*M'Millan* vs. *M'Neill*, 4 *Wheaton*, 209.

The charter granted by the British crown to the trustees of Dartmouth College, in New Hampshire, in the year 1769, is a contract within the meaning of that clause of the Constitution of the United States (art. i., sect. 10) which declares, that no State shall make any law impairing the obligation of contracts. The charter was not dissolved by the Revolution.—*College* vs. *Woodard*, 4 *Wheaton*, 518.

An act of the State Legislature of New Hampshire, altering the charter of Dartmouth College in a material respect, without the consent of the corporation, is an act impairing the obligation of the charter, and is unconstitutional and void.—*Id.*, 518.

No State shall, without the Consent of Congress, lay any Duty of Tonnage, keep Troops, or Ships-of-War in time of Peace, enter into any Agreement or Compact with another State, or with a foreign Power, or engage in War, unless actually invaded, or in such imminent Danger as will not admit of Delay.

ARTICLE II.

Executive power, in whom vested.

SECTION 1. The executive Power shall be vested in a President of the United States of America. He shall hold his Office during the Term of four Years,[1] and, together with the Vice President, chosen for the same Term, be elected, as follows:

Presidential electors.

Each State shall appoint, in such Manner as the Legislature thereof may direct,[2] a Number of Electors, equal to the whole Number of Senators and Representatives to which the State may be entitled in the Congress: but no Senator or Representative, or Person holding an Office of Trust or Profit under the United States, shall be appointed an Elector.

President and Vice-President, how elected.

[[3] The electors shall meet in their respective States, and vote by ballot for two persons, of whom one at least shall not be an inhabitant of the same State with themselves. And they shall make a list of all the persons voted for, and of the number of votes for each; which list they shall sign and certify, and transmit sealed to the seat of the government of the United States, directed to the President of the Senate. The President of the Senate shall, in the presence of the Senate and House of Representatives, open all the certificates, and the votes shall then be counted. The person having the greatest number of votes shall be the President, if such number be a majority of the whole number of electors appointed; and if there be more than one who have such majority, and have an equal number of votes, then the House of Representatives shall immediately choose by ballot one of them for President; and if no person have a majority, then from the five highest on the list the said House shall in like manner choose the President. But in choosing the President, the votes shall be taken by States—the representation from each State having one vote; a quorum for this purpose shall consist of a member or members from two thirds of the States, and a majority of all the States shall be necessary to a choice. In every case, after the choice of the President, the person having the greatest number of votes of the electors shall be the Vice-President.

[1] See Laws United States, vol. ii., chap. 109, sect. 12.

[2] See Laws United States, vol. ii., chap. 109.

[3] Vide Amendments, art. xii.

But if there should remain two or more who have equal votes, the Senate shall choose from them by ballot the Vice President.[1]]

Time of choosing electors.

The Congress may determine the Time of chusing the Electors,[2] and the Day on which they shall give their Votes; which Day shall be the same throughout the United States.[3]

Qualifications of the President.

No Person except a natural born Citizen, or a Citizen of the United States at the time of the Adoption of this Constitution, shall be eligible to the Office of President; neither shall any person be eligible to that Office who shall not have attained to the Age of thirty-five Years, and been fourteen Years a Resident within the United States.

Resort in case of his disability.

In Case of the Removal of the President from Office, or of his Death, Resignation,[4] or Inability to discharge the Powers and Duties of the said office, the same shall devolve on the Vice President, and the Congress may by Law provide for the Case of Removal, Death, Resignation or Inability, both of the President and Vice President, declaring what Officer shall then act as President, and such officer shall act accordingly, until the Disability be removed, or a President shall be elected.[5]

Salary of the President.

The President shall, at stated Times, receive for his Services, a Compensation, which shall neither be increased nor diminished during the Period for which he shall have been elected, and he shall not receive within that Period any other Emolument from the United States, or any of them.[6]

Oath of Office.

Before he enter on the Execution of his Office, he shall take the following Oath or Affirmation:

"I do solemnly swear (or affirm) that I will faithfully execute the Office of President of the United States, and will to the best of my Ability, preserve, protect, and defend the Constitution of the United States."

Duties of the President.

SECTION 2. The President shall be Commander in chief of the Army and Navy of the United States, and of the Militia of the several States, when called into the actual Service of the United States;[7] he may require the Opinion, in writing,

---

[1] This clause is annulled. See Amendments, art. xii.

[2] See Laws United States, vol. ii., chap. 104, sec. 1.

[3] See Laws United States, vol. ii., chap. 109, sec. 2. Now the first Tuesday in November.

[4] See Laws United States, vol. ii., chap. 104, sec. 11.

[5] See Laws United States, vol ii., chap. 109, sec. 9; and vol. iii., chap. 403.

[6] The salary of the President is twenty-five thousand dollars a year.

[7] The act of the State of Pennsylvania, of the 28th March, 1814 (providing, sec. 21, that the officers and privates of the militia of that State neglecting or refusing to serve when called into actual service, in pursuance of any order or requisition of the President of the United States, shall be liable to the penalties defined in the act of Congress of 28th February, 1795, chap. 277, or to any penalty which may have been prescribed since the date of that act, or which may hereafter be prescribed by any law of the United States, and also providing for the trial of such delinquents by a

of the principal Officer in each of the executive Departments, upon any Subject relating to the Duties of their respective Offices, and he shall have Power to grant Reprieves and Pardons for Offences against the United States, except in Cases of Impeachment.

He shall have Power, by and with the Advice and Consent of the Senate, to make Treaties, provided two thirds of the Senators present concur; and he shall nominate, and by and with the Advice and Consent of the Senate, shall appoint Ambassadors, other public Ministers and Consuls, Judges of the supreme Court, and all other Officers of the United States, whose appointments are not herein hitherto provided for, and which shall be established by Law: but the Congress may by Law vest the Appointment of such inferior Officers, as they think proper, in the President alone, in the Courts of Law, or in the Heads of Departments.

His power to make treaties, appoint embassadors, judges, etc.

The President shall have Power to fill up all Vacancies that may happen during the Recess of the Senate, by granting Commissions which shall expire at the End of their next Session.

May fill vacancies.

SECTION 3. He shall from time to time give to the Congress Information of the State of the Union, and recommend to their Consideration such Measures as he shall judge necessary and expedient; he may, on extraordinary Occasions, convene both Houses, or either of them, and in Case of Disagreement between them, with Respect to the Time of Adjournment, he may adjourn them to such Time as he shall think proper; he shall receive Ambassadors and other public Ministers; he shall take Care that the Laws be faithfully executed, and shall Commission all the officers of the United States.

Power to convene Congress.

SECTION 4. The President, Vice President, and all civil Officers of the United States, shall be removed from Office on Impeachment for, and Conviction of, Treason, Bribery, or other high Crimes or Misdemeanors.

How officers may be removed.

ARTICLE III.

SECTION 1. The judicial Power of the United States, shall be vested in one supreme Court, and in such inferior Courts as the Congress may from time to time ordain and establish.[1]

Judicial power, how vested.

State court martial, and that a list of the delinquents fined by such court should be furnished to the marshal of the United States, etc.; and also to the comptroller of the treasury of the United States, in order that the further proceedings directed to be had thereon by the laws of the United States might be completed), is not repugnant to the Constitution and laws of the United States.—*Houston* vs. *Moore*, 5 *Wheaton*, 1, 12.

[1] Congress may constitutionally impose upon the judges of the Supreme Court of the United States the burden of holding circuit courts.—*Stuart* vs. *Laird*, 1 *Cranch*, 289.

The Judges, both of the supreme and inferior Courts, shall hold their Offices during good Behavior, and shall, at stated Times, receive for their Services, a Compensation, which shall not be diminished during their Continuance in Office.[1]

To what cases it extends.

SECTION 2. The judicial Power shall extend to all Cases, in Law and Equity, arising under this Constitution, the Laws of the United States, and Treaties made, or which shall be made, under their Authority;—to all cases affecting Ambassadors, other public Ministers and Consuls;—to all Cases of admiralty and maritime Jurisdiction;—to Controversies to which the United States shall be a Party;—to Controversies between two or more States;—between a State and Citizens of another State;—between Citizens of different States;[2]—between Citizens of the same State claiming Lands under Grants of different States, and between a State, or the Citizens thereof, and foreign States, Citizens or Subjects.[3]

Jurisdiction of the Supreme Court.

In all Cases affecting Ambassadors, other public Ministers and Consuls, and those in which a State shall be a Party, the supreme Court shall have original Jurisdiction. In all the other Cases before mentioned, the supreme Court shall have appellate Jurisdiction, both as to Law and Fact, with such Exceptions, and under such Regulations as the Congress shall make.

---

[1] See laws of the United States, vol. ii., chap. 20.

[2] A citizen of the District of Columbia is not a citizen of a State within the meaning of the Constitution of the United States.—*Hepburn, et al.* vs. *Ellzey*, 2 *Cranch*, 445.

[3] The Supreme Court of the United States has not power to issue a *mandamus* to a *Secretary of State* of the United States, it being an exercise of original jurisdiction not warranted by the Constitution, notwithstanding the act of Congress.—*Marbury* vs. *Madison*, 1 *Cranch*, 137.

See a restriction of this provision.—Amendments, art. xi.

[4] The appellate jurisdiction of the Supreme Court of the United States extends to a final judgment or decree in any suit in the highest court of law, or equity of a State, where is drawn in question the validity of a treaty, etc.—*Martin* vs. *Hunter's lessee*, 1 *Wheaton*, 304.

Such judgment, etc., may be re-examined by writ of error, in the same manner as if rendered in a circuit court.—*Id.*

If the cause has been once remanded before, and the State court decline or refuse to carry into effect the mandate of the Supreme Court thereon, this court will proceed to a final decision of the same, and award execution thereon.

Quere.—Whether this court has authority to issue a mandamus to the State court to enforce a former judgment?—*Id.*, 362.

If the validity or construction of a treaty of the United States is drawn in question, and the decision is against its validity, or the title specially set up by either party under the treaty, this court has jurisdiction to ascertain that title, and determine its legal validity, and is not confined to the abstract construction of the treaty itself.—*Id.*, 362.

Quere.—Whether the courts of the United States have jurisdiction of offenses at common law against the United States?—*United States* vs. *Coolidge*, 1 *Wheaton*, 415.

The courts of the United States have exclusive jurisdiction of all seizures made on land or water for a breach of the laws of the United States; and any intervention of a State authority, which by taking the thing seized out of the hands of the United States' officer, might obstruct the exercise of this jurisdiction, is illegal.—*Slocum* vs. *Mayberry et al.*, 2 *Wheaton*, 1, 9.

In such a case the court of the United States have cognizance of the seizure, may enforce a redelivery of the thing by attachment or other summary process.—*Id.*, 9.

The question under such a seizure, whether a forfeiture has been actually incurred, belongs exclusively to the courts of the United States, and it depends upon the final decree of such courts, whether the seizure is to be deemed rightful or tortuous.—*Id.*, 9, 10.

If the seizing officer refuse to institute proceedings to ascertain the forfeiture, the district court

The Trial of all Crimes, except in Cases of Impeachment, shall be by Jury; and such Trial shall be held in the State where the said Crimes shall have been committed; but when Rules respecting trials.

may, on application of the aggrieved party, compel the officer to proceed to adjudication, or to abandon the seizure.—*Id.*, 10.

The jurisdiction of the Circuit Court of the United States extends to a case between citizens of Kentucky, claiming lands exceeding the value of five hundred dollars, under different grants—the one issued by the State of Kentucky, and the other by the State of Virginia, upon warrants issued by Virginia, and locations founded thereon, prior to the separation of Kentucky from Virginia. It is the grant which passes the *legal* title to the land, and if the controversy is founded upon the conflicting grants of different States, the judicial power of the courts of the United States extends to the case, whatever may have been the equitable title of the parties prior to the grant.—*Colson et al.* vs. *Lewis*, 2 *Wheaton*, 377.

Under the judiciary of 1789, chap. 20, sect. 25, giving appellate jurisdiction to the Supreme Court of the United States, from the final judgment or decree of the highest court of law or equity of a State, in certain cases the writ of error may be directed to any court in which the record and judgment on which it is to act may be found; and if the record has been remitted by the highest court, &c., to another court of the State, it may be brought by the writ of error from that court.—*Gelston* vs. *Hoyt*, 3 *Wheaton*, 246, 303.

The remedies in the courts of the United States at common law and in equity are to be, not according to the practice of State courts, but according to the principles of common law and equity as defined in England. This doctrine reconciled with the decisions of the courts of Tennessee, permitting an equitable title to be asserted in an action at law.—*Robinson* vs. *Campbell*, 3 *Wheaton*, 221.

Remedies in respect to real property are to be pursued according to the *lex loci rei sitæ*.—*Id.*, 219.

The courts of the United States have *exclusive* cognizance of questions of forfeiture upon all seizures made under the laws of the United States, and it is not competent for a State court to entertain or decide such question of forfeiture. If a sentence of condemnation be definitively pronounced by the proper court of the United States, it is conclusive that a forfeiture is incurred; if a sentence of acquittal, it is equally conclusive against the forfeiture, and in either case the question can not be again litigated in any common law for ever.—*Gelston* vs. *Hoyt*, 3 *Wheaton*, 246, 311.

Where a seizure is made for a supposed forfeiture under a law of the United States, no action of trespass lies in any common-law tribunal, until a final decree is pronounced upon the proceeding *in rem* to enforce such forfeiture; for it depends upon the final decree of the court proceeding *in rem*, whether such seizure is to be deemed rightful or tortuous, and the action, if brought before such decree is made, is brought too soon.—*Id.*, 313.

If a suit be brought against the seizing officer for the supposed trespass while the suit for the forfeiture is depending, the fact of such pending may be pleaded in abatement, or as a temporary bar of the action. If after a decree of condemnation, then that fact may be pleaded as a bar; if after an acquittal with a certificate of reasonable cause of seizure, then that may be pleaded as a bar. If after an acquittal without such certificate, then the officer is without any justification for the seizure, and it is definitively settled to be a tortuous act. If to an action of trespass in a State court for a seizure, the seizing officer plead the fact of forfeiture in his defense, without averring a *lis pendens*, or a condemnation or an acquittal, with a certificate of reasonable cause of seizure, the plea is bad: for it attempts to put in issue the question of a forfeiture in a State court.—*Id.*, 314.

Supposing that the third article of the Constitution of the United States, which declares, that "the judicial power shall extend to all cases of admiralty and maritime jurisdiction," vested in the United States exclusive jurisdiction of all such cases, and that a murder committed in the waters of a State where the tide ebbs and flows, is a case of admiralty and maritime jurisdiction; yet Congress have not, in the 8th section of the act of 1790, chap. 9, "for the punishment of certain crimes against the United States," so exercised this power as to confer on the courts of the United States jurisdiction over such murder.—*United States* vs. *Bevans*, 3 *Wheaton*, 336, 387.

Quere.—Whether courts of common law have concurrent jurisdiction with the admiralty over murder committed in bays, &c., which are enclosed parts of the sea?—*Id.*, 387.

The grant to the United States, in the Constitution, of all cases of admiralty and maritime jurisdiction, does not extend to a cession of the waters in which those cases may arise, or of general jurisdiction over the same. Congress may pass all laws which are necessary for giving the most complete effect to the exercise of the admiralty and maritime jurisdiction granted to the government of the Union; but the general jurisdiction over the place subject to this grant, adheres to the territory as a portion of territory not yet given away, and the residuary powers of legislation still remain in the State.—*Id.*, 389.

The Supreme Court of the United States has constitutionally appellate jurisdiction under the not committed within any State, the Trial shall be at such Place or Places as the Congress may by Law have directed.[1]

Treason defined.

SECTION 3. Treason against the United States, shall consist only in levying War against them, or in adhering to their Enemies, giving them Aid and Comfort.

No Person shall be convicted of Treason, unless on the Testimony of two Witnesses to the same overt Act, or on Confession in open Court.

How punished.

The Congress shall have Power to declare the Punishment of Treason, but no Attainder of Treason shall work Corruption of Blood, or Forfeiture except during the Life of the Person attainted.[2]

---

judiciary act of 1789, chap. 20, sect. 25, from the final judgment or decree of the highest court of law or equity of a State having jurisdiction of the subject-matter of the suit, where is drawn in question the validity of a treaty or statute of, or an authority exercised under, the United States, and the decision is against their validity; or where is drawn in question the validity of a statute of, or an authority exercised under, any State, on the ground of their being repugnant to the Constitution, treaties, or laws of the United States, and the decision is in favor of such their validity; or of the Constitution, or of a treaty, or statute of, or commission held under, the United States, and the decision is against the title, right, privilege, or exemption, specially set up or claimed by either party under such clause of the Constitution, treaty, statute, or commission.—*Cohens* vs. *Virginia*, 6 *Wheaton*, 264, 375.

It is no objection to the exercise of this appellate jurisdiction, that one of the parties is a State, and the other a citizen of that State.—*Id.*

The Circuit Courts of the Union have chancery jurisdiction in every State; they have the same chancery powers, and the same rules of decision in equity cases, in all the States.—*United States* vs. *Howland*, 4 *Wheaton*, 108, 115.

Resolution of the Legislature of Virginia of 1810, upon the proposition from Pennsylvania to amend the Constitution, so as to provide an impartial tribunal to decide disputes between the State and Federal judiciaries.—*Note to Cohens* vs. *Virginia. Notes* 6 *Wheaton*, 358.

Where a cause is brought to this court by writ of error, or appeal from the highest court of law or equity of a State, under the 25th section of the judiciary act of 1789, chap. 20, upon the ground that the validity of a statute of the United States was drawn in question, and that the decision of the State court was against its validity, &c., or that the validity of the statute of a State was drawn in question as repugnant to the Constitution of the United States, and the decision was in favor of its validity, it must appear from the record, that the act of Congress, or the constitutionality of the State law was drawn in question.—*Miller* vs. *Nicholls*, 4 *Wheaton*, 311, 315.

But it is not required that the record should in terms state a misconstruction of the act of Congress, or that it was drawn into question. It is sufficient to give this court jurisdiction of the cause, that the record should show that an act of Congress was applicable to the case.—*Id.*, 315.

The Supreme Court of the United States has no jurisdiction under the 25th section of the judiciary act of 1789, chap. 20, unless the judgment or decree of the State court be a final judgment or decree. A judgment reversing that of an inferior court, and awarding a *venire facias de novo*, is not a final judgment.—*Houston* vs. *Moore*, 3 *Wheaton*, 433.

By the compact of 1802, settling the boundary line between Virginia and Tennessee, and the laws made in pursuance thereof, it is declared that all claims and titles to land derived from Virginia, or North Carolina, or Tennessee, which have fallen into the respective States, shall remain as secure to the owners thereof, as if derived from the government within whose boundary they have fallen, and shall not be prejudiced or affected by the establishment of the line. Where the titles of both the plaintiff and defendant in ejectment were derived under grant from Virginia to lands which fell within the limits of Tennessee, it was held that a prior settlement right thereto, which would in *equity* give the party a title, could not be asserted as a sufficient title in an action of ejectment brought in the Circuit Court of Tennessee.—*Robinson* vs. *Campbell*, 3 *Wheaton*, 212.

Although the State courts of Tennessee have decided that, under their statutes (declaring an elder grant founded on a junior entry to be void), a junior patent, founded on a prior entry, shall prevail *at law* against a senior patent founded on a junior entry, this doctrine has never been extended beyond cases within the express provision of the statute of Tennessee, and could not apply to titles deriving all their validity from the laws of Virginia, and confirmed by the compact between the two States.—*Id.*, 212.

[1] Vide Amendments, art. vi.

[2] See Laws of the United States, vol. ii., chap. 36.

ARTICLE IV.

SECTION 1. Full Faith and Credit shall be given in each State to the public Acts, Records, and judicial Proceedings of every other State.[1] And the Congress may by general Laws prescribe the Manner in which such Acts, Records and Proceedings shall be proved, and the Effect thereof.[2]

Rights of States defined.

SECTION 2. The Citizens of each State shall be entitled to all Privileges and Immunities of Citizens in the several States.

Privileges of citizens.

A Person charged in any State with Treason, Felony, or other Crime, who shall flee from Justice, and be found in another State, shall on Demand of the executive Authority of the State from which he fled, be delivered up, to be removed to the State having Jurisdiction of the Crime.

Executive requisition.

No Person held to Service or Labor in one State, under the Laws thereof escaping to another, shall, in Consequence of any Law or Regulation therein, be discharged from such Service or Labor, but shall be delivered up on Claim of the Party to whom such Service or Labor may be due.[3]

Law regulating service or labor.

SECTION 3. New States may be admitted by the Congress into this Union; but no new State shall be formed or erected within the Jurisdiction of any other State; nor any State be formed by the Junction of two or more States, or Parts of States, without the consent of the Legislatures of the States concerned as well as of the Congress.

New States, how formed and admitted.

The Congress shall have Power to dispose of and make all needful Rules and Regulations respecting the Territory or other Property belonging to the United States; and nothing in this Constitution shall be so construed as to Prejudice any Claims of the United States, or of any particular State.

Power of Congress over public lands.

SECTION 4. The Constitution shall guaranty to every State in this Union a Republican Form of Government, and shall protect each of them against Invasion; and on Application of the Legislature, or of the Executive (when the Legislature can not be convened) against domestic violence.

Republican government guarantied.

---

[1] A judgment of a State court has the same credit, validity, and effect, in every other court within the United States, which it had in the court where it was rendered; and whatever pleas would be good to a suit thereon in such State, and none others, can be pleaded in any other court within the United States.—*Hampton* vs. *McConnell*, 3 *Wheaton*, 234.

The record of a judgment in one State is conclusive evidence in another, although it appears that the suit in which it was rendered was commenced by an attachment of property, the defendant having afterward appeared and taken defense.—*Mayhew* vs. *Thacher*, 6 *Wheaton*, 129.

[2] See Laws United States, vol. ii., chap. 38; and vol. iii., chap. 409.

[3] This is the clause of the Constitution on which is based the provisions of the Fugitive Slave Law of 1850. See page 501.

ARTICLE V.

Constitution, how to be amended.

The Congress, whenever two thirds of both Houses shall deem it necessary, shall propose Amendments to this Constitution, or, on the Application of the Legislatures of two thirds of the several States, shall call a Convention for proposing Amendments, which, in either Case, shall be valid to all Intents and Purposes, as part of this Constitution, when ratified by the Legislatures of three fourths of the several States, or by Conventions in three fourths thereof, as the one or the other Mode of Ratification may be proposed by the Congress; Provided that no Amendment which may be made prior to the Year one thousand eight hundred and eight shall in any Manner affect the first and fourth Clauses in the Ninth Section of the first Article; and that no State, without its Consent, shall be deprived of its equal Suffrage in the Senate.[1]

ARTICLE VI.

Validity of debts recognized.

All Debts contracted and Engagements entered into, before the Adoption of this Constitution, shall be as valid against the United States under this Constitution, as under the Confederation.

Supreme law of the land defined.

This Constitution, and the Laws of the United States which shall be made in Pursuance thereof; and all Treaties made, or which shall be made, under the authority of the United States, shall be the supreme Law of the Land;[2] and the Judges in every State shall be bound thereby, any thing in the Constitution or Laws of any State to the Contrary notwithstanding.[3]

Oath, of whom required, and what for.

The Senators and Representatives before mentioned, and the Members of the several State Legislatures, and all executive and judicial Officers, both of the United States and of the several States, shall be bound by Oath or Affirmation, to support this Constitution;[4] but no religious Test shall ever be required as a Qualification to any Office or public Trust under the United States.

---

[1] See *ante*, art. i., sec. 3, clause 1.

[2] An act of Congress repugnant to the Constitution can not become a law.—*Marbury* vs. *Madison*, 1 *Cranch*, 176.

[3] The courts of the United States are bound to take notice of the Constitution.—*Marbury* vs. *Madison*, 1 *Cranch*, 178.

A contemporary exposition of the Constitution, practised and acquiesced under for a period of years, fixes its construction.—*Stuart* vs. *Laird*, 1 *Cranch*, 299.

The government of the Union, though limited in its powers, is supreme within its sphere of action, and its laws, when made in pursuance of the Constitution, form the supreme law of the land.—*Mc Culloch* vs. *State of Maryland*, 4 *Wheaton*, 405.

[4] See Laws of the United States, vol. ii., chap. 1.

ARTICLE VII.

The Ratification of the Conventions of nine States shall be sufficient for the Establishment of this Constitution between the States so ratifying the Same. Ratification.

DONE in Convention by the Unanimous Consent of the States present, the Seventeenth Day of September, in the Year of our Lord one thousand seven hundred and Eighty-seven, and of the Independence of the United States the Twelfth. IN WITNESS whereof We have hereunto subscribed our Names.

GEO. WASHINGTON,
President, and deputy from Virginia.

NEW HAMPSHIRE.
JOHN LANGDON,
NICHOLAS GILMAN.

MASSACHUSETTS.
NATHANIEL GORHAM,
RUFUS KING.

CONNECTICUT.
WILLIAM SAMUEL JOHNSON,
ROGER SHERMAN.

NEW YORK.
ALEXANDER HAMILTON.

NEW JERSEY.
WILLIAM LIVINGSTON,
DAVID BREARLEY,
WILLIAM PATERSON,
JONATHAN DAYTON.

PENNSYLVANIA.
BENJAMIN FRANKLIN,
THOMAS MIFFLIN,
ROBERT MORRIS,
GEORGE CLYMER,
THOMAS FITZSIMONS,
JARED INGERSOLL,
JAMES WILSON,
GOUVERNEUR MORRIS.

DELAWARE.
GEORGE REED,
GUNNING BEDFORD, JR.,
JOHN DICKINSON,
RICHARD BASSETT,
JACOB BROOM.

MARYLAND.
JAMES M'HENRY,
DANIEL OF ST. THOS. JENIFER,
DANIEL CARROLL.

VIRGINIA.
JOHN BLAIR,
JAMES MADISON, JR.

NORTH CAROLINA.
WILLIAM BLOUNT,
RICHARD DOBBS SPAIGHT,
HUGH WILLIAMSON.

SOUTH CAROLINA.
CHARLES C. PINCKNEY,
CHARLES PINCKNEY,
JOHN RUTLEDGE,
PIERCE BUTLER.

GEORGIA.
WILLIAM FEW,
ABRAHAM BALDWIN.

Attest: WILLIAM JACKSON, *Secretary.*

AMENDMENTS[1]

TO THE CONSTITUTION OF THE UNITED STATES, RATIFIED ACCORDING TO THE PROVISIONS OF THE FIFTH ARTICLE OF THE FOREGOING CONSTITUTION.

ARTICLE THE FIRST. Congress shall make no law respecting an establishment of religion, or prohibiting the free exercise thereof; or abridging the freedom of speech, or of the press; or the right of the people peaceably to assemble, and to petition the Government for a redress of grievances. Freedom in religion and speech, and of the press.

[1] Congress, at its first session, begun and held in the city of New York, on Wednesday, the 4th of March, 1789, proposed to the Legislatures of the several States twelve amendments to the Constitution, ten of which, only, were adopted.

Militia.

ARTICLE THE SECOND. A well-regulated Militia being necessary to the security of a free State, the right of the people to keep and bear Arms, shall not be infringed.

Soldiers.

ARTICLE THE THIRD. No Soldier shall, in time of peace be quartered in any house, without the consent of the Owner, nor in a time of war, but in a manner to be prescribed by law.

Search-warrants.

ARTICLE THE FOURTH. The right of the people to be secure in their persons, houses, papers, and effects, against unreasonable searches and seizures, shall not be violated, and no Warrants shall issue, but upon probable cause, supported by Oath or affirmation, and particularly describing the place to be searched, and the person or things to be seized.

Capital crimes.

ARTICLE THE FIFTH. No person shall be held to answer for a capital, or otherwise infamous crime, unless on a presentment or indictment of a Grand Jury, except in cases arising in the land or naval forces, or in the Militia, when in actual service in time of War or public danger; nor shall any person be subject for the same offense to be twice put in jeopardy of life or limb; nor shall be compelled in any Criminal Case to be a witness against himself, nor be deprived of life, liberty, or property, without due process of law; nor shall private property be taken for public use, without just compensation.

Trial by jury.

ARTICLE THE SIXTH. In all criminal prosecutions, the accused shall enjoy the right to a speedy and public trial, by an impartial jury of the State and district wherein the crime shall have been committed, which district shall have been previously ascertained by law, and to be informed of the nature and cause of the accusation; to be confronted with the witnesses against him; to have Compulsory process for obtaining Witnesses in his favor, and to have the Assistance of Counsel for his defence.

Suits at common law.

ARTICLE THE SEVENTH. In Suits at common law, where the value in controversy shall exceed twenty dollars, the right of trial by jury shall be preserved, and no fact tried by a jury, shall be otherwise re-examined in any court of the United States, than according to the rules of the common law.[1]

Bail.

ARTICLE THE EIGHTH. Excessive bail shall not be

---

[1] The act of Assembly, in Maryland, of 1793, chap. 30, incorporating the bank of Columbia, and giving to the corporation a summary process by execution in the nature of an attachment against its debtors who have, by an express consent in writing, made the bonds, bills, or notes, by them drawn or endorsed, negotiable at the bank, is not repugnant to the Constitution of the United States or of Maryland.—*Bank of Columbia* vs. *Okely*, 4 *Wheaton*, 236, 249.

But the last provision in the act of incorporation, which gives this summary process to the bank, is no part of its corporate franchise, and may be repealed or altered at pleasure by the legislative will.—*Id.*, 245.

required, nor excessive fines imposed, nor cruel and unusual punishments inflicted.

ARTICLE THE NINTH. The enumeration in the Constitution, of certain rights, shall not be construed to deny or disparage others retained by the people. Certain rights defined.

ARTICLE THE TENTH. The powers not delegated to the United States, by the Constitution, nor prohibited by it to the states, are reserved to the states respectively, or to the people.[1] Rights reserved.

ARTICLE THE ELEVENTH.[2] The judicial power of the United States shall not be construed to extend to any suit in law or equity, commenced or prosecuted against one of the United States by Citizens of another State, or by Citizens or Subjects of any Foreign State. Judicial power limited.

ARTICLE THE TWELFTH.[3] The Electors shall meet in their respective States, and vote by ballot for President and Vice President, one of whom, at least, shall not be an inhabitant of the same state with themselves; they shall name in their ballots the person voted for as President, and in distinct ballots the person voted for as Vice President, and they shall make distinct lists of all persons voted for as President, and of all persons voted for as Vice President, and of the number of votes for each, which lists they shall sign and certify, and transmit sealed to the seat of the government of the United States, directed to The president of the Senate;[4]—The Presi- Amendment respecting the election of President and Vice President.

---

[1] The powers granted to Congress are not exclusive of similar powers existing in the States, unless where the Constitution has expressly, in terms, given an exclusive power to Congress, or the exercise of a like power is prohibited to the States, or there is a direct repugnancy or incompatibility in the exercise of it by the States.—*Houston* vs. *Moore*, 5 *Wheaton*, 1, 12.

The example of the first class is to be found in the exclusive legislation delegated to Congress over places purchased by the consent of the Legislature of the State in which the same shall be, for forts, arsenals, dockyards, &c. Of the second class, the prohibition of a State to coin money or emit bills of credit. Of the third class, the power to establish a uniform rule of naturalization, and the delegation of admiralty and maritime jurisdiction.—*Id.*, 49.

In all other classes of cases, the States retain concurrent authority with Congress.—*Id.*, 49.

But in cases of concurrent authority, where the laws of the States and the Union are in direct and manifest collision on the same subject, those of the Union being the supreme law of the land, are of paramount authority, and the State laws so far, and so far only as such incompatibility exists, must necessarily yield.—*Id.*, 49.

There is nothing in the Constitution of the United States similar to the Articles of Confederation, which excludes incidental or implied powers.—*M'Culloch* vs. *State of Maryland*, 4 *Wheaton*, 406.

If the *end* be legitimate, and within the scope of the Constitution, all the *means* which are appropriate, which are plainly adapted to that end, and which are not prohibited, may constitutionally be employed to carry it into effect.—*Id.*, 421.

The act of Congress of 4th May, 1812, entitled, "An act further to amend the charter of the city of Washington," which provides (sect. 6) that the corporation of the city shall be empowered for certain purposes and under certain restrictions, to authorize the drawing of lotteries, does not extend to authorize the corporation to force the sale of the tickets in such lottery in States where such sale may be prohibited by the State laws.—*Cohens* vs. *Virginia*, 6 *Wheaton*, 264, 375.

[2] This amendment was proposed at the first session of the third Congress. See *ante*, art. iii., sect. 2, clause 1.

[3] Proposed at the first session of the eighth Congress. See *ante*, art. ii., sect. 1, clause 3. Annulled by this amendment.

[4] See Laws of the United States, vol. ii., chap. 109, sect. 5.

Amendment respecting the election of President and Vice President.

dent of the Senate shall, in the presence of the Senate and House of Representatives, open all the certificates and the votes shall then be counted;—the person having the greatest number of votes for President, shall be the President, if such number be a majority of the whole number of electors appointed; and if no person have such majority, then from the persons having the highest numbers, not exceeding three on the list of those voted for as President, the House of Representatives shall choose immediately, by ballot, the President. But in choosing the President, the votes shall be taken by states, the representation from each state having one vote; a quorum for this purpose shall consist of a member or members from two thirds of the States, and a majority of all the states shall be necessary to a choice. And if the House of Representatives shall not choose a President whenever the right of choice shall devolve upon them, before the fourth day of March next following, then the Vice President shall act as President, as in the case of the death or other constitutional disability of the President. The person having the greatest number of votes as Vice President, shall be the Vice President, if such number be a majority of the whole number of Electors appointed, and if no person have a majority, then from the two highest numbers on the list, the Senate shall choose the Vice President; a quorum for the purpose shall consist of two thirds of the whole number of Senators, and a majority of the whole number shall be necessary to a choice. But no person constitutionally ineligible to the office of President shall be eligible to that of Vice President of the United States.

NOTE.—Another amendment was proposed as article xiii, at the second session of the eleventh Congress, but not having been ratified by a sufficient number of States, has not yet become valid as a part of the Constitution of the United States. It is erroneously given as a part of the Constitution, in page 74, vol. i., Laws of the United States.

VIII.

WASHINGTON'S FAREWELL ADDRESS.[1]

FRIENDS AND FELLOW-CITIZENS—

The period for a new election of a citizen, to administer the executive government of the United States, being not far distant, and the time actually arrived when your thoughts must be employed in designating the person who is to be clothed with that important trust, it appears to me proper, especially as it may conduce to a more distinct expression of the public voice, that I should now apprise you of the resolution I have formed, to decline being considered among the number of those out of whom a choice is to be made. I beg you, at the same time, to do me the justice to be assured, that this resolution has not been taken without a strict regard to all the considerations appertaining to the relations which bind a dutiful citizen to his country; and that, in withdrawing the tender of service which silence in my situation might imply, I am influenced by no diminution of zeal for your future interest—no deficiency of grateful respect for your past kindness; but am supported by a full conviction that the step is compatible with both.

The acceptance of, and continuance hitherto in, the office to which your suffrages have twice called me, have been a uniform sacrifice of inclination to the opinion of duty, and to a deference for what appeared to be your desire. I constantly hoped that it would have been much earlier in my power, consistently with motives which I was not at liberty to disregard, to return to that retirement from which I have been reluctantly drawn. The strength of my inclination to do this, previous to the last election, had even led to the preparation of an address to declare it to you; but mature reflection on the then perplexed and critical posture of our affairs with foreign nations, and the unanimous advice of persons entitled to my confidence, impelled me to abandon the idea.

I rejoice that the state of your concerns, external as well as internal, no longer renders the pursuit of inclination incompatible with the sentiment of duty or propriety; and am persuaded, whatever partiality may be retained for my services, that in the present circumstances of our country, you will not disapprove my determination to retire.

The impressions with which I first undertook the arduous task, were explained on the proper occasion. In the discharge of this trust, I will only say, that I have, with good intentions, contributed toward the organization and administration of the government, the best exertions of which a very fallible judg-

---

[1] See page 382. The original manuscript is in the possession of James Lennox, Esq., of New York city.

ment was capable. Not unconscious, in the outset, of the inferiority of my qualifications, experience in my own eyes, perhaps still more in the eyes of others, has strengthened the motives to diffidence of myself; and, every day, the increasing weight of years admonishes me more and more that the shade of retirement is as necessary to me as it will be welcome. Satisfied that if any circumstances have given peculiar value to my services, they were temporary, I have the consolation to believe, that while choice and prudence invite me to quit the political scene, patriotism does not forbid it.

In looking forward to the moment which is intended to terminate the career of my public life, my feelings do not permit me to suspend the deep acknowledgment of that debt of gratitude which I owe to my beloved country, for the many honors it has conferred upon me; still more for the stedfast confidence with which it has supported me; and for the opportunities I have thence enjoyed of manifesting my inviolable attachment, by services faithful and persevering, though in usefulness unequal to my zeal. If benefits have resulted to our country from these services, let it always be remembered to your praise and as an instructive example in our annals, that under circumstances in which the passions, agitated in every direction, were liable to mislead, amid appearances sometimes dubious—vicissitudes of fortune often discouraging—in situations in which not unfrequently want of success has countenanced the spirit of criticism—the constancy of your support was the essential prop of the efforts, and the guaranty of the plans by which they were effected.

Profoundly penetrated with this idea, I shall carry it with me to my grave, as a strong incitement to unceasing vows that Heaven may continue to you the choicest tokens of its benevolence—that your union and brotherly affection may be perpetual—that the free Constitution, which is the work of your hands, may be sacredly maintained—that its administration in every department may be stamped with wisdom and virtue—that, in fine, the happiness of the people of these States, under the auspices of liberty, may be made complete, by so careful a preservation, and so prudent a use of this blessing, as will acquire to them the glory of recommending it to the applause of every nation which is yet a stranger to it.

Here, perhaps, I ought to stop. But a solicitude for your welfare, which can not end but with my life, and the apprehension of danger, natural to that solicitude, urge me, on an occasion like the present, to offer to your solemn contemplation, and to recommend to your frequent review, some sentiments; which are the result of much reflection, of no inconsiderable observation, and which appear to me all-important to the permanency of your felicity as a people. These will be offered to you with the more freedom, as you can only see in them the disinterested warnings of a parting friend, who can possibly have no personal motives to bias his counsel. Nor can I forget as an encouragement to it, your indulgent reception of my sentiments on a former and not dissimilar occasion. Interwoven as is the love of liberty with every ligament of your hearts, no recommendation of mine is necessary to fortify or confirm the attachment.

The unity of government which constitutes you one people, is also now dear to me. It is justly so; for it is a main pillar in the edifice of your real independence, the support of your tranquillity at home, your peace abroad; of your safety; of your prosperity; of that very liberty which you so highly prize. But as it is easy to foresee, that from different causes and from different quarters, much pains will be taken, many artifices employed, to weaken in your minds the conviction of this truth; as this is the point in your political fortress against which the batteries of internal and external enemies will be most constantly and actively (though often covertly and insiduously) directed, it is of infinite moment that you should properly estimate the immense value of your national Union to your collective and individual happiness; that you should cherish a cordial, habitual, and immovable attachment to it; accustoming yourselves to think and speak of it as of the Palladium of your political safety and prosperity; watching for its preservation with jealous anxiety; discountenancing whatever may suggest even a suspicion that it can in any event be abandoned; and indignantly frowning upon the first dawning of every attempt to alienate any portion of our country from the rest, or to enfeeble the sacred ties which now link together the various parts.

For this you have every inducement of sympathy and interest. Citizens by birth or choice, of a common country, that country has a right to concentrate your affections. The name of AMERICA, which belongs to you in your national capacity, must always exalt the just pride of patriotism, more than any appellation derived from local discriminations. With slight shades of difference, you have the same religion, manners, habits, and political principles. You have in a common cause, fought and triumphed together; the independence and liberty you possess are the work of joint councils, and joint efforts, of common dangers, sufferings, and successes. But these considerations, however powerfully they address themselves to your sensibility, are greatly outweighed by those which apply more immediately to your interest—here every portion of our country finds the most commanding motives for carefully guarding and preserving the Union of the whole.

The *North*, in an unrestrained intercourse with the *South*, protected by the equal laws of a common government, finds in the productions of the latter, great additional resources of maritime and commercial enterprise and precious materials of manufacturing industry. The *South*, in the same intercourse, benefiting by the agency of the *North*, sees its agriculture grow and its commerce expand. Turning partly into its own channels the seamen of the *North*, it finds its particular navigation invigorated; and while it contributes, in different ways, to nourish and increase the general mass of the national navigation, it looks forward to the protection of a maritime strength, to which itself is unequally adapted. The *East*, in a like intercourse with the *West*, already finds, and in the progressive improvemement of interior communications, by land water, will more and more find a valuable vent for the commodities which it brings from abroad, or manufactures at home. The *West* derives from the *East* supplies requisite to its growth and comfort—and what is perhaps of still greater consequence, it must of necessity owe the secure enjoyment of indispensable *outlets* for its own productions to the weight, influence, and the future maritime strength of the Atlantic side of the Union, directed by an indissoluble community of interest as ONE NATION. Any other tenure by which the *West* can hold this essential advantage, whether derived from its own separate strength, or from an apostate and unnatural connection with any foreign power, must be intrinsically precarious.

While, then, every part of our country thus feels an immediate and particular interest in union, all the parties combined can not fail to find in the united mass of means and efforts, greater strength, greater resource, proportionably greater security from external danger, a less frequent interruption of their peace by foreign nations; and, what is of inestimable value! they must derive from union an exemption from those broils and wars between themselves, which so frequently afflict neighboring countries, not tied together by the same government: which their own rivalships alone would be sufficient to produce, but which opposite foreign alliances, attachments, and intrigues would stimulate and embitter. Hence likewise they will avoid the necessity of those overgrown military establishments, which, under any form of government, are inauspicious to liberty, and which are to be regarded as particularly hostile to Republican Liberty; in this sense it is, that your Union ought to be considered as a main prop of your liberty, and that the love of the one ought to endear to you the preservation of the other.

These considerations speak a persuasive language to every reflecting and virtuous mind, and exhibit the continuance of the *Union* as a primary object of patriotic desire. Is there a doubt whether a common government can embrace so large a sphere? Let experience solve it. To listen to mere speculation in such a case were criminal. We are authorized to hope that a proper organization of the whole, with the auxiliary agency of government for the respective subdivisions, will afford a happy issue to the experiment. 'Tis well worth a fair and full experiment. With such powerful and obvious motives to Union, affecting all parts of our country, while experience shall not have demonstrated its impracticability, there will always be reason to distrust the patriotism of those who in any quarter may endeavor to weaken its bands.

In contemplating the causes which may disturb our Union, it occurs as a matter of serious concern, that any ground should have been furnished for characterizing parties by *geographical* discriminations—*northern* and *southern*—*Atlantic* and *western;* whence designing men may endeavor to excite a belief that there is a real difference of local interests and views. One of the expedients of party to acquire influence within particular districts, is to misrepresent the opinions and aims of other districts. You can not shield yourselves too much against the jealousies and heart-burnings which spring from thase misrepresentations: they tend to render alien to each other those who ought to be bound together by fraternal affection. The inhabitants of our western country have lately had a useful lesson on this head: they have seen in the negotiation by the Executive, and in the unanimous ratification by the Senate, of the treaty with Spain, and in the universal satisfaction at that event throughout the United States, a decisive proof how unfounded were the suspicions propagated among them, of a policy in the General Government and in the Atlantic States unfriendly to their interests in regard to the *Mississippi:* they have been witnesses to the formation of two treaties—that with Great Britain and that with Spain—which secure to them every thing they could desire, in respect to our foreign relations, toward confirming their prosperity. Will it not be their wisdom to rely for the preservation of these advantages on the UNION by which they were procured? Will they not henceforth be deaf to those advisers, if such there are, who would sever them from their brethren, and connect them with aliens?

To the efficacy and permanency of your Union, a government for the whole is indispensable. No alliances, however strict, between the parts, can be an adequate substitute: they must inevitably experience the infractions and interruptions which all alliances in all times have experienced. Sensible of this momentous truth, you have improved upon your first essay, by the adoption of a Constitution of government better calculated than your former for an intimate Union, and for the efficacious management of your common concerns. This government, the offspring of our own choice, uninfluenced and unawed, adopted upon full investigation and mature deliberation, completely free in its principles, in the distribution of its powers, uniting security with energy, and containing within itself a provision for its own amendment, has a just claim to your confidence and your support. Respect for its authority, compliance with its laws, acquiescence in its measures, are duties enjoined by the fundamental maxims of true Liberty. The basis of our political systems is the right of the people to make and to alter their Constitutions of Government; but the Constitution which at any time exists, till changed by an explicit and authentic act of the whole people, is sacredly obligatory upon all. The very idea of the power and the right of the people to establish government, presupposes the duty of every individual to obey the established government.

All obstructions to the execution of the laws, all combinations and associations, under whatever plausible character, with the real design to direct, control, counteract, or awe the regular deliberation and action of the constituted authorities, are destructive of this fundamental principle, and of fatal tendency. They serve to organize faction, to give it an artificial and extraordinary force—to put in the place of the delegated will of the nation, the will of a party, often a small but artful and enterprising minority of the community; and, according to the alternate triumphs of different parties, to make the public administration the mirror of the ill-concerted and incongruous projects of faction, rather than the organ of consistent and wholesome plans, digested by common councils, and modified by mutual interests. However combinations or associations of the above description may now and then answer popular ends, they are likely, in the course of time and things, to become potent engines, by which cunning, ambitious, and unprincipled men will be enabled to subvert the power of the people, and to usurp for themselves the reins of government; destroying afterward the very engines which have lifted them to unjust dominion.

Toward the preservation of your government, and the permanency of your present happy state, it is requisite, not only that you speedily discountenance irregular oppositions to its acknowledged authority, but also that you resist with care the spirit of innovation upon its principles, however specious the pretexts. One method of assault may be to effect, in the forms of the Constitution, alterations which impair the energy of the system, and thus to undermine what can not directly be overthrown. In all the changes to which you may be invited, remember that time and habit are at least as necessary to fix the true character of governments as of other human institutions—that experience is the surest standard by which to test the real tendency of the existing Constitution of a country—that facility in changes upon the credit of mere hypothesis and opinion, exposes to perpetual change from the endless variety of hypothesis and opinion; and remember, especially, that for the efficient management of your common interests, in a country so extensive as ours, a government of as much vigor as is consistent with the perfect security of liberty, is indispensable. Liberty itself will find in such a government, with powers properly distributed and adjusted, its surest guardian. It is, indeed, little else than a name, where the government is too feeble to withstand the enterprise of faction, to confine each member of the society within the limits prescribed by the laws, and to maintain all in the secure and tranquil enjoyment of the rights of person and property.

I have already intimated to you the danger of parties in the State, with particular reference to the founding of them on geographical discriminations. Let me now take a more comprehensive view, and warn you in the most solemn manner against the baneful effects of the spirit of party, generally. This spirit, unfortunately, is inseparable from our nature, having its root in the strongest passions of the human mind. It exists under different shapes in all governments, more or less stifled, controlled or repressed; but in those of the popular form, it is seen in its greatest rankness, and is truly their worst enemy. The alternate domination of one faction over another, sharpened by the spirit of revenge, natural to party dissension, which, in different ages and countries, has perpetrated the most horrid enormities, is itself a frightful despotism. But this leads at length to a more formal and permanent despotism. The disorders and miseries which result, gradually incline the minds of men to seek security and repose in the absolute power of an individual; and sooner or later, the chief of some prevailing faction, more able or more fortunate than his competitor, turns this disposition to the purposes of his own elevation, on the ruins of public liberty.

Without looking forward to an extremity of this kind (which, nevertheless, ought not to be entirely out of sight) the common and continual mischiefs of the spirit of party, are sufficient to make it the interest and duty of a wise people to discourage and restrain it. It serves always to distract the public councils and enfeeble the public administration. It agitates the community with ill-founded jealousies and false alarms; kindles the animosity of one part against another; foments occasionally riot and insurrection. It opens the door to foreign influence and corruption, which find a facilitated access to the government itself through the channels of party passions. Thus the policy and the will of one country are subjected to the policy and the will of another.

There is an opinion that parties in free countries are useful checks upon the administration of the government, and serve to keep alive the spirit of liberty. This within certain limits is probably true; and in governments of a monarchical cast, patriotism may look with indulgence, if not with favor, upon the spirit of party. But in those of the popular character, in governments purely elective, it is a spirit not to be encouraged. From their natural tendency, it is certain there will always be enough of that spirit for every salutary purpose. And there being constant danger of success, the effort ought to be by force of public opinion, to mitigate and assuage it. A fire not to be quenched; it demands a uniform vigilance to prevent its bursting into a flame, lest, instead of warming, it should consume.

It is important, likewise, that the habits of thinking, in a free country, should inspire caution in those intrusted with its administration, to confine themselves within their respective constitutional spheres, avoiding, in the exercise of the powers of one department, to encroach upon another. The spirit of encroachment tends to consolidate the powers of all the departments in one, and thus to create, whatever the form of government, a real despotism. A just estimate of that love of power, and proneness to abuse it, which predominates in the human heart, is sufficient to satisfy us of this position. The necessity of reciprocal checks in the exercise of political power, by dividing and distributing it into different depositories, and constituting each the guardian of public weal against invasions by the others, has been evinced by experiments ancient and modern: some of them in our country and under our own eyes. To preserve them must be as necessary as to institute them. If, in the opinion of the people, the distribution or modification of the constitutional powers be in any particular wrong, let it be corrected by an amendment in the way which the Constitution designates. But let there be no change by usurpation; for though this, in one instance, may be the instrument of good, it is the customary weapon by which free governments are destroyed. The precedent must always greatly overbalance in permanent evil any partial or transient benefit which the use can at any time yield.

Of all the dispositions and habits which lead to political prosperity, religion and morality are indispensable supports. In vain would that man claim the tribute of patriotism, who should labor to subvert these great pillars of human happiness, these firmest props of the duties of men and citizens. The mere politician, equally with the pious man, ought to respect and to cherish them. A volume could not trace all their connections with private and public felicity. Let it simply be asked where is the security for property, for reputation, for life, if the sense of religious obligation DESERT the oaths, which are the instruments of investigation in courts of justice; and let us with caution indulge the supposition, that morality can be maintained without religion. Whatever may be conceded to the influence of refined education on minds of peculiar structure, reason and experience both forbid us to expect that national morality can prevail in exclusion or religious principle. It is substantially true, that virtue or morality is a necessary spring of popular government. The rule, indeed, extends with more or less force to every species of free government. Who that is a sincere friend to it can look with indifference upon attempts to shake the foundations of the fabric?

Promote, then, as an object of primary importance, institutions for the general diffusion of knowledge. In proportion as the structure of a government gives force to public opinion, it is essential that public opinion should be enlightened. As a very important source of strength and security, cherish public credit; one method of preserving it is to use it as sparingly as possible; avoiding occasions of expense by cultivating peace; but remembering, also, that timely disbursements to prepare for danger, frequently prevent much greater disbursements to repel it; avoiding, likewise, the accumulations of debt, not only by shunning occasions of expense, but by vigorous exertions in time of peace to discharge the debts which unavoidable wars may have occasioned, not ungenerously throwing upon posterity the burdens which we ourselves ought to bear. The execution of these maxims belongs to your Representatives, but it is necessary that public opinion should co-operate. To facilitate to them the performance of their duty, it is essential that you should practically bear in mind, that toward the payment of debts there must be revenue; that to have revenue there must be taxes; that no taxes can be devised which are not more or less inconvenient and unpleasant; and the intrinsic embarrassment inseparable from the selection of the proper object (which is always a choice of difficulties) ought to be a decisive motive for the candid construction of the conduct of the government in making it, and for a spirit of acquiescence in the measures for obtaining revenue which the public exigences may at any time dictate.

Observe good faith and justice toward all nations; cultivate peace and harmony with all; religion and morality enjoin this conduct; and can it be that good policy does not equally enjoin it? It will be worthy of a free, enlightened, and at no distant period, a great nation, to give to mankind the magnanimous and too novel example of a people always guided by an exalted justice and benevolence. Who can doubt that in the course of time and things, the fruits of such a plan would richly repay any temporary advantages which might be lost by a steady adherence to it? Can it be that Providence has not connected the permanent felicity of a nation with its virtue? The experiment, at least, is recommended by every sentiment which ennobles human nature. Alas! is it rendered impossible by its vices?

In the execution of such a plan, nothing is more essential than that permanent inveterate antipathies against particular nations, and passionate attachments for others should be excluded; and that, in place of them, just and amicable feelings toward all should be cultivated. The nation which indulges toward another an habitual hatred, or an habitual fondness, is in some degree a slave. It is a slave to its animosity or to its affection, either of which is sufficient to lead it astray from its duty and its interest. Antipathy in one nation against another, disposes each more readily to offer insult and injury, to lay hold of slight causes of umbrage, and to be haughty and intractable, when accidental or trifling occasions of dispute occur. Hence frequent collisions, obstinate, envenomed, and bloody contests. The nation prompted by ill-will and resentment, sometimes impels to war the government, contrary to the best calculations of policy. The government sometimes participates in the national propensity, and adopts, through passion, what reason would reject; at other times, it makes the animosity of the nation subservient to projects of hostility, instigated by pride, ambition, and other sinister and pernicious motives. The peace often, sometimes perhaps the liberty, of nations has been the victim.

So, likewise, a passionate attachment of one nation for another produces a variety of evils. Sympathy for the favorite nation, facilitating the illusion of an imaginary common interest, in cases where no real common interest exists, and infusing into one the enmities of the other, betrays the former into a participation in the quarrels and wars of the latter, without adequate inducement or justification. It leads also to the concessions to the favorite nation of privileges denied to others, which is apt doubly to injure the nation making the concessions; by unnecessarily parting with what ought to have been retained; and by exciting jealousy, ill-will, and a disposition to retaliate, in the parties from whom equal privileges are withheld—and it gives to ambitious, corrupted, or deluded citizens (who devote themselves to the favorite nation), facility to betray or sacrifice the interests of their own country without odium, sometimes even with popularity; gilding with the appearance of a virtuous sense of obligation, a commendable deference for public opinion, or a laudable zeal for public good, the base or foolish compliances of ambition, corruption, or infatuation.

As avenues to foreign influence in innumerable ways, such attachments are particularly alarming to the truly enlightened and independent patriot. How many opportunities do they afford to tamper with domestic factions, to practice the arts of seduction, to mislead public opinions, to influence or awe public councils! Such an attachment of a small or weak, toward a great and powerful nation, dooms the former to be the satellite of the latter. Against the insidious wiles of foreign influence (I conjure you to believe me, fellow citizens), the jealousy of a free people ought to be CONSTANTLY awake; since history and experience prove that foreign influence is one of the most baneful foes of republican government. But that jealousy, to be useful, must be impartial: else it becomes the instrument of the very influence to be avoided, instead of a defense against it. Excessive partiality for one foreign nation, and excessive dislike of another, cause those whom they actuate, to see danger only on one side, and serve to vail and even second the arts of influence on the other. Real patriots, who may resist the intrigues of the favorite, are liable to become suspected and odious; while its tools and dupes usurp the applause and confidence of the people, to surrender their interests. The great rule of conduct for us, in regard to foreign nations, is, in extending our commercial relations, to have with them as little political connection as possible. So far as we have already formed engagements, let them be fulfilled with perfect good faith. Here let us stop.

Europe has a set of primary interests, which to us have none, or a very remote relation. Hence she must be engaged in frequent controversies, the causes of which are essentially foreign to our concerns. Hence, therefore, it must be unwise in us to implicate ourselves by artificial ties, in the ordinary vicissitudes of her politics, or the ordinary combinations and collisions of her friendships or enmities. Our detached and distant situation invites and enables us to pursue a different course. If we remain one people under an efficient government, the period is not far off when we may defy material injury from external annoyance; when we may take such an attitude as will cause the neutrality we may at any time resolve upon, to be scrupulously respected; when belligerent nations, under the impossibility of making acquisitions upon us, will not lightly hazard the giving us provocation; when we may choose peace or war, as our interest, guided by justice, shall counsel.

Why forego the advantage of so peculiar a situation? Why quit our own to stand upon foreign ground? Why, by interweaving our destiny with any part of Europe, entangle our peace and prosperity in the toils of European ambition, rivalship, interest, humor, or caprice? It is our true policy to steer clear of permanent alliances with any portion of the foreign world; so far, I mean, as we are now at liberty to do it; for let me not be understood as capable of patronizing infidelity to existing engagements. I hold the maxim no less applicable to public than to private affairs, that honesty is always the best policy. I repeat it, therefore, let those engagements be observed in their genuine sense. But, in my opinion, it is unnecessary, and would be unwise to extend them. Taking care always to keep ourselves, by suitable establishments, on a respectable defensive posture, we may safely trust to temporary alliances for extraordinary emergences.

Harmony, liberal intercourse with all nations, are recommended by policy, humanity, and interest But even our commercial policy should hold an equal and impartial hand; neither seeking nor granting exclusive favors or preferences; consulting the natural course of things; diffusing and diversifying, by gentle means, the streams of commerce, but forcing nothing; establishing with powers so disposed, in order to give trade a stable course, to define the rights of our merchants, and to enable the government to support them, conventional rules of intercourse, the best that present circumstances and mutual opinion will permit, but temporary, and liable to be from time to time abandoned or varied, as experience or circumstances shall dictate; constantly keeping in view, that it is folly in one nation to look for disinterested favors from another; that it must pay with a portion of its independence for whatever it may accept under that character; that by such acceptance, it may place itself in the condition of having given equivalent for nominal favors, and yet of being reproached with ingratitude for not giving more. There can be no greater error than to expect or calculate upon real favors from nation to nation. 'Tis an illusion which experience must cure, which a just pride ought to discard.

In offering to you, my countrymen, these counsels of an old and affectionate friend, I dare not hope they will make the strong and lasting impression I could wish; that they will control the usual current of the passions, or prevent our nation from running the course which has hitherto marked the destiny of nations: but if I may even flatter myself that they may be productive of some partial benefit, some occasional good; that they may now and then recur to moderate the fury of party spirit, to warn against the mischiefs of foreign intrigues, and guard against the impostures of pretended patriotism; this hope will be a full recompense for the solicitude for your welfare, by which they have been dictated. How far, in the discharge of my official duties, I have been guided by the principles which have been delineated, the public records and other evidences of my conduct must witness to you and to the world. To myself, the assurance of my own conscience is, that I have at least believed myself to be guided by them.

In relation to the still subsisting war in Europe, my proclamation of the 22d of April, 1793, is the index to my plan. Sanctioned by your approving voice and by that of your representatives in both Houses of Congress, the spirit of that measure has continually governed me; uninfluenced by any attempt to deter or divert me from it. After deliberate examination, with the aid of the best lights I could obtain, I was well satisfied that our country, under all the circumstances of the case, had a right to take, and was bound in duty and interest to take, a neutral position. Having taken it, I determined, as far as should depend upon me, to maintain it with moderation, perseverance, and firmness.

The consideration which respects the right to hold this conduct, it is not necessary on this occasion to detail. I will only observe, that according to my understanding of the matter, that right, so far from being denied by any of the belligerent powers, has been virtually admitted by all. The duty of holding a neutral conduct may be inferred, without any thing more, from the obligation which justice and humanity impose upon every nation, in cases in which it is free to act, to maintain inviolate the relations of peace and amity toward other nations. The inducements of interest for observing that conduct will be best referred to your own reflection and experience. With me, a predominant motive has been to endeavor to gain time to our country to settle and mature its yet recent institutions, and to progress, without interruption, to that degree of strength and consistency, which is necessary to give it, humanly speaking, the command of its own fortunes.

Though in reviewing the incidents of my administration, I am unconscious of intentional error, I am, nevertheless, too sensible of my defects not to think it probable that I have committed many errors. Whatever they may be, I fervently beseech the Almighty to avert or mitigate the evils to which they may tend. I shall also carry with me the hope that my country will never cease to view them with indulgence; and that after forty-five years of my life dedicated to its service, with an upright zeal, the faults of incompetent abilities will be consigned to oblivion, as myself must soon be to the mansions of rest. Relying on its kindness in this as in other things, and actuated by that fervent love toward it, which is so natural to a man who views in it the native soil of himself and his progenitors for several generations; I anticipate with pleasing expectation that retreat, in which I promise myself to realize without alloy, the sweet enjoyment of partaking, in the midst of my fellow-citizens, the benign influence of good laws under a free government—the ever-favorite object of my heart, and the happy reward, as I trust, of our mutual cares, labors, and dangers.

UNITED STATES, September 17, 1796. GEORGE WASHINGTON.

INDEX.

THE END.

www.ingramcontent.com/pod-product-compliance
Lightning Source LLC
LaVergne TN
LVHW021050110826
845150LV00001B/35
9781425567866